THE VIOLENT DECADE

THE

VIOLENT DECADE

FRANK GERVASI

W•W•NORTON & COMPANY
NEW YORK LONDON

Printed in the United States of America.

The text of this book is composed in Times Roman,
with display type set in Neuland.
Composition and manufacturing by The Haddon Craftsmen, Inc.
Book design by Jacques Chazaud.

FIRST EDITION

Library of Congress Cataloging-in-Publication Data

Gervasi, Frank Henry, 1908–
The violent decade / Frank Gervasi. —1st ed.
p. cm.
Includes index.
1. History, Modern—20th century. 2. Gervasi, Frank Henry, 1908–
3. Foreign correspondents—United States—Biography. I. Title.
D443.G36 1989
909.82—dc19

ISBN 0-393-02464-4

W. W. Norton & Company, Inc., 500 Fifth Avenue, New York, N. Y. 10110
W. W. Norton & Company Ltd., 37 Great Russell Street, London WC1B 3NU

To my beloved wife, Georgia,
and, in memoriam,
To my dear son Tom Gervasi

CONTENTS

INTRODUCTION

This is the history in one man's retentive mind of a decade that molded the twentieth century. Those Americans and Europeans and Asians not killed in that decade and in the bloody year that followed, 1945, would be marked forever by those ten years. Giants emerged to stalk the world stage: Roosevelt, Churchill, Stalin, Hitler, Mussolini. They left their mark not only on their time but on us.

Frank Gervasi was one of the relatively small band of American correspondents in Europe in the 1930s. His first post in 1934 was Madrid, where he witnessed the beginings of the civil strife which was to sweep Spain, engulf it in civil war, and provide the Germans, Italians, and Soviets with a practice field for World War II.

From then until Culoz in southern France in 1944 he covered that campaign. His work led him to London, Bucharest, Cairo, Manila, and a half dozen other capitals at war. He saw soldiers of many nations under fire, and he himself underwent the lash of war.

Halfway through this fascinating book I wondered whether it would have any real appeal today. After all, it recounts events long inscribed in history books and endlessly debated by military and political historians. My answer is that it must have an appeal. To repeat, that war molded not only the thinking of the generation that fought it but those that followed it. The West Germans, at least, have accepted their crimes and have emerged as full partners in a new Europe. The Japanese have not. Until they do, how can they be welcomed into the community of nations?

Mr. Gervasi's ability to evoke a morning scene in Rome or a sunset in Cairo or a beach on the Mediterranean during the campaign in the Middle East gives the book a special poignancy. This is history written with great artistry.

A great many people have tried to picture London before and during the bombing. Ed Murrow on radio was one of the best. In print, few have come close to Gervasi's capsule treatment. Similarly, his descriptions of Cairo as British military headquarters during the long war against the Italians and Germans in what is now Libya, then called Cyrenaica, are excellent.

For students of those times the characterizations of Mussolini and especially of his relations with Hitler should be one of the most interesting parts of the book. Gervasi, an American of Italian origin from South Philadelphia, made even in Fascist Italy what the trade calls "good contacts." From them he learned a good deal about Mussolini, commonly called "Old Baldy" and his posturing son-in-law, Count Ciano.

From this knowledge there emerges a fascinating picture of the ramshackle Italian empire fashioned by the Duce, imbued basically by a love of Italian aggrandizement but increasingly by a desire to show Hitler that the Nazi was not the only dictator in Europe. Gervasi believes that Mussolini resented his, and Italy's role, as a minor partner in the Axis between Berlin and Rome and yearned for a more aggressive position. Hence the "conquest" of Ethiopia and of Albania and the later and costly invasion of Greece, from which Italy had to be rescued by the German Army and Air Force at great cost to Hitler's plans for the invasion of Russia.

Gervasi was one American correspondent who was never fooled by Mussolini. Yes, the trains ran on time. Yes, the Pontine Marshes were drained. But conditions in the south remained abominable for the poor. Despite il Duce's boasts, only the Italian Navy represented a modern force; the air force was flown from base to base to comfort Mussolini with flypasts, but it was woefully weak in numbers and modern equipment.

The villain in Gervasi's eyes was not Italy but Mussolini, and he gives ample evidence in some excellent, perceptive chapters that should be required reading for students of modern European history.

The war gobbled up Gervasi's attention as it did that of all reporters in Europe. He saw a great deal of it in the Mediterranean, particularly in the Middle East and Italy, and a bit in the Far East when the tide was going against the Allies.

These chapters will open the eyes of those who now regard the conflict in the deserts of Egypt and Libya as a walkover. After General Wavell's initial triumphs over the Italians early in 1941, the Germans, under Erwin Rommel, arrived and, until the early autumn of 1942, dominated the desert battlefield. Gervasi saw it at its worst. He also saw and appreciated the courage of the British soldier and junior officer and the incompetence and worse of the middle-rank staff officers who presided over the enormous headquarters in Cairo. All this is described in accurate and chilling detail. The reader will not soon forget Gervasi's visit to a field hospital where a young Italian lieutenant is dying of wounds and a British orderly and an Irish priest are helping him on his way. The Italian, Gervasi records, dies shouting not praise for il Duce but the old, familiar phrase *Mamma mia.*

Most of the rot and defeatism changed with the advent of Alexander and Montgomery. Alam Halfa and El Alamein were won. The former, as Gervasi accurately points out, is one of the least known and one of the most important battles of the war in Africa, one of the real turning points of the war in the desert and of World War II.

For Americans Normandy is a much more interesting and more glorious story than the long, costly, and basically unexciting campaign in Italy. It was Gervasi's lot to cover the latter. At the time, and in this book, he did a whale of a job.

The reader will see that he pulls no punches. He is unsparing in his criticism of General Mark Clark for his conduct of the Anzio campaign and of Winston Churchill for ordering it.

Gervasi also takes exception to Clark's generalship at Cassino. He is not alone there, although, as he says, "Several others share the blame." Clark's great error in the Italian campaign was to "go for Rome" and fail to cut off the retreating Germans. He entered Rome as a conqueror, but the Germans got away to fight a long, bloody campaign for nearly a year.

The war went on. So did Gervasi. He never lost his zest, although many did. In Sicily, Italy, and elsewhere along the way he was often without enough food or shelter. He did not pity himself. He had a story. He was first and foremost a reporter and a good one.

Then the tide changed. Gervasi was back in his beloved Rome but a far different Rome from the one he had known. The Allies had landed in Normandy. The Allies were moving into northern Italy. The Allies were about to land in the south of France. Gervasi gives a brilliant description of his part in that landing and what he found there: the prisoners of war released from the Germans; the French so long held by their German masters; the general sense of exultation. Brilliant passages.

Gervasi's was a pilgrimage during the most dramatic and hectic decade of this century. Few correspondents gave themselves so completely to their craft and to the war as did Gervasi. Fittingly he ended his pilgrimage with the Seventh Army under General Patch driving for Marseilles, which was liberated on August 23, 1944, eight days after the landings in southern France. By then, of course, the Normandy fight was about over and the drive on Paris about to shift to Berlin. Except for Hitler's last-gasp offensive in the Ardennes in December, the war in the west was all but won.

The big war and the small war. The reader will note that Gervasi keeps both in mind. He recalls how the French resistance, after Marseilles was taken, hunted out the Vichyites and killed them.

Gervasi ends his narrative at Culoz, where he found Gertrude Stein and Alice B. Toklas. The former gave him a ballad, which he treasured but which *Collier's,* for which he was then working, refused to publish. Thus he ended the war.

Since that war the United States has endured two other wars. The Korean

War has rapidly become a forgotten conflict, although in many ways it was a saga of American and Allied response to an extremely dangerous international situation. The Vietnam War has become a living part of our memory, kept alive by "professional" veterans, soldiers and former correspondents alike, who spend their days expiating upon the follies of that war and its political and military leaders. Certainly there were follies. There were in that war; there are in all wars. There are very few just wars.

One was the war Frank Gervasi describes, with great skill. Like most young men in the thirties, he realized that unless something was done about Hitler, Mussolini, and the Japanese, life would not be very easy for all young men or their families. So the war was fought. There were, as Frank justly points out, many follies. Fools and incompetents at times were in charge of great enterprises. But in the end good men triumphed.

The war was won. It changed the generation that won it. And to a degree only slightly understood, it changed succeeding generations. Hearing about this book, a young student at Columbia said recently, "I'd like to read that. My grandfather fought in that war, and it meant a lot to him and to my father and mother; maybe it means something to the country."

That, I think, is the basic message of Frank Gervasi's book. He is not a preacher. But he has given this generation a message. War *is* hell. No one knows that better than those who have been through it. But it also teaches.

Drew Middleton

FOREWORD

Printer's ink is as addictive as nicotine or alcohol, the common drugs of my time. Exposed to its insidious influence at an early age, I became a newspaperman and ultimately a foreign correspondent, one of the dwindling breed of print journalists who, from the mid-1930s to the mid-1940s, reported the revolutions and wars which radically altered the social, political, economic, even the geographic landscape of the world we know today.

Those were the violent years which spanned the Ethiopian War, the Spanish Civil War, the persecution of Europe's Jews, and the Second World War. This is a memoir of those years, the remembrances of a decade that embraced what I now think of as a cataclysm.

Webster's dictionary defines a cataclysm as "Any violent change involving sudden and extensive alterations in the earth's surface, hence, any upheaval, especially a social or political one." Such a phenomenon in nature, as we may imagine it, is a time when volcanoes erupt, earthquakes rumble, old mountain systems are broken down, new peaks and ranges thrust themselves upward, living creatures flee from destruction, and the very coastlines assume new shapes.

I realize now that the human world has been in the midst of a cataclysm since 1914, the first year of World War I, when I was only six years old. That war, its postwar troubles, the Russian Revolution, the Great Depression, the emergence in Europe of the Fascist and Nazi dictators, and the Second World War all were part of the process of violent changes which altered the very coastlines of human society beyond recognition, and for which "cataclysm" seems not too strong a word.

From the summer of 1934, when I went to Spain on my first overseas assignment, to the summer of 1945, when the Second World War ended, I had a grandstand seat, so to speak, at many of the events which reshaped the world of today.

I have long resisted a recurrent desire to describe what I saw, heard, and felt during those violent years, waiting to grow intellectually and develop perspective. I'm not certain that I have succeeded, but I feel the time has come to set down the recollections of my peripatetic journey through what was surely a cataclysm, hoping thereby to add to the sum of people's understanding of the history of my times.

ACKNOWLEDGMENTS

After several false starts I began writing this book some years ago at the insistence of the late Arthur Birnkrant—writer, scholar, teacher, and cherished friend—who persuaded me that my journalistic experiences during the violent decade 1935–1945 might have some value as an extended footnote to the history of those turbulent years.

Whatever the book's shortcomings, they might have been fewer had Arthur lived, for he had a keen eye for the discordant note, the misstatement of history, the flaw in composition. But he died too soon to see the work completed, and now I can only hope he would not have been disappointed in the result. To the departed Arthur, I am beholden for having set me to what proved to be a long and difficult task.

I am indebted also to Tom Wallace, originally my editor at W. W. Norton, for believing I should leave a scribbling on the walls of my time and for setting the book on the road to publication. To him and to Hilary Hinzmann, Tom's successor when he left editing for greener pastures, my warmest thanks for their help in reducing to printable dimensions what proved to be a monumental manuscript.

My deepest debt of gratitude, however, I owe to my late son Tom Gervasi for valuable data on weaponry and frequent editorial advice. Tom, who died while this book was in proof, was an accomplished writer, a former book editor, and an armaments expert. His moral support, and that of his older brother, Sean Gervasi, the economist, sustained me over the five years it took me to complete my work.

Also most helpful and supportive were my sister, Grace Beacham, and her husband, Robert, who found in the stacks of their hometown library in Chattanooga, Tennessee, bound volumes of *Collier's* containing stories I had written that refreshed my memories of the war years.

Among the first to suggest that I commit my adventures to paper was Dr. Lester Laudy Coleman, family physician and friend, and to him I am obliged for helping me overcome periods of doubt and depression.

Lastly, my thanks also to my agent, Glenn Cowley, for having arranged my fruitful meeting with Tom Wallace, and to Rochelle Mancini, for typing and retyping a manuscript that seemed never to end. I would never have finished it, however, without the encouragement and uncomplaining care of my wife, Georgia, who zealously guarded my health and privacy while I worked. To her, and to the departed Tom, this book is lovingly dedicated.

THE VIOLENT DECADE

PROLOGUE

I was exposed to the heady vapors of printer's ink for the first time at the age of ten, in hometown Philadelphia. It was early spring 1918, the final year of Woodrow Wilson's "war to make the world safe for democracy."

Around the corner from our brick row house on League Street, in Little Italy, Signor Guido Vitrone, a Socialist crony of my immigrant father, Eugene, produced *L'Opinione,* an eight-page left-wing Italian-language newspaper, circulation an uncertain eight thousand, in a shop on lower Eighth Street. Our other neighbors included a banker, a pharmacist, and, next door, a family of Neapolitan vaudevillians. But I remember best Signor Vitrone and his newspaper.

I would stop for hours, on the way home from school, to watch an elderly, hawklike little man in a green eyeshade operate the keyboard of the paper's single linotype with the virtuosity of a concert pianist and see a stream of printed pages flutter from the old-fashioned flatbed press. I longed to enter the printshop and learn how paper and ink were magically transformed into printed words.

On Saturday evenings and Sunday afternoons our hospitable home was usually filled with my rotund, overworked, but uncomplaining mama Teresa's innumerable relatives, and with gaggles of my darkly handsome, gregarious papa's radical friends. They came for Mama's good food and Papa's home-made wine, but also to talk about the war and Italy's unhappy role in it and to reminisce nostalgically about the homeland they had abandoned for a new and much different life in America. Hearing their reminiscences and anecdotes, I found myself dreaming of Italy much as I later learned that the Jews of the Diaspora dreamed of Palestine, the Holy Land of their origins.

At such times our home resounded to voices raised in heated arguments about the merits or demerits of the generals who were conducting Italy's war against the Austro-Hungarians—Badoglio, Cadorna, Diaz—and of the politicians responsible for it—Sonnino, Giolitti, Facta, Orlando. All the while the Victrola in the front parlor played arias by Verdi or Puccini or the wartime chorals of the *alpini,* the Italian mountain troops fighting in northern Italy. To this day those haunting melodies raise a lump in my throat.

One particular Saturday night my parents hosted a party for Signor Vitrone, a tall, lean, almost cadaverous Florentine who wore a broad-brimmed black hat and flowing red silk tie in the manner of our hero Garibaldi, and carried an ivory-handled sword cane. I recall many guests seated around the big oval table in our spacious dining room. A Tiffany lamp hung low from the ceiling and illuminated an array of antipasti: china bowls of green and black olives; platters of anchovies and tiny artichokes; salvers of thinly sliced salami, mortadella, and prosciutto; and crystal flagons of red wine. Then came spaghetti in tomato sauce, a joint of roast beef, a crisp salad of mixed greens, and other goodies, but I remember best the dessert. It was a sort of cake called a *cassata,* much like what I came to know years later as an English trifle. Its Italian version sparkled with candies that looked like silver ball bearings and glowed with candy flowers fashioned in red, white, and green, the Italian national colors.

I had already become a voracious reader of the afternoon papers Papa brought home from work every evening, and I had learned a lot about the war and the work of one Herbert Hoover. He was feeding the starving Belgian victims of Kaiser Wilhelm's spike-helmeted soldiery and as food administrator was mobilizing Americans to waste less food and produce more in Victory gardens. Sensitized by my reading, I regarded the abundance I saw on our table that memorable night as somehow immoral and certainly unpatriotic.

With the *cassata,* Papa served a bubbly Asti Spumante, of which I was allowed a scant half glass. The wine must have loosened my tongue, for in the midst of toasts to Signor Vitrone, I blurted: "Mr. Hoover wouldn't approve of all this." There was an embarrassed silence and a dark scowl from Father that held the promise of punishment, but Signor Vitrone smiled and gravely nodded approval.

"Your Francesco," he said, "is a thoughtful boy. He should become a journalist."

"Never," snapped Papa, who loved machines as a scholar loves books and who worked as a mechanic. "He will become the mechanical engineer I might have been had I been born in America." His gaze fixed on me as though to drive the words into my brain.

Our guest of honor was the last to leave that night—I fetched his hat and cane—and on the way out the door he asked my father's permission to allow me to visit him at *L'Opinione*. To my surprised delight, Papa agreed, and I was soon working happy hours after school and on Saturday afternoons as Signor Vitrone's copyboy. A kindly, learned man, he found time to drill me in Italian history, mostly the story of the Risorgimento, his country's mid-nineteenth-century struggle for unity and freedom from papal, Bourbon, and Austrian tyranny in the time of Garibaldi, Mazzini, and Cavour, respectively Stendhal's "Sword," "Soul," and "Mind" of Italy's eventual birth as a nation in 1861.

The editor also taught me Italian grammar and pronunciation. *Lingua toscana in bocca romana,* he kept reminding me, was the correct way to speak Italian, and he gradually eliminated most, though not all, of the accent I had acquired from my Sicilian parents.

My mentor also introduced me to Italian literature by obliging me to read aloud to him passages from Dante, the poet Leopardi, and the novelist Alessandro Manzoni. In fact, as a reward for my many months of unpaid services at the paper, he gave me his own well-thumbed, dog-eared copy of Manzoni's *I Promessi Sposi* (The Betrothed) prophetically inscribed: *"A Francesco, Futuro giornalista."*

Over the years, as his immigrant readers learned to speak and write English, Signor Vitrone's little paper lost circulation. By the time I was ready for high school in 1923, the paper had folded. The editor himself died in 1925—of consumption, people said—and his was the first funeral I ever attended, an impressive affair with an ornate black hearse drawn by two horses. There were many carriages and heaps of flowers, including a wreath from Papa and a small bouquet of white roses from me. To the departed editor I owed my introduction to journalism, much of my linguistic preparation, and, though unaware of it at the time, some of my liberal political views.

Although Signor Vitrone planted the seed of journalistic ambition in me, he was only partly responsible for my desire to fulfill that ambition as a foreign correspondent in Italy. My home life—language, customs, manners, even music—was quintessentially Italian. My boyhood heroes were both Italian soldiers. One was Giuseppe Garibaldi, the great liberator, whose Christ-like visage hung framed in oak over the upright ebony piano. Framed in ormolu on the piano was a sepia portrait of the other, my uncle Gennaro, my father's younger brother, a handsome man in his thirties with a high forehead, wide-set intelligent eyes, and a straight wedge of a nose upon which perched elegant pince-nez glasses. His firm mouth and clean-cut jaw suggested strength of character, a certain familial stubbornness, and a soldier's indispensable gift of command. Uncle Gennaro was a much-decorated major on the staff of Marshal Pietro Badoglio, fighting the Austro-Hungarians in 1918.

What made my soldier uncle particularly important to us all was that besides Papa, he was the sole family survivor of the earthquake which on December 28, 1908, destroyed Messina, my father's birthplace, and every living relative. At the time Gennaro was in Modena, in northern Italy, completing his studies at the Accademia Militare, his country's West Point. My parents were in Baltimore, where they landed from Sicily and resided briefly, before moving to Philadelphia. Had Papa and Mama tarried much longer in Messina, where they were married shortly before sailing, this book would never have been written.

Although Uncle Gennaro's letters were infrequent, they kept us in touch with Italy's struggle against its northern enemies, and he became my link with my ancestral homeland. He never failed to inquire after his *caro nipote Francesco,* but after the armistice and the Peace Conference at Versailles in 1919 his letters suddenly stopped. Father's letters went unanswered, and for several years we did not know whether Uncle Gennaro was dead or alive.

After 1922, and Benito Mussolini's *Marcia su Roma*—an event that upset my father and Signor Vitrone, who continued to frequent our house after his paper folded—Papa believed his monarchist brother might have come afoul of the Fascists' *squadristi.* How many these Blackshirt terror squads killed the world never learned.

In the summer of 1924, when Philly's newspapers printed the story of the murder of Giacomo Matteotti, the Socialist leader of Mussolini's opposition in the Chamber of Deputies, Papa and Signor Vitrone practically went into mourning. Both hoped, for a time, that the ensuing crisis would mean the end of Mussolini and his *fascismo,* but he survived to become absolute dictator. Both men, however, clung to their hope that Mussolini was "a passing phenomenon," as Signor Vitrone put it, "a Socialist turncoat who sooner or later will meet the end he so richly deserves." But of the two, only my father lived to see this prophecy fulfilled.

My nostalgia for Italy persisted through adolescence and my years at Southern High, South Philadelphia High School for Boys. I was by then an avid reader, not only of Philly's best dailies, the liberal morning *Record* and the conservative evening *Bulletin,* but also of national periodicals: H. L. Mencken's *American Mercury,* an exciting newsweekly called *Time,* the *Saturday Evening Post,* and *Collier's Weekly.*

In my last two years at Southern High my "required reading" included Scott, Dickens, some Shakespeare, and my favorite author, Joseph Conrad. In a manual on writing I read that to develop "style," aspiring writers should copy the work of the greats. I spent hours copying pages of *Lord Jim* on an ancient Oliver typewriter, but the only "style" I developed was the two-fingered method of typing I use to this day, sweating over every word, rarely certain whether the resultant sentences are cast in accordance with accepted rules of grammar.

I discovered Ernest Hemingway, Donn Byrne, and James Branch Cabell— "tell the rabble my name is Cabell"—whose *Jurgen* I read when I was about sixteen. I confess that I understood little of the sophisticated language he used to describe the events that occurred in Poictesme, his imaginary medieval kingdom, and I much preferred Hemingway, especially his short stories.

I should have read more, I suppose, but at Southern High I became heavily involved in sports, first as a participant, then as a reporter. During my junior and senior years, and for two years thereafter at college, I earned pocket money and considerably more covering local sports events for the *Inquirer* as a stringer paid at space rates: ten cents a printed line. My first piece for the paper occupied less than nine inches of space on a back page filled with ads, but on payday the man at the cashier's desk in the imposing Elverson Building on North Broad Street, where the *Inquirer* was published—and still is—handed me a brown envelope containing eighty-five cents. I recall a sense of accomplishment. I had actually written something, had it published, and been *paid* for it. I was euphoric. I hadn't been dreaming an impossible dream.

The *Inquirer*'s assistant sports editor assigned me to minor prizefights at a North Philly arena, downtown semipro basketball games, and prep school tennis matches out on the Main Line, where the bluebloods lived. By the end of my senior year in high school I was earning as much as six or seven dollars a week, riches enough to purchase a used Remington portable in a pawnshop, and to squire lovely Kathryn McGuigan, a blond Irish girl I had met at the New Students' League—a meeting place for aspiring poets and writers on Locust Street off Rittenhouse Square—to the movies uptown at the palatial Aldine, then Philly's finest motion-picture theater. Kay and I'd sit in the mezzanine, surreptitiously hold hands, and watch movies like *Love,* a confection more or less based on Tolstoy's *Anna Karenina* and featuring the glamorous new Swedish star Greta Garbo.

As I look back on such moments, I see that they marked the close of my formative years. I had much still to learn and unlearn, but I had arrived at the jumping-off point of my life. In the years that followed, I matriculated at college, dropped out, found my first full-time job as a reporter in the midst of the Depression, and rushed Kay into a marriage that was to endure thirty years before it dissolved in divorce. Always I had before me the dream of becoming a foreign correspondent and returning to the ancestral Italy I had come to know so intimately through my parents and Signor Vitrone.

My chance came in 1934. I had by then left Philadelphia for New York, to join the Associated Press at the fabulous salary of a hundred dollars a week. The AP had seen my work on the *Philadelphia Record* and hired me with the promise that I would eventually get to use my fluent Italian in the Rome Bureau. As the Depression deepened, however, the AP kept me in New York and reduced my salary to eighty-five dollars. By early 1934 I was ready to quit, except that Kay and I were now the parents of a blooming two-year-old, Sean, named for Sean O'Casey, one of our favorite authors, and I could not afford to lose my job.

Meanwhile, Matthew ("Matty") White, one of my few friends among the AP's top executives, resigned to join the Hearst Organization as editor in chief of Universal Service, a wire agency for morning newspapers, mainly those of the potent Hearst chain. I went to see him at his New York office, and after listening to my tale of disappointment and frustration at the AP, he promised to see what he could do about a job for me at Universal.

A few days later Matty called me to say that although there were no openings abroad, the agency needed a man in its Washington Bureau, "just the place to learn the ropes," he said, before going abroad. The job paid only eighty-five dollars a week, what I was earning at the AP. Was I interested? I certainly was, and in February 1934, shortly after my twenty-sixth birthday, I moved to Washington, for I had the solemn word of a man I knew I could trust that I would be sent to Rome or some other foreign bureau at the first opportunity.

I was soon immersed in the politics of Franklin Delano Roosevelt's New Deal, but my beat also had an international flavor, for it included the departments of State, War, and Navy as well as foreign embassies and legations. In August William Randolph Hearst—the Chief, as we Hearstlings called him— decided he wanted his own man in Spain, where the conflict of disaffected monarchists and the new Republican government was threatening civil catastrophe. At the time Universal depended on the coverage of Tomás Loayza, the bureau chief of Hearst's other and bigger agency, International News Service. Matty White recommended me for the job, and the Chief, who read every word of Universal's daily file, personally approved my appointment.

While INS served several hundred afternoon newspapers in direct competition with the AP and the United Press and therefore played by the industry rules, so to speak, Universal was the Chief's "baby," the conduit for his own anti-Russian and anti-Communist view of the world. But I did not know that then. I knew only that I was at last what I had always wanted to be—a foreign correspondent—headed for Rome, my private Jerusalem, by way of Madrid.

1

A BLOODY REVOLUTION

My wife, Kathryn, our small son, Sean, and I sailed for Spain from New York in the torrid mid-August of 1934. We traveled Hearst-style, first class aboard the Italia Lines' lovely flagship, the SS *Rex,* with two steamer trunks, three suitcases, a battered Remington portable, and a case containing books: a short history of Spain, Spanish-English and Italian-English dictionaries, and the two volumes I intended to read during the voyage. These were *Italy Under Mussolini,* by William Bolitho, and *The Fascist Dictatorship in Italy,* by the eminent Italian historian Gaetano Salvemini. Though I was physically bound for Madrid, my heart was set on Rome.

My mother had died the year before, but my aging, work-worn papa was on the pier to see us off. His was the last face I saw as the ship drew away from the dock the day I began what was to be a long, adventurous, often perilous journey through history. At parting, while he admonished me to "write often," I saw the hurt in his eyes, the lingering disappointment that I had not become the engineer he had wanted me to be. I felt a momentary twinge of regret, but waving farewell from the ship's rail, I surged with pride that I had succeeded in doing what I had set out to do.

The first day out, I received a radiogram from my editor, Matty White, informing me that my shipmates included Vittorio Emanuele Orlando, the former Italian prime minister, who had headed his country's delegation to the Peace Conference in Paris in 1919 and was one of the Big Four (the others were

Woodrow Wilson, Britain's David Lloyd George, and France's Georges Clemenceau) who had signed the Treaty of Versailles. The treaty was being denounced almost daily by Mussolini and Hitler, and Matty thought a talk with the anti-Fascist Signor Orlando might produce one of those "exclusives" which editors dearly love; they sell newspapers.

Orlando agreed to see me but refused to be formally interviewed for publication on any subject, least of all Versailles, Mussolini, or fascism. The Sicilian-born statesman was seventy-four years old, short—barely five feet two or three inches tall—with a full head of white hair cut *en brosse* and startlingly black bushy eyebrows and mustache. I invited him and his charming wife, Signora Augusta, to tea with Kathryn and me and our somewhat hyperkinetic Sean, who had just turned two.

The Orlandos were much taken with the boy, who was lively as a cricket, and when they discovered that he had not been baptized, Mrs. Orlando took charge. "He should be christened at once," she said. "I will make the arrangements."

The next day Sean was duly sprinkled with holy water by the vessel's chaplain with the Orlandos in the roles of godfather and godmother. Already registered as Sean David, my son became Sean David Orlando. His godparents presented him with a small sterling silver cup to commemorate the occasion. My family and the Orlandos were now linked by parafamilial ties sacred to all Italians but particularly so to Sicilians. To them, a *compare*—a word bastardized into *goombah* by Mario Puzo and others in popular literature—is virtually a blood relative.

During the remaining days at sea Orlando and I regularly paced the main deck every morning. However, the statesman steadfastly refused to be drawn into talking politics beyond confirming what I already knew—namely, that he had been in favor of Italian intervention in the Great War, had at first supported Mussolini, then withdrawn his support. I gathered that he had not been molested under fascism only because he no longer openly resisted Mussolini's policies. But on the fifth day, as Gibraltar loomed off our port bow, Orlando halted in his tracks, turned to me, and said: "Terrible things are happening in Europe. Democracy is in crisis on most of the Continent. It is dead in Italy, of course, and in Austria and Germany, but it is also dying in other countries. You are beginning your career at a most interesting moment and in a most fascinating place, Spain. She may be the next to fall. . . ."

The *Rex* entered the narrow strait between Europe and Africa and dropped anchor in the cobalt blue waters of the Bay of Gibraltar. The great rock, glowing like burnished bronze in the afternoon sun, was a magnificent sight, a formidable symbol of British imperial power.

Of the liner's several hundred passengers, fewer than twenty of us disembarked at Gib and were taken ashore at La Línea by a tender. As we landed, the *Rex*'s horn thundered a hoarse farewell, and the ship resumed course for Genoa, her twin screws churning a wide creamy wake.

Awaiting us on the quay was a man from Cook's, the travel agency which

tion. There, waiting on the platform, was another man from Cook's,
o greeted us effusively and led us and our baggage to a service bus from
Ritz, then, as now, one of the world's truly great hotels. At the hotel
assistant manager in tailcoat and striped trousers ushered us into what he
ed a small suite but what to Kathryn and me, children of working-class
ents, represented luxury beyond anything we had ever known, in fact
seen only in movies. Looking back, I am amazed at how easily we
usted.

I am even more astonished at how effortlessly I adapted to living and
king in a foreign capital. Within a fortnight, while we were still residing
he Ritz, I was speaking Spanish fluently, if not always grammatically, and
ing as much at home in Madrid as though I had been born there. I even
ed a piece or two that sounded as though I really knew what was happen-
in the country's capital.

This, however, was due less to my own reportorial skills than to the
erous help of others, mainly Tomás Loayza, the longtime INS correspon-
, whose office I shared on the ninth floor of the Palacio de la Prensa in
Plaza del Callao. Although I had read the current Universal file before
ing Washington, my ignorance of contemporary Spanish politics was abys-

Loayza was a Peruvian of Spanish-Indian parentage, a small, slender,
le-looking man in his mid-thirties with straight, jet black hair, hooded
, a soft voice, and courtly manners. The day following our arrival, he came
e hotel with an armful of roses for Kay, a street map of Madrid for me,
a rubber toro for *el niño*. Although unmarried, he loved children and
yed demonstrating to Sean the rudiments of the corrida with the toy bull,
paper cocktail napkin, and a toothpick. The boy was round-eyed with
der.

Loayza had many friends among the politicians of the various parties
sented in the Cortes, the Spanish parliament, and had built up a network
ormants not only in the capital but in key cities throughout the country.
new more about what was going on in Spain than any other foreign
paperman in town with the possible exception of his close friend and
v bachelor Henry Buckley, the wispy, ever-smiling Englishman who rep-
ted Reuters.

uring long sessions at the office or over drinks at Chicote's bar on the
Vía—a favorite haunt of journalists, politicians, bullfighters, and Ma-
better class of whores—Loayza schooled me in the complexities of
sh history and politics. Buckley often joined us, and between them they
ted a Spain with a glorious past, a turbulent present, and an uncertain
.

told them that I had met Orlando aboard the *Rex* and that he had
cted Spain might be the next European democracy to succumb to fascism.
wo friends nodded agreement, and Loayza said, "He was right. It is only
ter of time. . . ."

the Hearst Organization had hired to look after us. He h
the Rock Hotel, Gib's finest, and made reservations on
departing the next day from La Línea, on the internatic
Spain and British Gibraltar.

"First class all the way, señor," he said. "Those were
New York. In Madrid you'll be staying at the Ritz."

William Randolph Hearst, I decided, was a prince
was a view of the Chief that altered in time, alas, but (
late August 1934 when I stepped on Spanish soil, I cor
with gratitude.

The man from Cook's took us by taxi to the Rock
the night, and the next day saw us safely aboard the M
full of solicitude and advice.

"The train's departure may be delayed," he said. "I
and the bullfights start on time. By the way, don't dri
Order Agua Solaris from your conductor. And don't
pesetas [about two dollars] when you arrive in Mac
. . ." And he was gone.

I was excited at the prospect of working in Spair
through history like the blast of a trumpet and cor
hidalgos, heroic conquistadors, fierce Moors, fiery Gy
rial courts, and the clamor of battle. What American
the story of the Spanish Armada, of galleons sailin
treasures of the Indies, and the voyages of Columbu

But the Madrid assignment had come so suddenl
I had not had time to prepare myself and my family f
country. I knew some Spanish history, but nothing
drink. I wondered about housing and worried con
attention for my wife and son.

Nothing had prepared me for the Spain Kay and
ment window as the Madrid Express rocked and rolle
sooty journey across Andalusia, first through pleasar
trees, then steadily upward over spectacularly barrei
mountain country. What we saw was a Spain of poo
peasants working an arid soil; black-robed housew
wash on the rocky banks of feeble streams; gaunt wc
overalls and rope-soled *zapatas;* and shawled womei
in string-tied bundles or wicker baskets. And every
shiny, black patent-leather tricorne hats, armed w
arrogant.

The train arrived in the yards outside Madrid in
day. There was a long wait, a sort of quarantine peri
the south was permitted to enter the vast, smoke

My main concern during our stay at the Ritz was to find decently furnished, affordable living quarters. The few rentable apartments listed in the newspapers turned out to be either too large and expensive or airless, poorly equipped walk-up flats in the maze of narrow streets that rambled in all directions from Plaza Mayor, the heart of Old Madrid. I had begun to despair of making a home for ourselves when we met Margaret Palmer at a cocktail party at the American Embassy.

A small lady, fiftyish and the epitome of competence, Miss Palmer had lived many years in Madrid and knew everybody worth knowing. She apparently earned a living in Spanish antiques and for a modest fee finding and/or decorating apartments for English and American newcomers to the capital.

Two weeks to the day after our arrival in Madrid, Miss Palmer installed us in charming rooftop quarters which she herself had decorated. The flat was in a fine old five-story house at 15 Calle de Moreto, a quiet street behind the Prado Museum, with a large terrace and a lift that really worked. Its most attractive feature, however, proved to be Carmen Nuñoz, the cook who came with it.

Carmen was an Andalusian from Badajoz and physically straight out of Bizet, a truly beautiful women in her early thirties with lustrous black hair, luminous coal black eyes, and a luscious figure. Moreover, she was no mere *cocinera,* it turned out, but an invaluable source of information, for she had previously served in the household of the socialist leader and former premier Manuel Azaña. Politically she was an ardent socialist and trade unionist, and professionally she was an artist; she could make the best flan in all Spain, and her paella à la valenciana was a gastronomic work of art.

Carmen spent so much time looking after Sean that I soon found it necessary to hire a maid to help with the housework. Consuelo Menéndez was a husky, spinsterish blond woman in her mid-forties, a pious Madrileña with strong monarchist leanings. She rose daily before dawn to attend mass at a nearby church whose bells sounded the hours and the half hours. During most of her lifetime, according to her references, Consuelo had been a maid in the homes of aristocrats, and when socialist Carmen twitted her about her piety, she hotly responded that she prayed daily for the restoration of King Alfonso XIII to the Spanish throne.

Both were devoted to their pretty, physically fragile, and obviously inexperienced American señora, taught her "kitchen Spanish," and one or the other—usually the redoubtable Consuelo—always accompanied her to the hairdresser at the Ritz, the dressmaker in the Calle de Alcalá, or on afternoon walks with Sean in the Parque del Retiro.

Meanwhile, we cultivated the friendship of American and English colleagues, among them Rex ("Red") Smith and Eddie Knoblaugh, of the AP; Jaime Oldfield of the *London Daily Express,* and Jay Allen, of the *Chicago Daily News.* Kay and I often went on picnics with them and their wives in the nearby Guadaramas, dined out at places like Botín's—renowned for crispy roast suckling pig—or frequented all-night joints to hear flamenco and watch the dancing of that fiery Gypsy Miguel de Molinas.

My newspaper friends helped me orient myself to my new environment with the easy camaraderie and generosity that characterized journalism before television turned it into Show Business. Particularly helpful was Red Smith, of the AP, whose nickname, however, belied his politics. Most of his friends were right-wing politicians whom he and his wife, the stately Alice, often entertained at home.

It was at dinner at the Smiths one evening early in September 1934 that I met José Antonio Primo de Rivera, *El Jefe* (The Chief) of the Falange, the nascent Spanish Fascist party. Tall, thirtyish, unmarried, and almost prettily handsome with the delicate features of an aristocrat, José Antonio was the son of the late General Miguel Primo de Rivera, Marqués de Estella, who had staged a military coup in 1923 and ruled Spain as a dictator during the reign of Alfonso XIII. The king liked to introduce General Primo as "my Mussolini," but by associating himself with the overthrow of parliamentary government and linking his fortunes to Primo's dictatorship, the Bourbon monarch jeopardized his throne.

It was abundantly evident that José Antonio shared his father's belief in authoritarian rule. He expressed genuine admiration for Mussolini and Hitler, both of whom he had visited. "But neither leader," he said, "gave me much encouragement. Il Duce told me he saw no immediate hope for fascism in Spain, and der Führer indicated he was far too preoccupied with internal affairs to become involved in Spain."

Possibly because he frequently denounced in fervent tones the sad lot of Spain's *campesinos,* peasants who earned one peseta for a day's labor (about twenty-four cents in American money), José Antonio had a following large enough to win him a seat in parliament. This despite the fact that in Madrid proper his Falange Española numbered no more than a thousand members. Two years later his Fascist views placed him before a Republican (Loyalist) firing squad, and he was remembered as an early martyr to fascism's cause.

No more successful in organizing a Fascist movement was José Antonio's contemporary, Ramón Serrano Súñer, brother-in-law of General Francisco Franco. Serrano was a small, smiling, slender man with a black mustache who founded the Catholic youth group known as JAP, Juventud Acción Popular (Young People's Action party). His youngsters wore khaki breeches and leggings and adopted a Spanish version of the Italian Fascist salute, the right arm extended horizontally across the chest. But Serrano Súñer's efforts to stage impressive mass rallies invariably fizzled.

There were far more serious threats to the stability of the Second Republic. The shrewd, politically corrupt Alejandro Lerroux was maneuvering to supplant the republic with a regime more or less exactly like the monarchy but without a king. And José María Gil Robles, leader of the right-wing Catholic Action party, whom I succeeded in interviewing, told me that he wanted to set up "a corporate state on Austrian lines," actually a sort of clerical fascism. From all this, oddly enough, the army stood aloof.

My closest friend among the members of the Anglo-American press corps was Jay Allen of the *Chicago Daily News.* Scholarly, a lively conversationalist, and by far the most liberal of the lot politically, Jay and I spent hours discussing developments, comparing bits of news we had picked up here and there, and checking them with our various sources. Jay clearly saw the mission of the Spanish masses as "the conquest of poverty, disease, ignorance and social inequality." It was Jay Allen—a big, handsome, baby-faced man with brown hair whom women adored—who alerted me to the probability that Spain was on the verge of an upheaval of "major proportions, a great working-class uprising to prevent their country from going the way of Italy, Germany, and Austria.

"But I doubt they'll succeed," Jay prophesied one evening in late September. "The forces lined up against them—church, landowners, and eventually the army—are far too powerful."

At the beginning of October the moderate government of Premier Ricardo Samper fell on a vote of no confidence in parliament. It was replaced by a conservative regime led by Lerroux and Gil Robles, who moved to isolate the Socialists from power. The revolution began promptly at midnight on October 4, 1934.

But for Carmen, our cook, I would have missed the opening scene of the drama. I had dinner at home that evening, and while serving coffee, Carmen said she thought I had better hurry back to the office. Knowing her sources of information—the servants in the household of Señor Azaña—I listened attentively.

"A general strike has been called," she said sotto voce. "It will begin at midnight, and when it starts, so will the revolution." There was fire in her luminous black eyes. But how, I asked, would I know that the *huelga general* had actually started? "Watch the taxis in the Plaza del Callao," she said. "When they leave, it has begun."

I glanced at my watch. It was eleven-fifteen—even foreign residents dined late in Madrid, rarely before ten o'clock. If I hurried, I could just make it to my office. There were always several taxis in the Plaza del Callao waiting for customers when the nearby cinemas let out after the first show at one o'clock in the morning.

I flagged down a cab on the Castellana, reached the office at eleven forty-five, and telephoned Loayza. He wasn't at home, but the servant who answered the phone said he had left word that he was on his way to the Ministry of the Interior. I looked out the window at the plaza below. Half a dozen cabbies in their long gray denim dusters and visored caps were clustered about a man in civvies who was apparently giving them instructions.

At eleven fifty-five I placed a call to Hearst European headquarters in London, and when the night man came on, I told him to hold the line for possibly important news. Phone in hand, I returned to the window and shouted down to one of the cabbies: *"Qué pasa?"*

"Huelga general," he yelled back.

On the stroke of midnight the cabbies started their engines and drove off at high speed. The man in London was growing impatient and wanted to know what was happening. I was tempted to tell him to cable a flash to New York that a general strike was in progress, but the Hearst agencies' motto was: Get It First—but First Get It Right. I knew I probably had a "first" but wasn't certain it was altogether "right." I limited myself to relating what I had heard and seen and cautioned the London man to await confirmation. It came while he was still on the line.

Loayza burst into the room, breathless. Interior Minister Salazar Alonso had just told reporters that a general strike had been called by the UGT—Union General de Trabajadores—whose leader, Francisco Largo Caballero, was also secretary of the Socialist party and was known as the "Lenin of Spain."

"This is the real thing," I told London. "The elements of the left—anarchists, syndicalists, Socialists, Communists—fear that Gil Robles and his allies of the right mean to overthrow the republic and establish a Fascist or semi-Fascist dictatorship of some kind. There will be fighting."

I called home. Carmen answered the phone. I told her to tell the señora that I might not be back for a few days, and she said not to worry. There was plenty of food in the house, Carmen said, confiding that she had stocked the family larder with canned milk for the *niño* along with garbanzos, rice, sausages, and canned vegetables.

"We had to be prepared," she said apologetically, "because there will certainly be martial law."

In the early-morning hours of Friday, October 5, Loayza and I settled down to await developments—he in a huge, well-worn leather armchair, and I on a spavined mohair sofa that he had purchased secondhand years before for just such emergencies. By daybreak Madrid was usually alive with workers on their way to their jobs. Now the streets were deserted, the shops were shuttered, and all traffic had stopped. Madrid had ceased to function.

Reporters who hurried back to the office of Salazar Alonso found the minister solemnly dotting a huge wall map of Spain with colored pins—one color for deployments of the Civil Guard, other colors for the tough Assault Guards, aviation squadrons, and cavalry, infantry, and artillery units. His propaganda line was that there were "one million armed Socialists ready to bring down the national government and establish a Communist state." In the northern province of Asturias, he said, police had raided a secret cache of arms and discovered "a plot to overthrow the republic."

Subsequent events proved the rebels had at most a few hundred rifles and some machine guns. The troops quartered in any provincial city had more arms among them than all the Socialists in Spain. Both sides had plenty of handguns because Spain manufactured them in great numbers. Virtually every young Spanish male owned a pistol or a revolver. Leftists among the miners of Asturias, however, had tons of dynamite hidden away and knew how to use it.

But there was no doubt where the power lay. Lerroux had at his disposal the army, 120,000 strong including General Francisco Franco's Foreign Legion and its Moors, plus 30,000 hard-boiled Civil Guards, some 15,000 Assault Guards armed with machine guns and armored cars, 10,000 regular police, and about 12,000 *carabineros,* the Customs Guards.

There was more than a touch of naiveté in the Socialists' dream of creating a stable, social democratic Spain. They honestly believed that if they took to the streets en masse in classic revolutionary style, nothing could stop them. They were encouraged in this folly by the Socialist press and Largo Caballero, the stubby, idealistic boss of the UGT. At sixty-five Largo obviously had gone soft in the head.

A few pages are woefully inadequate to describe Spain's October Revolution of 1934. It was one of the great working-class uprisings in modern history, a desperate attempt by an ill-armed, poorly led, disorganized proletariat to preserve their democratic republic. And it led to the infinitely bloodier Civil War of 1936 to 1939, the dress rehearsal for World War II.

Someday, perhaps, a scholar will give the uprising of October 1934 the attention it deserves. Here I can only relate what I experienced while Spaniard fought Spaniard during the early autumn of the year that marked the beginning of my career overseas.

The fighting was fairly general throughout Spain, but centered mainly in Barcelona, Madrid, and Oviedo, capital of the mining province of Asturias. For the most part, with the exception of the Asturian miners, the revolutionaries fought with rifles, revolvers, a few machine guns, and some light cannon. They might as well have been armed with scythes and pitchforks.

In Madrid, Loayza and I heard the first shots, coming from the direction of the populous Puerta del Sol, shortly after the general strike started. Then a heavy, ominous silence descended upon the city, broken from time to time only by the ringing of one or the other of our two office telephones.

The first call, only minutes after midnight, was from the INS correspondent in Barcelona. He said the Generalitat, the headquarters of the provincial government, was under attack by the army and Civil Guards, but he was cut off before he could give further details. Loayza quickly tuned our office receiver to Radio Barcelona. The station was transmitting "El Segadors," the stirring Catalan nationalist hymn, plus occasional scattered incomplete news bulletins. Gradually, however, we managed to piece together the rather complicated story of what was happening.

In the sense that the first serious fighting occurred there, the revolution actually began in Barcelona, hotbed of anarchist syndicalism and capital of autonomous Catalonia. The region's government, headed by Luis Companys, leader of the leftist Liberal party, included Republicans and right-wing nationalists. It was an unstable combination at best, and some of its people were more interested in outright Catalonian independence than in preserving the republic.

Acting on the advice of his minister of the interior, Companys proclaimed the independence of Catalonia within a federalized Spain and called on the populace to rise against the central government in Madrid. When the regional army commander, himself a Catalan, declared that he was "for Spain," Companys's defeat was assured. On October 7, under army arrest, he appealed to his followers to lay down their arms. The revolution was over in Barcelona.

The fighting in Madrid was easily reported, for much of it took place right under our office windows. From the huge oval *ventana* of our bureau on the ninth floor of the Palacio de la Prensa, Loayza and I watched rebel forces being shot down by Civil Guards and Guardias d'Assalto, the tough Assault Guards. It was the first time I had ever witnessed violent death, or heard the soul-chilling whistle of bullets, the lethal chatter of machine guns, and the sharp, dry crack of bursting grenades.

At one point a detachment of Assault Guards entered our building, then one of Madrid's tallest, thirteen floors. They took up positions on our roof and at the windows of the upper stories in order to fire down on rebels occupying rooftops lower down. Our lights went out, and we worked by shielded candle-light. Snipers across the plaza from us shot out our window, and for protection Loayza and I, with the help of an office boy, dragged a heavy oaken bookcase across the open space to form a barricade.

One of the insurgents' principal objectives was the American-owned Telefónica, the tall, handsome building that housed the main exchange and offices of the International Telephone and Telegraph Company. The place was well guarded, but the attackers managed to come close enough to spray it with machine-gun fire before they were beaten off with some casualties. Amazingly, the telephone system, installed during the dictatorship of Primo de Rivera, continued to function efficiently throughout the uprising. Neither Loayza nor I had any difficulty reaching London or Paris periodically to dictate dispatches for relay to New York. Either capital could be summoned in five minutes or less, and I was able to keep in close touch with my family.

I had warned Kathryn to remain indoors when the shooting started, but overcome with curiosity, she went out on the terrace to "have a look." What she saw sent her scurrying back inside: On the rooftop opposite our house a servant was felled by a random bullet while taking in laundry that she had set out to dry in the warm early October sun. Sean was frightened by the noise far more than was evident at the time.

Fortunately, however, apart from the incident in the Calle de Moreto, neither Kathryn nor the boy saw any of the more brutal consequences of the fighting. They remained indoors, well cared for by Carmen and Consuelo. The cook, at considerable risk to herself while the city remained under martial law, foraged for food when necessary, and both she and the maid made sure that mother and son were safely tucked into their beds at night.

Loayza, who lived near the office and knew alleyways along which he could walk in comparative safety, occasionally went home to his own bed. I slept on the old sofa in the office and lived mostly on sandwiches, black coffee, and strong Spanish cigarettes brought to me by an obliging waiter from the nearby

Hotel Florida. He also provided me with towels, soap, and clean underwear purchased from someone living in his hotel. Luckily our office had its own lavatory.

On the fourth day the shooting suddenly stopped. The buses started running along the Gran Vía, and in our building the lights went on again and elevator service resumed. In the late forenoon of the lull I seriously considered hopping a bus and going home to look in on the family. One bus route would take me from the Plaza del Callao to the Prado, a short walk from the house. I could be home in fifteen minutes, and I was preparing to leave when there was a loud knocking at our office door as though someone were trying to kick it down. I flung the door open, and there stood Kathryn, her arms wrapped around a large, lidded copper pot.

I was furious, but before I could say a word, Kay, smiling sweetly, pushed past me with an impertinent toss of her head, deposited the pot on my desk, and took off the lid, filling the room with the sweet-sour aroma of my favorite food: frankfurters and sauerkraut. It was a gutsy thing to have done, and I said so as a prelude to a proper scolding, but Kay anticipated me.

"It was easy, really," she said, "and not at all dangerous. Carmen said it would be all right. She put me on the bus and told the driver to be sure to let me off at the Plaza del Callao. The driver was very nice. He took no fares from anyone. 'Free rides and free bullets for everybody today,' he said."

Loayza produced plates, knives and forks, and drinking glasses from a filing cabinet and sent the office boy across to the Florida for a bottle of Marqués de Riscal. We had a feast. I took Kathryn home, spent an hour or two playing with Sean, and returned to the office before sundown. The fighting resumed at nightfall.

In view of my upbringing, my sympathies were entirely with the rebels. I knew there were workers in Madrid, married men with families, earning a mere five pesetas—one silver duro—per day, little more than a dollar in American currency. Such families thought it quite a treat if they saw meat on their tables once a week.

An American executive at the Telefónica did not share my views. While helping me put an urgent call through to London one evening, he gratuitously informed me that he hoped Premier Lerroux would "give those Reds a good kick in the ass and put an end to their revolutionary nonsense." I am ashamed to say that I didn't argue with him. It was nearly four o'clock in the morning, and I needed that connection with London.

The bloodiest fighting took place in northwestern Spain, in Asturias. The mines there had traditionally been unsafe, the working conditions inhumane. The republic had won the loyalty of the miners—Communists in the main, with a sprinkling of anarchists—by raising pay and enforcing new safety measures and work rules. The miners feared Lerroux's new government would roll back these gains.

At first events went the miners' way. Fighting mostly with dynamite, by October 5 they had captured Oviedo, the port of Gijón, Mieres, and Trubia with its arms factory. Revolutionary committees were established to draft soldiers for the "Red Army," maintain order, and manage civil services. In the process the rebels committed a number of outrages. Church buildings were attacked, and several priests shot. At a town called Samè, seventy government soldiers were summarily shot after they had surrendered.

Madrid called on General Franco's Moroccan Tercio, the Foreign Legion, to quash the uprising. The rebels were first softened up with naval shelling and aerial bombing. Then the crack troops of the Tercio marched on Oviedo, Gijón, and the other rebel strongholds. By October 18 the rebellion was finished. Most of the deaths and injuries occurred after that date, as the Tercio drove home its victory by terror.

Late one afternoon, shortly after the end of hostilities, I was at home, having tea and chatting with Kathryn about family matters, when the doorbell rang. Consuelo answered the ring and came hurrying into the living room in a high state of excitement, eyes wide with fear.

"There are two men to see you, señor," she said. "They say they are from the Foreign Office, but I think they are policemen."

Kathryn paled. Frankly I was a little nervous myself. Loayza had just told me about his friend Luis Sirval, murdered in prison for writing about the atrocities in Asturias.

At the door two burly individuals in civilian dress, hatted and stony-faced, sternly informed me that I was under arrest and that I was to come with them, please. They produced very official-looking documents certifying their identities as security officers, and they made it plain that I was to go with them or be taken by force.

I told Kathryn, who had followed me to the door, to telephone the embassy at once, assured her it was probably only a routine check of correspondents, and said I would phone her as soon as I could.

A big seven-passenger car was at the curb, and I was relieved to see it already contained two friends: Rex Smith and Jay Allen. Knowing both to be incurable practical jokers, I immediately thought that this was another of their outrageous pranks. Once they had hired a shapely minor actress, one of the regulars at Chicote's bar, to present herself at the apartment and, in Kathryn's presence, pretend that I had engaged her as my secretary. I doubt that my wife ever really believed their subsequent explanation.

"Okay, you guys," I said, "fun's fun, but this is going a little too far. "

I saw at once by their expressions that this was no joke, and I got into the back seat with them. Both were as puzzled as I about what was afoot.

We drove for at least an hour to a grim-looking military barracks on the northern outskirts of the city and were led into a room crowded with about twenty other English and American correspondents, most of whom we knew. The air was close with the stink of sweat, fear, and tobacco smoke.

Presently a general in full uniform entered and sat behind a desk at the far end of the room. His mane of white hair and great white beard instantly identified him for Jay Allen.

"General Miguel Cabanellas," he whispered. "First-class Fascist prick."

In the expectant silence, sounds reached us from a distant part of the stone-walled barracks, probably its inner courtyard. They were the sounds men make when being roughly handled: groans; sharp cries of pain; unintelligible words of protest. Clearly prisoners were being beaten.

Then again silence. Cabanellas rose, hooked his thumbs into his wide black leather belt, and made a brief speech. He accused us of having "dishonored" the name of Spain in our dispatches during the "recent troubles." He said we had "grossly exaggerated" the strength of the rebellion against the authority of the central government and had given the impression abroad that Spain was "a land of murderers and cutthroats." He said he was recommending to the Foreign Office that our visas be revoked and that all of us be expelled.

With that the general turned on his heel and strode out of the room, leaving a civilian, Communications Minister Manuel Jalón, to deal with us as we began shouting protests and questions. Jalón raised his hands for silence and reiterated much of what the general had said, adding that our reporting had been "slanderous." Our accounts of the fighting, he said, had been "false and libelous to the honor of the nation, veritable journalistic atrocities." The minister repeated the general's expulsion threat and left in a chorus of angry shouts. Armed guards were posted at the doors.

"Bullshit," muttered Jay Allen, whom God had made a man and nature a reporter. "They won't expel us. They're just trying to scare us."

At that moment the room echoed to the distant sounds of a volley of rifle fire.

"Holy God!" someone gasped. "Firing squad!"

"Jay," I said, "if they *are* trying to scare us, they're doing a fine job as far as I'm concerned."

"Don't worry," Jay replied. "They'll hold us as long as they dare, then send us home. They've heard from our embassies by now. We'll be out of here soon enough."

Actually we were not released for several hours. Permission to telephone our homes was denied. We were allowed to use a smelly adjacent pissoir, and there was water in a filthy drinking fountain in a corner; but few of us dared do more than wet out lips.

It was nearly five o'clock in the morning before the two burly cops who had come to fetch me signaled me and my two companions to follow them outside. They drove us home in silence, I dózed most of the way, too weary to talk, emotionally and mentally exhausted by the idiotic episode.

A red-eyed Kathryn and the servants were waiting up for me. I gave them a lighthearted account of what had happened over an early breakfast of fresh fruit, hot rolls, and Carmen's café con leche.

None of us was expelled, and we later learned that the dispatches which had agitated the military had been written by a small horde of "distinguished" correspondents from abroad who had descended on Madrid when the rebellion erupted on October 4. In their accounts the uprising became a sort of reenactment of the French Revolution with the Puerta del Sol awash in the blood of innocents and rebel corpses strewing the streets.

On the night of the police roundup, however, the visiting prima donnas were in the south of France to cover a potentially far more important story: the assassination in Marseilles of Jean-Louis Barthou, the French foreign minister, and his royal guest, King Alexander of Yugoslavia. Barthou was one of the few European statesmen who were saying publicly that Adolf Hitler was not the "armed watchman" against communism that he professed to be but "an ambitious adventurer who dreamed of smashing the French and British Empires and leading Germany to world domination." He had invited Alexander to come to France to discuss a pact of mutual assistance against foreseeable Nazi aggression.

On October 10 Loayza and I, and most other resident Madrid correspondents, received urgent cables from our respective headquarters ordering that coverage of the rebellion in Spain—and its aftermath of outrages by both sides—be held to a minimum. The Spanish drama and its climactic episodes in remote Asturias were thus pushed off the front pages, and the full story of what was a seminal event of the Civil War that split the world into sharply divided democratic and Fascist halves went largely untold.

Meanwhile, General Franco, riding high as the government's instrument of vengeance against the "Red" revolutionaries, cut correspondents' telephone communications with the outside world and clamped a severe censorship on all cables. A special Foreign Press Committee was established to control the contents of our dispatches, which, when they moved at all, were reduced to unprintable gibberish.

For a time it looked as though the republic would be jettisoned in favor of a military dictatorship. But help for Spanish democracy came from an unexpected quarter. Gil Robles, who had consolidated all right-wing elements into a powerful party, the Confederación Española Derechas Autónomas (Autonomous Confederation of Spanish Rightists), or the CEDA, summoned the foreign press and made a startlingly welcome declaration.

"There will be no dictatorship in Spain!" he said. "We clericals will not permit the overthrow of the parliamentary regime!"

The army's leaders, including Franco, also about-faced and came out on the side of democracy, for the generals were aware now, after all the bloodshed, that their totalitarian views were not shared by their regular troops, whose ranks were drawn from the country's peasants and workers. In order to "pacify" the miners of Asturias, the generals had been obliged to bring in the Moors and the mercenaries of the Foreign Legion. In the circumstances, the army's commanders decided, it would have been unwise to attempt a military coup d'état.

Meanwhile, the quasi-African heat of summer gave way to the cold winds and frequent rain showers of November and December. Philip II, who was responsible for the Armada, was equally responsible for Madrid; he chose as bleak and monotonous a spot as could be found in all Spain, and as winter set in, the capital became a dreary place. In August and September we had often sat in the dappled shade of aromatic acacia trees on the sidewalk terraces of the cafés along the Gran Vía and the Castellana, sipped manzanilla, and nibbled a tapa or two of boiled shrimp, snow-cured mountain ham, or deep-fried slivers of fish. Now café life moved indoors and thereby lost much of its charm.

Nevertheless, crowds gathered as before in the Puerta del Sol, the throbbing heart of the city. In the early winter of 1934 Madrid was a city of one million inhabitants, and for the overwhelming majority of its citizens poverty was a way of life. Its biggest factory employed only a few hundred workers, and unemployment was visibly high and apparently incurable, for there were almost no industries. It was a city of whores, pimps, and bureaucrats, an unproductive capital whose main employer was the government.

With little to do at the office, I had time to take Kathryn to the Prado, the rose-colored palace a short downhill walk from our home. We spent many happy mornings marveling at the works of El Greco, Murillo, and Velázquez in the museum's collection but would remember best Goya's famous pair, *La Maja Vestida* and *La Maja Desnuda,* the clothed and unclothed portraits of the duchess of Alba, reputedly the artist's mistress.

In mid-December a telephone call from William Hillman, Universal's chief European correspondent, informed me that I was being assigned to his staff in London.

"You did well in Madrid," Hillman said, "but Matty White wants you here for a while before you go on to Rome. I don't know when that will be, but try to get here before the end of the year or as soon after Christmas as you can."

The Christmas Eve dinner that Carmen prepared was more like a wake than a festive occasion. There was no Christmas tree for Sean, but Loayza, our only guest on that cheerless evening, brought him a present, a fine set of red and green building blocks made of pressed Spanish cork.

We left for London via Paris a few days after Christmas. Loayza, Carmen, and Consuelo were at Norte Station to see us off, and leaving them was much like saying good-bye to close relatives. In only four months we had become a family. Kathryn was as tearful as the servants, and it was not until early the next day, when we glimpsed the rolling surf of the Bay of Biscay beyond San Sebastián, that our spirits rose.

2

FLEET STREET DAYS

There was no "man from Cook's" waiting for us on the platform at Victoria Station when we arrived in the late afternoon of December 31 approximately seven hours before the dawn of the year 1935. We were on our own now, and I confidently directed the cabby to take us to the Grosvenor, for I had heard Bill Hillman say it was "one of London's finest hotels."

Presently we found ourselves in a huge double room with bath. It was spotlessly clean and smelled of lavender and freshly laundered linen, but was as cold as an igloo and gloomy with heavy drapes and massive furniture, a far cry from the elegant "small suite" in Madrid's Ritz.

A call bell, however, brought Agnes, an elderly maid in a gray dress and starched white apron, and quick relief from the shivery unhappiness of our new surroundings. With the skill born of long practice, she soon had a coal fire going in the grate and a cot brought in for the "nipper." Meanwhile, she "organized" tea for Kathryn and me and hot milk for the boy, with whom she had instantly established cordial relations. His big eyes never left her as she carefully laid the coals with a huge brass tongs.

Later, when Sean had been put to bed after dinner, Agnes volunteered to "look in on the lad" while we went out. "You'll be wanting to see the New Year in with the crowds in Piccadilly Circus," she said. "It's a tradition, you know, and you do look a lonely pair, you do."

The press of Londoners in Piccadilly Circus reminded us of Times Square on New Year's Eve, and we greeted 1935 standing under a huge clock over a sign that advertised a nostrum called BILE BEANS. At the magic hour a great cheer went up, and the crowd started singing "Auld Lang Syne." We joined in heartily, kissed, and swore eternal love, and hurried back to the hotel to be with our son. I managed to find a cab on the edge of the crowd in Regent Street, and we were back at the Grosvenor in a matter of minutes. Sean never stirred when we entered.

On a small table beside the glowing coals in the grate we found an ice bucket containing a bottle of Lanson Brut, 1928, "Compliments of the Management." We toasted each other, fantasized hopefully about what the New Year might bring, heard Big Ben sound the first hour of the new day, and went to bed. . . .

When I reported for work at Universal's Fleet Street offices in Chronicle House two days later, I discovered we were staying at the wrong hotel. Bill Hillman had meant the Grosvenor House in Mayfair, not the Grosvenor in Buckingham Palace Road. He suggested we move at once, but I declined. The more luxurious hostelry might have central heating, but not an Agnes.

Shortly thereafter we moved into a furnished flat on the top floor of a three-story brownstone walk-up in the Tanza Road at the southern edge of Hampstead Heath, a middle-class neighborhood of civil servants, clerks, and professional people, mostly journalists. It was a shabby, musty place, meagerly warmed by smoky coal fires in only two of the apartment's five rooms, a smallish "master bedroom" and a chintzy, cramped "sitting room." A temperamental engine misnamed a geyser (pronounced GHEE-zer) provided a lukewarm trickle of water for baths and other household uses when it was fed the requisite number of two-shilling coins, and its appetite for those precious two-bob pieces was voracious.

After the bracing mountain air and abundant sunshine of Madrid sooty old London seemed unfit for human habitation. Hundreds of thousands of chimney pots belched smoke from as many coal fires, producing the dense fogs, greasy yellow billows of acrid mist, which blinded the entire city for days. One night in January, awakened by the smell and sting of smoke entering our bedroom through a partially opened window, we thought the house was on fire. We bundled Sean in a blanket and rushed downstairs only to find we were merely experiencing our first pea-souper. The crotchety landlady, roused by our cries of "fire," was not amused.

Mother and son periodically came down with heavy colds during the winter months, and in late February the three of us were abed simultaneously with influenza. I don't know how we would have managed without Mrs. Davidson, our Cockney servant, a work-bent widow who had lost her husband in the Great War. She shopped for food, cooked, did the housework, and played nurse for a weekly stipend of two pounds and ten shillings, somewhat less than twelve dollars in American money. It was a time of severe unemployment and widespread distress, and we felt guilty about paying Mrs. Davidson so little. But it was all we could afford, and English friends later assured us we had "overpaid" her; the "going rate" for domestics, they said, was only one pound ten, a little more than six dollars.

Daily except Sunday, my day off, my workday began at three o'clock and ended at midnight, when the last bus left for Hampstead from Ludgate Circus, a short walk from the Hearst Fleet Street offices. My work entailed culling the British press for news and editorial opinion and compressing into cablese the stories telephoned into the London Bureau by Universal's Continental correspondents, editing and rewriting them if necessary before relaying them to New York by wire.

I was definitely low man on the four-man staff of bureau chief William Hillman, a secretive man who had Hearst's ear and a sly way of letting me know that he personally held my future in his pudgy, well-manicured hands. He rarely sent me out on a story and kept me at much the same work I had done in New York in my AP days. There was a touch of sadism in Hillman's makeup that belied his affable manner, but I was determined not to give him cause for a negative report on my performance and did whatever was asked of me uncomplainingly, with such skill and diligence as I possessed. The job and the working hours it demanded, however, seemed to me to have been designed by Hillman to discourage me from continuing with my career.

I was wrong, of course. Actually I was dealing at last entirely with foreign news. I was learning what was happening in the key capitals of the time— London, Berlin, Rome, Moscow, Geneva—and acquiring some knowledge of the complex political landscape of a restive Europe. By the end of March it was evident even to a neophyte like myself that Nazi Germany represented a threat to Western democracy and that Britain, at least, was either unable or unwilling to deal with it.

The barbarities of the Nazi regime—its suppression of political parties and trade unions, its abrogation of free speech and assembly, its systematic persecution of the Jews—were being fully documented in the world press, including Britain's, and in the dispatches from William L. Shirer, our correspondent in Berlin. Yet the belief persisted in London that Germany represented a bulwark against communism, hence must be treated with diplomatic kid gloves, even sympathy.

Nazi sympathizers were seeded like raisins in a fruitcake throughout the British aristocracy. They included even a member of the royal family, the popular Edward Prince of Wales, already deeply involved in his historic romance with the acidulous Wallis Warfield Simpson. And Hitler's apologists numbered several prominent British journalists, among them G. Ward Price, of the *London Daily Mail.*

More than anyone else, perhaps, the man who personified the Britain of those days was Stanley Baldwin, leader of the Tory party and the real power in the "National" government of the fading old Labourite, Ramsay Mac-Donald, whom he subsequently succeeded as prime minister. Pipe in hand, stubby of stature and stubborn of will, Baldwin epitomized John Bull. He had the sure touch of the party politician in domestic matters but was not equal to the challenge of the likes of Adolf Hitler. In the face of German rearmament, Baldwin sat on his hands and did virtually nothing to prepare Britain militarily for the events that already could be discerned taking shape, however nebulously, upon the gray and darkening vista of the future. In Britain the ruling Tory clique rejoiced that Spain's right-wing elements had suppressed the uprising of the "godless Reds" in Asturias and thereby protected the considerable British financial interests in Spain's copper mines. Anti-Bolshevism remained the primary concern of British statesmen. In their view Moscow, not Berlin, was the "real enemy," and while they supported the principles of collective security espoused by the League of Nations, they showed little willingness to fight for them even at the political level. In the approaching spring of 1935, British policy, as I saw it reflected in the country's press, bespoke a vague pacifism that blunted serious consideration of how to deal with the threat to peace posed by Europe's dictators. Our correspondents were telling a different story.

According to the dispatches I saw from W.W. ("Bill") Chaplin, our Rome correspondent, Mussolini was preparing to make war on Ethiopia, amassing troops and building weapons and warships. The reports from Bill Shirer, in Berlin, were equally disturbing. They indicated Hitler was hardly the paladin of peace of his rabble-rousing orations to the German people. Actually, the Nazi dictator was systematically violating the restrictions imposed on Germany by the Treaty of Versailles. I remember Shirer reporting that Hitler had reintroduced conscription and created an army of thirty-six divisions—about five hundred thousand men—and was building a navy equal in size to one third that of Great Britain. They were not the actions of a man of peace, and in a subsequent speech the Nazi Führer uttered these "reassuring" words: "Whoever lights the torch of war in Europe can wish for nothing but chaos. We [Germans], however, live in the firm conviction that in our time will be fulfilled not the decline but the renaissance of the West. That Germany may make an imperishable contribution to this great work is our proud hope and unshakable belief."

I was taken aback, therefore, when, two days later, on March 18, the lordly *Times* of London, which I read religiously as part of my job, welcomed Hitler's "assurances" with what seemed to me to be be immoderate joy, for Hillman had told me the *Times* reflected the views of the British Foreign Office. The prestigious journal in its leader (the lead editorial) described the speech as "reasonable, straightforward and comprehensive.

"It is to be hoped," the paper said, "that Herr Hitler's speech will be taken everywhere as a sincere and well-considered utterance meaning precisely what it says."

The editorial marked the beginning of what proved to be the disastrous British policy of appeasement later actively pursued by Neville Chamberlain, Prime Minister Baldwin's successor.

Meanwhile, I longed to see the British parliamentary system of government at work from the press gallery of the House of Commons, meet the politicians, and circulate among the embassies, but Hillman kept me tied to the night desk. Occasionally I managed to take an hour off for supper and at the bar of the Falstaff, a dimly lighted, noisy pub up the road from the office, mingle with Fleet Street's newsmen. They were, however, a standoffish lot, more interested in their pints and small talk about salaries and working conditions than in discussing Britain's foreign policy. Oftener than not I ate my evening meal—a mutton chop or a rasher of bacon washed down with strong, well-sugared tea—at my workplace, answering phone calls from Shirer in Berlin, Alfred Tyernauer in Geneva, or Chaplin in Rome.

I felt increasingly certain I had fallen in disfavor with the Pickwickian Hillman. He had a way of talking out of the side of his mouth that I disliked intensely and often mimicked to the delight of our overworked office boy. I was sure the boss had caught me at it two or three times, and knowing him to be a vain man, I feared I had offended him. As the weeks became months, I resigned myself to staying on in London, sharpening my skills as best I could under the watchful, beady little eyes of Bill Hillman.

Moreover, I was fully aware that I still had much to learn. At twenty-seven, with less than a year's experience abroad, I was hardly what might be called a seasoned foreign correspondent. I was certainly not a Webb Miller, a John Gunther, a Vincent Sheean, or a Bill Shirer, the great ones of the generation half a decade or more ahead of mine. I particularly recalled with awe the expertise of my good friend Jay Allen, in Madrid, and curbed my impatience.

The only respite from the grind of desk work was a late April assignment from Hillman to write a series of mailers on the spread of fascism in Europe. The task sent me to a library in the Charing Cross and the files of London's leading newspapers. What emerged from about two weeks of intensive research was an abundance of material about the rise of authoritarian government throughout the Continent and the deepening cleavage between fascism and democracy. Although Mussolini maintained that his own *fascismo* was "not an export product," similar movements had sprung up in France, Belgium, Holland, Norway, Hungary, Romania, even neutral Switzerland and, indeed, Britain itself.

Naturally I concentrated on the nature and scope of the Italian phenomenon and on the life and times of Benito Juarez Mussolini, the man generally credited with having originated it.

I had completed my research on Italian fascism and had started work on Sir Oswald Mosley's movement in Britain when suddenly as news itself and in the same way, by cablegram, came orders from New York: PROCEED ROME SOONEST, cablese for "Leave for Rome at once."

I asked Hillman what I should do about the mail series he had requested.

"Keep your notes and write them up from Rome," Bill said. "Better dateline."

From what I had learned about Mussolinian fascism, I doubted this would be possible and said as much.

"Well," Bill said, smiling, "now you know what you're getting into."

I received the news of the transfer with mingled feelings. I had just begun to get my bearings in London and to appreciate it for the fascinating city that it is. There was so much I had not yet explored: the Houses of Parliament, Westminster Abbey, the Tower, the British Museum, the Tate Gallery.

"Damn it, Bill," I said, "I've never even seen the changing of the guard at Buckingham Palace."

"Next time," he said. "Get rid of your flat and get going."

A few days later we left London on the Golden Arrow for Paris, where we changed trains for Rome. Our baggage still consisted of only two steamer trunks, three suitcases, one elderly Remington portable typewriter, and a case of books.

When the Rome Express headed southward from Milan by way of Parma, Modena, Bologna, and Florence, I realized we were retracing the route Mussolini had taken on his spurious *Marcia su Roma* and traveling in much the same style: in a wagons-lits compartment paneled in polished mahogany inlaid with lemonwood, an overstuffed horsehair sofa that turned into a bed at night, and a tiny WC that had all the comforts except a shower bath.

3

FIRST IMPRESSIONS

I will remember always the Italy that burst into view in mid-May 1935, when the train emerged from the long Alpine tunnel at Modane on the first morning after leaving Paris, then rolled southward through Liguria along the deeply serrated western edge of the peninsula. It was the Italia I had heard described in childhood: dazzling sunlight, glimpses of blue sea, laboriously terraced mountainsides, groves of orange and lemon trees, miles of vineyards, and on distant hilltops stone houses huddled around the bell towers of churches.

But when the train stopped at Genoa, the country's most important port after Naples, I glimpsed another Italy, the Fascist Italy that was preparing to invade Ethiopia, which the Italians usually called Abyssinia. The station's platforms were crowded with troops in sun helmets and mustard-colored uniforms. They were being assembled for embarkation for Eritrea, Italy's colony in East Africa. All carried heavy backpacks and carbines as they shuffled off by twos. The scene depressed me.

My spirits rose again, however, in the early afternoon of the following day when I saw the bluish brown peak of Monte Gennaro, and I knew we were approaching the Eternal City, lodestar of my career. Soon after, with much screeching of the locomotive's whistle, the train entered the cavernous sheds of Rome's old Stazione Termini and we descended into crowds of *facchini* eager to help with our baggage.

There to meet us was Aldo Forte, the number two man in Universal's bureau. His boss, Bill Chaplin, the man I was replacing, was away on holiday. I had heard already about Aldo, and although I had been told that he was "a first-class newsman" and a "wonderful fellow," I was a little apprehensive. For he could, if he was a certain kind of man, make things very unpleasant for me. But the sight of him—short, compact, with a ready smile—was reassuring. I sensed at once that we would be friends, not competitors.

Like myself an American of Italian origin, Aldo was about my age but had lived most of his life in Rome, where his immigrant parents had settled after returning to Italy from Chicago in the early 1920s, before Mussolini had seized power. Aldo had an American accent and all the American slang, but he was Italian in his warmth of heart and charm.

Aldo escorted us to the Grand Hotel, adjacent to the nearby Baths of Diocletian, where we were installed in quarters as luxurious as those we had enjoyed in Madrid's Ritz. Later, over an early dinner in the hotel's sedate dining room, he endeared himself to us by his humor and his cynicism about fascism. Mussolini had fooled millions of Italians into believing his slogans about Italy's need for "a place in the sun" by conquering an empire in East Africa, but he had not bamboozled Aldo Forte.

I was comforted, for in Madrid and London I had developed strongly adverse feelings about fascism, and I had arrived in Rome less inclined to praise Caesar than to bury him. Aldo, obviously, was going to be my ally in covering Italy. He was careful, however, to explain the difficulties in the way of objective reporting of the Fascist scene.

"It's impossible," he said, "in fact, it's downright illegal to tell the truth when the facts don't jibe with the image of Italy that Mussolini wants to project to the outside world. To make sure, the regime has taken over every means of communication: the press, radio, newsreels, movies, even books."

During the first several days after our arrival, Kathryn and I and our sturdy toddler son explored Rome, usually with Aldo in the role of cicerone, learning the city's intricate geography and savoring every crumbling monument of its former greatness: the Colosseum, Arch of Constantine, Roman Forum, Campidoglio, Milvian Bridge, and Baths of Caracalla, noblest of ancient Rome's ruins. Like Henry Adams, we found Rome "seductive beyond resistance."

After raucous Madrid and grimy London, Rome—then a city of barely a million inhabitants—was a phenomenally quiet and remarkably clean place, a rather somnolent town, in fact, more like a provincial than a national capital. There were comparatively few automobiles, mostly big black Fiat and Lancia sedans, some obviously ancient but all well groomed, shining, and chauffeur-driven. Why so few cars in midtown Rome, we wondered, and why no horn tooting?

"Automobiles are very expensive in Italy," Aldo explained. "The only Romans who can afford them are moneyed aristocrats, bankers, cardinals, or privileged members of the Fascist hierarchy. The drivers don't sound their horns because Mussolini personally banned their use. He ordered all horns silenced one day when the honkings in the piazza under his windows in the Palazzo Venezia disturbed him at his work. So, no horn tooting, and Rome is as quiet as a tomb unless there's a mass rally or a Blackshirt parade."

Rome was as clean then as it was silent. The spacious piazzas, the road-ways, even the sidewalks were washed down nightly by brown-uniformed *spazzini* with high-pressure hoses. In fact, the very air of the city was clean and as intoxicating as the deceptively lighthearted wines that arrived daily at Rome's numerous *cantine* and *bottiglierie* from the vineyards of Frascati and other towns in the nearby Alban Hills.

We combined apartment hunting with our sightseeing, and in the busy Via dei Condotti, close to the Piazza di Spagna—then the heart of touristic Rome—we found exactly what we wanted: a well-furnished, airy penthouse with three bedrooms, central heating, and a maid's quarters. From its spacious terrace there was a glimpse of the piazza with its boat-shaped fountain—Bernini's *Barcaccia*—and a splendid view of the majestic upward sweep of the Spanish Steps, rising to the twin bell towers of the Trinità dei Monti, one of the most charming of Rome's several hundred churches. Keats had lived nearby, and diagonally across the street was the musty old Caffè Greco that boasted mementos of Mark Twain, Goethe, and Henry Adams.

With the apartment came Maria, the landlord's own *tuttofare,* or cook-maid of all work. She hailed from Venice, and though no beauty—she was a tall, angular woman whose upper lip faintly suggested a mustache—she turned out to be devoted and loyal, qualities much to be desired in a nation of domestic spies and tattlers.

Without Maria's help we might never have moved into 9 Via dei Condotti. Signor Feretti, the landlord, was the soul of civility during the preliminary negotiations, but by the time the lease was drawn up he had demanded—and received—three months' rent in advance, plus an equivalent amount as a deposit to cover possible damage to the apartment and its furnishings, the entire sum to be forfeited if we moved before the expiration of the one-year lease.

In addition, I had to pay him the equivalent of his own deposits to the telephone company and to the companies supplying gas, electricity and water, all also on a forfeit basis if and when the services were terminated. The process of completing the arrangements dragged on for days, but finally Signor Feretti allowed us to move into his premises.

The day we arrived, however, no water ran out of the taps, and neither the gas nor the electricity had been turned on. We found Maria complaining bitterly that her *padrone* had not kept his word but assuring us in staccato Italian with a heavy Venetian accent that she would see to it that matters would be put right.

Maria went to the telephone, which, fortunately, was in working order, and dialed her former employer's number. What she said in her throaty Venetian dialect I couldn't decipher completely, but I got enough of it to know that she was eloquently pleading our cause. Within an hour or two everything was functioning, and later that day Signor Feretti came in person to apologize for the inconvenience he had caused us by having failed to provide the promised services. Departing, he glared at Maria.

Meanwhile, I had learned at the War Ministry that my uncle Gennaro was now stationed in Tripoli. The moment we settled into our new home, I telegraphed him, inviting him to come stay with us at his earliest convenience. He replied immediately, expressing joy at hearing from me and advising me that he would be arriving for an extended visit August 5, the day his summer leave began. He was a full colonel now; his cable was signed "Colonello Commandante Centododicesimo Gruppo Automobilistico," which, Aldo explained, was either a motorized regiment or a transport unit.

Frankly, I was as anxious to hear what a high-ranking regular army officer had to say about his country's impending Ethiopian campaign as I was eager to embrace at last the man who for so many years had represented a living link with the land of my forefathers.

The apartment was within easy walking distance of the Hearst Organization's offices in the Galleria Colonna, the liveliest place in town, located on the Largo Chigi across the fashionable Via del Corso from the Palazzo Chigi, headquarters of Mussolini's Foreign Office. The *galleria* was—and still is— really a bifurcated arcade housing shops, a couple of banks, a cinema, two cafés, and a kiosk that sold magazines, lottery tickets, and foreign newspapers including, occasionally, the *Times* of London and the Paris edition of the *New York Herald Tribune,* often the only source of unadulterated news about the outside world. The imposing structure's two long arms were favorite meeting and strolling places for the city's whores, politicians, movie producers and actors, drug sellers and buyers, impresarios and flaneurs, all gesticulating, talking, arguing, and making an incredible amount of noise, punctuated by the sharp cries of vendors hawking the latest editions of local newspapers.

Our offices—shared by Universal, INS, and King Features Syndicate— were on the *galleria*'s mezzanine floor, their several windows looking outward on the noisy Largo Chigi on one side and inward on one branch of the even noisier arcade on the other. They were reachable by two short flights of dark stairway from inside the arcade next to the popular Café Picarozzi. To summon its waiters for freshly brewed espressos, sandwiches, or trays of tiny pastries, I had only to lean out my window and call down my order.

The Hearst "suite" consisted of two rooms, a rather cramped one occupied by Universal and an adjacent, somewhat larger chamber that housed INS and KFS. The floors throughout were bare parquet, and the brownish yellow walls were splotched with mildew and badly in need of paint. Much of the space in the smaller office was occupied by my desk, an enormous rolltop mahogany affair with numerous drawers and a secret hiding place for "sensitive documents." The massive, ornate piece had been bought at auction by a distant predecessor and had a pedigree: It was said to have once belonged to a princely member of the Chigi family.

A flattop desk for Aldo, a small table at which our office boy, Vittorio, sat next to the door, a couple of wooden filing cabinets with broken locks, two typewriter tables on casters, three or four uncomfortable chairs, and a bentwood hatrack completed the furnishings. I inherited the hatrack plus a large yellow silk pillow for my butt-sprung desk chair from David Darrah, the *Chicago Tribune* correspondent who had occupied offices on the same floor but had been expelled by the authorities shortly before my arrival. Darrah, one of the best correspondents ever to have worked in Rome, had committed the unpardonable error of writing the truth about the reluctance of some Italians to become warriors in Mussolini's Ethiopian adventure.

My office was a noisy, dingy, poorly lighted goat's nest that was to be my workplace for nearly four years. After a while, however, I no longer heard the racket outside my window as I worked. The air in my room usually smelled of coffee, chocolate, and freshly baked pastries from below, and eventually I came to like the place despite its many shortcomings.

The INS-King Features half of the Hearst team was Guglielmo Emmanuel, a handsome, silver-haired, cultured gentleman of the old school. A veteran Italian journalist, he occupied the larger, airier, neater office next to mine. Bill, as he was known to his American colleagues, was "a young sixty-five" at the time, and before the advent of fascism he had been the London correspondent of the prestigious *Corriere della Sera* of Milan.

Like Aldo, the genial Emmanuel had no love for fascism but remained an inactive anti-Fascist, one of millions of like-minded Italians skilled in the art of survival. Nevertheless, Mussolini's legions of secret police kept Bill under constant surveillance. Two agents, whom he dubbed Tweedle-dum and Tweedle-dee, watched his movements day and night.

Our *fattorino,* the office boy, Vittorio, served both agencies. He kept our two-room "suite" more or less tidy, ran errands, sorted the mail, and probably supplemented his meager wages by covertly working for the OVRA (Opera Vigilanza Reati Antifascisti), Mussolini's secret police. I first became suspicious of Vittorio when, only a fortnight after my arrival in Rome, the Hearst bureaus were raided.

Normally, at midday the hubbub under the high, vaulted arches of the *galleria*'s arcades was deafening. But on this particular day there were virtually no loiterers or strollers, and an ominous silence prevailed, indications that Mussolini's agents were in the vicinity in force. I sensed trouble even before I started up the dark stairs to my office.

I found the door locked. I could hear movement inside, however, and pounded on the door until it was opened by a short man in a dark suit and black felt hat whom I instinctively recognized as an OVRA operative. Aldo had taught me how to identify the breed: They invariably needed shaves, looked like unemployed undertakers, carried umbrellas, and were widely known and detested as *sbirri,* a contemptuous expression roughly akin to the use of "pigs" in recent times.

I pushed past the cop who had opened the door and saw two other *sbirri* rummaging through my desk and the contents of Universal's files. I burst into the room demanding to know, loudly and in English, what they thought they were doing. A fourth cop, better dressed than the others and obviously in command, strode in from the adjoining INS office and took me aside.

"You are not involved in this matter," he said in heavily accented but understandable English. "It is purely an Italian affair."

I disagreed and hotly demanded to be shown a warrant. "In such cases," Sbirro Number Four replied, "no warrants are needed. Anyhow, you are not in the United States now, you are in Italy, and we have our own way of handling matters of this kind."

"Perhaps so," I said, "but I will now call my embassy and inform my ambassador of what's going on here in the office of an American news agency."

He shrugged. I picked up the receiver. The line was dead.

"Pazienza," he said. "Service will be restored shortly."

The agents left minutes later, taking with them a batch of papers they had found in one of Bill Emmanuel's desk drawers.

A downcast Vittorio, who had remained discreetly in the background throughout the affair, informed me that the police had arrested Emmanuel and taken him away to Regina Coeli, the local slammer, only moments before my arrival on the scene.

As the boss *sbirro* had promised, the telephone was soon functioning again, and I called everyone I could think of who might help obtain Emmanuel's release. Our ambassador, Breckenridge Long, could do nothing: Emmanuel was an Italian subject. The pro-Fascist Swiss journalist who headed the Stampa Estera—the Foreign Press Association—promised to intervene but sat on his hands. Appeals from INS in New York were ignored by the Ministry for Popular Culture, a euphemism for the Ministry of Propaganda, then headed by Count Galeazzo Ciano, Mussolini's son-in-law.

Emmanuel remained in jail incommunicado for fifty-one days. His release was eventually obtained by his wife, Nellie, an elegant lady of noble birth, who appealed directly to an influential longtime friend in the Foreign Office. Bill emerged from Regina Coeli (Queen of Heavens) jail in high good humor, smiling, tanned from sunbathing in the prison yard, unbowed.

Prison was an old story with him, for he had frequently been jailed on suspicion of harboring anti-Fascist sentiments. This time, however, the charge had been treason, based on a telephoned message from one Giorgio Gaggiotini, the INS stringer in Naples, stating that many Neapolitans were opposed to the coming war with Ethiopia and describing how they had clamorously shown their displeasure with emotional scenes while their sons were being embarked for East Africa on their way to war. Women wept and shouted angry denunciations at the government as husbands, brothers, sons, and sweethearts trooped aboard Africa-bound transports.

Emmanuel had never sent the story but had kept his notes of his conversation with Gaggiotini in the desk drawer where the *sbirri* had found them. The agents had known exactly where to look. Who but our *fattorino,* I reasoned, could have informed them of where the notes were kept?

I was all for firing Vittorio on the spot, but Emmanuel vetoed the idea. The man had a wife and a flock of kids to support. Besides, Bill argued, what good would it do to discharge him? His successor almost certainly would be someone planted on us by the Propaganda Ministry, the Foreign Office, the Fascist party, or the OVRA itself. Latin logic laced with humanity prevailed, and we kept Vittorio on the payroll. We made certain, however, that thereafter no "sensitive" papers of any kind were left in the office.

After his release from jail Emmanuel was enjoined by the government from continuing as INS correspondent and was replaced by the veteran Hudson ("Buzz") Hawley, from our Paris Bureau. Gaggiotini, the source of Emmanuel's information, was arrested and held for some time but was released on his promise to refrain from working for INS or any other foreign news organization. We had difficulty replacing him.

Bill Emmanuel, however, remained on the Hearst payroll as the representative of King Features Syndicate, which supplied comic strips to Italian newspapers with Sunday supplements. Ironically, he also served as agent and distributor of periodic articles by Mussolini. The Duce's pieces, paid for at the rate of one dollar a word in gold, were actually written by his former mistress Margherita Sarfatti, a literate, charming, and once-beautiful Jewish lady whom I came to know well and with whom I enjoyed a longtime cordial relationship.

The Emmanuel and Darrah incidents showed me the true face of fascism and illustrated why the phenomenon was misperceived abroad. Its darker side simply could not be told, and the correspondent who dared describe it was subject to arrest and imprisonment if he happened to be an Italian, and to expulsion if a foreigner. In the case of the latter, censorship was curative rather than preventive. A foreign correspondent was free to write whatever he pleased, but if what he wrote displeased the authorities, he was promptly arrested and escorted to the frontier.

The truth about Italian fascism in the mid-1930s was that behind the facade of Mussolinian "modernization" of Italy—trains "running on time," monumental public works, the drainage of the malarious Pontine Marshes—so widely hailed abroad, millions of Italians lived in quasi-medieval squalor. The Mafia, which early in his dictatorship Mussolini was supposed to have "crushed" with vigorous "police action," continued to dominate impoverished Sicily and southern Italy, and banditry still prevailed in the rugged highlands of Sardinia.

In the wretched villages of the Mezzogiorno—the backward, plundered, neglected southern third of the country—the houses lacked even fireplaces for heating and cooking, to say nothing of running water and indoor toilets, and the bulk of the peasantry remained illiterate and ravaged by hunger and malaria. Agriculture, the mainstay of the national economy, improved only slightly despite the Duce's highly publicized *Battaglia del Grano* (battle of the grain) for making Italy self-sufficient in cereals. The price of bread remained high, so high that many people were eating cheaper corn and potatoes instead.

Furthermore, I soon learned, fascism's highly touted *stato corporativo* had failed to rectify the country's appallingly unequal distribution of wealth. Indeed, in the Fascist corporative state the rich became richer and the poor sank ever deeper into poverty. There was also a high rate of unemployment, even in agriculture, and discontent was widespread; but strict domestic censorship of the media prevented public airing of grievances.

It was an economically distressed but thoroughly regimented Italy, therefore, which in the early summer of 1935 prepared to embark on its Ethiopian adventure. It was to be a war to glorify a failing dictatorship, a war that would enable Mussolini to say that he, *il Duce del fascismo,* had given Italy its "place in the sun," an empire in East Africa.

The Ethiopia Mussolini coveted was a vast territory of some 350,000 square miles, almost as big as Texas and New Mexico combined. Nominally a kingdom under the emperor Haile Selassie, a small, fragile-looking man with steel in his backbone, the country was actually a loose feudalistic confederation of mountain tribes in a very backward state of civilization. Its seven or eight million inhabitants eked out a bare existence as herdsmen and farmers.

Italy had acquired the neighboring colonies of Eritrea, on the Red Sea, and Somaliland, on the Indian Ocean, in the nineteenth century and had aspired ever since to the intervening Ethiopian hinterland. An Italian attempt to conquer the country in 1896 ended in disaster at Adowa, where an Italian army was roundly defeated by Ethiopian forces. The failure rankled in Italian hearts, not least in that of Benito Mussolini, then thirteen years old.

In the spring of 1935, however, when Mussolini was a paunchy fifty-two and the unchallenged arbiter of the destinies of some forty-four million Italians, he was motivated only partly by a desire to wipe out the "stain" of the inglorious defeat at Adowa. His main objectives were to assert Italy's prestige as a "major power," resolve its deepening economic problems, and expand its overseas empire. He was obsessed with the idea of resurrecting Roman greatness. In the first speech I heard him make from his favorite rostrum, the balcony of the Palazzo Venezia, he declared: "Imperialism is the goal of all peoples who desire economic and spiritual expansion. Italy is an immense legion which marches towards a greater future. Nobody can stop her. Nobody will stop her!"

The fact that Ethiopia was a member of the League of Nations in Geneva did not deter Mussolini. He was determined, he said on that day, to make the country he called Abyssinia an Italian colony "with Geneva, without Geneva, or against Geneva." The huge crowd gathered to hear him cheered wildly.

The Duce had reason to believe that neither France nor Britain would seriously oppose his imperial aspirations. In January 1935 France's prime minister, Pierre Laval, had visited Rome in an effort to improve Franco-Italian relations against the growing German threat to Europe's peace. In the course of their discussions, the pro-Fascist Laval gave the Duce to understand that France would not oppose Italian ambitions in East Africa.

Three months later, when the heads of the British, French, and Italian governments met at Stresa, on Lago Maggiore, to unite against Germany, the British did not raise the Ethiopian question. In fact, when Mussolini read to the meeting the preamble of a resolution which ran "The Three Powers, determined to maintain the peace in Europe," he stopped and repeated with emphasis the phrase "peace in Europe." Neither British Prime Minister MacDonald nor Foreign Secretary Sir John Simon made any comment, and Mussolini took their silence to mean he could do as he pleased in Ethiopia.

By the end of May, soon after I had arrived in Rome, I was able to report that nearly one million Italians were under arms. The call-ups served, of course, to help Mussolini relieve his most troublesome problem: unemployment. Thousands of young men for whom fascism was unable to provide jobs at home were being sent to a distant war to die in battle or of malaria, dysentery, and the numerous other tropical diseases in which Ethiopia abounded.

Meanwhile, on June 18, 1935—a few months after Hitler had violated the Treaty of Versailles by creating what he called his "peacetime army" of thirty-six divisions—another event of surpassing importance occurred. Britain, without consulting France and Italy, its Stresa "partners," concluded an Anglo-German naval agreement allowing Hitler to build a navy of up to 35 percent of Britain's own naval strength. Mussolini turned the fury of the Fascist press against "Perfidious Albion."

From the point of view of British relations with Italy, nothing could have been more damaging than the seemingly capricious and ill-considered British decision to sign a naval accord with Nazi Germany which in effect condoned Hitler's rearmament in violation of the Versailles Treaty. Aware of the damage done by the Anglo-German naval deal, the British Foreign Office sent to Rome its rising young diplomat Captain Anthony Eden, minister without portfolio, and Britain's representative at the League of Nations, who was soon to become foreign secretary.

I was among the dozen or so British and American correspondents who met Eden at the heavily policed central railroad station when he arrived from Paris on the Rome Express in the early evening of June 23. He was only thirty-eight years old at the time, a handsome, meticulously tailored gentleman with a neatly trimmed guards mustache. He wore a homburg and carried an elegant attaché case which contained, he later revealed, "a most generous plan for settling peacefully Italy's dispute with Abyssinia."

As Eden presented it to Mussolini in two meetings the next day—and as I was able to report it on June 25 in my first major scoop out of Rome—the British plan gave Italy everything it could possibly have desired in Ethiopia except outright sovereignty over the entire country. But Eden, it developed, had come too late—Mussolini was already heavily committed to war with Ethiopia—and with too little. The Duce wanted the whole pie, not just a generous slice.

In the weeks that followed, the Fascist press intensified its anti-British campaign; the streets of Rome resounded to the anti-British shouts and the slogans of youthful demonstrators. Almost overnight, it seemed, Italy was ready to fight England as well as Ethiopia! By the third week in June many of Italy's transatlantic liners were being pressed into service as troop carriers, and Blackshirt units were sailing almost daily from Leghorn, Genoa, Naples, and Palermo.

Over the years Emmanuel had developed an excellent network of tipsters throughout the country; hence both INS and Universal were kept fully informed of the sailings *and* of the state of public opinion in the various ports. The people as a whole were uneasy. There was unrest and disapproval everywhere, in the moderately prosperous industrial north as well as in the poverty-stricken, predominantly agricultural south.

Remembering what had happened to Emmanuel and Darrah, however, I withheld the news of unrest and dissatisfaction, as did nearly every other resident foreign correspondent in Rome. To have transmitted it would have meant expulsion, which, in my own case, having only recently arrived, I dared not risk. I thought it prudent to await bigger news: an attempt on the Duce's life, perhaps, the collapse of the regime, or the possibility, however remote, that an outraged Britain, still Queen of the Seas, might go to war to prevent a Fascist conquest of Ethiopia.

Only in Rome was there any evidence of enthusiasm for the war with Ethiopia and, if the Duce so ordered, with "Perfidious Albion" as well. By August 5, the day Uncle Gennaro was due to arrive, there were far more soldiers in the streets and piazzas of the capital than civilians.

4

UNCLE GENNARO

The day dawned hot and humid. Two lone palm trees stood like motionless sentinels in the still air at the far end of the Piazza di Spagna opposite the British Consulate. The piazza itself was rapidly filling with troops, helmeted as though marching off to war, short, ugly bayonets projecting from their carbines, their hobnailed shoes scraping rhythmically on the lava-stone paving and obliterating the pleasant early-morning sounds of water splashing in Bernini's fountain.

The soldiers were assembling to "protect" the consulate against a "spontaneous" student demonstration planned for later that morning. From my terrace the gray-green helmets of the men in field uniforms looked like so many rows of cabbages ready for harvesting. They were so numerous and packed so closely not only in the piazza itself but in the approaches to it that I wondered how the relative from Tripoli, now known in the family as Uncle G, would manage to make his way from the railroad station. He had flown to Naples and was coming from there by train.

The hours dragged; the bells in the campaniles of the Trinità dei Monti sounded them on the hour and the half hour. Awaiting my uncle's arrival, I mentally reviewed the little I actually knew about him. My knowledge of the man was based almost entirely on what Papa had told me about him long ago.

As a young captain Uncle G had served as an aide to Field Marshal Pietro Badoglio in 1917, after the latter took charge of Italy's armies jointly with the inept Marshal Armando Diaz following the disaster at Caporetto. Badoglio, apparently, kept Uncle G on his staff mainly because he made an excellent partner at bridge, the marshal's favorite pastime. My uncle had never joined the Fascist party, probably accounting for his slow progress in the matter of promotions. He was in his mid-fifties and should have been a brigadier but was still only a colonel. Moreover, he was stuck in Libya, the graveyard of career officers of dubious loyalty to fascism and of Mussolini's rivals for power.

About my uncle's private life I knew only that in his youth, according to Father, he had been something of a Casanova and that in his middle thirties he had married a Jewish lady, Augusta Kurtzman, who had given him a daughter, Grace, named for his own mother, who had died in the Messina earthquake.

The traditional noontime cannon on the Vomero Hill sounded, church bells started ringing, and the hubbub in the piazza suddenly ceased. The demonstrating students departed, and the soldiers marched off to their barracks. The flower vendors returned to their stalls at the foot of the Spanish Steps, and when the bells stopped swinging, Rome was its somnolent, summertime self once more.

The only sounds now were the clippety-clop of horse-drawn carriages making the turn around the *Barcaccia* and the distant splash of the fountain's waters. I was contemplating how pleasant Rome could be even on a torrid early August day at high noon when the front doorbell rang.

Maria padded down the corridor from the kitchen to answer it, wearing a freshly starched white uniform reserved for special occasions. Kathryn and I waited, Sean fidgeting between us, in the wide arched doorway that separated the living room from the vestibule. Maria opened the door, and there he was: Uncle Gennaro, somewhat taller than I had imagined him, uniformed in immaculate summertime whites with much gold braid and a sunburst of ribbons over his left breast pocket.

Uncle Gennaro stepped into our home as though he had been away a long time and were entering his own house. He possessed the place at a glance, held his right hand at his temple in salute, bowed to Kathryn, then flung open his arms, saying in a voice that reminded me of Father's, "I have waited a long time for this moment." He embraced us each in turn, first Kathryn, then me. For Sean he had only a pat on his curly head and a muttered *"Che bel ragazzo."* This puzzled me; Italians were usually more demonstrative with children.

It was evident from the two scuffed brown leather gladstone bags he had brought that Uncle G fully expected to stay at least a fortnight. Maria and I carried them into the spare room down the hall, but our guest refused Maria's offer to help him unpack and indicated he wanted to freshen up before lunch. I showed Uncle the way to the bathroom and left him.

Physically, except for the matter of his height—he was a good three inches taller than my own five feet seven inches—Uncle G was exactly as I knew him from his photographs, somewhat older, perhaps, but the same tanned, sternly handsome soldier with a thick mane of steely gray hair, pince-nez, and a commanding presence that verged on the arrogant.

Over lunch Uncle asked, as Italian relatives will on such occasions, numerous personal questions: how much I earned, paid for rent, spent for food, even what we paid Maria. He seemed surprised by our replies and delivered a pointed lecture on frugality, explaining that he was able to manage his considerable household in Tripoli—a villa with three servants, all Arabs—on a monthly sum substantially less than what we were spending weekly. His salary as a colonel, he said, was only 2,450 lire a month, equivalent at the time to approximately $140, which, including my allowances for overseas service in what was considered a "hardship post," was about what I was earning weekly.

Throughout the meal our guest studiously avoided talking politics, especially when Maria was in the room. Obviously Italians had long since learned not to trust servants. I alluded several times to the morning's demonstrations and the debate over possible League sanctions against Italy which had already started at Geneva, but each time he looked blank, rolled his eyes toward the hovering Maria, and changed the subject.

"We'll talk later," he said, "after I have had my siesta. Perhaps we can meet at your office this afternoon. I'd like to see where you work."

At five o'clock, Uncle G, in mufti now, came to the Galleria Colonna. He wore a well-cut beige linen suit, blue shirt, dark blue necktie, and white Panama hat. Instead of his pince-nez, he carried a monocle on a long, narrow black ribbon and looked more like an aging boulevardier than the soldier I had met earlier. I introduced him to Aldo, who greeted him warmly in Italian; to Buzz Hawley, the new INS correspondent with whom he exchanged formal greetings in French; and to Vittorio, who snapped his heels together and stood at attention, looking like a serf before his squire.

Uncle suggested a walk unless I had urgent business to attend to. I didn't, and off we went.

Emerging from the *galleria,* we turned up the Via del Corso past the cinnamon-colored Palazzo Chigi toward the Piazza del Popolo. The street was virtually deserted, as, indeed, was the city itself. The Romans have better sense than to remain in town in August, when the heat and the humidity are almost unbearable, although the evenings are usually blessedly cool. July and August are the months of the scirocco, the south wind that rises in Africa, gathers moisture as it crosses the Mediterranean, and fills the Roman sky with low, gray, dampish clouds that drip what Norman Douglas called "death and putrefaction." On this day, however, no clouds, but hot, dry blasts. "Like Libya," my uncle said as we swung up the Corso.

It was a longish walk during which Uncle G stopped frequently to admire the gorgeous displays in the fashionable shops and talked about a livelier Rome of another era, the *bella Roma* of his youth, before the Great War, when he came to the capital on leave. He described a city of beautifully gowned "young women of good family" riding open carriages and flirting with youthful officers like himself.

Not until we reached the oval-shaped Piazza del Popolo, a magnificent old square which someone once described as the "public living room of the people of Rome," and were seated at one of the marble-topped tables outside (the

Valadier, where there was—and still is—a fine terrace overlooking Rome with the dome of St. Peter's and green Monte Mario in the distance. Over aperitifs, Uncle Gennaro resumed his story.

"It all happened in October 1917. Caporetto was a key position on the Isonzo River. Opposing us was a strong Austro-German force. And don't forget who was commanding them: Ludendorff, Germany's best general. We had General Cadorna. Count Luigi Cadorna. His father, Raffaele, took Rome in 1870, but the less said about his son Luigi the better.

"Well, we cracked at the first thunderous assault that was preceded by a barrage that seemed never to end. How I survived, I don't know. Men were blown to bits all around me. The slaughter was horrendous. Our troops were in a demoralized state and poorly led. The Austro-Germans captured two hundred thousand of our men, along with some fifteen hundred pieces of artillery. The retreat was chaotic, and we finally stopped at the Piave. The river was in flood, and the enemy couldn't cross. We were twenty-nine divisions against fifty. We made a stand there that should have wiped out the memory of Caporetto, but it hasn't. By the time the British and French help arrived, we had stabilized our front.

"In June we counterattacked. But we still had the swollen Piave to cross. We threw fourteen pontoon bridges across that damned river, and ten of them were swept away by torrential rains and floods. But by October the Austrians were tired, their empire was shaky, and we plunged ahead anew. We crossed the Piave. I must say the British were very helpful with their superb engineers. What followed was the Battle of Vittorio Veneto. The Austrians lost five hundred thousand prisoners and more than five thousand guns."

Twice during his stay with us Uncle Gennaro dined out but did not tell us where or with whom. He merely said he was invited out "for dinner and bridge," would be late coming home, and not to wait up for him. I guessed—correctly, it later developed—that his host was Marshal Badoglio, who owned a fine villa in the Via Bruxelles.

I kept late hours myself because of the six-hour time difference between New York and Rome and on one occasion arrived home shortly after Uncle had come in. I heard him splashing in the bathroom, and when he emerged, we had another long conversation in which, as usual, he did most of the talking. I poured myself a small brandy, lighted a cigarette, and listened. He delighted me by returning at last to the subject of Mussolini.

"Mind you," he said, "none of us really knew that with his ridiculous March on Rome in '22 a new epoch was beginning. Mussolini was seen then as just another politician, one of many leaders—more extreme than most, perhaps, more vehement in his language and in his writings—but it was assumed that eventually he would blend into the parliamentary, democratic landscape of a constitutional monarchy. Frankly it seemed to me at the time that he was merely giving us a new, more dynamic kind of politics, but I could never bring myself to join his party. I served king and country.

"I can tell you, if you promise not to print it now—someday, perhaps, but

original) Rosati's café—there was, and there still is, another Rosa
Veneto—did Uncle seem disposed to talk seriously about anythin
ideal place for private conversation; only scattered tourists occupie
tables, Americans, mostly, and a few Scandinavians, all drinking l
Peroni beer. We ordered espressos.

In civvies Uncle Gennaro was suddenly warmer, more human a
younger by five or six years, looked so much like Father that he
been his twin. I felt a surge of affection toward him that frankly,
experienced when we met.

I questioned him about fascism, Mussolini, the imminent war v
pia, and the burgeoning dispute with Great Britain. He described the
had spawned fascism as having been much like the country many
had depicted. More than most countries, however, he said, Italy was
disillusionment. Apparently the echoes of the Russian Revolution
recalled, were reverberating ominously throughout Europe but parti
Italy, Germany, and Hungary. Accordingly, communism loomed i
a distinct possibility.

"Of course," he said, "we Italians are not Russians. I doubt that
have arrested Victor Emmanuel and his family and executed the l
Bolsheviks did the Romanovs. But there were demonstrations, stri
ricades in the streets—unrest everywhere. In Milan, I remember,
about with a small Beretta under my tunic. It was worth your life t
in public in uniform. Those of us who had returned from the front—
battles on the Isonzo and the Piave—tired, beaten, though victorio
despised by the rabble, even spit upon. Premier Orlando had return
the Peace Conference in Paris without the rewards we had been pror
the Treaty of London. But surely you know about all that. . . ."

I said I did, but he continued as though wanting to make sure I unde
saying, "That treaty was signed in April 1915 and bribed us into a war fo
we were not prepared; we were poorly equipped for modern warfare ai
short of ammunition, medical supplies, food, winter uniforms—ever
But believe me, Francesco, by then it was a popular decision to enter t
on the side of Britain and France. The man in the street was heartily ir
of abandoning our alliance with the Austro-Hungarians and the German
the leading interventionist, of course, was our present Duce.

"For two and a half years we fought the Austrians in the Alps. Wh
British and the French were mired in the mud of Flanders, we fought in A
ice and snow and avalanches. We didn't advance much, but we tied down
Austrian and German forces that might have crushed the Allies on the we
front if they had been free to move. It was a contribution to the final vi
that was never fully appreciated or rewarded.

"The historians, particularly the British and the French, are foreve
minding us of Caporetto. Well, I was there. Let me tell you about it, bu
here. Let's go up into the Pincio, where we can see the sunset. . . ."

We took a *carrozza* for the uphill ride to the Pincio Gardens and the Ca not now—that at the time Badoglio saw the danger that *fascismo* represented. When Mussolini was still in Milan, trying to make up his mind whether or not it would be safe for him to go to Rome to challenge the government, the marshal asked the king's permission to stop him and his Camicie Nere with a regiment of infantry and a few machine guns. But the king refused. His Majesty said he didn't want any bloodshed! He feared starting a civil war! Too bad, in my opinion. But there you are.

"Now Mussolini is the most powerful man in Europe. He has imitators everywhere. This Hitler, for example, he's even more dangerous, I believe. But Mussolini is dangerous enough for the moment. He wants Abyssinia, and he'll get it. I doubt that he can do it with his Blackshirts. But I think we'll clean up Abyssinia in a year or less. After all, it'll be a war of bombers and tanks, heavy artillery, and machine guns against tribesmen armed mostly with spears and rusty old Enfield rifles. . . ."

I recall a long pause during which Uncle Gennaro rested his chin on his chest and seemed lost in thought. Then, leaning forward, he said: "What worries me most of all is the widening rupture with our old ally England. I doubt that she'll march against us now over Abyssinia, but if she does, God help us. Our navy is no match for hers, and we simply haven't the resources for a major war. No coal for our ships, and no oil for our planes, our tanks, our trucks, no iron to make steel, no copper, tin, nickel—anything.

"Nevertheless, England is doing more harm than good by opposing us at the League. She will push us closer and closer to Germany. An alliance between us and the Germans would be disastrous for Europe. I have read *Mein Kampf*—and I urge you to get your hands on a copy as soon as you can—and, believe me, that book spells doom for Europe. It projects a struggle between fascism and democracy. It could mean Germany *and* Italy against France and Britain. In such a struggle the richer nations would win in time. But it would mean a ruined Europe, and who can tell what would rise on the ruins?"

It was well after two o'clock, and we went out on the terrace for a breath of air. We could hear the water splashing in the *Barcaccia,* a pleasing sound, and in the pale moonlight the Spanish Steps and the Trinità dei Monti looked unreal, like a stage set.

Throughout his visit, Uncle Gennaro ate sparingly, particularly at break-fast, which invariably consisted of a plain roll and a small cup of strong, chicory-flavored coffee, the same as Maria prepared for herself. On his last day in Rome—a Sunday and Maria's day off—we treated him to an American breakfast: freshly squeezed orange juice, ham and eggs, buttered toast, and percolated coffee. He ate heartily and wondered aloud whether all Americans breakfasted so sumptuously every day. "Yes," I said, "when they can afford it." He was clearly surprised to learn that not everyone in America was rich. He did not pursue the subject, however, and I restrained my desire to tell him more about politics and economics in the United States. He had last-minute packing to do and a train to catch.

"You must tell me about America when you come to visit us in Tripoli," he said. "It is a jewel of a city, a model colonial capital with fine boulevards and luxurious hotels. I'll put you up at the new Uaddan, which means 'gazelle' in Arabic, and I doubt that even in your country there is anything as fine."

Later that morning, I took Uncle G to the station in a taxi in time for him to catch the noon *rapido* for Naples, where he was staying with friends before departing early the next day for Tripoli in an Ala Littoria flying boat.

On the way I told him that I would be going north in a day or two to cover the army's maneuvers in the South Tyrol. He seemed pleased. "Marshal Badoglio will be there," he said. "Should the occasion arise, make yourself known to him and give him my regards."

Uncle G had been curiously uncommunicative about his relations with the marshal during his visit, and I had begun to wonder if he even knew Badoglio. Hoping to draw him out, I asked him how long he had served as the marshal's aide during the Great War.

"I was his communications officer for two or three months," he said. "It was during that awful winter after Caporetto, and the other night while we were playing bridge after dinner, the marshal reminded me of an amusing incident that occurred while Gabriele d'Annunzio was visiting the front.

"Our famous guest was forever sending telegrams to friends, and they all came through my office, of course. Most of them were seen by Badoglio, and neither of us ever forgot the one that d'Annunzio sent to Eleonora Duse, *la divina Duse,* his great love of the moment. I can still quote the telegram exactly. It said: 'I kiss you my beloved where most you stink of woman.' "

Later, as we stood on the platform outside his compartment, Uncle Gennaro placed both his hands on my shoulders, stood me off at arm's length, and said: "I have always thought of you, dear nephew, as the son I never had and at my age will never have. You are very dear to me, so don't do anything foolish such as going off to Abyssinia to play war correspondent. It's going to be a dirty war in the world's dirtiest country. Promise me you won't go."

I replied that he was asking me to make a promise I couldn't keep. If my employers assigned me to cover the impending Ethiopian campaign, I couldn't refuse. "In a way," I said, "I, too, am a soldier and must go wherever I am sent."

Uncle Gennaro dropped his arms, smiled, and nodded understandingly, but I could see he was displeased. Stepping close, he embraced me warmly and whispered in my ear.

"In that case," he said, "be prepared to leave for East Africa as soon as the crops are harvested here in Italy. By late September or early October we shall be at war with Abyssinia."

With that Uncle Gennaro kissed me on both cheeks and stepped up into his compartment. He saluted smartly from the open window as the train pulled out, and I watched until the last carriage emerged from the shadows of the train shed into the bright sunlight beyond.

At home I found Kay on the terrace hard at work with an Italian-English dictionary and a grammar. She had already picked up some "kitchen Italian," but she was determined, she said, that when we went to Tripoli to return Uncle G's visit, she would be able to converse with him and his wife "instead of just sitting and smiling while you and they jabber away in Italian."

Two days later I went off to cover the annual army maneuvers being held along Italy's frontier with Austria, in the South Tyrol, former Austrian territory ceded to Italy after the Great War. The Italians called the area the Alto Adige, and had tried hard to Italianize and fascisticize it, but it remained preponderantly Austrian in language and culture and politically far more Nazi than Fascist.

5

THE FASCIST "WAR GAMES" OF 1935

Since Italy's emergence as a military power in the early 1930s the army's annual maneuvers were successively held along its Alpine frontiers with France, Austria, or Yugoslavia according to whether the Duce intended to intimidate Paris, impress Vienna, or frighten Belgrade with the growing might of Italian arms. In the summer of 1935 the war games were conducted on Italy's border with Austria to prove to the outside world in general—and to Adolf Hitler in particular—that Italy was capable of defending Austrian independence as well as its own territorial integrity against German aggression even while engaged in an impending imperialistic adventure in Ethiopia.

Normally the central figure in the exercises was King Victor Emmanuel. They involved, after all, *il reggio esercito* (the royal army), *his* army at least in name. But in 1935 the little king—he stood barely five feet four inches in high-heeled boots—was relegated to a secondary role in the show and was largely ignored by the swarms of foreign correspondents who covered the maneuvers which the Ministry of Press and Propaganda touted as the "most important in the history of Fascist Italy."

The king's role was usurped by Benito Mussolini, and during the last week in August I had my first good look at the corpulent dictator as warrior-leader of Italy's ground forces. He wore a steel helmet and the uniform of a plain corporal but behaved throughout the war games like a field marshal, a latter-day Caesar directing the movements of some five hundred thousand troops.

The maneuvers covered the entire South Tyrol, a magnificent area of rugged mountains, the Dolomites, that rise from green valleys to purple mists and lofty peaks snowcapped even in August. The mountains' lower flanks are heavily wooded, and their high plateaus and deep ravines hold some of the best grazing lands in all Italy. Beyond the Dolomites rise the Alps, a barrier of rock and snow and ice that invaders from the north historically found difficult to penetrate. Mussolini set out to prove that Italy could defend it with the weapons of modern warfare—tanks, armored cars, motor-drawn artillery—instead of with foot soldiers and mule-drawn artillery as in the recent past.

To cover the war games, which were conducted under simulated "combat conditions"—blackouts and tight security—I teamed up with the AP's chief of bureau, Andrew Berding, a competitor but also a close personal friend. Andy and I wanted to remain as free to move about as possible without having to depend on transportation supplied by the Press Bureau, so we hired a chauffeured Fiat sedan and daily drove to wherever Mussolini was performing for the newsreel cameras. Being autonomous, we could return to our base in Bolzano's Hotel Poste and telephone our stories long before the Duce's entourage arrived from its day's junket.

We soon discovered, however, that autonomy held its special perils. The narrow, winding Tyrolean roads had soft shoulders and were poorly paved. In the higher reaches there were often absolute drops of thousands of feet on one side and walls of sheer rock on the other. It frequently happened that between our car and eternity there was only a low wall of loose stones or a stubby concrete road marker and that our safety depended on the dubious skill of the driver in handling the bulky, top-heavy Fiat around hairpin curves.

Every day we started out early, rarely later than six in the morning, when the roads were still shrouded in heavy mist and slick with hoarfrost. Because our driver was invariably drowsy at that hour, travel in the awesome Dolomites was infinitely more hazardous than it might have been.

Mussolini hogged the show, carrying his audience with him. It consisted of a mile-long motorcade of officials, members of the foreign and domestic press, platoons of newsreel cameramen from every country in the world (except Ethiopia, of course), and the military observers from fifty nations. The United States was represented by Colonel Norman Fiske, a genial, gung ho cavalryman.

Andy and I went along a few times but soon tired of watching Mussolini's posturings—conferences with army brass at various field headquarters, inspections of units assembled in rear areas remote from the "combat zone," glimpses of the Duce scanning the terrain with field glasses—all strictly photo opportunities eminently unproductive of hard news. What we saw but could not report without risking expulsion was an egomaniacal peasant playing Caesar at the Rubicon.

Moreover, we had found it extremely difficult to keep up with the Duce's motorcade, which he led himself, driving a fast, apple red Alfa Romeo roadster. He drove recklessly at high speeds, sometimes hitting sixty miles an hour on rare stretches of straight road, and one day we found ourselves stranded in a thick, granular mist at an altitude of fifteen thousand feet or more after having nearly collided several times with approaching or passing army vehicles. The impenetrable fog not only obscured vision but muted the sounds of auto horns. Once we almost went over the side as we skidded around an unmarked curve.

The near accident caused the normally imperturbable Berding to explode. "This damned car is built for funerals," he said, "not for chasing after Old Baldy in his bloody Alfa Romeo. Let's call it a day. Tomorrow we'll try to find the king and see what he's up to. If we catch up with him, we might even get an interview."

We were after hard news or solid features, and so far the *grande manovre* had produced little of either.

Our search for His Majesty started at daybreak on the morning of August 26 with a sleepier-than-usual driver, whom we instructed to take us up into the actual "battle zone" where we had ascertained the king could be found. This meant driving for several hours, climbing sharply all the while. We knew we were in the right area when we began passing *alpini,* crack units with skis slung over their shoulders, their wind-burned faces thrust forward, as they sang a marching song I had often heard at home as a child. They were moving into position for the final phase of the maneuvers, their officers informed us, a mock battle between "invaders" and "defenders," and we were among the latter.

It was slow going for a while, threading our way through men and equipment; but farther on the road was clear, and we realized we were in the no-man's-land between the opposing forces. The sounds of machine guns firing quick bursts and the sporadic boom of artillery echoing and reechoing in the valley were audible above the noise our Fiat made as it ground along in low gear.

Approaching yet another hairpin turn, we entered a patch of thick fog and thought we heard the klaxon of an oncoming vehicle but couldn't be certain. Andy and I leaned forward, tense, for our driver had no clear view of the road and was steering with his head out the window to get his bearings.

Suddenly there was a screech of brakes and the gritty growl of wheels churning gravel. Simultaneously a huge open touring car, a long black Lancia, came briefly into view, shot past us going in the opposite direction, skidded downhill, slewed sideways across the road, and came to a halt about thirty yards behind us. Meanwhile, our Fiat had bumped to a stop on the soggy shoulder of the right side of the roadway inches from the edge of a mist-filled chasm; another foot or two and we might have plunged into space.

We looked back through our rear window, and there was the king, swathed in an army greatcoat, standing beside the seated, bulky figure of his friend and chief of staff Marshal Badoglio. His Majesty shook his fist at us, his prominent chin champing as though hinged and activated by springs, while Badoglio turned and glared at us. Both men seemed to be swearing fluently.

Andy and I gestured apologies as best we could, but before we could scramble out of our machine and make them in person, the king's driver had straightened out his vehicle and started downhill again. Had the incident involved Mussolini or some other Fascist bigwig, it might have had a different ending.

"Lucky for us that wasn't Old Baldy," said Berding, and I heartily concurred.

Neither of us, however, was ready to abandon the chase, and we decided to try to catch up with the royal Lancia.

With considerable backing and filling, our crestfallen but now wide-awake driver turned our car around and started back downhill. Minutes later we spotted His Majesty's vehicle parked on the right side of the road. Badoglio and a junior officer were standing behind the car talking, their breaths making puffs of chilled mist.

Meanwhile, the king, easily recognizable by his diminutive stature, stood spread-legged on the outer edge of the road—pissing into the valley below! I was for stopping to make myself known to Badoglio as Uncle Gennaro had suggested, but Andy scotched the idea.

"In the circumstances," he said, "we'd better just move along. Let's not push our luck."

Badoglio had looked up as our car approached, but if he recognized it, he gave no sign, and we drove on unchallenged. Looking back as we passed, we caught a glimpse of His Majesty buttoning up his fly.

Neither man, we noted, wore a steel helmet à la Mussolini.

Late that evening the officious colonel in charge of the foreign press implored us not to miss an "extraordinary military exercise" scheduled to take place at 9:00 A.M. the next day in the "battle zone."

Berding and I arrived in good time at the appointed place the next day and were delighted to find our mutual friend Colonel Fiske among the observers. With a cautionary wink he explained the "extraordinary military exercise": A regiment of infantry was to advance down a wooded mountainside, across a narrow valley, and up the far slope under *live* supporting fire from machine guns and artillery. The maneuver, it seemed, had been ordered by Mussolini to demonstrate "the skill and courage of Italian troops in actual battle conditions."

At nine o'clock there was the usual mist in the valley, and visibility was virtually nil. The signal to begin—a green flare to be fired by the Duce himself—was delayed until the sun had burned off the haze below. Conditions were not deemed appropriate until high noon.

When the flare went up, the shooting started, and the resultant noise was deafeningly impressive; but we could see little beyond a few artillery bursts on the "defenders' " distant slope.

Colonel Fiske, who happened to be standing between Andy and me and was following the "battle" with powerful field glasses, put down the binoculars with a puzzled expression.

"What's wrong?" I asked.

"They're shooting over the troops' heads," he said, "but the attacking team is moving too fast. Some elements are bound to run into their own fire. You can bet on it that there'll be accidents, maybe bad ones."

Back at press headquarters in Bolzano that evening, word spread among the correspondents that the exercise had resulted in four dead and at least as many wounded. The report was vigorously denied by a representative of the Ministry of Propaganda, but the reporters were not satisfied. Some swore they had seen several men carried off the field on stretchers.

Later the same evening a man from the Press Bureau in Blackshirt uniform held a press conference. He admitted that four men had been wounded, one mortally, and made a clumsy attempt to squeeze the last drop of propaganda value out of the tragedy.

"The moment the Duce learned that one of his soldiers had been seriously wounded by shrapnel," he said, "he rushed to the man's bedside at the hospital to comfort him. The dying soldier told his Duce how proud he was to have been wounded while serving with his unit."

Andrew Berding was not given to profanity or coarse language, but I distinctly heard him say, sotto voce: "Bullshit. What the poor bastard probably said was what all Italians say when they're hurting: '*Mamma mia!*' "

We subsequently privately confirmed from hospital records that the "extraordinary military exercise" had in fact cost four dead and four wounded from shrapnel bursts.

On the night of August 27 I scribbled these impressions in my diary: "I have just witnessed an insane military exercise. Old Baldy's promised war against Abyssinia hasn't yet begun, but it has already produced casualties. I wonder how many more young Italians and Abyssinians will die before long. . . . From all I have seen and heard in recent days, O.B. is not bluffing. He really means to make war on Abyssinia. . . ."

The climactic event of the war games was a highly theatrical mass review of about 140,000 of the half million troops who had participated in the maneuvers. The men were force-marched into the Valley of the Sun, near Bolzano, from points as far distant as sixty miles, an operation that took two days to complete.

The assembly was completed by four o'clock in the morning of the final day of the exercises, August 31. The men stood in close formations like so many planted trees hour after hour, eating their rations standing and performing their bodily functions in buckets passed among them. By noontime the sun was unbearably hot. Many fainted and were carried off in stretchers. Four more hours passed before Mussolini, the king, the diplomatic corps, and the correspondents took their places on the huge reviewing stand that had been built on a hillside overlooking the Valley of the Sun.

When I looked down from the section reserved for the foreign press, I saw a forest of troops, their helmets and bayonets glinting in the sun. The instant

Mussolini stepped forward to the microphone, the assembly roared the idiotic Fascist battle cry: "Aia Aia! A la la!"

Mussolini told the men he was canceling all leaves and calling an additional two hundred thousand to the colors "in order to face any eventuality that might arise." By then they and everyone else knew what the "eventuality" might be.

From that day onward the whole of Italy, but especially Rome, was subjected to an intensive propaganda campaign justifying war with Ethiopia. Prowar demonstrations and parades became a daily, almost hourly occurrence. Formations of Avanguardisti, the Fascist youth organization, marched along the Via del Corso singing "Giovinezza" and other Fascist hymns. Newsstands in Rome and the main embarkation ports—Genoa and Naples—sold picture postcards portraying beautiful, bare-bosomed Abyssinian virgins who presumably were eagerly awaiting the white soldier-lovers Mussolini was sending them. The most popular song of the time was "Faccetta Nera," a ballad extolling the beauty of the "Little Black Face" every soldier would find in the land he would conquer for the greater glory of Italy and Benito Mussolini.

At the same time Ethiopia was depicted as a sort of El Dorado where vast mineral wealth, including coal and petroleum, even platinum and gold, awaited development by its Fascist conquerors. Much was made of the fact that Ethiopia was ideally suited to the cultivation of grains, coffee, sugar, and cotton, hence was a natural outlet for Italy's "surplus population."

In the midst of the orgy of patriotism that preceded Italy's invasion of Ethiopia, a bit of comic relief was provided in Rome by Jimmy Donahue, the playboy cousin of Countess Barbara Hutton Reventlow-Haugwitz, the American heiress, then much in the news. She and her husband, the count, and a party of friends, including young Jimmy, were occupying the royal suite at the Grand Hotel. During one of the Blackshirt parades Donahue appeared on the suite's balcony overlooking the Via Vittorio Emanuele, one of Rome's main thoroughfares, made a speech in pidgin Italian à la Mussolini, and ended it with a shouted "Viva Ethiopia!" Adding insult to injury, he squirted seltzer water on the marchers. The offender was promptly arrested and escorted to the frontier by OVRA agents.

Because the count and countess were close friends of Mr. Hearst and Marion Davies, I was instructed by telephone from London to help them draft a statement apologizing for the incident. Count Haugwitz received me in gray silk pajamas and a black dressing gown with orange lapels and collar, looking slightly hung over. But he managed to help me cobble together a couple of paragraphs denouncing Donahue's behavior as "inexcusable" and apologizing to the Fascist government and the Italian people for the playboy's "prank."

6

FASCISM GOES TO WAR

On my return to Rome from the maneuvers Aldo handed me a cable from New York instructing me to have myself accredited to the Italian Expeditionary Forces, and by mid-September I was ready to become a war correspondent in Ethiopia. Quietly, without telling Kathryn, I had purchased what the Propaganda Ministry's Press Bureau told me I would need at the "front": pup tent, rubberized groundsheet, folding cot, bedroll, mosquito netting, water bottle, field boots, and other gear. Aldo helped me buy the stuff at Giampaoli, Rome's equivalent of New York's Abercrombie & Fitch.

Also required for accreditation were inoculations against typhoid and paratyphoid, smallpox, and tetanus. I put off getting the requisite shots until the last possible moment, however, and on the morning of September 15 I was glad that I had. Waiting for me at the office was a tall, broad-shouldered man with a mane of white hair and a patch over one eye. My visitor was the veteran journalist Floyd Gibbons, who had lost the eye in France while reporting World War I, and I realized at once that the Hearst Organization, probably on orders from the Chief, had in its infinite wisdom decided to entrust coverage of the impending war to far more experienced hands than mine.

Frankly I was greatly relieved. After what Uncle Gennaro had said about the kind of war the campaign would be, and what my doctor had told me about Ethiopia as a pesthouse of tropical diseases, an early eagerness to emulate Richard Harding Davis had waned considerably.

Gibbons arrived in Rome with two female assistants, a young blond "secretary" and an older woman, his "researcher." Both, he said, were to accompany him to the war zone to assist him in writing his articles for Universal Service and INS. But the ladies were only part of his fantastic scheme for reporting Italy's war against the Ethiopians.

Buzz Hawley, Aldo Forte, and I listened with astonishment as Gibbons outlined his plan. He proposed to charter an amphibious plane which, he said, he would base in Massawa, the seaport in Italian Eritrea, and would use for periodic flights over the battlefields to "obtain material" for his reports. At first we thought he was joking. We soon saw, however, that Gibbons was dead serious, and when he solicited our help in arranging for a plane, none of us had the heart to tell him he was dreaming the impossible.

I subsequently turned over my equipment to him and accompanied him to Giampaoli's emporium, where he bought hundreds of dollars' worth of additional gear for his expedition. We never saw Gibbons again, but he did manage to reach the war zone, courtesy of the Italian Air Force, after Hearst's pennywise management had vetoed his absurd scheme for covering the war from a private plane. The secretaries were left behind, haunted the sidewalk cafés on the Via Veneto for a while, and eventually went home to America.

Gibbons's first dispatch from Massawa was filed through my office shortly before hostilities began. It was an overlong, overemotive defense of Italy's need for "living space for its burgeoning population." He said the residents of "overcrowded Italy" required land on which to create "model farms" like those he had been shown by the the the smart propagandists of the Duce's Press Bureau in what were once the "malarious Pontine Marshes drained and reclaimed by Mussolini."

Gibbons, however, was soon replaced by more objective reporters: by my predecessor in Rome, Bill Chaplin for Universal, and H. R. ("Knick") Knickerbocker for INS. Both filed their dispatches through Paris and London, and I never saw what they wrote.

In the torrid summer of 1935 diplomatic efforts to forestall war, including offers of territory in British and French East Africa as well as Ethiopia, came to naught. "I am not a collector of deserts," Mussolini declared. At the League of Nations British Foreign Secretary Sir Samuel Hoare then called for sanctions, and Mussolini replied with a vicious propaganda campaign against Britain and the League, threatening war if sanctions were applied.

The British in turn sent ships into the eastern Mediterranean, apparently to deny Italy use of the Suez Canal in the event of war. The Duce blustered back. He knew it was safe to do so because his intelligence service had rifled the British ambassador's safe and discovered that Britain's warships were woefully unprepared for battle.

In the atmosphere of bluff and counterbluff the Ethiopian tragedy rolled inexorably on. Haile Selassie mobilized his country to repel invaders in late September, while Italy massed twelve divisions for attack and a bomber squadron led by Mussolini's son-in-law, Count Ciano. It included, as pilots, the Duce's sons, Vittorio and Bruno.

On the afternoon of October 2, 1935, Aldo Forte and I were in our office in the *galleria* checking the evening papers and sipping double-strength espressos to help us revive from too much Frascati at lunch when the air-raid sirens wailed. The hands on the wall clock stood at three-thirty and almost simultaneously Rome's thousands of church bells began pealing.

The deafening confusion of sound was the signal we had been alerted to expect for a spectacular mobilization of the Italian people to hear Mussolini speak. It was called the *Grande Adunata* (Great Rally), which everyone knew was the prelude to the invasion of Ethiopia. Loudspeakers had been installed in Rome's Piazza Venezia and in the public squares of every city, town, village, and hamlet in the country, where the people were ordered to gather when the sirens and bells sounded.

As always, the excitement was greatest in Rome. Leaving Aldo in charge of the office, I found the Via del Corso already jammed with black-booted Fascisti in their black uniforms and tasseled black hats, holding aloft black banners emblazoned with golden fasces, the bundle of rods enclosing an ax with the blade projecting, borne by the lictors of ancient Rome as a symbol of power. The Fascisti marched behind bands blaring their anthem, "Giovinezza," Puccini's more tuneful "Inno di Roma" (Hymn to Rome), or the popular, catchy "Faccetta Nera."

I joined the flow of marchers along the Corso to the Piazza Venezia, where the Duce would speak from his customary rostrum, the balcony of the Palazzo Venezia.

I elbowed my way to a spot on the edge of the grandiose Monument of the Unknown Soldier, beneath an equestrian statue and a conveniently located loudspeaker. From there I had a panoramic view of the piazza and of the balcony. Men, women, and children thronged the piazza and the streets leading into it. The Corso was packed all the way to the distant Piazza del Popolo. I had seen crowds in Rome before, but never anything like the pullulation of October 2, 1935. It must have numbered five hundred thousand, then approximately half the capital's inhabitants. Throughout the country some twenty million Italians were similarly assembled in their respective piazzas to hear their Duce's words, while the rest of the nation's forty-three million citizens sat by their radios.

In Rome a light, cold rain fell intermittently throughout the afternoon; but at dusk it stopped, and shortly after six o'clock, while there was still light to see by, Mussolini clad in the field gray uniform of a corporal of the Fascist militia, materialized on the balcony. A volcanic roar erupted from the crowd below. The incredible, inhuman sound lasted for about a minute before it subsided into a steady, rhythmic chant of "Duce! Duce! Duce . . ." For fully eight minutes—I timed it—the people chorused the title in a swelling, repetitive, mindless crescendo bordering on mass hysteria.

Meanwhile, the Duce, hands on hips, his heavy jaw thrust out, nodded approvingly and surveyed the crowd as though making eye contact with it.

Then, stepping back, he signaled for silence. The crowd obeyed instantly, like a chorus responding to a choirmaster's direction, and Mussolini, in a voice thick with rage, declared: "A solemn hour is about to strike in the history of our nation. With Ethiopia we have been patient for forty years. *Ora basta* [Now, enough]!"

The crowd broke into frenzied cheers. Again Mussolini had to wait while the people in the piazza waved banners, cheered, and resumed their "Duce" chant for another full minute. Once more he prodded old wounds. He reminded them that in World War I Italy had lost six hundred thousand dead and a million wounded but in return had received "only the crumbs of the rich colonial booty." Now, he said, those same powers that had grabbed the lion's share of the spoils planned to "suffocate Italy with sanctions."

"To sanctions of an economic character," Mussolini shouted, "We will reply with discipline, sobriety, and sacrifices. To sanctions of a military nature, however, we will reply with acts of war. . . ."

Thunderous cheers greeted his words and persisted until the orator again signaled for silence.

"Italia," Mussolini roared, so loudly that his voice cracked, "arise and let the cry of your determination soar to the skies and reach our soldiers in East Africa—they who are about to fight! Let it be a salute to our friends and a warning to our enemies. Let it be the cry of Italy—the cry for justice and victory!"

There was a moment of utter silence. Then came a roar of approval even greater than the one that had first greeted the Duce.

The Piazza Venezia became a lake of waving handkerchiefs and banners while Mussolini stood, hands on hips, nodding acceptance. Suddenly he raised his arm in the Fascist salute, turned, and was gone.

A light rain began falling, and the crowds oozed homeward in slow-moving streams.

Early the following morning Mussolini's legions in Eritrea, under the command of General Emilio de Bono, longtime Fascist, forded the shallow Mareb River along the border, invaded Ethiopia, and headed for Adowa, a city of about fifteen thousand souls. That afternoon Adowa was heavily bombed by Ciano's squadron. Vittorio Mussolini, who took part in the attack, likened the bombs dropped on the city to "beautiful red flowers blossoming in the desert sands."

News of the bombing was released to Rome correspondents at 1:15 A.M. the next day. Late-night demonstrations were strictly forbidden by law, but the capital went wild when the people learned from their radios that Ciano had bombed Adowa. Although it was raining, the streets quickly filled with cheering, singing Blackshirts, and the cafés did a lively business in espressos and brandies. The demonstrations kept Aldo and me at the office until dawn.

From our tipster on one of Rome's major dailies, I learned that Ciano's planes had hit several nonmilitary targets, including a clearly marked hospital, causing heavy casualties, among them many women and children. His paper, my informant said, had just received instruction not to refer to the incident.

By October 6 the Italians had occupied Adowa, and the Romans again swarmed into the streets shouting, *"Viva il Duce,"* and "On to Addis Ababa!," the Ethiopian capital. There were no announcements of Italian casualties to dampen their ardor.

The Romans sobered down somewhat four days later, however, when the General Assembly of the League of Nations found Italy guilty of "overt aggression" and voted to impose sanctions on the aggressor. But the proposed sanctions specifically excluded several of the most essential ingredients of modern warfare, including oil. Moreover, the date set for applying the sanctions was November 18, thus affording the Fascist government ample time to accumulate stocks of petroleum, aviation fuel, and other strategic materials.

In advance of the League deadline, Mussolini negotiated a series of highly advantageous barter agreements—with Argentina for meat, Brazil for coffee, Hungary for wheat, Switzerland for precision instruments—in exchange for some cash but mostly oranges, olive oil, wine, and long-term credits. The most important of his deals was a trade pact with Germany.

From Hitler's Reich, Italy received fabricated steel, chemicals, and coal, which was almost as vital as oil because most Italian vessels, freighters as well as warships, were coal burners. Italy paid in citrus fruits and other agricultural products, and I recall that oranges, for example, suddenly virtually disappeared from Rome's markets and that prices for the poor grades available quintupled from twenty cents a kilo to a dollar. Vegetables and meat also became scarce and expensive, and the Italians' standard of living took a sharp drop. Prices rose alarmingly, and before long Italy's economy verged on the catastrophic; gold reserves fell, and currency in circulation tripled.

Sanctions, however, worked perceptibly in Mussolini's favor. The prewar grumbling subsided, and the people's anger turned away from the regime toward *le sanzionisti* (the sanctionists), especially "Perfidious Albion." Mussolini deftly used every League action to create animosity toward Great Britain and mounted a strong propaganda counteroffensive. A national boycott was decreed against the products of all nations participating in the League's efforts "to stifle Italy's economy."

Soon even sensible Italians were saying, "Mussolini is only asking for what was due us for our sacrifices in the Great War." I became convinced of the effectiveness of Mussolini's propaganda when Bill Emmanuel, an astute and intelligent man who had suffered greatly at the hands of the Fascisti, came to me with eyes burning with hatred for Britain and declared, "England has no right doing this to us."

Meanwhile, mobs stormed daily through Rome, shouting insults against the British and obliging shopkeepers and bars to remove from their shelves all goods imported earlier from England. Gordon's gin disappeared from Charlie's bar in the Albergo Ambasciatori on the Via Veneto, and correspondents were deprived thereafter of his justly famous martinis. The Hotel Eden changed its name to Albergo Paradiso, and on restaurant menus a dessert known as zuppa inglese became zuppa imperiale.

At the time the United States was Italy's main supplier of airplane motor fuel, and on the country's armistice day—November 4—I happened to be passing the American Embassy and witnessed an unusual demonstration. Thousands of university students in those absurd varicolored peaked hats that marked them as undergraduates had gathered to thank the *Stati Uniti* and the American ambassador, Breckenridge Long, who had consistently advised Washington to stay out of oil sanctions, for their friendly attitude. The students chanted, *"Viva l'America!"* and even attempted to sing our national anthem, but few of them knew the tune or the words well enough to get beyond the first few bars. The demonstration, I later learned, had been personally ordered by the Duce.

Russia, meanwhile, was Italy's chief source of fuel oil for its transatlantic liners and some of its newer warships, but there were no demonstrations of gratitude outside the Soviet Embassy. In Geneva Moscow's commissar for foreign affairs, Maksim Litvinov, repeatedly denounced fascism's aggression against Ethiopia and kept reminding the "craven democracies" that "peace is indivisible." His words fell on stony ground—and his government made no move to deprive Italy of oil.

When sanctions failed to slow down the Fascist drive into Ethiopia, much less halt it, the League proposed to expand the list of embargoed items to include oil, coal, pig iron, iron, and steel. The matter was still being hotly debated in Geneva when I learned from French and Soviet diplomatic sources that the Italian government was secretly negotiating with an Anglo-American-Dutch consortium to ensure itself adequate and continuing supplies of oil and gasoline. In the course of my investigation I discovered that my friend and competitor G. Stewart ("Stu") Brown of the United Press was working on the same story with British informants. Our paths crossed accidentally, but we decided to work together.

Stewart had had years of experience covering the machinations of the League before coming to Rome and knew far better than I that our story would cause a furor in Geneva when we broke it. Since millions of dollars' worth of oil were involved, publication might also have serious repercussions on Western stock exchanges. For days we talked with friendly bankers, engineers, commercial attachés, and others directly or indirectly involved in the complex deal, taking care to meet only in out-of-the-way cafés and bars not frequented by other correspondents to compare notes.

The story as we finally pieced it together was that an Italian subsidiary of Standard Oil, Italo-American Oil, Inc., based in Genoa, acting in concert with British and Dutch interests, had agreed to furnish Italy with oil against credits totaling ninety million dollars, a huge sum in those days. The agreement, we learned, was to become effective the moment the League voted oil sanctions, tentatively set for December 12.

Still uncertain of the accuracy of our findings, Stewart and I took them to our mutual friend the American ambassador. Breck Long was a tall, canny, Lincolnesque Missourian who was well informed on the inner workings of Italian politics and diplomacy. Almost two years before Mussolini invaded Ethiopia, Long warned Secretary of State Cordell Hull that il Duce was planning a major military action of some kind in East Africa. He had noted unusually large shipments of lumber, barbed wire, cement, and steel reinforcement rods to Eritrea and rightly concluded that the materials were meant for the construction of military roads and installations. But Washington poohpoohed the idea and scolded Long for spending too much money on cables detailing the shipments. The State Department began taking serious notice of Long's dispatches only when he started reporting excessive troop movements. And it took him very seriously indeed when he reported that Mussolini meant what he said about going to war if oil sanctions were imposed.

The ambassador, more politician than diplomat and always willing to talk "off the record" to American correspondents, smiled knowingly when Stewart and I told him what we had unearthed. He confirmed our story in all its essential details, adding, "Look, boys, I've sold my oil stocks. I don't want to be accused of profiting from foreknowledge." It was the green light Stewart and I had hoped for, and on the way to our offices we agreed that Stewart would break the story for the UP's afternoon clients and I would send it for Universal's morning newspapers.

When the story hit the front pages on December 3, it was immediately and vehemently denied in New York by the president of Standard Oil of New Jersey, in Rome by the Foreign Office, and in London by British oil executives. "A preposterous tale" some called it. Yet at a meeting of the Fascist Grand Council held the next day, Mussolini told his ministers to "rest easy, the League will not impose oil sanctions on us." Furthermore, orders had gone out to the Fascist press earlier to "soft-pedal news concerning oil imports in order not to disturb important negotiations now under way." We obtained copies of the order from cooperative Italian newsmen.

Mulling the matter over later in the paneled, leathery comfort of Charlie's dimly lighted bar, Stewart and I wondered whether we had scored a genuine scoop or had been manipulated by vested interests into sending a story designed to torpedo oil sanctions. We tended to believe we had been gulled, for when the proposed extension of sanctions subsequently came to a vote in the League's Committee of Eighteen, only ten members expressed willingness to participate. We concluded that Britain, France, and Russia, as well as the United States, had never really wanted the League to impose oil sanctions. Such an embargo might have brought Mussolini's war to a standstill, saved Ethiopia and collective security, and vindicated the League, but it would have been bad for business.

The day the League's sanctions went into effect, November 18, 1935, Mussolini appealed to the women of Italy to contribute their wedding rings and gold jewelry to help defray the rising cost of the war. Although the flow of oil and other essentials remained unimpeded, Italy was effectively cut off from the world's financial markets and desperately short of gold for conversion into foreign currencies with which to help pay for imports.

The wives of peasants, factory workers, clerks, and aristocrats solemnly marched to the Monument of the Unknown Soldier in the Piazza Venezia and in an elaborate ceremony, which I attended, dropped their offerings into rows of upturned steel helmets. It was good opera, and the women loved it. Each contributor received in exchange for her gold ring an iron one appropriately inscribed on the inner surface. Roman women alone turned in 250,000 rings.

Some ten million women took part throughout the country, most of them wearing the black clothes they reserved for funerals and churchgoing. When the rings were melted down and turned into bars, the country's gold reserves were reportedly augmented by 20 percent. The gold thus recovered was valued at $120 million.

Prominent among the contributors were Rome's Jews. There was no overt racism, no "Jewish question" in the kingdom of Italy in 1935. In reply to Mussolini's appeal, a delegation of leaders of the Jewish community went to Fascist party headquarters in the Palazzo Braschi, bringing with them the gold of their synagogue: the hand-wrought gold menorah, a solemn symbol of Judaism; the long, fingerlike gold pointer with which ceremonial readings of the Torah are followed; and, most symbolically of all, the solid gold key of the Ark, resting place of the Torah, the two-posted scroll of the five books of Moses. All these holy things were melted down into yellow bricks to be hurled at fascism's enemies. The treasure's bearers had their pictures taken with a local Fascist boss.

So many young Jews volunteered for service in Ethiopia that the regime was obliged to provide a rabbi to serve their spiritual needs at the front and to build a synagogue for them in their rest area behind the lines.

Meanwhile, after an initial rush into Ethiopia that by the end of November enabled the Italians to claim they had conquered a huge chunk of Haile Selassie's empire—a portion about the size of Vermont and Rhode Island combined—General de Bono's campaign bogged down.

Irked by de Bono's apparent lack of soldierly skill and by persistent rumors of dissension in the general's staff, Mussolini recalled him in mid-December and replaced him with Marshal Badoglio. Spurred by a stream of orders from Rome, Badoglio quickly reorganized his forces, replacing Fascist field commanders with regular army officers, and in mid-January 1936 launched his offensive. On May 5, less than four months later, the old marshal was at the gates of Addis Ababa and Emperor Selassie fled to safety in London.

Four days later, in the early afternoon of May 9, there was another grand rally in the Piazza Venezia, this time more military than civilian. I found a convenient spot directly across from the Duce's balcony and heard him proclaim to a delirious crowd of civilians and cheering troops the conquest of Ethiopia and King Victor Emmanuel III's assumption of the title of emperor of the conquered country. When the cheers subsided, Mussolini intoned: "Lift high your banners, your weapons, and your hearts, O legionnaires, to hail the reappearance of the empire on the sacred hills of Rome after fifteen centuries."

Exultation filled the piazza, and every public square in Italy, for the nation was celebrating peace regained, national pride restored, and the end of military humiliations.

It was Benito Mussolini's finest hour.

7

LIFE UNDER FASCISM

For days after the war ended in Africa, Rome resounded to the strains of Fascist hymns, the rhythmic thump of drums, and the blare of trumpets. Student demonstrators filled the streets and piazzas, shouting "Viva il Duce!" and cheered obscenely when hundreds of Ethiopian captives were marched through the Arch of Constantine in a restaging of the imperial conquests celebrated in Roman times.

Meanwhile, the cult of Duce—the word always printed in block letters as DUCE—was being actively promoted by fascism's stage managers. Benito Mussolini was depicted in articles and editorials in the Fascist press as the charismatic leader par excellence. His scowling bigger-than-life visage appeared increasingly on huge posters and billboards, in profile to emphasize his manly jaw, in uniform and wearing a steel helmet to accentuate his warlike demeanor.

The most blatant expression of his charisma—in the word's original Greek meaning of "magic power"—was the slogan "Mussolini Is Always Right" emblazoned on public buildings throughout the land. In a sense, that was all the Italians knew or needed to know, and the impression was widespread abroad that the Duce enjoyed the unqualified admiration of the entire nation.

Whether the adulation was genuine or as universal as fascism's propagandists wanted foreign observers and correspondents to believe, I frankly did not know at the time. Ever since my arrival in Rome in the spring of the previous year I had been working twelve to fourteen hours a day, learning my way about the labyrinthine Fascist bureaucracy and trying to keep abreast of events. Although I had heard enough wartime grumbling to be fairly certain that not *all* Italians marched to the beat of Mussolini's drum, I had been far too busy with office routine to circulate among the people to catch their real mood.

Indeed, I rarely even had time to play with Sean, who was growing like a backyard weed and needed a father's companionship, or to take Kathryn to a concert, the opera, or a movie. Our social life was limited to infrequent dinners out with fellow American correspondents and their wives and occasional cocktail parties, the standard entertainment of the small American colony.

Socially my colleagues and I lived in a tight little world peopled by our own kind, a tiny cosmos of American diplomats, journalists, and businessmen and a few retired Italophiles. These elderly longtime residents preferred Rome to Seattle or Kansas City and lived handsomely on dollar incomes from stocks and bonds. They admired the Duce for having "made the trains run on time" and heartily approved of fascism because it opposed communism and stood for "law and order."

When the war ended, the flow of news slackened sufficiently to enable me to try to explore the Fascist society that Mussolini had created. For weeks I walked the streets, rode buses and trolley cars instead of taxis, and frequented working-class restaurants, cafés, and wineshops. I met garage mechanics, masons, electricians, telephone installers, carpenters, stenographers, railway station porters, waiters and barmen, and grizzled jehus who drove the city's several thousand horse-drawn carriages.

The results of my inquiry were depressing. The Romans, I quickly discovered, were actually *afraid* to talk even among themselves and were doubly fearful in the presence of *un giornalista americano.* Mussolini seemed to have succeeded in cowing into silence the descendants of those spirited Italians who had fought for freedom and national unity under Mazzini, Garibaldi, and Cavour.

The few whom I managed to engage in conversation in the cafés and wineshops of plebeian Trastevere and other working-class quarters on the city's periphery talked guardedly, constantly looking over their shoulders to make certain they weren't being overheard. Nevertheless, this smallish sample, numbering no more than about thirty out of some two hundred citizens with whom I made contact, provided a glimpse into the poverty and misery in which most of the capital's workers lived.

They complained of the high cost of bread and the other staples of their diet; they rarely saw meat on their tables more than once a month. Most were barely making ends meet on wages that averaged the equivalent of less than two dollars a day. Their main complaint, however, was having to live in cramped quarters. Couples with five or six children occupied the standard three-room flats which the regime's public housing program provided in jerry-built high-rise walk-up apartment houses, unbearably hot in summer, they said, and never sufficiently heated in winter.

A few attributed their misery to "corruption in high places," but none held Mussolini responsible for it. "If the Duce knew there were grafters in the regime," they said, "he would hang them from the nearest lamppost." In their eyes, their Duce was the incorruptible godhead of fascism, the father figure who would solve all their problems.

All with whom I succeeded in establishing a relationship—individually over an espresso in a workingman's café or a *quartino* of cheap wine in a carter's cantina—depended heavily on the minimal benefits they received from the rudimentary welfare state which Mussolini, a renegade Socialist, had created. It provided old-age pensions, workmen's compensation for illness or disability, low-cost medical and dental care, free education for children through age sixteen, reduced fares on public transportation, cut-rate tickets for cinemas and theaters, and, most important of all, "family allowances," meaning bonuses for additional babies, a benefit that mainly served the Duce's military aims. The only requirement for these rewards was membership in good standing in the Fascist party or in any one of the various workers' syndicates created when Mussolini outlawed free trade unions early in his dictatorship.

On the whole, social security benefits under fascism were modest, and the system was far less advanced than in Scandinavia. But none of my reluctant informants regretted the loss of individual liberties involved. In fact, conformity seemed to them a small price to pay for the modest measure of social security they enjoyed.

Numbered among the country's leading conformists, and particularly favored by the regime, were Italy's journalists. A former newspaperman himself, Mussolini understood the value of a supportive press. Members of the Sindacato dei Giornalisti, therefore, were among the nation's best-paid workers, the salaries of topflight editors and reporters often equaling the substantial stipends of cabinet ministers. In addition, they received cut-rate first-class air and railway transportation, free theater tickets, reductions in rents and taxes, and many other favors.

The result was a press that obsequiously reflected the Duce's policies and dutifully suppressed unpleasant truths. Strikes and protest demonstrations, for example, were illegal, hence few and far between. But when they happened, they were not reported in the newspapers, so that the impression the general public got from the print media, at home and abroad, was one of labor contentment in the Fascist state. The American expatriates whom I met at cocktail parties and who sang Mussolini's praises for running "an orderly society" were unaware of the fact that crime was nonexistent simply because it was never reported.

Actually Italian newspaper readers loved crime news, and editors were frequently tempted to print such items in hopes of increasing circulation. Crime statistics were never available, but in the year 1935–1936 the Ministry of Propaganda was obliged to issue four thousand censorship orders killing reports of crimes ranging from petty theft to murder, and four hundred fines were levied against newspapers that had repeatedly violated the rule against publication of items dealing with forbidden subjects, which included references to lovers' quarrels, domestic disputes, broken homes, train wrecks, floods, and other public calamities.

Three sailors were killed and several others were injured aboard the liner *Conte di Savoia* during a particularly stormy Atlantic crossing. I sent the story and was severely scolded by a lower-echelon functionary of the Propaganda Ministry's Press Bureau. Not a word appeared in the Italian press. "Publication of such items," I was told, "could give the false impression that the Italian people have not yet reached the level of maturity which would allow them to face reality with a strong and virile spirit!"

But the heavy hand of Propaganda Minister Dino Alfieri, who invariably acted on orders from the Duce, failed to squelch entirely the critical faculties—or the integrity—of many of the nation's premier journalists. Some, like Virginio Gayda, editor of Rome's powerful *Giornale d'Italia,* were taken in by the regime and slavishly served Mussolini's dictates. But a substantial number, among them Sandro Sandri, Paolo Monelli, Gian Gaspare Napoletano, and Luigi Barzini, Jr., conformed reluctantly and merely out of the sheer need to survive.

On the whole, Italian newspapermen were probably Europe's most frustrated journalists. They didn't particularly mind having to write things in praise of the regime which they knew to be gross exaggerations of the truth, but they deeply resented having to suppress real news. Daily, sometimes several times a day, orders came *orally* from Mussolini's Press Bureau telling editors what they could or could not print or what they should emphasize or minimize. They were never permitted, for instance, to publish in full the texts of the Duce's speeches or of his interviews with visiting foreign journalists; they could print only the carefully edited versions disseminated by Agenzia Stefani, the government's official wire service.

Of the half dozen Italian newspapermen I saw more or less regularly, the most interesting was the cynical, darkly handsome Barzini, of Milan's *Corriere della Sera.* Luigi, Gibom to his friends, had lived in the United States, had studied journalism at Columbia University, and wrote English and Italian with the same fluid skill. More outspoken than most of his colleagues, he once described Mussolini to me as "the personification of the secret longings of the overwhelming majority of Italians."

Not even the courageous Gibom, however, would talk politics on the telephone; a censor might be listening. Like everyone else, Luigi had a healthy respect for the OVRA. A chance remark that could be construed as anti-Fascist might mean prison or a stretch in *confino,* banishment to one of the rocky Lipari Islands off the north coast of Sicily, where dissidents were sent for extended periods, sometimes for life.

The secret police penetrated every nook and cranny of the society, an invisible army of upwards of a hundred thousand OVRA agents, plus countless thousands of paid "volunteers": waiters, doormen, servants, cabbies, barmen, office boys, prostitutes, and others who supplied the raw intelligence of their daily reports. Foreigners in general, and foreign correspondents in particular, were closely watched.

The OVRA knew what time I left home for my office and what time I returned, where I lunched and with whom, what foreign mail I received (and its contents!), and the number (and often also the names) of my guests at parties. Like all my colleagues, I was demoralized by the uncomfortable feeling of being constantly under surveillance but soon found it was useless to complain to the Press Bureau; its functionaries vehemently denied the OVRA even existed.

Those of us who gathered regularly for a leisurely drink in the upholstered comfort of Charlie's bar or bellied up to the plain zinc bar at Rampoldi's, in the Piazza di Spagna, for a beer and a sandwich took care never to refer to Mussolini by name. He was always "Old Baldy," "the Big Boy," "Mr. Brown," or "His Nibs," and we often used baseball or football terminology, even schoolboy pig Latin to convey our meanings. For invariably there was someone close enough to overhear what was being said: the barman himself, a waiter, or perhaps a stranger who sidled up offering black-market lire for dollars, a sure sign of an agent provocateur setting a trap.

Mussolini's all-pervasive police system was run by Arturo Bocchini, a man of medium height, stocky, heavy-jowled like his master, almost foppishly elegant in dress and manner, and as ruthless as Hitler's Himmler. Endowed with a prodigious memory for names and faces, Bocchini was the Fouché of the Fascist regime and the most powerful man in Italy after the Duce himself. Unlike Napoleon's chief of police, however, he nourished no political ambitions and was content to remain a supercop whose mission was to protect Mussolini's life and rout out subversives, real or imaginary.

The OVRA was highly departmentalized and had branches everywhere, including Argentina and the United States, where its agents kept watch over numerous professors and students of Italian nationality and regularly reported on their views and attitudes. Like Hitler's Gestapo and Stalin's OGPU, the OVRA also had many female agents who acted as spies and propagandists. They were generally to be found in the smarter cafés and nightclubs, in the posh dining cars of first-class trains, and at important social functions attended by foreign diplomats and correspondents.

It was Bocchini's men who had arrested my friend Bill Emmanuel. Shortly afterward, I met one of Bocchini's Mata Haris at a diplomatic cocktail party. Lisa, a luscious brunette in her early thirties, was less a spy than a propagandist assigned to entice me into becoming a friendly supporter of the regime.

After our brief encounter at the party, during which we sipped Manhattans tête-à-tête and flirted outrageously, Lisa often came uninvited to my office in the Galleria Colonna to "chat" about the virtues of the corporative state and the benefits workers derived from Italy's "highly advanced" social security system. She was intelligent, knowledgeable, and, had I chosen to become "involved," eminently "available." But warned off by the experienced Emmanuel, who alerted me to the possibility that because of my Italian name and background I was considered pliable material, I avoided entanglement. There were sultry Roman afternoons, however, when temptation almost overcame my instinct for self-preservation.

For foreign journalists, the OVRA was merely a nuisance one learned to live with, but for most Italians it was a terroristic organization that dominated their lives from dawn to nightfall, from cradle to grave. It was responsible in the mid-1920s for the flight abroad of anti-Fascist politicians, intellectuals, and some ten to twenty thousand ordinary citizens who refused to live on their knees under the dictatorship of Benito Mussolini. Many went to Paris, where they founded an anti-Fascist newspaper, *Libertà e Giustizia*.

Obviously, not all Italians who detested fascism and cherished freedom fled. Hundreds of thousands of dissidents remained behind out of sheer necessity or love of country. Like Bill Emmanuel, they never joined the party and, like my son's godfather, former Premier Orlando, offered no active resistance to fascism. They were upper-middle-class lawyers, doctors, engineers, scientists, businessmen, and teachers, and they constituted the "passive enemies" of the regime, tolerated as long as they "behaved" themselves. But they lived in terror of the OVRA; even in the privacy of their homes few dared criticize the Duce and his works in the presence of their servants unless the latter were old retainers and virtually members of the family. And none freely used the telephone to express political views.

Only the Italian peasants were not unduly bothered by Bocchini's men. The rural masses were truly second-class citizens, servile and resigned, particularly in the south in what had been the Kingdom of the Two Sicilies in Bourbon times. In central and northern Italy traditional folk cultures continued to give some dignity and meaning to their lives, and the regime wisely refrained from interfering with their customs beyond encouraging the production of more children. But south of Rome the peasants were much like the blacks in the American South in the mid-1930s, though with a far less expressive popular culture. Fascist propaganda, with its boastfulness and its scoffing at death, was especially alien to people for whom death was the most meaningful reality in the world, its presence constantly evoked in the black mourning clothes of the work-bent women. In homes often shared with donkeys or goats there were pictures of the Madonna and the saints, but rarely of the king or Garibaldi, and never of Mussolini.

It was really the bourgeoisie that felt the brunt of OVRA terrorism, and my American colleagues and I were nothing if not bourgeois in our life-style. Moreover, because we were foreigners and journalists, we were singled out for special attention. We worked and lived, therefore, in an atmosphere of ceaseless surveillance, intimidation, and harassment. But we were all young, adventurous, and resilient, and we stubbornly refused to allow Signor Bocchini and his *sbirri* to interfere with our work or our pleasures.

Individually and collectively American correspondents lived well in Mussolini's Rome, even during the Ethiopian War and its aftermath of League of

Nations sanctions, which caused prices to rise and the deplorable disappearance of imported English gin and scotch whiskey. On our dollar incomes we maintained living standards we could not have afforded in Chicago, New York, or Washington. Rents were reasonable—I paid sixty dollars a month for the charming furnished penthouse in the Via dei Condotti—and servants were considered well paid at fifteen dollars a month, plus, of course, the cost of their uniforms (white for day, black for evening) and their keep. Most not only shopped for food, cooked, and served but cleaned the living quarters and laundered *la signora*'s undergarments.

For the first time in our lives Kathryn and I could afford tailor-made clothing, dine in style in fine restaurants, and buy the best seats at concerts, the opera, or the movies. A seamstress made Kathryn a stunning evening gown for eighty dollars, and Sonneman, the Jewish haberdasher-tailor across the street from where we lived, charged me sixty dollars for a handmade summer suit.

On weekends there were family picnics with the Berdings, the Browns, and other colleagues, at the nearby beaches at Ostia or Castel Fusano, both only a short ride from Rome by car or electric railway, or excursions into the mystic Roman Campagna and its grape-garlanded towns: Frascati, Albano, Nemi, and Rocca di Papa in the Alban Hills. They were delightful places at any time except winter but were at their best in the early autumn, after the grapes had been harvested. Then flowers and glistening vine leaves, mellow sunlight, and the aroma of new wine commingled in the joyous festivals that marked the season and that were infinitely more evocative of Bacchus than of Bocchini.

One of our favorite pastimes in any season was going to the movies at the Quirinetta, a small, intimate midtown cinema off the Corso which seated no more than a hundred persons, was luxuriously furnished with armchairs for seats, and showed American, British, and French films in their original versions without subtitles: *Camille, My Man Godfrey, Mr. Deeds Goes to Town,* and *La Kermesse Héroïque.*

On summer evenings there were outdoor performances of *Aïda* and other operas in the Baths of Caracalla, the great stone bathing place where the ancient Romans, in white togas, gathered to cleanse their bodies and revel in the latest gossip. Only in the ancient baths, with their gargantuan stage, can *Aïda* be properly produced with elephants, camels, and a cast of hundreds.

Delightful in spring and autumn, Rome is unbearably hot in summer, especially in July and August. Kathryn and the boy sweltered through one summer in 1935 but were visibly suffering the heat and humidity of early July of the following year. I sent them north to Zell am See, a lakeside resort in the Austrian mountains with Stu Brown's wife, Helen, and their two small children. There would be no language problem; the Browns had served in Vienna before being posted to Rome, and Helen had fluent German. But it would not be a happy holiday for my wife.

8

THE CHIEF'S VISIT

In the early summer of 1936, following a welcome lull, the work load at the office was suddenly and dramatically increased by reports that Pope Pius XI was ill. The pontiff was seventy-nine years old and, according to our Vatican informant, might not long survive what appeared to be a chronic heart ailment. The situation required mounting a round-the-clock "death watch," for which I needed additional staff: a man to work the midnight to 9:00 A.M. shift. But my repeated requests for permission to hire someone fell on deaf ears in New York and London. From both places, in fact, came ominous warnings that unless Universal Service's bureau chiefs managed to hold down operating expenses, Mr. Hearst's pet news agency might be shut down.

The thought of being beaten by my competitors on so big a story as the death of the pope, however, was almost more than I could bear. Both the Associated Press and the United Press had ample staffs of trained American personnel in addition to experienced Italian assistants and could easily divide their workdays into eight-hour shifts. Aldo Forte and I simply couldn't handle the swelling flow of news, so when the opportunity arose one day to take on Michael Chinigo—an engaging, ever-smiling young American of Italo-Albanian origin who, incidentally, claimed kinship to Albania's King Zog—I hired him on the spot without consulting anyone and paid him out of my pocket.

Michael had attended Yale before coming to Italy to study medicine at the

University of Rome and after two years of medical studies had decided to become a newspaperman. Fluent in Italian and knowledgeable about medicine, he was just the man to help cover the increasingly important Vatican beat. Moreover, he indicated he had "private means" and while serving his apprenticeship was willing to work for twelve dollars a week, all I could afford until I persuaded management to let me transfer him to the regular payroll.

In the early morning of July 14, shortly after my family had left on their Austrian holiday, I was awakened by severe pains in the groin. A pulled muscle, I thought, having played tennis the day before. But the pains persisted and were accompanied by nausea. I called as loudly as I could for Maria. Then, remembering I had given her the day off to visit relatives, I called the office from my bedside telephone. I described my symptoms to Michael, who listened attentively, then said, "Sounds like appendicitis. I'll be right over."

Michael arrived within an hour with a doctor friend, who examined me and muttered something in Italian that sounded like "peritonitis." Between them they managed to wrap me in a dressing gown and hurried me by taxi to a private hospital where the doctor operated. Because of complications that arose during surgery, it looked as though I might not survive, and Michael telephoned Kathryn to return to Rome at once. I was surprised to see her at my bedside when I regained consciousness but happy that she stayed, helping with bedpans and other unpleasant duties during the miserable postoperative period, for the sisters who ran the place seemed always to be at vespers or matins when needed. A few days later, assured that I was out of danger, she returned to Zell am See, where she had left Sean in the care of Helen Brown. Departing, she said, "Michael probably saved your life. . . ."

On the morning of July 19, 1936, as I was preparing to leave the clinic, Michael brought me a cable from New York ordering me to "proceed at once" to Madrid, where a Fascist uprising, led by General Franco, was in progress against the Republican government following the assassination by left-wing guerrillas of José Calvo Sotello, one of the more popular leaders of the Spanish right. I dictated a reply explaining what had happened to me and that according to my doctor, I probably would not be fit enough to travel for at least another ten days.

I deeply regretted my inability to rush to the big story that I had sensed was developing in Madrid. Frustrated and angry at being immobilized, I pondered what roles Mussolini and Hitler might play in the unfolding drama. It seemed to me an excellent opportunity for them to make trouble for Spanish democracy. The basis for Italo-German political and military cooperation, and intervention, in European affairs had already been laid at Feltre, in northern Italy, where Mussolini and Hitler met secretly sometime early in 1936—soon after the Führer opened the Winter Olympic games at Garmisch-Partenkirchen—and reached an "understanding" that was tantamount to a mutual assistance pact.

I sent the story of that meeting on February 10, and the *New York American,* "flagship" paper of the Hearst chain, had headlined it sensationally: DUCE

HAS PACT WITH HITLER. The story was vehemently denied by both Rome and Berlin, and I was summoned to the Propaganda Ministry for a *lavata di testa* (literally "headwashing," meaning scolding), which correspondents got whenever they sent news deemed "false" or "tendentious" but not sufficiently serious to warrant expulsion.

In any event, my dispatch was amply confirmed less than a month later, on March 7, 1936, when Germany reoccupied the Rhineland, which had been demilitarized by the peace treaties of 1919. The zone's reoccupation by German forces was also prohibited by the Locarno agreements of 1925, whereby Germany, France, Belgium, Britain and Italy mutually "guaranteed" the peace of Europe, a stipulation which Hitler had accepted and had promised to respect. By the treaties of Versailles and Locarno the French were entitled to regard German reoccupation of the Rhineland as an act of aggression and were empowered to take steps to expel Hitler's forces alone or in concert with the other signatories. But none of the Western "guarantors" moved a muscle.

Clearly the Ethiopian War had paved the way for Germany to secure Italy's cooperation in what was to become first the Rome-Berlin Axis, then the famous—or infamous—Pact of Steel and had made possible Hitler's boldest step since assuming power in 1933. Yet another milestone along Europe's road to cataclysm was passed, but the Western powers slept and dreamed of peace.

After Kathryn returned to Zell am See, I recuperated in a seaside pension at Anzio, the picturesque fishing port and resort town on the Tyrrhenian coast about thirty-five miles south of Rome that became a major battlefield in World War II. Ten days of sunbathing, long walks on the volcanic black sands of Anzio's beaches, plenty of good seafood, and an excellent dry white wine from nearby Nettuno worked wonders. By early August I was fit again and returned to work. The first thing I did was to persuade London to let me put Michael Chinigo on the payroll.

My sickbed hunch that Mussolini and Hitler would be tempted to help stir the witches' caldron in Spain proved correct. While I was convalescing, I learned the Duce had sent a vigorous protest to the Madrid government charging that five Italians had been assassinated by "Red terrorists" in Barcelona. Meanwhile, the Italian Air Force and Navy were preparing to attack the city; eighty or more Caproni bombers were poised for takeoff at a Sardinian base, and a naval squadron was proceeding toward the Catalonian coast, carrying marines for a possible landing at Barcelona "to protect the lives and property of Italian residents there."

Italy's protest paralleled one made earlier by Adolf Hitler, who had sternly admonished the Madrid government against "acts of barbarism" following the alleged execution of four Germans by "a radical Catalonian firing squad." Fortunately I had developed a good source in the Spanish Embassy, a Captain Gallegos, a staunch Republican, who assured me there had been *no* executions of Italian or German nationals. Obviously the two dictators had found—or manufactured—a reason for armed intervention in Spain on the side of General Franco and his Fascist insurgents.

I checked the information Captain Gallegos gave me with other diplomatic sources—Colonel Robert ("Robbie") Stone, at the British Embassy, and Leon Helfand, the Russian chargé d'affaires, both close friends—while my INS colleague Hawley made corroborative soundings at the French Embassy. Satisfied that the story as related to me by Captain Gallegos was true, I sent a long, carefully constructed dispatch to New York on August 7. It made page one in the *American* under a headline that proclaimed: ALL EUROPE UNEASY: DUCE INTERVENTION IN SPAIN FEARED.

I expected a sharp reaction from the Propaganda Ministry, but none came. What did come on the morning of August 9 was a cable from New York advising me that Mr. Hearst and "a party of friends" were arriving in Naples aboard the SS *Rex* on August 13. I was to meet the ship, of course, and make myself available to the Chief, who had requested that I arrange an audience with the Duce for him.

Mr. Hearst was accompanied by Marion Davies, two toy dachshunds, and a gaggle of male and female guests drawn from what was then called café society, the equivalent of today's jet set. Wearing a newly acquired double-breasted powder blue suit of ersatz linen, I boarded the ship and met for the first time the impressive William Randolph Hearst.

He was a strikingly handsome man and huge, at least an inch or two above six feet, broad in the shoulders and deep in the chest, but with long, somewhat spindly legs, inadequate, I thought, to support such a massive superstructure. The really surprising thing about him, however, was his voice. I had expected a basso profundo to match his physique and importance, but he spoke in thin, almost squeaky tones. In his summer-weight dark suit and white shirt with a narrow blue-black necktie, he looked more like an evangelical preacher than one of America's most influential publishers.

With Mr. Hearst in his stateroom was Colonel Joseph Willicombe, a short, stubby, penguinesque man, the Chief's secretary and alter ego. He introduced me, pronouncing my name correctly, but my employer got it wrong and said he was pleased to meet Mr. "Gervaski."

In an adjoining stateroom I met the gorgeous Miss Davies and her dachshunds, which she thrust into my arms with a gracious smile as she prepared to follow me to the gangplank. I held the squirmy creatures in the crook of my left arm as I assisted Miss Davies with my free hand.

Miss Davies wore flouncy white from head to toe under a floppy white hat and walked slowly, carefully, as though stepping on hot rocks. This was due, I saw, to the high heels she was wearing. As we progressed uncertainly down the gangplank, one of the dachshunds piddled gently, warmly on my jacket. The bloody little beast must have been pissing hydrochloric acid, for his emission left an irremovable stain.

I saw the party and their luggage through customs and into the several limousines waiting to transport the Chief and his guests to the Hotel Excelsior, where appropriate suites overlooking the magnificent Bay of Naples and plumed Vesuvius had been booked in advance. I promised Willicombe that I would see what I could do about the audience with Mussolini which Mr. Hearst had requested, handed the dachshunds over to Miss Davies, and took my leave. If the lady noticed what one of her pets had done to my brand-new suit—by then it was a clearly visible dark stain that ran from about the top button to the hem of the jacket—she gave no sign.

On August 24, my diary tells me, the Hearst party came to Rome and checked in at the Grand Hotel. A call from Joe Willicombe informed me that the Chief wanted to see me and had requested that I come to dinner that evening. Dress, informal; time, eight o'clock. The invitation included Mrs. Gervasi; Kathryn had returned from Austria but could not attend; the maid Maria was taking her mid-August holiday, and Sean was still too young—he had just turned four—to be left alone.

There were no cocktails or preliminaries, and dinner was served promptly in the privacy of the dining room of the ornate royal suite occupied by Mr. Hearst and Miss Davies. As a result of Kathryn's absence, the guests numbered thirteen.

The Chief sat at the head of the table, and I could see he was greatly disturbed, fidgeting, glowering, and muttering to himself. I caught a look of annoyance directed at me and nudged Willicombe, seated next to me at the lower end, for an explanation. He said that Mr. Hearst considered thirteen at dinner "unlucky." I offered to leave, half rising to do so, but Willicombe restrained me, saying, "The Chief wants to see you for a chat."

In the meantime, Miss Davies had left her place to hover over the Chief from behind his chair, whispered in his ear, and patted his shoulders with both hands before resuming her seat. Mr. Hearst seemed reassured, and dinner proceeded without further ado. The guests' dinnertime conversation never included me, and what I overheard of it was gossipy prattle about the Hollywood and Broadway friends of those present. Of the many names dropped during the chitchat, the only one I recognized was that of Elsa Maxwell, the reigning queen of café society in the 1930s and 1940s.

After what seemed an interminable meal, I followed Willicombe into a small parlor adjoining the Hearst suite. The Chief was waiting for us standing before a marble-topped Venetian table. He looked up from a letter he was reading as we entered. He had something to say to me and said it without preamble. "Young man," he said, "you have given important information to the enemy."

"I'm sorry, sir," I said lightly, "but I didn't know we were at war."

"We are always at war with communism," he said, sternly. "You have given the Reds in Spain important information, and the people here are greatly disturbed about it.

"Now then, I want you to send nothing which will offend the people here. I believe Signor Mussolini is a great man. I believe he has done great things for Italy. Send nothing which could in any way be of comfort to the Communists.

I recalled kindly Joe Willicombe's words: "just go on doing your stuff as before." That was not journalism but at best truth refracted through the prisms of fascism. "Of course," the Chief had said, "don't distort the news." I chuckled at that. What was pouring out of Rome and Berlin was distorted news, the only kind available.

I could think of no other course of action as a corresspondent in Rome beyond striving for the truth despite the obstacles created by the Fascist regime. I vowed to try to put fascism in perspective, to reveal it for what I knew it to be, an evil force in European affairs, though how I would accomplish this, frankly, I had no clear idea.

More than two months later I received a letter from Mr. Hearst dated October 16, 1936. Written on the stationery of St. Donat's Castle, his place in South Wales, it said he was about to leave for America and was writing to say good-bye and to thank me for my kindness while he was in Rome. The last three paragraphs confirmed that he meant every word he had said to me that unforgettable August evening in the Grand Hotel. He wrote:

> The fight which the Duce is making for orderly government and the preservation of civilized conditions is not merely for Italy—not merely for Europe, but for the Western Hemisphere as well.
>
> It is my hope that all thoughtful, capable and creative people in every civilized land will unite to stem the flood of riot, revolution and destruction which is miscalled communism, and which means merely common disaster.
>
> When occasion offers, please express to the Duce my admiration and best wishes.

In fairness to Mr. Hearst, however, he was not alone in his admiration for Signor Mussolini. He was only one of a distinguished company that included Mahatma Gandhi, George Bernard Shaw, Winston Churchill, Sir Oswald Mosley, and Rabindranath Tagore, to mention only those who readily come to mind. England's David Lloyd George and George Lansbury, incidentally, were similarly captivated by Herr Hitler.

By the end of the summer of 1936 General Franco's right-wing revolution in Spain had assumed the dimensions of a cruel and relentless civil war. The revolt was checked in Madrid and Barcelona but was eminently successful in garrison towns in the south. Only one in ten army officers remained loyal to the state.

While the Madrid government raised a "people's militia," it also tried to buy arms abroad, as any government has the right to do. But Britain and France decided not to sell arms to either side and sponsored a policy of nonintervention, which they justified on grounds that the war in Spain might become a clash of rival ideologies, Fascist versus Communist, and spread

"You can tell the people here those are my orders to yc
use us at any time, tell them they can. Send anything they
Of course, do not distort the news."

I was speechless. I could hardly believe what I had just I
I could say a word, Hearst dismissed me with a smile and a c
and left the room. Willicombe, sensing an outburst on my pai
and led me out into the hall.

"Joe," I said, almost choking with anger, "how the hell ca
what he says and *not* distort the news? I thought Universal was
not a propaganda pipeline—"

"Relax, Frank," Willicombe said. "The Chief didn't mear
sounded. Anyhow, just go on doing your stuff as before—"

"Sorry, Joe," I replied. "I'm quitting. I've had offers—"

I was bluffing, of course. I had had no offers and hadn't the
where I could get another job, certainly not as a bureau chief i
European capital.

"Don't do anything foolish," said Willicombe with the air of a
giving fatherly advice. "Just be patient for a while, and you wor
Some big changes are in the air, and my hunch is that you're ir
promotion and a raise in pay. So take it easy. Promise me you w

I nodded agreement, and we shook hands.

I walked to the office and typed in my loose-leaf diary the mair
what Hearst had said to me.

The next day the Press Bureau phoned to say that the Duce was
to see Mr. Hearst at the moment but that Mussolini would be only t
to receive him on his next visit to Rome. I relayed the message to
Willicombe, who replied that it was "just as well." The party was lea
Munich in the morning and would go on to France and England fror
The freeloaders from Broadway and Hollywood were getting the gran

On a quiet, rainy Sunday afternoon shortly after the Hearst party's
ture, I reread the Chief's instructions about how I should conduct my
Universal's correspondent in Mussolini's Rome, wondering what
prompted them. I could only assume that the Italian Embassy in Washii
had complained about the tone and content of my dispatches since my ar
in the spring of 1935.

Reviewing my file, I made a sickening discovery: I had been unwittii
doing exactly what I had been instructed to do—namely, serving as a chan
of communications between fascism and readers in the United States. Th
were exceptions: an early story about Italy's abandonment of the gold st:
dard, another dealing with the new cordiality between Rome and Berlin, a
finally the disclosure of Italo-German intervention in the Spanish crisis whic
already had assumed the dimensions of all-out civil war. Otherwise, my di
patches had been based almost entirely on official communiqués, the publi
pronouncements of the Duce, and the editorials in the controlled press.

beyond the country's borders. The United States also accepted the nonintervention policy, even after it had become clear that Franco was receiving military supplies as well as troops and air support from Italy and Germany.

Meanwhile, the Soviet Union declared that it would not be bound by any policy of nonintervention and began sending the Madrid government military supplies and technicians as well as field officers and aviators. Spain quickly became the proving ground for new weapons and techniques and the ideological battleground for volunteers from a dozen democratic countries, including the United States. The American contingent was known as the Lincoln Brigade.

General Franco, however, was receiving powerful support from yet another source besides Mussolini and Hitler: the Vatican. Pope Pius XI had no divisions to offer Franco; but he could lend moral assistance, and he did. Papal declarations denouncing the Madrid government for waging a "Communistic cataclysm of bestiality" against the church in Spain appeared almost daily in the Vatican's official organ, the *Osservatore Romano*.

On August 19 the *Osservatore* declared editorially that the Madrid government had "confessed its inability to control the armed mobs which have perpetrated the most atrocious public crimes of arson, murder and theft" against the church's property and clergy. On August 25 the paper printed official charges of "executions and barbaric torture of Catholic priests, nuns and students surpassing even the horrors of the French Revolution."

Citing "unimpeachable" Vatican sources, Universal's competitors were beating me consistently with stories about Spanish Republican "atrocities": the tarring and burning at the stake of the bishop of Sigüenza; the murder of the bishops of Jaén, Lérida, Segovia, and Barbastro; the alleged herding of nuns, monks, and students aboard a ship scuttled and sunk by "Red terrorists" at Cambrilla. Atrocities were undoubtedly being committed in Spain by both sides, but I found it odd that in the reports emanating from the Vatican the names and actual numbers of the victims were rarely mentioned. One report, for instance, merely said, "Nuns were forced to flee in many places." How many nuns? What places? The Vatican had no acceptable answers.

At this point Aldo Forte resigned to join the staff of the United Press at considerably more money than he had been getting from INS. Until then I had left coverage of the Holy See in his hands; Aldo had reliable Vatican sources whom he had cultivated over the years.

I now turned the job over to the genial Michael, who possessed the necessary diplomacy to deal with hypersensitive prelates and the knowledge of Italian required to decipher the ecclesiastical subtleties of the *Osservatore Romano*, often the only source of reliable foreign news, for it was beyond the reach of Mussolini's censors. Our coverage did not improve substantially, however, until I negotiated a deal with Monsignor Enrico Pucci, the self-appointed public relations representative of the Holy See.

For a modest fee of twenty dollars a month each, the monsignor had been supplying Universal and INS with a daily bulletin, typed on yellow onionskin paper, containing "inside information" on the daily routine of the pope, the personages the Holy Father received in audience, texts or excerpts of his more important speeches, tips on who might or might not be made a cardinal, and, most important, the state of the pontiff's health. More often than not, however, our copy of the bulletin reached us too late in the afternoon to be of much use. Also, since our copy was the twentieth or thirtieth that came out of Pucci's typewriter, it was frequently barely readable.

Determined to improve our coverage, I invited the monsignor to lunch at the Sora Rosa, a nearby trattoria which specialized in charcoal-broiled fish and served the best Frascati in town. Even in clerical garb the tall, bulky monsignor looked worldly, sophisticated—and greedy. Something in the dark eyes behind thick lenses and the sensuous mouth under his graying black mustache told me that here was a man who could be bought.

By the time we had finished the antipasto and drunk our first *litro* of Sora Rosa's well-chilled Frascati we had a "deal." The Hearst offices would receive Pucci's bulletin before noon daily, and it would be one of the readable top copies. His fee, of course, would be doubled to eighty dollars monthly, but in addition, he would place at our disposal a young assistant who would supply the Hearst offices with "special coverage," meaning information about the health of the pope.

The aged pontiff was reportedly suffering from a variety of life-threatening ailments. I could not afford to be scooped on the death of the pope whatever the cost. We agreed on a price for the "special coverage" but left open the delicate matter of the size of the bonus in the event Pucci & Company produced a scoop on the pope's death. On that ghoulish note we attacked a bowl of fruit and a *quarto* each of Frascati, then ordered coffee and brandy.

To test the monsignor's ability to deliver the goods, I asked him to arrange for me to follow the pope through a day's routine in order that I might see for myself if it was true that, as Pucci himself had reported, Pius XI was "wan and enfeebled" as a result of worry over what was happening to the church in Spain. The monsignor arched a bushy eyebrow dubiously, but he telephoned that same evening to say that he had obtained permission for me to visit the pope at his summer residence at Castel Gandolfo, a twelfth-century village overlooking Lake Albano in the Alban Hills. It had been arranged, he said, that I participate as a spectator in the public papal audiences planned for the next day.

For two hours on the morning of August 28 I was able to observe the pope in action as he received in turn groups of churchmen, foreign pilgrims, and visiting peasants from various parts of Italy. The audiences took place in the great central hall of the palace begun by Urban VIII, pope from 1623 to 1644, and later enlarged by Alexander VII, Clement XIII, and Pius IX.

I knelt with the faithful as Pius XI entered the audience chamber, his step feeble, tentative, and slow. He was gowned in white, a golden cross gleaming on his breast, and hesitated briefly, as though gathering strength, before mounting the four shallow steps of the scarlet and gold dais upon which the papal throne was placed. He stood before the throne as he was about to sit down, breathed deeply, and pressed his left hand to his breast. The crowd applauded and cheered.

I was barely ten feet from him when, with a rustle of silk, the pope rose to speak. His voice, unaided by a public-address system, was indistinct and barely audible. After intoning a prayer and blessing the assembly, he descended from the dais haltingly, placing both red-sandaled feet squarely on each step before taking the next. Holding himself erect, he left the chamber, followed by his equerry and applause and shouts of *"Viva il papa!"*

Later that morning I talked with Dr. Antonio Folchi, the pope's physician. He confirmed that the pontiff walked with difficulty, perspired freely, and slept little. Organically, however, Dr. Folchi said, the pope was suffering from no serious ailment, merely from the accumulated frailties of his advancing years, adding, "He is as well as any man on the verge of eighty, and having his cares and responsibilities, can be expected to be."

The pope was obviously every bit as "wan and enfeebled" as published reports had indicated. The difficulties which the church was having in Spain undoubtedly weighed upon him. But the editorial efforts of *Osservatore Romano* to depict him as virtually a martyr of the Spanish Republic seemed to me a bit farfetched. Born Achille Ratti in 1857, in bucolic Desio, near Milan, Pius XI—scholar, linguist, librarian of the famous Ambrosiana of Milan—was of rugged stock and in his youth had been a renowned climber of Alpine peaks. He was to survive a series of illnesses before his death in 1939.

The pope, as I saw on the morning of August 28, 1936, was undoubtedly in failing health, however, and my visit to Castel Gandolfo alerted me to the need for establishing within the Vatican the relationships which would ensure that I would not be scooped when the end came. I could not rely on Monsignor Pucci alone.

Because I was still shorthanded after Aldo Forte's departure, I appealed to Hillman in London, who responded by sending me Alan Cranston, a tall, lean, athletic-looking young man, prematurely bald at twenty-two, and green as grass in the newspaper business. He was teaching himself the language with the help of *Italian in Three Months,* and by the time he reported for duty in the late summer of 1936 he had acquired a vocabulary of approximately a dozen words.

Alan, however, had all the earmarks of a "quick study," and at Hillman's suggestion I put him on the payroll at twelve dollars a week, barely enough for room and board at a students' hostel in the Via dei Serpenti. I shifted Michael to late-afternoon hours, and assigned Alan to overnight duty—midnight to 9:00 A.M.—figuring that he could use the hours between rare telephone calls from tipsters to improve his Italian.

On quiet Sunday mornings Alan was often our guest at home for American-style breakfasts of pancakes or waffles with sausages, and we became lifelong friends. A Californian, he talked endlessly and enthusiastically about his home state's virtues and showed a keen interest in national and international politics. I was not unduly surprised when, years later, Alan was elected to the United States Senate as a Democrat and subsequently sought his party's nomination for the presidency.

The Cranston I knew in the summer of 1936 was an adventurous youth thirsting for knowledge about the world around him. The statesman in him was not yet discernible, perhaps, but the qualities that would make him a leader were clearly evident in the manner in which he took hold of his duties at the office, so much so that I never hesitated leaving him in charge over the ostensibly more experienced Michael.

Meanwhile, the tedium of Fascist propaganda was relieved from time to time by unintentionally funny editorials in newspapers, especially the Rome afternoon daily, the *Giornale d'Italia,* edited by the wispy, unsmiling Gayda, often cited by the foreign press as the Duce's "spokesman." One of Gayda's panegyrics urged all Italians to eschew neckties. "They constrict the neck," he wrote, "thereby impeding the free flow of blood to the brain and reducing the wearer's capacity to enjoy the poetry, dynamism and mystique of Fascism."

In the same paper there appeared on December 20, 1936, an article announcing the forthcoming publication of *Argento Vivo (Live Silver)* featuring "100 per cent Italian cartoons for children. We must be done with comic strips recounting the adventures of [American] redskins and gangsters. . . . An Italian spirit will henceforth animate the poets and writers of this new newspaper; Italian humor will inspire its cartoonists. . . . Italy is not only the most beautiful country in the world; it is also the most imaginative."

Shortly after the paper began publication, a comic strip featuring Mickey Mouse, sold in Italy by Hearst's King Features Syndicate, was banned as "anti-Fascist." I had to appeal to Count Ciano himself to have the ban rescinded.

One of the funniest decrees ever issued by the regime, however, originated with the fanatic Achille Starace, the athletic secretary of the Fascist party. In January 1937 he ordered immediate cessation of all handshaking. "It is un-Fascist," he said. "Henceforth, the Fascist salute will replace the bourgeois handshake. Violations will be recorded in the individual dossiers of party members." Starace's order had intelligent Italians laughing for months.

Meanwhile, the *Official Gazette* published a far more serious decree which provoked no laughter anywhere, for it was indicative of an emerging racism. The decree, from the pen of Mussolini himself and signed by the king, outlawed marriages in Ethiopia between blacks and whites, Whites marrying blacks would be subject to prison sentences ranging from five to ten years and to heavy fines. It also punished whites cohabiting with blacks with jail terms of from one to five years plus fines.

The decree marked the beginning of a campaign whose announced objective was "purification of the Latin race," but there was worse to come. The drive for "racial purity" was bound to affect the welfare of Italy's Jews, the classic scapegoats of dictators mired in political, economic, and social difficulties.

9

ANTI-SEMITISM REARS ITS UGLY HEAD

Suddenly, in the early spring of 1937, as Rome drew ever closer to Berlin—almost overnight, it seemed—Italy had a "Jewish problem." The country had always had its anti-Semites, especially among clericals and reactionaries, but anti-Semitism was never a national characteristic as it was in the countries of central and eastern Europe.

Jews had been part of Italy's social, political, and economic fabric for some two thousand years, the first Jews having arrived in Rome in 138 B.C. as the Maccabean emissaries of the kingdom of Judah to the Roman Senate. Protected by Julius Caesar and more or less tolerated by his successors, the Roman Jews were later subjected to the caprices of Christian emperors and suffered considerably in the heyday of the popes. They remained free to live where they chose, however, until the reactionary Pope Paul IV confined the Jews of Rome to a ghetto soon after his election in 1555.

But during the Risorgimento of the middle decades of the nineteenth century they were liberated and restored to full citizenship, and the Italian Jewish community, never numerous but by far the oldest in Europe, became thoroughly integrated in its country's life, supporting its domestic and foreign policies, and fighting in its wars. Always adaptive, Jews accepted fascism and gave freely of their blood and treasure during the Ethiopian War.

Nevertheless, in March 1937 the country's Jews, who numbered only about forty-four thousand in a national population of approximately forty-three million, became the target of a campaign of vilification and terrorism led by

Roberto Farinacci, Mussolini's minister of the interior, the most fanatical of the regime's small but highly vocal band of anti-Semites. The vehicle for his racist fulminations was a newly created newspaper called *Il Tevere* (the Tiber), founded and nourished with Nazi German money.

In an editorial published on March 30, 1937, Farinacci attacked the country's Jews as "a people in conflict with Italy's destiny." He deplored their "disproportionate numbers in literature and the professions" and attributed current unrest among Italian intellectuals to Jewish influence. "The attitude of revolt in our intellectual world," Farinacci wrote, "can only be explained by some defect in the purity of our blood."

The language was turgid, but Farinacci's meaning was clear: The Jews were responsible for the spreading disaffection in the wake of the unprofitable Ethiopian War and Fascist Italy's increasing entanglement in Spain. Sensing danger to the relatively small Jewish community—its members totaled no more than one-tenth of 1 percent of the population—I cabled extensive quotes from Farinacci's abusive editorial. To my dismay, the subject was virtually ignored by Universal's client newspapers; in the few clippings which I received later my story was cut to three or four short paragraphs.

In my view, Farinacci's diatribe against Italy's Jews signaled a most important development: the probable adoption by Fascist Italy of Nazi Germany's anti-Semitic policies as proclaimed in the Nuremberg Laws of 1935. Clearly editors back home either had failed to perceive its significance or didn't care. Perhaps, I reasoned, they needed more information, and I sought it from Farinacci himself. An interview with him was arranged for me by the Press Bureau.

Farinacci received me in his office in the gloomy Ministry of the Interior wearing his Blackshirt uniform complete with black Sam Browne belt and decorations. He was a bulky man in his middle fifties who had volunteered for service in Abyssinia, where he had lost his right arm, not in battle but while "fishing" in Lake Tana with hand grenades. One had exploded prematurely, and his forearm was shattered up to the elbow. It was replaced by a prosthetic device that ended in a gloved artificial hand. Nevertheless, he was awarded his country's highest honor for valor on the battlefield, the *medaglio d'oro,* roughly equivalent to Britain's Victoria Cross and usually awarded posthumously.

In an "interview" that was really an anti-Semitic monologue, Farinacci characterized the Jews as constituting "a problem that must be eliminated. Fascist Italy," he said, "does not want this problem, and its solution is the separation of the Jews from the life of the nation." To my question about how the "separation" might be accomplished, the super Fascist smiled knowingly and declared that the "necessary steps" were being considered by the regime's Grand Council—of which he was a member—and would be made public "in due course". He assured me, furthermore, that the impending policy had the wholehearted approval of the Duce.

My interview with Farinacci was never published. New York's response to it was a cable stating: YOU ARE FISHING IN TROUBLED WATERS. I was indignant. The rebuff was indicative of uninterest in what I considered to be a crucial development in Fascist policy, symptomatic of Italy's drift toward closer relations with Nazi Germany. Again I was strongly tempted to quit my job.

But resignation was out of the question. Apart from the fact that no other job was available—I had already put out feelers to the United Press with negative results—Kathryn was pregnant again and having a difficult time. She was being well looked after, however, by one of Italy's foremost obstetricians, Professor Artom, whose practice included members of the royal family.

The baby was due in the latter part of July, and I reserved a private room for Kathryn's accouchement in the Anglo-American Hospital, where the staff spoke English. It was near where we now lived in the Via Rovigo, the lease on our Via dei Condotti apartment having expired. Our new home was an airy floor-through flat on the first floor of a two-story villa with a garden, an extra bedroom that could be converted into a sunny nursery, and a railed balcony from which we could see a corner of the brown walls of Villa Torlonia, the Duce's palatial residence on the Via Nomentana.

Weary of living with "other people's things," we furnished the new flat ourselves with a few antiques bought at auctions and good copies of English and Venetian pieces made for us at reasonable prices by Italian craftsmen. It was the first real home we had known since Kathryn and I were married, but it represented yet another reason for not quitting my job. To furnish the apartment, I had had to borrow heavily from the office, and I couldn't quit before paying off my considerable debt.

In the meantime, Sean, now nearly five was ready for kindergarten. Italian friends recommended a school run by German nuns in the Piazza di Spagna, but when Kathryn took the boy there to register him, she was horrified to find in the entrance hall a huge framed portrait of Adolf Hitler flanked by swastika flags, past which fair-haired moppets marched, making the Nazi salute. For a day or two afterward my wife and I seriously discussed the pros and cons of pulling up stakes and returning to the United States. In the end, however, we decided to stay where we were and teach Sean his ABCs at home with the help of a correspondence course.

The Rome that had been the lodestar of my journalistic ambitions had begun to pall, but I could not bring myself to leave it. I was torn between a desire to escape and an eagerness to discover more about fascism and its creator, Benito Mussolini. I was conscious of occupying a front-row seat at an engrossing drama. The Duce was its central character, but its denouement I could only dimly perceive.

One night, dining under the stars at an outdoor restaurant on the Via Appia, a fortune-teller told me that I would live to see "the death of the Pope, the fall of the monarchy, and the streets of Rome running in blood." All this in a conspiratorial whisper from the mouth of a bearded man with the burning eyes of a prophet. I half believed him because, I confess, I wanted to.

In the months following the Ethiopian War, Mussolini became engaged in a duplicitous diplomatic game, striving, on the one hand, to reestablish friendly relations with Great Britain and, on the other, to enhance his military prestige by achieving a clamorous success on the battlefields of Spain. A friendly Italian newspaperman told me that during the final stages of the Ethiopian campaign they had received instructions from Mussolini himself to cease all propaganda attacks against Britain. The Duce was keen to resume cordial relations with London, for he still regarded Germany with apprehension, aware that once Hitler reoccupied the Rhineland in March 1936, his next move might threaten Austria and bring him to Italy's border.

The obstacles in the way of a genuine rapprochement with the West in general and with Britain in particular, however, were formidable. In Paris the spring elections of 1936 had produced the leftist Popular Front government headed by Léon Blum with which Italy found it difficult to do business, and in England resentment still simmered over Mussolini's flouting of the League of Nations by making war on Ethiopia. Nevertheless, the Duce clearly preferred an alliance with the Western powers to one with an increasingly powerful Germany. Although he referred often to the "Axis" as having been "born" in 1936—in his secret meeting with the Führer at Feltre—Italo-German relations had not yet crystallized into a formal partnership.

But neither the British nor the Italians were truly prepared to forgive and forget. Britain deeply resented Mussolini's threats and high-handedness during the League of Nations sanctions fight. And while Mussolini wanted better relations with Britain and an end to sanctions, Spain promised what he craved most of all, another military victory. In this hope he was encouraged by Hitler, who, differing from his generals as he often did, took a rosy view of Italian military competence.

Mussolini had promised the Spanish right arms and money in 1934. With Franco's rebellion against the Republican government, the time was ripe to fulfill his promise. On July 24, 1936, two Italian aircraft made a forced landing on Moroccan soil, and vigilant newsmen made the fact known to the world. From that point onward the Duce cast prudence aside. Men and money and weapons were rushed to Franco's assistance in an ever-increasing flow.

At that critical juncture in the regime's history, on June 9, 1936, Mussolini appointed as his minister for foreign affairs his son-in-law, Count Galeazzo Ciano. At the time Ciano deeply revered the Duce, whose militant style he aped.

Ciano was the only member of the Fascist hierarchy with whom I developed a relationship that vaguely approximated friendship. His office in the Palazzo Chigi was diagonally across the Via del Corso from mine in the Galleria Colonna, and I enjoyed fairly frequent access to him, not because he liked me but because I represented a news agency whose owner was regarded in Rome as a supporter of the regime's anti-Communist policies. Although I never communicated to Ciano or anyone else in the government Mr. Hearst's instructions to me to make Universal Service available as a channel for its propaganda, the foreign minister was well aware of them.

Ciano was thirty-five when I first met him, a handsome man of medium height with glossy black hair, a smooth olive complexion, a heavy chin, and an arrogant manner. Onstage, in full Blackshirt uniform, booted and wearing his fezzed black headpiece, he looked faintly ridiculous, for he was perceptibly knockkneed. In well-tailored mufti, however, he cut a dashing figure.

Frankly I was kindly disposed toward him when we met soon after the Duce installed him in the Palazzo Chigi. Although a Fascist from his high hairline to the tips of his well-polished shoes, he frequently demonstrated a pro-Western turn of mind. He professed, for instance, a fondness for my favorite American poet, Walt Whitman, and a leather-bound volume of *Leaves of Grass* occupied a place of honor next to Niccolò Machiavelli's *The Prince* on a bookshelf behind his desk. He told me he ranked Abraham Lincoln above all other American presidents as "probably the purest embodiment of the democratic ideals of the nineteenth century," a man who had "faced successfully the most terrifying event with which a statesman can be confronted: civil war." Moreover, Ciano hinted from time to time that he was not entirely in accord with his father-in-law's pro-German policies. (I realize in retrospect I was probably being conned by an expert.)

Ciano's official office in the Palazzo Chigi, as befitted Fascist number two, was almost as imposing as Mussolini's own vast Sala del Mappamondo (Hall of the Map of the World) in the Palazzo Venezia, but he preferred working in a small adjoining study comfortably furnished in fine nineteenth-century Italian and English pieces. Two tall windows overlooked the Piazza Colonna and a view of the sculptured column that serves as a pedestal for a statue of Marcus Aurelius, one of the noblest in the long line of Roman emperors, a man who loved peace but whose reign was plagued with constant wars.

Until he married Edda Mussolini, the Duce's slim, elegantly gowned and expensively bejeweled daughter, Ciano was virtually unknown to the public. Italians knew more about the private lives of Neville Chamberlain, Léon Blum, and Hermann Göring than they did about the Duce's sleek-haired, suntanned son-in-law. They soon divined, however, that Mussolini had handpicked Ciano as his eventual successor, though most critics held that his only qualification for the job of foreign minister derived from his having married the boss's daughter, a strong-willed woman much given to exerting her considerable influence on both father and husband. Ciano seemed not to mind, explaining: "A clever husband always takes his wife's advice when he knows it to be sound." About his role as foreign minister, Ciano stressed that Mussolini was the "grand maestro" of his country's foreign policy. "He strikes a chord," Ciano said, "and I write the theme, then submit it for the Duce's approval."

Like Mussolini, Ciano was a nonsmoker and a teetotaler but, unlike the Duce, was neither a vegetarian nor intensely athletic. Although fond of fencing and swimming in the open sea—I often saw him on the beach at Castel Fusano, where he maintained a private cabana for entertaining members of the diplomatic corps—he admitted to me that he was "a bit lazy about sports." He was in the bad books, therefore, of Party Secretary Starace, a devotee of physical fitness who obliged fascism's leaders to engage in vigorous calisthenics and outrageous athletic competitions, including jumping through fiery hoops.

One of the basic appeals of fascism was that it would make Italians braver, stronger, and better all-around performers as individuals and as a nation, especially in warfare. It was the regime's goal, as Ciano confided in one of his rare moments of candor, "to turn our nation of mandolin players into good soldiers." Fascism came closest to fulfilling this aim during the Ethiopian War, but from then on growing numbers of disillusioned Italians complained of the war's consequences: rising prices, food shortages, and severe unemployment.

For the jobless, however, the only employment the Fascist state could offer was a chance to die "fighting communism" on Franco's side in Spain, and a story I sent disclosing the magnitude of Italy's assistance to the insurgents almost wrecked my carefully cultivated but always precarious relationship with the foreign minister.

The flow of Italian men and weapons to help Franco gain a quick victory over the Spanish Republicans began in the late winter of 1936. Troops who had seen service in Abyssinia were being demobilized on their return from East Africa and encouraged to "volunteer" for duty in Spain. At first, long queues formed outside the Fascist party headquarters in the Palazzo Braschi in the Piazza Navona, where a mysterious "Señor Martínez," whom I was never able to track down, offered high pay and bonuses to men willing to fight in Franco's legions. Very soon, however, the stream of unemployed veterans, peasants, workers, and anti-Communist zealots slowed to a trickle. Those enlisting came singly or in twos and threes.

Hopes of raising six divisions, about ninety thousand men, to help Franco overwhelm Madrid's Republican defenders were unrealized. By the end of the year the invisible Señor Martínez had succeeded in raising only eighteen thousand foot soldiers and some five thousand "specialists," comprising airmen, tankers, mechanics, chemical experts, and ambulance drivers. They were for the most part poorly trained, ill armed, and poorly led, mere cannon fodder. Predictably, their performance on the battlefield left much to be desired, and Mussolini realized that to achieve the military success he wanted, he had to turn the job over to the regular army. This, however, had to be done in utmost secrecy, for the Duce had accepted "in principle" an agreement with France and Britain to refrain from direct intervention in the Spanish Civil War.

A tight censorship was clamped down on all troop movements, but Universal's informants on newspapers in Rome, Genoa, and Naples managed to provide a weekly log of troop sailings destined for Spain. By mid-February 1937 I was fairly certain that approximately seventy thousand infantrymen, including many Askari—Libyan Arab soldiers whom Franco would pass off as Moors from Morocco—had landed in Spain with large quantities of small tanks, field artillery, ammunition, and supplies. It took me more than a month to check the information with my sources in the American, Russian, and British embassies.

Colonel Robbie Stone, the British military attaché, confirmed my data in virtually all details and added a few of his own. The troops being sent to Spain, he said, were not exactly being impressed into service but were given little choice; only married men with families to support were allowed to stand down. All were being paid double army pay, he said, and were being given "insurance policies" covering death and injury as an added inducement.

Colonel Stone, it developed, had been feeding information similar to mine into the War Office for some time, hoping that his superiors would persuade Whitehall to protest Mussolini's violation of the nonintervention agreement. But Robbie's efforts had failed to arouse John Bull from his deep sleep.

On March 31, satisfied that my story was airtight, I telephoned it to London. There a Hearst client paper, Lord Beaverbrook's *Daily Express,* gave it smashing front-page play, and Labour backbenchers in the House of Commons loudly demanded to know why the facts reported from Rome by a journalist had not been made available to them by His Majesty's government.

In Rome Propaganda Minister Dino Alfieri denied my story and ordered my expulsion. Before his directive could be carried out, however, I flew to London—less to escape arrest than to secure uncensored communications with Joseph V. Connolly, president of the Hearst wire services and of King Features Syndicate. He extracted assurances from the State Department that if I were punished in any way for "a factual presentation of undeniable news," Washington would lodge a strong protest.

What good *that* would do me, I had no idea. But heartened by the knowledge that I had the backing of the government of the United States, I hurried back to Rome. Kathryn was at the end of the fifth month of her troubled pregnancy, and I was determined to fight the expulsion order by every means possible.

Half expecting to be arrested when I landed at Ciampino Airport, I was greatly relieved when I wasn't. The next day I called on Ciano and explained to him my wife's "delicate condition," pointing out *en passant* that if anything untoward happened to her or the baby, the resultant publicity would be bad for Italy's cherished "image" as a modern, civilized society. Ciano said I had "greatly damaged" Italy with my story, whose accuracy, oddly enough, he did not question, but he promised to reverse Alfieri's order. This he did within the hour, but I recall a sinking feeling in the pit of my stomach as I emerged from the medieval Florentine gloom of the Palazzo Chigi into the bright sunlight of the Corso that I now owed Galeazzo Ciano a favor, and I knew he would not hesitate to ask it. I wondered, dimly, what it would be. I was not kept long in suspense.

Meanwhile, Kathryn was quite ill and bedridden much of the time as a delightful Roman spring turned into the usual hot, sticky summer. For all foreign residents, having a baby in the Italy of the 1930s presented problems. Kathryn was a brave young woman, but she understandably had balked at the idea of giving birth in an Italian hospital where she would have language difficulties and where, generally speaking, standards were far below those maintained in comparable institutions back home. Hence, our choice of the Anglo-American Hospital, one of the best of the several private clinics founded in Rome by church groups and warmly endorsed by the prestigious Professor Artom.

But on the afternoon of July 23, 1937, when Kathryn knew her time had come and was taken to the hospital, her obstetrician, Professor Artom, was nowhere to be found. Being Jewish, and warned from high places that Italy's anti-Semitic decrees were being pondered by the Fascist Grand Council, he had quietly left Italy with his family and his Jewish staff.

Who, in the circumstances, would deliver Kathryn's baby? The hospital talked vaguely about an available midwife but had no staff obstetrician.

The problem was solved by my assistant, Michael Chinigo, the former medical student. Making the rounds of Rome's best hospitals, he located a young Italian doctor who had delivered successfully scores of babies during the Mussolinian baby boom, and he rushed him by taxi to Kathryn's bedside late that night. Unfortunately the doctor spoke no English. Worse, he knew nothing of his patient's history and delivered Kathryn of a baby boy without the help of the anesthesia which Dr. Artom had specified in her case.

The boy was born at approximately 5:00 A.M. on July 24. We named him Eugene, for my father, and added Michael as an honorific middle name. But the newcomer would be known thereafter as Tommy because his brother, Sean, seeing him for the first time, dubbed him Tommy Tucker after the nursery rhyme character.

Two days after Tommy was born, I received a letter from the local Fascist party headquarters. The authorities were pleased to know that a new baby had arrived in the Gervasi household but wondered why his older brother, then not yet five, had not been registered for the Balilla, the Fascist children's militia whose members were parading around Rome, carrying wooden rifles and singing "Giovinezza" at the tops of their childish sopranos.

I informed the officials involved that although my name was Italian, my citizenship was American and that I had registered the new baby as an American citizen the moment the consulate opened the day after the boy's birth. And Sean, I reminded them, was American-born, a fact duly recorded in his passport. I never heard from them again.

But I did hear from Ciano.

Throughout the summer of 1937 Ciano was the Duce's point man in efforts to negotiate an amicable relationship with Great Britain. But Mussolini was well and truly trapped by the confusion of his many aims. Negotiations in one area were bound to conflict with those in another. Mussolini wanted an end to British and French sanctions; he wanted British and French recognition of the Italian conquest of Ethiopia. He wanted to check German designs on Austria; he wanted friendly relations with Hitler without a formal alliance. He wanted military glory in Spain but found himself hopelessly overcommitted and bogged down.

It was during this crucial time in the development of Italy's foreign policy that on August 4 I was summoned to the Palazzo Chigi and handed what purported to be an "exclusive interview" with Count Ciano. In it the foreign minister declared: "The way was now open for an Anglo-Italian rapprochement to provide a stabilizing element for a European peace." I was both stunned and pleased, amazed by Ciano's method and, frankly, inwardly pleased that I had in hand what was obviously a big story, front-page stuff. I was also aware that I was being used.

The questions and answers were written out for me. All I had to do was write a lead and a few interpolative paragraphs, and, *voilà*, I had an "exclusive" interview with the second most important man in all Italy. Ciano's statement followed an exchange of letters between British Prime Minister Neville Chamberlain and Mussolini and preliminary negotiations in Rome between Ciano and British Ambassador Sir Eric Drummond, a golfer for whom the Italians had gone to the trouble and expense of building an eighteen-hole course on the Via Appia.

The alleged interview was widely distributed by Universal Service at home and abroad under an "All rights reserved" copyright line. It was mostly diplomatic pap, but it contained one significant paragraph: "Italo-German friendship would in no way be interfered with by an understanding between Rome and London. Quite on the contrary. One of the fundamental tenets of the Rome-Berlin Axis is, in fact, the collaboration of all nations which desire to do so in the supreme interests of peace and civilization."

Also interesting, if somewhat disconcerting to me personally, was my discovery the following day that Ciano had given the identical "interview" to the Rome correspondent of the *Times* of London. In short, I had been had.

Later, feigning as best I could profoundly wounded professional pride, I complained to Ciano that my "exclusive" interview was given not only to the *Times* but also to every major newspaper in Italy. The Turin newspaper, *La Stampa,* among others, splashed it all over its front page, even making my by-line part of the streamer headline.

Ciano pretended not to understand at first, then blamed the slipup, if any, on the Propaganda Ministry, which apparently had received a copy of my interview from the Palazzo Chigi and had distributed it for what it was—a handout.

"But after all," said Ciano defensively, "you did have it exclusively for the United States, didn't you?"

I had to agree that was true enough but asked a favor to assuage my injured feelings. Ever since coming to Rome, I said, I had been trying to obtain an interview with the Duce. It was not Mussolini's policy to give interviews to resident correspondents, a privilege reserved for visiting big-name journalists like the *London Daily Mail*'s monocled G. Ward Price, who believed the sun rose and set on Mussolini and Hitler. Ciano promised to see what he could do. I seized the opening to suggest that an appropriate occasion for the kind of interview I had in mind might be the upcoming fifteenth anniversary of the Fascists' March on Rome on October 28. Ciano pulled at an ear, smiled, and nodded approval. He said he would talk to Dino Alfieri.

August became September, but no word from Alfieri. Ciano either had not taken kindly to my proposal or had forgotten it. I resigned myself to the idea that I probably would never interview Mussolini. I was bitterly disappointed, for I had hoped to study the man at close quarters and judge for myself if he in fact possessed the personal magnetism that inspired the adulation of the masses, especially women.

The state of Mussolini's health and the details of his personal life were among fascism's best-kept secrets, but it was common knowledge that the Duce was a compulsive womanizer whose sexual proclivities he and his secret police went to great pains to conceal.

Most foreign correspondents knew, for instance, but dared not write, that in the autumn of 1936, when the Duce was at the apogee of his power and popularity, he had resumed a longtime liaison with Clara Petacci, a young, rather vacuous, but ravishingly pretty brunette. Claretta, as the Duce called her, was half his age, with green eyes, long, straight legs, a delightfully husky voice, and those large, heavy breasts that he liked in his women.

From conversations with the few gossipy members of the elite of Roman society who attended the frequent diplomatic cocktail parties, it was not difficult to piece together the story of Claretta's origins, how she met Mussolini, and the role she played in his life at a time when he was struggling with fateful preoccupations: rapprochement with England, victory in Spain, and Hitler's mounting threat to the independence of Austria.

Some of my informants were patients of Clara's father, Dr. Francesco Petacci, a Vatican physician whom one source described as "a decent, honest man, completely absorbed in his extensive upper-class practice." The rest of his family consisted of his wife, Giuseppina, a large woman reputedly as amoral as she was ambitious; Clara's younger stagestruck sister, Miriam; and a greedy older brother, Marcello.

Mussolini first met Claretta on the road to Ostia, the seaside resort near Rome, sometime in the summer of 1932 and never forgot her. The Duce was driving his scarlet two-seater Alfa Romeo roadster when one day he sped past the Petaccis' chauffeur-driven open touring car. Clara, then in her early twenties, stood up on the back seat, waving excitedly and shouting, "Duce! Duce!" The susceptible Mussolini stopped, got out of his car, and walked back to where his security people had halted the Petacci vehicle. Clara trembled with excitement when the Duce spoke to her and invited her to come visit him if her parents approved.

The Duce, too, was smitten, but two years passed before he saw Claretta again. In the interval she had married an Italian Air Force officer, from whom she obtained a divorce of dubious validity in Budapest in 1934. She felt free to visit the Duce when he telephoned her home one day in the early summer of 1936 and repeated his invitation to come visit him at the Palazzo Venezia. Mama Petacci posed no objections, for she saw at once the possible pecuniary advantages to be derived from a "serious relationship" between her beautiful daughter and Italy's most powerful man.

The young divorcée became a frequent visitor at the Palazzo Venezia, always entering by a side door in the Via degli Astagli and going up in a private elevator to a cozy apartment on the topmost floor, where the Duce periodically visited her, sometimes for only a few minutes, to copulate urgently between meetings with Fascist bigwigs or other important visitors waiting below in the anteroom to the lofty Sala del Mappamondo where he worked.

Fidelity in love, however, was never one of Mussolini's strong points, and he was as unfaithful to Claretta as he had been earlier to his wife, Rachele, and to his Socialist principles. In March 1937 Mussolini became embroiled in a scandal that not even the adroit Bocchini and his OVRA could conceal. The woman in the case was an actress with journalistic ambitions and good connections in the French Foreign Office who traveled under her stage name, Magda Fontanges. She came to Rome in January, ostensibly to interview the Duce for a Paris newspaper, La Liberté, but in reality to entice him into an affair, and she stayed two months. A blowsy, curvaceous blonde in her early thirties, she had openly announced in Paris that she would not leave Italy until Mussolini had made love to her, and there was good reason to believe she succeeded, for on her return to Paris she publicly boasted that during her Roman sojourn "the Duce had me twenty times."

When her overly explicit account of her meetings with Mussolini later appeared in print, the Duce made it known to Bocchini and to France's Ambassador Charles de Chambrun that Mlle Fontanges was no longer welcome in Rome. Hustled out of Italy and forbidden to return, Mlle Fontanges reacted violently. First she tried to poison herself. Then, on March 17, while Chambrun was entraining in Paris to return to Rome after a visit to the Quai d'Orsay, Mlle Fontanges shot and wounded him in his ample derriere.

After her arrest more than three hundred photographs of the Duce were found in the actress-journalist's apartment, and at her trial she testified that she had shot Chambrun because he had caused her "to lose the love of the most wonderful man in the world." Mlle Fontanges got off lightly; she was sentenced to one year's imprisonment for "malicious assault with a deadly weapon."

Of the many relationships with women in Mussolini's life—and the list of mistresses and casual amours is long, dating back to his earliest days as a Socialist revolutionary—the only one he eventually legalized was his liaison with Rachele Guidi, the simple peasant girl who gave him a daughter, Edda, in 1910. Rachele, a fair, well-built girl with good peasant features and the allure of vibrant good health, was eighteen at the time. In September 1915 she gave birth to a second child, Vittorio, and later that year Mussolini married her in a civil ceremony at Treviglio.

Mussolini had just turned fifty-four when Claretta, twenty-six, entered his life. Although not yet an old man, he was obviously no longer the youthful, vigorous Duce of the March on Rome, and one of the few Italian newspapermen who saw him in person from time to time, confided that Mussolini had begun to show signs of wear, as though prematurely aged by his intense life, his poor health, and his numerous amours.

That was the Mussolini I wanted to meet face-to-face, but as August became September, and still no word from Alfieri, I felt increasingly certain that I would never have an opportunity to satisfy my curiosity. Before the month was out, however, I saw him in action in a new role—as Hitler's partner—not in Rome but in Berlin.

10

THE FORGING OF THE AXIS

The first public indication of Fascist Italy's partnership with Nazi Germany came in November 1936, soon after the end of the Ethiopian War, when Mussolini returned to Milan, the city where he was first a Socialist agitator, then an eloquent advocate of Italian intervention on the side of the Allies in the Great War of 1914–1918, and shortly thereafter the Fascist paladin of anticommunism. It was this theme he now took up in the most warlike speech I had ever heard him make.

From a podium specially built for the occasion and facing Il Duomo, the city's multispired cathedral, the Duce shouted in a cold fury that fairly choked his words: "The time has come to end communism. It is no wonder if today we hoist the old flag against bolshevism. But it is our flag, we were born under this flag. We fought under it. What is called bolshevism and communism today is only a form of supercapitalism in its most ferocious expression."

The Duce coupled his attack on communism with a warning to Great Britain to "keep hands off" Italian interests in the Mediterranean, declaring that if an attempt were made to violate "Italian rights" in the "Middle Sea," Italy would "rise as one man, ready to fight." He implied that the conflict would quickly spread through Europe. "A bilateral clash would be unthinkable," he said, "for a bilateral clash would soon become a European war."

Mussolini then disclosed that recent meetings between Ciano and Hitler had resulted in a new anti-Bolshevik Italo-German pact. "The Berlin conversations," he said, "have produced an understanding between our two countries over certain problems which had become particularly acute. The understanding is embodied in written documents, duly signed agreements. But this Rome-Berlin alignment is not a diaphragm, but rather an axis around which can revolve all European states animated by a desire for peace."

Those words were the only conciliatory phrases in a very thorny speech. Peace with England and France, Mussolini made it clear, was possible only if those countries formally recognized Italy's conquest of Ethiopia as "an irrevocable fait accompli."

And so was born the Rome-Berlin Axis. In my diary that night I wrote: "Europe has passed another milestone on the road to chaos; Old Baldy has sold out to Hitler."

Mussolini thereafter made only intermittent efforts to retrace his steps. One attempt culminated in the signature of the so-called Gentlemen's Agreement with England of January 2, 1937, wherein both countries disclaimed any desire "to modify or see modified the *status quo* as regards national sovereignty in the Mediterranean." The accord was designed to assuage British fears that Italy sought a territorial foothold in Spain—a base or bases from which to harass Britain's imperial lifeline—and guaranteed all nations "freedom of transit" through the "Middle Sea." A second effort was the exchange of letters between Mussolini and Chamberlain that resulted in the eleventh-hour rapprochement with Britain negotiated by Ciano and announced in his "exclusive" interview with me.

On September 24, 1937, Mussolini and an impressive delegation of members of the Fascist hierarchy—attired in dressy uniforms specially designed for the occasion, booted, spurred, plumed, and bemedaled—entrained for Munich for the Duce's prearranged rendezvous with Adolf Hitler. Scores of Italian journalists went along, as did a few Rome-based American correspondents, myself included. I looked forward to seeing Germany for the first time, and observing the Führer and his henchmen in action in their native habitat.

It would be the second formal meeting between Rome's Big Caesar and Berlin's Little Caesar, Hitler having come to Venice in the summer of 1934 to meet Mussolini at a particularly lonely moment in the Führer's diplomatic life. He had bolted Geneva the previous autumn by way of emphasizing his claim to equal armaments, was in bad odor everywhere, needed a friend, and saw the likeliest one in Benito Mussolini. The Venice meeting with the Duce was Hitler's first venture in international visiting, but the encounter was poorly arranged on the German side, and the results were far from satisfactory for either participant. Mussolini, for his part, formed a thoroughly unfavorable impression of his German colleague. "Instead of speaking to me about current problems," the Duce later told French Ambassador André François-Poncet, "he recited to me entire chapters from *Mein Kampf,* that boring book which I have never been able to read."

However, more than two years had passed since, much Italian and German blood had been spilled in Spain, and the jaws of events had pressed them closer together. When they met this time, the arrangements had been made by German masters of the art of political showmanship. Hitler was determined not merely to impress his guest but to overwhelm him with the military power of Nazi Germany, with German efficiency in the production of the tools of modern warfare, and with the unflinching devotion of the German people to their Führer.

Ostensibly the Duce was going to Germany to witness the fall maneuvers of the Nazis' armed forces. Actually, however, as we all knew, he was journeying to Germany to consolidate his partnership with Adolf Hitler, whom he once saw as an imitator but now recognized as the most powerful man in Europe—next to himself, of course. When Hitler liquidated Storm Troop leader Ernst Röhm and his coterie of homosexuals only a fortnight after the two dictators had met in Venice in 1934, Mussolini denounced the Führer as "a cruel and ferocious character" who reminded him of Attila. "The men he killed," the Duce shouted to his sister Edvige, "were his closest collaborators, men who hoisted him into power. It is as if I were to kill with my own hands [Italo] Balbo, [Dino] Grandi, [Giuseppe] Bottai . . . ," naming those who had "marched" with him to Rome in 1922. But it was 1937 now, and he needed Hitler just as, to a degree, the Führer needed him.

The train left Italy at Brennero, wound northward through the Brenner Pass, crossed Austria via Innsbruck, and entered Germany. I was suddenly conscious of being in a land which I had learned to fear in childhood, during *la grande guerra* of 1914–1918. I remembered vividly the wartime propaganda cartoons of spike-helmeted "Huns" skewering Belgian babies on long bayonets.

The landscape that flowed past the window of my wagons-lits compartment was strikingly beautiful, much like an endless park, meticulously kept, hedges trimmed, neat little farmhouses surrounded by well-tilled acres, peasants pausing at their work to wave at the passing train, great forests cleared of underbrush, and on distant hillsides toy villages clustered about church spires.

Troops were everywhere, guarding bridges, grade crossings, viaducts, and approaches to stations, as well as on railway platforms. Except for the people in the fields, I saw no one not in some kind of uniform. A nation had been mobilized for the Duce's visit to Germany.

In the train shed at Munich the troops wore no spikes on their helmets, but they looked fierce enough to me as they lined up at present arms like so many giant figurines poured out of the same mold, stony-faced, expressionless, soldiers, I thought, who would love war for war's sake. The Germanic lust for battle hung in the very air of Munich, palpable, unmistakable, exactly as Hitler had meant it to be.

In the old Bavarian capital, after seeing the Brown House and inspecting Hitler's apartment, the Duce lunched with the topmost leaders of the Nazi party, then was treated to a parade of labor troops carrying long-handled spades instead of guns, formations of the Hitler Youth, and group after group of party organizations in their various uniforms. The Königsplatz resounded for hours to the tramp of marching Teutons. From the reviewing stand, Mussolini surveyed it all with evident admiration. He had never before seen anything of the kind. Some of us thought we caught a look of envy on his mobile features as he watched and nodded approvingly.

The next day, traveling by special train, the dictators went to Mecklenberg to witness the most elaborate military maneuvers ever held in Hitler's Germany, and the day after came a visit to Krupp's works at Essen. There the Duce saw the giant enterprise working full blast to produce guns, tanks, every conceivable weapon of modern warfare. He came away visibly excited not only by the immensity of the industrial complex that dwarfed anything Italy possessed but by the disciplined efficiency of the workers themselves.

Three days of indoctrination in Germany's military and industrial power were followed by the nation's welcome to the Duce in Berlin. Never had the capital witnessed such a display. A special railway station had been readied on the city's outskirts, near the Olympic Stadium. The two Caesars arrived in separate special trains from Essen, split-second scheduling making certain that for the last few miles the two trains ran on parallel tracks to underscore the parallelism of their respective "revolutions." Just before they pulled into the station, Hitler's train sped ahead to ensure that the Führer would be on the platform in time to greet his arriving guest.

From the station at the Heerstrasse along the straight, broad highway leading into the heart of Berlin, the two dictators rode through a valley of German and Italian flags. Special care had been taken to turn Unter den Linden into a spectacular setting for a triumphal march. Four rows of towering white pylons, each alternately surmounted by Fascist and Nazi symbols—the Roman fasces and the German swastika—lined the great thoroughfare, and its buildings were draped with thousands of billowing yards of Italian and German bunting.

Vast crowds were assembled along the sidewalks. Nearly a million spectators had been brought in from the provinces in special buses and trains to pay their vociferous respects to the visitor from Rome. Offices and shops closed at 4:00 P.M., and the following day was declared a public holiday in Mussolini's honor.

The security precautions were rigorous. SS formations from all over Germany, some sixty thousand strong, lined the route three and four deep. Plainclothesmen circulated among the crowds, behind which roamed squads of special police with Doberman pinscher and German shepherd dogs. There had been rumors of a plot to kill Mussolini (or Hitler!), and the Germans took no chances. The Gestapo rounded up two hundred "undesirables" and arrested two alleged "ringleaders." Four accomplices, we were told, were being hunted. Armed launches even patrolled the distant Spree.

Mussolini had expressed a desire to "meet the German people" and speak to them in their own language. In compliance a mammoth demonstration was organized for the next day on the Maifeld, an immense sports field near the Olympic Stadium. There nearly a million Germans were assembled, men and women, each carrying rations for a day. They began arriving at four o'clock in the morning and were lined up in solid phalanxes in front of the official tribune, where they stood, waiting, for nearly twelve hours before Mussolini and Hitler arrived in a drizzling rain shortly before nightfall.

Salvos of *"Sieg heil"* rose in mighty roars from the crowd as the principals appeared. Then, after an introduction by the Führer, the Duce spoke from a carefully prepared German text. The Duce's German, I was told, was "atrocious," but his audience cheered at appropriate moments, probably on prearranged signals. Because he was moved by the spectacle before him, Mussolini's oratorical pace accelerated perceptibly as he went, so that his words became for the most part unintelligible.

The gestures and facial expressions with which he mesmerized his Italian audiences were wasted on the Germans. Most could not see them through the drizzle that soon became a downpour, and those who could, I was told, thought them comical.

The rain turned the Duce's manuscript into a sodden mass, but the orator kept bravely on, proclaiming that his visit was no mere diplomatic episode but a manifestation of "solidarity between two revolutions with a common purpose." Mussolini took care to profess a desire for peace but warned that it would be fruitless for anyone to attempt to divide Italy and Germany. It was part of Fascist ethics, he declared, to be loyal to one's friends and to march with them to the end. "Henceforth," he said, "one hundred and fifteen million souls would be indissolubly united, and the gigantic manifestation on the Maifeld would bear witness to this truth to the world."

I watched the proceedings from the tribune directly behind and to the right of the raised rostrum from which the Duce struggled on with his speech through the rain and the resultant distortions in the loudspeaker system. I had an excellent view of the gigantic field and its rows of German faces, an almost solid mass of rain-soaked Teutons standing rigid as statues, arms swinging upward in unison to salute and shout again and again their *Sieg heil.*

Then the crowd burst into a thunderous rendition of "Deutschland über Alles" that managed to drown out the noise of what had become a full-blown rainstorm.

The elaborate ceremonials attending the Duce's visit had taken up so much time that there was little left for serious discussion of outstanding issues.

The day after the Maifeld demonstration, Mussolini and Hitler did meet with their respective foreign ministers, Baron Konstantin von Neurath and Count Ciano, but the subsequent communiqué contained little helpful information. After a final military review, during which the Wehrmacht's elite formations goose-stepped smartly under Mussolini's chin for an hour or more, the Duce returned to Rome.

The feeling among most members of the Anglo-American press contingent was that the show had accomplished its purpose. It had impressed upon Benito Mussolini the fact that Adolf Hitler had become Europe's dominant statesman and the arbiter of its future.

The making of history was now in the hands of the apostles of violence. Neither dictator believed in peaceable and orderly transformation of existing conditions by negotiation and agreement. Both considered war a noble and ennobling objective and regarded peace as a sign of "democratic decadence."

The overall story of Mussolini's visit was handled by Pierre ("Pete") Huss, the INS bureau chief in Berlin. The only item I managed to file resulted from a tip from a member of Ciano's entourage indicating that the Duce had invited Hitler to visit Rome in the near future.

Although Mussolini and Hitler constantly inveighed against communism, in reality the Bolshevik threat that had seemed so real to the Italians, the Germans, and most Europeans in the 1920s had been smothered by the Nazi-Fascist tide that had spread throughout the Continent during the 1930s. I charted the process on a map which I had pasted on the wall above my typewriter. On it I had crayoned with a black *F* those European states which had succumbed to fascism or nazism and with a red *D* those which had remained democratic.

As of the end of September 1937, my map showed that fascism or nazism had irradiated the whole of Europe, in most cases with Italian or German money and political support. In addition to Italy and Germany, totalitarian governments patterned along Italian or German lines were in power in Portugal, Poland, Austria, Hungary, Bulgaria, Romania, and Greece, with Spain teetering on the abyss. They closely resembled one another in the repression of individual liberties, the banning of opposition parties, and the abolition of parliamentary institutions.

Some, among them Portugal and Austria, had borrowed various features of Mussolini's corporative state. Others, such as Hungary, Romania, and Poland, had also instituted German-style anti-Semitic legislation, with Italy soon to follow suit.

Only ten out of twenty-seven European nations remained democratic in the sense that their different political parties honestly competed for office and that their citizens could think and behave much as they pleased. These were Britain and France; Holland, Belgium, and Switzerland; Czechoslovakia and Finland, and the three Scandinavian countries.

As I pondered my map on my return to the office, the conclusion seemed inescapable that the fascistization of Europe was making rapid progress and would lead inevitably to a clash between the Western democracies and the Nazi-Fascist bloc.

Meanwhile, I did not know whether I had a job. Universal had been losing money, and Mr. Hearst's accountants had decided to fold it. Some of the best foreign correspondents in the business, among them my good friend Bill Shirer in Berlin, were fired. But while Bill soon wound up with Edward R. Murrow's newly created team of CBS radio journalists, I had nowhere else to go and stayed on at Universal waiting for the ax to fall.

Much to my surprise, however, I was promoted to chief of bureau for INS, the senior service, with a small increase in pay. I was delighted, not because of the promotion or the raise—although with a new baby the extra fifteen dollars a week were most welcome—but because I felt I was no longer bound to the disturbing "instructions" which the Chief had imparted the year before. Though I had observed them only in the breach, I was always aware of them whenever I sat at my typewriter. Unlike Universal Service, INS was a hard-hitting, highly competitive news agency with several hundred clients in the United States and abroad, not a propaganda vehicle, and I was happy to represent it.

An interview with Mussolini, I thought, would be a fine way to start my new career with INS. I pressed my case with Alfieri's ministry, solicited the help of Ciano's office, and waited.

11

EIGHTEEN MINUTES WITH THE DUCE

I had seen Benito Mussolini in action dozens of times since the spring of 1935. He adored having the foreign press trailing about with him when he bared his torso in the broiling sun to thresh wheat among the peasants of the Pontine fields, stood spread-legged atop a tank to address troops at maneuvers, or jumped his white horse over low hurdles in the garden of his residence, Villa Torlonia. Once during one of these periodic junkets I was introduced to him by the officer in charge of the party of correspondents as "the representative of the Hearst press," and on two similar occasions we had exchanged greetings; but I had never talked with him.

In preparation for my hoped-for interview, I studied the biographical notes I had compiled in London, a compendium to which I had added data accumulated since about the Duce's home life, his relationships with his principal aides, his public behavior and other minutiae.

I had gleaned much of the material in conversations with foreign diplomats who professed to know what was going on behind the walls of the Palazzo Venezia or Villa Torlonia, though how much of it was mere gossip, malicious prattle, or hard fact I could not be certain. Some of my information came from a few friendly Italian newspapermen who were in daily contact with members of fascism's inner circle and rang true.

My notes indicated that lately the Duce had become highly intolerant of bad news; the password among high-ranking Fascisti was: "Tell Mussolini only what he wants to hear." He was now incapable, furthermore, of disciplining the profiteers who had sprung up like poppies in a wheat field during the Ethiopian War. When the postwar financial scandals were brought to his attention, he replied that he considered such thievery comparable only to the "petty pilfering of the housemaids who dip into their employers' grocery money for a few lire for themselves."

The notes revealed other chinks in the Duce's armor. Mussolini was as susceptible as any other Italian, for instance, to the superstition that certain individuals were *gettatori del malocchio* ("throwers of the evil eye," meaning "bearers of bad luck"). This was why the Duce never received ex-King Alfonso of Spain, renowned throughout the land as the all-time champion *gettatore*. To counter the baleful consequences of a mere glance from the former monarch, Italian women fondled amulets, crossed themselves, and muttered incantations. Italian men performed other rituals ranging from covertly touching their genitals to, best of all, plucking a pubic hair.

During most of the Civil War in Spain Alfonso occupied the Royal Suite in the Grand Hotel awaiting the day of Generalissimo Franco's triumph over Madrid's Republican defenders and, he fondly hoped, of his return to the throne. Although he and Mussolini had common interests and, presumably, much to talk about, Alfonso was never invited to the Palazzo Venezia. Whatever negotiations went on between them were safely conducted by intermediaries. In the matter of the *malocchio* the Duce pursued a policy of "better safe than sorry."

I found nothing in my hodgepodge of anecdotes and other scribblings to inspire good questions for Mussolini, and I had almost given up hope of ever seeing him when, in mid-October, I received a call from Guido Rocco, the head man at the Press Bureau, informing me that the Duce had "graciously consented" to grant me an interview but on "certain conditions." I was to submit written questions dealing "only with nonpolitical matters" to which the Duce would reply in writing. Mussolini could not receive me in person; he was "far too busy" and could not spare the time. Naturally I balked.

"What you are suggesting," I said, "is not an interview. Besides, I'm not sure I understand what you mean by nonpolitical subjects—"

"Well," Rocco replied, "you could ask him how it feels to be the Duce of forty-three million Italians, what his daily routine is like, something perhaps about his home life. You know, the kind of questions that bring out his personality. American readers like that sort of thing; I believe."

"I could write that kind of story out of my files," I said. "But unless I am permitted to see His Excellency in person and am allowed to ask him a few spontaneous questions, I see no point in submitting a questionnaire. Anyhow, I'll think about it."

That was how matters stood for several days while I drafted a dozen questions along the suggested lines, including one about the Duce's diet that would indicate the truth or falsity of persistent reports that he suffered from chronic ulcers. The questionnaire completed, I sent it by messenger to Rocco, who returned the typewritten replies two days later, on October 24.

The answers to my innocuous questions were so terse and so clearly reflected annoyance that I was sure Mussolini himself had dictated them. He described himself as "The guide, the head, and at the same time the servant of the people." He rose daily at seven o'clock, he said, shaved or not, "as the mood takes me," rode horseback in the grounds of the Villa Torlonia, then had breakfast, "plenty of milk with only a dash of coffee and, perhaps, a roll." He frequently lunched at his desk, "mostly on fruit," he said, adding that he never touched wine except at formal dinners. "My diet," he said, "consists almost entirely of fruit and vegetables, boiled or raw, with sometimes a little poached fish." Did he ever talk over affairs of state with his wife, Donna Rachele? "No, never!" he wrote.

And so the "interview" went. It told me nothing startlingly new except that in view of the blandness of his diet, the Duce almost certainly suffered from ulcers or some other serious gastric disorder.

I telephoned Rocco, thanked him for the prompt replies, and reiterated that unless the Duce received me in person, I had at best only a mildly interesting feature story that would receive little attention and was, in fact, hardly worth sending, a statement which, of course, was not true. In the early autumn of 1937 anything Mussolini said was news.

Later that same day Rocco called back to inform me that the Duce had agreed to receive me "in audience" and that I would be free to ask him a few questions, proving once again that in journalism as in life itself persistence pays. The "audience" was set for the following day, October 27, on the eve of the fifteenth anniversary of Mussolini's March on Rome.

My appointment was for four o'clock at the main entrance to the Palazzo Venezia, where Alfieri himself was to meet me to conduct me to the Duce's office on an upper floor, the one with the famous balcony. I walked up the Corso from the Galleria Colonna, mentally rehearsing my questions. The Duce had been saying recently that he envisioned the creation "soon" of a Fascist Europe, perhaps a Fascist world. I would ask him how he thought this could be achieved. I would try, also, to extract from him his view of the immediate future. Would there be peace or war?

Waiting for Alfieri, I took in the immensity of the Piazza Venezia, the stage Mussolini had chosen for his dramatic pronouncements to his people. The Palazzo Venezia itself is an impressive structure, topped by battlements and surmounted by a tower. It is dwarfed, however, by the imposing monument at the far end of the square, the tiered architectural horror variously known as the Monument of the Unknown Soldier and the Vittoriano, the edifice that commemorated Italy's emergence from the Risorgimento in 1870 as a united nation, a constitutional monarchy under Victor Emmanuel II, father of the present king. The monument had stubbornly refused to acquire the russet patina characteristic of Rome's other public buildings, and we foreign correspondents called it the white typewriter. But it remained a stark reminder that for half a century Italy had been a democracy, and I was about to meet the man who in 1922 had destroyed the parliamentary government it symbolized.

Alfieri arrived punctually, nattily attired as always in his well-fitting uniform of black *orbace,* a tweedlike material used exclusively for the uniforms of Blackshirt officials and party leaders, his boots mirror-bright, and looking his devilishly handsome best. Alfieri was the fashion plate of the Fascist hierarchy, by far its most elegant, though not its most intelligent, member. He preceded me athletically up the broad stone steps leading to the entrance to the Sala del Mappamondo, once the reception hall of the Austro-Hungarian rulers of pre-Risorgimento Italy, now the immense, cavernous, shadowy office where the Duce worked in self-imposed lonely splendor.

The Sala del Mappamondo seemed at least sixty feet long, about forty-five feet wide, and two stories high, but the architectonic effect of its columned walls made the great hall seem even larger than it really is. From the center of the ornate vaulted ceiling hung a chandelier with innumerable lights; but they were not turned on, and the place was more like an unlighted setting for Puccini's *Tosca,* the scene in which Tosca stabs Scarpia, than an office.

The sala, I noticed at a glance, was virtually unfurnished except for Mussolini's massive table desk to the right of the room's monumental fireplace in the wall farthest from the imposing entrance. Behind the desk there was a chair for the Duce, and two straight-back chairs flanked the fireplace, over which the decorators had immured a gilded Roman lictor framed in a sculptured laurel wreath. The chairs, however, were for occasional distinguished visitors—Mahatma Gandhi, Ramsay MacDonald, Pierre Laval, Maksim Litvinov—but there were none for his collaborators or his Fascist leaders, who in his presence were always required to stand, and I saw at once that no arrangements had been made for seating Alfieri and me.

The minister's heels resounded sharply on the waxed stone floor as we walked the twenty paces toward stage right, where Mussolini sat working by the light of a table lamp with an ornate, domed shade. But for the rhythmic thwack-thwack of Alfieri's bootheels, the place was silent as an underground cave.

If Mussolini heard our approach, he gave no sign but continued leafing through a thick, leather-bound folder, stopping at each page to scrawl a signature—a large, imperious *M,* I later learned, to signify approval. The Duce did not look up until we were about ten feet from him. He did not rise and obviously could not offer me a seat. I took a tentative step forward, but Alfieri restrained me and remained standing stiffly beside me, clearly the underling before his master.

I had expected to find Mussolini as I had always seen him before, in uniform, black shirt and tunic or army field gray-green, but he wore a double-breasted business suit of a dark material relieved by a white shirt and a polka-dotted necktie. I was seeing him for the first time as a civilian, and a rather rude one, I thought, for he had no word of greeting or recognition. The simplest Italian peasant would have shown a visitor more courtesy. Instead, Mussolini folded his thick arms across his chest and leaned back in his leather-upholstered thronelike swivel chair, and as he did so, a shaft of yellowish light from the mullioned window at his left—like an amber spotlight manipulated by a stagehand—illuminated his bald pate.

In that position the Duce looked fixedly at me for a moment, then made a gesture—an upward lift of his massive chin—instantly recognizable as an invitation to speak, a gesture that as much as said, "Well, what have you to say for yourself?"

I said the first words that came to mind: "Thank you, Excellency, for replying to what must have seemed to you very elementary questions."

"Frankly," he said with a scowl, "I didn't like them."

"Frankly," I retorted, glancing at Alfieri, "neither did I. It seemed to me that the anniversary of your March on Rome should be the occasion for an important message to an anxious world that daily only hears talk of war."

Mussolini leaned forward, arms resting on his desk, and scowled his best scowl.

"Why is it," he asked, "that they persist abroad, especially in your country, in attributing to me the dramatic pose of the standard-bearer of the cause of war? There is nothing dramatic about me. I am the antithesis of the dramatic."

The Duce's eyes bulged bigger than I had ever seen them, and he spread his arms in an actor's gesture of feigned innocence. Then, suddenly calmer, and with studied sincerity, he said: "The situation in Europe as a whole is far from rosy. But you may tell the world that Italy wants peace. That *I* want peace. We have much work to do, and to accomplish it, we need a long period of peace."

Reminding the Duce that he had predicted the emergence "soon" of a Fascist Europe, perhaps a Fascist world, I asked: "How will this process of fascistization take place? Through a series of internal revolutions? As a result of external pressures? Or through sheer necessity to meet changing social, economic, and political conditions?"

He nodded affirmatively during my brief recital, the suggestion of a smile crossing his heavy features.

"It will come," he said, "through a spontaneous realization within each individual nation that they must come together to make common cause against communism. Fascism is not an export product manufactured in Italy, but a European phenomenon, a revolt of the plain people against the threat of international bolshevism."

With that Mussolini reopened his folder. Alfieri tugged at my sleeve to indicate my time was up. Frankly I was relieved. I had the story I wanted. I had heard Europe's leading warmaker, fresh from his meeting with the Continent's most dangerous warmonger, solemnly declare he desired only peace.

I stepped back and bowed. Mussolini nodded. Alfieri saluted smartly, Fascist style, turned on his heel, and marched me toward the sculptured double door through which we had come. As we neared the exit, Alfieri, always the sycophant, whispered, *"Adesso facciamo al Duce un bel'saluto fascista."* He stopped, spun around, snapped his heels together smartly German style, and gave his stiff-armed salute. I merely bowed politely a second time, arms straight down by my sides, in the direction of the distant desk and the hunched figure behind it. Mussolini never even looked up.

Visibly annoyed with me for not having obeyed his instructions to give the Fascist salute to the Duce, Alfieri left me in the anteroom to the Sala del Mappamondo and went about his business.

I glanced at my wristwatch. It was 4:20 P.M. I had spent perhaps eighteen minutes, give or take a minute or two, in the presence of the man who held in his spatulate fingers the destiny of Italy and its forty-three million people. I lingered a few minutes to inspect the medieval weapons displayed under glass in a row of cases: cudgels; daggers; sabers; a pair or two of dueling pistols. Were they intended to intimidate visitors? I wondered. An elderly flunky in a tailcoat ushered me down the stairs and out into the broad piazza, where I slipped him a hundred-lire note—worth then about five dollars—before I turned left into the Corso and headed toward the Galleria Colonna and a waiting typewriter.

On the way I tried to sort out my impressions. I was aware of having seen face-to-face a deeply troubled man, a Mussolini struggling with problems for which he probably had not found answers. Indecision was evident in his big, round eyes, red-rimmed as though he had not slept well the night before.

Mussolini had just turned fifty-four but looked at least ten years older, his complexion sallow, his manner weary. I had observed him many times before, when he was invariably at his best, in uniform and surrounded by his ever-present retinue, swaggering, posturing, enjoying hugely his role as the *Duce* of his worshipful people. I had no reason to doubt their affection for him. I had seen women hold up their babies to him to be touched, had heard crowds hail him with frantic shouts of "Duce! Duce! Duce!" For fifteen years he had given them a grandiose spectacle, and they loved it. Had he not made Italy a great power, feared by its enemies, a nation now being wooed by Adolf Hitler's powerful Germany?

Nevertheless, I wondered now why masses of Italians, an intelligent and perceptive people, followed his leadership so blindly. I had seen not a super-man up there in the corner of the Sala del Mappamondo but a rather ordinary-looking, lower-middle-class Italian utterly lacking in charisma. Dared I say so in the story I was hastening to write? By the time I climbed the back stairs of the *galleria* to my office on the mezzanine floor I had put the thought out of my mind. I had too much at stake now to risk an expulsion order that this time surely would not be rescinded. Better play the game a little while longer, I decided.

The resultant "interview" as it appeared in the morning newspapers of October 28 was widely and profitably distributed by INS. Our London client, Lord Beaverbrook's *Daily Express,* gave it front-page display, and so did the Nazi party organ in Frankfurt. The Italian newspapers ignored it, probably on orders from the Duce himself, for the next day, Thursday, October 28, all available newsprint was to be devoted to extolling fascism's virtues on the occasion of the regime's fifteenth anniversary.

measures aimed at reforming their character and style. They included, in addition to the abolition of handshakes, the mandatory use of the Roman salute in all forms of friendly greetings; the substitution of the traditional *lei* in formal address with either the Latin *tu* or the more respectful *voi;* and the introduction in the Royal Italian Army and the Fascist militia of the German goose step. Oblivious of the antagonism and ridicule which his blatant mimicry aroused, Mussolini called the unnatural and awkward step the *passo romano,* but by any name it was the Prussian parade step, difficult and exhausting to perform and ridiculous unless perfectly executed, something for which nature never intended Italians. Shorter and stockier, as a rule, than Hitler's Teutons, the goose-stepping Italians managed to look more like waddling ducks than marching troops. Mussolini, however, stoutly defended the goose step as his own creation and was enormously proud of it.

Not surprisingly, one of the sharpest critics of the Prussian parade step was King Victor Emmanuel, who did not hesitate to make known his objections. To the royal annoyance, Mussolini scornfully replied, "Naturally he doesn't like it, and for the same reason he doesn't like riding a horse—because he has to use a ladder to mount the beast."

During the early months of the following year corpulent Fascist militiamen could be seen practicing the *passo romano* on playing fields and parade grounds, preparing for Hitler's impending visit. Eventually a few hundred troops, enough to form a special drill unit in a parade, got the hang of it sufficiently to satisfy Mussolini that they would not disgrace themselves when marching past the Führer.

Such manifestations of Germanophilic rapture in Rome encouraged Hitler, however, to undertake new and daring adventures. Fully cognizant, now, of his ascendancy over Mussolini, the Führer prepared to fulfill what he had described in *Mein Kampf* as his "heart's most burning desire, the union of my beloved country, Austria, to the common Fatherland, the German Reich."

There were party rallies in the public squares of every town and village
the land, with uniformed Blackshirts parading to martial music, flags wavir
and church bells pealing everywhere, church thus joining state in celebrati(
of what was really fascism's triumph over parliamentary government in 192
The day's climactic ceremony, however, took place in Rome, where more tha
a hundred thousand party functionaries from all over the country converge
to hear their Duce speak. As in my interview, his theme was peace, but h
preached a strange version of it that promised future violence.

Ironically the Duce spoke from a specially constructed platform before th
Vittoriano. In full Blackshirt regalia, Mussolini stood in the company of ⱡ
delegation of Nazis headed by Rudolf Hess, Adolf Hitler's deputy, and no one
who heard him speak that day could possibly think of him as a man of peace
or doubt that he had allied Rome irrevocably with Berlin.

With Hess at his side, Mussolini denounced the peace treaties of 1919,
demanded the return to Germany of the African colonies which it had lost
after the Great War, poured scorn on the "bleating shepherds of the reactionary, so-called great democracies," and revealed that "an ever-closer solidarity"
was developing between Italy and Germany and their two peoples.

"Peace," the Duce declared, "will be fascism's watchword as it enters the
sixteenth year of its existence. But if peace is to be fruitful and lasting, it is
necessary that bolshevism be eliminated from Europe."

A few days later, on November 6, at Hitler's urging, Italy officially joined
Germany and Japan in "a solemn covenant against the Communist International," the so-called Anti-Comintern Pact which Germany had already
formed with imperial Japan, and the pattern of friendship between Duce and
Führer began assuming definite and final shape.

Then, on December 11, 1937, I stood with thousands of uniformed Fascisti
in a cold, steady drizzle in the Piazza Venezia to hear the Duce announce from
his balcony the "historic decision" to lead Italy out of the League of Nations,
again under pressure from Hitler, who had taken that step more than four
years earlier. Mussolini declared that Italy was "fully armed on land, sea and
in the air" in preparation for the European war which, like Hitler, he now saw
as "inevitable."

Exactly forty-four days before, the Duce had sought to assure the world,
through INS, that he was "a man of peace." Now he envisioned war as
"inevitable." Only then did I realize why my interview with the dictator had
not been reproduced in the Italian press. Mussolini simply did not want his
people to think of him as "a man of peace," and I had unwittingly helped him
mislead public opinion in the United States, Great Britain, Australia, wherever
INS had client newspapers. This knowledge dimmed somewhat my enjoyment
of the scoop I had engineered.

In subsequent weeks it became increasingly apparent that Mussolini's German visit had sealed his friendship with Hitler and snapped shut the lock on
the chain that bound him to the Führer.

Mussolini resolved to "Prussianize" the Italians and to that end introduced

12

ANSCHLUSS AND WORSE TO COME

In the early-morning hours of March 12, 1938, the tanks of Hitler's Wehrmacht rolled across the Austrian frontier from their bases in Germany.
By one o'clock that afternoon, accompanied by the Führer himself, the
newly created German Army's forward units had reached the Brenner
Pass, gateway to Italy.

Alerted to what was happening by an INS tipster on the *Giornale d'Italia*
who had access to the teletyped bulletins of Stefani, the official Italian news
agency, I rushed by cab to the Press Bureau in the Via Veneto. The boss,
Alfieri, was unavailable—he was at Palazzo Venezia conferring with Mussolini—but Jack Bosio, one of his lesser but more personable aides, had news
of major importance.

"The Duce," he said, "has ordered the mobilization of several divisions at
the Brenner Pass on a full wartime basis."

"Does that mean Italy will oppose Germany's move?" I asked.

"I doubt it," Bosio replied with, it seemed to me, a touch of bitterness.

"I can assume, then," I said, "that Italy will offer no resistance."

"Your guess," Bosio said, "is as good as mine."

"Okay, Jack, "I said. "But off the record, how do you *personally* feel about
having the Germans on the Brenner instead of Austrians?"

Jack Bosio, a nice young fellow, really, although a *fascista* in every inch
of his tall, slim, athletic body, turned thoughtful.

"Well," he said, stroking his chin ruefully, "my father fought the Austrians
and the Germans in the last war. Need I say more?"

I pressed Jack no further, thanked him, and left. I was sure Mussolini's "mobilization" was a colossal bluff, a repetition of the "show of strength" he had put on back in the summer of 1934, when Austrian Nazis had assassinated the diminutive Chancellor Engelbert Dollfuss. I was in Washington then and remembered that the Duce had marched his troops up to the Brenner Pass, then marched them down again. Had the Italians fought then, they might have changed the course of history, but they were now history's prisoners, not movers, and the history maker was Adolf Hitler, not Benito Mussolini.

The day Hitler sent his newly created Wehrmacht into Austria was the first time since 1914 that German troops had invaded another European country. It was a Saturday, but Mussolini learned what Hitler was up to only late on Friday evening, fewer than twelve hours before the Wehrmacht violated the Austrian frontier. The details were brought to him in a letter from the Führer by Prince Philip of Hesse, a Nazi sympathizer and husband of Princess Mafalda, a daughter of Italy's king. The letter was not made public at the time, but German sources made sure that newsmen were apprized of its arrival and most of its contents.

The next morning, Sunday, March 13, at a hastily summoned conference at the Press Bureau, a spokesman confirmed that Mussolini had received the letter and had "accepted" the Führer's explanation of the momentous event. He added that Italy had rejected "purely tentative" proposals from Britain and France for joint action to restrain Germany.

"Italy," he said, "is no more prepared to fight for Austrian independence than are Britain and France."

"Then why," someone asked, "has Italy mobilized troops at the Brenner Pass on a wartime basis?"

To this the spokesman replied, enigmatically, "Frontiers must be defended."

I came away from the briefing with a gut feeling that Mussolini resented Hitler's behavior—not because Germany had invaded Austria but because he had not been consulted beforehand. The Duce had long since wearied of "mounting guard over Austria," and had so informed Joachim von Ribbentrop, the Führer's new foreign minister, back in November 1937, when Mussolini was still euphoric over his visit to Germany and ready to do anything to please his friend and partner. At the time, however, Mussolini and Hitler had agreed that neither Germany nor Italy would do anything about Austria— or anything else involving Axis policy—without prior consultation, an agreement the Führer had chosen to disregard. German tanks were already rolling toward the Austrian frontier when the Duce read the Führer's explanatory letter on March 11.

Knowing that the Italian people would react unfavorably when they awakened on Sunday morning and learned that for the first time in history they would have as next-door neighbors a people they historically regarded as enemies, he ordered the mobilization of troops on the Brenner Pass. The addition of the phrase "on a wartime basis" was purely a propaganda ploy, for like every other correspondent and military attaché in Rome, I was certain Italy had no intention of using force against the Wehrmacht, and before the sun had set on Sunday, March 13, one of the oldest states in Europe had ceased to exist.

Nevertheless, Italy's mobilization, phony or not, caused a flurry of speculation abroad that Mussolini might, after all, live up to his oft-repeated pledge to uphold Austrian independence, and late that Sunday afternoon I received a call from Bill Shirer asking me to participate in a CBS radio network show dealing with the "crisis."

Bill called from London, suggesting that I arrange for shortwave transmission facilities with Ente Italiana Audizioni Radiofoniche (EIAR), which had headquarters in Turin and an office in Rome. Phone calls to both places elicited negative replies: It was too late in the day to make the necessary arrangements, and "It's Sunday, you know, everyone's day off." Disgusted and discouraged, I telephoned Bill and told him the outlook for completing a hookup in time to meet his tight schedule was grim.

But Bill had a solution. "We'll take your story over a line to Geneva," he said. "Tell EIAR to order the lines for you and be sure to reserve a studio in Rome."

"I'll try," I said, but knowing the Italians, I doubted I would succeed. But Bill said that he would get after the Swiss at his end and that if all else failed, I should phone my story to London, and he would read it from there. "New York," he added, "is anxious to know what Mussolini is going to do."

"You know damned well what he's going to do," I said. "Nothing. He's marched his men up the hill, and he'll march them down again."

"Sure," Bill said. "Same as Chamberlain here in London. But New York, Frank, wants to hear it from you, speaking from Rome. It'll sound more effective than if I say it here from London."

Bill's efforts and mine to clear a direct line from Rome to Geneva came to naught, but I did manage to write a piece and dictated it to a stenographer in London in Bill's BBC studio. It was nearly 3:00 A.M. my time when I finished dictating. I have no idea what I said, but I do remember receiving a check for my services—fifty dollars, I think it was—from CBS sometime later and warm thanks from Bill Shirer.

Mussolini's acceptance of Austria's demise as an independent entity dismayed and alarmed the Italian people. They had been schooled over the years in the belief that, in the Duce's own words, "The independence of Austria, for which Dollfuss died, is a principle for which the Italians have fought and will continue to fight." They knew instinctively that the presence of a strong and militant Germany on their Alpine frontier spelled danger.

Having no recourse to a free press or the right of assembly, they vented their resentment by sending thousands of anonymous letters to Ciano and Mussolini protesting the Anschluss. Not since the murder in 1924 of Socialist leader Giacomo Matteotti, who had dared denounce fascism from the floor of the Chamber of Deputies as "an association of criminals," had any event so damaged the Duce's popularity and prestige as his acquiescence in Hitler's Austrian coup.

There was rancor also within the Grand Council, but Mussolini—not too convincingly, I learned—assured its members that Italy had nothing to fear from Germany. "The Axis has proved itself," he said, according to published reports, "and the two nations, whose unification has been parallel in time and method, united as they are by an analogous conception of the politics of living, can march forward together to give our tormented continent a new equilibrium."

Those sentiments were reflected in the press, which received orders to minimize the negative aspects of the Anschluss, but the Italians had become experts at reading between the lines of official communiqués and the scribblings of Fascist editorialists. They knew that by condoning the Anschluss, Mussolini had taken yet another step toward a new European war. Of this I was personally certain, as were my colleagues in London, Paris, and Berlin.

My Berlin counterpart, Pierre Huss—somewhat overjubilantly, I thought—confided that "Czechoslovakia is probably next, old boy. . . ."

Mussolini was not as "satisfied" with the turn of events in Austria as his spokesmen in the Ministry of Propaganda led correspondents to believe. Throughout the preceding winter the Duce had been aware of the imminence of a new German assault on Austrian independence, and early in 1938 he had decided to resume negotiations for a rapprochement with Britain. He found a ready partner in Neville Chamberlain, to whom he sent a friendly message through Lady Ivy Chamberlain, the widow of Sir Austen Chamberlain and the British prime minister's sister-in-law.

Lady Ivy, whom I interviewed on February 21, was a tall gray-haired woman of imposing schoolteacherish presence. She had traveled widely in Italy, liked the Italians, and held Mussolini in high esteem. She and her husband had been frequent visitors at the Palazzo Venezia until his death in 1937. While she would not specifically confirm that she had been acting as an intermediary between the dictator and Prime Minister Chamberlain, she left no doubt in my mind that she had been instrumental in bringing the two parties together.

"I am a believer in the traditional friendship of Italy and England," she said over tea at the Grand Hotel, "and I shall do all in my power to bring about a better understanding between Italy and our government. I believe in peace—a peace established on a realistic basis. I feel that my brother-in-law is working along realistic lines."

Anglo-Italian negotiations were resumed late in February and, while welcomed by Chamberlain, were bitterly opposed by Anthony Eden, the foreign secretary, who correctly doubted Mussolini's sincerity and resigned in protest. His resignation followed a heated argument between him and Chamberlain in an unusual Friday night cabinet meeting at 10 Downing Street on February 19. The cabinet had not violated the sanctity of the British weekend since the abdication of Edward VIII! The departure of Eden—"that sworn enemy of Italy" the Duce had called him—pleased the Italians, and the talks proceeded through the period of the Anschluss and beyond.

On April 16, in the magnificent Victory Salon in the Palazzo Chigi, Count Ciano and Sir Eric Drummond, now Lord Perth, the British ambassador, signed what was trumpeted as the "Anglo-Italian Pact of Friendship" that "ended three years of strained relations between London and Rome." Possibly because I had been involved in helping Ciano clear the way for the agreement with his August 1937 "interview," I was among the few American and English correspondents invited to witness the ceremony.

The seven-thousand-word agreement, which included a protocol reestablishing Italo-British friendship and eight separate documents for settling the various points at issue between the two countries, was signed on a massive sextagonal Venetian table. From its pink marble top rose a tall bronze statue of a winged victory, and the diplomats affixed their signatures under the shadows of its wings cast by klieg lights while movie cameras whirred and still cameras clicked.

The appended documents covered all the points at which Anglo-Italian interests touched. Freedom of transit in the Mediterranean was reconfirmed, and annexes contained agreements regarding the exchange of military information and the renunciation by both parties of hostile propaganda. The most important provision, however, deferred the pact until Italy withdrew its military forces from Spain and Britain recognized Italy's conquest of Ethiopia. Thousands of Blackshirts—many of whom three years before had stood outside the British Embassy shouting, "Down with Britain"—gave a thunderous ovation to Count Ciano and Lord Perth when they appeared on the balcony of the Palazzo Chigi minutes after the pact was signed.

But seven months would elapse before the conditions which brought the pact into force were met, and by that time—November 1938—the accord had lost whatever minimal significance it might have possessed. It was another grand charade in Fascist diplomacy, and quick to recognize it as such was Winston Churchill, who denounced it as "a complete triumph for Mussolini."

Meanwhile, on March 30, Mussolini had himself promoted to the rank of marshal of the empire, a title simultaneously conferred by law on the king-emperor, and personally took charge of elaborate preparations to greet Hitler, due to arrive in Rome on May 3. The Duce was as anxious to impress the Führer as the latter had been to impress him.

By then Benito Mussolini had become the increasingly impotent junior partner in his alliance with Hitler. In his fear of political isolation in the European scheme of things and in his craving for greatness, he had embraced Adolf Hitler, once the Duce's imitator, now his master. The reversal of roles was the really big story of the fateful year 1938, but one of many stories we couldn't tell from Rome.

It was not possible to write from Rome that Anschluss had been the price Mussolini had had to pay for the royal reception he had received in Germany and for the substantial material and political help which Hitler had provided during Italy's Ethiopian War, the event which I believed then—and still believe—set off the explosive forces leading inexorably to the Second World War.

By the annexation of Austria, Germany substantially increased its military potential both in terms of manpower and the acquisition of such valuable natural resources as iron and magnesium. It was still not too late, however, to stop Hitler, and the Soviet Union proposed a general conference of all interested states, large or small, to lay plans for collective resistance to any future German aggression. This suggestion the British government rejected as inopportune since "it might seem like organizing Europe into two ideological blocs." That, of course, was idiotic; the Continent was already divided into ideological blocs. To confirm this, I needed only to glance at the map I had pasted on the wall above my typewriter.

Studying it one day and reflecting on what I had read in *Mein Kampf* about Hitler's designs for Europe's future, I started making plans to send Kathryn and the boys home for Christmas. If a general war erupted as a result of Hitler's next aggressive act—against Czechoslovakia, as Pete Huss, my well-informed Berlin colleague, had hinted—I wanted to be certain of my family's safety.

The Anschluss in March 1938 had brought German troops to the Brenner Pass, the gateway to Italy. Now preparations for Hitler's state visit in May went forward in an atmosphere of official elation and civilian disquiet. Mussolini was eager to show off his domain. The people knew that if the Italian Tyrol were not next after Austria in Hitler's campaign to amalgamate all of what he called Greater Germany, it was because Czechoslovakia's Sudetenland lay easier to hand. There would still be war, at Germany's side rather than against it. When hundreds of Italian-speaking German tourists began to appear in Rome in January, even before the Anschluss, many Romans saw them as Hitler's advance guard. Indeed, they were, most of them, sent by the Gestapo to plan security measures and test the welcome Hitler could expect in May.

If the common people could have spoken freely, the welcome would have been icy. After the Anschluss I saw the fear of war reflected in the faces of people of all sorts—journalists, shopkeepers, bank tellers, waiters, barkeeps, cabbies—and heard it echoed in their guarded comments. Among those who feared that the future held another war was my barber in the Via Sistina. He had fought in *la grande guerra,* and remembered its cost in blood and political consequences.

"Un altra maledetta guerra sara la rovina del'Italia [Another damned war

will be Italy's ruin]," he muttered into my ear during my monthly haircut. "*E lei, comme la pensa* [And what do you think]?"

I sensed he merely wanted reassurance, and I lied. "Just another political crisis," I replied. "It'll pass like a summer storm."

A swift run of news stories varied the pressure of those gloomy days. Gabriele d'Annunzio, the poet-adventurer who commanded a revolutionary government in Fiume from September 1919 to January 1921, died on March 1. I wrote the obituary myself and gave him a good send-off. D'Annunzio deserved credit, if that is the right word, for designing the rituals and emblems of fascism and much of its rationale as well. Mussolini attended the funeral, appropriately enough.

Many stories originated in the Vatican, which required more careful watching than ever, for the pope was being kept alive now by pain-killers and stimulants, and his doctors had despaired of his life. Nevertheless, the stubborn pontiff worked on; he even found the strength and courage to send General Franco a sharp note criticizing him for bombing Barcelona and other Republican civilian centers.

Pius XI also took to task Theodor Cardinal Innitzer, the archbishop of Vienna, for accepting Nazi rule on behalf of the Austrian clergy. The cardinal's avowal of loyalty to Nazi Germany, the pope held, did not have the approval of the Holy See.

The story that caught the eye of INS editors in New York, however, originated in a routine telephone call from our INS tipster, a local newspaperman in Naples. The liner *Conte di Savoia* had just arrived bearing Leopold Stokowski. The famous conductor, our informant said almost as an afterthought, was accompanied by "a very beautiful lady" listed on the ship's manifest as Miss Marguerite Gustafsson, of Swedish nationality.

"Gustafsson," Alan Cranston mused. "Rings a bell. I think it's Greta Garbo."

"Nonsense," I said. "What would a gorgeous creature like her want with a temperamental orchestra leader twice her age?"

But Alan set me thinking. If the lady really was Garbo, we had a story of the kind most appreciated by Hearst editors: illicit romance, May-December love, pictures galore. I couldn't take a chance.

I called our tipster in Naples and questioned him closely about what he had seen and heard when the *Conte di Savoia* docked the night before, February 27.

"Miss Gustafsson," he said, "wore a floppy hat that shadowed her face. I could see, though, that she was *una bellisima signorina,* a very, very beautiful lady. She moved like a princess. . . ."

I gave him no hint that the woman might be the Divine Garbo. I wasn't about to have him scoop INS.

I sent Michael Chinigo to Ravello, the mountain resort where Stokowski and the lady had gone. He drove through the night and early the next morning,

March 1, reported that he had located the couple in the Villa Cimbrone, a magnificent Renaissance residence overlooking the sea south of Naples. Stokowski and the lady, Michael said, were in total seclusion, but he had made "certain arrangements."

Later that same day Michael telephoned that the lady had sent her secretary out to the local cobbler with a pair of walking shoes to be fitted with new rubber heels. He had bribed the shoemaker—he had a flair for that sort of thing—and read the name of the shop (I. Miller, Fifth Avenue, New York City) and the serial number imprinted inside.

I cabled this vital intelligence to New York, requesting an urgent reply. New York wired back within an hour that the shoes had been sold some months before to Miss Greta Garbo, adding: SMELL SWELL FRONTPAGER RUSH DETAILS REGARDS.

It was indeed the kind of story that sold newspapers, especially those served by INS, mostly afternoon papers hungry for circulation.

I phoned the details to London that evening and received in return even warmer congratulatory telegrams from New York than those I had gotten for my interviews with Ciano and Mussolini.

Within twenty-four hours the Villa Cimbrone was besieged by the world's press. Reporters and photographers from every capital rushed to chronicle what the Hearst papers headlined as A LOVE IDYLL MORE ROMANTIC THAN ANY GARBO FILM.

For several days the villa was surrounded by armed police to prevent reporters and photographers from invading the grounds. Its occupants remained virtual prisoners, unable to emerge to enjoy the luminescent stretch of coast between Sorrento and Salerno along the Amalfi Drive.

Meanwhile, apparently Miss Garbo appealed for help to Hollywood gossip columnist Louella Parsons, a power within the Hearst Organization. For on the third day of the siege I received an urgent cable from Mr. Hearst himself with explicit instructions to CALL OFF THE WATCHDOGS and how to go about it. I was to persuade Stokowski and Garbo to agree to a mass press conference in exchange for privacy—after "selling" the idea to the correspondents at an INS cocktail party!

I got through to Stokowski, who sourly recalled a piece I had written about him years before in the *Philadelphia Record.* He agreed to the Chief's plan, but only if there were no photographs and Miss Garbo and he saw the reporters separately.

Most of the fifty-odd reporters and photographers involved were staying at Ravello's Hotel Palumbo, where I invited the lot to cocktails as guests of INS. When I felt they had had enough to drink and were in a receptive mood, I read them the cable from Mr. Hearst and pleaded for their cooperation. The reporters in the crowd, who had already wrung the story dry, readily agreed to "call off the dogs" in exchange for a gang interview, but the frustrated photographers howled. They were outnumbered and outvoted, however, and the press conference was held in the softly lighted spacious salon of the palatial Villa Cimbrone.

As arranged, the maestro appeared first, casually attired in a dark blue summer-weight suit with a white cravat around his long, skinny neck. He stood before the huge, sculptured fireplace at the far end of the room and in a reedy voice skillfully parried all questions about a romance between him and Miss Garbo. Standing there, figuratively naked before the reporters, he was not the imposing figure who bullied Philadelphia audiences from the podium but an apprehensive sexagenerian. He said nothing worth inscribing on history's walls except, perhaps, that he liked jazz, which he believed derived from the music of the islands of Bali, "the finest music in the world." When the reporters had no more questions, he made a small bow, turned, and vanished through a curtained doorway.

Minutes later Greta Garbo entered the room. There was an audible, collective gasp of admiration, even a few spontaneous handclaps, for she was surely the most beautiful creature any of us had ever seen. Her glossy golden hair was parted in the middle and fell straight to her shoulders. She wore a tailored navy blue silk ensemble—a double-breasted jacket over pleated trousers—and at her throat she had loosely knotted a filmy canary yellow scarf that draped down to her slim waist. The effect was electric.

Garbo advanced into the center of the room and sat stiffly in an armchair, knees together, hands cupped in her lap, eyes darting about our faces. I thought of Joan before her inquisitors. In the throaty voice we all knew from her films, she denied most emphatically all reports of a romance between her and the maestro, adding that she intended to retire from filmmaking in a year or two. Only then, she said, when she could consider herself "a private person" would she give any thought to marriage. She had come to Italy on a holiday, she said, with someone who knew the country well and was teaching her much about its history and culture, and she begged everyone to allow her to enjoy her trip.

"I vant only to be left alone," she concluded in her small, resonant voice, and the reporters pressed no further. At the curtained doorway Garbo turned, smiled ineffably, swept the room with her eyes, and was gone.

The press called off the siege of the Villa Cimbrone as promised but pursued the couple wherever they went—Naples, Capri, Amalfi. Reports of an impending marriage followed them to Tunis and beyond.

In the meantime, however, far more important news was in the making, and I had staff problems again. Alan Cranston had decided to quit, and I wondered how INS Rome was going to deal with Hitler's visit and keep watch on the pope's condition with only Michael and myself to handle the job.

Alan had the makings of a first-class newspaperman: curiosity, boundless physical and mental energy, love of adventure, and, above all, respect for truth. But in the approaching spring of 1938, after many months of hard work for small pay, he realized that it would take him too long to go where he wanted to go in the newspaper business: the top. He lacked the connections he would have developed had his career begun in America instead of Europe. More important, perhaps, he had begun thinking in terms of a life in politics and government. He didn't like what he saw of fascism in Italy and was profoundly disturbed by what was transpiring in the world at large.

Alan had dropped hints about quitting back in the fall, but I talked him into staying on while I tried to persuade New York to authorize a substantial raise for him or to place him in a better paying job elsewhere in Europe. The months dragged on, and Alan remained at his post mainly out of personal friendship, to help me deal with the mounting crush of news.

Shortly after the Stokowski-Garbo story broke, Alan had had enough. He wanted to "get moving," as he put it, and see something more of the world before returning to California and becoming "part of the stream of things instead of floating on it." He hankered to become the first American foreign correspondent to visit Ethiopia since its conquest by the Fascists, and I made the necessary arrangements with the Foreign Office on Alan's promise that INS would have first rights to whatever he wrote.

Alan sailed for East Africa from Naples on March 7, 1938, and shortly after his arrival there wrote me jubilantly: "The government is breaking its neck to give me a favorable impression of Italy's progress in empire-building. They met me at the dock, put a car with a soldier-chauffeur at my disposal, and booked me into the best hotel in Massawa; drove me up to the capital, Asmara, threw some poor devil out so that I'd have a good room; gave me an immediate audience with the governor. . . ."

The future California politician had no illusions, however, about why he was being treated so royally. "Fortunately," he wrote later, "I realize it's not *I* they're interested in but INS and its hundreds of papers. . . . I've met every big shot in the Empire, including the Duke of Aosta, in the first interview he's granted since becoming Viceroy last December."

The elaborateness of the preparations for the Führer's visit revealed the spirit of emulation in Mussolini's relations with Hitler. He plainly wanted to give his friend an even more impressive and grandiose reception than he had received in Germany.

To ensure a warm welcome, all Germans residing in Italy, and all Italians of Germanic origin—virtually the entire population of the South Tyrol—came under official compulsion to be in Rome when Hitler arrived. Special trains and buses from the north arrived almost daily, disgorging Nazis, and by mid-April there seemed to be more Germans in the streets of the capital than Italians.

On May 1 some fifty thousand Nazis, many in brownshirt uniforms, others in civilian dress, waving swastikas, chanting *"Sieg heil,"* and singing the odious "Horst Wessel Lied," paraded through Rome's main thoroughfares. Some wore native Tyrolean costumes, but all had come on orders from German consulates, the travel and living expenses of the poorer elements defrayed by assessments levied on their wealthier compatriots.

On the outskirts of Rome I watched parties of sullen workmen building a new railway station near San Paolo Fuori le Mura. A foreman explained it was being built only to permit a triumphal drive into the city when Hitler arrived. In fact, the entire country was being modified—at a cost of twenty-five million dollars, I later learned—in Mussolini's attempt to show the Führer the "new face" Italy had acquired under fascism.

Houses along the railway from the Brenner Pass to Florence, Rome, and Naples—the three cities Hitler was due to visit—were freshly painted and lavishly decorated with swastikas and Fascist symbols. In the cities the poorer houses along the streets where the parades would pass were given false fronts like so many stage sets, reminding a friend of mine, an anti-Fascist Italian historian, of the Potemkin villages of the time of Catherine the Great's visit to Russia's new lands in the south in 1787.

In Florence, Rome, and Naples sixty thousand army reserves were recalled to duty to help in the extraordinary police work entailed in the scheduled celebrations. An additional hundred thousand Italian soldiers were called up for deployment along the railway line from the Brenner Pass to Naples to guard against saboteurs while patrols of German detectives checked every bridge and culvert for explosives.

The troops who were to participate in the various reviews were carefully selected and formed a special corps. As many of its members as were capable of executing the *passo romano* were mobilized to show Hitler that Italians, too, were militaristic. They wore brand-new uniforms and were armed with the best weapons available in Italy's depleted arsenals.

A cynical Italian newspaperman friend, with whom I watched a platoon of troops rehearsing the German goose step on a soccer field one afternoon, remarked out of the side of his mouth, *"Mi sembra che abbiamo scambiato il Passo del Brennero per il passo romano* [Seems to me we've swapped the Brenner Pass for the German goose step]."

By May 2, on the eve of Hitler's arrival, Rome was ablaze with swastikas, German and Italian flags, and Fascist symbols. There was little joy anywhere, however, least of all in Rome's ghetto, where many of the capital's Jews lived. Here, too, swastikas and fasces were in evidence, but the residents themselves were either under house arrest or in what the authorities insisted were "luxurious detainment centers." My request to be allowed to visit one was denied.

Detained, also, were more than seven thousand Jews throughout the country, many of them refugees from recent Nazi persecution in Germany and Austria. All were considered a potential threat to the safety of the Eminent Visitor from Germany and were rounded up by the Italian police, acting on lists provided by the Gestapo.

13

HITLER'S VISIT

Painters and decorators were putting the final touches on the Stazione Ostiense when I visited it in the early afternoon of May 3, 1938, a few hours before the arrival there of Adolf Hitler and his entourage for the extravagant ceremonies that would celebrate, in effect, the mating of Italian fascism to German nazism.

Workmen lugged into place wooden planters filled with flowering blooms and greenery, swabbed and polished the terrazzo paving, brightened metalwork, and dragged rolls of crimson carpeting to wherever they would be needed when the visitors arrived. All toiled silently, like automatons, intent upon whatever they were doing, replying to queries with shrugs, grunts, or enigmatic smiles.

From what I observed that afternoon, Romans were not in their best mood and would give the Germans at most a cool reception, although the slogans painted on banners in brilliant letters told a different story. VIVA IL FÜHRER!, they said, VIVA IL DUCE! and VIVA L'ASSE ROMA-BERLINO! By sundown the railway station which the Duce had caused to be built beyond the Porta San Paolo to provide his friend with a triumphal entry into Rome was ready to receive the Eminent Visitor.

The station still smelled of fresh paint and drying plaster when Hitler and his suite arrived at 8:00 P.M. Of the Führer's official family only Air Marshal Göring was missing; he had stayed behind in Berlin to run Germany during his master's absence. My assistant, Michael Chinigo, watched them descend in order: Hess, Ribbentrop, Goebbels, Himmler, and, among others, General

Keitel, men whom history would arraign as some of the archcriminals of the cataclysm of 1939–1945.

On the station's platform to greet the Führer was the king, who, according to protocol—and to Hitler's evident dismay—was to be his host in Rome. The Führer had been led to believe that Mussolini—and only Mussolini—ruled Italy, and he was visibly irritated when, on descending from his train, he was received by Victor Emmanuel III and his regular army brass while the Duce, Ciano, and their entourage stood respectfully aside.

The king was the one element Mussolini had been unable to change in anticipation of Hitler's visit. Actually, the Führer should have been pleased, for the monarch was more Nordic than most Italians, his Austro-Germanic ancestry clearly discernible in his small blue eyes. In them, however, Hitler accurately read dislike, and the Eminent Visitor behaved accordingly: He rudely seated himself first in the horse-drawn royal carriage that took him and the king to the Quirinal Palace behind an escort of mounted cuirassiers in gleaming silver breastplates and plumed gold and silver helmets.

The triumphal procession into the city proper through the Aurelian wall at the Porta San Paolo seemed endless. The Germans had come in unexpected numbers. Hitler's retinue, which included battalions of Nazi journalists in party uniforms, filled four special trains. Mussolini and those in attendance during his trip to Germany, I recalled, had required only a single train.

The procession proceeded past the Pyramid of Sestius and the Protestant Cemetery where Keats and Shelley are buried, then up the broad Via dei Trionfi (Street of Triumphs) to the Colosseum. There, as the royal carriage approached, Hitler was greeted by a fabulous display of fireworks.

The ancient structure, ghostly in the half-light of the gathering Roman dusk, suddenly came alive in a spectacular explosion of sounds and colors. Hitler stood up in the carriage for a better view and remained standing, excitedly clasping and unclasping his hands until the vehicle was well past the Colosseum, then turning for a last look and gesticulating at the king, who nodded in apparent agreement but remained seated, looking straight ahead.

As I observed the scene from the elevated roadside press stand, it occurred to me that the Führer might have been reminded of the Reichstag fire—the mysterious blaze that helped propel him to power in 1933—as he gazed upon what seemed to be a Colosseum being consumed by flames. I said so in my account of the event, and the single sentence earned me a stern rebuke from Alfieri's Ministry of Propaganda, plus a warning that a repetition of such "tendentious reporting" would mean the loss of my credentials for covering *la visita del Führer in Italia.*

Hitler was demonstratively unhappy that night at having been quartered in the Quirinal, the royal palace, and the king, for his part, found his guest personally repugnant. He told members of his court that the Führer was addicted to stimulants and narcotics, and they, in turn, gleefully spread the story at every opportunity. I heard it myself from Contessina Memmi, a minor lady-in-waiting to the queen.

Meanwhile, Pope Pius XI, saddened by the wholesale display of the "hooked cross" of Nazi Germany throughout the capital, showed his displeasure by closing the Vatican Museum for the duration of the Führer's visit and retiring to his summer palace at Castel Gandolfo. There, on May 4—commemorative of the Catholic Day of the Holy Cross—the pontiff publicly voiced his regret that "the banner of another cross, which is not the cross of Christ," should have been raised in Rome.

Nevertheless, Mussolini's carefully staged and expensive celebration of fascism's marriage to nazism achieved its aim. While more Mediterranean and less Wagnerian than Hitler might have liked, it impressed the Führer with its parades, its folkloristic peasant dancing in the Villa Borghese, and the audible enthusiasm of the crowds wherever he went. He could not have known that much of the "enthusiasm" was manufactured. Along the Via dei Trionfi on the day of his arrival, for instance, microphones had been set up at intervals under the grandstands to pick up and magnify the cheers and applause that came to him over hidden loudspeakers. Fascist claques were strategically located among the spectators to stimulate the acclamation.

May 5 was spent in Naples, where Mussolini put on a grand display of Italy's sea power. From the railway station to the quay where the Duce and an array of admirals in gold-braided dress whites awaited their arrival, king and Führer drove through a valley of flags and cheering tens of thousands of Neapolitans, a warmhearted emotional people who love a good show more than most Italians. At least half the city's million citizens turned out to line the route and make themselves heard. Politically more monarchist than Fascist, their cheers were really for their king rather than for his pink-cheeked guest, but Hitler basked in the warmth of their reception, smiling and bowing, and for once seemed pleased, I thought, to be in the monarch's company.

The highlight of the naval review, which I witnessed from the fantail of a trim destroyer, was a spectacular performance by a fleet of thirty submarines which simultaneously submerged and surfaced, like so many trained dolphins, collectively diving then breaking water in perfect unison. The maneuver, the subsequent parade of battleships and sleek cruisers, and the sham battle that followed with guns roaring impressed the Führer, who as yet had no sizable navy of his own. He came away from the spectacle—staged on the smooth blue waters of the Tyrrhenian Sea outside the Bay of Naples—persuaded that whatever its deficiencies on land and in the air, on the sea, at least, Italy could make a valuable contribution to the military potential of the Rome-Berlin Axis.

In Rome the following day, May 6, Mussolini showed Hitler a sample of the eight million men whom the Duce boasted he could mobilize for war. Mussolini beamed, but Hitler looked on expressionless as thirty thousand Italian troops paraded with their tanks, artillery, armored cars, poison gas dispensers, and flamethrowing units. The equipment was Italy's best but brought no approving nod from Hitler. He also remained impassive when a formation closed the show with an Italian rendition of the *passo romano* which had Mussolini frowning darkly because the marchers were not always in step with the music.

But when Hitler boarded his train on May 9 to return to Germany after a brief visit to Florence, he was sure of the Italian dictator's undying friendship and cooperation in all his objectives, including the dismemberment of Czechoslovakia, which the Führer was already pondering. On the station platform there was an affectionate farewell. As the two leaders shook hands, the Duce said, "Henceforth no force will be able to separate us." Hitler's eyes, I noticed, glistened with tears of gratitude.

Thanks to Alan Cranston, I was now involved in a minicrisis of my own. Haile Selassie, the former emperor of Ethiopia, now in exile in England, had named me, William Randolph Hearst, and INS in a libel suit resulting from what Alan had written during his Ethiopian junket. He had flooded the New York office with articles describing the barbarism prevalent in pre-Fascist Ethiopia, and his pieces were widely printed by INS client papers—at home by the Hearst chain and in England by the *London Evening Standard.*

The dispatch that caused the trouble resulted from Cranston's sensational interview with Ras Hailu, a suborned tribal chieftain whom the Italians installed as the puppet ruler of an Ethiopian province. Hailu admitted to Alan that for years before the Italians invaded his country, he had conspired with Mussolini for the overthrow of Selassie. Messages between him and the Duce were intercepted by the emperor's secret police, and Hailu wound up in jail.

"They threw me into prison," Hailu said, "then captured a nephew of mine and sawed him in half in a public place to show what happened to traitors."

The conspiracy was important news, for until Hailu revealed it to Alan, the Italians had been stoutly maintaining that they had invaded Ethiopia to put an end to Ethiopian raids and acts of aggression against Italian Eritrea. The fate of the "nephew" added the macabre detail which prompted the circulation-hungry *Evening Standard* to feature it prominently in its street posters and headlines. Selassie's solicitors promptly filed suit for about half a million dollars.

I cabled Alan, then still in Addis Ababa, for substantiation of Hailu's charges, and he questioned the rascally ras a second time. Hailu, however, changed his story: The victim was not his nephew but his son, and the latter had lost only a leg, not half his body. The renegade chieftain's statement was of no help in defending the suit and Selassie won his case in a London court where lese majesty was undoubtedly a factor.

The ex-emperor was awarded damages in the amount of fifteen thousand dollars from the *Standard* and seventy-five thousand dollars from INS. I was absolved of responsibility because Alan's stories had been distributed by New York, not Rome.

From a purely humanitarian point of view, the most important result of Hitler's Italian sojourn was the sudden revival and intensification of fascism's campaign against the Jews, started the year before but allowed to lapse. Anti-Semitism flared anew in infinitely more virulent form, and what most Italians had previously dismissed as merely ranting suddenly became in the early spring of 1938 an extension southward into Italy of Nazi Germany's racial theories.

To please Hitler, Mussolini had sold out Austria. For the same reason he was now prepared to sacrifice his country's comparatively small minority of Jews, only forty-four thousand in all, though they had been part of Italy's social fabric for more than two millennia.

Back in February, 1938, three months before Hitler visited Rome, the only member of the Fascist hierarchy who seemed genuinely concerned that Italian anti-Semitism might adversely affect his country's relations with the West in general and with the United States in particular, was Galeazzo Ciano. The young foreign minister may have been many things—vain, pompous, arrogant—but he was neither unintelligent nor totally insensitive.

Early in February Ciano invited me and Paul Cremona, of the *Christian Science Monitor,* for a chat in his study at the Palazzo Chigi. He wanted to know how we felt personally about the anti-Jewish editorials and articles already appearing in the Italian press, and what we American journalists believed the reaction would be if Italy followed Germany's example in its treatment of the Jews.

Ciano's summons might have been inspired by the fact that at the time Italy was trying to negotiate a substantial loan in Wall Street and needed America's goodwill. At any rate, Paul and I unhesitatingly told Ciano that we, as journalists representing American news organizations, were shocked by what we had been reading and jointly suggested that Italian emulation of German anti-Semitism would arouse indignation, outrage, and anti-Italian feelings in the United States.

"Also," I added, "it would imperil Italy's efforts to obtain loans and credits from American bankers."

To this, Ciano replied, with some annoyance, "They won't lend us the money anyhow, no matter what we do about the Jews."

Actually, however, Ciano seemed less interested in what Cremona and I had to say than in assuring us that the Italian government had no intention of persecuting the country's Jews. "They number only about forty thousand among more than forty-three million," he said, "less than one-tenth of one percent of our entire population. Therefore, they do not constitute a danger to the state." The anti-Semitic diatribes in the press, he indicated, were being printed "merely to please Berlin."

A few days later, February 16, Ciano's office published its *Informazione Diplomatica*—an authoritative bulletin on foreign policy usually written by himself or Mussolini—which categorically denied that the Italian government entertained any intention of taking political, economic, or moral measures against the Jews. At first glance, it seemed that my friend Cremona and I had struck a blow for justice and decency in our meeting with the foreign minister.

Farther down, however, the statement said the Fascist government "reserved the right to watch the activities of the recent Jewish immigrants"—meaning German and Austrian Jews who had recently escaped Nazi terrorism—to "ensure that the influence of the Jews in the national life was not disproportionate to the numbers." As an example of political cunning and bad faith, I decided, the document was worthy of the quill of Machiavelli, and I remembered, then, that Ciano often cited *The Prince* in describing his approach to politics and relations between states.

The devious statement understandably increased the fears of the Jewish community. Its leaders knew that anti-Semitic legislation had been drafted and awaited only approval by the Fascist Grand Council to become law. In fact, Ciano himself must have known this when he summoned Cremona and me to his office; he was a member of the Grand Council. In my diary that night I wrote: "G. C. lied to Paul and me the other day, or he was obliged to yield to *forza maggiore*. . . . The Germans, maybe, or Old Baldy himself."

The Jews were stunned by the sudden revival of the government's anti-Semitic policies. As recently as 1935, when Mussolini's legions invaded Ethiopia, the Jewish community's leaders had every reason to call the Fascist society their own. There were Jews in the Chamber of Deputies and in many leading positions not only in the government but in the party itself. Until the formation of the Axis, in fact, Italy was one of the few remaining European countries where Jews could live their lives not only as full citizens but also, if they wished, as observant Jews.

When the Ethiopian War was won, Italian Jews declared themselves proud and joyful of the victory and saw to it that Benito Mussolini received God's blessing in their synagogues as well as more gold for his Fascist coffers. And Italy's Jewish leaders nodded approvingly, later, when their country went to war in Spain and their young coreligionists marched off to fight—and some to die—at the side of Franco.

But by early 1938 all the Jewish gold, all the Jewish prayers, and all the Jewish blood suddenly counted for nothing. Italy's "Jewish problem" had been growing behind closed doors for some time before Hitler's arrival in Rome, but the Duce's adoption of an anti-Jewish foreign policy and the strengthening of the Rome-Berlin Axis resulting from the Führer's visit exacerbated it. The style and content of the resurgent anti-Semitism led me to believe that the Fascists were not simply imitating the Nazis, but that racism per se was a fundamental element of fascism itself whatever its national color: Italian black, German brown, or Russian red.

In the wake of Hitler's departure—he left with crocodile tears of gratitude and public assurances that Germany would thenceforth "regard the frontiers of the Alps . . . as forever inviolable"—came almost daily anti-Semitic editorials and articles in the press and a spate of pseudoscientific racist books in the bookstores. It was correctly assumed that the Duce personally approved of the campaign when his own newspaper, the Milanese daily *Il Popolo d'Italia*, printed a rave review of Professor Paolo Orano's lurid anti-Semitic tome *Gli Ebrei in Italia*.

Mussolini was known to have nourished his ill-informed resentment against the Jews by reading Nietzsche, and it was easy to find evidence of anti-Semitism throughout his career. As a young man he had written that "the inversion of moral values in our times has been the principal work of the Jewish people." More recently, in an editorial in *Il Popolo* in September 1937, he referred to the United States as "a country of blacks and Jews, the forces which will disintegrate civilization," adding, "The races playing an important role in the future will be the Italians, the Germans, the Russians and the Japanese. Other countries will be destroyed by the acid of Jewish corrosion."

In his *personal* relationships, oddly enough, a younger Mussolini had shown no sign of racial bias. Both Angelica Balabanoff and Margherita Sarfatti, the two women who early in his career exercised the greatest influence in his life, were Jewish. A prominent Jewish banker, Joseph Toeplitz, and his Banca Commerciale paid most of the expenses incurred on the March on Rome. A Jew, Aldo Finzi, held office in the Duce's first cabinet, and another, Guido Jung, was his finance minister for many years.

The explanation for Mussolini's dichotomy toward the Jews who had contributed generously to his rise to power lay in his flawed character. Betrayal and opportunism were the constants of his career, and these two characteristics became increasingly apparent after 1935.

Until then, when he was opposing Hitler's aspirations in Austria, expediency coincided with his goals, and he had every reason to avoid friction with the Jews. The Ethiopian War, however, brought about a deterioration of relations between fascists and liberal Jews living abroad, who condemned the Italian aggression. Before the war Mussolini had been at pains to demonstrate that fascism's "Latin humanity" was superior to "Nazi barbarism." But after the Ethiopian conquest, Italy moved toward Germany, and the Duce stopped emphasizing the differences between the two regimes. He concentrated on demonstrating their ideological similarities and identity of purpose.

Mussolini soon convinced himself that to cement an alliance with his obviously more powerful partner, he had to eliminate any dissimilarities between the policies of their two countries. The Italians had to be made to feel that they, too, were "Aryans," and shortly after the Führer's visit, Mussolini launched his campaign to "Aryanize" his people.

On July 14 the Ministry of Propaganda distributed to the press a manifesto, ostensibly produced by a panel of "leading university professors" but clearly reflective of racist influence in language and content, declaring that Italy's population was Aryan and its civilization, moreover, distinctly so. It was an absurd document, entitled "The Defense of the Race," which proclaimed the existence of a "pure Italian race," ordered Italians to declare themselves "openly race-conscious," and asserted that Jews did not belong to the Italian race. Written in stilted, pseudoscientific language, the opus was used as the text for an obscene, garishly illustrated exhibit staged by Farinacci in a midtown hall caricaturing Jews as a subhuman species one stage removed from apes. Many Italians who saw it privately pronounced it "revolting."

The only *public* denunciation of the Fascists' sudden fervor for "Aryan purity," however, came from the ailing pope. He characterized the campaign as "detestable . . . illustrative of the spirit of separatism and exaggerated nationalism . . . a disgraceful imitation of the racism of Nazi Germany." The Duce's response to the pontiff's attack was a shallow denial that fascism had "imitated anything or anybody."

Later, on September 1, Mussolini personally decreed the expulsion of all Jewish residents domiciled on Italian territory since 1919. The decree affected about half the country's forty thousand-odd registered Jews and applied to all, regardless of whether or not they were Italian citizens, a cruel blow to many refugees from Nazi persecutions in Austria and Germany.

The next day, September 2, another Mussolinian edict banned all Jews from the teaching staffs of state or state-affiliated schools and from all scientific, literary, or artistic institutions. This meant that one out of every twelve of the universities' permanent professors had to abandon his chair—particularly in science, medicine, and the law—and indirectly struck at Enrico Fermi, the nuclear physicist who had just been nominated for a Nobel Prize.

Fermi, Roman-born, and as Italian as Galileo, had been teaching at the University of Rome since 1927 and by 1938, at the age of thirty-seven, had become one of the world's leading scientists in his field. He was not Jewish, but his petite, vivacious wife, Laura, was, as were his ablest assistants and members of his staff of researchers.

Appalled by the decree laws which the government seemed to be issuing almost daily, the couple—accompanied by a mutual friend who knew of my interest in the fate of the Jewish community and of my frustrations in attempting to project its difficulties in print—came to my office one day shortly after publication of the latest *decreto* to inquire whether I had any information beyond what had appeared in the press. In a closed society, however, I had little more knowledge than they and was unable to add to what they already knew. I could only volunteer the opinion that the regime's "Aryanization" program was no mere political ploy to curry favor with the Nazis—a view held by most Western diplomats at the time—but had become irrevocable Fascist doctrine.

Present during my brief meeting with the handsome, gentle couple was my friend and former colleague Bill Shirer, who happened to be in Rome on CBS business. He reminded me recently that I suggested to the Fermis that if they were going to Stockholm for the Nobel ceremonies, they would be well advised not to return to Rome. On this point, however, I must trust Bill's memory, for I have no recollection of having made that suggestion. I do remember saying to the Fermis, though, that if necessary the American Embassy might help them expedite their departure.

A final series of anti-Semitic decrees came into effect on October 28, 1938, and automatically turned Italy's Jews into second-class citizens. No Jew was to be allowed to serve in the armed forces or to function as a teacher, lawyer, journalist, doctor, banker, broker, or member of the Fascist party. Special elementary schools were to be established for Jewish children, and the universities were closed to Jewish students.

Among the Italians the decrees intensified opposition to fascism. A people who had not known anti-Semitism in more than a century could not learn overnight to hate a defenseless minority so small that one would have had to knock on a thousand doors to find the home of a single Jew. Since the overwhelming majority of Italians felt sympathy for the Jews, enforcement of the laws was on the whole lax. Nevertheless, there were a number of tragic incidents, including a few suicides.

Many Jews followed the example of our obstetrician who had disappeared when Kathryn went into labor with Tommy and left the country, often with the help of the Vatican where, for a price, passports could be obtained. Others made elaborate preparations to depart, liquidating real estate holdings, businesses, and household goods for cash, which they converted into transportable gold coins, black-market dollars, or gems.

When a Jewish friend, whom I shall identify only as Gustavo, learned I intended returning to the States in the near future, he brought me, for safekeeping and eventual delivery to him in New York, a ten-carat diamond. Gustavo had prospered on Rome's bourse as a broker and was arranging travel documents for himself, his wife, and their small daughter.

"When I sell this in your country," he said, "I shall have money enough to start a new life. . . ."

Nothing the Fascists did during my residence in prewar Italy—not even the Ethiopian War or the Blackshirt intervention in Spain—depressed me quite as much as their persecution of the Jews, a people I had long since learned to admire and respect. The plight of the Jews touched me deeply and confirmed me in my decision to remove my family and myself from Mussolini's Italy at the earliest opportunity.

Especially frightened, and with good reason, were Jews of lesser means. Sonneman, the Jewish haberdasher-tailor in the Via dei Condotti, was full of anxiety one day in late April when I stopped in his shop to buy a shirt and some socks. "I can smell war in the air I breathe," he said, "and I want to leave Italy before it comes." But he was having difficulty obtaining American visas for himself and his family and begged my help. I suggested that he see my friend John Wesley Jones in the U.S. Consulate. Our government was not being particularly helpful to Jews fleeing from the Fascists and the Nazis in 1938, but I knew Johnny to be a compassionate man who might find ways to cut through the red tape.

Sonneman, whose given name I never learned, had changed the sign over his shop to read "Son & Man" when the regime's anti-Jewish decrees were promulgated, but the disguise hadn't helped trade. The place was being boycotted, and Sonneman was losing money. "I don't know how much longer I can hold out," he said as I was leaving. "Soon I may not have money enough to go to America or anywhere else. . . ."

By early May a mood of impending doom had descended upon Rome, for by then even the most illiterate peasant knew from listening to Radio Roma's propaganda about the turmoil among the Sudeten Germans of Czechoslovakia that the future held war. The normally lively table talk at the cafés in the Galleria Colonna was subdued, and there was none of the customary gaiety among the diners in the restaurants. The Via Veneto was alive with spring flowers, dazzling sunshine, and sparkling fountains, but the faces I saw were sober, unsmiling, even grave.

14

THE GATHERING STORM

From all subsequent accounts the advance of the German Army to the northern end of the Brenner Pass in March 1938 meant little more to the average American than did the assassination of an Austrian archduke in Sarajevo in July 1914, the event that triggered a four-year world war.

The Europeans, however, have a highly developed sense of history, and the presence of Nazi troops at the Brenner sowed disquiet throughout Europe, particularly among the Italians, who, after the Austrians, were the people most directly affected. When Germany occupied Austria, they knew without the help of an official communiqué that Czechoslovakia must be next on Hitler's timetable.

Nor did they need to be told that a German invasion of Czechoslovakia, Central Europe's last remaining democracy, would mean another European war. By the time the Germans marched into Austria, Italy's most literate citizens had read *Mein Kampf.* It was available in the bookstores in garish paperback editions featuring the swastika and the brooding idealized face of its author, Mussolini's friend. After reading it, most adult Italians, many of whom had fought in the first *grande guerra,* concluded with Latin logic that another was brewing.

"Ciao. Ci vediamo in qualche ossario [So long. See you in some boneyard]" became a common form of farewell among the more cynical. I first heard it used by a portly Roman businessman in parting from a counterpart complete

with paunch and briefcase. They had been holding an animated conversation within earshot of where I sat at Rosati's sipping an espresso one afternoon in early May. Other passersby must have overhead, for very soon the expression was a tiresome cliché.

At the time the news was all bad. What I read in the papers and heard on the radio daily became increasingly alarming. Hitler had massed troops on the borders of Bohemia and Moravia, the Czech provinces where most Sudeten Germans lived, and the Führer indicated he meant to "liberate" them by force of arms. The Czechs responded by mobilizing four hundred thousand men, and for several days in early May it seemed war would erupt at any moment.

I hurried to the British Embassy to see Colonel Stone, my most reliable informant on military affairs. Robbie, good friend and source of much of the information that had gone into my early scoop disclosing Italian intervention in Spain, poured me a sherry, and advised me to relax.

"The balloon is not about to go up just yet," he said. "The Czechs have a well-equipped, well-trained army of thirty-five to forty divisions, and Hitler's generals will think twice about tackling them. The German Army isn't battle-ready. And anyhow, in Europe wars never start in the spring. They always begin in late summer or early autumn, after the crops are harvested. Look for action sometime in late September or early October. My guess is that Hitler will try to bully the Czechs into giving him what he wants without having to fight for it. Of course, if they don't oblige, he'll go to war. . . ."

As Robbie foresaw, the crisis subsided in mid-May. When the Czechs mobilized, the British—and Czechoslovakia's French allies—issued stern warnings. Hitler withdrew his army from the Czech borders and publicly sought to reassure the Western powers of his peaceful intentions. But as always happened when frustrated, Hitler was furious. He intensified his campaign of subversion and propaganda in the Sudetenland. The Germans branded the Czechs Europe's "plague carriers of bolshevism" and the perpetrators of "unspeakable atrocities" upon the "helpless" Sudeten Germans. In Rome my colleagues and I followed the resultant war of words with sinking hearts and an increasing awareness that Czechoslovakia, Central Europe's last remaining democracy, was doomed, and with it what passed for peace in Europe.

Most of us, I believe, saw more clearly than our employers that the Axis powers jointly represented a direct threat to the peace of Europe, perhaps the world. Communism, however, not fascism and nazism, remained the bugaboo of American and British press lords. It was also the bête rouge of many Western statesmen, especially the British. Their so-called Cliveden Set of eminent old-school-tie politicians regarded Europe's dictators—Franco, Mussolini, and Hitler—not as enemies of democracy but as stalwart defenders of Western civilization against the spread of bolshevism.

The gap in staff created by Alan Cranston's departure was filled by Cecil Brown, who was sent down to Rome from Paris, where he had landed a job with INS in January 1938 after roving the Continent for several months as a free-lance journalist. With Cecil's arrival the INS Rome Bureau had for the first time an experienced crew capable of the speed, accuracy, and professionalism required for wire agency work, Michael Chinigo having developed into a first-rate newsman.

Older than Cranston and a born newspaperman, Cecil was a welcome addition to the Rome staff at a critical time. He had visited Czechoslovakia and brought with him a fund of knowledge about how the Nazis had infiltrated the country and prepared it, through subversion and propaganda, for Hitler's next advance into Europe's heartland. The Sudeten Germans, Cecil said, had long since fallen under the influence of a pro-Nazi movement organized by Hitler's surrogate, Konrad Henlein, at whose urging the Sudetens repeatedly claimed they were being "terrorized" and "oppressed" by the Czech authorities.

Henlein's real concern, Cecil said, was to help his master in Berlin join Bohemia and Moravia to the expanding Third Reich, so named to recall past German greatness in the time of the First Reich, or Holy Roman Empire (962–1806), and the glories of the Second Reich in Bismarck's time (1871–1918). Cecil had spent some time in the Sudetenland. He confirmed Robbie Stone's view that militarily Czechoslovakia would prove a "hard nut for Hitler to crack" and agreed with him that the Führer would now wage a "war of nerves" to gain his ends.

Events proved both Robbie and Cecil right, and the Western powers soon found themselves embroiled in what became known as the Munich Crisis of 1938. It began with the annual Nazi party's rally at Nuremberg, an event known to the Germans as their *Parteitag* and to the rest of the world as the National Party Congress.

Since 1933, the year of Hitler's rise to power, the Führer had used the occasion to increase international tensions, stimulate European fears of bolshevism, and intensify hatred of the Jews. No expense was spared to make every *Parteitag* bigger, noisier, and gaudier than the previous one with grand displays of Nazi military power and skill and party discipline and enthusiasm. Each party day had its theme: In 1936 it had been "Honor"; in 1937, "Labor"; and in 1938, appropriately enough, it was "Greater Germany."

I had never covered a Nazi party congress, but I had read accounts of previous ones and was aware of their importance as guides to German policy. On the morning of September 12 the two newspapers I read every day at breakfast—Milan's *Corriere della Sera* and Rome's *Messagero*—described the 1938 *Parteitag* as the biggest, most important ever, attended by 1 million uniformed, wildly enthusiastic Nazis who eagerly awaited the speech their beloved Führer would make at the closing ceremonies.

Although Hitler's speeches were rebroadcast in Italian by Radio Roma, I wanted to hear this one in German with all its Hitlerian inflections. Not knowing German, I persuaded a German-speaking Swiss journalist to come to the office and translate for me—for a fee, of course. The first forty minutes or so were a torrent of mingled self-adulation and self-pity, boasts of German military skill and prowess, dire warnings about Bolshevik designs on Europe, and vilification of the Jews.

Then, after abusing Czechoslovakia's President Eduard Beneš in what the translator said was the "most scurrilous language" he had ever heard Hitler use, the Führer disclosed his sinister designs. He reiterated his demands for "self-determination for the German people residing in Czechoslovakia—a right of which they were robbed by a certain Mr. [Woodrow] Wilson at Versailles," and added these ominous words: "In no circumstances shall I be willing to regard with endless tranquillity a continuation of the oppression of my German compatriots in Czechoslovakia."

The Swiss and I agreed that Hitler's closing statement was tantamount to an ultimatum and that after hearing their Führer's words, the Sudeten Germans could be expected to clamor more violently than ever for "union with the fatherland." Our shortwave receiver was still tuned to Radio Berlin and blaring martial music following Hitler's speech when our office phone rang.

It was our informant at the *Giornale d'Italia* with word that his paper was receiving reports from its own correspondents and Stefani, the Italian news agency, stating that outbreaks of "unprecedented violence" had erupted in Bohemia and Moravia. Sudeten Germans were pouring into the streets in various cities, attacking Czech army barracks and police stations, and looting and burning public buildings. The Czechs, the dispatches said, had declared martial law and were moving to suppress the demonstrations.

Before going home to dinner that evening, I telephoned Pete Huss, my INS colleague in Berlin, for his interpretation of what was happening in Germany and in the Sudetenland.

Our conversation was conducted mostly in sports jargon—"My pitcher is playing hardball" that sort of thing—but Pete confirmed my impression that Europe was sliding rapidly toward war. The Germany he described was already virtually an armed camp, with about 1.5 million troops deployed from the North Sea to the Danube. The railway leading to the Czech frontier was being hurriedly double-tracked for transporting men and weapons. The armed forces were on full alert, and some 400,000 laborers drafted from industrial centers were completing the German fortifications—the West Wall—opposite France's Maginot Line.

After the Führer's belligerent speech, Huss agreed, only an unforeseeable diplomatic miracle could avert another disastrous European war. And war, the dictators had conditioned us to believe, would mean massive air raids on civilian centers and the probable use of poison gas, the "ultimate weapon" of the First World War.

The prospect was terrifying, and at home that night, when Kathryn and I were alone after the boys had been put to bed, I told Kay she had better start packing. The thought of what might prove to be a long separation didn't appeal to her in the least, and she wept a little. . . .

For the Italians—for all Europeans, in fact—the summer of 1938 proved to be the last peaceful one they were to know for six long years. During most of it they were kept in the dark about what their Duce would do. Daily, between monitoring the transmissions of the BBC London and Radio Paris on my shortwave radio, I made the rounds of my sources at the British, French, and American embassies, and everywhere the consensus was that Mussolini was playing Hitler's game to the hilt, but no one had any clear idea of what, if anything, he intended doing. At the Press Bureau of Alfieri's Ministry of Propaganda, which masqueraded under the official title of Ministry of Popular Culture, we were fobbed off with statements that the Duce was "vigilantly following developments" but were given no hard facts.

Those of us who were responsible for keeping American readers informed about what was happening in Italy were almost as much in the dark as the Italians. Like them, we were obliged to depend more on intuition than on what passed for information in a closed society. The stuff of our dispatches derived from the inspired and often misleading news items and editorials in the Fascist press and the written or verbal assurances of the genius in the Palazzo Venezia who spoke only his version of the truth.

The first clue we had to Mussolini's intentions came on the morning of September 14, forty-eight hours after the Führer's rabble-rousing speech at Nuremberg, with publication on the front pages of all of Italy's newspapers of the text of the bulletin called *Informazione Diplomatica*—the regime's vehicle for imparting to the public its major decisions in the area of foreign policy—declaring: "Only a radical solution, on the basis of self-determination [Hitler's words], can put an end to the Czech crisis." The Duce thus confirmed to the Italian people that if war came, he would support Hitler.

But whatever hopes they may have entertained that Mussolini intended merely political support were dimmed with subsequent publication of a second *Informazione Diplomatica* which declared, "The Europe created by the Treaty of Versailles is in its final agony," and predicted the "rise of a new Europe, a Europe of justice and reconciliation of all peoples." Those of us who knew that the bulletins reflected Mussolini's personal views and were often written by the Duce himself concluded that in the event of war Italy would fight on Germany's side.

Mussolini personally confirmed this later in a speech he made at a huge rally in Trieste. Mussolini stated flatly that Italy would be Germany's ally in the war that might result from the Czech crisis. "We hope," Mussolini said to cheering tens of thousands, "that in these final hours a peaceful solution can be reached. . . . But if this does not happen, let it be known that Italy's place is already determined."

I was in almost hourly contact by telephone with my INS colleagues in other European capitals, mostly London, the bureau to which I usually telephoned my stories, and, by exchanging information, could arrive at an approximation of the truth about what was happening during that fateful summer of 1938. By mid-September my fellow correspondents and I had concluded that Europe stood on the brink of the abyss.

When I telephoned my story to London about the stand Mussolini had

taken at Trieste, Bill Hillman came on and filled me in on developments in
England. Britain and France, he said, were mobilizing. In London itself the
people were digging trenches in Hyde Park and the government was distributing gas masks. Hospitals were being made ready to receive air-raid victims, and
a first-aid station was even being established in Buckingham Palace. Public
buildings were being shielded with sandbags, and the British Museum had
begun hiding its priceless treasure in bombproof underground storage.

Bill also had hopeful news. His sources in the Foreign Office had informed
him that the French premier, Édouard Daladier, had prevailed upon Prime
Minister Chamberlain, to attempt to negotiate a settlement of the Czech crisis
personally with Hitler. The meeting was scheduled for the very next day at
Berchtesgaden.

"And what's more," Bill said, "the PM is *flying* to Germany. He hates
planes and has never flown before. That should give you some idea of the
gravity of the situation."

So began the unfolding of the Munich Crisis of September 1938, a time of
uncertainty and alarm during which almost all Europeans held their collective
breaths. Exactly half a century has elapsed since those hectic, frenzied days,
but I still feel the anxiety and fear that for a fortnight dominated our lives.

In the early morning of September 16 my bedside telephone roused me out
of a sound sleep at home. It was Bill Hillman with bad news.

Chamberlain had been rudely received by Hitler and on his return to
London had told Bill and other correspondents that he had found the situation
"more acute and more urgent" than he had believed. Hitler had angrily
informed Chamberlain that there could be peace with Czechoslovakia only on
Germany's terms: "self-determination for the Sudeten Germans," meaning
surrender of Bohemia-Moravia to the Reich. Hitler apparently had made it
clear to Chamberlain the alternative was war and demanded that his wishes
be met by no later than 2:00 P.M. on Wednesday, September 28. He subsequently extended the deadline to October 1.

On Monday evening, September 26, at eight o'clock, I tuned in BBC
London on my Telefunken shortwave radio at home and heard Chamberlain's
historic speech to the British Empire. The elderly prime minister spoke in a
high-pitched, quavery voice. His speech was that of a weary statesman who
had abandoned all hope of peace and was appalled at the prospect of war
arising from what he called "a quarrel in a faraway country between people
about whom we know nothing."

Chamberlain had just finished speaking when Bill Hillman phoned me to
tell me that the prime minister, determined to avert war if humanly possible,
had instructed the British ambassador in Rome, Lord Perth, to request Mussolini's intervention to save peace. The Duce, delighted to be cast in the role
of peacemaker, readily agreed and proposed to his Axis partner a conference
of four powers—Britain, France, Germany, and Italy—to resolve the Czech
crisis. The following day Tuesday, the Führer cabled invitations to Chamber-

lain, Daladier, and Mussolini to meet with him in Munich the very next day, Wednesday, September 28.

Word that Mussolini was going to Munich to "make peace" spread through Rome with the speed of a windblown brush fire after a long drought. How the people in the streets knew that the Big Four were meeting in Munich the next day before any announcement over the radio or the appearance of the late editions of the afternoon papers, I never learned. I saw pedestrians rush to pay station telephones to tell families and friends the good news. There were shouts in the piazzas of *"Mussolini ha salvato la pace* [Mussolini has saved the peace]!"

By three-thirty that unforgettable Tuesday afternoon the Galleria Colonna was filled to overflowing with cheering, laughing, gesticulating Romans. The noise was deafening. I could not be jubilant at the prospect of Czechoslovakia's demise, which I was sure would be the end result of the conference, and I crayoned another fat, black *F* on the map on the wall above my desk.

My office phone rang while I was writing a cable describing what I had seen. It was Bill Hillman calling from London for precisely such a story. He said he had just come from the House of Commons where jubilant parliamentarians were celebrating. I told him what was happening under my windows in the *galleria*, and he described a similar, though more subdued, scene in Fleet Street.

"Nobody here seems to realize," he said, "that the conference only postpones the inevitable. Anyhow, be sure to cover the Italian delegation. Huss has made a reservation for you at the Vier Jahreszeiten. Will you be flying to Munich?"

"No," I replied. "The press office phoned a few minutes ago to say the Italian delegation is leaving by train this evening at six o'clock. There will be a place for me on the wagons-lits reserved for the correspondents."

"In that case," Bill said, "I'll tell Pete to meet you at the station."

I thanked him and rang off. It was four-thirty. I'd have to hurry. I phoned Kathryn to pack me an overnight bag and have it ready for me when I came by in a taxi. She, too, had heard the news and was elated. Did this mean she and the boys could stay on in Rome?

"No, darling, it doesn't," I replied, and hung up.

I made it to the Stazione Centrale with minutes to spare.

On the platform Mussolini, resplendent in uniform, was visibly delighted with his new role of savior of the world's peace. He was jaunty and chatted amiably with a handful of party bigwigs who bad come to wish him Godspeed.

Ciano, however—also in uniform, as were the Italian journalists and other members of the delegation—seemed somewhat subdued, I thought. His last words before departing, tossed over his shoulder to a friend while entraining were "may the prayers of Italy go with us."

15

THE SORDID BETRAYAL

E n route to Munich on the night of September 28, 1938, Benito Mussolini was in high good spirits. He had earned Adolf Hitler's gratitude for his support of Germany's "case" against Czechoslovakia, and he was being hailed at home and abroad as the savior of Europe's peace. Moreover, according to the few Italian newsmen who had access to the Duce's entourage and presumably had inside information, the dictator believed that by his eleventh-hour intervention in the crisis he not only had averted war but had also regained his ascendancy over the Führer.

This was the theme which Italian journalists stressed in conversations with foreign correspondents over food and drink in the dining car that separated the deluxe carriages of the official delegation from the rest of the special train as it hurtled north through the night toward Germany. The Italian reporters' contention that their Duce had reasserted his authority in Axis relations seemed to me a labored effort to counter the increasingly widespread belief abroad that since the Anschluss Mussolini had become Hitler's vassal.

Their arguments sounded plausible enough. Without the Duce's intervention, they said, the conference toward which we all were hastening would not be taking place. Only Mussolini, they maintained, could reason with the headstrong Hitler; only his sponsorship had made the talks possible, and only on condition that Mussolini himself attended them had the Nazi dictator agreed to them at all. Hitler, moreover, had even allowed the Duce to choose the meeting place.

The insiders were right on one point: Mussolini had certainly earned the Führer's thanks for his support of Germany's demands on Czechoslovakia and thereby probably averted war. But the Duce's help merely meant that Hitler could now acquire the Sudetenland without having to fight for it, and if the Führer followed a recent suggestion of Mussolini's for disposal of the Czech "problem," Czechoslovakia would cease to exist altogether.

The Duce's stand on the Czechoslovakian question had been broader than Hitler's throughout the crucial week preceding the Munich Conference. While the Führer was publicly simply demanding the Sudetenland as his "last territorial claim in Europe," Mussolini was asking for plebiscites in each of Czechoslovakia's national groupings, thus laying the groundwork for the dismemberment of that country.

In a speech Mussolini gave to cheering thousands at Treviso, in northern Italy, on September 21, only days before the Munich Conference, he said, "If today Czechoslovakia finds herself in a situation that might be called delicate, it is simply because she was *not*—and by now we can say *was*—simply Czechoslovakia, but Czecho-Germano-Polono-Romanio-Slovakia, an artificial state created at Versailles of many different nationalities. It is a counterfeit state, a monstrous geographic configuration, *lo stato mosaico numero uno* [the number one mosaic state]."

Recalling these words, I concluded that the country's fate was preordained. I assumed—correctly, events would prove—that at Munich Czechoslovakia would cease to exist as a politico-geographic entity and Germany, having already acquired Austria would become potentially the strongest power on the Continent.

And if that happened, could a new European war be averted or be long delayed? I thought not and made a mental note to hasten my family's departure for home, if possible, when I returned to Rome.

Those were the melancholy broodings I took with me to bed on the night of September 28. My compartment was at the end of the car, over the noisy trucks, a fact that helped make sleep a long time coming.

Early the following morning Hitler met Mussolini's train at Kufstein, on the old Austro-German frontier, about seventy miles southeast of Munich. It was a courtesy designed to demonstrate to the world in general—and to Chamberlain and Daladier in particular—that he held the Italian dictator in high esteem, but it was also an opportunity for Hitler to show Mussolini exactly how he intended to "liquidate" Czechoslovakia.

After boarding the Duce's train with Prince Philip of Hesse, Hitler invited Mussolini to come across to his own carriage, and the two dictators continued the journey together in Hitler's train.

I later learned from Filippo Anfuso, Ciano's close friend and *chef de cabinet,* that during the trip Hitler did most of the talking while the Duce listened attentively, "unsmiling and as magisterial as a Buddha." The Führer, he said, boasted that Germany's army was ready and that he fully intended to liquidate Czechoslovakia no matter what was decided at the conference.

Huss met me as planned at Munich's Hauptbahnhof, rescued me from the throng of uniformed Germans and Italians at the station, and led me to a taxi. The streets on the way to the hotel, I saw, were crowded with people in festive mood, among them many soldiers, all of whom, however, were in field gray-green. No troops in SS black or Storm Troops brown. How come? Pete grinned.

"All formations are in battle dress today," he explained, "ready to march if this so-called conference turns out to be a flop as the man sincerely hopes. He's spoiling for war, and my sources tell me that he's sore as a boil at the way things have turned out."

Why then the relaxed atmosphere? The civilians, at least, seemed to be celebrating peace, not war. Pete laughed at my ignorance.

"We're at the tail end of the Oktoberfest," he said, "the annual beer binge in this brewing capital of Bavaria. Everybody's in a good mood. They'll be even gayer tonight, after they've had a *Mass* or two. . . ."

We stopped at the palatial Vier Jahreszeiten on the Maximilianstrasse only long enough for me to shower and change, then headed for the Führerhaus in the Königsplatz where the Big Four were to meet in Hitler's suite of offices on the second floor. The Führer was already there after having deposited Mussolini and Ciano in the palace where he had quartered them in style. Chamberlain and Daladier awaited a summons to the meeting at their respective hotels, the Regina and the Bayerischer Hof.

Hastily convened and ill prepared in virtually every respect, the meeting was a disorderly affair. Unlike any major international conference in recent history, it had no chairman, no agenda, no agreed-upon procedure, except the one preordained by the two dictators. Its most shameful aspect, however, was the absence of Czechoslovakia's President Beneš, whom Hitler had expressly refused to admit.

The conference was held behind closed doors, and reporters were pointedly excluded. But we were allowed to inspect the premises before the meeting began and to witness the arrival of the principals. As host the Führer and his entourage arrived first. Then came Chamberlain and Daladier and, finally, Mussolini.

The Führer, I noted, greeted Chamberlain and Daladier coolly but went out of his way to be cordial when Mussolini and Ciano arrived a few minutes later. He came halfway down the broad red-carpeted stairs, welcomed the Italians with calculated warmth, and personally conducted them upstairs to meet the prime minister and the premier, who were waiting in an anteroom where a table was set with drinks and snacks. After halfhearted handshakes with Chamberlain and Daladier, the Duce thrust his hands into his pockets and moved off to a corner, where the Nazi leaders quickly gathered around him, leaving the others to their own devices. The atmosphere was one of vague embarrassment. The French, particularly, seemed ill at ease.

Chamberlain sought out Mussolini and thanked him profusely for all that he had done to bring about the meeting; but the Duce was rudely unresponsive, and their rather one-sided conversation petered out as the participants began assembling in Hitler's commodious office, where the conference started at approximately 12:30 P.M. Present, in addition to the four chiefs, were Ribbentrop and Ciano; Daladier's adviser, Alexis Léger, secretary-general of the French Foreign Office; Chamberlain's counselor, the dour Sir Horace Wilson; and Paul Schmidt, the Führer's schoolmasterish interpreter.

With me in the spacious second-floor hallway of the Führerhaus to witness the gathering of the principals were Pete Huss and Luigi Barzini, Jr., of the *Corriere della Sera,* one of the few Italian journalists *not* in uniform. Barzini was a man of wit and style. Unimpressed, he regarded the scene coolly with an amused smile, and when the Big Four and their retinues had disappeared into the meeting room, he remarked, in English, "It's a tableau right out of Madame Tussaud's wax museum in London, which is probably where they'll all wind up some day. . . ."

Hitler, I later learned from my Italian sources, opened the proceedings with a few grudging words of thanks. Then, talking fast and excitedly, his voice rising and falling, he announced that he intended taking action against Czechoslovakia unless the conference acted quickly. "Action," he said, repeatedly thumping a fist against an open palm, "must be taken at once." Chamberlain and Daladier spoke briefly. Then the Duce affirmed the need for a "rapid and concrete" solution of the current crisis and to that end produced a "document" which, with only minor modifications, coincided with the desires of the German government.

What followed seemed to me an appalling mixture of farce and tragedy.

As the day wore on, more and more people invaded the chamber where the fate of Czechoslovakia was being decided, and the hallway outside turned into something like a railway station corridor on the eve of a holiday weekend. Ambassadors and aides bearing drafts and counterdrafts shuttled back and forth between Hitler's office and the typists' room. To complicate matters further, the building's telephone system broke down, and the delegations had to resort to sending messages to their respective hotels by car.

During the hurly-burly, while the doors to the conference room were open, Mussolini distanced himself from the discussions. I caught a glimpse of him, hands in pockets, moving about with a detached air. Of the four chiefs he was the only one not wholly dependent on the interpreter, and he stopped to chat with Chamberlain in halting English, with Daladier in fluent French, and with Ribbentrop in careful German. He seemed to be showing off for the monolingual Hitler, who observed him closely, laughing when the Duce laughed, frowning when he frowned.

Hitler's attitude, I surmised, was motivated partly by his admiration for Mussolini and partly by his dislike for the whole business. He had envisaged a military, not a diplomatic, victory and brooded while his friend from Rome assumed the main role in an affair in which he as Führer of the Third Reich visibly wanted no part. Despite his display of intractability, however, Hitler seemed to me nervous and oddly unsure of himself. Much of the time he sat on a divan by a wall, nervously crossing and uncrossing his legs and glancing frequently at his watch like a baleful timekeeper.

The sycophantic Ciano, watching his father-in-law playing peacemaker, could not conceal his admiration. "His great spirit," he wrote afterward, "always ahead of events and men, had already absorbed the idea of agreement and while the others still wasted their breath over more or less formal problems he had almost ceased to take an interest. He had already passed on to, and was meditating, other things." For all his apparent detachment, however, the Duce made no effort to conceal his satisfaction that matters were proceeding much as he had hoped they would. "I'm sure," he told an Italian journalist when the Big Four paused for dinner, "that I have saved Europe."

By that time the first steps toward the dismemberment of Czechoslovakia had been taken and were communicated by Ribbentrop to Pete Huss and the other correspondents covering the German delegation. The Germans could start occupying the Sudetenland on October 1 and would complete the occupation in stages by October 10.

Huss brought me the unhappy news at the Hotel Regina, where the British delegation was staying and where all afternoon I had been trying to see two Czech officials who were virtual prisoners of the Gestapo in a room on an upper floor. They were Dr. Hubert Masarik, who had been flown in from Prague as a result of Chamberlain's successful appeal to Hitler, and Dr. Voytech Mastny, the Czech minister to Berlin. The guards had turned me away, and I was still haunting the place when a British Foreign Office functionary, Frank Ashton-Gwatkin, arrived to inform the Czechs of what was happening to their country. I attempted to intercept him, but he brushed past me.

Masarik and Mastny protested the action taken by the conference loudly enough to be heard in the hallway, but Ashton-Gwatkin icily reproved them for not seeming to understand "how hard it had been to negotiate with Hitler." The British diplomat, on the other hand, seemed incapable of comprehending how difficult it was for the Czechs to accept the result of those negotiations.

At about ten o'clock Ashton-Gwatkin conducted the two Czechs to the suite of his superior, Sir Horace Wilson, to have the bad news graphically confirmed. Wilson, Dr. Masarik told me afterward, handed them a map showing the areas which the Czechs were to evacuate within the next forty-eight hours. When the Czech envoys began voicing objections, Wilson abruptly cut them off, turned his back on them, and left the room. They got no sympathy from Ashton-Gwatkin. "If you do not accept," he told them, "you will be obliged to settle your affairs with the Germans absolutely alone." He assured them that the French were utterly uninterested and shared the views of the British.

The various translations of the Munich Agreement were finally completed at about 1:00 A.M. on September 30. The only comic touch in the dreary affair came when the Big Four sat down to sign Czechoslovakia's death warrant and there was no ink in the monumental inkstand. It was quickly provided, however, and the betrayal of Central Europe's only democracy by its French ally and British friend was duly formalized.

In its final version, the agreement, as released to the press, called for German military occupation of the Sudetenland to start on October 1 and be completed by October 10 under rules to be decided by a so-called International Commission. This largely fictitious body, which would include a Czech delegate, would be responsible for arranging plebiscites in those areas where the ethnographic composition was in doubt and for delimiting the frontiers of the new rump Czechoslovakia.

Lastly, the accord stipulated that "all existing installations" in the territories surrendered to the Germans remain intact. From the verdict of the Big Four, of course, the Czechs had no appeal, and they were so informed.

The task of collating the documents as the conference ended fell to the amiable and conscience-stricken André François-Poncet, the French ambassador to Berlin. As he sorted the papers, Ciano heard him exclaim: *"Voilà comme la France traite les seuls alliés qui lui s'étaient restés fidèles* [This is how France treats the only allies who have remained faithful to her]."

Hitler was visibly triumphant when I saw him emerge from the Führerhaus at about 1:30 A.M. on the momentous September 30, 1938. His face was flushed and set in a wide grin as he descended the steps to street level, accompanied by Göring, Hess, Ribbentrop, Goebbels, and General Keitel. The Führer's movements were jerky, as though he were containing himself with difficulty; he seemed to want to leap with joy.

Directly behind him, and hurrying to catch up to share in the noisy acclaim of the huge crowd that had gathered on the sidewalk outside the Führerhaus behind the newsmen, came Benito Mussolini. Smiling broadly under his black tasseled cap, he personified smug self-satisfaction.

Chamberlain, too, seemed pleased at the outcome, and only Daladier looked depressed. Surrounded by the resplendent uniforms of the Nazis and Fascists, the Briton and the Frenchman—attired in the somber dark gray mufti of diplomacy—looked to me like a pair of weary morticians after a hard day's work.

Before leaving Munich, the British prime minister had a private meeting with Hitler, according to a handout given to all correspondents, and the two signed a brief declaration stating that the Munich accord was "symbolic of the desire of our two peoples never to go to war with one another again." It expressed a resolve to settle all other questions arising between the two countries by consultation and to continue with efforts "to remove possible sources of difference and thus to contribute to the peace of Europe."

Munich, therefore, was expected to mark the beginning of a new and peaceful era in Anglo-German relations. Ostensibly Neville Chamberlain took home not merely an agreement with Germany over Czechoslovakia but a commitment to settle all future differences between Britain and Germany amicably without resort to force.

On his return to London and the acclaim of Parliament, the press, and the people, the prime minister waved the single sheet of paper bearing the two signatures, his own and Adolf Hitler's, and jubilantly proclaimed that he had achieved "peace with honor . . . peace in our time." The dissenters were few, but at least one was prophetic. His name was Winston Churchill.

"We have suffered total and unmitigated defeat," he said in Parliament. "The German dictator instead of snatching his victuals from the table has been content to have them served to him course by course."

In France, Daladier, too, was acclaimed as if he had scored a diplomatic triumph rather than suffered a diplomatic reverse of the first magnitude. Many Frenchmen, however, shared the sentiments of the Socialist leader Léon Blum, who admitted, "We have probably avoided war, but I feel torn between cowardly relief and shame."

In Italy I saw Mussolini the "peacemaker" hailed with frenzied enthusiasm, and there were no dissenters. In fact, the Duce's return home was a triumphal progress from the Brenner Pass all the way to Rome. At every station and grade crossing, even along the railway lines crowds, among them many men and women on their knees, gathered to acclaim him as an *"angelo della pace* [angel of peace]."

The king, who was vacationing at his country estate at San Rossore, met our train at nearby Florence and stood on the station platform to add his personal congratulations to those of the nation. The Duce looked flattered and outwardly pleased, but inwardly, he was deeply disturbed and angry.

It had annoyed him to see those Italian peasants kneeling in the crowds along the route. The realization that they were giving prayerful thanks for peace galled him, for he saw in the act a renunciation of war, and Nietzsche had taught him that "The man who renounces war renounces a grand life." Mussolini despised pacifists, and it would be difficult for him to retain Hitler's esteem, or to make with conviction those warlike gestures to which he was becoming increasingly addicted, with a nation of pacifists behind him.

In Rome some two hundred thousand citizens had gathered outside the Central Station in the vast Piazza Esedra, and gave him a rousing welcome when he emerged to enter his waiting limousine. He had not seen such enthusiasm since the proclamation of the empire.

Shortly after our arrival I rushed to the Piazza Venezia, where, as I had anticipated, Mussolini appeared on his balcony in response to the persistent clamor of "Duce! Duce! Duce!" in the crowded square. Hands on hips, he looked over the sea of upraised faces, disdain plainly visible in the curl of his lower lip, the thrust of his massive chin, his arched eyebrows.

"We lived memorable hours in Munich, and we worked for peace," he declared.

There were more cheers and shouts of "You have saved the peace of the world!"

"Well," Mussolini roared back, "isn't peace what you wanted?"

As a longtime Mussolini watcher I detected contempt in his voice, but to the Duce's rhetorical question the crowd replied with a thunderous *"Si!"*

Mussolini nodded knowingly, raised his arm in the Roman salute, turned, reentered the palace, and did not reappear to acknowledge the continuing ovation.

The Duce returned home determined to shed his peacemaker image, his head filled with expansionist, imperialistic ambitions inspired by German militarism. He was bent on hardening the Italian people and infusing them with the spirit which characterized German military success. To achieve this, he ordered even his top-ranking ministers to set a national example by taking part in strenuous mass calisthenics, footraces, and swimming contests and in performing such difficult stunts as leaping through flaming hoops.

Mussolini entrusted the task of organizing and directing these idiocies to the slender, athletic, and widely detested Achille Starace, who was not only secretary-general of the Fascist party but also an exalted lieutenant general in the Fascist militia. He specialized in indoctrinating young Italians in Fascist ideology and making them physically fit for war. As vain as Göring, Starace was an avid collector of decorations and the butt of many anti-Fascist jokes.

One story current in the hectic post-Munich days had it that Starace presented himself at a meeting in Mussolini's office one morning without the gaudy splash of medals he was fond of wearing on all occasions. "How does it happen, Achille, that today you are not wearing your decorations?" the Duce asked.

Starace, embarrassed, glanced nervously at the bare front of his natty black tunic and exclaimed, "By Bacchus! I forgot them. I must have left them on the coat of my pajamas."

It seemed to me that Mussolini's very character had been affected by his association with Hitler, by his unwilling but growing dependence upon him, his reluctant admiration of him, his patent jealousy of him. It was common knowledge that whereas in the past he had been willing to listen to advice and occasionally even to criticism of his policies, now the Duce attacked with venom anyone who presumed to advise him or to question his political judgments. He was furious with Italo Balbo when the latter proposed at the October 26 meeting of the Grand Council that full citizenship be granted to the Arabs in Italy's African colonies. Mussolini denounced the idea as a flat contradiction of the country's racial policy and mentally marked Balbo for future "liquidation."

Meanwhile, to create the environment of crisis Mussolini required for "Prussianizing" the Italians and dragooning them into acceptance of Nazi Germany as their friend and ally, he needed an enemy. He chose France, which at that time appeared to be disorganized by internal political turmoil after Daladier had cravenly assisted in the dismemberment of Czechoslovakia. The French premier was also in difficulties for having decided to recognize Italy's conquest of Ethiopia and having appointed a new ambassador to Rome—the elegant, monocled François-Poncet—to be accredited to the king.

In this, as in the Munich affair, Daladier followed the lead of Chamberlain.

During a conversation with Mussolini at the Führerhaus, the British apostle of appeasement offered to bring into force the Anglo-Italian Pact of Friendship of April 1938 by recognizing the Fascist conquest of Ethiopia a concession dear to the Duce's imperialistic heart, in exchange for Italian withdrawal of a mere ten thousand volunteers from Spain. Mussolini feigned reluctance but accepted in principle, and the necessary negotiations were satisfactorily concluded in Rome by Ciano and Lord Perth on November 16, when the British ambassador presented new credentials at the Palazzo Chigi addressed to Italy's miniemperor, Victor Emmanuel III. At the same time it was arranged that Chamberlain, accompanied by Lord Halifax, should visit Rome early in January 1939.

Unfortunately for Mussolini, however, whatever political profit he might have derived from the restoration of friendly relations with Britain was dissipated by the unbridled attacks he chose to launch against France. The Duce hated the French, whom he described to Ciano as "a nation ruined by alcohol, syphilis, and journalism."

The anti-French campaign, orchestrated in the streets and piazzas by the ubiquitous Starace and in the press by Propaganda Minister Alfieri on orders from Mussolini, had begun months earlier, but I saw it intensified after Munich. The day before Ciano and Perth signed the Anglo-Italian accord, I recalled, a group of war veterans concluded their annual congress in Rome with a march to the Piazza Venezia. Mussolini made his customary appearance on his balcony to receive their acclaim and was greeted with cries of *"Savoia! Nizza! Tunisia!"*

The shouts puzzled me. *Savoia* was vaguely understandable: It was the name of Italy's ruling house, and it had been the soldiers' battle cry—*Avanti Savoia!*—in the Great War. But Savoy coupled with the names of two other French-held regions—Nice in the Alpes-Maritimes and Tunisia in North Africa—obviously had deeper significance. To me, the cries smacked of the kind of irredentism Hitler had used against the Sudeten provinces of Czechoslovakia.

True, Nice and Savoy had been Italian long ago, before Napoleon's time. Tunisia, however, had never known Italian sovereignty, though it did have a substantial number of citizens of Italian origin. The 1936 census showed Tunisia with 106,568 French inhabitants and 94,389 Italians—more Italians, incidentally, than all the Europeans in Libya. Apparently, Mussolini still regarded Tunisia as an outlet for Italy's surplus population, because unpacified Ethiopia, like the arid wildernesses of Italy's other colonial possessions—Eritrea, Somaliland, and Jubaland in East Africa—had proved worthless as living space for Italian settlers or as markets for Italian goods. This was demonstrated when fifteen shiploads of colonists headed for Libya in 1938 instead of Ethiopia.

The anti-French campaign culminated on the afternoon of November 30, 1938, in a speech by Foreign Minister Ciano that I heard him make before the Italian Chamber of Deputies, which was meeting for the last time pending its transformation into a new Chamber of Fasces and Corporations.

Ciano delivered his speech with Mussolini sitting in the front row. He reviewed the situation leading up to the Munich Conference, praised the conclusion of the Anglo-Italian Pact of Friendship as an important factor for consolidating peace, and then said: "This consolidation is the objective of our policy and we intend to pursue it with tenacity and realism, combined with that circumspection which is indispensable if we intend to guard with inflexible firmness *the interests and national aspirations of the Italian people.*"

At the words "national aspirations" Superfascist Starace jumped to his feet and led the Blackshirt deputies in chorused shouts of "Tunisia! Tunisia!" From the Blackshirt spectators in the public galleries came strident cries of "Djibouti! Corsica!" It was an astonishing performance, I thought, Mussolini's way of telling his countrymen and the world that Italy had territorial aspirations independent of Germany's and that he was fully capable of acting without the advice and consent of the Führer.

The Duce evidently coveted not only Nice, Savoy, and Tunisia but also Corsica, the birthplace of Napoleon, which the French had held since the island's surrender by the Genoese Republic in 1881, and Djibouti, French Somaliland's gateway to Ethiopia by reason of the railway that connected the Indian Ocean seaport with Addis Ababa.

I saw the elegant François-Poncet peer through his monocle from his seat in the diplomats' gallery at the cheering deputies, his face inscrutable, set as though he were playing high-stakes poker with crooks. The French ambassador, newly transferred from Berlin, was aware that the demonstration in the chamber had been staged for his benefit. I knew from word passed on by a friend in the editorial offices of a leading Rome daily that the deputies had been instructed to "shout Italian demands" at a signal from Starace, though what they might be my source either did not know at the time or dared not tell me.

Later, in his speech to the Grand Council, the Duce revealed what he called the "immediate goals of Fascist dynamism," and they included new and even more outrageous demands. He announced his intention of taking Albania, Tunisia, and Corsica, of moving Italy's French frontier westward to the line of the Var River, and of annexing the Italian-speaking Swiss province of Ticino since Switzerland, he said, "has lost her cohesive force and is destined one day, like so many little countries, to be disrupted." Lastly he solemnly pledged everyone present to utmost secrecy. "Anyone revealing what I have just said in whole or in part," he warned, "will have to answer to the charge of treason."

Mussolini was dissembling, for he had already ordered leading Fascist editors in key cities to start clamoring for Nice, Corsica, and Tunisia, and the clamor began the next day, December 1, with an editorial by his favorite journalistic spokesman, Virginio Gayda, in the *Giornale d'Italia,* which reached 350,000 readers daily and was closely watched by foreign correspondents for clues to the Duce's policies. Gayda undoubtedly spoke for Mussolini that day when he wrote, "The Italian nation, solidly behind its government, is ready for anything. It is ready to march, if necessary, even against France."

Every editorial trained seal in the land followed Gayda's lead in demanding fulfillment of Italy's claims against France. The hullabaloo sparked a flurry of well-organized "spontaneous" demonstrations by students, who hurled insults at France and echoed on crude placards the "demands" for Nice, Corsica, and Tunisia being shouted by the headlines. In Rome impressive cordons of police guarded the French Embassy in the Palazzo Farnese, the city's most beautiful Renaissance building. But while the demonstrators in the magnificent piazza were appropriately vociferous, I noticed that they never tried to force the police barriers; most of them seemed to me to be not as angry at France as they were happy at having cut classes.

Then, early in December, while the anti-French campaign was still in full cry, the government issued a decree making it virtually impossible for foreign correspondents to function. The order, which had originated with Mussolini, prohibited all members of the Fascist Journalists' Syndicate from working for foreign employers.

Of the American news agencies, the hardest hit was INS. The AP retained the exclusive use of Stefani, the official government news agency with which the AP had a long-standing contractual exchange agreement. The UP was not affected by the new ruling because the agency itself was incorporated as an Italian organization whose staff members were automatically inscribed in the Journalists' Syndicate.

INS, on the other hand, was cut off from its correspondents in Venice, Milan, Bologna, Naples, and Palermo and from local Rome tipsters who were in touch with the inner workings of the regime. At a stroke the decree destroyed the network of stringers and informants which Bill Emmanuel had created over the years and which I had expanded since 1935. "Old Baldy," said Cecil Brown, "is trying to put us out of business." Suddenly the telephones stopped ringing.

The day the ruling was made public, I lodged a vigorous protest with the Ministry of Propaganda but got no satisfaction. I was merely told that as of January 1, 1939, INS could no longer employ Italians in any news-gathering role. Finally, after several heated encounters with lesser functionaries, I managed to see Signor Rocco, Alfieri's deputy in charge of the foreign press, who confided that the decree had been promulgated "in the interests of national security."

From this slender clue I deduced that Mussolini planned a major coup of some kind, probably a war, and feared that Italian journalists working for Western agencies or correspondents might pass on vital information of a military nature. But a war against whom? The French? The idea was absurd. Apart from the fact that Italy was utterly unprepared to make war against a major power—and this was known to every military attaché in every foreign embassy in Rome—it was now winter, the wrong season for starting a war in Western Europe.

Rome itself was already in the rainy grip of the *tramontana,* the icy wind from the snowy slopes of the Apennines that renders life in the capital miserable from mid-November to mid-March. Until spring Italy from Rome to the

Alps, and most of the Continent north of the Alpine barrier, would be drenched in rain or blanketed with snow. Mussolini's generals knew, even if the Duce did not, that "every mile is two in winter," and his commanders, however servile, were not all stupid.

Nevertheless, war was in the air, and I wanted my family out of harm's way, for I was dead certain now that the European war the dictators were planning would begin soon, at the latest within a year, probably in the late summer or early autumn of 1939, after the harvest.

During the first week in December 1938, at the height of the Duce's anti-French campaign, Kathryn and I sorrowfully dismantled the apartment in the Via Rovigo that had been our home for two years, the first real home we had known since coming abroad.

We hated parting with our possessions, but foreign correspondents were not encouraged to sprout roots abroad, and INS would not pay for the cost of transporting our belongings back to the States. So we sold everything at a loss in what had become a buyers' market, for Jewish residents were practically giving away costly antiques and bric-a-brac in their haste to leave the country. Kathryn managed to salvage only the household linens and silverware, which she packed in the trunks she was taking with her. With her, also, would go the large diamond which my Jewish friend Gustavo had entrusted to my care.

On December 7 Michael and I took Kathryn and the boys to Naples by train and boarded them on the *Rex.* They were going to her parents' home in Philadelphia, where they would arrive in good time for Christmas, the first but not the last that I would miss in their company. Waving good-byes to a bravely smiling wife, a stoic Sean, and a tearful Tommy, I wondered when I would see them again. In a passing moment of panic it occurred to me that if war came while I was still in Rome, we might be separated for a long, long time.

Before their departure I had cabled New York requesting permission to accompany my family on the home leave due me after three years' service overseas. I had been abroad four years and four months at the time, and was overdue for a stateside holiday. The cabled reply read: SORRY BUT DUE TO TUNISIAN CRISIS CANNOT COMPLY PRESENTLY.

I returned to Rome and my new "home"—a musty single room and bath in the Albergo Ambasciatori—reluctantly resigned to the idea that a foreign correspondent cannot have a normal family life.

16

A COOL RECEPTION FOR CHAMBERLAIN

Early in the new year 1939 the Fascists' anti-French campaign suddenly subsided in anticipation of Neville Chamberlain's arrival in Rome on an official visit to which Mussolini had grudgingly agreed at Munich. Anglo-Italian "friendship" was too tender a plant to be exposed to the simulated fury of student demonstrators inveighing against Britain's traditional ally, and by January 11, the day the prime minister was due to arrive, the capital's streets and piazzas were free of peak-capped hooligans shouting imprecations at the French.

Nearly a month before Chamberlain's scheduled arrival, Mussolini told Ciano that he believed the anti-French agitation had gone far enough "for the time being" and ordered "a little sand" poured on the mounting flames of anti-Gallic sentiments. "If matters continue at this rate," he said, "we shall be obliged to make the cannon speak, and the time has not come for that."

The abominable Starace was thereupon instructed to cool the ardor in the streets and to make certain that Chamberlain and his foreign minister, Lord Halifax, received a correct but chilly reception. The Fascist party secretary carried out his instructions precisely, almost—it seemed to those of us who participated in the resultant ceremonies—to the point of deliberate insult.

The Englishmen were greeted at the Central Station with restrained courtesy by Mussolini and Ciano, both in uniform, as were Starace and Alfieri and a few other Fascist dignitaries. The entire staff of the British Embassy turned out, but except for the ambassador himself its members were relegated to the role of applauding spectators. Then the tall gray-haired Chamberlain reviewed a guard of honor. The prime minister in tailcoat and striped trousers, sartorially the antithesis of Fascist militarism, strode sedately down the line of youthful black-garbed soldiers who wore small daggers at their hips which they presented on command with a flourish that suggested a threat.

There was some handclapping and waving of tiny Italian flags by the citizens lining the Via Nazionale on the way to the Palazzo Venezia, but none of the inspired cheering or fabricated enthusiasm that had welcomed Adolf Hitler. Starace had found plenty of swastika flaglets to distribute among the Führer's sidewalk welcomers, but not a single Union Jack was to be seen when the Italians welcomed Great Britain's prime minister.

The guests arrived in the late afternoon and within an hour went into conference with their hosts in Mussolini's office. Later that evening we were told that the meeting had accomplished little of importance, the participants having merely made what the diplomats call "a tour of the horizons." That night, however, at a state banquet in the Palazzo Venezia, both Mussolini and Chamberlain invoked "peace with justice" in postprandial speeches. While the Duce did not specify how he thought peace might be ensured, Chamberlain said he hoped "a just and peaceful solution of current international difficulties might be found through negotiation," and in an effort to clear the air for the following day's conclusive conversations, the prime minister took pains to flatter Mussolini. Speaking for himself and Lord Halifax, he said: "It is a real pleasure to both of us to see with our own eyes the new Italy, powerful and aggressive, which has risen under Your Excellency's guidance and inspiration."

The formal dinner was followed by a reception in the Palazzo Venezia, attended by uniformed Fascist officials, the more pro-Fascist elements of the Italian aristocracy, and the domestic and foreign press in the enormous, high-ceilinged salons of what had been the imperial Austrian Embassy before World War I. The five hundred or so guests were convoked to provide a glittering background of evening gowns and tailcoats for the visitors.

Properly attired in white tie and tails—I had had them tailored by Sonneman for an important papal reception at the Vatican the year before—I circulated among the guests, inching my way toward the Duce to see him in a better light than I had seen him in the dimly illuminated Sala del Mappamondo. For this occasion the Duce had eschewed his habitual uniform for sober full dress like nearly everyone else. I noticed, however, that his outfit was old-fashioned, poorly cut, and at least one size too small for him. He had gained weight, and his tailcoat was held together at the front with two buttons linked by a silky elasticized cordon. Seeing him hatless at close range for the first time, my eyes were drawn to the thick mole, an excrescence about the size of a dime, on the crown of his bald head.

What I saw was not the theatrical Duce with the flashing eyes and dramatic gestures of his public appearances, but an aging would-be Napoleon in black broadcloth turning perceptibly green with age, a sort of Caesar in hand-me-downs. He moved about in an attitude of scowling boredom, stopping to exchange a few words with high-ranking Fascist underlings while his guests were being given a conducted tour of the salons which contained an exhibition of ancient armor and weapons.

It was a dull party. Spirits and champagne might have helped, but the hosts served only a fruit punch mildly spiked with an Italian wine. It did little to enliven the proceedings.

The party given by the British in return for the Duce's first-night hospitality, however, was a totally different story. Held in their embassy building on the Via Venti Settembre, it was easily the outstanding event of Rome's social season of 1939 and the last for many years to come. It began with a formal dinner for Mussolini, Ciano, and the Fascist elite and as before was followed by a reception for all of us who had been invited to the Palazzo Venezia affair.

The British Embassy, while appropriately elegant for the occasion, was also smaller and infinitely more conducive to conviviality than the austere salons of the Duce's palace. More important, perhaps, excellent scotch whiskey and vintage French champagne—both virtually unobtainable in Rome since sanctions—flowed freely.

Mussolini and Ciano left early, but the foreign minister's wife, Edda, and everyone else stayed late, and by midnight the brilliantly lighted embassy ballroom was a scene of somewhat boozy gaiety. Everyone had a good time, including the normally starchy Achille Starace, who came in uniform complete with what looked like a square foot of medals.

Before Chamberlain's arrival Starace had let it be known that "good Fascists" were not to dance the Lambeth Walk, an athletic dance step then as much the rage in Rome as in London. At his instigation the obedient press had denounced it as "a Negroid dance, fit only for a people whose princes knit," reference to the fact that the former prince of Wales, now duke of Windsor, liked to relax by knitting sweaters.

Starace's edict, however, was invalid in the British Embassy, and at the height of the festivities the orchestra played the forbidden music. There was some apprehension among the most cautious Italian guests, but they quickly overcame their inhibitions when they saw Starace, of all people, prancing and leaping through the intricate steps of the dance he had condemned, though his was, to be sure, a fascistized version of the Lambeth Walk. At the point where the dancer flings arms upward and jerks thumbs backward with a Cockney "Oi!" Starace raised both arms in the stiff Roman salute and shouted in Italian the Fascist battle cry "A Noi!," medals bouncing on the chest of his full-dress uniform.

Richard ("Dick") Massock, the AP bureau chief, grabbed my arm and whispered, "Too bad Mussolini left when he did. Had he seen this exhibition, he might have been less bored than he was at his own party, and Starace might be out of a job."

"Amen," I said, and we headed for a refill at the bar.

Politically the Chamberlain visit was totally unproductive. The prime minister failed in his attempts to persuade Mussolini to negotiate his differences with France, to induce him to withdraw additional troops from Spain, and to preserve the status quo in the Mediterranean. From Chamberlain's flabby proposals, the Duce concluded that the prime minister was concerned to maintain peace at almost any price and responded accordingly. French-Italian relations, he said, had been "poisoned by the Spanish Civil War," and until it ended—in a Franco victory, of course—no agreement between Rome and Paris was possible.

As matters stood, the visit merely confirmed Mussolini's recently taken decision to complete a military alliance with Germany. He sensed, correctly, that the British were more interested in detaching him from Hitler than they were in winning the friendship and support of Italy. To Ciano, it was revealed later, the Duce spoke of his British visitors with disdain bordering on contempt. "These men," he said, "are not made of the same stuff as the Francis Drakes and the other magnificent adventurers who created the British Empire. These, after all, are the hired sons of a long line of rich men, and they will end by losing their empire."

And to demonstrate his loyalty to the Axis, Mussolini instructed Ciano to give German Ambassador Hans Georg von Mackensen a copy of the transcript of the Anglo-Italian conversations. Ciano also telephoned Ribbentrop to assure him that Mussolini's meeting with Chamberlain was "a fiasco, absolutely worthless."

Yet Chamberlain believed his mission had been a resounding success. In an interview he gave me shortly before his departure for London, the aging prime minister said he was "very satisfied" with the results of his conversations with Mussolini. He and the Duce, he said, had succeeded in "building a bridge" between Italy and England "for the peaceful solution of outstanding European problems."

As Chamberlain left Rome with Halifax the next day, January 14, he told a group of Anglo-American reporters who had come to see him off, "We leave more than ever convinced of the good faith and goodwill of the Italian government."

Mussolini and Ciano were at the station to say good-bye to the prime minister and his foreign secretary. Chamberlain's eyes filled with tears as the train moved out to the strains of "For he's a jolly good fellow" sung by a group of British residents. They had come to bid farewell to the tired, well-meaning man of sixty-nine who, whatever his shortcomings, nevertheless represented the British people of 1938—a people anxious to avoid war at any cost, save freedom.

In all fairness Chamberlain had few cards to play against the dictators. He was heir to the complacency and military weakness passed on to him by his predecessors, Ramsay MacDonald and Stanley Baldwin. He had only recently begun a serious effort to rearm Britain, and then only slowly, in 1937. Fortunately, however, MacDonald and Baldwin both had started expanding and modernizing the Royal Air Force upon which the burden of defending Britain would soon fall.

Mussolini belied the "good faith and goodwill" mentioned by Chamberlain in his parting remarks by promptly resuming with renewed vigor his anti-French campaign. Meanwhile, the French reacted to the Fascist "demands"—these now included a share in the ownership of the Suez Canal—with more Gallic wit than caution. What I read in the French press touched the sorest possible spot on sensitive Italian skins: It ridiculed the danger of a war with Italy by asserting that "it would take at least ten able-bodied Italians to lick one retired old Frenchman." The Rome newspaper *Il Tevere,* notorious for its pro-German and anti-Semitic editorial policy, retorted that "forty-four million Italians spit in the face of the Third Republic." Childish stuff, but it accurately reflected the Italians' reaction to slurs on their valor.

Mussolini soon stirred up yet another European crisis. His press ground out propaganda designed to lay the blame for an eventual Franco-Italian shooting war on France. The newspapers reached a curious conclusion: Italy's increasing population, they said, gave it certain claims on France; unless those claims were satisfied, Italy would be justified in using force; ergo, France would be responsible for starting an Italo-French war!

Hitler gave his full support to this strange logic, declaring in a speech to the Reichstag and rebroadcast by Radio Roma that if Italy were attacked for any reason, the Third Reich would stand by it, although the Führer must have known that France had no intention of attacking Italy; he was again skillfully employing the threat of war with all its horrors. The Big Lie was Hitler's most powerful weapon, and he used it to the full to dragoon, to frighten, to subvert.

In Italy the only voice raised against the idiotic process belonged to Pope Pius XI. But the voice was fading. Though once a sturdy climber of mountains, the pontiff was dying.

17

THE DEATH OF PIUS XI

In November 1938 Pius suffered three heart attacks, and the papal household despaired of his life. His personal physician, Dr. Amintore Milani, implored him to rest, but he refused. "The pope must be a pope and not stay in bed," Pius protested, and continued working within the limits of his failing energies. By early December Pius was so ill that his doctor often slept in the papal bedchamber to be near his august patient.

Nevertheless, on December 24 the pope overruled Dr. Milani's objections and had himself helped from his sickbed into a chair to receive those members of the College of Cardinals who traditionally called to pay their respects on Christmas Eve. To his doctor's continued remonstrances, Pius replied, "My son, this may be my last Christmas, and I have work to do."

It was my first Christmas Eve away from my family, and I spent it reporting the papal reception of his cardinals. For admission to the ceremonies I was obliged to wear tails, but with black tie and black vest and looking, Michael Chinigo remarked when I returned to the office to write my story, "just like a headwaiter."

The ailing pontiff used the occasion to make a brief but pointed speech denouncing fascism and nazism and their respective leaders for wanting, as he put it, "to ride roughshod over everyone and everything." He reiterated his distress at having seen Rome emblazoned during Hitler's visit with "that crooked cross hostile to the cross of Christ."

The pope's main target, however, was Mussolini, whom he accused of having repeatedly violated the Lateran Treaty of 1929 that had established friendly relations between church and state after a long hiatus. The accord was by far the greatest single achievement of his papacy and by the same token the most important political accomplishment of Mussolini's career. In fact, the problem of how church and state could coexist was the only problem the Duce ever solved.

The historic Concordat, as the treaty was known, settled the Roman Question, the estrangement between church and state that had endured for fifty-nine years, ever since the troops of the newly proclaimed constitutional Kingdom of Italy marched into Rome on September 20, 1870, in the climactic event of the Risorgimento. The new government's capture of Rome, then the temporal as well as spiritual seat of the pontiff, made the pope a prisoner of the Vatican. The Concordat, however, restored his temporal privileges by granting him sovereignty within the territorial boundaries of the Holy See, a complex of buildings behind St. Peter's covering about a hundred acres.

The treaty handsomely compensated the church financially for the loss of Rome and its considerable territories in the Papal States, confirmed the Roman Catholic faith as Italy's sole religion, and provided for recognition of the Italian state by the Holy See. Most important, perhaps, the accord healed the long-standing rift in the nation's conscience. Although united geographically and politically in 1870, the Italian people had remained divided in their loyalties between pope and king. But the treaty enabled the monarch to say, in his crown speech at the inauguration of Parliament on April 20, 1929, that the "spiritual unity of Italy" had at last been achieved.

Yet conflicts between church and state persisted. Differences cropped up periodically, and in 1937 and 1938 a new issue arose between the Vatican and the Palazzo Venezia. The dispute stemmed from Fascist Italy's Nazi-inspired racial program which by prohibiting marriages between "Aryans and non-Aryans" encroached on the church's zealously guarded prerogatives governing matrimony. In the church's view, the only valid unions were those it sanctioned.

As one of the most stalwart defenders of the church's authority who had ever sat on the Throne of Peter and who decried persecution in any form, Pius XI felt obliged to speak his mind on the sad state to which relations between the Vatican and his beloved Italy had fallen. To that end he had laboriously prepared at risk to his health a major speech and had summoned to Rome all the nation's bishops to hear it on the tenth anniversary of the conclusion of the Lateran Treaty on February 11, 1939.

Pius regarded his throne as the "sacred repository of all truth," and it was of vital importance to him that he be able to deliver his speech. So when he became ill with what was at first diagnosed as "a mild influenza" in the early days of February, he submitted willingly to Dr. Milani's insistence that he remain in bed and do no work until fully recovered. He was determined to live long enough to be able to address his bishops on the auspicious occasion of the anniversary of the great conciliation between church and state. The speech, alas, was never given.

Of all men, only the pope dies in elaborate ceremony. Its rituals prescribe, among other things, that the pontiff, in his last hour, must confess, like any secular Catholic, and he recites word for word, syllable for syllable, the declaration formulated by the Council of Trent in the sixteenth century.

At approximately 5:00 A.M. on Friday, February 10, in the grayish half-light before dawn, Lorenzo Cardinal Lauro was seen hurrying across the cobbled Courtyard of San Damaso to the pope's palace. He was the pontiff's confessor, and at that hour he could have but one mission. An INS informant, whom I had planted in the heart of the Vatican, recognized him, guessed why he was hastening to the papal residence, and alerted my office.

Michael Chinigo, the former medical student, who was on overnight duty, opened a line to London and summoned Cecil Brown on another telephone. INS was able to handle the story of Pius XI's long illness and death, thanks mainly to Michael's knowledge of medicine, which had given the agency a series of remarkable scoops.

An important link in the INS's network for covering the Vatican was an employee in the pharmacy of the Fatebene Fratelli, which prepared the medicines Dr. Milani prescribed. Copies of the prescriptions were promptly made available to INS, and from them Michael could deduce what ailed the pope. When Dr. Milani ordered adrenaline, for instance, we knew the patient was suffering from heart disease, and INS was first to tell the world the Holy Father had suffered an attack of angina pectoris.

By 5:20 A.M. that fateful Friday, as the pope lay abed in his sparsely furnished chamber on the third floor of his palace, Cardinal Lauro had received the pontiff's confession. Dr. Milani bent over his patient and heard him sigh, "We have so much to do. . . ." The pope uttered no other word and fell into a coma. A sacristan intoned the moving prayer for the commendation of the soul to God, Proficisere anima cristiana (Depart, Christian soul).

The bluish light of an approaching dawn suffused the courtyard below as Rome's purple-robed resident cardinals, hastily summoned by telephone, alighted from their black limousines. Halberd-bearing Swiss Guards stood immobile as statues on either side of the entrance to the palace and along its murmurous corridors.

Upstairs the penitentiaries of St. Peter had arrived to dress the pope in his robes of state and, while waiting to begin their funerary work, sang the psalms of penitence, their voices filling the bedchamber. The cardinal camerlengo, sixty-two-year-old Eugenio Pacelli, the pope's secretary of state—and his unspoken choice as successor to the Throne of Peter—knelt apart on a purple pillow, praying and awaiting his turn in the unfolding ritual.

At 5:31 A.M. Dr. Milani found no heartbeat. The pope was dead.

The telephone rang in the INS office. Cecil Brown took the call: *"Il papa è morto. . . ."* The news was flashed instantly on the open line to London.

Meanwhile, in the Vatican, the ritual attending the death of the pontiff proceeded in accordance with centuries-old formality.

In the papal bedchamber the penitentiaries interrupted their psalms to place a white veil over the pope's face, now composed in death. Cardinal Pacelli, robed in violet mourning, approached the bed, in his hand a small silver mallet.

The penitentiaries uncovered the face, and Pacelli tapped the broad, placid forehead three times with the mallet, pronouncing with each tap not the dead man's chosen pontifical name but the name his mother had given him on the day of his baptism: "Achille Ratti, are you alive or dead?"

Then Pacelli broke the room's tomblike silence with the words: "The pope is truly dead."

All those present fell on their knees and recited the de profundis.

The prayer over, a papal servant removed from the pope's finger the ring of Peter the Fisherman and gave it to Cardinal Pacelli for safekeeping until the first session of the Sacred College, when his papal symbol of authority would be broken to signify the end of the pontificate of Pius XI, priest, Alpinist, scholar, linguist, and surely one of the greatest in the long line of popes.

I was not in Rome the morning the pope died but was sound asleep in my room at the Savoy Hotel in London. Early in February the New York office had granted me a breather from Axis politics in lieu of home leave after I had assured my editor, Barry Faris, that my presence in the Rome Bureau was not necessary to guarantee an INS scoop in the event the pope died. I was confident that the arrangements I had made with our Vatican informants would enable Chinigo and Brown to deliver the news of the pontiff's death ahead of our competitors, the AP and the UP. I knew it would be my head if the people involved let me down, but I wanted very much to celebrate February 5, my thirty-first birthday, with old friends in London, where, among other things, I hoped at last to see the changing of the guard at Buckingham Palace.

Everything functioned according to plan, and when the night desk man at the INS London office awakened me from a deep sleep moments after the pope's death, his first words were: "Congratulations. We were way ahead with the flash." I dressed hurriedly and taxied the short distance up the Strand to our Fleet Street offices. Cecil Brown was still on the phone, dictating a running account when I arrived.

Cecil was describing the scene in the St. Peter's Square, where the *campanone,* biggest of St. Peter's many bells, was tolling the news across the tiled and lichened rooftops of the Eternal City. Over the open line I could hear the big bell's basso profundo summoning the populace and could envision Rome's inhabitants—rich and poor or merely curious—making their way to the vast square and filling the great paved area within the extended curving arms of Bernini's colonnades, a silent multitude cloaked in grief.

I worked all morning at the office, transcribing Cecil Brown's dictated story into cablese and filing it in short takes to New York. Then I lunched with

Bill Hillman at the Savoy Grill. Over our lamb chops and a bottle of Burgundy we discussed staff arrangements for coverage of what I knew would be the elaborate ceremonies attending the papal funeral and the subsequent election and coronation of his successor.

Bill was as pleased as I about how well the Rome Bureau had functioned, and I extracted from him the promise of raises in pay for Chinigo and Brown, both of whom were overworked and underpaid. For myself I requested only his approval of home leave as soon as possible after the final episode in the papal coverage, the coronation. To Hillman's question about the possible identity of the next pope, I unhesitatingly replied: "Pacelli." From my now-excellent Vatican sources I had learned that the papal secretary of state was Pius XI's *papa in pectore,* the prelate he secretly hoped would succeed him.

Bill accompanied me to Victoria Station and saw me off on the Rome Express.

Arriving in Rome in the early evening of the next day, a Saturday, I recalled the excitement of a similar arrival in the spring of 1935, when the Eternal City was still the shining goal of my journalistic ambitions. It had lost much of its magic over the years, and with my family far away in America I was homesick and depressed as I stepped down from my wagons-lits compartment when the train pulled into the Central Station. I was cheered, however, to find Michael Chinigo waiting for me on the platform. He handed me a sheaf of cables.

I read the messages in the cab on the way to the office and found that the complicated, and expensive, mechanism I had set up to ensure an INS beat on the pope's death had worked to perfection. The cablegrams said that the agency had delivered the news ahead of its competitors everywhere. We beat the AP and the UP into New York by at least six minutes and by eight minutes into Sydney, Australia.

The most meaningful telegram came from San Simeon, and was signed by the Chief himself. It said: NO STORY COULD HAVE BEEN MORE IMPORTANT. GERVASI AND THE WHOLE SERVICE DESERVE GREATEST CONGRATULATIONS.

I had grown fond of Pius XI, the "Pope of Peace," and regretted his passing as deeply as any Roman.

At first, in 1935 and 1936, when I saw him bless Italian Fascist troops drawn up in the Piazza San Pietro before they left to slaughter ill-armed tribesmen in Ethiopia and to help Franco demolish democracy in Spain, I mentally ranked Pius with Mussolini and Hitler as an enemy of peace.

In time, however, I came to see him as he really was: a lone antagonist of both fascism and nazism who devoted the last years of his life to a losing struggle against racism in general and anti-Semitism in particular. In the summer of 1938, when it became evident that the Fascists really intended to ape the Nazis's racist doctrines, I was present when Pius XI told four hundred teachers in an audience at his hillside villa in Castel Gandolfo that Italy's anti-Semitic doctrine was "a great and serious error, which touches the steps of the altar, and touches Catholic doctrine."

On his return to Vatican City shortly thereafter, the pope did what no other contemporary world leader had had the courage to do. In his fine, scholarly hand Pius wrote two letters, one to Mussolini and the other to King Victor Emmanuel. He appealed to them to refrain from promulgation of the anti-Semitic decrees that awaited formal ratification by the Fascist Grand Council. Only the king replied, promising the "greatest consideration" to the pope's objections. It was a vain promise. The legislation became effective.

The pope was also grieved by the Fascist party's persecution of Catholic Action, the lay organization that dealt with education and social welfare. Its freedom of action was ensured by the Concordat, but Blackshirt bullyboys had raided the organization's headquarters at Venice, Turin, Bergamo, and Milan, confiscating records, destroying furniture, and defacing photo portraits of the pontiff.

"Catholic Action," I had heard the pope say on several occasions, "is the apple of our eye." But fascism was jealous of the organization, and in 1938, following the example of Hitler's anti-Catholic campaign in Germany, Mussolini set out to destroy the organization. The raids by Fascist gangs on Catholic Action branches throughout northern Italy marked the resumption of the old struggle between church and state for the loyalties and spiritual welfare of the country's young people.

The quarrel dated back to 1931, when similar violations of the Concordat caused Pius XI to issue an encyclical denouncing Fascist doctrine and policies as a revival of "pagan worship of the state." On September 2, 1931, after months of tension and negotiations, the pope and Mussolini made peace. The Duce gave the church the right to have priests in the schools and chaplains in the Fascist organizations. The church, for its part, agreed that Catholic Action should refrain from all political activity.

For a time thereafter Pius XI and Benito Mussolini were on relatively good terms. But in 1938 fascism's adoption of Nazi anti-Semitism again gave rise to friction between the pope and Mussolini, the Fascist press resumed its sniping against Catholic Action, and Blackshirt gangs raided the organization's headquarters as vigorously as they had in 1931.

The pope, meanwhile, contested equally vigorously the right of the Fascist state to forbid the mixed marriages of Jews with so-called Aryan Italians and to punish any who contracted or performed such marriages. The Concordat specified that marriages celebrated by a priest should be recognized by the civil authorities, and the Vatican held to the view that in Italy the propriety of a marriage was a matter for the church to decide.

In his last Christmas Eve address to the cardinals the pope was obliged to say that Catholic Action was being molested everywhere in Italy, and made it plain that he knew Mussolini was behind the attacks. "The zeal in the [Fascists'] 'lower ranks' clearly shows," he said, "that permission and encouragement come from above." The Fascist decrees forbidding the marriage of

Jews and Aryans, he reiterated, violated the Concordat and caused "real and serious preoccupation to the head of Catholicism and the custodian of morality and truth."

The Duce must have known, for his spies were everywhere, that the speech the pope had wanted to make in February contained a strong denunciation of the regime's violations of the Lateran Treaty. But the outside world never learned its contents. The pontiff had left the text on the desk in his study in the Vatican in several typed copies. Pius was not yet in his grave when the story leaked out of the Vatican that pro-Fascist prelates in Cardinal Pacelli's entourage had confiscated and destroyed them all as soon as His Holiness was pronounced dead.

The undelivered text undoubtedly would have contained the strongest denunciation of fascism and its leader ever made from within Italy itself. Few of us in Rome doubted that the time and energy the pope consumed in preparing it, working nightly when he should have been resting, hastened his death.

18

HABEMUS PAPAM

To chronicle the funeral of Pius XI and the moving and grandiose events that followed, William Randolph Hearst caused to be assembled in Rome three of the most distinguished writers England could provide. They were Alfred Noyes, poet; Hilaire Belloc, poet-essayist-biographer; and Hugh Walpole, best-selling novelist.

In charge of this pride of literary lions was Bill Hillman, who had engaged their services and subsequently supervised their journalistic output in Rome. Each was to write a daily article describing and interpreting the momentous happenings they witnessed: the dead pope's interment and the election and coronation of his successor.

Hillman could not have chosen three more physically and temperamentally diverse individuals.

Noyes was a convert to Catholicism and best known, perhaps, for a book in which he attempted to prove that Voltaire was a Christian. He was tall, thin, somewhat thorny, and reserved. I saw very little of him throughout the three weeks between the services attending the pope's burial and the crowning of the new pontiff.

Belloc, the Anglo-French author of innumerable essays and poems, was also the renowned biographer of Marie Antoinette, Richelieu, and Napoleon, and in his black inverness cape and beret he looked more like a French revolutionary than a man of letters. He was short, squat, and as self-sufficient as a one-man safari, carrying in the inner folds of his capacious outer garment a salami, a loaf of bread, and a bottle of red wine whenever he was called upon to stand in St. Peter's Square or in the basilica itself to observe and report. He was a superb journalist and, unlike the others, needed no help, for he was, among other things, the very Catholic wearer of the papal rank of knight commander of the Order of St. Gregory, which gave him access where the rest of us were excluded.

I saw Belloc only twice during his well-paid labors for the Chief. The first time was to bring him a bottle of rare port that I had managed to scrounge from an English friend, half of which he consumed after a sumptuous lunch in the dining room of the Albergo Ambasciatori. The second occasion found us pressed together like two kernels of corn in the dense crowd in St. Peter's Square while awaiting the appearance of the new pope following his coronation. But for Belloc, who supplied thick slabs of salami and coarse peasant bread from the inner recesses of his magnificent cape to sustain me, I would have collapsed from hunger during the long wait.

Of the three, the one I saw most often and with whom I struck up a close and enduring friendship was Sir Hugh Walpole, a big, full-chested, florid man with thinning reddish hair who wore a pince-nez, could quote Keats and Shelley in a melodious voice, and personified what I most admired in British gentlemen: civility. Quick to anger at rudeness or injustice, he was as quick to forgive and forget. The most delightful thing about him, apart from his gentleness, was his insatiable curiosity about anything and everything.

I saw him flare up only once. It happened shortly after the body of Pius XI, encased in its triple coffin of cypress, lead, and elm, had been laid to rest in the bowels of the basilica. That ceremony covered, he thought he had completed his assignment until the election took place nearly three weeks later. How, he wanted to know, could he possibly write *every day* when there was *nothing* to write about?

Walpole arrived at the INS office in the Galleria Colonna that memorable morning fuming and insisting that he had *not* contracted to write *daily* pieces but only articles dealing with the funeral, the election, and the coronation. Hillman disagreed.

"No, Sir Hugh," he said, "your contract calls for daily articles."

"I didn't contract to do that," said Walpole.

"I think that you did," said Hillman. "You agreed to write every day beginning with the funeral and ending with the coronation. And *in between* those events."

"And that might be how long?" Walpole asked, turning to me.

"Very probably three weeks," I replied. "Today is the twenty-third of February. The cardinals from abroad will not arrive much before the first of March. I should say that the coronation will be around the twelfth."

Walpole's pince-nez quivered with righteous anger. He indicated he was ready to "pack it in" and return to London. Hillman soothed him.

"It won't be so bad," he said. "We'll all help you."

"But I can't write about *nothing at all!*"

"That," was Hillman's rejoinder, "is what journalists have continually to be doing."

Walpole looked about him like a trapped creature, hating the ugly utilitarian INS office, loathing Hillman and me. But only for a moment. Suddenly he was all smiles and graciousness. Taking a deep breath, he said: "This day one hundred and eighteen years ago Keats died. I'm going with Noyes to visit his grave."

That was the morning Walpole and I became friends. He sensed that I was on his side in his argument with Hillman, and as he departed, he gave me a broad smile that expressed gratitude and an unspoken acknowledgment that we would be allies in our common effort to give Mr. Hearst his money's worth.

I had read *Vanessa,* one of the four volumes of Walpole's immensely popular *Herries Chronicle,* and over lunch the next day told him how much I admired (and envied) his straightforward, easy-flowing style, great descriptive powers, and talent for evoking atmosphere. I was embarrassed by his reaction. He was as pleased as though he had received praise from a qualified critic.

I understood his difficulty in finding something to write about during the long hiatus between the funeral and the conclave that would elect the new pope. But he would have no difficulty finding subjects, I told him. There were topics concerned in one way or another with papal affairs, I said, and he would have no trouble writing a daily essay.

"For instance," I said, "we can go up into the Alban Hills and visit Castel Gandolfo, the village where the late pope liked to spend his summer holidays. There is an astronomer there who knew and loved Pius. . . ."

Walpole beamed upon me with genuine affection, and a day or two later we motored up to Castel Gandolfo.

Hillman took care of the trio of literary giants whom we called, among ourselves, the "trained seals." My job was to run the bureau with the help of the able Cecil Brown, who manned the desk in the Galleria Colonna, while the indispensable Michael assisted me in my main task: to get the name of the newly elected pope to the outside world before anyone else. This was not easy.

A new pope is elected by the conclave of cardinals voting in strictest secrecy in the Sistine Chapel. The tradition of centuries requires that the results of the cardinals' deliberations be announced by wisps of smoke.

Each ballot is burned in the electoral chamber in a small sheet-iron stove from which a chimney stretches up through the ceiling of the Sistine Chapel into the open sky. As soon as any cardinal receives two thirds of the votes of any meeting of the conclave, a thin white smoke—caused by mingling dry twigs with the paper ballots—issues into the sky from the narrow tubular chimney, and the whole world knows that a new pope has been elected. When there is no election, the smoke is black from the damp straw mixed with the ballots.

For about an hour after the positive signal that a new pope has been "made," the identity of the pontiff remains a closely held secret until an official appears on the balcony of St. Peter's and proclaims the name. After that there is again a pause while the new pope is arrayed in his white robe (white garments in three sizes are held in readiness) before appearing in front of his people.

My task was to know that it was *white* smoke issuing from the chimney protruding from the roof of the Sistine Chapel and somehow to obtain, before anyone else, the identity of the new pope. My preparations to meet these fundamental requirements for a major double scoop struck Hugh Walpole as "romantic and decorative," and in retrospect, I suppose they were.

To make certain that we would have a good view of the setting, I rented a second-story room, exactly opposite St. Peter's in a priests' lodging house that Walpole said "might have been a hideaway, in a spy story or romantic novel." Outside, it was innocent enough, a shabby house with a shabby door and in front of it a ruin of stones and rubble where some houses had been destroyed to further Mussolini's plans for a great wide road from St. Peter's Square to the Castel San Angelo.

Walpole found himself climbing rough stairs toward a room full of ugly Madonnas and crucifixes and paper flowers, a room that was for some reason being repainted. Down a passage on the left was a kitchen, and this place fascinated Sir Hugh because it was "human and lively, and hugged, with enjoyment, an enchanting smell of good cooking." Inside, a stout priest, sleeves turned up, rocked pans over a slow fire, absorbed and contented.

Up another short slight of stairs were the bedrooms of the priests, and it was one of the larger of these that I had hired. There was a bed, above it the picture of a Madonna and Child; a tin washstand; and a table with two telephones, a shortwave radio, and a typewriter. There was also a sofa and a chair. Opposite, in full and perfect view, were St. Peter's, the square, the Vatican, and the fatal chimney.

To make certain there would be no mistake about the color of the smoke that would issue from that distant, slightly askew tube with its tiny cap, I purchased a powerful telescope of the kind popular with amateur astronomers and set it up on its tripod in the center of our room. When I looked through it, the chimney was as brilliant and dramatic as the pointing finger of fate. I had decided that if I were not the first human being to see the white smoke threading out of that chimney, I had failed in the whole purpose of what I meant to be my last assignment in Rome.

To make doubly sure that I would see the smoke the moment it began issuing from the tube, I posted on the wall opposite the chimney a friendly priest who would sight its emission before anyone in the square. Thoroughly briefed by me on the importance of his role, he was to signal Michael, who would be standing by a pillar midway between our hideaway and the basilica. Michael, in turn, would wave his hat to me, whereupon I would alert London instantly on an open line that a vote had been taken. If the smoke I saw in my telescope was white, we'd have a scoop of a few seconds, maybe minutes.

On the fine morning of March 1, when the conclave began its labors, only Walpole and I were in our room. Michael was at his post in the square, and our cleric-watchman was at his rooftop position. I alternately looked at Michael with field glasses and stared into the eyepiece of the telescope. The only life in the square during the hours before noon was provided by the inevitable pigeons, a few loiterers, a taxi or two, a procession of priests, and some tourists clustered about a gesticulating guide.

Shortly after noon my telephone rang. It was Cecil with word that Mussolini had called up two classes of reservists.

I switched on the shortwave radio. In cultured Oxonian tones a Berlin broadcaster was pouring out German propaganda about "the Führer's love for all Germans, wherever they may be, in the lost plains of China or in the darkest depths of Africa. . . ." I turned the thing off.

Twice that first day, in midafternoon and again toward sundown, the chimney emitted thin streams of *black* smoke. The conclave had failed to elect a pope, and the widowed church remained without a husband.

There had been much discussion on how long the conclave would last. Some conclaves had lasted months. My sources, however, all agreed this one would be short. The seriousness of the international situation demanded a new pope as soon as possible.

But who of the sixty-two cardinals present would be elected?

The question was one which Monsignor Pucci, the Vatican spokesman whom I had bribed to give INS first call on Vatican news, Michael, and I had discussed at length in recent days. The monsignor and Michael argued in favor of Elia Cardinal dalla Costa, of Florence, the favorite candidate of the Fascist regime, as the one least likely "to meddle in politics" and likeliest to succeed Pius XI. Neither Pucci nor Michael thought Pacelli would be the successor because he had been the pope's secretary of state. "They never elect anyone who has held that position," they said.

Walpole and I had seen photographs of all the cardinals in the double-page spreads in the newspapers and studied their portraits. We divided them into three categories: the Worldly, the Fleshly, and the Spiritual. Some of the cardinals looked like goats and satyrs; other, like sharp little small-town lawyers; still others, like aging matinee idols. The only one who fell into the Spiritual category in our view was Eugenio Cardinal Pacelli. The church needed him precisely because he was a diplomat. He had served as papal nuncio in Munich. He knew Hitler. Yes, it had to be Pacelli, I decided, and Walpole agreed. "That's the man for me," he said.

On the morning of March 2 the crowd began gathering early, arriving first singly and in pairs, then in family groups. By noon the colonnades of the basilica held within their vast quasi-circular embrace at least a quarter of a million men, women, and children, among them many nuns and priests. Those who were unable to press themselves into the arms of their mother church formed a dense black mass down the slope from St. Peter's Square and filled the wide Via della Conciliazione all the way to the Tiber.

Of Rome's entire population, it seemed, only those whom infirmities or duties kept away had failed to make the pilgrimage to where Peter was martyred for his Christianity. Many in the crowd knelt in prayer, as though beseeching those cardinals enclosed in the conclave to do something that would help save the world—to choose a man who would, in his own time and fashion, be God's man.

By their presence in such numbers—it was a Wednesday, a working day— the people must have known instinctively that this was the day the successor to Pius XI would be chosen. They stood or knelt for hours, their numbers increasing steadily, all gazing steadfastly at the dove-colored facade of the basilica, hoping that from the conclave would emerge one who would arrest Europe's drift toward war.

At precisely 5:28 P.M. came a puff of white smoke, as from a cigarette, then a steady stream, distinctly, unmistakably *white*. Into my telephone's mouthpiece I screamed—yes, screamed—"Flash. Pope elected."

I swung the telescope around to Michael, who was waving his hat frantically. I leaned out the window and signaled my acknowledgment with a handkerchief.

The crowd in the square came alive in a mighty roaring cheer unlike any I had ever heard Italians make before in the Piazza Venezia or anywhere else. The people had come to the piazza of their free will. No one had summoned them to appear in a "spontaneous" demonstration of affection. It was a roar of genuine joy and collective relief.

It would be some time before the people knew the name of the new pope, but already there were shouts of *"Viva il papa!* Viva Pacelli. . . ."

Pacelli! Pacelli! Pacelli!

The name hung in the air as though the wishes of those many hearts in the piazza were suddenly vocal. Groups of priests in the crowd started singing a psalm in somber, measured Gregorian. The sound of the singing grew and was picked up and carried to the very outskirts of the crowd.

Suddenly the doors of the balcony over the portals of St. Peter's opened. The crowd saw a tall cross of sparkling gold come forward, held by a prelate. Behind it in violet robes came Camillo Cardinal Caccia Dominioni. He stretched out his hands, and there was instant silence. He spoke in Latin into a battery of microphones, and loudspeakers carried his voice to the multitude: "I give you tidings of great joy. *Habemus papam* [We have a pope]"—the crowd emitted a great cheer—"the most eminent and reverend Eugenio Cardinal"—renewed and tremendous cheers, for there was only one Italian cardinal named Eugenio—"Pacelli, who has taken upon himself the name of Pius the Twelfth."

The sound that welled up from the crowd was deafening. From within the basilica a choir sang the papal hymn. Priests in the square struck up an impromptu Te Deum.

Minutes later the tall, thin figure of Pius XII—the Man in White—appeared on the balcony, and he imparted his first apostolic benediction on the waiting multitude. His gestures were ample, his voice was strong as he concluded, *"Et Spiritus Sancti descendat super vos et maneat semper."*

The crowd had hardly responded with "amen" when "vivas" accompanied by the pope's name filled the air. The square became a sea of waving handkerchiefs, and the pope, having first blessed the diplomatic corps massed atop the colonnades, retired.

The crowd slowly dispersed, repeating *"Habemus papam!* [We have a pope]," and the bells of St. Peter's, tolling festively, awakened, one after another, the bells of all the several hundred churches in Rome. They chanted in bronze and silver, and the whole countryside responded. Churches throughout the Catholic world soon echoed them.

The thoughts and feelings of the others—Belloc, Noyes, Hillman, Michael—I never learned. But Walpole and I, who were together much of the time between the election of the new pope and his coronation on March 12, knew we had participated in a truly momentous event. Hundreds of thousands of Romans had stood in St. Peter's Square, almost hand in hand, joyful and happy, believing in God and believing in peace.

"Had we who stood there been given the ruling of the world," said Walpole, reflecting later on the events of that afternoon, "and stayed permanently in the spirit and temper that we then experienced, there would be no more fighting, no more lust of selfishness and cruelty of desire. For an instant, believing in God, being willing to put his precepts into practice, we saw clearly, we knew the *only* law. . . ."

At that single moment of time it seemed ridiculously easy. Love God? Love thy neighbor? Why, of course. What was there to prevent it? Let us all share and share alike. Let us meet in a world conference and say: "What do *you* want, Herr Hitler? What are *your* needs, Signor Mussolini? Certainly you can have this or that. But instead of tanks and planes and bombs, let us make new schools, and houses for the poor, and hospitals for the sick."

The day after his election Pius XII broadcast an appeal for peace in his first public pronouncement. Seated on his gilded throne in the Sistine Chapel under Michelangelo's frescoes and wearing a white hat, the pontiff delivered his address after receiving the traditional oath of allegiance from each of the sixty-one red-robed cardinals who had elected him. Addressing himself "to those leaders to whom fall the high honor and grave weight of guiding people along the ways to prosperity and progress," the pope issued "an invitation to peace."

I found the speech disappointingly vague. As I listened to it on the radio, and when I read the official text later, the address seemed to me to contain little to nourish the hopes of those tens upon tens of thousands who had stood in St. Peter's Square to await his emergence as pope. He spoke of peace not as the product of reason but as "the sublime gift of heaven" and "of the immense ills which travail the world" as merely a "vision" rather than a reality stemming from the policies of Hitler and Mussolini.

I decided Pius XII would be no more successful than his predecessor in stemming the drift toward war.

How potentially more effective would have been a papal pronouncement threatening excommunication of the two great sinners of the time. It seemed to me that Pius XII missed a God-sent opportunity to rally the whole civilized world against the dictators and perhaps cause them to pause in their headlong rush to disaster.

Pope Leo XIII, speaking in a different political context in 1878, shortly after Italy's unification, defined the papacy as "the hope of Italy and the whole world." But the pontificate inherited by Pius XII seemed more nearly to fit a definition by Thomas Hobbes, the seventeenth-century English philosopher. "The papacy," he wrote, "is the ghost of the deceased Roman Empire, sitting crowned upon the grave thereof."

There was, however, one small consolation. The conclave had not produced the pope desired by Mussolini and Ciano. Their candidate, the malleable Cardinal dalla Costa, was never seriously considered in the balloting.

Nevertheless, the Duce sent Pius XII a message of "reverent homage," and the pope, in turn, invoked upon him "divine aid." It did nothing to turn Benito Mussolini away from his chosen path. The Vatican had no divisions, no tanks, no planes.

Walpole, meanwhile, had begun the first pages of what was to be his last novel, *Roman Fountain*. Among its most effective chapters were those dealing with the pope's election and his subsequent coronation. Between the two events there was time for recreation. Hillman and I took him one evening to a musical revue that Hugh found remarkable for its lighthearted but friendly mockery of Mussolini and to a soccer match between Roma and Lazio that surprised the Englishman for the low quality of the play.

At other times Walpole and I lunched at out-of-the-way restaurants and talked—about America and England. It was the only area in which we found ourselves in conflict.

Hugh loved America, where he had lived nearly half his fifty-five years, and had many friends there, especially in Hollywood, where he had worked on films with Frank Capra, George Cukor, and David O. Selznick. But while he was fond of America for its vitality, humor, and idealism, he was critical of what he called its "cheap journalism" and its political system, which seemed to him "unworthy of so great a country." Too often, he said, America blunted its idealism by allowing unworthy citizens to come to power. He was thinking of Warren G. Harding and the Teapot Dome scandals and of Herbert Hoover and the Great Depression.

Most of all, Walpole was distressed by the fact that although the United States had helped create the League of Nations in 1919, it had refused to participate actively as a member and thereby had missed "a superb opportunity" to play a leading role as a world power. In his view, America had done nothing since to help the world and had pursued "selfish and short-visioned policies."

Inwardly I agreed with him, but I felt compelled to remind him that

England's record as a world power had left much to be desired. It had abandoned Czechoslovakia, a desertion that had helped bring Europe to the brink of war. At the time I saw England as a nation whose great history was behind it and whose word was subtle and double-minded, its ruling upper classes a patronizing lot, snobbish and supercilious. This roused Walpole to insist that with all its faults and mistakes England had a quality that belonged to no other country in the world: stubborn courage in the face of adversity. "The future world," he said, "will need her and will use her." History would prove him right.

For all our differences, Walpole and I liked and enjoyed each other. He awed me as a man of letters who was on speaking terms with the literati of his day, and he, in turn, seemed genuinely interested in me. He questioned me closely on what I hoped to do with my life. His interest stemmed, I think, from the fact that he believed I resembled physically his good friend Frank Capra, the Hollywood director, like myself an American of Sicilian origin.

Walpole encouraged me to leave daily journalism for more creative literary work, such as writing for the screen. He knew that I hoped to return to the States soon, ostensibly on home leave but actually to seek other employment, and gave me warm, handwritten letters of introduction to Capra, Cukor, and Selznick. He vastly overrated my talents, but I gratefully accepted the letters shortly before he completed his last chore for Mr. Hearst, the pope's coronation.

I never took advantage of Walpole's kind effort to turn me into a film writer; I was profoundly aware, at thirty-one, of having too much to learn about my own trade to try to master another.

The coronation of Pope Pius XII took place on March 12, and the next day, Walpole's fifty-fifth birthday, he left Rome for Florence. His departure helped hasten my own decision to return home, although spring was in the air and Rome was at its loveliest.

19

VALE, ROMA

Early in March, shortly after the elevation of Pacelli to the papacy, I cabled Barry Faris, my editor in New York, requesting permission to return to the States, pointing out in my telegram that I was long overdue for home leave. Anticipating a favorable reply—Faris was a reasonable man as well as one of the sharpest newspapermen I ever worked for—I booked passage on the *Conte di Savoia,* sailing from Naples on March 20.

I had had enough of life in a racist police state and had long since wearied of tapped telephones, of having my mail read by strangers, and of being spied on virtually day and night. I sorely missed my family and ached with homesickness, but there was another equally compelling reason: America now summoned me as obsessively as had ancestral Italia during my youthful gropings for identity in the bigoted, exclusivist America of Harding, Coolidge and Hoover—the America of the Ku Klux Klan, the lynchings in the South, the Palmer raids, the persecution of Sacco and Vanzetti.

Time had erased the bitter memories of those years, and I longed now to return to the land of my origins, for I knew at last where my roots really lay. My adolescent love affair with Roma was over, and the time had come to say, "Good-bye, fair city, I'm going home."

Of the many Italian friends I had made I would sorely miss two: Dr. Giorgio Mattoli and Ercole Graziadei. Kathryn and I had met Mattoli aboard the *Rex* on our way to Spain in 1934, and through him had met Ercole, his wife, Emma, and their teenaged daughter, Paola, when we arrived in Rome in the spring of 1935. The two men were among the few upper-class Italians who could trust their servants—old retainers in both cases—and in their homes talked freely about the iniquities of *il fascismo.* They constituted educational islands of sanity in an Italy gone berserk, and over the years Ercole, Giorgio, and I became almost as close as brothers.

Mattoli, a well-to-do bachelor—I recalled his flirtation with pretty Betty Kern, the daughter of composer Jerome Kern aboard the *Rex*—was a successful young cardiologist and owned a fine villa on a hilltop at Anzio, where we and the Graziadeis often went for summer weekends of noisy, sumptuous dining al fresco in the villa's garden and, at times, hilarious horseplay: mini-races through the spacious grounds in Topolino Fiats and water battles with garden hoses and buckets.

Usually, though, we went sailing in Giorgio's ketch and swam in the clear turquoise waters of Anzio Bay or went fishing off adjacent Nettuno. The evenings were spent in good talk under the stars on the villa's terrace, from which, on Saturday nights, we had a fine view of the weekly fireworks display in the seaport below. I would miss Giorgio not only because he had kept me in good health despite too many cigarettes and too much strong coffee but because he had the gift of laughter. He was short, round, and jolly and shed fascism's slings and arrows as easily as ducks shed raindrops.

Ercole was a tall, slender aristocrat from Mantova, in northern Italy, the eminent lawyer son of the Socialist leader of the opposition in the Chamber of Deputies back in the early 1920s during democracy's losing struggle against the Fascisti. Giorgio was only two or three years older than I, but Ercole was in his middle fifties. Well read, multilingual, and widely traveled—as a young man attached to an official delegation he had visited Moscow in 1923 and met Lenin—Ercole survived fascism much in the manner of my son Sean's godfather, Orlando, simply by not overtly opposing the regime.

We met often in his offices in the Via Veneto for long talks during which he instructed me in the origins and doctrines of fascism. "A spurious nationalist revolution against the nonexistent threat of bolshevism," he said, "financed by a handful of moneyed industrialists to suppress the trade unions." He was among the many of his class who had read *Mein Kampf* and saw it as Hitler's blueprint for the conquest and domination of Europe, "an ambition," Ercole said, "that sooner or later will bring him into conflict with the Western democracies." Ercole believed the Anschluss was "the Sarajevo of another great war."

The day I booked passage on the *Conte di Savoia,* I invited both Ercole and Giorgio to a farewell lunch at our favorite restaurant, the terrace of the Casina Valadier in the Pincio. Giorgio couldn't come, but Ercole said he'd be there the day I suggested: March 16. I couldn't have chosen a less propitious time had I tried.

The day before—the Ides of March, incidentally—German troops poured into Bohemia and Moravia. They met no resistance, and at nightfall Hitler himself marched into Prague with the pomp and fanfare of a conquering Caesar. The morning papers, Milan's *Corriere della Sera* and Rome's *Il Messagero,* covered their front pages with the ominous news. Radio Roma, meanwhile, filled the air with bulletins. One said the Führer had issued a proclamation to the German people declaring that the Sudetenland had belonged "for a millennium to the *Lebensraum* of the German people" and proudly proclaiming, "Czechoslovakia has ceased to exist."

Deprived of all but one of our INS informants by the January decree forbidding Italian journalists from working for foreign news organizations (the exception was a trusted member on the staff of Virginio Gayda's *Giornale d'Italia,* whom I could not immediately reach by telephone), I spent all morning trying to ascertain what the regime's reaction to the startling development might be. A quick check of my sources at the British and American embassies elicited only puzzled dismay that the Führer had violated the Munich accords.

At the Ufficio Stampa on the Via Veneto, where I stopped on my way to the Villa Borghese and my rendezvous with Ercole, the officer on duty, a man named Straneo, would only say, "Well, it would seem that Herr Hitler has done it again." I took that to mean that the Führer, who had failed to inform the Duce of his move into Austria, had again acted unilaterally without advising his Axis partner beforehand. But when I pursued this possibility with Straneo, he responded by saying, "A lovely *primavera* we're having, isn't it?"

He was right. I had never seen Rome lovelier. Spring had come earlier than usual to the Eternal City. The stands of the flower vendors along the Via Veneto glowed like painters' palettes with roses and daffodils and irises from the greenhouses of the Italian Riviera, and the fountains sparkled in the bright Roman light, a crystalline light I would find later only in Jerusalem. The gardens in the Pincio were fragrant with early-blooming jasmine and wisteria, but the premature arrival of a glorious Roman spring failed to lift my spirits, for I was more than ever certain that Europe was on the road to war.

Ercole had preceded me, and I found him seated at a table for two in a far corner of the terrace, his back to me and bent over a copy of the *Corriere,* the country's closest thing to an honest newspaper. He turned when he felt my hand on his shoulder and looked almost as downcast as I felt.

"Well," he said, shaking hands, "it seems you were wise to have sent Katerina and the children home when you did. The war you and I have feared since the Anschluss lies just over the horizon. Old Baldy, as you call him, must be furious, but there's not a line in the *Corriere* to indicate what he's thinking. Then again, that's to be expected, isn't it?"

We ordered charcoal-broiled chicken and a wine from the Castelli to go with it, and Ercole, an expert at reading between the lines of official communiqués, a talent common to most literate Italians of his generation, said he saw in the morning's sensational news proof that Hitler believed he could dominate Europe unchallenged, that Britain and France feared his military superiority.

"But he is wrong," Ercole said. "At some point, and probably in the very near future, the Western powers will realize Hitler must be stopped. And *voilà!* Another *grande guerra,* in which I doubt that our ambitious Duce will remain neutral. We betrayed our alliance with Austria-Hungary and Germany back in 1915, when we joined Britain and France in Wilson's 'war to save democracy,' but he wouldn't allow that to happen a second time. His vanity, his pride, his ambitions would not permit it. . . ."

We reminisced awhile about the good times we had had at Giorgio's villa at Anzio, and Ercole remembered a particular Saturday night in August 1935, only days after we had met. He reminded me that while watching the fireworks, we all were startled by a small voice crying, "I don't like revolutions." Turning, we saw Sean, in pajamas, standing in the doorway leading to the terrace, tearful and obviously frightened.

The noise had awakened the lad, and his mother and I realized for the first time that the revolution in Spain had traumatized him far more than we had imagined. Kathryn rushed to him, swept him up in her arms, and carried him back to bed, where she stayed until he was again sound asleep. The boy had just turned three, but he was to be a militant pacifist the rest of his days.

Our luncheon ended on a somber note. Frown lines had suddenly creased Ercolino's broad brow while we were having coffee and enjoying the view. I asked him what was troubling him.

"Frankly," my friend said with unaccustomed solemnity, "I'm afraid. Not for myself and family alone, but for my beloved Italy, her people, her treasures. And I'm afraid for Europe, this wonderful Europe, the heartland of Western civilization. The last war bled us white only a generation ago. Another war, now that the airplane has become war's dominant weapon, may destroy us completely. . . ."

Later, as we embraced at parting, Ercolino said, far more prophetically than either of us could have known, "Gervasino, it wouldn't surprise me in the least if the next time we meet you are in your country's uniform. I can't imagine that America would allow the Fascists and the Nazis to conquer Europe unopposed. . . ."

Waiting to hear from Faris, I decided that in the event of an unfavorable reply I would quit and go home anyhow, in "tourist third" instead of first class, if need be, though resigning from INS would mean having to find another job, and jobs in the newspaper business, I knew from soundings I had made, were as scarce as they had been when I left Penn. It never crossed my mind to go to Hollywood and use the letters Walpole had given me to Capra, Cukor, and Selznick. I wanted to stay in journalism, a trade I loved and one in which I hoped to prosper, perhaps by writing for the popular magazines—*Saturday Evening Post, Collier's, Liberty, Life*—that in the 1930s flourished in the great middle ground of literature between newspapers and books. It was the escape from agency work that my friend Paul Gallico had suggested when he visited me in Rome in the late spring of 1938.

Gallico, a big man physically and in other more important ways, was one of America's best sportswriters and had recently left journalism to write fiction. In fact, he had just completed his first novel, *Adventures of Hiram Holliday,* which his agent had submitted for serialization in *Cosmopolitan* magazine, a Hearst publication, and he was eagerly awaiting a cabled rejection or acceptance, "the difference," he said lightly, "between poverty and affluence." At the moment he was nearly broke.

Paul made my office his headquarters, and one day, while I was struggling with a mailer about how the octogenarian Pope Pius XI was carrying on the business of the church though sorely beset by the infirmities of his advancing years, Paul riffled through my voluminous file on the subject. Suddenly he blurted, "Hey, Francesco, you've got a dandy magazine piece here for any one of the big weeklies—*Liberty,* or *Collier's,* maybe even the *Saturday Evening Post.* Why don't you write it and make yourself some real money?" I replied, lamely, that the idea had never occurred to me and that, anyhow, I didn't know how. "Easy," he said, "I'll show you."

"Magazine readers want to be entertained as well as informed," he said, and instructed me in the technique of writing for that audience. Establish a theme, he said, and develop it with illustrative material, quotes, anecdotes, and colorful detail. I followed his instructions, completed the article, sent it off to his agent, and forgot about it.

The next day Paul arrived at the office beaming. *Cosmopolitan* had bought the serial rights to *Adventures of Hiram Holliday* for fifteen thousand dollars. "Let's celebrate," he roared, and we did—with a two-day holiday in Naples that included a climb to the sulfurous brim of Mount Vesuvius and a late afternoon's fishing from a rowboat in the bay. The boatmen, a father-and-son team with good voices, sang Neapolitan folk songs while we fished for sardines, which they cleaned and deep-fried in olive oil in a shallow iron pot set on a charcoal-fired brazier in the bow. The fish, served on tin plates with fragrant slabs of lemon and garlic bread, accompanied by a light wine from Sorrento, kept cool in clay amphorae under a tarpaulin, made a meal Lucullus might have served at one of his banquets.

Paul returned to the States a day or two later, and years passed before we met again, but we kept in touch. He was delighted when *Liberty* bought my article and sent me a copy he'd picked up at a newsstand, the issue of August 13, 1938. The agent subsequently sent me a check for $685, the largest amount of money I had ever received at any one time.

Months later, as I awaited Faris's reply to my plea to allow me to come home. I wasn't as worried about the future as I might have been. I had material for at least half a dozen more articles, and I was confident my family wouldn't starve if Faris obliged me to resign by insisting I remain at my post. But he didn't. A family man himself, Barry must have sensed how much I missed my wife and kids, for he cabled: COME HOME AT YOUR EARLIEST CONVENIENCE STOP KAY AND BOYS SEND LOVE STOP REGARDS.

During the few remaining days before sailing, I made a round of parting calls at the American and British embassies, had farewell drinks with Ralph and Aldo Forte, dinner with Cecil Brown, and said good-bye to Giorgio Mattoli over a quiet meal at his home.

Two days before sailing for home I made the last of my round of parting calls—at the Palazzo Chigi to say good-bye to Count Ciano. My friend Luigi Barzini, Jr., had warned me that the foreign minister was annoyed with me. "*Gervasi parla troppo* [Gervasi talks too much]," Ciano had said to Gibom, from which I surmised that Ciano had learned that I had conveyed to my friends in the American Embassy the gist of our conversations about Italy's role in Spain and its racist policies.

Nevertheless, Ciano received me readily enough when I requested an appointment for a farewell visit. I found him leaning on the broad sill of one of the tall windows of his inner office, arms folded, gazing thoughtfully down on the Piazza Colonna below. He straightened and gave me a rather stiff, formal smile as I crossed the threshold behind his uniformed flunky. We shook hands, a very un-Fascist thing to do under the new rules; but he did not offer me a chair, and I knew this was going to be a brief meeting.

I started the conversation by remarking that Franco-Italian relations appeared to be worsening by the minute. In recent days there had been anti-French demonstrations in Genoa, Milan, Florence, Naples, Palermo, and Rome—all over Italy—by university students bellowing the usual "demands" for Tunis, Savoy, Corsica, and the Suez Canal and proclaiming their readiness to "march" against France to fulfill them. "The situation," I said, "would appear to be serious—"

Before I could say more, Ciano interrupted with a gesture that as much as said the topic didn't interest him in the least, and Italians can say more with a movement of the hands, a shrug of the shoulders, or a facial expression than any other people in the world except, perhaps, the Arabs.

"*Parliamo d'altre cose* [Let us talk of other things]," he said. "So, you are going back to America. On home leave, I understand. But you will return to Rome, of course?"

"I think not," I replied, evenly and looking him straight in the eye.

Ciano's eyebrows arched, his chin lifted. He was silently asking me to explain.

"Well, Excellency, if I do return to Rome," I said, "it will probably be in the uniform of an American soldier. I'm convinced there will be war, and in that event—"

Ciano cut me off. "Nonsense," he snapped, in English, adding, in Italian, "*Le pluto-democrazie non faranno mai la guerra* [The plutocratic democracies will never make war]. Never."

With that, Ciano frowned and stared past me. I recall an inner conviction that he did not believe what he had just said. I broke the brief but embarrassing silence with the first words that came to mind. "You may be right, Excellency, as always. . . ."

Ciano smiled as though enjoying an inner joke. "The only man in Italy who is always right," he said, "is the Duce. *Solo lui ha sempre raggione.*"

Our good-byes were perfunctory, downright chilly, in fact. We shook hands.

I never saw him again.

I left the Palazzo Chigi thinking, *Well, he did not deny there would be a war. He merely rejected the idea that the democracies would fight.*

The cannon on the Vomero that daily signaled high noon sounded as I was leaving the Palazzo Chigi and crossed the Corso to the Galleria Colonna. At the office Michael Chinigo handed me a cable from Kathryn wanting to know when I was coming home. I dictated a reply and went for a leisurely lunch alone at my favorite restaurant, Ranieri's, in the Via Mario dei Fiori.

After lunch I took a long, relaxed walk about the city I had called home for three years and ten months, cherishing every moment, feeling deeply Rome's mystique. A *carrozza* took me up the Janiculum for a farewell look at the city from the heights where in 1849 Garibaldi had vainly defended the short-lived revolutionary Roman Republic proclaimed by the Risorgimento's "other Giuseppe," Mazzini, the one Stendhal had called the "Soul" of Italy's struggle for unity and independence.

It was early afternoon, and except for a dozen sleeping cats, the piazza atop the tallest of Rome's seven hills was deserted, for it was the hour of the siesta, when Romans slept after heavy midday meals. I was alone with the noble equestrian statue of Garibaldi, the hero, looking much as I remembered him from the oak-framed engraving that had hung in the parlor of my childhood home in League Street, in South Philly.

I lingered long on the Janiculum to fill my eyes and memory with my favorite view of the Eternal City. From its heights Rome seemed removed from both earth and luminescent sky, a suspended polychromatic vision of greens and golds, brilliant slashes of white, and every shade of brown from deep sienna to cinnamon and saffron, a radiant jewel bisected but curiously enhanced, rather than flawed, by the dark, winding stain made by the Tiber.

How remote Rome seemed that afternoon from the realities of a Europe already well launched on the road to war. It was unthinkable that this splendid city's crumbling monuments, noble campaniles, stately palazzi, magnificent cathedrals, and museums filled with the treasures of centuries should ever become targets for the warplanes of fascism's enemies. Incredible, yet distinctly within the realm of the possible, for Benito Mussolini seemed to have lobotomized the Italians.

Under Garibaldi and Mazzini and Cavour, the Italians had fought long and courageously against Austrian, French, Spanish, and papal tyranny to make a united nation of free men—the constitutional monarchy of 1870. But this once-democratic people had allowed themselves to be reduced to supine submission to the will and dictates of a power-mad ex-Socialist politician. What they needed was another Risorgimento, but who would lead it? Who dared challenge the man who was "always right"? No one chanced even to contradict him, much less attempted to overthrow him. The Duce was firmly established in power and completely, if resignedly, accepted by the overwhelming majority of the people, hence, I concluded, they would remain faithful to the dictum painted on every wall: BELIEVE! OBEY! FIGHT!

Clearly an unbelievably tragic fate awaited Italy, a country guided and dominated by a man sick in mind and body, for Benito Mussolini was no longer the "young and vigorous" Duce of the 1920s and early 1930s. The man I had seen at the British embassy party only two months before, in January, had aged considerably since I interviewed him in the fall of 1937, and rumors were rife in Rome that he was taking morphine to ease the pain of recurrent stomach cramps. He was only fifty-six, but visibly old beyond his years, a man whose thinking was grounded less and less on reason, more and more on expediency.

In recent years, by linking Italy's destiny with Germany's, Mussolini had reduced his country to the early-fourteenth-century Italy of Dante's *Purgatorio,* "Ah, servile Italy, thou inn of grief, ship without pilot in a mighty storm, no longer queen of provinces, but a brothel."

Sadly I turned away from the Roman tableau of sharp lights and lengthening shadows. The sky was afire now with the orange-red flames of sunset, and I imagined the Eternal City itself in flames.

It was early evening by the time I returned to the Galleria Colonna, intending to clear out my desk in preparation for my departure. The atmosphere in the *galleria* at the hour of the *aperitivo* was dejected. After the uplift provided by the accession to the papacy of one of their own sons the Romans seemed to have reverted to their pre-Munich gloom, as though suddenly conscious their destiny would not be decided by the Roman-born new Vicar of Christ but by the schemer in the Palazzo Venezia who had suddenly resumed and intensified his quarrel with France.

Waiting for me at Picarozzi's café, at a table close to the steps leading up to my office, was the informant on the *Giornale d'Italia* whom I had tried earlier to reach by telephone. He was a small, slight Sardinian with dark eyes and black hair who looked more like an Arab than an Italian and since 1936 had been carried on the INS payroll as "Augur," the code name he chose when I hired him during the hullabaloo over sanctions. He was the only survivor of the January 1939 "purge" of Italian journalists working for foreigners, and he had been Augur so long I had forgotten his real name. I strongly suspected he was a member of the Communist underground who had burrowed his way into a staff job close to his boss Gayda, Mussolini's mouthpiece. The information he provided was rarely off the mark, and I kept him on the payroll, paying him always in cash for services rendered in a relationship that was risky for us both but worth it.

Tonight Augur had important news. Hitler had declared a "protectorate" over the Sudetenland and taken Slovakia, too, under his benevolent protection. He had also allowed Ruthenia, which formed the eastern tip of Czechoslovakia, to be taken over by the greedy Hungarians. "They had been waiting like jackals on the province's borders for a signal from Berlin," Augur said.

Meanwhile, he said, Prince Philip of Hesse, Hitler's messenger, had arrived by air from Berlin and delivered a verbal message to Mussolini relaying the Führer's explanation of his coup. Word had come to Gayda's paper from the Palazzo Venezia that the Duce was furious. "Every time Hitler occupies a country," he shouted after Philip had left, "he sends me a message."

Augur doubted, however, that Mussolini would abandon his alliance with Hitler. The instructions to Gayda from the Palazzo Venezia were to play up the demonstrations against France and to underscore Italy's readiness to fight for Tunisia, Savoy, Corsica, the Suez Canal.

"But Italy has no intention of attacking France," my informant said. "Not yet, in any case. Our military correspondent, who covered the war in Ethiopia and has just returned from Spain, has been alerted to be ready to go to Albania. The war in Spain, by the way, is almost over. . . ."

I didn't find it necessary to inform Augur of my own travel plans, which were to leave Rome for Naples the next day.

The *Conte di Savoia* cleared the harbor at Naples and swung gracefully onto her westward course through the Mediterranean, the sea Mussolini insisted on calling *mare nostrum* though it belonged to all humankind, for it had cradled three great faiths—Judaism, Christianity, and Islam—and everything we held dear as Western civilization.

I was elated at being homeward bound at last and looked forward to reunion with my family after so many months. Nevertheless, it was with a deep inner anguish that I stood on the boat deck and watched plumed Vesuvius recede in the distance. In those moments I realized I was leaving not Mussolini's Italy but a beloved mistress: Italia.

True, I had found no kinship with the Italy of the Fascisti, but I had come to know and love the Italy of a host of giants in every imaginable field: art, science, literature, architecture, philosophy, music, statesmanship, navigation, and, yes, remembering Garibaldi, even warfare. Leaving *that* Italy now, I was almost overcome with nostalgia for it, and I realized that however American I might be, a part of me would be forever Italian.

Over the years I had resolved the matter of my identity. I knew now who and what I was, but I was inwardly aware of an enigma. Why, I asked myself, had I been drawn to a land other than the one of my birth? I had no answer then, at thirty-one, in the early summer of a career that would take me around the world, through the cataclysmic war of 1939–1945, and beyond.

Pondering the question now, uncomfortably near the end of my career, I am inclined to believe that there is no answer and that some of us remain wanderers, in transit all our lives, seeking a haven that somehow remains out of reach.

For some years, however, actually until the advent of McCarthyism, the "haven" was the liberal, progressive, moralistic America that had emerged with Franklin Delano Roosevelt and the New Deal. My longish residence abroad in the oppressive climate of fascism had revived and intensified my love of country, and it was with a tightness in my throat that I gazed at Manhattan's serrated skyline on my return home in the early spring of 1939 as the *Savoia* slid quietly into New York Harbor to await her pilot.

Setting foot once more on American soil that ash gray late March morning of my arrival, I vowed never to leave it again. A foolish vow, as it turned out, for the requirements of my trade made me a wanderer again sooner than I knew. But on the magic day of my homecoming, feeling much like a prodigal who had expiated his sins in self-imposed exile, I thought only of how fortunate I was that my parents had chosen to make their home in Emerson's America, "another name for opportunity, a land whose whole history appeared like a last effort of divine Providence on behalf of the human race."

I was aware, of course, of the imminence of war in Europe. At the time Adolf Hitler stood at the head of the Continent's most powerful nation with conquest in his eye and malevolence in his heart, especially toward the Jews, whose destruction he had already begun. He had amply demonstrated his ability to bully the democracies into submission and pick off his targets one by one, and he now awaited an opportunity to pounce on his next victim. The Balkans, the Ukraine, Poland, perhaps even France and Britain lay temptingly before him. His aim to master them menaced Europe and implied a threat to the United States.

In Rome I had seen the threat clearly enough and had indicated as much when I told Count Ciano that if I returned to Italy after my home leave, it would probably be in the uniform of an American soldier. But during my seven-day crossing of the seemingly limitless and protective ocean, I persuaded myself that the impending conflict was strictly a European affair, a faraway imperialist struggle of no immediate concern to my country. America, I unperceptively concluded, could and should remain aloof from "Europe's war" in blessed neutrality.

After checking in at the INS office on arrival, I hastened to Philadelphia to collect my family, my mind set on making a home for ourselves as close to the soil as possible. Aboard ship I had fantasized a small farm somewhere within commuting distance of New York, but like American neutrality in the looming war, it was to remain an unrealized dream.

20

BETWEEN PEACE AND WAR

Kathryn and the boys looked pale and sickly when I fetched them at my sister Clementine's home in North Philly. They had suffered debilitating recurrent colds during the bitter winter months since Christmas and obviously needed fresh air and sunshine. "Take them to Florida," my sister suggested, and I did, in the extravagant style to which a Hearst expense account and the low-cost Italian economy had addicted me.

For a month we lazed on Miami's beaches, feasted on southern cooking, and made long, exhilarating trips in a rented Ford convertible, driving nearly always with the top down. Once we drove to Key West via the spectacular overwater causeway and on another occasion crossed the fabulous Okefenokee Swamp, an adventure that delighted the kids. They marveled at the area's giant tupelo trees, bald cypresses festooned with Spanish moss, mysterious stretches of oily dark waters, and exotic wildlife, especially the alligators sunning themselves on the swamp's sandy hummocks.

By the time we returned to New York and checked into the St. Moritz in a suite overlooking Central Park, mother and children had regained their Mediterranean coloring and robust good health, but I was nearly broke. Pullman fares to and from Miami, car rental, and first-class hotel accommodations for four had proved to be far more expensive than I had anticipated. Although my INS salary covered current living expenses, I now needed money with which to make a permanent home for us. To earn it, I followed Paul Gallico's advice and turned to writing magazine articles.

Working nights and on my days off, I wrote four pieces in as many weeks, and my agent, Harold Matson, a fair-haired Swede with kindly blue eyes, infinite faith, and a talent for marketing the written word, sold all four. One, entitled "Save America First," in which I said that war was imminent and that I believed the United States would do well to remain aloof from Europe's quarrels, was bought by Hearst's *Cosmopolitan*. A second was a profile of Virginio Gayda, Mussolini's megaphone, and found a home in *Vanity Fair*. Two others—one headed "The Care and Feeding of a Dictator" and the other a pastiche about ex-King Alfonso and his presumed propensity for casting the "evil eye"—both were fortuitously placed with *Collier's Weekly* in a sale that changed the course of my career. The four articles earned me approximately four thousand dollars, money enough to enable Kathryn to go house hunting.

Friends with children had suggested Bronxville, in nearby Westchester County, as an ideal community in which to raise kids, and there Kathryn soon found a two-story brick Dutch colonial house with a front lawn, fine old shade trees, and a big, grassy backyard. She furnished the place tastefully—with the help of a decorator and generous credit terms from Bloomingdale's department store—and by early summer we had roots at last in our own country as firmly planted as our new home's shrubbery and tall maples.

It wasn't the "small farm" of my shipboard dream, but for Kathryn and me—remembering our asphalted, treeless row house childhoods in South Philly—the house on green and pretty Bronxville's Homesdale Road represented fulfillment of desires long deferred and sanctuary for our children against a predictably chaotic world. For while we were vacationing in Florida, the long ordeal of the Spanish people ended in a Fascist victory, and peace was running out in Europe like sand in an hourglass.

The "peace in our time" proclaimed by Neville Chamberlain after the dismemberment of Czechoslovakia in September 1938 lasted barely six months.

Soon after he had swallowed Czechoslovakia, Hitler seized Memel from Lithuania and raised demands for Danzig and the Polish Corridor. The horrible realization now at long last spread in Britain and France that the Führer's most solemn guarantees were worthless, that his designs were not limited to repatriating Germans, but reached out to all Eastern Europe and beyond, and that he could never be appeased. In April—on Good Friday, to be exact—Mussolini, his partner in aggression, took over Albania.

The Western powers began to make military preparations in earnest. Britain, changing its Eastern European policy at the eleventh hour, now gave a guarantee to Poland—under the worst possible circumstances, the military bastion of Czechoslovakia having been already surrendered, and the Soviet Union alienated from the West by its exclusion at Munich.

In the summer of 1939 the British and the French desperately tried to form an anti-German alliance with Russia. Poland and the Baltic States, however, proved stupidly unwilling to allow Soviet armies within their borders, even for the purpose of defending them against the Germans. There the matter rested until the end of August. The "Polish question" lay like a ticking time bomb while Hitler inveighed against "encirclement" and renounced Germany's ten-year nonaggression pact with Poland.

In the meantime, when my two months' leave expired at the end of May, INS asked me to return to Rome, but I temporized, pleading the need to establish a home before undertaking another overseas assignment. Actually, apart from having no desire to resume my former post, then in the capable hands of Cecil Brown, I wanted more time with my family. I was certain there would be war in Europe before the leaves turned in Bronxville, but I had no intention of becoming a war correspondent if I could possibly avoid it; the years had somewhat cooled my ardor for adventure.

Pending what INS hoped would be my return to duty abroad—Paris was temptingly mentioned as an alternative to Rome—the agency assigned me to the cable desk in New York, helping an overworked Jack Oestreicher rewrite and expand the swelling flood of dispatches from our overseas correspondents. I missed being in the field, but throughout the summer of 1939 I was ideally situated to observe the approach of war as it was reflected in the voluminous incoming file from our bureaus in London, Paris, Berlin, Warsaw, and other European trouble spots.

I enjoyed being a suburbanite. Working decent hours at last—roughly 9:00 A.M. to 5:00 P.M.—I could play with the kids when I came home from the office on the 5:27 out of Grand Central, take them to Saturday matinees at the local movie, and preside over Sunday afternoon cookouts on the charcoal grill in our spacious backyard. Radio, which was rapidly assuming importance as a news medium, was already in its heyday as an entertainment medium, and the family regularly gathered before our shining new Magnavox radio-phonograph to laugh with Amos 'n Andy, Fred Allen, Edgar Bergen and Charlie McCarthy, Fibber McGee and Molly, and other hilarious comedy programs. After the boys were put to bed, Kathryn and I listened to the depressing news or tuned in a broadcast of classical music in a happy togetherness we had rarely known while living abroad.

I even enjoyed commuting to Manhattan. The daily ride to and from work gave me time to read the newspapers whose front pages recorded under big black headlines not only the fearsome trend of events in Europe and Asia but also our own country's fluctuating, uncertain, anomalous state of mind and to hear the views of talkative fellow commuters from the village I now called home.

Bronxville was, and still is, the epitome of suburbia. In the summer of 1939 it was also a metaphor for isolationism, a community populated almost entirely by conservative, well-to-do Republicans who hated Roosevelt, abominated the New Deal, and resented the president's reported desire for an unprecedented third term in office. Most of all, they agonized over FDR's advocacy of a "firm stand" against Europe's increasingly rambunctious dictators. While I defended his domestic policies, I found myself in agreement with my fellow villagers in their opposition to our embroilment in the impending conflict in Europe.

In mid-July, while war clouds piled ever higher on Europe's horizons, INS became increasingly insistent that I return to my beat overseas, and I was in a quandary. *Collier's Weekly,* on the strength of the two articles it had bought earlier, commissioned a third and offered me a staff job as an associate editor with a roving assignment abroad at substantially more money than INS was paying me. I was torn between accepting the offer and loyalty to the agency which had stood by me in my difficulties with the Fascist regime and was responsible for such prominence as I had achieved as a journalist.

My dilemma was resolved by Joe Connolly, president of INS, when I told him of the *Collier's* offer, a guaranteed yearly income of ten thousand dollars plus a fee for each article I wrote. INS couldn't give me a raise; the agency was operating in the red. "But don't worry, Frank," Connolly said, "I'll work something out," and he did.

To make up the difference between my salary and what *Collier's* had offered, Connolly arranged that I should write six articles a year for *Cosmopolitan,* a monthly Hearst magazine. Moreover, I was told, I would replace H. R. Knickerbocker, the chief European correspondent, who was returning to the States to fulfill a long-standing lecture engagement. Believing I had made a deal that satisfied both my growing financial needs and my conscience, I accepted and agreed to leave as soon as possible for Paris, where I would be based.

It never occurred to me at the time that I had undertaken a double assignment and would be serving two masters, INS and *Cosmopolitan,* involving not only a prodigious amount of work but possible editorial conflicts between daily journalism and the magazine variety. But at thirty-one I thought I had the best of two worlds, and as steamy July became torrid August, the yen for movement and adventure reawakened, and I looked forward to covering the biggest of all possible stories, a war.

Roosevelt knew war was coming and spent the ill-omened spring and summer of 1939 trying to persuade a reluctant Congress to repeal or amend the country's neutrality legislation so as to allow Britain and France to obtain the weapons and ammunition they needed to resist Axis aggression. The Neutrality Act—adopted as a temporary measure in 1935 on the eve of Italy's invasion of Abyssinia, strengthened during the Spanish Civil War, and made permanent in 1937 while Japan ravaged China—forbade the sale of munitions and the granting of loans to belligerents.

The president was not the hot-eyed warmonger depicted by his isolationist critics, and he hoped as desperately as they that the United States would not be drawn into the impending conflict. But he foresaw with considerably more clarity than they what the consequences to this country would be of an Axis domination of Europe. He knew that the rigidities of the Neutrality Act had done infinitely more harm to the victims of aggression than to the aggressors in Ethiopia, Spain, and China.

In mid-May the president summoned House leaders to the executive mansion and told them that in his opinion, repeal of the arms embargo would make an Axis victory less likely if war occurred, indeed, might even prevent war.

His words fell on deaf ears. Representative Hamilton Fish of New York, one of the more vociferous of the isolationists, told the House that what the president suggested would "make the United States the slaughterhouse and arsenal of all nations, particularly Great Britain."

Hoping to foster Anglo-American friendship, Roosevelt persuaded King George VI and Queen Elizabeth to pay a state visit to the United States in June. The occasion stirred suspicions in the isolationist breast of Congressman George Tinkham that while the two ruling families munched hot dogs at a picnic at Hyde Park, "an entente of military understanding" had been "secretly forged" between the two countries.

During those terminal weeks of peace Britain and France, ill prepared for war, were buying planes, guns, ammunition, and other supplies from America. But if war came, they would be cut off as belligerents under the Neutrality Act. Failing to obtain outright repeal, Roosevelt and his administration strove to have the act amended so that the hard-pressed democracies might buy our weapons and war matériel on a cash-and-carry basis, whereby the buyers transported the goods in their own ships and paid for them in hard cash. The provision would have been particularly beneficial to Great Britain with its powerful navy, big merchant marine, and large gold reserves.

Roosevelt believed with Secretary of State Hull that Hitler would strike in September, and on July 18 he invited Vice President John N. Garner and Senate leaders to the White House for a frank discussion of the steadily worsening European situation. The senators were warned of war's imminence and of the urgency of a cash-and-carry amendment to help the democracies. The response of isolationist Senator William Borah was characteristic. "There will be no war this year," he said, adding with startling insolence, "I have my own sources of information and they are superior to those of your State Department," whereupon Garner turned to the president and said, "Well, Captain, we may as well face the facts. We haven't got the votes, and that's all there is to it."

Wearily Roosevelt replied that he believed he had done his best and that the Senate would have to shoulder the responsibility for refusing to take action to protect the nation's security.

Congress adjourned on August 5 without having changed its mind about the Neutrality Act, and the president went to Campobello on vacation.

Through the rest of the month the air remained filled with tension and dread. Yet, locally and nationally, the familiar concerns of a noncrisis world continued to occupy us all.

Crowds swarmed the World's Fair in New York, displaying an almost morbid curiosity in the Polish pavilion and freely patronized the gorgeous Italian pavilion, which featured an excellent restaurant. The Yankees, behind the bat of a gentleman with the euphonious Italian name of Joe Di Maggio, led the American League and held the attention of the baseball world.

On Broadway *Hellzapoppin,* a wacky musical comedy, did a brisk business with summer visitors. Block-long lines formed outside a movie theater to see

Judy Garland and friends—the Tin Woodman, the Scarecrow, and the Cowardly Lion—in *The Wizard of Oz.*

The looming crisis had not yet affected prices. I bought the kids a 78 rpm recording of the nation's number one song hit—Judy Garland's "Over the Rainbow"—for thirty-five cents. Needing a summer-weight Palm Beach suit while August was at its stickiest, I found one at Weber and Heilbroner's for $15.50 including minor alterations. The real estate agent through whom we had rented our house thought I might be interested in buying a house and offered me a white stucco two-story affair on a hillside lot on Bronxville's Sagamore Road, diagonally opposite from a mansion owned by Ambassador Joseph Kennedy, for a mere $8,800. I wasn't yet ready for home ownership, nor did I yet want to own a car, but a local used car dealer tried to talk me into one for $625. Fond of Thomas Wolfe, I bought his new best seller, *The Web and the Rock,* at our Main Street bookstore for $3.95.

Meanwhile, at Newport News, the president's wife, Eleanor Roosevelt, christened the *America,* the biggest merchant vessel ever built in the United States. The president's mother, Sara Roosevelt, her European tour cut short, arrived on the liner *Washington,* posed for photographers, and was borne away to Hyde Park in a limousine. Twenty-one passengers returning from Europe on Pan American Airways' American Clipper, one of the great flying boats then in service, told excitedly of "feverish" defense preparations abroad.

The isolationists still held sway. In St. Louis a radio station cut off news commentator Dorothy Thompson when she dared criticize Adolf Hitler. In Boston delegates to the annual encampment of the Veterans of Foreign Wars applauded Senator Henry Cabot Lodge and Marine Major General Smedley Butler when they called for a neutrality policy strong enough to keep America out of any European war. Americans should be allowed to fight, the feisty Butler shouted, for only two things, "defense of their homes, and the Bill of Rights."

The INS office in New York was a bedlam of clattering teletypewriters. From our London Bureau came word that the House of Commons cheered Prime Minister Chamberlain's pledge that Great Britain intended to resist Nazi aggression. A dispatch from Moscow said the Russians were massing troops along the country's western frontiers. Did this mean, we wondered, that the Soviets were preparing to fight Germany?

As the pawns on the European chessboard moved into position in preparation for Armageddon, the place of only one major European power remained unclear. That power was the Soviet Union, with which the British and the French tried desperately through the spring and summer to form an anti-German alliance.

When the negotiations began back in April, the Russians had favored a triple alliance of Britain, France, and the USSR which would have guaranteed the Baltic States—Lithuania, Latvia, and Estonia—as well as Poland and Romania. The Anglo-French negotiators, clinging to what was left of international propriety, refused to throw Poland and the Baltic States to Stalin as they had recently thrown Czechoslovakia to Hitler. But since the Poles, in 1920, had conquered far more territory than the Allies had meant them to have, pushing their eastern border deep into White Russia, almost to Minsk, the Anglo-French scruples seemed to the Soviets needlessly delicate.

The Russians did not relish having Germans launch an attack on them from a point as far east as Minsk. They feared, too, and with reason, that what the British and French really wanted was for Russia to take the brunt of a Nazi attack. They considered it an affront that the British had sent a Foreign Office career official as negotiator to Moscow whereas the prime minister himself had thrice flown personally to Germany to treat with Hitler.

Waving aside Anglo-French pleas, the Soviets signed a treaty of nonaggression and friendship with Hitlerite Germany instead. The Nazi-Soviet Pact of August 23, 1939, stupefied the world. Communism and nazism, supposedly ideological opposites, had come together. The pact was recognized as the signal for war as all last-minute negotiations failed.

The news had a shattering effect in the ranks of the radical left in the United States. The discovery that their immaculate Communist motherland had bedded down with the Beast of Berlin was more than most left-wingers and fellow travelers could stomach. Thousands of converts traded their faith for outright revulsion and abandoned the party as well as the creed.

When I telephoned my Socialist father in Philadelphia and told him what had happened, he was speechless for fully a minute, then said: "I never trusted Stalin, but frankly I didn't think he'd do anything like this. It only proves that his regime is as wrongheaded as Mussolini's and Hitler's. Birds of a feather. Red fascism, black fascism, brown fascism. They're all alike. But mark my words: Hitler will turn on Stalin someday. . . ."

The Germans invaded Poland on September 1, 1939. Britain and France were now bound to come to Poland's aid. In a last desperate hope they waited two more days, and during the lull I was on my way back to Europe. Destination: Paris.

I was to have sailed on the French liner *Normandie*; but that great ship never left New York, and on short notice INS arranged for me to fly from Port Washington in the early forenoon of September 1. I had packed some days before and prepared Kathryn and the boys for my departure, telling them untruthfully that I was sure there would be "another Munich" and that therefore, I would certainly be home by Christmas. Tommy and Sean seemed reassured, but not Kathryn. She knew, as I did, that we probably faced a long separation.

On the slip at Port Washington, I held Kathryn in my arms a long moment, kissed the boys, and stepped aboard the flying boat that was to take me on the greatest adventure of my life, the second European war in a generation, soon to become a world war.

21

AND SO TO WAR

In the hiatus between uncertain peace and undeclared war, the Clipper hopscotched across the Atlantic toward neutral Portugal. It was a splendid aircraft, stable in flight and much like an airborne yacht with every imaginable comfort (except showers) for about thirty passengers, although on this trip it carried fewer than half that number. Shortly after takeoff, seated in groups of four at tables in the salon amidships, we lunched on jellied consommé, roast beef with Yorkshire pudding, a green salad, vanilla ice cream, and excellent coffee.

The passengers included only four Americans—Ned Buddy, a Pathé News executive, and his cameraman, Arthur Menken; Rolland Gardner, an architect with headquarters in Paris; and myself. The others were a mixed bag of uncommunicative foreign diplomats and two elderly, expensively gowned women. One was Schiaparelli, the famous Parisian couturiere, and the other a mysterious lady in severe black traveling incognito. Both kept to themselves throughout the journey and successfully resisted my efforts to interview them.

Flying only during daylight hours, we made a first overnight stop in Bermuda and a second, the following day, at Horta, in the greenish brown Portuguese island group known as the Azores. Early the next morning, September 3, 1939, we took off for Lisbon, and several hours later, at precisely 11:15 A.M. ship's time, word came over the plane's radio that Britain and France, true to their pledges to Poland, had declared war against Germany. But there was no turning back. Both Europe and the Clipper had passed the point of no return, and Captain Winston, an unforgettably handsome man who might easily have doubled for Clark Gable, kept his big four-motor craft on course for Lisbon.

As we cruised at eight thousand feet above the ocean in dazzling sunlight, the journey was as comfortable and pleasant as any I had ever experienced on one of Europe's crack trains. But exhausted by days of tension and restless nights at the Pan American hostels in Bermuda and Horta, I was still asleep when Ned Buddy thrust his blond head through the curtains of my Pullman-like berth, shook me awake, and croaked excitedly, "Wake up, Frank. It's started. As of right now, Britain and France are at war with Germany."

I thanked Ned drowsily and turned over, but sleep would not return. I was excited, yes, but neither surprised nor alarmed. I lay in my bunk for a while, thinking nostalgically of home and family and remembering that almost up to the moment of my departure Kathryn had insisted that she and the boys should accompany me to Europe. In her understandable desire to keep the family intact come what may, she had envisioned a cottage somewhere in the English countryside or, preferably, in her ancestral Ireland, where she and the children would live while I "commuted" to the war! A lovely, romantic, and utterly impractical idea against which I argued hotly, and I was happy now that I had prevailed.

I rose, dressed hurriedly, and at one of the tables in the ship's salon typed a brief note to Kathryn on Clipper stationery in which I said, among other things, that I had not been shocked by the news from London and Paris. "Actually," I wrote, "I felt as though I had at last solved a complex problem in calculus after a long involvement in mathematical formulae."

Shortly afterward Captain Winston began his descent, and we could see luminous pastel-colored Lisbon framed in the ship's side windows. As we descended, we overflew the anchored vessels of many nations, neutrals and belligerents. One of the latter, a rusty old freighter, flew the ugly bright red and black swastika flag of Nazi Germany.

Winston brought the Clipper down to a smooth landing on the pale waters of the Mar de Palha, the wide estuary of the Tagus River, then taxied upriver to the landing slip in the heart of the city, aglow now in the blazing late-afternoon sun. We had been in the air twenty-six hours—five from New York to Bermuda, fourteen from Bermuda to Horta, and seven from there to the Portuguese capital.

At the dock the uniformed Portuguese officials who examined our passports seemed puzzled that we should be coming to Europe when so many Europeans were clamoring to leave it. The place was crowded with people seeking passage on westbound Clippers, for Lisbon had become Europe's escape hatch and overflowed with refugees. Many were Jews who had managed to escape from Austria and Czechoslovakia ahead of the advancing Nazis.

The flight from the east had quickly assumed the proportions of an exodus, a sudden, unheralded arrival of tens of thousands of frightened, unhappy people in search of safety, food, and shelter. Some came without passports or papers of identification, but to Portugal's credit very few were refused entry although not all who sought admission were genuinely in flight. All besieged the offices of shipping companies in an effort to get away either to the United States or to South America. Queues waited hours, from daybreak until nightfall for vacant berths on ships. Fantastic sums were offered for space; as much as five hundred dollars were being bid for a third cot in a two-berth cabin.

Refugees with means filled the better bars and hotel lounges and created, by their presence and strange languages, an atmosphere of mystery, intrigue, and fear. The newcomers were French, Germans, Belgians, Poles, Czechs, Romanians, Bulgarians, Dutch, Austrians, and others, including a sprinkling of Americans and Britons. They ran the gamut of occupations from displaced cabinet ministers to mere adventurers with bejeweled mistresses. Generally, however, they were a tragic lot who wanted only to get away from old Europe and its blackouts, its promise of bombs and hardships and death, and to begin new lives in some faraway place in the New World, preferably in the United States of America.

Lisbon was already a haven for one of war's major growth industries, espionage. Spies had been gathering in the Portuguese capital since before the Anschluss, and now they and the wealthier fugitives filled the city's better hotels as well as the even more luxurious hostelries of nearby Estoril, a sort of Portuguese Monte Carlo where Italian and German agents touched sleeves at the gaming tables with their British and French counterparts, Turkish merchants, Greek shipping magnates, and Swiss bankers.

In the princely Restaurant Avis, in Estoril, where Ned Buddy and I dined that evening, we saw rich Jews, identifiable by their reserved manners and furtive glances, and self-important Gestapo agents in mufti. My companion, new to Europe, was impressed that I could spot the Nazis, but it was easy: They wore small swastika buttons in the lapels of their well-cut jackets and ostentatiously smoked expensive cigars with their brandies.

Early the next morning Buddy, Menken, Gardner, and I hastened in a body to Cook's to try to obtain accommodations on the Sud Express leaving Lisbon at 3:10 P.M. that day for Irún, on the Franco-Spanish frontier, where we hoped to connect with a Paris-bound train the following day. The travel agency's office, a biggish room with a long mahogany counter at the far end, was jammed wall to wall with Europeans bidding for space on ships bound for England, the United States, Brazil, Argentina—anywhere away from Europe. It was bedlam. People waved sheafs of banknotes and documents as they tried to elbow or bribe their way forward toward the few harassed clerks behind the counter.

We milled about in the hot, crowded room for nearly two hours before Gardner, in fluent and authoritative Portuguese, succeeded in enlisting the services of one of the clerks, who, encouraged by the promise of a substantial tip, provided us with two double compartments on the wagons-lits to Irún. But he could do nothing for us beyond that point.

"The French," he said, "have closed their border."

This was bad news. How would we get to Paris?

"Don't worry," said Gardner. "I have friends at Hendaye."

Buddy and Menken looked blank, but I was relieved. I recalled that during the Spanish Civil War Hendaye, just across the International Bridge from Irún, was where in the early autumn of 1936 the pro-Franco British ambassador to Spain, Sir Henry Chilton, had set up his embassy in a grocer's shop after Franco's Nationalists had driven the Republicans out of the Basque country. Like St.-Jean-de-Luz, farther up the coast, it was a black-market center where, for a price, anything could be had from a forged passport to a carload of small arms. The town was famous also for a pale, potent liqueur called Fleurs de Hendaye.

"My friends will organize something," Gardner assured us. "If there's no train for Paris out of Hendaye, there might be a bus. Or we could hire a car. Hell, I'll buy one if we must. . . ."

Gardner, a balding, soft-spoken man in his early forties with a paunch, soft hands, an ingratiating smile, and a gift for languages—he was as fluent in Spanish and French as he was in Portuguese and English—suddenly acquired new stature in our eyes. Buddy and Menken were typical newsreel men—tough, cynical, and virtually monolingual—and, like myself, had hitherto been inclined to look upon Rolland Gardner as something of a nuisance, an effete American Francophile who had attached himself to us uninvited. We now regarded him as our potential savior. Moreover, he knew Paris as well as the rest of us knew Manhattan.

In Portugal, as in Spain, trains rarely left on time. Surprisingly enough, however, the Sud Express departed promptly at 3:10 P.M. on September 4 and by nightfall had crossed the narrow butt end of the Iberian Peninsula and arrived at Elvas, a green and pretty town, untouched by the war that had raged ten miles east at Badajoz. There we were boarded by Franco's dour customs guards, who searched our baggage and our persons and might have invalidated our Spanish visas but for the ingratiating ways of Rolland Gardner and his skill in appeasing the inquisitors' venality with a carton of Camel cigarettes.

Despite the rude welcome at Badajoz, I was happy to be on Spanish soil again. Like other travelers who have visited Spain before Portugal, I infinitely preferred the former as more vital, though dirtier. Spain, not Portugal, had produced Velázquez and Goya. The Portuguese I had seen in Lisbon and Estoril had looked pale and docile, bearing little resemblance to the great mariner ancestors that had given them an empire. They had bowed easily to fascism under António de Oliviera Salazar, whereas the Spanish had fought for nearly three years to preserve their republic.

Rolland Gardner, my roommate—since he was more than ten years my senior and decidedly unathletic, I had yielded him the lower berth in our compartment—shared my excitement about being in Spain again. But we were destined to see very little of it during our jouncy, bouncy, sooty nightlong journey northward from Badajoz, with innumerable unexplained stops between stations, via Cáceres, Salamanca, and León to Oviedo, then eastward along the coast of the Bay of Biscay to Irún, where we arrived only three hours late shortly after noon on September 5. There our troubles began in earnest. Franco's frontier guards were as reluctant to allow us to leave the country as his minions at Badajoz had been unwilling to permit us to enter it.

In the drab, bullet-pocked customs shed—Irún had been stoutly defended by the Republicans until it fell to the Nationalists on September 4, 1936—the overzealous guards inspected the contents of our luggage item by item, including the soiled linen. They were particularly interested in Menken's two cameras—one for stills and a 16 mm Mitchell for movies—and my brand-new lightweight Swiss-made Hermès portable typewriter, which I had bought in New York on the eve of my departure. They demanded papers proving that the cameras and the typewriter had been purchased abroad, not in Spain. If we were unable to produce such documents, the cameras and typewriter, they said, were subject to confiscation or payment of an exorbitant "export tax."

Noting that I was about to explode with anger at the outrageous demands, Gardner quietly intervened. He asked to see the officer in charge and was reluctantly conducted to an inner room, where he remained for nearly half an hour. When he emerged, preceded by the smartly uniformed young comandante, both smiling affably, I knew we would soon be on our way, and we were. In fact, two of the comandante's men were ordered to help us carry our baggage across the bridge to Hendaye. There the French douaniers greeted us warmly and directed us to a nearby restaurant, where we found clean rest rooms for a much-needed washup and welcome food and drink at a sidewalk table shaded from the blazing early-afternoon sun by a striped awning.

Buddy, Menken, and I assumed that Gardner had paid dearly for our passage to freedom, and offered to share the cost. Gardner smiled.

"It didn't cost me a sou," he said. "To begin with, this particular officer was incorruptible. Moreover, he was a reasonable man, and when I explained to him that the cameras and the typewriter were the tools of your trade as journalists, he seemed to understand. But what touched him was the magic word 'Paris.'

"His younger sister had married a local Rojo—a Red—meaning, of course, a Republican, and when the Nationalists captured Irún three years ago, she fled with her husband and the city's thousands of citizens across the International Bridge to Hendaye. He showed me her picture, a beautiful girl of twenty or so. He had had one letter from her from Paris, but not a word since. They were very close as children in Burgos, and now he and she are the only ones left of their small family. Their parents died recently, and an older brother was killed during the war fighting for Franco's Nationalist Blancos.

"The comandante gave me his sister's name and the only address he had for her in Paris. I promised to do everything I could to locate her and to let him know, through the Red Cross or by whatever means possible—a messenger, if necessary—how she is faring. And I will, too. I've got connections in Paris. . . ."

As he had indicated in Lisbon, Rolland Gardner also had "connections" in Hendaye. After confirming that regular train service to Paris had been suspended and that all of Hendaye's buses had been requisitioned by the French Army, still in its early stages of mobilization, he went off in search of a garage owner with whom, he said, he had "done business from time to time." He returned within the hour with a squat, sturdy-looking, grizzled Basque in a blue beret and clean gray coveralls whom he introduced as Meurice.

Meurice, it developed, had a big Citroën touring car in good running order with new Michelin tires which he offered to rent us, with himself as chauffeur, for five hundred dollars plus the cost of gasoline, oil, and incidentals en route, *tout compris.* We readily agreed. The trip would cost us, we figured, not much more than first-class accommodations on the *train de luxe* that ran no longer, and we set off for Paris that same afternoon, September 5, after stocking the car with bread, sausages, cheese, wine, bottled Évian, and a flask of Fleurs de Hendaye.

To avoid the military traffic and the southward flow of refugees on the main highway (A-63), Meurice wisely headed northward along the narrow coastal road to Arcachon, where we stopped shortly after nightfall to dine on the town's famous oysters and a fine fish soup.

Late that moonless night we pulled into blacked-out Bordeaux, a silent, gloomy city, whose citizens moved about lighting their way with flashlights. There were few people in the almost deserted streets, however, and those we passed walked with stooped shoulders, a dejected-looking lot carrying gas masks in black tin cylinders. The silence was broken only by the beep-beep of an occasional auto horn and the hurrying heel sounds of pedestrians. It struck me that the French had lost the war before it had really begun.

Meurice, who knew the city well, groped his way about in the blackout from one hotel to another. Every one of them—the Grand, the Normandie, the Splendide—was *complet,* full up. No rooms anywhere, not even in the second-class hotels. Our driver, however, had a solution: Madame Michaud's place, a bordello on the northern outskirts of the city, just off the main road to Paris. He assured us we would be welcome there.

The establishment smelled of cheap perfume and Lysol, but the two rooms with double beds which Madame Michaud offered were clean, had small adjoining bathrooms, complete with bidets, and were unoccupied. Their occupants had taken the night off, and Madame Michaud, a well-formed, bosomy woman in her middle fifties with red hair and the suggestion of a mustache on her upper lip, was only too happy to accommodate the American clients of her *cher ami* Meurice. Judging by the looks exchanged between her and our chauffeur, none of us doubted with whom *he* would spend the night. Gardner and I shared one room, Buddy and Menken the other, leaving word with Madame before retiring that we be awakened for an early start.

I was almost asleep when I felt the bed shaking perceptibly and heard Gardner chuckling. To my muttered inquiry about what the hell was so funny, he replied, laughing: "How are you going to explain to your good wife in

America that you spent your first night in wartime France in a whorehouse in Bordeaux?"

Meurice again chose the less traveled secondary roads for the daylong journey from Bordeaux to Paris mainly, he said, because gasoline would be easier to find. We crossed the broad Gironde at Libourne and continued by way of Périgueux and Limoges, where we stopped for lunch, then on to Paris via Châteauroux, Vierzon, Orléans, Étampes, and Arpajon. The route lengthened the trip by at least a third, but we traversed a France tourists rarely saw, a green and pleasant countryside of farmers tilling well-kept fields, harvesting crops, or tending vineyards already heavy with fruit.

My memory of that seemingly endless ride—it was past midnight in the small hours of September 7 when we reached the outskirts of Paris—is a montage of the spires and domes of the cathedrals and abbeys we passed at Périgueux, Limoges, and Orléans and, in between, of cavalry patrols trotting from farm to farm requisitioning draft horses; of old women and mere boys pasting mobilization orders on telephone poles and walls; of women in black placing flowers on monuments to the dead of the Great War in every town and village we passed; of shawled young women praying at wayside shrines; of men in civilian clothes but wearing heavy hobnailed military shoes with fiber suitcases at their feet sitting at tiny marble-topped tables with their girls or their wives and children at cafés near railway stations, not smiling, waiting.

The remembrance, only slightly dimmed by time, is of France, bled white by the Great War of 1914–1918, preparing to go to war again for the second time in a generation, but quietly, almost reluctantly, it seemed to me, an impression that was confirmed over and over again in palpably nervous, blacked-out Paris, where we found our way to *centre ville* and my hotel, the France et Choiseul, in the Rue St.-Honoré, only by following the silvery ribbon of the Seine.

Paris had the jitters. Autos filled with people and baggage were rushing out of town, hoping to beat the daytime traffic jams. In the darkness there were many collisions, cars scraping one another, men cursing and arguing as only Latins can. The streetlamps, hurriedly splashed with bluish paint, gave only a dim, ghostly light, and pedestrians lighted their way, as in Bordeaux, by turning their flashlights on and off as they went.

Because I had stayed at the France et Choiseul several times before, the concierge found me a room. Gardner said he was within walking distance of his apartment, Menken and Buddy were going on to the Hôtel Scribe, where most foreign correspondents were staying, and a red-eyed Meurice said he was turning right around and heading for home. He left as soon as we had settled our accounts with him, and the rest of us had our last drink together, successive swigs from what remained of the sticky-sweet Fleurs de Hendaye.

Of my three American companions, the only one I ever saw again was Menken, whom I met years later, in Rome. Whether Rolland Gardner found the sister of the Nationalist comandante at Irún, I never learned. I like to think that he did, but I believe that like thousands of other victims of Spanish fascism, the young woman and her husband wound up in a camp for Republican refugees somewhere in France and were overtaken by the tragic events that followed.

The sudden blast of an air-raid siren bounced me out of bed at noon. The sound rose to a shrill crescendo but lasted only a few seconds and subsided to a low, distant growl. A test, obviously, but nonetheless scary when heard for the first time. Wide-awake after five or six hours' sleep, I rang for breakfast.

The elderly waiter who brought rolls, butter, marmalade, and tepid café au lait confirmed that the sirens were tested daily at twelve o'clock. I noticed that he was wearing his wartime medals on a small enameled metal bar in the lapel of his frayed frock coat. Yes, he said, he had fought in the last one—years of mud and *merde,* he said—and early that very morning, before coming to work, he had accompanied his only son to the Gare de l'Est, where the men were departing for the Maginot Line. I encouraged him to tell me what he had seen at the *gare.*

"It was not like when I went to war in 1914," he said. "*Tout est changé.* There's not the same esprit. No bands playing, no flowers, no flags. Only fathers, mothers, wives, and sisters saying their good-byes, crying a little, waving handkerchiefs as the trains pulled out. . . ."

I could see he didn't want to talk and let him go. But later, after I had showered and dressed and he came to collect the tray, he opened up a little. Few Frenchmen, he said, were thrilled about going to war again. He reminded me that only twenty-five years ago almost to the day, in September 1914, he himself had been among the hundred thousand troops rushed to the front in taxicabs and buses to help Marshal Joffre stop the Boche at the Marne.

"The last time," he said, "we fought to save France, to save Paris. But now we fight for . . . for . . . Danzig? I don't even know exactly where it is. Last time we fought for *liberté.* Today we fight for Daladier. *Pas la même chose. Tout est changé . . .* "

It took me nearly an hour of walking to reach the INS offices in the Rue Caumartin. The few buses in circulation were filled to overflowing, and there were no taxis. Many had been requisitioned by the army, and others had been hired to take Parisians out to the country. Since the government had requested everyone who could to leave Paris, the evacuation which had begun even before France formally declared war was still in progress. The streets were bumper to bumper with taxis and private cars piled high with baggage, babies' cribs, bedding, and boxes stuffed with food.

The luggage shops were doing a brisk business, as were the news vendors at the kiosks. Buyers snapped up copies of Léon Blum's *Populaire* and the two Communist dailies, *L'Humanité* and *Le Soir.* Posters were pasted on walls everywhere. One, entitled APPEL IMMÉDIAT, summoned Frenchmen to arms. Another, headed AVIS À LA POPULATION, warned that "enemy bombs may be *redoubtable*"—a euphemism for horrendous—told the people what to do in the event of a gas attack, and instructed them about blackout procedures.

It was the Parisian midday break for lunch, and the sidewalks were crowded with people, nearly all of whom carried gas masks, slung over shoulders or stuffed into handbags. Conscripts in uniform and steel helmets hurried through the crowds, lugging the blanket rolls and bundles of socks and handkerchiefs they had been ordered to bring from home. Brasseries and cafés were filled, mostly with older Frenchmen, talking, arguing over beers or Pernods.

I stopped at a brasserie for a beer and eavesdropped. The phrase I heard most often was: "*Eh bien! Maintenant il faut en finir* [This time we must put an end to it]." Neither on that occasion nor on many similar ones during my sojourn in Paris did I hear a Frenchman utter the words *democracie* or *fascisme.* The French, it seemed to me, were not going to war to save democracy or to extirpate fascism but merely to fight an old enemy: Germany, the Boche. I heard no echoes of the Gallic patriotism I had read so much about.

Kenneth Downs, the INS Paris Bureau chief, was expecting me. Unlike most newspapermen, he smoked cigars instead of cigarettes, and I found him in a cloud of blue postluncheon smoke in his inner office. He was a stubby westerner from Montana with straight brown hair, an inscrutable smile, and a curt manner.

"Cable for you," he said. "Came in this morning."

The wire was from Barry Faris and instructed me to report to Bill Hillman in London.

"I thought I was going to work out of Paris," I said, adding somewhat lamely, "I was supposed to replace Knickerbocker when he returned to the States to lecture."

"Yes, I know," said Ken. "But there's been a change in plans since you left New York. Knick is staying on to cover the war. INS wouldn't let him off the hook. After all, he's our biggest by-line. . . ."

Ken could have added, with reason, that it had been presumptuous on my part to think that I could have filled Knick's shoes. But he didn't, and I was grateful.

Nevertheless, I was shaken. I realized I had made a bad bargain with the Hearst Organization and was tempted to quit then and there, but I decided to wait until I got to London and could communicate more easily with my agent, Hal Matson, and, perhaps, *Collier's.*

I left for London on the boat train from the noisy, chaotic Gare du Nord at 11:50 A.M. the next day, September 8, crossed the Channel through a cordon of British destroyers, and arrived at Victoria Station in the early evening. A telephone call to the INS office in Fleet Street informed me that I had been booked into the modest Strand-Palace.

During the taxi ride to the hotel I saw that the English were taking the war far more seriously than the French. The blackout in London was the real thing, much blacker than in Paris and rigorously respected. Not a pinpoint of light anywhere, yet the traffic of double-decker buses, private cars, army vehicles, and taxis moved smoothly, without incident. Londoners, too, I noted, were carrying gas masks, and most also had their tin hats.

After checking into the hotel, where I had a room without bath that was little more than a glorified broom closet, I groped my way down the Strand and up Fleet Street to the INS offices in Chronicle House. At one corner, a woman's voice called out, "Hello, darling," and its owner lit up her painted face with her flashlight.

"Not tonight, lovey," I said, and hurried on, looking for the entrance to the Falstaff, my favorite pub. I found it and ducked in. I needed a quick drink, an old friend even more.

The long bar was crowded with Fleet Streeters, none of whom I knew well enough to speak to, much less confide in. The air was filled with newsmen's lamentations of the botch the Ministry of Information was making of its handling of the war news. I listened while sipping my sherry, then reemerged into the blackout for the short walk to Chronicle House and what I hoped would be a friendly meeting with Hillman.

Hillman quickly confirmed my growing suspicion that the arrangement I had worked out with the Hearst Organization through Joe Connolly had foundered on the rocks of office politics. INS had no definite assignment for me, he indicated, except a return to duty on London's cable desk. Thus tied down, I would be unable to fulfill my obligations to *Cosmopolitan*. I was sure, now, that I had been a fool not to have accepted the *Collier's* offer. I returned to my hotel in a dark mood and spent a sleepless night berating myself for my cupidity.

The next morning I sent the cable that changed the course of my career. It was addressed to Charles Colebaugh, the managing editor of *Collier's*, whom I had met briefly in New York, and it said, simply: IF YOU STILL WANT ME EYE CAN MAKE MYSELF AVAILABLE IMMEDIATELY STOP REACHABLE STRANDPALACE HOTEL REGARDS.

The magazine's reply came three days later, on the morning of September 12. It was signed by William L. Chenery, the editor in chief, as well as by Colebaugh, and appointed me Western European correspondent on the same generous terms they had offered originally in midsummer.

I wired my acceptance, cabled the good news to Kathryn and Hal Matson, and hurried down to the INS offices to inform Bill Hillman that I was quitting and why. He expressed neither surprise nor regret but wished me good luck and slyly confided that he, too, was contemplating a major change in his own career. (I later learned that he had been secretly negotiating with *Collier's* for some time and in mid-October became the magazine's Mr. Fixit as general European manager.) *Collier's* subsequently reimbursed INS for my travel expenses and deposited fifteen hundred dollars to my credit in Barclay's Bank for my current needs.

I celebrated my new job and its welcome affluence by moving from my stuffy little room in the Strand-Palace into an airy room in the Dorchester, in Mayfair's Park Lane, where I had a fine view of green Hyde Park, and could watch the army's sappers installing antiaircraft guns and giant searchlights and digging trenches. The first of the many barrage balloons designed to protect London from low-level bombing already floated lazily in the blue September sky, turning slowly in the light wind. They resembled tethered hippos and seemed unequal to the task for which they were intended, but they provided, nonetheless, a vague sense of security in a suddenly uncertain world.

Having said farewell to daily journalism and its Damoclean deadlines, I had time now to revisit the London I had known back in 1935, explore it more extensively than I ever had, and get the "feel" of England's greatest city at war. I was disappointed at first. At the National Gallery the Gainsboroughs and Van Dycks were gone into safekeeping, and I strolled through empty halls past discolored squares and oblongs where the pictures had hung. At Buckingham Palace the sentries had mothballed their red coats and shakos, and they mounted guard in utilitarian khaki battle dress minus hordes of tourists with cameras.

By taxicab and afoot I visited what earlier had been for me terra incognita, the East End: Aldgate, Whitechapel, Bethnal Green, Stepney, Wapping, Limehouse, and the curiously named Isle of Dogs. They were (and still are) working-class neighborhoods of monstrous rows of serried two-story houses, one exactly like the other, not unlike those of my South Philly boyhood, but much smaller and infinitely more like mere hovels. They housed the men and women who worked in nearby factories and the draymen, dockers, and porters who toiled on the Thames's numerous docks.

The area that fascinated me most, possibly because of its odd name, was the Isle of Dogs, a peninsula formed where the Thames makes a large loop as it winds southward around Stepney and Limehouse before resuming its eastward course to the sea. An old history of London informed me that the isle took its name from the fact that King Henry VIII and several monarchs before him kept their hounds there.

In 1939 it was where the figurative Master Henry Hawkins—'Ennery 'Awkins to his pals—had lived in a sooty brick receptacle he called 'ome until Chamberlain declared war on Adolf Hitler. On that day 'Ennery was removed to a safe place in the country, out of reach of the anticipated bombs, along with nearly seven hundred thousand other children from London's slums. Simultaneously the English language acquired a new word—evacuees—and the English society a new problem, one of such poignancy that not even British understatement could disguise it as anything less than the beginning of a major social revolution.

The great evacuation was a colossal task, ably accomplished in fewer than three days by the London County Council under the direction of the hard-nosed socialist member of Parliament Herbert Morrison. But restrained, polite enthusiasm and self-congratulatory exclamations of "Mahvelous! Simply mahvelous!" subsided quickly when the expected German bombs failed to come. Dr. Goebbels had scared the British into believing that London's skies would be filled with thousands of Nazi bombers dropping steel-encased death, fire, and destruction the moment war came. When the bombs failed to come, Britain's moneyed ruling classes, playing hosts to those hitherto separated from them by the rigid walls of birth, education, and money, had time to reflect.

The correspondence columns of the *Times* were soon filled with letters expressing annoyance, regrets, exasperation, even disgust at the sudden dose of sociological medicine Chamberlain had forced down their throats in the national emergency. Following the first flush of emotional satisfaction at what they had undertaken, Britain's upper classes discovered that a per diem of one shilling and sixpence (about thirty cents) for lodging individual evacuees was insufficient and loudly demanded increases. The government's evacuation bill at the time already amounted to the sterling equivalent of nearly two million dollars.

Startling truths began to emerge about the nation's social disrepair. The children had been removed from their homes so hurriedly that there had been no time for medical examinations. Some were found to be "verminous, infected with impetigo, ill-mannered and barely house-broken." The *Times* tried to disguise the fact that some children were lousy by saying their heads were "in a zoological condition."

Clearly, when Chamberlain took the final, fateful step along the road to war, he dug up the Isle of Dogs and uprooted Wapping, Limehouse, Stepney, and St. George's in East London. He scooped 'Ennery out of his house in dismal Billson Street and sent him into the green countryside, where he learned, among other things, that milk came not from bottles but was "squirted out from under blinkin' cows." The prime minister unwittingly drove a spading fork deep into the complacent greensward of the upper classes' existence and turned up clods of unpleasant things.

I took my East End findings to my friend Hugh Walpole, whom I hadn't seen since we covered the election and coronation of the pope in Rome in March. He was waiting for me in his apartment in the Athenaeum. Sir Hugh had just joined his district's air-raid patrol (ARP) unit and had his armband, white helmet, and gas mask handy. He listened to what I had to say about the deplorable conditions on the Isle of Dogs and admitted he had never seen the place.

"But don't be downhearted," he said. "This war for all its foreseeable horrors will have beneficial results for British workers: better housing, sanitation, education, everything. The children who are now in the country will learn to love the land again. Not all, certainly, but probably a great many will want to raise sheep instead of sweeping chimneys, to mow hay instead of selling newspapers at street corners, to be yeomen on the land instead of porters in Covent Garden.

"You'll see. A lot of good will come out of this war. It may be the best thing that's happened to England since the invention of the power loom that gave us the Industrial Revolution. We'll probably remake England because we've found your Master Hawkins so incredibly dirty. . . ."

When we parted, Hugh handed me a gift, a box containing the four leather-bound volumes of his *Herries Chronicle,* each with a touching inscription. I never saw him again, for when the bombs finally came some months later, there was far more work for him as an air-raid warden than his elderly heart could stand. He died on duty.

In my letter home that night, I wrote, "England is calm, determined, but grim. Its people, however, are as courteous and kind as ever, and the words 'This England' have a new meaning for me. . . . I'm happy to say that I believe I am beginning to understand this country and to love it. . . ."

22

BRITANNIA AND THE PRESS

My cabled credentials from *Collier's* included instructions to "proceed as soon as possible to the front for a vivid picture of the war." Accordingly, I applied at the newly created Ministry of Information for accreditation to the British Expeditionary Force as a war correspondent. I might as well have requested membership in Boodle's, White's, or any one of London's exclusive men's clubs, the turf of British aristocracy.

The retired Guards Brigade colonel, a red-faced man well past middle age with a formidable mustache, who received me at the ministry and examined my papers had never heard of *Collier's*. A veteran of the First World War recalled to service as a press officer, the colonel was stuffy, utterly ignorant of a journalist's needs, and clearly disinclined to be helpful. He looked upon all newspapermen as a "bloody nuisance" and regarded all foreign correspondents, including Americans, as potential spies.

"Sorry, old boy," he said, "but this will take time. *Collier's Weekly,* eh? Three million subscribers, you say. Sounds impressive. We'll see what we can do. You'll be hearing from us. You're at the Dorchester, right? Meanwhile, I suggest you learn the regulations, have your uniforms tailored, and assemble your kit. . . ."

Days passed with no word from the mustachioed colonel or anyone else at the ministry.

In the meantime, on the advice of friends, I visited Moss Bros., in New

Street, near Covent Garden, an establishment that outfitted those officers in His Majesty's forces who couldn't afford Bond Street tailoring. I spent an afternoon and about two hundred dollars there assembling the "kit" recommended by the firm's obliging clerk, a rather servile elderly man in striped pants and cutaway, who assured me he had similarly equipped a number of British correspondents headed for BEF headquarters "somewhere in France."

The kit included an off-the-rack cavalry officer's uniform complete with flaring breeches, fine leather boots, a Sam Browne belt and visored cap, plus a sleeping bag, bedroll, water bottle, and washbasin. Trying on the uniform, I looked like an older, pudgy version of the ten-year-old Philadelphia schoolboy who had pestered Papa for a "soldier suit," but minus any insignia of rank, not even the correspondent's gold-embroidered *C* that had been decreed by the ministry for the cap. What I saw in the tall mirror looked faintly ridiculous, and I was glad to resume my civvies.

I could have had the stuff I'd bought sent to my hotel but decided to take it with me in the event of a sudden summons from the colonel with the preposterous mustache. Wearing the officer's cap to reduce by one the bulky bundle I was carrying, I emerged at dusk into busy New Street and collided with a beefy territorial sergeant in battle dress. He came to a full stop, drew himself up to attention, and saluted me smartly in the stiff-fingered, waggling British manner. In a clumsy attempt to acknowledge the salute, I dropped the basin and bedroll.

"Here, let me help you, sir," the sergeant said, gathering up my gear and flagging down a passing cab. "Off to the war, I see. Well, good luck, sir," he said.

"Thanks, Sergeant," I said. "And good luck to you, pal."

The sergeant grinned broadly as he shut the cab door behind me, saluted again, and said, "Welcome aboard, Yank."

I recall a sense of embarrassment and guilt. London was full of soldiers reporting for duty or waiting to be marched off somewhere. America was still far from being "aboard." Only a few days before, on September 6, President Roosevelt had proclaimed America's neutrality, as required by law, and thereby placed an embargo on arms and munitions. Earlier, in a fireside chat to the nation, he had said, "Let no man or woman falsely talk of America sending armies to European fields."

The British had found small comfort in the news out of Washington during that lovely late summer of the September of 1939, and England's aloneness already was as real as the balloons in the sky, the protective sandbags at the entrances of the city's public buildings, the crosshatchings of gummed brown paper on its plate glass windows, and the nearly impenetrable blackouts of London's nights.

The English had known for a long time—ever since Louis Blériot flew the Channel in the summer of 1909—that they no longer lived on an island protected by a moat. In 1939 they realized that their highly concentrated population centers—London, Liverpool, Manchester, Coventry—were vulnerable to air attack. When war was declared on that unforgettable Sunday, they expected gas as well as bombs, hence the ubiquitous gas masks which even crusty old admirals and generals carried and the rectangular splotches of mustard-colored "detector paint" on His Majesty's scarlet mailboxes everywhere. The paint, it was said, would change color if there were poison gas in the air.

As a people the English hated the war and instinctively dreaded its consequences but were determined to "get on with it." This was especially true, I found, among the working class. Its members were staunchly behind the war effort, hoping the war would end in more democracy and real "people's rule" at home. They were audibly disturbed when twenty-two Laborite members of Parliament signed a manifesto calling for an early armistice as Poland began disintegrating before the might of German armor and air power.

The news from Poland, what there was of it, was all bad. By mid-September the Germans had almost reached Brest-Litovsk and surrounded Warsaw. The rapid collapse of the Poles gave rise to rumors that Britain, still too weak to make violent war, would welcome possible German offers of an armistice.

Londoners hungered for word that the BEF and the Royal Air Force were fighting back, but there was none, for between them, the War Office and the Ministry of Information had decided that this war would be a newsless episode in the history of the twentieth century. The country's great dailies were unable to provide the news the people wanted, partly because little was happening at the so-called front but mainly because of the rigid censorship under which the press operated.

Pessimistic predictions about the effects of bombings of large cities, the fact that many Conservatives in high places still admired Hitler, the determination of a substantial portion of the wealthier upper classes to escape from any unpleasantness, and the damned censorship combined to produce a lack of understanding of what the war was about. As the days stretched into weeks, there developed a palpable decline in morale and a vast, all-inclusive boredom. Foreign correspondents began describing the state of affairs as the phony war, or *Sitzkrieg,* and blamed the Ministry of Information.

The real culprits, however, were the Colonel Blimps in the War Office and their retread equivalents in the Ministry of Information, who had secretly concluded that the system for controlling news and the war correspondents would be exactly the same as in 1914–1918. There would be only a limited number of correspondents at GHQ, in France, supervised and escorted by conducting officers and allowed to send back to their papers only carefully censored dispatches on subjects unlikely to depress the morale of the folks at home. The "hard news" for the press—meaning the War Office communiqués—would be supplied by an official "eyewitness." On the important propaganda front Britain was preparing to fight the new war precisely as it had fought the old one.

This deplorable state of affairs stemmed from the Emergency Powers (Defense) Act which authorized the government to do virtually as it pleased to prosecute the war, without reference to Parliament. Every press, commercial, or private message leaving the "sceptered isle" by mail, cable, wireless, or telephone was censored. Everyone, particularly newspaper editors and correspondents, was strictly prohibited from "obtaining, recording, communicating to any other person or publishing information which might be useful to the enemy."

The rigidity of the censorship and the catholicity with which it was applied produced a memorable crisis in Fleet Street eight days after Britain and France declared war on Germany.

On Monday night, September 11, a war extra gestated on the presses of the *Times, Daily Telegraph, Daily Herald, News Chronicle,* and *Daily Express.* Trucks waited at the circulation exits of the papers' printing plants to carry the special edition to every corner of slumbering London and to waiting provincial trains.

The dailies had hard news at last, information ending the news drought that had set in since September 3: The first contingents of the British Expeditionary Force had landed in France! It was really true, therefore, that England would be fighting side by side with its Gallic ally in a struggle to the finish with Nazi Germany. The war extra was to have dispelled a widely held belief, expertly nourished by Dr. Goebbels, that Britain was ready to fight Hitler only to the last Frenchman.

But the special edition never reached its intended readers. News of the BEF landings had been cleared for release by the ministry's blue-pencil wielders at 8:52 P.M. that Monday, but at 11:38 P.M. the ministry changed its collective mind. Permission to publish the information was rescinded, and Scotland Yard was ordered to impound the war extra, which by that time had come off the presses and was ready for delivery.

The ministry's orders were as explicit and precise as a king's proclamation, and Scotland Yard did its duty. Squad cars roared out into the night. Bobbies pounced on the freshly bundled batches of ink-wet newspapers as they were being tossed onto the waiting trucks. Shouts of "Extra! Extra! Tommies Land in France!" died in the throats of those few Cockney newsboys who had managed to obtain copies. Newsies who objected were told, "Here, give us them papers. Orders, me lad. Shut your trap or in you go."

The following morning some two hundred journalists—Fleet Street editors and subeditors and a fair sprinkling of foreign correspondents, including this writer—descended upon the ministry's offices in the twenty-story gray monolith of London University, then the city's only skyscraper, demanding to know who was responsible for what a British reporter dubbed the "biggest balls-up in the history of Fleet Street."

We were received by a tall, thin, aristocratic gentleman in a winged collar, striped pants, and a morning coat who didn't know a deadline from a clothesline. He politely regretted the "unfortunate incident" but offered no acceptable explanation. Instead, he tried to entertain his restive audience with anecdotes, including one about how his cook made bread pudding.

Pressed to explain an action that had cost the morning newspapers money and prestige—the afternoon papers carried the story on September 12 and scooped their matutinal competitors on their own story—the ministry's spokesman finally suggested that news of the BEF landings in France might have given "vital information to the enemy." His astonishing reply brought a roar of laughter from the newsmen. Word of the landings, which, incidentally, had begun the day war was declared, had already been broadcast throughout most of the world on the afternoon of September 11 by the French radio.

The spokesman's recital was interrupted by Tribly Ewer, of the Labourite *Daily Herald,* dean of British diplomatic correspondents, a sardonic, beetle-browed Fleet Streeter widely respected for his outspoken criticism of Labour as well as Conservative politics. Ewer rose and made a speech that warmed the hearts of his British and American colleagues.

"Our country," he said, "is engaged in a war, not a tea party. Upon the shoulders of this ministry's censors rests the heavy responsibility of providing England and her friends with the truth of what is happening at the front and of preventing everyone concerned from becoming thoroughly bored by the war for lack of factual information."

Ewer sat down to approving shouts of "Hear! Hear!" from his British colleagues and cries of "Attaboy, Tribly!" from his American friends.

Until the night of September 11 nobody had paid much attention to the Ministry of Information, which, though planned as a shadow ministry as early as the spring of 1938, had come into being only two days before war was declared. Thereafter, however, the alert British press went to work, and when someone in the House of Commons revealed that in less than a month the ministry's staff had grown from a mere dozen to a notorious 999, Fleet Street dubbed it the "Ministry of *Nein! Nein! Nein!*," in a Germanic jibe at its negativeness, and variously referred to it thereafter as the "Ministry of Misinformation" and the "Ministry of Mysteries."

Accordingly a Public Relations Section was hastily created as part of the Intelligence Section of the BEF, and the War Office urged the major newspapers to nominate correspondents to accompany the BEF. While they were being vetted to weed out potential spies, however, "Eyewitness" would provide basic coverage.

This time "Eyewitness" was not an army officer, as in World War I, but a journalist. The man chosen for the job was Alex Clifford, formerly Reuters' chief correspondent in Germany, whom I met later in the Middle East and admired as one of the two best British correspondents of the war, the other being Alan Moorehead, of the *Daily Express.* Clifford left London on September 19 to join the BEF, but he had a thin time of it. A month passed during which he produced nothing of interest or importance for the British press and nearly went out of his mind trying to find something to write about. Apart from the fact that very little was happening, his dispatches were rendered useless by the army's overcautious field censors.

It is axiomatic that when journalists have nothing to write about, they are inclined to exercise their imaginations and engage in what was known in the trade as "sucking stories out of their thumbs." In this period, American readers were fed a steady diet of half-truths, poisoned statistics, rumors, and rumors of rumors. In American headlines the French advanced daily in the Saar but by the end of the week had "retreated to prepared positions." Phony stories appeared about a second Battle of Jutland, the breaching of Belgian dikes, the piercing of the German's Siegfried Line, and fierce dogfights over the Channel between fighter planes of the Royal Air Force and the Luftwaffe, all fairy tales to fill space and justify expense accounts.

Meanwhile, the British were still examining the credentials of applicants for accreditation and trying to decide such vital issues as whether the insignia on their uniforms should be a *C* or, as some malicious army officers insisted, a *W.C.,* the letters to be found on the doors of toilets in pubs and public buildings. In the end we were accorded a gold-embroidered *C* for our headgear and the words "War Correspondent" spelled out in gold letters on green shoulder tabs.

The Ministry of Information continued to be the target of criticism for some time, especially after members of the House of Commons disclosed that of the ministry's huge staff, only forty-odd had ever been professional journalists. The former employment of its "information experts" ranged from professorships in music appreciation to resident lectureships in Christian relations. Their ignorance of journalism and of what constituted "news" was dramatically illustrated one day when John Gunther, veteran correspondent of the *Chicago Daily News,* asked for a copy of a leaflet dropped by the RAF over Germany and was told he could not have it because publication of the text "might give the enemy vital information." Two million copies of that leaflet had been dropped on Germany. Clearly something was terribly wrong with how the British were handling their propaganda.

The days became nearly a fortnight before I got word from the red-faced colonel at the ministry that my application for accreditation to the BEF had been approved. But when the first group of fifteen British and nine American correspondents left for France on October 10, I was not among them. I complained bitterly to the colonel, who said he was sorry, but he had no transportation for me. I would have to wait a bit longer and go with the next lot, for whom, he said, he was "organizing transport, conducting officers, censors, dispatch riders, and telegraphists.

"I'll let you know," he said, "when the arrangements have been completed."

"And when might that be?" I asked.

"Sorry," he said, "military secret," and I could see he wasn't kidding.

Impatient, now, to produce the "vivid picture of the war" *Collier's* had requested, I tried the Royal Navy and was flatly told it had no room on its ships for correspondents. The Admiralty seemed intent on seeing the war through without them just as it had during World War I.

Meanwhile, I learned that the RAF, whose pamphlet raids over Germany had become the butt of jokes about how it was fighting a war called "Mein

Pamph," had created its own Press Office under Wing Commander Stanley Bishop, a former star reporter on the *Daily Express,* where I had many friends. One of them, René MacColl, had been called into service as a conducting officer under Bishop with the rank of flight lieutenant.

René had often visited me in Rome when I was stationed there for INS, and I took my case to him. He was instantly sympathetic. The RAF, he said, was anxious to have its role in the war "properly publicized," and when he offered to fly me to the Advance Air Striking Force base in France I accepted with alacrity. I would see action at last! MacColl promised to call me in a day or two, when he had assembled what he called "the proper mix of noncompetitive correspondents"—in other words, a group of reporters who would provide the broadest possible coverage.

In the meantime, the army got wind of the RAF's offer to fly reporters to France and was furious. It threatened to withdraw accreditation from any correspondent who accepted the RAF's hospitality. This deterred most British newspapers, including the *Times,* from accepting the RAF's offer, but I refused to be intimidated. I had had enough of the red-faced colonel in the Ministry of Information.

In addition to myself, MacColl's "mix" included two other Americans—the great Walter Duranty, who was British-born but represented the New York-based North American Newspaper Alliance, better known as NANA, and Bill Henry, who was doubling in brass for the *Los Angeles Times* and the Columbia Broadcasting System—and reporters from the *Daily Express,* Allied Newspapers, Reuters, the BBC, and an Australian news syndicate. The army refused to allow us to wear our correspondents' insignia in what the Australian correspondent denounced as "an unforgivable act of bureaucratic nonsense."

Minus insignia, but in uniform, we took off for France on October 12 in an old trimotor plane normally used to carry tourists back and forth between London and Paris. The plane had a fine galley amidships and an amply stocked bar, and Flight Lieutenant René MacColl proved to be an excellent host.

23

THE ELUSIVE WAR

From the plane the "war zone" was a pastoral patchwork of haystacks, grazing cows, plowed brown fields, and green meadows. Vineyards were mauve with fruit, and the chalky walls of red-roofed villages shone yellow and bronze in the late-afternoon sun. Peasants looked up from their toil, squinted skyward, and returned to harvesting grapes or digging up root crops. Neither the scars of the war called Great nor wounds of the new one were discernible. A more peaceful landscape could have been painted only by Millet.

Northward under a tumble of cloud and cyclamen-tinted mist lay the Maginot Line, built along France's eastern frontier from Luxembourg to Switzerland at a cost of five hundred million dollars, and there Frenchmen manned their guns and waited. In those days the remarkable *Ligne Maginot* seemed to ensure the peace of Western Europe. It was built of masonry and steel, a series of formidable forts connected by deep underground tunnels, and it was highly regarded as a defensive wall . . . in those days.

If the published communiqués were to be believed, the French were gnawing at German territory a bit, then returning to their fabulous *ligne* when counterattacked by the enemy. The latter, however, apparently was far too busy mopping up Poland to mount any serious attack against the French. "Stalemate" was how the "situation" was characterized for us by Lieutenant MacColl, a condition that endured for some time to come.

Why the Anglo-French air forces had not attacked the Germans while the latter advanced into Poland was not explained by MacColl or anyone else. Not a bomb fell from British or French planes; not a shot was fired in anger on the western front. This surprised and delighted the Germans, who thus had time to sharpen their warmaking skills and increase the power of their armored punch behind their western frontier.

The German line was a series of staggered interdependent positions so placed as to bring to bear a deadly crossfire on any force that penetrated the area. This was the vaunted Siegfried Line, rushed to completion since 1937 with as many as half a million men engaged in constructing it during the 1938 crisis. Though differing in construction, both the Siegfried and the Maginot had this in common: a progressive stiffening of defense against an assaulting force, with the intention of wearing it down to the point where it would be destroyed before the main fortifications had been pierced.

It was against these positions that the French armies began to move when the war began. On September 5 a French communiqué announced: "Our troops have made contact everywhere on our frontier between the Rhine and the Moselle." During the next ten days they occupied an area of about a hundred square miles within the no-man's-land between the two fortified frontiers. The advance, however, was marked by caution, a clear determination to avoid any reckless waste of life and to complete each stage of the operation before proceeding to the next. It was warfare by the book, but the Germans were rewriting the book.

By the time Polish resistance collapsed the French had taken only the advance outposts of the Siegfried Line, and the main fortifications still lay ahead. With Poland gone, Germany was free to move the bulk of its armies against the West. By mid-October a series of local offensives had been launched against the French, who scuttled back to what the communiqués called "prepared positions."

While the French were retreating, British troops were moving across the Channel in a steady stream. On October 11, the night before I left for France with MacColl's party, Leslie Hore-Belisha, Chamberlain's secretary of state for war, announced that during the five weeks since September 3 some 158,000 men had been transported to France, and he strongly implied more were on the way.

My colleagues and I aboard the transport that was taking us to the "front" therefore had every reason to believe we would see action. We did not know then and could not have known—given the rigidity of British censorship—that England's army, navy, and air force were critically short of ammunition and that Conservatives in high places were still thinking in terms of a "negotiated peace" with Hitler. With the notable exception of Winston Churchill, who now ran the Admiralty, the leadership was still in a defeatist mood. Most important, perhaps, we did not know that the Royal Air Force had been prohibited by the cabinet from bombing any enemy targets, not even German submarines!

Our pilot fired a final signal rocket in confirmation to ground crews and ackack batteries below that we were a press plane from London, not some overbrave Luftwaffe bombardier come to drop a few bombs on a British air base, and we landed bumpily on one of the new airfields which the British had improvised of metallic landing strips "somewhere in France." An impressive number of these fields, we were told, was scattered throughout the "battle zone," each so skillfully concealed as to be "invisible to the enemy." The one where we landed was invisible by virtue of being nonexistent; there were no hangars, no fighter planes arrayed wing to wing and ready for combat, no bombers being loaded for action.

Even before we were hustled into a makeshift barracks for strong tea and hard biscuits while waiting for the bus that was to take us into Rheims—where the Royal Air Force had established its headquarters—I began to doubt I would be able to produce the "vivid picture of the war" my editors wanted. There was no "war," but there were plenty of posters depicting Adolf Hitler with one oversize ear and captioned: A WOMAN LOVED, AN UNGUARDED WORD, A COMRADE DEAD, HITLER SERVED.

In the smoke-filled vehicle en route to the hotel where we would be quartered, the press officer who had taken us in hand assured us that Britain's fighter planes would prove infinitely superior to the Germans' Messerschmitts when, eventually, they went into action. There was much talk about *enemy* shortages of raw materials, particularly steel and gasoline, and about the fact that for the Germans the war had started with rationing cards for the citizenry.

We were also told that camouflage had already become one of war's major weapons and that the enemy—variously identified as the "Hun," "Jerry," or the "Boche" in the conducting officer's briefing—might find that what looked like hangars and other airfield paraphernalia from the air might really be papier-mâché dummies. The officer warned us, however, that we would not be allowed to say so in our dispatches. "Vital gen, that," he said, "strictly off the record and for your own information."

Then why tell us? I thought, but said nothing, content to be at the "front" at last.

Of the correspondents in the bus only Walter Duranty had been here before, and as we entered the outskirts of Rheims, he remembered "piles of smoldering timber and dusty mortar." The little church we had just passed on the edge of town was a rubbish heap in 1914, he said, with its crucifix askew on its battered altar.

Sitting in the back of the bus, speaking in low, nearly inaudible tones almost as though talking to himself, Duranty bemoaned the prevalent policy of drift and inaction in the leadership of the Western Allies. "France is in danger because both its flanks on either side of the Maginot Line are exposed," he said. "And Britain is in danger because it's no longer an island. The Allies have prepared to fight old-fashioned trench warfare. There won't be any. This one will be a war of tanks and planes. . . ."

The bus drew up before the town's best hotel, the Lion d'Or, where we were quickly assigned rooms and shepherded into the bar. The place was charged with cigarette smoke, laughter, and the loud babble of men all talking at once.

RAF officers in gunmetal blue uniforms were ranged two and three deep at the breast-high mahogany bar. Among them were a few British reporters in their new khaki uniforms, looking like captains but behaving like raw cadets just let out of school.

Duranty and I shouldered our way to the bar, ordered champagne, and listened to the talk around us. A young RAF flight lieutenant who might have been nineteen or twenty leaned heavily against the bar and raised his eyes to look hard at a taller, much older officer. He spoke with a public (that is, private) school accent and voiced old-school-tie ideas about war.

"Now look here," the younger man was saying, "bombing women and children is out. Why can't we fight this war properly? I don't mind dropping a few bombs on a bridgehead or a factory, old boy, but cities, no. Babies live in cities, old boy. I don't mind knocking off a few troops in trenches, if it comes to that—military objectives and all that sort of thing—but bombing women and children, no. Bad show, that."

The older man had three stripes on the cuffs of his sleeves and under his silver wings a double row of ribbons, two with encrustations that bespoke heroics in the Great War. He talked down to his junior officer in a cold, flat voice.

"Our mission in this war," he said, "is to paralyze the productive capacity of the Boche. And the only way we can do that, old son, is by bombing his production centers, meaning cities. Do you think Jerry is going to be squeamish about the doing the same to us? Remember Warsaw? Remember Barcelona?" The senior officer put his arm about the younger man's shoulders and said, "You were born four hundred years too late. You're a knight on a white horse. The days of chivalry belong to the distant past. . . ."

Arm in arm, the two pushed their way through the crowd in the bar, into the gluey yellow light of the lobby, and out into the street, headed for their mess and dinner.

MacColl's charges were dining as a group at a nearby restaurant. Duranty knew the place and knew the way. The man fascinated me. He liked to talk, especially about wars, blood, and women, and he did it extremely well, though he was, I thought, something of a name-dropper. Dorothy Thompson, Louis Fischer, Sinclair Lewis (to whom he referred as Red) and H. R. Knickerbocker were among his many friends, and all managed to enter his conversation.

I knew Duranty only through his work as the *New York Times*'s longtime Moscow correspondent. George Bernard Shaw, I had read somewhere, once described him as the "king of reporters." But his real ambition was to write fiction. He had written several short stories, one of which had earned him one of the annual O. Henry prizes. I looked up to him, however, as a sort of dean of my trade, wise, experienced, and witty. He had lost a leg in a railway accident and walked with the aid of a cane.

It was about seven-thirty o'clock when we left the Lion d'Or for the restaurant, and the shopkeepers along the main treelined street were pulling down the shutters of their shops. In the deepening darkness the clatter of falling shutters was the signal to townspeople to pull down their own blinds, draw their blackout curtains, and seal themselves into their tight little individual worlds for the night. The obliteration of all lights was rapid and systematic. French patrols clumped through the streets to make certain no lights showed.

The streets through which we walked became black caverns filled with shadowy life. Men and women moved about with the uncertainty of the newly blind, in twos and fours, rarely alone. There was a low hum of disembodied voices and the scrape, scrape of hobnailed boots against the stone paving.

A girl's laughter, sudden and startling as the unexpected tinkle of tiny bells, caused us both to stop and peer hard to see to whom the throaty music belonged. Duranty wondered aloud whether she was a blonde or brunette, adding, "Of course, there's only one way of telling, really. . . ." We never saw her but caught a whiff of perfume as she passed, her heels clicking smartly out of step with the sharp ring of a man's boots.

"Officer, probably," Walter said. "Nothing doing there. But the evening is young. Dinner, first."

A dispatch rider on a motorcycle shattered the silence into sharp fragments; then it was quiet again except for the shuffle of invisible feet. The motorcycle's headlamp made a faint bluish glow in the distance, turned a corner, and disappeared.

There were no stars and the moon was hidden by thick, low-lying clouds. The wind barely rustled the leaves of the trees that lined the street. "Good night for an air raid," Duranty said. But there was no air raid that night, not even the wail of a siren.

The light in the crowded restaurant stung the eyes after the street's blackness. The long, narrow room was filled with British colleagues who had preceded us and with RAF officers and their French counterparts sitting at long tables set end to end along three sides to form a great U. The food had not yet been served. Everyone was still drinking, talking, laughing. The atmosphere was one of collective excitement.

Oddly, only the few women in the place seemed calm. Back of the cashier's desk which dominated the room from near the entrance behind a sort of pulpit sat a black-haired Madonna with a pale face and long, tapering fingers. She handled the running of the restaurant with an amazing economy of movement, her eyes darting this way and that, speaking quietly and firmly to a platoon of pink-cheeked waitresses who bustled about in black frocks under spotless white aprons. The women all behaved as though ours were the most normal of well-regulated worlds.

The town's mayor sat with us as the guest of honor of the British and American correspondents who had come to write about the First World War of the Air. *Monsieur le maire* wanted to know "When is America coming in?" Duranty, who sat next to him and to whom he addressed the question, smiled enigmatically and shrugged.

The set meal began with a pâté, which was followed by a potage, broiled chicken, pommes frites, an assortment of undercooked vegetables, a tarte de fruits, and indifferent coffee. The wine, a red *vin du pays,* flowed freely, and so did the war talk, mostly about the last one.

The mayor, a taut little man in his thirties, didn't remember much about the Great War except that it had killed his father and two maternal uncles. He said he was worried about the sudden influx of British troops, but the RAF wing commander, who had more or less taken over the town from him, patted him affectionately on one shoulder and made a little speech.

"Ah, *mon frère,* " he said, "it is nothing. Think! In a year or two we shall all be gone, and you will stand on the steps of your Hôtel de Ville, shaking hands with me with tears in your eyes, telling me how sorry you are to see us go. And I will embrace you and tell you how sorry we are to go. . . ."

Everybody laughed and applauded.

Then the field censor, senior in rank and years to all the other British officers, rose to make a toast. He was a tallish stick of a man with four stripes on his sleeves and a burst of ribbons under his pilot's wings. He was a Scot with sparse, curly gray hair, blue eyes, and a crisp manner. He raised his glass, and everyone stood up, brimful glass in hand.

"To liberty, gentlemen, and to victory in a just cause. May it be justly won and a peace justly made. And may man never thereafter fight against man."

We all said, "Hear! Hear!" and drained our glasses.

The Scot excused himself and left early, pleading "urgent business at the base."

"That man," an officer sitting next to me confided when the Scot had gone, "fought in the last war. He went up day after day in an open cockpit plane with only a helmet and a fur-lined leather jacket to protect him from the cold. He had no machine gun. He carried a carbine, and he squeezed as many bullets as he could into the calf straps of his boots. He would sit up there doing a top speed of perhaps seventy miles an hour, and then he'd come down on a German, potting him with the carbine. He got a few that way until he was shot down himself finally. He barely managed to get his chute open in time. . . ."

The enemy didn't come that night, or the next, or the night after that. By then the threat of a raid ceased being a brain-numbing business, and gas masks and tin hats were left behind in our billets. The regulations said they had to be within five seconds' reach at all times, but we took no notice and scurried around in vain, trying to find something to write about.

The correspondents weren't allowed to visit the stations of the RAF's Advanced Air Striking Force in France, and only AASF officers were permitted to talk to air crews. Anyhow, the RAF did no "striking" while we were in Rheims, and after a week of idleness and champagne hangovers, we all were ready to return to London.

Duranty disappeared nightly, returning at dawn. On the morning before our departure he handed me a wad of francs, asked me to buy a dozen roses, and take them to a certain lady at an address on a sealed envelope.

Walter, I found, had given me money enough for *two* dozen roses, and I took them to the place he had indicated. It was the finest whorehouse in Rheims. I stayed long enough in its red-damasked salon to have coffee with the grateful lady herself. Duranty, I decided, was an incurable romantic with an excellent taste in women.

I said as much to Walter in the bus on our way to the plane that took us back to London in the early afternoon of a misty October day. He acknowledged the compliment with a wry smile and a faraway look in his eyes.

The absence of large-scale air warfare in the West was the biggest surprise of 1939. Although the RAF bomber units stationed in France were only 250 miles or so from the centers of German heavy industry engaged in making munitions—twice the distance of German planes from British factories—they were barred from attacking such targets, even troop concentrations, lest they might invite massive reprisals from the Luftwaffe.

The day war was declared, I later learned, British reconnaissance planes took seventy-five photographs of units of the German fleet. The next day twenty-eight Wellington and Blenheim bombers took off to attack the enemy ships. Seven bombers were lost in the assault, which managed, however, to damage the battleship *Admiral Scheer.* Other daylight raids were made on German naval bases, but the heavy losses incurred from both antiaircraft fire and Luftwaffe fighter patrols made them too costly to continue.

Meanwhile, the RAF's Coastal Command incessantly patrolled the coast during the harsh winter of 1939–1940, aiding materially in protecting British shipping. At the same time bombers flew over Germany as far as Berlin, dropping not bombs, however, but millions of propaganda leaflets written, Bill Shirer later told me, "in crummy German." Nevertheless, the leaflet raids provided valuable flight training for the deadly work ahead.

In drizzly London in late October 1939, with winter in the offing, the war continued to have a strange, almost dreamlike quality. Lloyd's was laying odds that it would be over by Christmas, but knowledgeable British friends were of the opinion that by the time the season of "Peace on Earth, Good Will to All Men" came around the war would be an all too active nightmare.

Gasoline rationing was already in effect, and the rationing of foodstuffs was imminent. Generous allowances were promised, and there were soothing statements from government sources that margarine was better for one's health than butter. The *Daily Express* was opposed to rationing altogether, arguing that food was plentiful and that the people should not be made to feel the pinch when there was no need.

Editorially, however, there was more talk in the newspapers about "war aims" than about ways and means of fighting and winning the war. A clue to what Englishmen were thinking about the war's objectives was provided by Commander Stephen King-Hall, purveyor of a widely read newsletter. It had conducted a survey which indicated that Britons wanted the war to result above all in "the preservation of freedom at home and abroad" and the

creation of a postwar world "freed from war through international cooperation."

Disaccredited as a war correspondent for having accepted the RAF's offer
to fly to France, I had no choice but to try to find the elusive war elsewhere.
I decided to go to Holland, which, a look at the map told me, might well be
next on Hitler's program.

The Nazi dictator's long-awaited appeal for peace, delivered on October 6,
after he and Stalin had gobbled up Poland, had made little news in London
since it was no more or no less than was expected. Speaking in the Reichstag,
Hitler said, "Germany has no further claims against France. . . . I believe that
there can only be real peace in Europe and throughout the world if Germany
and England come to an understanding. . . ."

Reading the lengthy excerpts in the *Times* of London, I thought the speech
might go down well in France, where I knew there was little enthusiasm for
continuing the war, but I doubted that the British would fall for it. Chamberlain proved me right six days later, when he told the House of Commons, "No
reliance could be put on the promises of the present German government," and
indicated that the wrongs done to Czechoslovakia and Poland would have to
be put right first before there could be any talk of a "negotiated peace."

My editors still wanted a "vivid picture of the war," however, and I
concluded that I might find it in Holland. On the map Holland looked every
bit as vulnerable as it eventually turned out to be, and I flew to Amsterdam
in a neutral KLM plane, leaving my expensive kit in storage at the Dorchester.
What prompted my decision was a published report that the Germans were
massing troops on the Belgian and Dutch borders for a flanking attack on
France through the Low Countries.

The report was substantiated on November 1, when the Dutch government
proclaimed a "preliminary state of siege" in certain frontier districts. Five days
later Leopold, the king of the Belgians, paid a sudden visit to Holland's Queen
Wilhelmina at The Hague, and the following day, November 7, the two sover-
eigns sent to the belligerent powers a peace proposal and an offer of their good
offices for arranging a negotiated settlement.

I had every reason to believe that in the Netherlands I would finally catch
up with the elusive war. Instead, I found a deceptive land of plenty. There were
no shortages of food or drink, and the Dutch ate and imbibed heartily. Nor
did they seem to feel a pinch of guilt over their good fortune. They were
exercised about being cut off by British naval blockade from their colonies, and
they worried about shortages and the loss of business to come.

Meanwhile, they worked industriously to defend their country from Hitler.
In doing so, the Dutch looked back hopefully to their experience in the First
World War, when Kaiser Wilhelm sidestepped Holland and invaded France
via neighboring Belgium instead. The reason why, a young captain in Holland's engineering corps told me, was this.

Some months before his imperial armies attacked in the fateful summer of

1914, the kaiser invited Queen Wilhelmina—then a plump, sweet-faced, but spunky matron in her mid-twenties—to observe his troops in maneuvers. Intending to impress and intimidate the Dutch queen, the kaiser called her attention to a strapping, goose-stepping unit of his elite Prussian Guard.

"Look, Your Majesty," the German emperor said ominously, "they are all nearly seven feet tall."

Undaunted, the queen replied, "Yes, Your Highness, but the fields of Holland can be flooded to a depth of eight feet."

Whether this story was apocryphal or not, the Dutch had let the sea in past their dikes on at least one occasion. In 1574, when Leiden was besieged by the Spanish troops of the duke of Alba, William the Silent opened the dikes and flooded the enemy out. Having studied a little civil engineering at Drexel in Philadelphia, I persuaded myself, foolishly, that the Dutch could employ this stratagem nationwide against the Germans. And so I cabled in a hopeful story for *Collier's.*

I was still in Amsterdam, hoping to be sent to Finland to cover the only shooting war then in progress, when *Collier's* wired: COME HOME FOR CHRISTMAS IF YOU CAN. Disappointed, I sailed for New York on the Dutch liner *Statendam.*

24

TURMOIL ON THE HOME FRONT

While waiting my turn in the pushy crowd of porters and debarking passengers competing for taxis outside the *Statendam*'s West Side wharf, I debated whether to go straight home to Bronxville or check in at *Collier's* first. When a cab finally became available, its grumpy driver decided the matter for me. "I don't make out-a-town calls," he growled, and I told him to take me to 250 Park Avenue, the magazine's headquarters. I would telephone Kathryn from there, I thought, and take a train later from nearby Grand Central.

I was eager to see my wife and the boys, of course, but I was also anxious to learn why I had been invited to "come home for Christmas" instead of being sent to Finland. I was tormented by the possibility that I was summoned home to be told I hadn't made the grade.

In my lifelong struggle with the simple declarative sentence, I had developed deep-seated doubts about my skill as a writer, was never satisfied with anything I wrote. I was certain that what came out of my typewriter would have been vastly better had I finished college, read more in the classics, and worked harder at developing clarity and rhythm. Since joining *Collier's*, I habitually questioned the quality of my output, uncertain whether the thousands of words I cabled from England, France, and Holland were worth the considerable expense of transmission, even at the lowest available rate: night press collect. The piece from Amsterdam, for instance, ran to more than four thousand words and must have cost the magazine the better part of a thousand dollars.

I had reason to be concerned about my future, for while I had received no complaints about mounting cable tolls or the size of my rather hefty expense accounts, neither had I received any glowing telegrams about my work. In fact, until I saw in print my piece about the Dutch and their "water stratagem" in the December 23 issue I had bought on arrival that morning, I had no assurance that anything I had written had been published.

On the way to the office I studied the magazine's masthead and was pleased to see myself listed as its correspondent in France, and in distinguished company: Walter Davenport, politics; Quentin Reynolds, sports; Kyle Crichton, screen and theater; W. B. Courtney, Germany; Martha Gellhorn, Scandinavia; Jim Marshall, the Orient; William Hillman, European manager. To 3.1 million subscribers to *Collier's,* "The National Weekly," those names were household words, and they were also familiar to the millions more who read the magazine in barbershops and the waiting rooms of lawyers, doctors, dentists, and chiropractors.

Of the writers listed on the masthead, I knew personally only the ubiquitous Hillman, Bill Courtney—he had visited me in Rome in 1936 while en route to the Ethiopian War for *Collier's*—and Quent Reynolds, another former Hearstling. Quent had quit INS several years before I did and had recommended me highly to Colebaugh when the latter was considering hiring me. It was an eclectic company—an elite of the print journalism of the time—and I wondered if I would fit in.

Whether I did or not depended, I believed, on the editor in chief, Bill Chenery, and the managing editor, Charley Colebaugh. I had met them only briefly during the summer before they hired me by cable in September. I remembered Chenery as a tall, distinguished-looking but rather stiff-necked Virginian with a Phi Beta Kappa key dangling from his watch chain. I recalled Colebaugh as a short, compact, middle-aged Scot with bespectacled blue-gray eyes, neatly barbered silvery hair, and a quick smile.

Both men prized good writing and knew better than most editors what made an interesting magazine article or what constituted publishable popular fiction of the genre produced by Faith Baldwin, Frederick Hazlitt Brennan, Octavus Roy Cohen, and other novelists whose work *Collier's* regularly serialized. Proof of Chenery's and Colebaugh's acumen lay in the fact that *Collier's* was flourishing against heavy competition from the older, stodgier *Saturday Evening Post.* Like the latter, "The National Weekly" was an editorial "mix" of light fiction and close-to-news nonfiction, but unlike the conservative *Post, Collier's* plowed the liberal side of the field. Although Chenery was a hidebound Republican, the magazine had been an early opponent of Prohibition, one of the leaders in the fight to repeal the Volstead Act, and remained a staunch supporter of Franklin D. Roosevelt and his New Deal.

Colebaugh and the secretarial staff seemed to be the only occupants of the editorial offices when I arrived shortly after nine that morning, threaded my way past rows of busy typists to the managing editor's glassed-in enclosure, and stood in his doorway. He was in shirt sleeves, engrossed in a manuscript, and looked up in wide-eyed surprise when his secretary announced. "Mr. Colebaugh, look who's here." His astonishment at seeing me told me at once that he hadn't received my cable from Amsterdam advising him—and through him my family—that I was returning on the *Statendam.*

Colebaugh greeted me so warmly that my doubts about whether I had "made the team," apprehensions I had carried like so many rocks all the way from Holland, began dissolving. He motioned me to a chair, said he was glad to see I had survived "all that rich food and Dutch gin," and chided me for not having cabled him that I was coming home. I assured him that I had, but the message, I said, probably was never sent because it stupidly contained the name of my ship and the date and port of its departure.

"Well," said Colebaugh, "when we didn't hear from you, Chenery and I decided you had gone off to Finland on your own. Good thing you didn't. I assigned Martha Gellhorn to *that* war, and the temperamental Mrs. Ernest Hemingway wouldn't have liked it at all if you had shown up on *her* turf."

Colebaugh had just received Miss Gellhorn's first story from the Russo-Finnish front, "a colorful, beautifully written piece," he said, "but a bit long." He planned to use it in the next issue and had headed it "Blood on the Snow."

"How does the title strike you?" he asked.

"Sounds perfect," I said. "It's evocative, but I hope the blood is mostly Russian." I detested the Russians at the time. I believed with many of my colleagues that Stalin's nonaggression pact with Hitler had made possible Germany's attack on Poland and precipitated what promised to become the second world war in my lifetime.

"There's plenty of Russian blood in Martha's story," Colebaugh said, handing me a copy of her manuscript, "but lots of Finnish blood, too. Here, read it as soon as you can and let me know if you think it can be trimmed. Now, come say hello to Chenery. . . ."

Chenery occupied the adjoining office, a spacious, fully enclosed corner room with walnut-paneled walls and wall-to-wall carpeting that bespoke authority and comfort. Its occupant was in pensive mood, gazing out a window at the gray, snow-laden sky, turning as we entered.

"Welcome aboard, Mr. Gervasi," he said, shaking hands cordially, "and welcome home." In the next breath he startled—and delighted—me by asking when I intended going back to Europe. My fears about my future at *Collier's,* obviously, were unfounded.

"The war is sure to begin in earnest in the spring," he said, "and we'll want you back there before then. Perhaps you should go to Italy and find out what il Duce is up to, if you can, then take a swing through the Balkans before the guns roar and the bombs fall."

He asked whether I was satisfied with the financial arrangements *Collier's* had made. I assured him I was—the magazine was paying me substantially more than twice what I had been earning at INS—thanked him for bringing me home for the holidays, and wondered aloud what I had done to deserve such thoughtful treatment. The two men exchanged glances.

"For one thing," Chenery said in his best executive manner, "we wanted to have a good visit with you, get to know you better personally. Also, since the war in Europe was in the doldrums, we decided you might as well come home and spend the holidays with your family. Mrs. Gervasi, by the way, has been calling from time to time for news of you. She said she hadn't heard from you since you left England. I assume you've called her?"

I admitted I hadn't, and Colebaugh led me to a cubicle containing a desk, a typewriter, a telephone, and two chairs. It would be my workplace, he said, while I was in New York.

"Here you are," he said, pointing to the phone. "Now call your wife."

I rang our Bronxville number, but there was no reply. I figured that Kathryn and the boys were out doing the family's Christmas shopping and mentally pictured them at F.A.O. Schwarz's fabulous Fifth Avenue toy store inspecting model trains and steam engines and Erector sets.

The gray sky framed by my window held the promise of snow, and I hoped it would produce a white Christmas. The Westchester village we called home would be charming dressed in white, and I envisioned a crackling fire in the living-room fireplace, a tree sparkling with ornaments, and under it a mound of gaily wrapped gifts. I was suddenly, painfully homesick.

I was deep in Miss Gellhorn's vivid account of the Russo-Finnish fighting when a familiar baritone voice intoned, "Welcome back, Frankie," and I knew it belonged to Quentin Reynolds even before I looked up into his smiling Irish face.

"Everybody loved your stuff, kid," he said, "especially that first piece from London about the evacuees. Come on, I'll show you around. Most of the guys are in by now. It's nearly lunchtime."

Quent introduced me to the pixieish "Davvy" Davenport, the magazine's senior writer and an authority on domestic politics; the ebullient Kyle Crichton; the scholarly fiction editor, Kenneth Littauer, and his assistant, Max Wilkinson; and the solemn Jim Marshall, just back from the Far East. They were a lively, talented, humorful bunch who freely spoke their minds in conversation and in print and were to become my friends during some of the happiest, most productive years of my life. As Jim Bishop wrote later about his time as an associate editor at 250 Park Avenue, "incredibly bright was the world at *Collier's* magazine."

The one star in the *Collier's* firmament for whom I was to develop a special fondness, and with whom I was to enjoy a lasting and rewarding friendship, was Kyle Crichton. Tall, spare, with stooping, broad shoulders, a sharp tongue, and a booming voice, he was intolerant of fools, dissemblers and reactionaries. Kyle could and did write about anything and everything for *Collier's*, and he held the record for versatility by having interviewed Marlene Dietrich, Henry Ford, and the Marx Brothers all in the same week.

Crichton was the magazine's most militant liberal and in the past had also regularly written for the *New Masses* as "Robert Forsyth." When the latter's real identity became known, the complaints from the magazine's big-money advertisers sowed panic among the business-minded members of *Collier's* board of directors, some of whom believed Franklin Delano Roosevelt was a Communist. Chenery was urged to "fire that pinko fellow traveler" on his staff, but the lanky Virginian had his own inflexible code of fair play. He handed Crichton's critics copies of everything Kyle had written for *Collier's* over the years and challenged them to find a single subversive phrase or sentence. They found none, of course, and Crichton kept his job, much to the magazine's benefit and Chenery's credit.

I finished reading Miss Gellhorn's piece from Helsinki, envying her powers of description. She made me see and feel the horrors of the Russo-Finnish struggle then raging on the Karelian Isthmus, a sub-Arctic hell where winds howled at thirty below zero and thousands of young Finnish and Russian soldiers lay dead, frozen in fighting attitudes, some locked in mortal combat. I returned the article to Colebaugh and told him I thought it should be run as written.

"It would be sacrilege to cut it," I said. "She writes better than her husband."

Colebaugh smiled, slid off his glasses, thanked me, and said, "How about lunch? Normally it's Dutch treat, but today it's on the house." I accepted after calling home once more. I let the phone ring almost a full minute before hanging up.

On the way out Colebaugh and I were joined as though by prearrangement by Davenport, Reynolds, Crichton, Wilkinson, Littauer, Jim Marshall, and Bill Chessman, the burly art editor, to whom I was introduced as the "new boy on the block." Lunch, as many of my future *Collier's* lunches would be, was in the grill room of the Marguery Hotel, a few steps up Park Avenue from the office. It was preceded by drinks in the restaurant's adjoining bar, an inviting bistro which everyone called "Magoory's Saloon." The first round was a toast to me, the newcomer. A second was pledged to "those brave Finns who are giving the Russians hell."

I was apprehensive that during lunch I might be asked questions about the war in Europe that I couldn't answer, but I needn't have worried. The table talk over food centered almost entirely on American politics with our house expert, Walter Davenport, holding center stage. Everyone listened attentively, for Davvy had predicted before anyone else Alf Landon's crushing defeat by Mr. Roosevelt in 1936 and was known to have friends among the kingmakers in both political parties.

"FDR is keeping everybody guessing about whether he'll run for a third term," Davvy said, "but you can bet on it that when the chips are down, he'll be his party's candidate. What's more, he'll win come November. The New Deal may have lost a lot of its glow and practically all of its novelty, but FDR has lost none of his charisma or political clout."

Pressed by Crichton to name Roosevelt's probable Republican opponent,

Davvy mentioned a man who had gained national attention in 1935 as one of Big Industry's most effective opponents of the New Deal's Public Utility Holding Company Act and its invasion of the power field with the government-owned Tennessee Valley Authority. "I wouldn't be surprised," Davvy said, "if the GOP puts up Wendell Willkie, and I think he'll give FDR a run for his money." Colebaugh suggested Davvy do a piece about him, to which the writer replied, "Working on it, Charley."

On our way back to the office Crichton, in jovial mood, wondered aloud what Jim Marshall and I and other *Collier's* war correspondents would do for a living when the war ended.

"We won't have to worry about that for a long time," Marshall replied. "It'll be a long war, Kyle, long and bloody. . . ."

"You believe that, too?" Kyle asked, turning to me.

"I'm afraid so," I replied, and Crichton, suddenly serious, said he hoped we were both wrong.

In midafternoon I called Bronxville again and, receiving no reply, acted on a hunch. It occurred to me that Kathryn, unaware that I was coming home, might have taken the boys to hometown Philadelphia, where we both had gaggles of relatives. A phone call to my sister Clementine elicited a mild scolding for my "long silence" and confirmation of my presentiment. Clem had invited Kay down for the holidays, but she and the boys were staying with a favorite niece of ours, Ruth Malone, and her husband, Jim, in suburban Upper Darby.

Despite the change in scene, Christmas turned out to be much like the picture-book one I had fantasized, memorable for the happy reunion with Kathryn and the boys and the hospitality of the Malones in their big, rambling Dutch colonial house in suburbia. The holiday was complete with a cozy fire in the spacious living room, a tall tree glittering with ornaments, piles of gaily wrapped presents for everyone, and a fine turkey dinner over which gentle Jim Malone presided. The house rang with the hubbub raised by the children, our own Tommy and Sean, and the Malone's irrepressible Molly, as pretty a colleen as I would ever see. There were also enough uncles and aunts and cousins, it seemed, to cast a Gilbert and Sullivan operetta.

Unforgettable, too, was an all-too-brief visit with my father, Eugene, at my sister's home in North Philly. I had not seen him in nearly five years and found him older and grayer but still militantly Socialist—he planned to vote for Norman Thomas in November—and deeply concerned with the course of events abroad. Like many Americans, Papa was enraged by the Russian invasion of Finland but doubted that the Finns could resist much longer.

"Stalin," he said, "is as ambitious as that other dictator Hitler. Speaking of dictators, do you think Mussolini will honor his pact with Hitler or stay on the sidelines as a neutral? If he's as smart as he's supposed to be, he'll break with Germany and join the Allies. Italy has a history of switching sides in war. . . ."

I told him I doubted that Mussolini would split with Hitler, but I hoped to find out what il Duce was up to when I returned to Europe after the holidays. Papa then asked if I thought America could stay out of the war if Italy joined Germany and set out to make "a Nazi-Fascist Europe." I said I hoped so, for I hadn't yet shed my belief that what was happening on the other side of the Atlantic was essentially a European quarrel and my conviction that the Allies were fully capable of turning back the German threat. My father was visibly displeased.

"That's isolationist talk," he said angrily. "I hear it all the time on the radio, and it's a lot of nonsense. Sooner or later, you'll see, America will be in it, just like the last time. I'm glad my grandsons are still children. But you, Francesco, you are of military age. You might be drafted. . . . Well, you always did want to be a soldier. Remember how you pestered me for a soldier suit when you were a boy? I still have the picture of you in the officer's uniform that client of mine made for you in his shop. . . ."

I assured Papa that if America entered the war, I probably would be in it as a correspondent, not as a soldier.

After we had said our good-byes—Italian style, with embraces and kisses and dewy eyes—I asked Papa whether he had heard from Uncle Gennaro, my boyhood hero. His face darkened, and he shook his head negatively. It was, I could see, a subject he did not wish to talk about. Obviously the brothers had quarreled. I never learned what had passed between them, though I suspected that Papa thought Gennaro had embraced fascism.

Before returning to New York, I stopped in at the *Record,* where my career began and where a boozy editor once told me I would never "make it" in journalism. The newsroom looked shabbier than when I last saw it, and there had been many staff changes. But three old friends—Dave Wittels, Morris Glazer, and Jesse Laventhol, who had taught me a lot about reporting and writing news—were still at their desks. They had followed my work in *Collier's* with evident pleasure and plied me with questions, most of which I admitted I couldn't answer. All three were Jewish, and wanted to know if I thought the Germans would win the war.

"The mere thought of a Nazi victory," said Wittels, the paper's star rewrite man, "sends cold shivers up and down my spine. If what Hitler's done in Germany is any indication of his plans for Europe's Jews, he will slaughter them by the thousands."

I argued that although it might be a long war, the Allies would win in the end and cited the reasons then current among Western "experts."

Glazer, the eldest of the three and the *Record's* financial editor, solemnly disagreed. He envisioned an Allied victory *only* if America entered the war, but he saw little chance of that happening. The country, he said, was predominantly, even overwhelmingly, isolationist and wanted no part of the war in Europe. Among other reasons, there was widespread resentment over the failure of most European nations to repay the debts they incurred during the

First World War, and the popular consensus was that the United States should avoid involvement at all costs.

"We had our fingers burned once," Glazer said, "pulling Europe's chestnuts out of the fire, and now the people are saying, 'Never again.' Anyhow, they believe that America is big enough, smart enough, and strong enough to go its own way and that its interests would best be served by minding its own business. They're for all-out help for Finland because it was the only country that regularly paid the installments due on the debts it incurred in the old war—on time and in full, with interest. But generally speaking, the people, especially the pragmatists in the business community, are for treating both sides impartially in the matter of selling them supplies and weapons.

"It's a cockeyed situation, but that's how it is. The isolationists in Congress, the clergy, and the press are determined to keep America out of the war. If they prevail, and they are a powerful bloc, the Germans will prove you wrong because they, not the French, have the best army in the world. Unless Hitler is stopped somewhere along the line, we'll have a nazified Europe."

America's opposition to involvement in Europe, Glazer reminded me, was almost as great as its aversion to involvement in the ongoing war in Asia, where Japan was overrunning China. In that conflict, geographically and ethnically remote, the Chinese had our sympathy and best wishes, but not much more.

I returned to New York and my friends at *Collier's* much sobered by what I had heard from my peers at the *Record* and aware that I had a lot to learn about my country's state of mind while the "phony" war extended into 1940. I devoted the rest of my time at home to studying the views and techniques of the godheads of isolationism, at once a political doctrine and a cult whose high priests would profoundly influence the course of national affairs.

Isolationism became the stuff of the news and editorial columns of such powerful newspaper combines as those owned by the McCormick-Patterson group and my old boss, William Randolph Hearst. Meanwhile, pacifists argued that the only way to prevent war was to have nothing to do with it, and the Communists charged that Britain and France were fighting merely to preserve imperialistic capitalism.

The isolationist cause was taken up by the reigning folk hero Charles Augustus Lindbergh, who seemed to have developed friendly feelings for nazism during his visits to Germany and who often spoke of the "futility" of opposing what he saw as the "wave of the future." The popular air idol of other days repeatedly warned that the American people had no stake in the war and should keep their hands clean.

While Lindbergh was merely wrongheaded and the senatorial isolationists were political opportunists, their patriotism was unimpeachable. Isolationism, however, had spawned a small host of popular spellbinders whose motives were somewhat less than patriotic and in some cases downright subversive.

The rabble-rousers included pro-Nazi spokesmen like Father Charles Coughlin, the Detroit "radio priest," and the Reverend Gerald L. K. Smith.

The radio audiences of these two demagogues numbered in the many millions, and their public meetings drew tens of thousands of impressionable, ill-informed, often barely literate farmers and workers. The Catholic priest and the Protestant minister used their pulpits and microphones to fan those flames of chauvinism and bigotry that have always burned naturally at the American grass roots.

The orators' tirades on the radio, to which I listened at every opportunity, shook my isolationist sentiments and opened my eyes to the extent to which fascism and nazism had penetrated the American political scene. The speakers' harangues spoke of "evil hidden forces" which were "dragging America into a foreign war" and blatantly identified those forces as Jewish. Such talk had a familiar ring; I had heard it before in Rome, Munich, and Berlin, and it dawned on me that Father Coughlin and the Reverend Smith were merely using isolationism as a club to belabor Roosevelt and bring down his "liberal-internationalist New Deal" in order to make way for an America patterned after Mussolini's Italy or Hitler's Germany.

More easily identifiable as subversive were several organizations operating on the lunatic fringe of American politics. They included the Christian Front, the Silver Shirts, and the German-American Bund, whose isolationism was a shield behind which they actually plotted an eventual Nazi-Fascist takeover of the United States.

A powerful new combination of southern and eastern Democrats, however, was taking shape in Congress in support of President Roosevelt's policies. They were joined in the country at large by many of the nation's leading intellectuals, and by such open-minded Republicans as Henry L. Stimson and Frank Knox. They led the fight against isolationism and stimulated support of the president's call for all possible aid to the embattled Allies "short of war."

As the new year began, the Finns continued to beat back heavy Russian attacks, but on February 1, 1940, the Finnish president, Kyösti Kallio, begged Moscow for "an honorable peace to end the senseless, barbaric slaughter." His appeal signaled the impending collapse of Finnish resistance.

In the meantime, the weeks passed without any eruption on the western front. Hitler planned his future strategy and honed his Wehrmacht and Luftwaffe to blitzkrieg sharpness. At the same time Britain and France toiled frantically to rearm and build up their defenses, but they fatuously continued to cherish the desperate hope that Hitler had sated his territorial appetite in the West and would turn southeast toward the Balkans, the historic direction of German imperial ambitions.

It was in this climate of uncertainty abroad and at home that early in February I said good-bye to Kathryn and the boys and sailed for Genoa on the SS *Washington* with instructions to "take a swing through the Balkans after casing Italy."

In my baggage I carried a horseshoe, a going-away present from Jim Marshall, who knew better than most of us at *Collier's* what it meant to be under enemy fire. Jim had been one of several foreign correspondents on board the U.S. gunboat *Panay* in December 1937, when it was bombed and strafed by the Japanese while the vessel was on a routine patrol in the Yangtze River. The attack resulted in heavy damage and a number of casualties, but Jim escaped without a scratch and attributed his good luck to the horseshoe he gave me the day I sailed. I was to cherish the U-shaped bit of rusty iron through the remaining years of the violent decade that had begun with the Ethiopian War in 1935.

25

NEUTRALITY, ITALIAN STYLE

An icy wind swept down from the snowcapped Apennines above Genoa and frosted the nose of the *Washington* as the liner slid through the great port's wartime antisubmarine net and snuggled up to her assigned dock with the help of squat little tugs. The merchant ships of a dozen nations lay stem to stern at other berths, loading and unloading cargo, their busy booms rising and dipping against a gray mist of smoke from their boilers.

A few destroyers, a flotilla of torpedo boats, and a squadron of amphibious Caproni bombers tethered wing to wing in the inner harbor attested to Italy's readiness to assert its claim to supremacy in the sea which Benito Mussolini called *mare nostrum*. Otherwise, it was a peaceful scene, with the Union Jack and the Gallic tricolor snapping in the brisk breeze from the stern poles of British and French freighters.

From the *Washington*'s hurricane deck I looked for German flags but saw none. This was surprising, but more surprises awaited me ashore. Gone from the walls and facades of the port's grimly utilitarian buildings, for instance, were those brave slogans that only a few months before had shouted, "Viva Hitler" and *"Viva l'Asse Roma-Berlino."* Now, I noticed, the brash words had been painted over, as though the Fascist regime wished to expunge such Germanophile thoughts from Italians' minds. Had the Duce, I wondered, undergone a change of heart about his alliance with the Führer? There were audible and visible indications that he had.

Mario, the *facchino* who shouldered my baggage—suitcase, bagful of reference books, and typewriter—thought so, and so did the barman at the Mira-mare Hotel and the waiter in its sparsely populated dining room. All three, in various ways, verbally and with eloquent gestures, indicated they believed the Rome-Berlin Axis was *finito* and expressed pleasure at being able "to hold up our heads again as Italians."

I recalled, however, that Genoa had never been a Fascist stronghold and that back in 1935 and 1936, when Blackshirt legions were departing to make war on Ethiopia, the port was often the scene of antiwar demonstrations, even illegal work stoppages. Mario and the others, I decided, were merely engaging in wishful thinking or seeking to please an American visitor by telling him what they thought he wanted to hear in exchange for generous tips. I gave little weight to their assurances that the Axis was *finito* or, as one of them, thinking in German, had put it, kaput.

Fortunately I had other sources of information in Genoa, cultivated during my years as INS bureau chief in Rome: editors and reporters on local newspapers, industrialists and businessmen, whom I interviewed over lunches, drinks, and dinners during my stay in their city before going on to Milan. Most of them confirmed that the disappearance of the blatantly pro-German slogans was not an accident but part of a deliberate campaign to persuade the Italian people and, of course, the Western democracies, that Italy would remain aloof from Hitler's war.

Mussolini, my Genoese informants said, needed time to "digest" newly conquered Albania; stabilize the situation in Ethiopia; bring the army, navy, and air force up to strength; and, most of all, repair the ravaged Italian economy. Italy desperately needed foreign exchange for its imports, and the Duce planned to acquire it with a pet project of his: an immensely impressive international exposition—a sort of super world's fair—to be held in Rome in 1942 to commemorate the twentieth anniversary of his March on Rome. The event would attract millions of tourists, he believed, and replenish fascism's depleted coffers.

Gaudy posters announcing the exposition were prominently displayed on Genoa's walls and billboards and provided evidence that for at least three years Italy had no intention of going to war. Fair buildings were already under construction on the outskirts of Rome in the stark modernistic architectural style favored by the Duce. The project, to be known as EUR—Esposizione Universale Roma—was only one of several indications pointing toward continued Italian neutrality.

Another was the recent changing of the guard, a high-level cabinet reshuffle, that excluded from fascism's ruling hierarchy its known pro-German elements. The shakeup occurred early in November, two months after the war started, and lent added credibility to Italy's "nonbelligerency."

The men dropped from the cabinet were Achille Starace, the widely detested Fascist party secretary; Dino Alfieri, the thoroughly incompetent minister of propaganda; and two generals, the inept undersecretary for war Alberto Pariani and the corrupt undersecretary for air Giuseppe Valle. All four had been frequent visitors to Berlin, where they were feted and flattered by Air

Marshal Göring, shown troops marching with mechanistic precision and assembly lines turning out bombers and fighter planes at the rate of a thousand a month. They became persuaded that Italy and Germany together could conquer Europe and returned to Rome imbued with the idea that Italy's destiny was inexorably linked to Germany's.

The foursome's highly publicized dismissal was greeted with approval throughout the country but was particularly welcome in the industrial north, where it was interpreted as proof of a dramatic 180-degree turn in Fascist policy away from closer relations with Germany and war.

"In the democracies," a veteran Genoese journalist explained, "a new cabinet portends a new policy. In our totalitarian society a new policy requires a new cabinet. The Duce's purge of the hierarchy's pro-German, anti-Western elements has caused us to conclude that the Rome-Berlin Axis was an aberration of Mussolini's best forgotten."

Visible behind the upheaval, my Genoese informant agreed, was the fine Italian hand of Galeazzo Ciano, who replaced both Starace and Alfieri with close personal friends. Starace's post as Fascist party secretary, the most important position in the regime after those of premier and foreign secretary, was filled by Ettore Muti, a tough, burly Blackshirt in his mid-thirties, who looked like an American Leatherneck, had won numerous medals as a daring fighter pilot in Ethiopia, Spain, and Albania, and was devoted to Ciano. He was essentially a soldier, not a politician or an executive, but could be counted upon to run the Fascist party exactly as Mussolini and Ciano wanted.

To replace Alfieri, Ciano chose Alessandro Pavolini, a darkly handsome newspaperman, who was also a pilot and had flown with the foreign minister in Ciano's squadron, La Disperata, in Ethiopia. My Genoese source believed Pavolini would make a far more efficient propaganda minister than Alfieri, who wore his Blackshirt uniform with dash and elegance but knew practically nothing about journalism or the art of molding public opinion.

With handpicked surrogates running both the Fascist party and the Propaganda Ministry Ciano obviously had strengthened his position in the government and greatly enhanced his capacity to influence Italian policy against further involvement with Berlin. And it was Ciano, my informants confirmed, who persuaded Mussolini to fire Pariani and Valle, the former for having misled the Duce into believing the army was composed of "happy warriors ready to fight Britain and France" and the latter for having failed miserably to produce an air force worthy of the name.

Although I had long been aware of Italy's military inadequacies, during my swing through the industrial north I learned the true extent of the deficiencies in the country's armed forces. Retired army officers to whom I was introduced by mutual friends in Genoa—and who talked freely when assured they would not be quoted—said Mussolini's army of *otto milioni di baionette* was an "idle boast." Italy had neither the 8 million men nor the bayonets, they said, and they estimated the army's strength at no more than 1.7 million troops, most of whom were poorly equipped. Some infantry units, they said, still carried World War I rifles, were short of ammunition, and were shoddily uniformed.

The wars in Ethiopia and Spain, they said, had stripped the army of weapons, particularly artillery, aircraft, and vehicles. During the Spanish Civil War, for instance, Italy sent General Franco nineteen hundred field guns, several hundred planes, and thousands of trucks. Because of graft and corruption in high places, they said, replacements had been slow in coming.

Later, in Milan, where I arrived by train in the evening of February 21 in a swirling snowstorm, I talked with industrialists who described Italy's war-making potential as "not much better than—if as good as—it was in 1915," the year Italy quit the Triple Alliance to go to war against its former allies. The worst deficiency, they said, was in air power.

This surprised me because the air force was reputedly the best branch of the Fascist armed services. I recalled that at the height of Italo-British tensions in 1937 and 1938 Mussolini had boasted that Italy would "darken the skies over London with bombers." At the time Italy was believed to have the "finest air armada in Europe" with upwards of three thousand first-line warplanes.

"That may or may not have been true then," my informant replied, "but it is certainly not true now. I doubt that our air force totals more than a thousand aircraft, which is why Mussolini fired Valle. For some time the general tricked the Duce into believing we had thousands of planes by flying squadrons from one airfield to another in advance of Mussolini's inspections. Then, one day, the Duce made a surprise visit to a military airfield near Turin, where fighter planes were based against a possible attack from France. Instead of the many squadrons listed in General Valle's memorandums, Mussolini found only a dozen or so scattered aircraft. Exit Valle, who faces a court-martial. . . ."

There were serious deficiencies, also, in the armored forces. Italy's L-35 tank was described as too light—a mere three and a half tons—and too vulnerable for modern warfare, its armor so thin as to be "easily penetrable by machine-gun bullets." A tanker referred to it as *tascabile,* something one could put into one's pocket.

Clearly Italy was economically and militarily unprepared for war, and none knew this better than Galeazzo Ciano. He had his own network of spies and counterspies and was aware that the people, especially in the industrial north, were anti-German and more disposed to fight on the side of Britain and France than as allies of Nazi Germany. He knew, for instance, that on the morning of September 2, 1939, the day after Hitler had "liberated" Danzig and begun military operations against Poland, early risers on their way to work in Milan's factories found crudely drawn posters on the walls declaring: ITALIAN WORKERS WILL NOT FIGHT ALONGSIDE THE BUTCHERS OF OUR FELLOW WORKERS IN POLAND.

Ciano had met with his Nazi opposite number, Ribbentrop, at Salzburg on August 11 and had tried in vain to persuade him and through him Adolf Hitler that Germany could obtain whatever it wanted from Poland by the same techniques used in the dismemberment of Czechoslovakia. Ciano warned that it would be impossible to localize a conflict with Poland and that in such an event Germany could expect no help from Italy.

More pertinently, he reminded Ribbentrop that Italy needed at least three years to prepare for war, a condition which had been agreed upon between them when they signed the Rome-Berlin military alliance in May 1939. Ribbentrop had blandly consented, adding that Germany itself would not be ready for war for four or five years. But when they met again in August, only three months later, Ciano found Ribbentrop obdurate, and the Italian foreign minister left Salzburg convinced that what the Führer wanted was not Danzig and the Polish Corridor but all-out war.

On his return to Rome Ciano alerted the Duce to Germany's perfidy and set into motion his plan to keep Italy out of the war. He began by persuading Mussolini to inform Hitler that Italy's support in the event Germany attacked Poland would have to be limited to purely "political and moral" assistance unless Germany immediately made available supplies of raw materials and weapons. The list of Italy's requirements, which Milanese industrialists helped compile, was described by one of my sources as *formidabile*. It included 7 million tons of oil, 6 million tons of coal, 2 million tons of steel, 1 million tons of lumber, 17,000 military vehicles, and no fewer than 150 antiaircraft batteries to protect Italy's war plants, most of which were located in and around Turin and Milan within reach of French bombers.

Italy's "shopping list," which Ciano later described as "big enough to choke a bull if a bull could read," caused Hitler to delay his attack on Poland from August 29 to September 1 but otherwise had little effect on the Führer. Two days later, when Britain and France entered the war, Mussolini, rejecting the more explicit word "neutrality" preferred by Ciano, proclaimed Italy's "nonbelligerency" and fell into a deep, sullen silence.

In the absence of any guidance from Rome, Italy seethed with rumors. Some Italians predicted the imminent collapse of the Rome-Berlin Axis. In Milan a group of university students carried a large tree trunk into the Galleria Vittorio Emanuele, in the heart of the city, sawed it into four sections, and left the pieces there, each bearing one of the four letters that spelled A-S-S-E (Axis).

Simultaneously, in a wave of anti-Fascist sentiment, the people engaged in the wildest kind of wishful thinking: Some said the Duce had been physically incapacitated by a heart attack or a stroke; others said he had been shot by King Victor Emmanuel or by Field Marshal Badoglio. Mussolini had ways of quashing such subversive scuttlebutt. Having been a newspaperman, he knew that mere denials would only have served to confirm the rumors to a congenitally skeptical people. So he had himself photographed visiting the king, appearing in public with the marshal, and engaging in strenuous calisthenics before newsreel cameras with members of his entourage.

Then, in what everyone said was a masterstroke, the Duce used the grapevine to spread a story which he knew would be accepted as fact by supporters and opponents alike, for Mussolini was aware that while few Italians believed what they read in the papers or heard on the government radio, they all swore by what came to them as news over the "people's telegraph."

The Duce fed into the grapevine an astonishing story. He was widely quoted as having confided to his private secretary that "Italy will be dragged into this war only by the hair on my head."

In the closed Fascist society there were many things about Mussolini that the Italians didn't know; but every man, woman, and child was aware that he was as bald as a pomegranate, and the people were much relieved to learn that their country would be drawn into Hitler's war only by the hair on their leader's cranium.

Within twenty-four hours coded cables went out from the foreign embassies and legations in Rome—including our own—telling the world at large that Italy would remain neutral.

Meanwhile, the Duce's personal popularity registered new highs on the seismographs of Italian public opinion. Stock prices soared; shipowners in Genoa, Naples, Leghorn, and Trieste profited handsomely by chartering their "neutral" vessels to British and French shippers; and Italy's industries flourished.

Britain was still allowing coal to reach Italy through the blockade, and French orders for textiles, machinery, and shell casings placed with Italian manufacturers during the five months since the war began totaled, I was told, an unbelievable three hundred million dollars. During the last week of February 1940 Italy seemed to be enjoying Swiss-style fat-cat neutrality, a condition most of my informants believed would continue.

What persuaded the Italians of the industrial north that they would not be called upon to bear arms against Britain and France and that the Rome-Berlin Axis had become a dead letter of Fascist diplomacy was a speech Count Ciano gave before the Chamber of Deputies on December 16, 1939. Its main theme was German treachery. Ciano accused Germany of having violated the Italo-German Anti-Comintern Pact by secretly signing its treaty of nonaggression and friendship with Russia. Italy, Ciano said, learned of the Russo-German pact only on the evening of August 21, fewer than forty-eight hours before it was signed in Moscow on August 23.

Ciano then charged that Germany also had violated the terms of its military alliance—the Rome-Berlin Axis or Pact of Steel—signed with much fanfare in Berlin in May 1939.

The pact had stipulated that Germany and Italy would refrain from military action of any kind long enough to allow each of the signatories time to complete internal political and economic preparations for war. The period of peace required by the two allies was defined in the pact as three years for the Italians and from four to five years for the Germans. Because Germany had let down the Duce by jumping into war prematurely, Ciano said, Italy's declaration of nonbelligerency instead of outright neutrality was more than the Führer had any "juridical right to expect."

The speech, the complete text of which I found in the files of the *Corriere della Sera,* filled the paper's entire front page and was acclaimed not only in the north, my Milanese friends said, but throughout the country as Ciano's "funeral oration over the remains of the Rome-Berlin Axis." The press was instructed to give the speech maximum display to stress its importance, and three days later the country's editors were ordered to report all war news "with complete impartiality."

The Germans never forgave Ciano for his anti-German speech, and in the light of subsequent events it seems fair to say that when the Duce's son-in-law spoke on December 16, 1939, he signed his eventual death warrant.

On January 3, 1940, Mussolini wrote to Hitler to inform him that everything Ciano had said expressed his own views and sharply criticized the Führer for having abandoned the anti-Bolshevist cause by signing a pact with Stalin. "Until four months ago," the Duce wrote, "Russia was your world enemy number one; she cannot have become, and surely is not [now] your *friend* number one." He encouraged Hitler to turn east instead of west in his search for lebensraum, the "living space" the Führer said he needed for the German people.

About the war itself, Mussolini expressed himself pessimistically. While he did not believe that the Western powers would ever compel a Germany "assisted by Italy" to go down to defeat, he was not certain, he said, that Britain and France would be brought to their knees or that a wedge could be driven between them because the United States would never permit the total defeat of the European democracies.

Mussolini's reference to the United States as a possibly decisive element was a rare and startling admission. I had good reason to believe the Duce knew very little about America; he had always lumped the United States with the plutodemocracies that would "never fight." Apparently he knew better now; two of them, Britain and France, had gone to war against a Nazi regime that threatened the destruction of European democracy. It must have occurred to the Fascist dictator as he penned his letter to his Nazi counterpart that the United States could not be counted out of the conflict if and when Italy entered it.

As February became March, however, there were no indications in northern Italy that the country would abandon its neutral role. On the contrary. On March 6, shortly before I left Milan for Budapest, the Italian government signed a new trade agreement with France and was negotiating a similar accord with Great Britain.

It was a strange, almost unbelievable situation. Factories at Breda and Turin were turning out motors and trucks for the British armed forces. The munitions plant at Terni was making shell casings and small-arms ammunition for the French. Manufacturers had explicit instructions to fill Allied orders before meeting requests from domestic sources, even the Italian Army. Meanwhile, Milanese exporters told me it was "virtually impossible" to obtain from the government in Rome export permits authorizing the shipment of goods to the Third Reich.

But while the Italian people, and visitors like myself, were being encouraged to believe Italy would remain on the sidelines during Hitler's war against the Western democracies, Ettore Muti, the new Fascist party secretary, was traveling about the country, explaining to people gathered in the piazzas that the regime was as anti-Bolshevik and antidemocratic as ever and telling them to hold themselves ready to defend their country in war. What Italy wanted, Muti told the Italians in speeches and press releases, was an eventual *Pax Romana,* which he defined as a *pace con baionette* (peace with bayonets).

In the meantime, the life-style of the Milanese had changed little since the war began. In every store, office, and public building signs were posted saying, QUI NON SI PARLA DI POLITICA O DI ALTA STRATEGIA. QUI SI LAVORA (HERE ONE DOES NOT TALK OF POLITICS OR HIGH STRATEGY. HERE ONE WORKS), but war and peace remained the main topics of conversation. There were two meatless days a week, and in the restaurants what appeared on the menus as "veal stew" was usually made with rabbit meat. The meat shortage, however, didn't affect working-class Italians; they couldn't afford meat anyway. They lived on pasta, bread, and vegetables, all still plentiful.

Gasoline was strictly rationed, and the well-to-do grumbled that they had been obliged to garage their cars. Most of all, they regretted the total disappearance of coffee, imports of which the government had prohibited to save foreign exchange. The ersatz substitute, compounded of charred barley laced with chicory, was virtually undrinkable and sharply curtailed the leisurely café life of city-bred Italians accustomed to drinking several espressos or cappuccinos daily.

Otherwise life in northern Italy went on much as before. A dressy audience filled Milan's famous La Scala for a performance I attended the night before I left for Budapest. Normally after the opera they would have filled the grill room of the nearby Hotel Continental, but restaurants were now obliged to close at midnight. It was one of the few "hardships" the Milanese endured in the awful winter of 1940.

The world at large still hoped Mussolini might throw his weight in favor of a negotiated peace. As the winter wore on and Hitler's blitzkrieg in Poland gave way to the phony war, during which nothing happened on the western front, there was a resurgence of optimism that "real war" might be averted.

Typical of this attitude was the mission which President Roosevelt entrusted to Undersecretary of State Sumner Welles in mid-February. Welles was to visit the capitals of all the belligerents and report to the president on the possibilities of negotiating a just and lasting peace. The envoy's first stop was Rome, on February 16, while I was still in Genoa. In his conversation with

Welles, I learned later, the Duce strongly supported the German point of view but did not exclude the possibility of a negotiated peace, provided it was concluded promptly while the belligerents' armies were still inactive.

Welles proceeded to the other capitals, then stopped in Rome on his way back to the United States. It was in the middle of March, and the atmosphere had changed. Fearful lest Mussolini be persuaded by American arguments, Hitler had sent Ribbentrop to Rome to tell the Duce in rather strong language that Italy's place was at Germany's side, and Welles now found Mussolini firm in his solidarity with his Axis partner. The Duce, Welles concluded, had decided to "cross the Rubicon."

Unable to fly to Budapest because of the foul weather, I traveled by train in a wagons-lits compartment on the deluxe express to Trieste, which subsequently became, at Ljubljana, in Yugoslavia, part of the fabled Orient Express. The second night of the long journey, as the train entered the snowbound Magyar plain and skirted frozen Lake Balaton, I dined in a wagon-restaurant peopled with effete Romanians, sturdy Serbs, mustachioed Greeks, and sinister-looking Turks. Nearly all were accompanied by wives or mistresses gowned, perfumed and coiffed as for a state banquet or ball.

At dinner I shared a table with a very beautiful and very pregnant Hungarian lady who, it turned out, occupied the compartment adjoining mine. She evidently had a portable phonograph, and I fell asleep listening to American music. Clearly audible through the partition was the voice of Bing Crosby singing, "Good night, little skipper, good night. . . ."

26

BLOOD ON
THE BALKAN MOON

BUDAPEST

This incredibly beautiful Hungarian capital was still in the grip of the terrible winter whose rigors were at least partly responsible for the several postponements of Hitler's plans to attack in the West.

From my window in the Dunapalota Hotel in Pest, I looked down on a snowscape in white, slate-gray, and black, a vista as sharp and stark as an etching. The snow was head-high in the streets and mantled the rooftops and cornices of the ornate old-world government buildings that crowned the Castle Hill on the far bank of the frozen Danube. The celebrated stream was merely a great white ditch into which men, hooded and booted against the bitter weather, dumped handcart loads of the snow they had shoveled off the sidewalks.

But soon it would be spring. Then the river ice would begin breaking up, and the Danube, classic highway of invasion from north and east, would become navigable again. Could the anticipated blitzkrieg, I wondered, be far behind? And what then? Could Hungary and those countries of southeastern Europe known as the Balkans—Yugoslavia, Romania, Bulgaria, Greece, and Turkey—resist the Germans or fall like so many tenpins before the mighty Wehrmacht and the powerful Luftwaffe?

Much the same questions were in the minds of the Hungarians and the people of the troubled and troublesome Balkans, the historic "cockpit of Europe," where, at Sarajevo, the first Great War began only days after a Serb terrorist, Gavrilo Princip, on June 28, 1914, shot to death the archduke Francis Ferdinand, heir to the Austro-Hungarian throne. Was another Princip lurking in the shadows to give Hitler cause for hurling his blitzkrieg into Hungary and the Balkans when the Danube was free of ice again?

I was awed by the Danube, Europe's longest river after the Volga. What a lot of history it had seen as it flowed an erratic 1,770 miles from its sources in Germany's Black Forest mountains to the Black Sea, first through Czechoslovakia, Austria, and Hungary, then through the three Balkan countries of Yugoslavia, Bulgaria, and Romania, where it became the Romanian border with the Soviet Union before forming a marshy delta at the sea's edge below Odessa.

More than a thousand years had passed since the warlike Magyars, distant cousins of the still-embattled Finns, came out of the Urals on their Mongol ponies, crossed the tall Carpathians, and entered the Danube's broad valley to establish what became Hungary. Through seemingly endless wars that had stained the river with the blood of Germans, Turks, and others, the Magyars saw their country grow into the great Austro-Hungarian Empire, then watched it shrink in the hands of the victors in the twentieth century's first great war.

Logically the river should have united the lands of its watershed, but logic was always in short supply among the region's seventy or eighty million inhabitants. In the approaching spring of 1940 Hungary and the Balkans were a disunited, quarrelsome lot far more eager to settle old grievances than to unify in concerted resistance to an attack from the Goliath in the north.

The vulnerability of the Danubian countries stemmed from the fact that they possessed in considerable abundance what the Germans most needed for ultimate victory: food and raw materials. Of the latter, the most important were Hungary's bauxite and Romania's oil—i.e., aluminum for Göring's warplanes and petroleum to keep them flying. All the countries involved sought refuge in neutrality or in tacit alliances with whichever side, the Allies or the Germans, their leaders believed might win the new war. Safety lay in unity and military strength, but they had neither, for they were all the more or less misbegotten creatures of the peace treaties of the First Great War, born of the wreckage of the Austro-Hungarian Empire and the spoils of the Ottoman Empire of the Turks.

Nearly all seethed with revisionist ambitions for territorial aggrandizement at the expense of one or another of their neighbors, and all were intensely, almost pathologically nationalistic, anti-Semitic, pro-Fascist or pro-Nazi, and ill prepared to fight anybody. They preferred to sell their cattle, grains, fruits and vegetables, olive oil, hemp, lumber, tobacco, bauxite, chrome, and petroleum to the highest bidders—the Allies or the Germans—and be left in peace.

This was especially true of the farmers, shepherds, goatherds, and miners, who constituted the bulk of the population. They remembered vividly the ravages of the old war, and they wanted no part of a new one. They prayed for peace as fervently as they prayed for rain during one of their periodic droughts, but on starlit nights they saw blood on the moon and knew peace was at best only a pious hope.

Hungary was the most exposed of the Danubian nations; it lay athwart Germany's path to the country's grains and bauxite and, ultimately, the Romanian oil Hitler so desperately needed. It was no secret in Budapest that the Wehrmacht could roll across Hungary without feeling much more than a slight bump. Unprotected by mountains, dense forests, or broad rivers, the Magyars' homeland was as flat as the potato pancakes the peasants made in their straw-thatched stone huts on the great Danubian plain.

Yet, though faced by Germans on their northern and western frontiers, and on the east by the much-hated Russians, the Magyars put on a brave front. Whether they were aristocrats twirling amber-colored Tokay wine in stemmed glasses in a noisy Budapest nightclub or peasants ladling paprika-reddened stew in their dirt-floored huts on the steppes, the Magyars talked of resisting "the Nazis or the Bolsheviks" as fiercely as centuries before their ancestors had resisted Attila the Hun.

Hungary's leaders admitted, however, that as a result of the restrictions imposed by the Treaty of Trianon after World War I, the country had little to fight with. Its military "strength" consisted of seven poorly armed infantry divisions and one of horse cavalry, about seventy thousand men in all. Its navy was made up of a few small river gunboats, and the air force totaled about two hundred old planes supplied by the Italians. Compulsory military training had been introduced in 1937; but Hungary's eleven million inhabitants could produce only six hundred thousand men of military age, and few were trained troops.

Under Admiral Nicholas Horthy—an admiral without a fleet who ruled as regent a kingdom without a king—Hungary was a thoroughgoing dictatorship, one of Europe's worst, in fact, renowned for its violent nationalism, hatred of Jews, and suppression of liberals, pacifists, and socialists. The regime was almost indistinguishable from that of Nazi Germany or Fascist Italy.

Ironically, however, Hungarians owned the distinction of having been the first people in continental Europe to achieve a human rights charter. Back in 1222, only seven years after England's King John signed Magna Carta, the Magyars wrested from their own wicked King Andrew II a similar document called the Golden Bull, conferring on the nobles the *ius resistendi* (right to resist) whenever the monarch broke the pact.

In modern times the only Hungarian to invoke the Golden Bull was a Communist, Béla Kun, who in March 1919 set up a Soviet republic that lasted only four months. It was crushed by a counterrevolutionary movement headed by Admiral Horthy and General Julius Goemboes, who idolized and tried to emulate Mussolini. Horthy and Goemboes were responsible for Hungary's horrendous White Terror, during which thousands of Jews were tortured and murdered on the pretext that they were Communists.

With Kun's downfall Horthy tried to reestablish the monarchy, but when the idea proved unpopular, he proclaimed himself regent in 1920. Twenty years later he was as firmly in power in Budapest as Mussolini in Rome or Hitler in Berlin.

Horthy was a tall, craggy, inscrutable man of seventy-two and reputedly anti-German, but during our brief encounter he kept his anti-Nazi feelings to himself. The admiral, however, didn't bother to disguise his hatred of the Russians, an animosity all Hungarians shared. Until Hitler stopped the traffic, Horthy told me, he had allowed about three thousand Hungarians to go to Finland to help their "remote cousins" fight Stalin's Red Army.

The Hungarians were also unanimous in their irredentist claims to territories lost in World War I, principally Transylvania, which was awarded to Romania for its minimal assistance to the Allies in World War I, and Voyvodina, which became part of northwestern Yugoslavia.

What Horthy & Co. really wanted—and hoped to regain with the help of the Axis powers—was Transylvania, where Horthy was born, as were virtually all other members of the Hungarian hierarchy, among them the wily prime minister, Count Paul Teleki. All were dispossessed landed aristocrats from Transylvania and hated the Romanians at least as much as they loathed the Russians.

Count Teleki, a tall, spare, gray man with a perpetually worried look, tried to persuade Italy and Yugoslavia to join Hungary in a defensive alliance against Germany. He journeyed often to Rome to confer with Mussolini and Ciano but eventually realized that the Italians would be of little, if any, help in staving off the Germans. Although Italy desired a predominant position in the Danubian Basin, Teleki saw that Mussolini—for whom the Hungarians had named a street in Budapest—was not prepared to offer any strong opposition to German penetration of the Balkans.

"Hungary," one of Teleki's closest aides told me in an interview, "is fully aware of the difficult moment in which we find ourselves and has adopted an attitude that harmonizes with superior European necessities. Our country is patient. It has a thousand years of history, and it therefore can wait."*

I interpreted this to mean that the Duce and Ciano had persuaded Teleki that Hungary's territorial demands would be satisfied only if Budapest joined the Rome-Berlin Axis and contributed to an ultimate Nazi-Fascist victory.

Meanwhile, Hungary continued to sell bauxite to Germany at the rate of 560,000 tons a year, along with hogs, wheat, corn, horses, and beef. The country went without meat twice a week, but meatless days worked no hardship on the upper classes. They dined well on venison, boar, pheasant, and

* In 1941, when Germany marched against Yugoslavia through Hungary, Teleki committed suicide.

duck, wallowed in gypsy music, and filled to capacity such nightclubs as the honky-tonk Arizona, where tables rose and fell at the touch of a button and the platter-shaped dance floor spun around and around under tricky lighting.

Watching the tableau, I almost forgot that on Hungary's steppes peasants were earning the equivalent of fifteen cents a day in American money, rarely tasted meat, and lived like serfs, their lives regulated by the needs of the soil. It was a contrast between haves and have-nots that I was to find throughout the Balkans.

BUCHAREST

The Danubian countries—specifically, Hungary, Yugoslavia, Romania, and Bulgaria—had become a chessboard upon which both the Germans and the Allies were playing out a desperate political-economic game. What Germany wanted at the time was not actual possession of the area's lands as much as assurance that their products would remain fully available; invasion was too likely to interfere with production and frustrate the purpose which it might have served. So long as the countries involved continued to trade with it, Germany's policy was to support their neutrality while trying by intrigue, threats, and political blackmail to bind their economies to the ultimate service of the Reich.

The focal point of German pressure—and of Allied counterpressure—was King Carol's Romania, fabulously rich in grain, lumber, and, most important of all, petroleum. Romania virtually floated on the stuff that Hitler needed for Europe's burning. Germany wanted it, and the Allies were doing their best to prevent it from falling into German hands.

Hitler had only two important sources of oil beyond the frontiers of Germany and the lands it had acquired as a result of Munich and the successful Polish campaign: Romania and Russia. However, the single-track Russian railroads, already congested with troops and supplies for the Finnish front— and in preparation for operations in Bessarabia—could not move oil to Germany even if Russia had it to spare. American oil engineers who had recently visited the Soviet Union told me in Budapest that the country's production was behind the previous year's schedule. Since early September Russia had stopped exporting petroleum.

The worst winter Europe had experienced in nearly a century had complicated Hitler's supply problem. He could not have foreseen that the Danube would freeze weeks before it usually did and stay frozen nearly a month longer than usual. The two single-track railway lines that ran through German and Russian Poland, moreover, remained almost inoperable from November to the end of February; the passes in the Carpathians, normally more or less open even in midwinter, were blocked with snow and ice.

By the terms of a German-Romanian trade agreement signed in December 1939, Berlin was supposedly assured of a minimum of 130,000 tons of crude a month. But the January 1940 deliveries amounted to only 26,000 tons. The shortfall was mainly due to transportation problems. The frozen Danube prevented transport by that route, and the Allies had prepared for the spring thaw by chartering all available barges. Movement of oil by rail through Galicia, then controlled by Russia, was so unreliable that toward the end of January Germany obtained permission from Moscow to put its own technicians in charge in an attempt to remedy what had become a critical situation. Germany, it was estimated, required at least 20 million, tons of oil a year for its war machine but was getting only a fraction of the amount it needed, and only at premium prices.

Allied competition in the form of preemptive buying shot the price of Romanian crude up from seventeen dollars a ton to forty-seven dollars, and German pressure for increased shipments met with Anglo-French counterpressure. Nearly 80 percent of the Romanian fields were owned by British, Dutch, American, and French consortiums, and when a petroleum commission was set up in mid-January to regulate the industry, the Allies saw to it that no oil from British- and French-owned companies went to Germany. The following month the Allies clamped down on Romania's trade by cutting off shipments of rubber, metals, and manufactured goods and wrung from King Carol's government a promise that it would ban all further deliveries of aviation fuel to the enemy and would reject Berlin's demands for an increase in its petroleum quota.

In the early stages of the war the pliable Romanian government favored the Allied cause and further complicated Hitler's oil difficulties. Bucharest imposed heavy export taxes on cereals and vegetable oils, which also strictly rationed Germany, and increased freight rates on all shipments to the Reich. Then Romania called up its military reserves, thereby hampering agriculture and substantially reducing the amount of farm produce available to Germany. In March Carol's kingdom had under arms about 1.6 million troops, virtually every man of military age in a population of 18.8 million. Ostensibly Romania was preparing to resist a German invasion.

From what I had heard in Budapest, however, the Romanian Army could offer little opposition to the Wehrmacht. Its officers, I was told, wore corsets to disguise their paunches, rouged their cheeks to give them color after nightlong debauches, and doused themselves with eau de cologne instead of washing. With few exceptions the Romanian officers with whom I came into contact in Bucharest fitted the malicious Hungarian description almost perfectly. They were a swashbuckling lot in fancy old-world uniforms who epitomized the corrupt regime of their dictatorial ruler, King Carol, who in turn was ruled by his longtime mistress, the once-beautiful Magda Lupescu.

Western military experts doubted Carol's army could hold off the Germans for more than a week or ten days. Some went so far as to suggest that the Romanians, poorly armed, poorly trained, and poorly led, would not fight at all because the country was wormy with fascism.

Romania was still an almost totally agrarian society with a corrupt aristocracy, a small middle class, and a vast proletariat of repressed, poverty-stricken peasants who were easily drawn into the ranks of the Iron Guard, an antidemocratic, anti-Semitic movement with close links to the dominant Greek Orthodox Church. Romania's prime minister, General Ion Antonescu, whom I remembered as his country's military attaché in Rome a few years back, rose to power with the help of the proscribed but still powerful clerico-Fascist Iron Guard. Antonescu was inclined to look to Italy for support against Germany *and* Russia.

The belligerents continued to maneuver for favorable diplomatic and economic advantages in Danubian Europe, but the evidence was mounting almost daily that the Allies were losing the game. After the British had blown up a cargo vessel and two barges carrying oil to Germany on the lower Danube, Berlin obtained the right to participate in "policing" the river. This put the Nazis in complete control of the Danubian traffic as the river's ice started to break up with the onset of spring.

At the same time German "tourists" began appearing in unusual numbers in Bucharest. They seemed far more interested in Romania's border fortifications and extensive oil fields, however, than they were in the sights of the Romanian capital.

I left Bucharest depressed by everything I had seen and heard, skipped Sofia and the Bulgaria of King Boris, and headed for Athens by way of Belgrade. I was convinced, by then, that the Danubian countries, possibly all the Balkans, would soon become a battlefield. History, nature, and geography, it seemed to me, had decided the area's fate in the Second Great War.

BELGRADE

Here my spirits rose somewhat. The dowdy Yugoslav capital at the junction of the Danube and Sava rivers had named no street for Mussolini, and the country, I recalled, had courageously participated in sanctions against Italy when the Duce sent his Blackshirt legions into Ethiopia. Furthermore, Mussolini's image in newsreels elicited jeers, laughter, and those rude labial sounds known to New Yorkers as Bronx cheers.

Of the Danubian countries only Yugoslavia, according to British military experts, was capable of offering more than token resistance to a German attack. The kingdom had an army of nearly two hundred thousand tough mostly Serb troops, a trained reserve of more than a million men, and a sizable air force of about seven hundred planes. Strategically, it owned a mountainous, eminently defendable terrain slashed by deep valleys with swift-flowing rivers.

Yugoslavia, however, lacked homogeneity. Also born of the ruins of the Austro-Hungarian and the Ottoman empires, the kingdom was a boiling hodgepodge of Serbs, Slovenes, Slovaks, Montenegrins, Macedonians, Bulgarians, Ruthenians, and Czechs. Among its nearly fourteen million inhabitants— mostly poor peasants, miners, and lumbermen—there were even some Hungarians, Germans, Gypsies, and Turks, each with grievances.

Yugoslavia's titular ruler was a mere boy of seventeen, Peter II, king in succession to his father, Alexander I, murdered with Barthou in Marseilles in October 1934. The real ruler was the regent, Prince Paul, a cousin of Alexander's. His task after Alexander's assassination was to unify the country, but he never managed it. From the beginning of his regency Yugoslavia was torn by domestic quarrels, the dominant one being the historic division between the Serbs and Croats, constituting between them about two thirds of the entire population.

Whether Serbs and Croats would make common cause when the Germans attacked was anyone's guess. My hunch was that the Serbs would fight but that the Croats and Slovenes, their allies to the north, probably would sit on their hands if they could. Nevertheless, the outlook for resistance in the rough terrain of Yugoslavia looked far brighter than in Hungary or Romania.

There was no night flying in Europe in those days, and the Italian Ala Littoria flight for Athens out of Belgrade made an overnight stop in Rome, where I checked in at my sometime home, the Albergo Ambasciatori, on the Via Veneto. There was no time for serious "pulse taking," but it was evident that the atmosphere in the Fascist capital had deteriorated in Germany's favor.

At the hotel, where the only tourists in residence were Germans, my old friend Charlie, the barman, was glumly uncommunicative, a sure sign that the secret police had warned him not to talk to foreigners. In the early-evening hour of *l'aperitivo,* when normally the Via Veneto would be crowded with strollers, there were few pedestrians and the famous boulevard's several cafés were half empty. With nightfall the street was dimly lighted, and motor traffic practically ceased.

At Ciampino Airport early the following morning there were more armed carabinieri on duty than normal, and decidedly unfriendly officials scrutinized my passport, personal belongings, and papers so thoroughly that I thought my tour of the Balkans might end in a Fascist jail. I was greatly relieved when I was at last allowed to pass through the gate to the tarmac to board my plane, a trimotored Caproni transport of the kind Mussolini liked to fly for the benefit of photographers. There were only five other passengers, all Italians.

Aboard the nearly empty plane, after a blue-uniformed steward offered me hard candy from a wicker canister, I scribbled a note in my pocket diary: "The smell of war is in the air in Italy."

ATHENS

On the eve of the deluge Greece was an anomaly. The cradle of democracy rocked a despotic dictatorship.

Ostensibly the country was a constitutional monarchy under the pro-British George II, who had spent many of his fifty years in exile in London, where he lived comfortably in a royal suite in Brown's Hotel, in Dover Street. Actually, however, the Greece that had given Western civilization its enduring concepts of self-government was a totalitarian state run by General John Metaxas, a dictator in the Mussolinian mold.

George had ascended the Greek throne in 1922, when he was thirty-two years old, but he ruled only briefly. He was ousted in 1923 by an uprising led by Eleutherios Venizelos, the grand old man of Greek republicanism. He regained the throne in November 1935, when the aging and ailing Venizelos failed in his final attempt to establish a Greek republic and General George Kondylis, a longtime royalist conspirator with a murky past, conveniently arranged a plebiscite in favor of the monarchy. Venizelos fled to Paris, where he subsequently died.

King George's return, however, failed to resolve the long-standing antagonisms between Greek royalists and republicans. In January 1936 a general election resulted in a virtual tie between the two parties in which the balance of power in Parliament was held by a Communist bloc of fifteen delegates. In the ensuing political chaos General Metaxas emerged as the "man on a white horse," and the pliable George accepted him as prime minister of a new right-wing royalist government.

On the pretext that the Communists were planning a general strike to paralyze the country, Metaxas proclaimed martial law and with George's consent began ruling by decree à la Mussolini. By the end of December 1936 Greece had become the world's newest totalitarian state. The king himself, however, remained staunchly pro-British, for he was a cousin of Princess Marina, the wife of the duke of Kent, and was thus linked to England's ruling house of Windsor.

In 1939 the Metaxas government accepted Britain's guarantee of military assistance in the event Greece was attacked by either Italy, its traditional enemy, or Germany, and the dictator wisely rejected Italian efforts to persuade him to renounce Greek ties to Britain. Apart from the fact that Britain owned or controlled at least two thirds of the Greek economy, Metaxas knew that the country's overwhelmingly peasant population was anti-Italian and anti-German.

This was especially true of Greece's tobacco farmers. Most of their crop, then the country's main source of income, was bought by Britain and the United States for cash on the barrel head, whereas German purchases were paid for in aspirin, cheap radios, and household utensils.

The Greeks I met in Athens—among them Dr. Bellis, a dentist who relieved me of an impacted molar—were universally pro-British and even more decidedly pro-American. Almost everyone—taxi drivers, waiters, storekeepers, local newsmen—had relatives somewhere in America. Several gave me letters to brothers, uncles, and cousins for mailing when I left the country.

After the Russians defeated the Finns in mid-March, the Allies—and the neutral Turks—made important military moves in the eastern crescent of the Mediterranean. The veteran French General Maxime Weygand was already in command of what was being billed in dispatches as "a vast army of democ-

racy" in Lebanon and Syria, which France then ruled under a League of
Nations mandate, and the British landed thirty thousand Anzacs at Suez to
reinforce their garrison in Palestine, which, with Transjordania, constituted
the area of the British mandate. The Turks, meanwhile, mobilized troops on
their northern frontier in the Caucasus, and strenuous diplomatic efforts were
being made by London to persuade them to join the Allied cause.

A friendly military attaché in the British Embassy in Athens told me that
the Russian victory over the Finns had removed any immediate prospect for
creating an Allied northern front against Germany, and the existence of the
impregnable Siegfried Line had made it necessary to find some other, more
promising area from which to launch a coordinated attack against the Germans. The Allies—particularly the British, I gathered—had decided therefore
to create a powerful army in the Middle East with a twofold objective: (1) to
protect the West's vital oil resources in the area and (2) to act as a potential
counterforce to an anticipated Russo-German pincer movement toward the
Middle East by way of the Caucasus and the Balkans.

I decided that the Middle East was the place for me to be. Getting there,
however, proved somewhat more difficult than I had imagined. There was no
plane service, direct or indirect, to Beirut, where Weygand had his headquarters, or to Cairo, where the British command was located. But an obliging Mr.
Hill, manager of the American Express Company office in Athens, solved my
problem. He booked me on a Romanian vessel, MS *Transylvania,* a Black
Sea-Mediterranean cruise ship sailing for Beirut via Suez from Piraeus, the
great port city southwest of the Greek capital, where, I was told, I would have
a two-day wait for the ship's departure.

In Piraeus I found accommodations in a modest waterfront hotel. It was
several cuts below the Grande Bretagne, where I had been staying in Athens,
but I had a magnificent view of the city's blue Phaleron Bay and time to ponder
all that I had seen and heard and felt since my arrival in Genoa aboard the
Manhattan in early February only a few weeks earlier.

I was depressed by everything I had learned in the countries south of
Germany: their evident military helplessness, their poverty, their political
disunity in the face of probable invasion by the Nazis from the north or the
Russians from the east, the greed and apparent unconcern of their pleasure-
loving upper classes, and, above all, the anti-Semitism of their universally
antidemocratic regimes. Indeed, with the possible exception of Greece, all
seemed to me to be potential allies of the Axis powers rather than friends of
France and Britain when hostilities resumed after the long winter hiatus.

I was certain of only one thing: The war was about to resume at any
moment, though probably against the will of all or most of the peoples involved. I wrote my wife:

So far, I've found no one in the so-called neutral camp who really wants
this war. The Dutch, I know from having been in Holland, are anxious
to stay out of it, and so I believe are their neighbors the Belgians, as

well as the plain people everywhere—in Hungary, Romania, Yugoslavia and Greece, even Italy, where the decision to go to war will not be made by them, of course, but by one man, Old Baldy. Want it or not, war will come to them anyhow. I don't know when, but soon, maybe even before this reaches you . . . I'm doubly glad now that I sent you and the boys home after Munich.

27

WEYGAND THE "FIREMAN"

The fat money changers who boarded the *Transylvania* at Suez at the end of the ship's first day's run offered Middle East currencies for dollars at bargain rates, and I assumed these shrewd merchants in foreign money knew something I didn't. They were invariably ahead of the news, never behind it, and the Armenian with fingers like so many sausages who sold me a batch of limp Syrian notes had an explanation. "American dollars," he said, "are much in demand by Jewish refugees."

I had become aware of the phenomenon in Piraeus, where Jews fleeing from Central and Southeastern Europe were gathering by the thousands. They filtered down through the Balkans from as far away as Poland and filled the port city's cheaper hotels and boardinghouses, awaiting transportation to freedom in Palestine, the United States, or one of the Latin American countries.

I was tempted to leave the *Transylvania* at Suez and go to the Holy Land by rail but decided to wait until after visiting Lebanon and Syria.

The next morning, when the *Transylvania* docked at Beirut, then a gleaming Levantine city deservedly known as the "Pearl of the Middle East," the drop in the value of the local currency seemed to have yet another explanation. A French-language Lebanese newspaper shouted in bold headlines that the Russians were massing troops along the Turkish and Iranian frontiers for a springtime offensive against the West's oil resources.

Dispatches from various capitals—Damascus, Teheran, Baghdad—elaborated the theme that the Soviets, only two weeks after their victory over the Finns, were bent on fulfilling the ancient czarist dream of reaching the warm waters of the Mediterranean by forcing its eastern gateway, the Turkish-held Dardanelles. I wondered at the time whether the stories were true or merely Allied propaganda to justify a Franco-British military buildup in the Middle East. True or not, the news obviously was creating a stir among the Lebanese; the Arab vendor on the quay where the ship docked sold his papers almost faster than he could make change.

I congratulated myself on having arrived in the Middle East at an apparently propitious moment to see General Weygand, commander of the French forces in Lebanon and Syria, and settled happily into Beirut's luxurious beachfront Hôtel St.-Georges where the efficient Mr. Hill had booked me an enormous double room. It had a balcony overlooking the Mediterranean and a bath as big as a skating rink.

The phones didn't work very well, but after an hour's efforts I got through to the press office in the état-major and requested an interview with Monsieur le Général Weygand at his earliest convenience. Later that afternoon a call from the general's aide, Lieutenant Fouchet, informed me that my request had been submitted and that I would receive a reply "in a day or so."

The French consul who issued my visa for Lebanon-Syria in Piraeus had given me a brief official biography of General Weygand. He was born in Brussels in 1867, making him seventy-three in 1940, and I mentally questioned whether a man of his advanced years had the mental and physical vigor to hold off the Germans or the Russians in the Middle East. Weygand had learned his soldiering at St.-Cyr, France's West Point. In World War I Weygand served as chief of staff to Marshal Foch and in that capacity helped stop the Germans at the Marne.

Weygand was also credited with having "saved Warsaw and Poland from the Bolsheviks" in 1920, and in 1931 he became chief of staff to the French Army, a post he held until 1935. By that time he had reached retirement age but was so highly regarded as a soldier that the government waived the retirement rule to keep him in uniform. Foch was reputed to have said, "When France is in danger, send for Weygand."

The laudatory details contained in the official bio were amply confirmed by Lieutenant Fouchet, who called on me at my hotel. He was a dashing young officer whose mirror brown handmade boots and tailored uniform bespoke St.-Cyr and a commission in a crack regiment of horse cavalry. Over syrupy Turkish coffee on the hotel's sun-drenched terrace he provided additional data.

Monsieur le général, he said, was "a very young seventy-three" who rode his Arabian horse every morning before breakfast, still played a snappy game of tennis, and put in eighteen hours of work every day, including Sunday, when he took time off to attend mass after his horseback ride. An author of three books on the science of warfare, Weygand was a member of L'Académie Française and an avid reader. He was currently reading Margaret Mitchell's *Gone with the Wind* in French translation.

Weygand had served in Lebanon and Syria before, from April 1923 until November 1924, during which he imposed French authority in the turbulent region which France had received as a League of Nations mandate following the Allied victory over the Turks in World War I. The conditions Weygand had found, Fouchet said, were "intolerable."

The streets of the principal cities—Beirut, Damascus, Aleppo, and Tripoli—were unsafe, and the mountainous hinterland swarmed with wandering bandit tribes that lived by plundering travelers along the trade routes. Caravans required heavily armed escorts to fight their way along the three hundred miles from Damascus to Baghdad. But only thirty days after Weygand arrived as high commissioner, his aide said, the caravans no longer needed armed protection, and travelers could go alone, on camelback or by bicycle, wherever they pleased. Women could walk the streets of cities and towns in complete safety.

Moreover, Weygand had caused dirt roads to be paved and new roads to be built, desert areas to be irrigated, and houses and barracks to be constructed. The Christian Arabs and Jews who dominated the economy grew to respect and even like Weygand because with political stability came profits, and there's nothing like the music of a jingling till to soothe the souls of merchants.

Fouchet admitted that the methods Weygand had used to pacify the country were "severe." The general had imposed his will with firing squads. How many tribesmen were executed during the nineteen months of Weygand's regime as high commissioner Fouchet couldn't say, but he guessed they probably numbered "in the hundreds."

"Force was a language the Arabs understood," the young officer said. "As a result, *monsieur le général* was widely respected as a strong administrator and admired for the many improvements he made."

A somewhat different Maxime Weygand emerged, however, from my subsequent talks with local Arab newsmen, French-speaking Muslims, and English-speaking Christians, a few of whom were graduates of the American University of Beirut. All knew the general personally or by reputation and saw him not as a paladin of progress but as the cruel embodiment of French colonialism. The veterans among them remembered particularly the severity with which Weygand foisted French rule over resentful Arabs who had been promised independence, not French colonial domination, for their contribution to the Allied victory in World War I. According to my informants, the general had used the firing squads far more freely than his aide had indicated. Not "hundreds," they said, but thousands had fallen before the rifles of the general's troops of the Foreign Legion.

Arab resentment of French hegemony persisted through the 1930s, when it was nourished by antidemocratic Axis propaganda and money from Berlin and Rome. With the exception of Lebanon's Christian and Jewish minorities, who remained loyal to the Allied cause, the area's huge majority of Muslim Arabs hoped to achieve through an Axis victory in World War II the independence denied them after World War I.

After several meetings with Weygand's aide, during which he told me, among other things, that the general was his own censor and read every word journalists cabled out of the country, Fouchet took me on a two-day tour of northern Lebanon and western Syria in an army vehicle driven by an Arab soldier with a mania for speeding around blind curves. During our travels I saw a number of tented encampments that suggested the presence in the area of thousands of French colonial troops: ebony black Senegalese; wild Circassians, who rode and shouted and looked like Russian Cossacks; Bedouin units mounted on camels; hard-riding spahi horsemen in colorful flowing capes; detachments of meharist Algerians, some Moroccans, and a few Malagasy from Madagascar.

I saw nothing to substantiate published reports that Weygand was assembling a "vast army of democracy." The only units that had the look of well-trained and disciplined soldiers were elements of two regiments of the Foreign Legion, whose precisely stacked rifles and immaculate camps were impressive. I saw no tanks, artillery, or planes, however, and, when I asked why not, got in return a blank stare from Fouchet.

Finally, one bright morning, as I was having an early breakfast on the hotel terrace and wondering when, if ever, I would get to see Weygand, Fouchet came to tell me that *monsieur le général* would receive me *immédiatement.* I gulped down a last bite of croissant with my café au lait and accompanied the aide to headquarters.

At the entrance to the three-story building that housed the état-major, the two brown-skinned spahi hussars in red, white, and blue capes who flanked the doorway saluted smartly, rifles held at present arms. We climbed the stairs to the top floor and Weygand's soundproofed suite, and on the way up Fouchet told me the general was "very upset" about the fact that the Finns had been obliged to submit to the Russians for lack of support from the Western powers. I made a mental note to ask Weygand his reaction to the Russian victory.

A sign on the wall of Weygand's outer office said, in French: SILENCE. YOU KNOW NOTHING. THEREFORE SAY NOTHING.

How true, I mused. I certainly knew very little about Weygand's "army of democracy," surely nothing I dared cable at thirty-five cents a word to *Collier's.* Just to write "General Maxime Weygand" would cost more than a dollar. I hoped, however, that the general would say something worth cabling about how he intended to defend the Middle East from German or Russian attack.

Waiting to be ushered into the commander's presence, I resisted a temptation to light a cigarette, for the aide had warned me that *monsieur le général* was a nonsmoker. After a fidgety half hour a buzzer sounded, and Fouchet motioned me to follow him.

Of the many high-ranking Allied field commanders I was to meet in the years ahead, Weygand remains etched in memory as the most uncommunicative. My "interview" with him in his Spartan study—uncarpeted floor, plain, uncluttered desk, two nondescript chairs for visitors, portrait of Marshal Foch on the wall behind where Weygand sat—produced all the professional satisfaction I might have derived from a chat with the very late King Tutankhamen.

The general rose to his full five feet eight inches, greeted me politely in French, then sat down and waited for my questions. I looked into a lean, leathery face—much like a professor's, I thought—with wide-set brown eyes, a balding pate rimmed with nicely clipped gray blond hair, and a neatly trimmed brownish mustache. From all that I had heard about him I had expected to see a dashingly romantic figure, a character out of *Beau Geste*. But although Weygand was in uniform, he looked more like a pedagogue than a soldier.

I asked the general how he felt about the Red Army's victory over the Finns.

"It would be strange indeed," Weygand replied, "if at my age I didn't have ideas of my own about things. . . ."

There was a long pause during which I waited for the general to continue, but it became apparent that he wasn't going to share those "ideas," whatever they might be, with a reporter.

Could the general give a perplexed journalist any indication of the size of the French forces in Lebanon and Syria and what their mission might be—offensive or defensive?

"No, I cannot," he replied. "Numbers and objectives are military secrets. But you have visited our camps. How many troops would you say there are?"

I said I thought there might be as few as twenty thousand or as many as half a million. Weygand pursed his lips and raised his eyebrows but said nothing.

At long last, perhaps out of pity, the general volunteered a few words.

"*Moi, je suis un pompier* [Me, I'm a fireman]," he said in a metallic, though not unpleasant, voice. "If a fire breaks out anywhere, I shall put it out. I am a soldier at the command of my superiors in Paris."

And where did the general think the fire might erupt? In the Low Countries? The Balkans? The Middle East itself?

Weygand answered with an imperceptible smile and rose to indicate the "interview" was over. At Penn I had an English professor who dismissed classes abruptly. His name was—Cornelius Weygandt! I almost asked if they were related but held my tongue.*

---

* Years later I learned there was a mystery about the circumstances of Weygand's birth. Possibly because he was born in Belgium, some said his father was King Leopold II. Other sources said he was really the son of the archduke Maximilian, quondam emperor of Mexico, and yet others that he was actually the out-of-wedlock offspring of a Belgian Jewish businessman who had a gardener named Weygand. In September 1940, after three months as minister of national Defense in Pétain's Vichy government following the fall of France, Weygand was sent to Algeria as governor-general. Washington and London both entertained hope he might defect to the Allies. The Germans thought so, too, and in 1942 they imprisoned him for three years. After the war, so did the French. Released, he wrote his

That evening, aware that Weygand himself would read every word I wrote, I cabled *Collier's* a routine and, I blush to say, very hokey piece about the great "Desert Warrior." I reread it now in shame and sorrow.

But although Weygand's "vast army of democracy" in Lebanon and Syria proved to be more myth than reality, the Middle East was far from lost. Having read Allenby's memoirs, I sensed that the area would become one of the major battlefields of World War II.

I moved on to Palestine, where not only the British but also the Jews were building armies. The Jews, I found, were also laying the foundations for something more, a future nation.

Postscript: On the tenth day of May, 1940, five weeks almost to the day after my brief, unproductive meeting with him, General Maxime Weygand was summoned to France to "put out a fire." For in the morning of that fine spring day Hitler launched his long-delayed blitzkrieg in all its anticipated fury. German troops poured into Holland, Belgium, and Luxembourg and were soon deep in French territory.

Nine days later, on May 19, with the Allied armies in retreat and the French forces disintegrating like shale under the hammerblows of the Wehrmacht's armor, Weygand succeeded General Maurice Gustave Gamelin as chief of the Allied high command. He proved a poor choice, for he lacked experience as a field commander. His outmoded "linear defense" to hold the Germans' "penetration in depth" proved inadequate and led to the rout of the French Army.

---

memoirs, *Recalled to Service,* in 1952 and died in obscurity in 1965 at the age of ninety-eight.

28

ZION DEFERRED

I had wanted to visit Palestine for some time but never had the opportunity until I found myself next door, in Lebanon.

Since the end of World War I, when Palestine became a stepchild of the British Empire as mandated territory, the land that had cradled Judaism and Christianity—and was sacred also to Islam—had become the scene of bloody strife between Jews and Arabs. The Jews fought to regain their long-lost sovereignty in the domain of their biblical kingdoms of Israel and Judah, and the Arabs struggled to prevent it in a land they claimed was theirs by right of possession and religious affiliations.

In late March 1940, six months after the outbreak of World War II, I looked forward to visiting the charismatic scene of what seemed to be almost a war within a war. Apart from a desire to walk in the steps of the giants of the Bible, I wanted particularly to see whether the Zionists had succeeded in establishing in Palestine the Jewish homeland which England had promised them in the crucial third year of the First World War but had expediently recanted on the eve of the Second.

I had become interested in Zionism in the late 1930s, when it became abundantly evident that in the anti-Semitic Europe of Hitler and his contemporaries the Jews were an endangered species. Their main, perhaps their only hope of sanctuary in the dawning wartime world of the 1940s was a state of their own in the land of their origins such as England had promised the Zionists in 1917.

England's pledge came in a letter from Arthur James (later Lord) Balfour, Britain's foreign secretary, dated November 2, 1917, to Lord Rothschild, eminent Zionist and head of the distinguished financial house that bore his name. It stated, in brief, that "His Majesty's government views with favour the establishment in Palestine of a national home for the Jewish people . . . it being clearly understood that nothing shall be done which may prejudice the civil and religious rights of the existing non-Jewish communities. . . ."

With this statement, inscribed in the history books as the Balfour Declaration, England apparently undertook to reverse the Diaspora, the dispersion of the Jews to the four corners of the world by their Roman conquerors A.D. 70. From it, the Zionists hoped, would flow the return of the Jews to eventual nationhood and safety from persecution in the land that had cradled their faith.

Hailed by the Zionists as a renewal of the political connection of the Jews to Zion and the land of Israel, the declaration was vociferously denounced by anti-Zionists—Jews as well as Gentiles—and, of course, by Arabs, to whom the idea of Jewish nationhood in the Holy Land was (and still is) an act of unpardonable injustice to the territory's Arab population. Actually the declaration was a triumph of expediency over morality, a not uncommon phenomenon of power politics, for even as the British were promising the Jews a homeland in Palestine, they were also encouraging Arab nationalism as a means of hastening victory. As soon as the war ended, Syrian nationalists declared Palestine to be "Southern Syria" and demanded its inclusion in a vast Arab state with its center in Damascus.

By then, however, the Zionist task of turning an unremarkable piece of Mediterranean real estate—consisting largely of desert, rock, and marshlands—into a viable Jewish nation had already bugun. But so had Arab resistance to the Jewish presence, and to defend themselves against Arab strikes, riots and terrorism, the Zionists organized a hard-hitting underground defense force known as the Haganah.

By the early spring of 1936 what had been merely sporadic Arab violence directed mainly against the Zionist establishment had developed into an organized nationalist insurrection aimed principally, though by no means exclusively, against British authority. The uprising lasted nearly three years and coincided significantly with Nazi and Fascist successes in Ethiopia, Spain, Austria, and Czechoslovakia.

The insurrection, which entered the history of mandatory Palestine as the Arab Revolt of 1936–1939, frightened the appeasers then still in power in London and undoubtedly influenced a dramatic about-face in British policy in the Holy Land. After Munich, Neville Chamberlain's government realized that a new major war was imminent and decided that the Holy Land's restive Arab nationalists—and the remainder of the Arab world as well—had to be appeased lest they join Britain's enemies in the looming conflict. Thus in May 1939, four months before the Germans invaded Poland, Britain's Colonial Office issued a white paper which threatened to extinguish the Zionist dream of a national homeland.

The white paper limited Jewish immigration to Palestine to ten thousand a year for five years, severely restricted the sale of Arab land to Jewish buyers, and proposed the creation by the year 1949 of an independent Palestinian state with an Arab majority but linked to Great Britain politically and economically.

From the Zionist point of view, the white paper was an act of appeasement comparable in its iniquity with the one committed earlier at Munich, for it could not have come at a more crucial moment. Tens of thousands of Jews were fleeing the Nazi-Fascist racism then rampant in Czechoslovakia, Hungary, Romania, Italy, Yugoslavia, Austria, and Poland. Thousands more waited in vain in Mediterranean ports to take them to the Promised Land.

After what I had seen of so-called Christian regimes in the Europe of my time, I had concluded that the Jews, whom I respected and admired as a dynamic, enlightened people, were infinitely more sincerely dedicated to the human values inherent in democracy than their Christian tormentors. Since the rise to power of Adolf Hitler in 1933, I had become persuaded that the Jews needed a homeland of their own more than at any time since the Inquisition expelled them from Spain in 1492.

In the early spring of 1940 I was anxious to see how the Zionists in Palestine were coping with the new obstacles to Jewish nationhood created by the white paper. Admittedly, however, I undertook the task as a partisan of what I believed to be a just cause.

Tel Aviv, where I arrived shortly before noon on a Saturday, the Jewish Sabbath, was only a few hours' ride from Beirut on the smelly train that ran southward along the picturesque Levantine coast and linked the Lebanese "Pearl of the Middle East" with distant Cairo to the southwest.

The lone vehicle available at the dismal station in Tel Aviv was an elderly Chevy sedan. Its owner-driver was a fat, middle-aged Arab in a faded gray duster and battered visored cap who identified himself as Ahmed Mazjoub, official guide, and showed me a dog-eared document to prove it. He assured me his car was roadworthy and after some haggling over the fare consented to take me to Jerusalem.

The narrow and strictly utilitarian British-built tarmac road leading to Jerusalem ran through Ramla, on the coastal plain southeast of Tel Aviv-Jaffo. Ramla was the only city the Arabs had ever founded in Palestine, established A.D. 716 by a caliph named Suleiman, who built marketplaces, fortifications, and a great mosque with a famous blue tower. On Ahmed's recommendation we stopped to inspect the unexceptional ruins.

Later, at a café where Arabs in galabias played a noisy form of checkers known as *sheshbesh,* sipped coffee, or smoked water pipes called nargilehs while listening to whiny Arabic music blaring from a radio, Ahmed informed me that before 1936 a large community of "Jews—too many Jews" had lived in Ramla, but by 1939, during what he called "our three-year revolution," they all had been "driven out." He meant, of course, the Arab Revolt that had inspired the British white paper. Ramla, he added in the course of his routine guide's spiel, was captured by the Crusaders in the year 1096.

"But they didn't stay long either," he said with obvious relish. "We drove them out in less than three years. They fortified the city, but the fortifications were destroyed by our great Saladin in the twelfth century, and from then on Ramla was always an Arab city. Napoleon came in 1799, when he was trying to conquer Palestine from the Turks. But we pushed him out, too . . . just like someday we will push out the British and the Jews. . . ."

At an outdoor Arab restaurant, where we lunched on thinly sliced lamb from a rotating spit, served with grilled tomatoes and hot pita bread, Ahmed confided that he was a member of the outlawed Istiglal, the Arab independence party founded in 1932 by the notorious anti-Semite Haj Amin el-Husseini, soon to become Hitler's helper in the latter's genocidal "final solution" of the "Jewism problem."

At Ramla the road turned eastward from the coastal plain and upward into the Judean hills toward Jerusalem. On the way Ahmed, having determined that I was neither English nor Jewish, let it be known that he hated Palestine's British overlords but detested the Jews even more.

"We were better off under the Turks," he said. "The British promised us independence after the big war in 1919, but instead of freedom, they gave us colonial oppression and lots of Jews. Those Jews! They own every piece of land worth having. And that's not right. That's not the justice the British promised us. . . ."

Ahmed was silent for a while after I reminded him that the Arabs had sold the land to the Jews and received good gold in return. After deep thought and a few near misses with British military vehicles coming downhill along the winding ribbonlike road, he said, "Yes, but if the Jews keep on coming, there will be no land left for us . . . only this . . ." and he indicated a stretch of deforested hills that flanked the road on the right.

I ignored Ahmed's remark and directed him to the very British King David Hotel in Jewish West Jerusalem, opposite the YMCA and its imposing, phalliclike bell tower. I had a couple of martinis at the bar, showered and rested after the long, hot trip, and scribbled a few notes in my diary on what Ahmed had said.

Then I stepped out onto the balcony of my fourth-floor room to take in the view looking east toward Old Jerusalem. I was enthralled by what I saw and somewhat baffled by what I felt.

I beheld a city more evocative of the past than Rome itself, and I experienced an inexplicable sense of kinship with a place that I had never seen before yet that was vaguely familiar, as though I had seen it in another lifetime. I felt I'd been caught in a time machine that had transported me back into some distant yesterday. But which one? The burning of the Second Temple of the Jews? Christ's crucifixion? Muhammad's ascension?

In the light of the afternoon sun Old Jerusalem was a city of gold and silver enclosed in the skewed rectangle formed by its surrounding walls. Visible from where I stood were the Citadel with David's Tower, the golden dome of the Mosque of Omar, and the silver dome of the el-Aqsa Mosque.

Contained within the walls' crenellated ramparts, my guidebook told me, were the Church of the Holy Sepulchre, Golgotha, Calvary, the Via Dolorosa, and, somewhere nearby, the Garden of Gethsemane, scene of the agony and arrest of Jesus. Clearly the absurdly small space held monuments sacred to Judaism and to both its daughter religions, Christianity and Islam.

For more than a thousand years before its capture by the Romans A.D. 70, Jerusalem had been the capital of an Israelite empire. Then followed Roman rule, Byzantine rule, and again Jewish rule. The years 638 to 1099 marked the Muslim period, but the Arabs ruled from Baghdad and Ramla and Damascus, not from Jerusalem. The Turks, Tatars, Mamelukes, and Crusaders all came and went until in 1917 General Allenby conquered it with the help of his Jewish units.

As I looked down upon the Old City's agglutination of bell towers, domes, and spires, it occurred to me that Jerusalem contained the explosive elements of contention for a long time to come, perhaps forever. Three of humankind's great faiths could claim it. But which, I wondered, had prior right to sovereignty in a place sacred also to the others?

To whom did Jerusalem "belong" in the year 1940? The answer did not lie in the Old Testament, the New Testament, or the Koran. Nor could it come from the British, the city's most recent conquerors and its masters in wartime 1940. Whatever the ultimate decision, it would have to be postponed until the world was at peace again sometime in the clouded, distant future.

Impatient to explore the holy places before the muezzin's sundown call to Muslim prayer, I walked across the shallow valley that separates modern Jerusalem from the Old City and entered it by the noble Damascus Gate. After wandering rather aimlessly through crowded, shop-lined streets and cobbled Arab souks that stank of donkeys' droppings and uncollected garbage, I found myself at the Western ("Wailing") Wall.

As I stood for the first time before those massive tawny stones which ancient masons had laboriously squared with primitive tools and fitted together without benefit of mortar, it struck me that the ruin established beyond question the primacy of Judaism's claim to the Holy City, ergo to the Holy Land itself.

Moreover, religious Jews in considerable numbers had lived in Palestine since time immemorial—not all Jews were dispersed by the Roman conquest— and could claim a lien on sovereignty in the Holy Land that preceded by several hundred years the coming of the Arabs with the rise of Islam at the turn of the seventh century A.D.

The mostly secular-minded Jews I met in Tel Aviv, Haifa, and Jerusalem, however, took the view that they had a right to Palestine not for religious reasons or because they were born in Palestine but because no other country would have them. They were Zionists bent on making a nation out of swamp, desert, and rock and, for the most part, were inclined to look upon the Arabs as squatters or intruders from neighboring, less prosperous Arab states. For them, the moral dilemma implicit in the phenomenon of Jews occupying Arab land lay in the distant future.

In 1940 some thirty-two thousand British troops mounted guard over the Holy Land, and there was peace. But the peace was palpably only a truce which even the most sanguine Zionists knew would be broken when the war ended or when the British left the territory to its own devices in 1949 as proposed in the white paper.

Over the years both Arabs and Jews had increased in numbers. In 1922, according to the official census, Palestine had 757,182 inhabitants, of whom only 83,794 were Jews. By 1940, however, the Arabs numbered about 800,000 and the Jews 400,000. The Arab increment was attributable to a higher Arab birthrate as well as to local immigration from adjacent Arab lands. The increase in the Jewish population, on the other hand, was due mainly to the heavy influx of refugees from Hitlerism.

Jewish immigration had apparently benefited the Arabs by creating an improved economic and social climate. Thousands of Arabs found employment on Jewish settlements, where for the first time in their lives they were paid decent wages. Furthermore, they were treated as equals in Jewish hospitals, where they went for treatment of their many ailments: trachoma, tuberculosis, and the almost infinite variety of intestinal diseases common to the Middle East.

The prosperity of the Palestine Arabs became, in fact, the envy of their brethren in sparsely inhabited Trans-Jordan. In 1933 the emir Abdullah, the country's British-appointed ruler, entered secret negotiations with the Zionists on the possibility of large-scale Jewish immigration into the area east of the Jordan River. But the talks were nipped in the bud by the British military authorities, who from the outset obstructed rather than helped Jewish implementation of the Balfour policy.

Meanwhile, the Jews wisely strengthened their hold on Palestine by making huge purchases of land from the small but wealthy class of Arab and Turkish effendis, the landowners. Many were gentry living luxuriously in Beirut, Paris, or Cairo while their peasants, the fellahin, were paid coolie wages, slept in mud huts with their animals, if they owned any, burned dried camel dung for fuel, and usually died before reaching the age of thirty-five.

By the end of 1935 the Jewish National Fund—with money raised mainly in the United States from working-class Jews—had bought 250,000 acres of land for the the fantastic sum of $21,010,400, equivalent to about $84 an acre for land not worth one tenth the amount. Much of it was scraggy, stony desert and soggy swamp. But the Zionists irrigated the land if desert, cleared it if rock-strewn, drained it if swamp, and made it bloom with orchards and crops.

Except for those improvements, however, Palestine remained much as it had been for centuries and as it largely remained when I saw it in 1940: a fertile coastal plain; patches of green where Zionist hands had rebuilt ancient terracings against erosion; then rock and dun-colored desert. The Dead Sea, as I glimpsed it from atop Mount Scopus above Jerusalem, lay like a great greasy blue-green puddle in the distance, at the southern end of the Jordan River, a reservoir of Palestine's only mineral wealth: potash for fertilizer.

But even as the Zionists went about the business of building their national homeland with plow and hoe, they were obliged to defend it over and over again with rifle and grenade against Arab marauders. Despite the uncertain conditions created by the Arab Revolt and, subsequently, the white paper, some sixty thousand immigrants managed to enter Palestine between the spring of 1936 and March 1940 both legally and illegally. The "illegals" were the beneficiaries of a traffic in human lives that had sprung up in the eastern crescent of the Mediterranean mainly as a result of the restrictions imposed by the new British policy.

As racial nihilism radiated outward from Germany throughout Central and Southeastern Europe, the resourceful Zionists contrived ways and means of bringing in refugees in spite of the new regulations. The agents of a well-organized network in the affected areas helped the fleeing Jews reach Mediterranean ports in Greece and Turkey. There they were loaded onto ships whose Levantine owners were far more interested in profits than in saving lives. For berths in the dark, stinking holds of their often unseaworthy vessels they charged as much as four hundred dollars a head for a passage normally costing only sixty dollars for a first-class cabin with bath, which was what I had paid for my longer trip on the *Transylvania* from Piraeus to Beirut via Port Said.

The ships ran the British naval blockade and sailed as close as they dared to the Palestinian coast at points where, by prearrangement, small boats went out from shore to meet the incoming vessels and take off their passengers. At first the British, aware that the immigrants were mostly sick, frightened, penniless people without passports or official papers of any kind, closed their eyes to the traffic. They banned it, however, when the Arabs protested, and it became a criminal offense for local Jews to help the refugees. Shore patrols of Tommies were set up, and the arrivals, when caught, were hauled off to internment camps.

Some of the vessels carrying "illegals" were fired upon by British shore batteries and forced back onto the open seas. But the piratical shipowners were making far too much money to be discouraged even by gunfire, and they often risked their ships and the lives of their passengers by beaching their vessels. Despite the dangers of the voyage and the likelihood of internment, the immigrants kept coming.

The immigrants believed they were responding to a higher mandate than the one held by Palestine's imperial overlords. Written into the "passports" issued to them by the Jewish underground's agents was a passage from the Book of Ezekiel: "And they shall dwell in the land that I have given unto Jacob, my servant, wherein your fathers have dwelt; and they shall dwell therein, even they, and their children, and their children's children, forever."

And so the Jewish underground kept bringing them in, by the dozen, by the hundreds, the new arrivals making an ideological virtue out of hard work, bare-handed toil to win back Palestine from the neglect of centuries.

When the war started, Palestine's Jews were caught on the horns of a dilemma. On the one hand, they had to support Great Britain in its struggle against Hitler's Germany, for there was no other protector in sight. On the other hand, they could not accept Britain's policy of appeasement of the Arab world, for this would have meant endangering the lives of an ever-increasing number of Jews in Europe. Some 200,000 Jewish lives were at risk in Austria, as were the lives of 117,000 Czech and 136,000 Slovak Jews in Czechoslovakia and of hundreds of thousands more elsewhere in Europe.

The dilemma was resolved by the formidable David Ben-Gurion, chairman of the Jewish Agency, which represented the World Zionist Organization in Palestine and abroad. He declared: "We shall fight the war as if there were no White Paper, and the White Paper as if there were no war." Ben-Gurion's twofold policy resulted in the arrival in Palestine of about twenty thousand "illegals" during the first five months of World War II.

Ben-Gurion was, and remained for many years, the driving force behind the Zionist Socialist movement in the Holy Land. This secular Jew, who, I later discovered, couldn't recall when he was last in a synagogue, was a short, squat man with an mane of unruly white hair, brooding eyes, and a leonine expression. He seemed to have been hewn from the gray-black rock that covered much of the denuded hills of the Palestine of his time and resembled portraits I had seen of the French revolutionary Maximilien Robespierre.*

The day Britain declared war against Germany, Palestine's Jews, responding to Ben-Gurion's dictum, showed their willingness to aid Britain's cause by registering virtually en masse for military service. All told, 136,033 members of the Jewish community—85,781 men and 50,262 women, almost the entire Jewish population between the ages of eighteen and fifty-four—volunteered. But the British were reluctant to accept Jewish help. As a high-ranking British officer put it, "the recruitment of Palestinian Jews would cause more trouble among the Arabs than it was worth."

However, the shortage of British manpower, especially of service personnel, soon made itself felt throughout the Middle East, and the authorities appealed to the Jewish Agency to assist them in recruiting pioneer companies, men to dig latrines and trenches, construct fortifications, and build roads. The Jews were obviously being offered menial jobs, and the Jewish Agency rejected

* Born plain David Grün in Poland in 1886, he emigrated in 1906 to Palestine, where he changed his name to Ben-Gurion ("son of the lion cub" in Hebrew) and worked as a farm laborer. In 1915 he formed the country's first Jewish trade union. Expelled by the Turks for pro-Allied sympathies shortly after the start of World War I, he helped raise a Jewish Legion in the United States and served with the British in the Palestine campaign against Turkey. In 1930 he founded the Mapai (Labor) party, and by the time World War II erupted he headed the shadow government of the Jewish state-to-be.

the appeal. The British later requested volunteers to serve in transport companies and engineering units, as mechanics, RAF ground crews, and service personnel in the navy, and the agency agreed although the British steadfastly refused to accept Palestinian Jews for combat.

The readiness of the Jews to participate in the struggle against a common enemy raised hopes that the white paper policy would be suspended at least for the duration of the war, but these hopes were soon disappointed. The mandatory government, then headed by Sir Harold MacMichael as high commissioner, persisted in its campaign against refugee boats arriving from Europe. When it became apparent that the internment of new arrivals would not stop the flow, the government began deporting them to distant places like Mauritius.

The beginning of the war also coincided with the introduction of repressive measures against the Jewish community's defense force, the Haganah. Although the British army had gladly accepted its help in putting down the Arab Revolt, the organization was forced to resume its original underground defensive character. Thereafter its members trained secretly at night in remote areas to avoid British sentries and Arab spies. More than forty Haganah troops were arrested while participating in a clandestine officers' training course and sentenced to five years' imprisonment.

The British demanded the surrender of the Haganah's arms and conducted searches for weapons in Jewish villages and settlements throughout the country. There was no serious British attempt to disarm the Arabs, however, and security remained one of the Jewish community's paramount problems. All Jewish villages were fortified with barbed-wire fences, strongpoints, and searchlights and wherever necessary were reinforced with Haganah fighters.

But the Haganah continued to strengthen its forces. By early April 1940 it numbered about ten thousand men, all well trained in guerrilla warfare by the pro-Zionist British captain (later general) Orde Wingate. The Jews were preparing to fight the Germans if they succeeded in invading the Middle East or the Arabs after the big war ended and the British went home.

Meanwhile, the flow of refugees via the underground route continued almost unabated. Although few of the newcomers had ever worked on the soil, they found employment on the numerous farm cooperatives, known as moshavot, that had sprung up along the coast between Tel Aviv and Haifa, filling jobs that Arabs had abandoned during the insurrection. The result was a spectacular increase in farm output. I visited several moshavot and was surprised to learn that the Jewish community was able to meet its needs for vegetables, fruit, poultry, eggs, and other foods.

More surprising was what I saw on the faces of the immigrants working on the farms. Gone, now, was the look of fear I had seen on Jewish faces in Italy, Hungary, Romania, Yugoslavia, and, most recently, Piraeus. I came away with a feeling that in Palestine a new breed of Jew was emerging and that despite the innumerable obstacles created by the war, a new Jewish nation was rising on the ruins of the old.

The newcomers also replaced Arabs in the ports, on construction sites, and in the quarries where stone was being cut for the massive building program the Jewish community had undertaken. In the new western portion of Jerusalem, a leafy quarter known as Rehaviah, I saw a great building boom was under way, financed mainly by well-to-do immigrants from Germany. Jerusalem held seventy-six thousand Jews, about 60 percent of the city's population.

When I visited it in 1940, Tel Aviv was already a sprawling caramel-colored minimetropolis of more than 150,000 Jews and a budget that exceeded the combined budgets of twenty-two other municipalities. In Haifa, where the construction of Palestine's first modern port had been completed in 1933 (in 1940 it was being used as a base by the British navy), the Jewish population had tripled to 50,000, about half the city's total.

In the meantime, in the cities and their environs modern industry was coming into being, based mainly on the production of foods, textiles, and building materials. In the industrial sector the new arrivals also found employment, though the greatest beneficiaries of the "illegal" immigration, apart from the agricultural settlements, were the defense forces: the Haganah and its auxiliaries.

The increment in Jewish military strength, actual and potential, pleased Ben-Gurion, for he knew the day was bound to arrive when Palestine's Jews would be called upon to fight to realize their dream of nationhood in the Holy Land. If all went according to British plans as outlined in the white paper and as urged by Sir Harold MacMichael, there would be a national government in Palestine after the war, a government based strictly on population figures that would make the Arabs automatically the ruling majority.

Sir Harold, a Colonial Office visionary, thought in terms of an eventual federation of Middle Eastern states, each of them independent but tied to Britain politically and economically. He was a brilliant, morose man whose word was law in Palestine and who brought to his high office wide experience in colonial administration in the Sudan and Tanganyika. He was seldom seen in public and was known in Jerusalem as the "Old Man on the Hill" because his house was on a hilltop near the city. The site happened to be the Hill of Evil Counsel where in Roman times the decision was made to arrest and prosecute Jesus.

Sir Harold was an ardent advocate of the recommendations made in 1937 by a British royal commission to partition Palestine into two states, one Islamic and the other Jewish. Jerusalem was to be "internationalized" neutral territory under British protection. For the Jews, it would have represented Zion without Zion. Anyhow, the Arabs rejected the proposal. They, too, wanted Jerusalem.

In my diary on my last day in Palestine I wrote what turned out to be a fairly accurate forecast of what happened in the Holy Land some years later: "Lots of people are going to be killed in these parts some day because, obviously, Britain cannot impose a plan for the solution of the political and religious antagonisms between Jews and Arabs against their separate wills."

Among the many friends I made in Palestine, two endeared themselves by the warmth of their hospitality and their patience in answering my questions about their country. They were Harry Zinder, the young correspondent of the Associated Press in Jerusalem, and his lovely brunette wife, Hemdah. In acquiring their friendship, I more than doubled my mental resources, for to them I owed much of what I had learned about Palestine's troubled past and present.

Harry was born and educated in America, but Hemdah was born in Palestine of a European father and a Sephardic mother. It was while Hemdah, her dark eyes glowing, related the touching story of the Marranos, the Iberian Jews who had embraced Christianity to avoid persecution during the Inquisition but who had secretly practiced Judaism, that I decided to go next to Spain to see what was left of the country after the Civil War.

"Good idea," said Harry. "You can write your Palestine piece out of Madrid. You'll never get it past the censors here or in Cairo."

We parted promising each other to "keep in touch" but inwardly doubting we would ever meet again. I had known the Zinders barely a fortnight, but saying good-bye to them was like leaving close relatives, or friends of many years. The night I left their cozy flat in the two-story stucco house in Rehavia, Hemdah took me in to see their child, Oren, asleep in his crib. The baby was not yet a year old, and the sight of him lying on his belly filled me with longing for my own "babies," Tommy and Sean.

Leaving Palestine by air proved somewhat more difficult than entering it by rail from Lebanon. The British and French airlines were heavily booked far in advance and gave priority to military personnel. But the Italians were still flying out of Tel Aviv, and I managed to obtain a seat on an Ala Littoria flight to Madrid via Rome.

Takeoff was delayed fully half an hour while the British security police inspected my baggage for secret recesses that might hold "important documents." Harry had warned me this might happen, and I had taken care to "hide" government handouts and clippings from the English-language newspaper, the *Palestine Post* (later the *Jerusalem Post*), where they could be "discovered." The more substantial material, typed on onionskin paper, was taped to my chest under my shirt.

The burly civilian inspector at the airport, an Arab, was obviously contemplating a body search when the waiting plane's Italian pilot burst into the customs shed to complain of the delay. The inspector grudgingly let me go but confiscated the handouts and the clippings.

On our way to the plane the pilot said his was probably the last flight Ala Littoria would make "for God only knows how long." He wouldn't say why, but the answer came a few days later. On April 2 Italy adopted measures providing for civil mobilization in wartime.

29

THE SPAIN
FRANCO WROUGHT

Aware of the extent of Italian help to Generalissimo Franco's Nationalist cause during the Spanish Civil War (the eighteen planes that ferried his Moors from Tetúan to the mainland in the opening phase of his insurrection had come from Italy, a story I couldn't cable from Rome at the time), I expected to find a devastated Spain. I had not anticipated, however, the prostrate Spain I found on my return in the early spring of 1940, barely thirteen months after the fighting ended.

When I left Spain in the winter of 1934, the country was still a republic, its democratic institutions intact. But the Spain I saw on my return was politically as Fascist as Italy or Germany and physically a hollow shell of its former self. In Madrid I saw many Madrileños living like rodents in the bombed and shelled houses they were too poor or too weary to repair.

As I prowled uncertainly among the rubble of what had been the neoclassic buildings of Madrid's University City, where the Loyalist Republicans had bravely repulsed repeated Nationalist attacks, it occurred to me that the devastation I saw all around me was probably what much of Europe would look like after the Germans launched their long-awaited blitzkrieg.

The ragged, grizzled old watchman who led me over the ruins, making certain by word and gesture that I didn't pick up a shard for a souvenir, told me that during the fighting the besieged ate first the flesh of horses and mules, then dogs and cats and in the end subsisted on parched corn. But the big problem, he said, was water. The defenders ran out of water long before their food gave out. "*Y los heridos pedián aqua,*" he muttered, "*siempre agua* [And the wounded called for water, always water]."

Fascism's victory over Spanish democracy had cost the country about six hundred thousand dead on both sides (some put the figure at "more and a million") and at least as many more in wounded, but the burden fell heaviest on the Republicans. Of these, I learned, some five hundred thousand were exiles who had fled across the Pyrenees into France, where they were herded into refugee camps, or had found sanctuary in Latin America or the United States.

Approximately two hundred thousand additional Republicans languished in Nationalist jails as political prisoners, and every day from twenty to thirty were executed as traitors while tearful families gathered outside the grim walls of the prisons to learn the fate of fathers, husbands, brothers, sons, and sweethearts in a twentieth-century Spanish reenactment of England's seventeenth-century Bloody Assizes. Nearly all officers of the Republican armed forces had been shot when captured, usually machine-gunned at the lips of their graves.

Food was scarce and of poor quality even at the Ritz, where I stayed, and hungry men, women, and children gathered outside the hotel's tall iron railings daily to beg for bread or money. I remember even now their pinched faces as they stared into the hotel's main dining room while I breakfasted on a fried egg and coarse bread the morning after I arrived.

Later that day, and for several days thereafter, I searched in vain for Tomás Loayza, my former colleague at INS, our cook, Carmen, and maid, Consuelo. All three, like so many Spanish Republican friends, seemed to have vanished without a trace, though I learned later that Loayza had returned to his native Peru and was working in Lima for an American news agency.

Staying at the Ritz at the time were the duke and duchess of Windsor. I was in the dining room the day they gave a cocktail party for a few highborn Spanish ladies and gentlemen and saw the headwaiter bring in a trayload of hors d'oeuvres. The duchess inspected the appetizers and imperiously waved them away as evidently unfit for human consumption. The waiter passed me on the way back to the kitchen, and I saw that what the duchess had rejected were tiny squares of toasted bread topped with bits of *jamón de serrano,* snow-cured mountain ham. The duchess wanted caviar, which was unavailable. I didn't stay to see how the matter was resolved but left the dining room with an enduring dislike for the woman for whom Edward had abandoned a throne.

Also stopping at the Ritz was Louis Huot, the European representative of Press Wireless, whom I had met in London. By bribing the concierge with American money, we managed to hire a Citroën in good condition for a trip to Barcelona to see what the Civil War had done to the Republican countryside.

Traveling along secondary roads, we drove through town after town that

The Spain Franco Wrought 2 6 5

had been badly mauled by Italian or German bombers and Nationalist artillery. We stopped from time to time to talk with survivors, who were trying to put together the pieces of their shattered lives. Everywhere we found such a deep, abiding hatred for the Nationalists and their foreign allies that Huot decided what Spain needed was "not a dictator but a faith healer."

One of the most severely damaged of the many villages we passed was Fraga, located on the Cinca River near where the stream flows into the Segre, not far from Saragossa, a key Republican city during the fighting. Fraga must have held at least two thousand inhabitants. The houses were heaps of rubble, and at least half their occupants had been killed by German and Italian bombers. Huot and I counted one thousand crosses on a burial mound atop a hill near what had been a town.

Between Madrid and Barcelona we must have passed fifty small towns, villages, and hamlets. Not one of them had escaped the demolition bombs of Franco's helpers or the shells of Nationalist artillery. We also drove through silent, deserted villages that seemed to have escaped the bombs and shells. Their walls on either side of the narrow, winding road were intact. After we passed one of these "intact" villages, the road rose on a hillside. We looked back at the village. It wasn't there. Only the walls remained. The innards were gone. The village looked like an incomplete stage set.

There were soldiers in every habitable town, invariably more troops than people. They were needed to police a Republican zone whose loyalty to the New Spain was in doubt, but they had also been mobilized for a possible Spanish entry into the bigger war on the side of the Axis.

In Barcelona, which had been badly damaged by Nationalist air raids, there was a lot of war talk at the marble-topped tables of the sidewalk cafés along the Ramblas and the city's other boulevards. The talk was not about the Civil War but about the impending European war. It was furtive talk, and conversations were in whispers across the tables with the foreheads of the participants nearly touching. The Spaniards wondered what their country could possibly give Germany in the way of assistance. They knew that their army was in patches and in no condition to go to war.

It was no secret to any Spaniard, from the richest grandee who had returned to his acres down to the humblest campesino, that Spain was physically, financially, morally, even politically bankrupt. One word passed across the café tables was more ominous than "war," and that word was "revolution." Huot and I talked to monarchists who thought Franco should be overthrown because he had failed to restore the monarchy, as he had promised early in his rebellion, and to Falangists who believed he should be liquidated because his efforts to install the corporative state had not been sufficiently vigorous.

In Barcelona, however, most Catalonians bemoaned the loss of their quasi-independence as citizens of the autonomous state they had achieved under the republic. They also lamented the widespread unemployment.

Workers could obtain employment only if their papers were in order, meaning that they had to belong to the Falange or to the prescribed syndicates whose members had to be approved by the party and the political police, a virtual impossibility for former Republicans. Work was scarce anyhow because of the lack of raw materials to keep the mills running and to rebuild damaged houses and factories.

Aware of the unrest that smoldered under Spain's Nationalist facade like an unquenchable peat-bog fire, Franco talked of "empire" and the country's reconquest of Gibraltar. Spain hadn't owned the Rock for more than two and a half centuries, but Franco hoped to regain it with an Axis victory in World War II and seemingly was preparing to climb onto the Italo-German war wagon.

When I arrived in Madrid, I had asked a Foreign Office official whether Spain had designs on Gibraltar. "We lost Gibraltar once," he said, throwing out his chest. "We don't intend to lose it again."

Over manzanilla and a skimpy tapa of boiled shrimp at one of Barcelona's better bars, a local journalist gave us a graphic account of the Catalonian capital's torment under German and Italian bombs in mid-March 1938. For seventy-two hours the big Capronis and Heinkels hammered the city while hundreds of thousands cowered in the subways. Others fled to the hills. Hundreds were killed, and hundreds more were wounded.

The bombing had been exceptionally destructive, and our informant believed the Germans had experimented with new explosives. We were shown the streets in which entire apartment houses had been demolished, and others badly damaged. The Republicans had practically no bombers and only a third as many fighter planes as the enemy. Nevertheless, Barcelona continued to resist for fully another year.

Meanwhile, neither Britain nor France did anything to save the Spanish Republic. Nor did the United States.

Everything I saw and heard and felt in Spain, but particularly in Barcelona, brought on what soon became an acute depression. It was evident from what people said that horrendous atrocities had been committed on both sides. Nearly 150 churches were destroyed, I learned later, mostly by the anticlerical Republicans, and more than 4,000 were badly damaged.

But again the brunt of the atrocities fell on the Republicans, the plain working-class people of Spain whose Nationalist enemies were encouraged and supported by the Catholic Church. In Barcelona, as in every town we passed on the way from Madrid, the mourners were not Nationalists but Republicans.

The number of Republican rank and file executed for various crimes after the war—from church burning to merely serving the republic administratively—was estimated by our journalist friend at no fewer than 100,000 by the end of 1939. I later learned that Count Ciano, visiting Franco in July 1939, reported 200,000 Republicans in prison, with "trials going on every day at a speed I would call summary. . . . There are still a great number of shootings. In Madrid alone between 200 and 250 a day; in Barcelona 150; in Seville 80."

On our return trip to Madrid we stopped at Toledo, where a handful of Nationalist cadets under a Colonel Moscardo had held the Alcázar for seventy-two nightmarish days and nights against the bombs, shells, machine-gun fire, dynamite, and flames from gasoline poured over its defenses and ignited by the Republican attackers. The Alcázar, one of the finest examples of medieval Moorish architecture in all Spain, looked like any downtown bank or office building in the final stages of demolition. Franco had decreed that it not be restored (it eventually was) but remain as it was after the Republican siege as "a monument to the fury of the Reds."

I wanted to forget Spain as quickly as possible but found that I couldn't.

Huot and I flew to Lisbon. From there he went on to London and I took the first available Clipper home. I was overwhelmed by loneliness for my family and a desire to return to normality after seeing what had happened to Spain.

30

WHILE EUROPE BURNED

In my absence the boys had grown like weeds in an untended garden, but not even the joy of seeing them again could erase from my mind the destruction and human suffering I had witnessed in Spain. My depression deepened. I imagined the whole of Europe reduced to the shambles I had seen in Fraga, and I counted graves in my sleep.

Of my colleagues at *Collier's* only the perceptive Kyle Crichton understood the significance of what had happened in Spain, where democracy was extinguished because Britain, France, *and* the United States had failed to go to the assistance of the republic. Unless America soon intervened in force on behalf of the Allies, I argued hotly at editorial conferences, the Germans would win the war. "Paris and London," I said, "will look like Madrid and Barcelona."

In April the Nazis had taken Denmark and Norway with ease, but it never occurred to anyone I talked with later in New York that the Germans would attack Holland and Belgium. At the always spirited luncheons at the Marguery the consensus was that the Maginot Line would keep the Nazis out of France. On *that* score no one had any doubt.

The war news, which soon bore out my gloomy view of the future, did nothing to lift my spirits. In May the Germans overran the Netherlands and Luxembourg and delivered their main attack in Belgium. Nothing, it seemed, could stand against their armored divisions and dive bombers, the dreaded Stukas, and I berated myself for a gross error in judgment: I had left Europe much too soon. The shooting war I was supposed to be covering was happening at last, and I was three thousand miles away.

Charley Colebaugh, however, seemed not to mind. In fact, he said he was glad to have someone handy for assignments on our side of the Atlantic. I was grateful for his tolerant attitude but inwardly resentful that he had sent Quent Reynolds to Paris to replace me. Quent's excellent stories were being featured on the magazine's cover nearly every week. I seethed inwardly with low, meanspirited envy.

Toward the end of May Colebaugh sent me to Washington to see what the Roosevelt administration was doing about strengthening America's defenses. It was doing a great deal, I found, against heavy opposition.

Legislation providing nearly two billion dollars for defense was already pending when Hitler invaded the Netherlands. Following that unhappy event, the president requested an additional appropriation of another billion dollars. Projects providing for the creation of a two-ocean navy as well as compulsory military training based on a selective draft were in the works. A gigantic preparedness program that would cost an additional ten billion dollars or more was in full swing.

But it was an election year, and the administration had to tread as carefully as though walking through an uncharted minefield. The isolationists were still giving "that man in the White House" a hard time and threatened to withhold approval of FDR's defense plans.

Meanwhile, in France, the Nazis took the British and French by surprise. Skirting the northern end of the Maginot Line, German mechanized divisions drove across the Ardennes Forest and raced toward the Channel ports. British and Belgian forces, and some French divisions, were cut off from the main French armies and fell back upon Dunkirk. The Belgians capitulated, and the British could now only hope to salvage their broken units.

On Dunkirk's beaches ten British divisions assembled along with the greater part of the French Army and were taken aboard rescuing vessels of every conceivable type, from cruisers and destroyers down to private yachts, motorboats, even some rowboats which swarmed across the Channel from England. No fewer than 224,000 British and 123,000 French soldiers were brought safely across the Channel, but they arrived in England with only their rifles and a few Bren guns.

Winston Churchill, who had succeeded Neville Chamberlain on May 10, the day the Nazis invaded Holland, admitted that the Allies had suffered "a colossal military disaster," reminded everyone that wars are not won by evacuations, and, in the finest of his many great wartime speeches, promised England would "fight on . . . never surrender."

I was still in Washington the day Mussolini declared war on Britain and France. Having made certain that Hitler had defeated France, the Duce announced he was ready to march with his Axis partner "against the plutocratic and reactionary democracies of the West who had hindered the advance and often threatened even the existence of the Italian people." This was an outrageous statement. I was visiting at the time at the home of Stu Brown, who had left his United Press job in Rome to become director of the American Red Cross, and neither of us could remember a British or French "threat" to the "existence" of the Italian people. We both heard with satisfaction President Roosevelt's denunciation of Mussolini's act: "On this tenth day of June, 1940, the hand that held the dagger has struck it into the back of his neighbor."

Italy's entry into the war meant that Mussolini was convinced of Germany's total victory in France and of Britain's early defeat. I wondered how Italy's participation would affect Uncle Gennaro. What role would he play? Would I ever hear from him or see him again? I tried in vain to put thoughts of him out of my mind.

On the day Italy entered the war, German motorized units were within thirty-five miles of Paris. They launched a smashing offensive at the hinge of the Maginot Line and the defensive line which General Weygand, the uncommunicative fellow I had interviewed in Beirut, had established south of the Bresle River. The Nazis' attack proved completely successful, and on June 13, the French government having moved to Tours, Paris itself was occupied. Historic Verdun fell two days later, and by then both Weygand and Pétain were convinced that further resistance was useless.

On June 22 France sued for peace, and an armistice was signed. On the radio I heard Bill Shirer describe how Adolf Hitler danced with glee.

The fall of France stunned me. I remembered the reluctance with which Frenchmen went to war on September 3, 1939, and knew that France was no longer its former self. Nevertheless, it had still been considered a great power, and its collapse in approximately thirty days left the Western world aghast.

Under the terms of the armistice, the northern half of France was occupied by the Germans. The Third Republic, its capital now in Vichy in the unoccupied southern half, was transformed by the vote of a confused and stunned Chamber of Deputies into a totalitarian state headed by the octogenarian Marshal Pétain and the cynical, unscrupulous politician Pierre Laval, Mussolini's friend.

The Third French Republic was dead; the very slogan *Liberté, Égalité, Fraternité* was banned from official use. Pétain, Laval, and their pro-Nazi henchmen proceeded to collaborate with the Nazis and to integrate an authoritarian France into the Nazi "New Order" in Europe. I feared for the many Jews who had fled earlier to safety in France from Central and Eastern Europe.

Britain now faced the enemy alone.

That summer the isolationists in Washington were as vocal as ever. I read with dismay the Republican party's platform for the coming convention to select a presidential candidate. Although it came out strong for equal rights for women, blacks, Indians, and Hawaii, nothing in it reflected an awareness of the world-shaking events occuring in Europe.

President Roosevelt foresaw what the consequences to the United States would be of an unopposed Nazi victory in Europe and that our best, long-run hope of survival lay not in bland neutrality but in doing everything possible to avert the catastrophe of Hitler's conquest of Britain. The president's powers to help Britain, however, were limited by the Neutrality Act of 1935. Its most pertinent prohibition in 1940 was that it forbade the shipment in American vessels of war materials to any belligerent. The prohibition meant nothing to the Germans since they now had abundant sources of food and raw materials in a Europe which Hitler dominated as completely as Napoleon had in 1807.

For the British, however, the barriers in our neutrality legislation foreshadowed their strangulation. Britain's production and raw material resources were limited, its merchant marine was suffering a fearful toll from Nazi submarines and bombers, and its supply of gold, the only coin for cash-and-carry purchases in the United States, was running low.

President Roosevelt's hand was also being restrained during the early months of 1940 by the realities of the political campaign. The year marked the end of his second term, and while he refused to say whether or not he planned to run for an unprecedented third term, he felt he had to protect its eventual candidate against charges of "warmongering" and "interventionism." Moreover, the overwhelming majority of the American people did not want war. Roosevelt knew this, and as a leader and a politician he had to respect their sentiments.

But by early summer the American people were coming around to the belief that we should give the British all the help we could "short of war"— weapons, munitions, food—even at some risk of involvement in the actual fighting. After a swing through the Middle West, the heartland of isolationism, Walter Davenport, our political editor, assured me my fears of continued American neutrality were unfounded.

"We'll soon be in it right up to our necks," he said. "The American people are beginning to realize that they have a big stake in the final outcome of the war in Europe."

Meanwhile, the newspapers and the radio carried distressing news of massive German air raids on Croydon, Tilbury, Coventry, and London. In August, while Nazi warplanes rained death and destruction on English cities, Winston Churchill announced Britain's readiness to cede bases to the United States in exchange for much-needed naval help. Shortly afterward Mr. Roosevelt gave the British fifty overage but reconditioned destroyers for the right to build American bases in Newfoundland, the Bermudas, and the British Caribbean islands.

In announcing the deal, President Roosevelt characterized it as the "most important act" by an American president since Thomas Jefferson completed the Louisiana Purchase in 1803. This implied that we had acquired a ready-made Caribbean "empire," and *Collier's* sent me down there to inspect it.

On the move again, visiting strange lands and people, I snapped out of my depression. I spent the months of October and November playing inquiring reporter in the islands of the Lesser Antilles that dangle like a necklace between Puerto Rico and Trinidad and enclose on the east the Caribbean Sea, America's own Mediterranean, or *mare nostrum*.

Mr. Roosevelt, or his administration's spokesmen, had exaggerated. The bases-for-destroyers deal was not even remotely comparable to the Louisiana Purchase. The United States, I found, had not acquired any *territorial* rights in the islands but had merely obtained ninety-nine-year leases on certain islands—Antigua, St. Lucia, Jamaica, the Bahamas, and Trinidad—on which we could build and maintain bases that would cost American taxpayers many millions of dollars.

Of all the bases involved, with the possible exception of Bermuda and Newfoundland, Trinidad was by far the most important. This lush green island, rich in oil, at the southernmost extremity of the Lower Antilles, lies within sighting distance of the continent of South America.

What made Trinidad particularly attractive as a base, apart from its strategic location, was the Gulf of Paria, a deep, quiet blue harbor capable of taking our biggest warships. Its smooth waters were eminently suitable, also, for the flying boats of our shore patrol. There was plenty of land, furthermore, for military and naval installations.

But my visit was premature. In most cases the sites for our bases had not yet been selected. There were a thousand details to be worked out, including the question of extraterritoriality for the Americans eventually to be stationed on them. Land was yet to be condemned; final surveys were yet to be made.

Certain things were clear, however. The United States, historically a Pacific power whose eastern defenses were entrusted to the British navy, had become overnight a two-ocean power. It was also evident that the cost in money would be considerable. The sum of $25 million had already been appropriated for the preliminary work on Trinidad, but American engineers on the spot told me that the final cost would be in the neighborhood of $120 million for Trinidad alone. The bill for all the bases Uncle Sam planned to build would run into several hundred millions, and I wondered whether a reluctant isolationist Congress would approve.

In the meantime, the islanders, who numbered about 2.5 million on territory whose combined area roughly equaled that of Maryland plus New Jersey, welcomed the anticipated arrival of tens of thousands of Americans. They mistakenly believed they would be shedding their British nationality for American citizenship and everything that implied: higher wages; decent housing; better schools; sanitation. Many declared themselves eager for the change.

This was particularly true on Trinidad, whose calypso troubadours raised their black faces to the flat, distant autumn moon and sang improvised songs invoking the favor and protection of Uncle Sam.

On the night of November 9, three days after Mr. Roosevelt was overwhelmingly elected for a third term, I sat on the broad veranda of the Queen's Park Hotel in Port of Spain and as a visiting American journalist was serenaded by the minstrels of Iere, one of the island's leading calypso groups. In very free verse, they sang of their gratitude to the American people for having chosen Mr. Roosevelt over Wendell Willkie.

The calypsos somehow managed to rhyme "Roosevelt" with "liberty" and "Washington" with "Lincoln" and made the hot, sticky tropical night quiver with their ballad of thanksgiving to the millions of Americans who had voted for "Franklin-Dee instead of Mister Will-Kee, for thus was the world saved for democra-Cee."

To an American who happened to agree with them, it was sweet music, though decidedly bad poetry.

31

TO ENGLAND IN A BOMBER

I had been home nearly nine months, and on my return to New York from the Caribbean, Colebaugh said it was high time I went back to England and the war. He was recalling Quentin Reynolds, who had been through some of London's worst bombings and fire storms since Hitler's blitz began and needed a rest. Furthermore, the war was spreading into the Middle East, and it was decided that after Christmas I should go to London, then proceed to Cairo.

Christmas in our snug harbor in Bronxville was one of the happiest we would ever know, complete with the traditional tree, toys, eggnog, turkey, the crackle of logs in the fireplace, and the white silence of the snow. Sean, now nearly ten, and Tommy, just over four, were excited about their new sled. I didn't tell them, or their mother, that I was leaving until after we had celebrated the New Year.

Kathryn was frightened at the prospect of another long separation, imagining that this time she might not see me again, and Tommy was tearful. He buried my field glasses in the soft earth under the shrubbery, thinking that if I didn't have them, I couldn't leave. Sean was his usual stoic self, but I could see that he, too, was disturbed at the news of my impending departure.

Transportation to England had become a problem. Transatlantic Clipper flights to Lisbon were booked solid through April, with all space reserved for high-level American and British "brass" and diplomats. In the week or ten days during which I assembled warm clothing and obtained the necessary visas, it was decided that I should return to the war in one of the twin-engine Consolidated PBY bombers which were being flown to Britain from Bermuda. The British used the amphibious planes to patrol their coasts and the North Atlantic. About this change in my travel plans I said nothing to the family.

Many wires had to be pulled in Washington and London to arrange for a civilian to be flown as a passenger in a military aircraft, and it was late January before all arrangements were completed. I flew to Bermuda from Baltimore after being assured by the British air attaché in Washington that I had been cleared for the trip.

I was to have departed a day or two after my arrival in Hamilton, but in fact, I waited three weeks for the big bomber to be groomed for the flight and the crew to be trained. The delay was due to the disorganization that plagued the early days of Anglo-American cooperation, British red tape, interservice rivalry, and the low level of British mechanical aptitude.

The Canadian Pacific Railroad Company and the British Overseas Airways Corporation had contracted with the planes' manufacturers to ferry the bombers from Bermuda to England. They had hired crack American fliers— pilot Clyde Pangborn and navigator Bernt Balchen—to handle the job at good salaries and generous expense accounts. But Pangborn and Balchen never flew one of those bombers. First the Royal Air Force stepped in and said it'd fly the planes. The Royal *Canadian* Air Force then claimed its airmen should do the work.

The snarl of orders and counterorders delayed the flights until the Air Ministry in London intervened and ruled that the task be shared by the RAF and the RCAF. If it hadn't, the planes would have remained in Bermuda until the Gulf Stream changed course. But interservice rivalries were only part of the story.

After I had waited a week, a Canadian pilot friend tipped me off that we were getting away the very next morning. But at the moment of departure at dawn the following day he told me the trip had been called off. A generator had burned out; someone had forgotten to lubricate its bearings. It would take at least a fortnight for a new one to arrive from the Consolidated factory in Los Angeles.

Delays followed one upon the other. One was due to the fact that the radio receiver was asnarl, and nobody knew how to repair it. Then two or three of the flying boats were damaged by pilots practicing crash landings, as though knowing how to perform such a maneuver on the North Atlantic in winter would have done anyone any good. But it was written in an instruction manual that crash landings had to be practiced before a flight.

Finally, one rain-lashed morning, I crawled, cold and scared, into the belly of one of the PBYs. Just before takeoff someone shoved under my nose a paper wherein I declared I wouldn't write anything about the flight. Certain that more sensible officials in England would revoke it, I signed the paper. I wasn't sure I would see England again anyway.

We bounced heavily on the dark waters of Hamilton Bay. We had four hundred gallons of spare gas on board in long, round tanks, trussed up on two-by-fours. We strained into the air with the reluctance of an inanimate teakwood log but soon were somewhere over the North Atlantic.

Below us the sea was like hard, polished lava, blue-black, treacherous, evil-looking. Above us was a heavy overcast, gray and hard, and as the pilot lifted the ship to bore through it to quiet air, snow sifted along the fuselage with the shushing noise of sand slithering on tin. But if the effort strained the motors, they gave no sign and turned with a full-throated, imperturbable moan. I silently blessed the skilled American hands that had made them.

The navigator was an earnest young man in his early twenties who had seemed shy and diffident on land but was now as self-assured and poised as a well-trained pointer under its master's gun. He shot the feeble sun with his sextant, made rapid calculations on a pad, and penciled a tiny dot on his chart.

"Tomorrow," he said, "we will be in England," and he said "England" with reverence.

I was excess baggage and envied the crew. All had something to do, but I didn't.

The pilot, after he had lifted the ship to its cruising altitude, had to watch George. George was the automatic aviator, the gyropilot, and George was nearly perfect. But from time to time an unexpected updraft or downdraft twisted the controls ever so slightly out of George's mechanical hands and the flesh-and-blood pilot had to make minute corrections with the knobs on the instrument panel.

The navigator was the busiest man on board, constantly checking our progress. Our two radio operators never left their instruments, and the engineers watched those motors, one on duty, one off and asleep on the single bunk aft. I particularly envied the younger of the two engineers. He was very young, maybe twenty, and he slept soundly; for him the flight was a great adventure.

The rest of us had families to whom we had written "last" letters from Bermuda. We wanted very much to survive the journey and knew that we might not. We had twenty-four hours of flight ahead of us through heavy weather and through German air patrols off the coast of England, and we were thoroughly cognizant of our danger.

It was cold in the big plane. The ship had none of the refinements of a transatlantic Clipper, no heater, no soundproofing, and the toilet was a crude bucketlike affair aft. We had donned soft flying suits, like overalls, and over these a windproof, waterproof jumper and a Mae West, a life jacket, in case we crashed into the sea. We didn't bother with parachutes, figuring that if we ever needed them anywhere west of Land's End, they wouldn't do us any good anyway. Nobody could survive hitting that undulating slab of blue-black lava below.

We set our course for Pembroke Dock, Wales. We couldn't use our radio to obtain signals to assist in plotting our course. What ships there were below wouldn't have replied anyway. But one hundred miles east of New York we obtained fairly accurate bearings on the big broadcasting stations. Beyond that point the navigator, Lieutenant Neil Guthrie, was obliged to rely on instruments and inboard calculations. We might as well not have had a radio. It would be useless until we neared the British coast. Then incoming signals would help us come into Pembroke Dock. We couldn't send; that would have given away our position to lurking Nazi fighters.

Morale was good aboard ship. The two radio operators smoked and joked and helped pass the hours. I don't believe either of them slept all the way over. The bunks aft were crowded with boxes and gear of all kinds which we were taking to England for the RAF. The floor of the fuselage was cluttered with the arms and cables of a heavy, cumbersome beaching gear used to haul the big plane up on a ramp for repairs or stowage. The gear weighed a thousand pounds, and it wasn't lashed.

We had a cold roasted turkey on board and forty dollars' worth of sandwiches, apples, oranges, coffee, and tomato juice. We ate at frequent intervals to help while away the hours.

The ship's skipper was Lieutenant Peet, a Canadian, a big fellow with a confident manner who had flown over his country's lakes, forests, and mountains for years. He wasn't too familiar with PBYs, but he said planes are all alike once you get them off the water or the ground. He said it was no trick at all to switch from a landplane to a seaplane such as ours. I thought he was crazy; but he definitely seemed to know what he was doing, and anyhow, it was too late to do anything about it.

For an hour or so, though, I wished Pangborn and Balchen were flying the ship, but after that I knew that Peet and Guthrie would see us through all right. They were just plain Britons doing a job for about twenty-five dollars a week and their keep. Yet what they were doing would have been epochal in the time of Charles A. Lindbergh.

Having nothing to do, no specific task to perform, and knowing that it was entirely possible that the crew and I might die, I meditated and soon found myself accepting death without a quiver in my diaphragm. I packed into every moment an exquisite enjoyment of being alive, pressing my elbows close to myself, flexing my biceps, opening and shutting my hand before my eyes and pondering what mysterious force had engineered this wondrous ability of mine to move muscles at my command, to feel warmth inside my flying suit.

I slid back the panel of the hood over the copilot's seat I occupied and gloried in the icy wind whipping my face, thinking all the while of small, familiar things: the sounds of a quarrelsome fire in the fireplace back home, the turmoil the boys made upstairs at bedtime, a table set with white linen and silver and crystal, and the intoxicating smell of damp earth in the spring.

I thought of my wife, warm and dear in my arms, and of Sean's quivering excitement when I gave him what he wanted most, a wire-haired pup that he named Christopher. I remembered the feel of Tommy's pudgy arms about my neck when he realized I was leaving home again.

I thought of Bronxville friends who had become dear to me: the Nelson

Perrys, the Vince Maloneys, and the Reverend Harold Hohly, the Episcopalian pastor who had tried so hard to persuade me to join his church. I was sorry now that I hadn't. I might have found great comfort in believing in his God. . . .

The bomber bored on through the night, and daybreak found us bouncing in strong headwinds. We climbed high into thin air to avoid them, and we thought our lungs would collapse. More than ever I wanted to contribute in some way to keeping that plane of ours in the air and headed toward England, but there was nothing I could do except keep out of the way in the cramped quarters.

I tried to sleep but couldn't and for hours watched the navigator at work. The radio was still of no use to him; the Germans might pick up our signal, take bearings on us, and intercept us. England would be minus a plane, and six lives would be lost. Our lives, important only to us and to those they touched.

Off the coast of England we hit an overcast so dense it might have been a snowbank, and we couldn't see anything but shredded whiteness streaming in ribbons from the propellers. Then, suddenly, the navigator said to the pilot, "Okay. Down we go," and we dropped through a thick mist alive with the light of the morning sun. We scanned the sky for enemy planes but saw none. And then we saw snowbound England, brown and rolling and green in places, and everybody lighted cigarettes except the engineer who was too near the gas tanks. The navigator was a boy again. His job done, he suddenly looked very tired and very young.

The PBY landed on smooth water and taxied up to a landing slip, where I was met by a British civil servant in a bowler hat with many forms for me to fill. He examined my passport carefully and solemnly advised me that it was invalid; I had forgotten to sign it. But a red-faced captain of the Scots Guards and a pleasant little RAF intelligence officer vouched for me, and the officious civil servant allowed me to sign my passport in their presence.

The crew and I celebrated our arrival with hot tea and brandy, after which we lunched on lamb stew.

I had made it to Pembroke Dock, Wales, and Lloyd's of London had bet *Collier's* heavy odds, as war insurance rates went, that I wouldn't.

The crew went to sleep, but I had to get to London as quickly as possible. Before departing on an afternoon sleeper, however, I had time for a pint or two with the Scots Guards captain in a local pub. The place was full of Welshmen, sturdy people with thick bodies, big workers' hands, and broad, honest faces. They were good to see after Bermuda's snobbish colonials. They told me they were working harder than ever in their mines and factories and fields, and I saw they took joy in their work.

Usually reticent, the Welshmen warmed when they spotted me for an American, talked freely, and made me feel at home. They joked about Woodbine cigarettes' being hard to get and groused that chocolate and candy had vanished from the shops, but they were a determined lot and ready for "those bawstids the Jerries" if they decided to come.

At train time the captain accompanied me to the station and saw me off with a "Good luck, old chap."

The countryside that rolled past my window might have been my native Maryland under a thin coverlet of snow. I looked out at every station but couldn't tell where I was. The English had adopted a sort of national anonymity to befuddle the expected invaders. They had removed or blacked out the place-name signs from all railway stations. They had also taken down road signs and traffic indicators that might identify towns, villages, hamlets, and crossroads.

German parachutists, I concluded, would have a rough time of it in England. Tailors' shops and the shops of apothecaries, fishmongers, and greengrocers had removed or obliterated signs bearing their towns' names. Village inns, too, had changed their identities. It would be useless for the Germans to look for the Golden Swan in Tunbridge Wells, even if they knew they were in Tunbridge Wells.

It was all very reassuring, somehow.

The sleeper conductor, who resembled Churchill, worried that an air raid might interfere with his train's journey and delay our getting into London, but there was no raid that night. When he brought my tea in the morning and later when he helped me with my bags, we talked and became great friends. He was probably sixty, but there was an indestructible quality about him that was exquisitely British. He said it was a "shyme" those "Eyetalians" had decided to enter the war. He was sorry, he was, for they were such nice people. "But those bloody Germans," he said, "they're the livin' end, they are. Real bawstids . . ."

From Paddington Station to the Savoy Hotel I squirmed and twisted in the taxicab to see what the Luftwaffe had done to London. There were no visible wounds, and for a moment I thought I was awakening from a bad dream. There hadn't been a war. I was waking up in the same taxi I had taken to the Savoy from Victoria Station when I had come up from Rome to escape the depressing effects of life under fascism. No taped windows. No sandbags. Then I saw a bobby wearing his "battle bowler," and I was back in reality with the thump of falling into bed in a dream.

It was Sunday, and London was still asleep at 9:00 A.M.

At the Savoy I stripped off the clothes I had worn during twenty-one hours and forty-three minutes of flight plus an overnight train ride, showered and shaved, put on a suit which the hotel's valet pressed for me himself as a special favor, then walked about in the area I knew so well—down the Strand and up Fleet Street to the old INS office.

If I hadn't known England was at war, I couldn't have believed it was from what I saw. The lovely Wren church that stands where the Strand ends and

Fleet Street begins was intact, as beautifully fragile as ever. I expected to find a chaos of ruin and found instead a solid, substantial center-city London. But I had seen only a small portion of it and reserved judgment.

The next day, however, I knew I would not eat steak and kidney pie again at the old Cheshire Cheese; it was gone, bombed out. So was the place in Fleet Street where I used to buy pipes and tobacco. And my favorite pub, the Falstaff, had been hit. So had St. Paul's, and the docks, the Isle of Dogs, Lambeth, and Limehouse, and I saw how badly London had been hurt.

32

BRITAIN'S UNCONQUERABLE WORKERS

The magnitude of the devastation visited upon England by Hitler's Luftwaffe during the historic Battle of Britain was appalling. In the London area alone, I was told at the Ministry of Information, upwards of a million dwellings had been destroyed or severely damaged, and 375,000 people rendered homeless, mostly in the East End, where the great city's workers lived.

History's first great air battle lasted about six months, from early May 1940 through December, and had continued, though with diminishing intensity, well into the first quarter of 1941, causing, I was told, more than forty thousand casualties. But thanks to a few young men of the Royal Air Force in Spitfire and Hurricane fighter planes, Germany's attempt to overwhelm Britain by air power had failed. The defenders richly deserved, therefore, Churchill's memorable tribute: "Never in the field of human conflict was so much owed by so many to so few."

But if Hitler's bombs had failed to bring Britain to its knees, they had nevertheless radically altered the lives of its people, particularly of its millions of workingmen and women, and the changes were nowhere more evident than in Stepney, one of the several workers' quarters in London's populous East End where, on an earlier visit, I had met Charlie Brickett, a gasworks pipe fitter, and Minnie Cotter, a widowed lathe operator in the plant's machine shop.

Stepney, then still a borough of Greater London (now part of Tower

Hamlets), was a city in itself, about as big as Bridgeport, Connecticut, and a good three-mile ride from the Savoy along Mile End Road, Commercial Road, and Burdett Road through Limehouse. All the way, on either side, I saw the obscene remains of what had been houses, stores, markets, schools, infirmaries, churches, wineshops, pubs, news vendors' stalls. Entire blocks equal to the row houses of Philadelphia or Baltimore were razed, turned into heaps of rubble by Hitler's Heinkels. Most of the churches were stumps of bell towers, their walls peeled off, exposing fire-blackened arches and flying buttresses looking like the charred ribs of prehistoric beasts.

Off the main roads, in the winding, narrow streets, the houses stared at me with burned-out eyes like those I had seen in Madrid and Barcelona. Row on row of those sooty warrens that had served as homes for London's East Enders had been rendered uninhabitable or had been obliterated. The figures the Ministry of Information had given me came to life, and it was obvious that Hitler's raiders had not been seeking military targets but had been bent on breaking civilian morale. They had deliberately bombed homes, schools, churches, and hospitals in order to terrorize the civilian population into submission. Well, they had failed.

It was lunchtime at the gasworks' "feeding center"—it was located in a nearby parish church—and when I arrived, Charlie Brickett was standing on a rough bench, shouting that the food was bad, there wasn't enough soap in the washroom, and the towels there were filthy. A few voices called out, "Hear! Hear!" in agreement; but most of the others shouted him down, and stubby little Minnie Cotter, a sturdy woman in denim coveralls with a red bandanna wrapped turbanlike about her hair, dissented with a sharp "Y'r off y'r nut, Charlie Brickett."

The lunch I shared with Charlie, Minnie, and about a hundred of their fellow workers at one of the long board tables was very good—a deep bowl of mutton stew made with potatoes, carrots, and cabbage; pudding with stewed prunes; unbuttered thick slices of good white bread; strong tea sweetened with saccharine—during and after which we talked. They told me of fearful nights on which it seemed the whole of London was burning, and I asked, of no one in particular, whether perhaps it might be best for England to quit fighting and come to terms with Germany while some of London still remained intact.

The chorus of negatives almost blew me off my bench, but the most direct reply came from Brickett, a burly fellow in his mid-fifties dressed from neck to ankles in the livery of his trade: oil-stained gray denim dungarees and greasy cap. "Well, now," he said in a voice dripping scorn, "you're talking pure nonsense, chum. We're not quitting, not 'arf, we ain't."

He was seconded by a hollow-cheeked older man with a grimy yellow scarf tied ascot fashion around his scrawny neck. "Look 'ere, Yank," he said. "I 'eard your question. You just give us the guns and tanks, and ships to carry 'em in, and we'll fix this 'Itler bloke for ye. Put that in yer paper and tell it to Mr. Roosevelt."

And what did they think of Roosevelt? Their replies, individual and collective, strongly indicated that after the man they called "our Winnie" they believed Mr. Roosevelt was the greatest man in the world, a sort of latter-day Moses who would lead the American people out of their isolationist wilderness. When everyone had quieted down, Minnie Cotter, sitting next to me, whispered, "I do wish, though, that Mr. Roosevelt would hurry things up a bit," from which I gathered that behind the brave front there was a bit of weariness, a fatigue born of sleepless nights in smelly air-raid shelters and of long daylight hours spent toiling at routine tasks.

I came away from my meal with British workers—men who wore their caps while they ate and for whom a "washup" meant a dip of the hands in cold water and a quick wipe on their trousers (few were as fussy as Charlie Brickett about cleanliness)—with renewed confidence in England's ability to stand fast until we provided the tools of victory. For one thing, their capacity for improvisation was far greater than I had imagined, and so was their ability to organize communal services.

The feeding center in Stepney was an example of both aptitudes. At first, during the May to December blitz, when gas and water mains and the conduits carrying power lines were being ripped up by the Nazis' bombs, women cooked stews and heated water for tea in field kitchens contrived from scraps of sheet iron and a few salvaged bricks. Coal had to be scrounged by parish priests and was carried in barrows or dragged in gunnysacks by schoolchildren. Now, in the early spring of 1941, the feeding center had a mobile field kitchen, much like those used in the army, provided by the municipality.

In London alone there were three hundred such mobile kitchens, in addition to emergency canteens and centrally located restaurants to take care of workers' needs in the industrial area. And the workers were getting far better food and at lower cost than they got before the war, when they earned an average of only eight dollars a week, half their average wartime wage.

The meal I had in Stepney was typical and cost ninepence (about fifteen cents in American money) and equaled in quantity and quality a fifty-cent blue plate special in one of our chain restaurants back home. Standard prewar midday fare for a British workingman was a portion of greasy fish-and-chips wrapped in newspaper and a mug of tea which filled him up but didn't provide a balanced diet and cost a shilling (about twenty-five cents). Now fish-and-chips had doubled in price to two bob (fifty cents) and couldn't easily be had anyway; scores of fish-and-chips shops had been bombed out.

The mobile kitchens, especially designed for their work, had become permanent affairs, protected by brickwork or reinforced concrete so that cooking could go on during the worst raids. Meanwhile, I noticed, the people of the East End of London had become as blasé about eating while the bombs fell as had West Enders about dining, wining, and dancing in the smart hotels while sirens wailed, bombs crumped, and antiaircraft guns pumped shells skyward at the invaders overhead.

During the lull that followed the infernal September–December bomb and fire bomb blitz the British, normally given to a muddle-through philosophy, radically reorganized and vastly improved feeding methods and menus, as well as the air-raid shelters, which, however, were still inadequate in size and numbers. The shelter situation would have become far more serious except that everyone had come to regard the raids, and the banshee wails of the sirens that preceded them, as part of wartime life.

The Savoy, I remember, had a fine deep shelter where dinners were served during raids. I dined there on several occasions while German bombers were trying their best to obliterate the area in which my hotel was located in the Strand. The Portuguese waiter who brought the food and wine perspired freely and crossed himself at every opportunity between trips with his trays as the building shook from close-by blasts. But the British diners, I noticed, seemed oblivious of the hell raging overhead. I recall, however, that my hand shook as I poured myself another glass of Bordeaux to go with my very chewy mutton chop.

Charlie Brickett and his mates in Stepney represented the proletariat of British workers, men and women who toiled for weekly wages ranging from eighteen to twenty dollars. In Coventry a few days later I met the aristocrats of England's working classes. Here the typical worker was a skilled mechanic—the operator of a milling machine, for instance—who earned an average of forty dollars a week, more than double what Charlie found in his weekly pay packet. Moreover, unlike Charlie, he lived not in a sooty two- or three-bedroom warren but in a six-room row house with a postcard-size patch of garden, was considerably better educated and more articulate than Charlie, proud of his trade and not much given to grousing.

One of the leaders of Coventry's workers, the head of his plant's engineering union, told me frankly that he and his colleagues were fighting for the postwar socialization of Great Britain.

"We believe," he said, "that production in this country must eventually pass into the hands of the people. What we want to see after this ruddy war has been won is the extension of our precious political democracy into the area of economic democracy." The tall, angular Englishman didn't even remotely resemble my father, but he certainly sounded like him.

Actually, British workers had been talking in that vein for decades. After the Scandinavians they were probably the industrial world's most socially conscious individuals, and it suddenly struck me that England's future depended no longer upon a few brave young men in fighter planes but upon the ten or eleven million English men and women who toiled to help provide the weapons of ultimate victory. They represented Britain's civilian army, working on the farms and in the mills, shipyards, mines, and munitions factories, and were as completely in the war as those youngsters in Spitfires and Hurricanes or the men and women who were waiting for the Nazi invaders on the chalk cliffs of embattled Dover.

The deputy chairman of a sheet metal workers' union in Coventry left no doubts in my mind that the Tory Britain where men and women chased foxes, played tennis on velvety turf, and shot grouse on the moors was headed for socialism after the war ended.

"The trades union movement," he said between puffs of his pipe, "is distinctly a socialist movement. We're no party to the continuance of existent inequality in the distribution of material wealth. And we're definitely thinking about the future. Make no mistake, our biggest concern aside from winning the war is what's ahead. We won't tolerate unemployment or the least sacrifice in our privileges as free men."

Coventry was (and still is) Britain's Detroit. Clearly, the million pounds or so of bombs that the Luftwaffe had dumped on the industrial city had failed to shake its residents from their dream of a new world. In fact, they had clung to it more fiercely than ever. As one citizen put it, "We know damn well that if we don't win this war, we'll be worse off than before."

Coventry, a city of some 250,000, took a terrible beating on November 24, a clear, moonlit night with no haze and with visibility at fifteen miles. The center city was laid waste, more than five thousand houses were destroyed or damaged, and St. Michael's, the cathedral, was left in flaming ruins.

Before leaving Coventry, I stopped by the cathedral, what was left of it. It reminded me of the Alcázar in Toledo, but merely as a ruin. The Alcázar was, after all, a military target. There were no guns of any kind defending St. Michael's that awful night of the blitz. Citizens said they would rebuild it after the war.

At the end of February, after seventeen months of war, Britain had begun to feel the effects of a labor shortage and started training women to replace men as operators of the machines that were producing weapons. Forty-two training schools were created throughout the country. The women were to be paid while they were being trained and then to be moved into semiskilled jobs, thus releasing the men for more skilled work.

Revolutionary schemes were also evolved by Captain Oliver Lyttelton, president of the Board of Trade, who called for mobilization of nonessential industries—producers of gloves, hosiery, shoes, hats—luxuries as well as necessities. Hands "freed" from such work were to be more usefully employed making guns, ammunition, and other paraphernalia of war. A half million, perhaps as many as a million additional men would thus be thrown into the British war effort or made available for military service.

To check my observations of the attitudes of England's workers and to ascertain whether they knew where they were headed, I called on Father St. John Groser in his vicarage in Stepney's Watney Street. A tall, godly man, spare of frame with white hair and sharp features, he was known in his parish as the "Saint of Stepney." Of the borough's two hundred thousand inhabitants, he knew at least several thousand by name.

"They're not really thinking much right now," Father Groser said. "They're thinking only of survival and of the absolute necessity of seeing this ugly business through. If they're thinking at all about the future, it's in terms of security and of holding on to the gains they've made in terms of the social legislation which protects them through their trades unions. They're wary of all labor leaders after Ramsay MacDonald deserted them, but they trust their present minister of labor, Ernest Bevin."

The workers didn't read much, and their relaxation took the form of "a bit of gab over a pint of pale ale" or a game of darts in their favorite pub. Nevertheless, they knew what the war was about.

Another Anglican clergyman, Father Carter of the Bow Common parish, who looked after the spiritual needs of thirteen thousand people (he also saw they got coal, food, and blankets), told me the war had stimulated a revival of interest in religion. Not in the camp meeting "revivalist" sense but in a sincere search for kinship with God the Supreme Being.

Father Carter confirmed what Father Groser had said, and what I had observed, that if there were to be any appeasement of the dictators, it would not come from Britain's working classes. Nor was their determination to "see it through" entirely attributable to fatter pay packets. Actually, despite higher wages, they weren't much better off economically than before the war because prices had risen sufficiently to absorb the increases in wages. Moreover, the bombings meant loss of sleep and loss of personal property: furniture; clothing; family possessions.

The consensus among parish priests, schoolmarm Ruby Hodges, and a social worker named Miss Grenfell down in Old Highway by the docks was that the determination of England's workers to resist stemmed from their realization that the triumph of the Axis powers would mean annihilation of their personal liberties.

Miss Grenfell ran a settlement house for children in what had been politely known as a house of ill fame but that had become a place where kids got milk and gaily colored paper with which to make cutout pictures. Miss Grenfell, of the Labrador Grenfells, had spent twenty years in the East End, and she knew what her children's parents thought about the war.

"There are no appeasers in Stepney," she told me. "They're as scarce here as capitalists."

Her settlement house had been bombed a few days before I visited Miss Grenfell; but she had got the place fixed up, and the day I called on her, children between the ages of five and thirteen were learning to sing the song called "Jerusalem." In the midst of a rehearsal staged for my benefit, the siren moaned low and high and low and high, but the kids went right on singing a bit louder than before "till we have built Jerusalem in England's green and pleasant land."

Clearly the war in England had become a people's war. It had turned England inside out, much as my friend Hugh Walpole had told me it would months before in the autumn of 1939, when scared Londoners were frantically digging trenches and sending their children to safety in the country. The novelist had told me then that Britons would remake Britain and would set right the inequalities in its social system that had existed for centuries and produced the literature of Dickens.

Sir Hugh had stood in his library, surrounded by Gauguins and Matisses and sculptures by Epstein, whose work he fancied very much, and it seemed a lifetime ago that he had predicted his country's social revolution. Frankly I had doubted him then, but I knew now, fifteen months later, that he was right. The social upheaval began when the children were evacuated out of the London area, and Britons found them ill fed, poorly clothed, verminous, and diseased.

England had come a long, long way since then. Its physical defenses still left much to be desired, a condition that would continue until America gave more help, but there were no doubts in my mind about its moral armament. I was sure now that Germany would never conquer the British Isles. I became even more certain after visiting Dover.

Nowhere in England, not even in London, was the stubbornness of the British spirit more evident than in Dover, the ancient resort town on the strait opposite Calais. Situated where the rolling downs of Kent suddenly break off and spill into the Channel in great chalk white cliffs, Dover, normally home to some forty thousand souls, was being hit during the blitz not only from the air but also by German long-range guns emplaced along the French coast.

The bombardment continued into the early months of 1941, and when I was there in late February, the townspeople were still being subjected to shelling and fully expected the Germans to come any day, for Dover was historically the "key to England," the place where the Romans had landed when they began their conquest of the British Isles.

From the battlements of lichened old Dover Castle, atop the cliffs, Dover-ites kept constant vigil. On clear days they could see the coast of France, an irregular purple strip on the horizon between the blue-gray of the water and the smoky gray of the sky. On good nights they could see the spurts of flame from German guns at Calais, Boulogne, and Dunkirk, long before they heard and saw the explosions as the shells hit a house, school, or church in the town below.

Every hit was recorded on a huge map in Major John Martin's bombproof control room in the police station, and a glance at it told me why Dover was called Hell's Corner. Red pins for bombs and blue pins for shells splashed the entire map, and I wondered how any residents had survived. The answer was twofold. All but about six thousand of the inhabitants had been evacuated, and those who remained had become acclimated to the incredible noise of the sirens, the crump-crump of bombs, the scream of shells, and the crunch of falling bricks and mortar. In Dover, more than anywhere else, I expected the citizens to go about in helmets and carrying their gas masks. But fewer than half the people did. Like Londoners who queued up for the movies while bombs fell, Doverites had become conditioned to living in hell.

I was amazed, after looking at Major Martin's map, that there was anything left of Dover. On a tour of the town, however, I passed rows of houses intact and all alike, their architectural monotony broken only by the slope of the streets. I stood atop a hill and looked down at regiments of chimney pots marching away, smoking as they went. Overhead, fat barrage balloons floated watchfully in a blue sky. I walked past prosperous-looking red-brick houses with brown tile roofs, sparrows twittering under the eaves, and waist-high cedarwood gates set in ivy-covered stone walls. Children played in the streets. No compulsions could separate the kids from their parents any more than the latter could be blitzed out of their homes no matter how badly damaged. Mothers sunned babies in prams.

How, I wondered, had so many Doverites survived? The answer was the catacombs, long natural tunnels in Dover's cliffs where entire families holed up for the night, sleeping in tiers in pipe-framed bunks. Major Martin, a retired artilleryman of sixty-three with a tobacco-stained mustache and a mane of white hair, was very proud of those catacombs, which he had caused to be floored with planks and fitted with sanitary facilities, an emergency hospital, and field kitchens. Those shellproof and bombproof shelters were better than anything I had seen in London and could accommodate six thousand people though fewer than half nightly bothered to use them.

There was plenty of food in Dover. I saw three butcher shops filled with meat—chops and steaks and those "joints" the English love. In Mother Brown's emergency feeding center in a convent, where the homeless were taken after a raid or a particularly bad shelling, I had my first really sweetened coffee since my return to England. There was plenty of sugar in Dover because the rest of England knew that Dover had been "taking it" and the people there had to want for nothing.

There was also another Dover, a town of entire streets of blasted houses, smashed roofs, and charred shells of buildings. The esplanade along the short arc of beach where in peacetime middle-class English folks strolled in the sunshine on weekends was deserted. The beachfront hotels were boarded up, their bed and breakfast signs askew. In one window, though, there was a canary in a cage, kept there by a pair of stubborn householders who even had their brass door knocker polished and front steps scrubbed.

When Winston Churchill said that all England would fight against the invader, he knew what he was talking about. I met a normally peace-loving little old lady who waited for the Germans with bottles of vitriol which she intended to pitch at them as they skulked beneath her window. Another kept pots and pans of water boiling for similar use, and a girl had armed herself with a slingshot and was seriously considering poisoned darts. Some citizens of Dover were sharpening knives and oiling old pistols and shotguns. Others had stores of ground glass and arsenic and plans for using them against the enemy.

In Paris in the spring of 1940 there wasn't much will to fight. In Dover, in the approaching spring of 1941, it was an entirely different story. The town and its people personified the stubborn British spirit which was one of the country's major resources.

33

LONG VOYAGE TO WAR

T he Middle East now loomed as the ground war's most important theater, and about two months after I had left New York, Charley Colebaugh cabled me to "proceed with all possible haste" to Cairo. I hated to leave London but was glad for new adventures and new scenes.

Air transportation was by secret and circuitous routes and strictly reserved for high-ranking military personnel. I had no choice but to make the long sea voyage to Cape Town, South Africa. There, if lucky, I might find a plane to take me to Cairo, and the Ministry of Information arranged for me to sail from Liverpool on March 11 on the SS *Themistocles*.

The night I left for Liverpool, March 10, London took a bad beating from the Luftwaffe. From the direction of the sounds I guessed my friends in the East End were being hit again. I pictured Charlie Brickett huddled in a stinking Stepney shelter and cursing "them bawstids" overhead.

Searchlights prodded long, impatient fingers into the night sky, and flak fell like heavy rain, bits of it pinging off the cab's roof on the way to the railway station. The taxi, slow and smelling of old leather, moved through dark, deserted, unfamiliar streets, and I realized the cabby was wisely driving a roundabout course to avoid the roads used by ambulances and fire-fighting equipment.

At the station ghostly figures materialized in the dim, yellowish light under the sooty marquee. One of the figures, an elderly porter, took charge of my two pieces of luggage and my typewriter while I gave my cabby a one-pound note, double his fare. The air outside smelled of cordite and coal smoke.

The train waited forlornly in the station's cavernous shed, its engine breathing asthmatically, sounding the way I imagined a tired old dragon might sound when resting after great exertions. The porter deposited my baggage in my compartment. I tipped him a half crown for his trouble. He said, " 'Ank-yousir, 'ank *you,* " and was gone.

I heard the roar of planes overhead, hurrying planes, flying high. They might have been those damned Junkers Ju 88s going home after their dirty work or British fighters returning to base. Anyhow, the raid was over. The sirens moaned their welcome all clear.

I shucked off my outer clothing and climbed into my berth in my underwear. I was asleep in minutes and awoke the next morning in Liverpool.

It was cold in the long, dismal, dimly lighted shed of the Liverpool dock where Cape-bound passengers assembled for customs examination. The censors got us after the bag searchers had finished. They read every scrap of printed, typed, and written material we had. Most of the travelers were considerate; they took along only their most important private papers. I couldn't be; I had the rough draft of a book I had been working on in my spare time, outlines for several *Collier's* pieces, and biographical material on a number of important Tories, some of it not very complimentary. It was the kind of stuff I would have gone to great pains to hide from censors in Rome or Berlin.

It took my censor, a schoolmarmish lady with a sad, tired smile, more than an hour to go through my papers. She was intelligent and considerate and handed back my material with the same sad smile and wished me a good voyage.

Before embarking, we deposited our gas masks, tin hats, and ration cards with an official who rechecked our passports and stamped them.

The *Themistocles* was an old hooker with a scrofulous black hull and a bluntly utilitarian superstructure daubed brown. Her bridge sagged, and she looked sea-weary. She might have been any old tramp steamer as she lay glued to her dock by the sulfurous mist that enveloped the harbor while coal thundered into her bunkers and cargo came over the side.

Aboard ship an amiable deck steward conducted me to what he called my stateroom on the boat deck. It was really a tiny cabin equipped much like a first-class compartment on a train, with a bunk but minus a toilet. A washstand that folded down from a bulkhead completed the sanitary arrangements. The "conveniences," the steward said, were at the far end of the corridor forward. I could have a "bawth," he said, provided I took care to "book in advance." He had no idea when we would sail.

All through the morning and most of the afternoon we loaded coal, and topside the ship was filthy with coal dust. The vessel's deck machinery moved with noisy senility. Hooks pivoted rheumatically on their samson posts. Cones of steam spit into the river Mersey's mist from leaky gaskets on the winches. Blocks complained with rust.

I leaned over the boat deck's forward rail, watching the first mate as he supervised the chaos of loading. The packing cases, drums, and barrels that plunged into the open hatches in rope-net slings were stenciled with the words "Britain Delivers the Goods." I wondered what odds a Broadway bookie would lay that we would actually deliver those goods. If mines didn't get us, and if we escaped enemy torpedoes and bombs, we were fair game for German sea raiders, and against *them* we carried a futile four-inch gun on our poop deck.

I asked the first mate, a tall, lean, middle-aged Scot, what *Themistocles* could do in the way of speed. He said old "Tommy's Testicles" would average "maybe nine knots." He smiled, for he knew what I was thinking. The kind of German submarine that lay between us and Cape Town could do fifteen knots on the surface and nine submerged, fast enough to catch convoy stragglers or lone oldsters like ourselves.

"But don't worry," the officer said, flicking coal dust from the lapel of his blue tunic. "We've got an extra quarter knot up our sleeve." It was his laconic way of saying only luck and good seamanship would see us through without the added protection speed might have given us. The "extra quarter knot" was as much good to us as an extra mile would be for an airplane when fifty miles were needed.

"This ship," he said, "was built in 1911. She'd have been junked if only the numskulls in the government had listened to Churchill. If they had, we wouldn't be fighting the Battle of the Atlantic. But when the war started, this old tub and hundreds like her were pressed into service."

The Battle of the Atlantic was one Britain had to win before any other, for it would decide whether the guns, tanks, and planes from democracy's arsenals, at home and in the United States, reached the fighting men on the battlefronts. It was a struggle for the maintenance of the transport lanes without which production would be futile, and ultimate victory doubtful.

Lacking warships, the British converted their newest merchant ships into armed vessels mounting six-inch guns and carrying depth charges and antiaircraft guns. Their unarmored hulls made them no match against enemy shells, bombs, and torpedoes. More than a dozen such vessels had already gone down since the war began. Among them were the *Rawalpindi* and the *Jervis Bay.* Both died fighting heroically, but many others were ambushed and sunk on the high seas before they could even aim their guns.

Most of those armed merchantmen were modern vessels of from ten thousand to seventeen thousand tons, built since 1925. They were designed to replace ships like the ten-thousand-ton *Themistocles* for the Mediterranean service to India via Gibraltar and Suez, or the Cape run to Australia and New Zealand, carrying freight and passengers on the Royal Mail schedules calling for speeds of up to seventeen knots, with as much as five knots in reserve. They were the vessels which in 1940 and 1941 should have been delivering Britain's goods at high speed but instead were carrying a large share of the burden of fighting because a few lack-vision politicians had failed to heed the advice of an old Tory imperialist named Churchill.

Meanwhile, the supremely important task of delivering the goods had fallen upon the slow old three- to five-thousand tonners that plowed the seas laboriously in convoys, fell behind in heavy weather, and were sniped at daily by Nazi U-boats. In fact, most of the four million tons of shipping that Britain had lost since the war started consisted of ships too slow to keep up with their escorts. Great vessels like the *Empress of Britain* and the *Lancastria* had gone down, too, but they were the exception rather than the rule. Most of the dead soldiers in the Battle of the Atlantic were ships such as the *Themistocles* and smaller.

Toward nightfall, our ports battened and blackened out, we moved to midriver and took our designated place at the head of what seemed to be a huge convoy. The decks had been flushed of coal dust with high-pressure hoses, and *Themistocles* was as clean as she would ever be.

The first woman I saw on board was a pretty brunette. She looked lonely. I offered her a cigarette and lighted it for her, and we leaned together on the rail, staring down into the greasy river water, not speaking, and she must have wondered, as I did, whether we'd get out of port and into the Irish Sea without being bombed.

I was about to suggest a drink in the bar aft, but three Australians beat me to it. They were three of the biggest, brassiest, and healthiest-looking men I'd ever seen. I left the field and the brunette to the Aussies.

In the salons and corridors there was a whispery hubbub of subdued voices. Several children cried and whimpered; others ran about laughing and making a rumpus. The grown-ups were very quiet. No two persons knew each other unless they were married or related. Besides, nobody felt much like talking, and I returned to the boat deck, where the ship's fat lifeboats were swung outward ready for release.

There was a full moon blurred by the lifting mist. I could barely make out the outlines of Liverpool's taller buildings and the long black shadows of the docks when I heard the city's sirens signal an imminent raid. Their wail rolled across the Mersey like the distant cries of a woman in labor, rising, falling, rising, growing in volume and urgency. I saw the blue bursts of bombs and heard their complacently destructive grunts as they struck. Days later, at sea, we heard the casualties had been heavy that night.

I thought we were to sail as part of a big convoy, but we were only three ships—*Themistocles* and two smaller vessels—as we sailed at dawn the next morning, steaming down the brown Mersey past the hulks of vessels killed by mines or enemy bombs into the Irish Sea. We moved slowly and as cautiously as you'd walk in an unfamiliar dark room. In those waters the enemy had dropped magnetic mines, cute devices that exploded when they came within the magnetic field generated by a ship. We carried electrical equipment which neutralized the vessel's magnetic radiations, but you couldn't always be sure it worked. And the Germans had lately begun using a new kind of deadly toy, an acoustic mine that detonated at the sound of a ship's mechanical heart. Against this kind of sudden annihilation we carried only our prayers, and in my case the horseshoe Jim Marshall had given me long ago.

It was cold on deck, so cold it congealed in lumps in my pockets. The 210 ship's passengers were ordered to boat stations for the first of innumerable boat drills. We were given life preservers, four large, thick oblongs of cork jacketed in coarse brown canvas, with a hole in the covering for the head and straps that came under the arms. They tied on with strings across the chest.

I looked skeptically at the preservers, and the officer in charge of the drill confided, "They blinkin' well ain't much good. Get waterlogged in twenty-four hours, they do, but you'd die in twenty of exposure in the North Atlantic, so what's the odds?"

He'd started speaking with the air of a man with superior knowledge but wound up with the manner and tone of voice of a man who'd made a new and shocking discovery for himself. He turned to help a short, thick youngish woman with a pretty face adjust her life preserver. She carried an eight-month-old boy on her hip, clutching him with both hands. Her smile couldn't overcome the concern in her large blue eyes. I had a disturbing image of her going down the Jacob's ladder to a pitching lifeboat.

Some of the crew who came up from the engine room, stokeholds, and galleys for the drill had good life jackets: blue canvas vests stuffed with kapok, with tiny red lights on the thick collars so they could be seen in the darkness. The men played at lighting them, as they would do before going over the side in a lifeboat or leaping into the water if we were torpedoed. You could jump fairly safely in one of those vests, but you couldn't jump in one of those Board of Trade things issued to the passengers. The impact would send the blocks in front or those behind, depending on how you landed in the water, crashing against your neck with sufficient force to snap it.

My informant told me all this while I practiced quick tyings on of the strings, and I told him to shut up. He was persistent, however, confiding, "There's a way of beating gettin' your neck broke. Look 'ere," and he showed me how to jump while grasping the two front blocks firmly with the hands, holding my elbows close to my body. "But don't forget to bring your knees up to your elbows when you hit the water," he said. "That'll help you to hold on to the cork blocks."

I thanked him for the instructions, for like everyone else aboard *Themistocles* when we sailed, I was dead certain we'd be torpedoed.

The next day we were on the open sea. She was old, that ship, but she was what sailors call "a great sea boat." The vessel rose and fell gently in that breathing motion which a good ship owns and which bespeaks a well-designed hull, good seamanship, and careful stowage of cargo. The foothills of doom that roll across the wintry North Atlantic were soft dunes for her bows.

Two "Churchills"—a couple of those fifty destroyers Franklin gave Winston—flanked us to port and starboard. A heavier British destroyer of the *Tribal* class surged ahead under a cockade of bluish black smoke. A lithe, fast AMC (armed merchant cruiser), as fastidious as a collie worrying plow horses into a barn, shepherded the sterns of our ship and its lone companions.

A blinker aboard the AMC signaled incessantly, ordering alterations in course, speed, or formation. In wartime the course of ships is ordained not by the sun and the stars but by the known or suspected positions of enemy submarines and raiders. Sometimes we ran in a tight V like three ducks, sometimes we spread out, and frequently we steamed Indian file.

The little Churchills, identifiable by their four slim funnels and low hulls, scudded off on mysterious missions in daytime; but by nightfall they were always back, and our skipper, who allowed me occasional visits to the bridge, told me, "Great little ships. They're old but still fast enough for the job. And my, how we need them! They'll make all the difference in the world. It's unprotected convoys that go down, and if we could spare the ships to guard our cargo carriers, we'd win the Battle of the Atlantic practically overnight, and that means we'd win the coming battles in the Egyptian desert." (The Italians had just invaded Egypt.)

Once we heard depth charges some miles away off our port side. Our steward's telegraph—the ship's grapevine that linked the wireless room, engine room, bridge, and passenger decks with news, misinformation, and plain every-day gossip—reported that an enemy submarine had been sunk. The Churchill did look fatter and somehow pleased with herself when she returned, but there was no way of knowing for certain whether she had got her sub.

One morning, about ten days out of Liverpool, we found ourselves alone— three ships at some distance from each other—on a desolate disk of gunmetal blue water. Gone were the two Churchills and their bigger cousin, but most of all we missed that fussy collie, the AMC, which was, I recall, the classy *Winchester Castle,* originally built for the fast fortnight's run to the Cape from Plymouth, carrying the Royal Mail. The last message the AMC had winked at us was to proceed toward port independently, with good-luck messages added. The crews thereafter practiced daily with the antiaircraft guns and manned the four-inch gun on the poop deck, which suddenly assumed the importance of a battery of eights.

The day before our escort left us, I watched a tall, slender Englishwoman with a thick halo of blond hair, holding a ten-year-old boy by the hand, wave a life preserver at a figure aboard one of the two other vessels in our tiny convoy. The ship was less than two cable lengths away, and I aimed my field glasses at the figure of the man and saw he was a naval officer, at least a commander, possibly a full captain, by the glint of gold on the visor of his cap as he moved in the bright sunlight.

The steward's telegraph confirmed that he was a British naval officer en route to a new command in the Far East. The woman and the boy were his wife and son. The three were to have sailed together but couldn't for service reasons. They would be rejoined in Singapore, Hong Kong, or Bombay.

The second day we were on our own we sighted a neutral Spaniard, white-hulled, distant and as unreal as though she had been cleverly scissored from white tissue paper. That night we heard gunfire off our starboard bow. We saw star shells trace dim patterns at the rim where sky and sea meet. There was nothing we could do. To have gone to the assistance of one of our ships in distress would have meant inviting disaster.

Down in the stokehold the men poured on coal. Somehow the corpulent chief engineer, a jolly fellow with four greasy gold stripes on his sleeve, cajoled two whole extra knots out of *Themistocles*'s sclerotic engines, and we thought her old heart would burst with the effort. But we got away. The grapevine reported that the victim of the attack we had seen from afar had gone down. It was the vessel that carried the Englishwoman's husband.

The lady remained in her cabin for two days, and the skipper went down to see her, one of the rare times he left the bridge. When the lady reappeared on deck, composed and remote, we all tried to pretend we knew nothing. The boy took it well, though I caught him staring sadly off to sea from time to time. He kept to himself even more than his mother did, and as the voyage progressed, he seemed to grow older daily.

The day we crossed Cancer into the flat cobalt-hued waters of the tropics, a wireless message from the Admiralty in London reported German raiders in our vicinity. The grapevine had it they were the *Gneisenau* and the *Scharnhorst,* but we learned later that wasn't true. It was all too true, however, that German raiders were on our trail. The bulletin on the board beside the purser's office reminded us there was "Still danger of enemy action. Wear warm clothing. Be prepared to quit ship at the signal."

But the news didn't prevent tweedy Englishmen from stomping incessantly on deck for exercise while the younger folk plunged into deck sports in the most animated shipboard competitions I had ever seen. At night, we sat in the smoking room, played cards, drank bottled ale, and sang wartime songs, some oldies dating back to World War I, some new.

We sang to keep our courage taut as we described a geometry of furtiveness to keep out of harm's way, running zigzag, changing course and pace every five, ten, or fifteen minutes to confuse the enemy and avoid his torpedoes.

Then, somewhere between Cancer and Capricorn, we awakened one morning with the world red with the nascent sun to find that we had slowed down to about three knots. My cabin steward, with customary quasi-accuracy, said, "Our bloody rudder's gone." Well, we had not lost our rudder, but the strain of zigging and zagging over some twelve thousand miles of sailing to accomplish only half the distance toward where we were headed had proved too much for the old ship's steering mechanism. A pin as thick as a man's wrist in the vessel's steering quadrant had snapped like a matchstick.

We were suddenly becalmed, our rudder useless, with Nazi subs and raiders all around us. I thought of the Ancient Mariner and of his "painted ship upon a painted ocean." We steered by spinning our engines, revolving our starboard propeller to swing to port, and our port screw to veer to starboard.

The skipper didn't dare stop the ship completely. An enemy, hovering just beyond the rim of the horizon, might see our smoke and come roaring down on us, and we'd have been as helpless as a wooden decoy in a duck pond.

The chief engineer sweated off twenty pounds in the keel of the ship, squirming his beery bulk into tight places to repair the broken gear. It took him twenty-three hours. Then we were under way again, first at six knots, then full speed ahead.

For several days we ran lightly, easily, and once we must have come close to land, for some of us landsmen thought we smelled honeysuckle on the heavy night air, but an Irishman insisted it was hawthorn.

We sailed under skies profligate with stars by night and yellow with molten sunlight by day. Life aboard ship lost some of its grimmer aspects. We stopped rehearsing how to grab up warm clothes, brandy bottle, and life preserver in the darkness that would come when an enemy torpedo killed engines, dynamos, and men below the waterline.

The passengers gathered on the tarpaulin-sheltered veranda deck to listen to newscasts from London. The Englishwoman was there when the radio told us that a Spanish vessel had picked up two boatloads of survivors. There was the flicker of a hopeful smile on the lady's lips, and we danced that night under the light of a new moon.

One evening the polished voice of the BBC's London newscaster said Germany had invaded Yugoslavia and Greece. The Yugoslav national anthem was played, and we all stood solemnly at attention, swaying with the ship's roll. It was April 6, and we had been at sea twenty days but were still many days out of Cape Town. The next day came word that the British had occupied Addis Ababa, meaning that Mussolini's "African empire" had fallen. We cheered and sang "God Save the King."

That night a ship moved past us on a parallel track headed northeast toward New York with all her lights blazing. It filled us with amazement that ships could sail at night with lights on. We couldn't even smoke a cigarette on deck unless there was a moon, when it wouldn't matter. But you can see a cigarette's glow three hundred yards on a moonless night and the flare of a match a thousand yards. The lighted vessel was American, and I wondered how much longer my country's ships would be able to sail the seas with lights aglow. She was on the track sailed by the ships that Roosevelt was sending into the Red Sea and up to Suez with weapons and munitions to help Britain hold the Middle East.

Soon we were in the swelling Cape rollers and knew we were approaching our destination. But we moved slowly, with extreme caution, for the waters off the Cape of Good Hope were seeded with mines probably planted by the Japanese, our skipper said. They alone, except for the Portuguese, sailed those waters in addition to the Americans and the British.

The Japanese would be obliged to attack America's Cape route to the Red Sea and Britain's imperial lifeline to Australia, New Zealand, and India in what I saw at the time as the "possibly imminent Battle of the Pacific," and I so recorded in my diary for April 8. I wrote:

> Severed from her imperial extremities, the heart that is England would be a heart without a body, and England would die. Similarly, an America severed from democracy's battlefronts (in the Middle East) would render futile the tremendous efforts of the American people to prevent the catastrophe of a German victory. It isn't pleasant to contemplate, but it's the horrible truth, however, that Britannia's command of the seas is only relative. . . . Her fleets must fight in the Mediterranean, patrol the North and South Atlantic, and the Pacific and Indian oceans, the Tasman Sea and the Red Sea; and even for Britannia that's just too many waves to rule. . . .

Those of us who had sailed for more than a month to reach the Cape from Liverpool on a journey that was normally a thirteen-day run never at any time felt that Britannia ruled the seas. Our ship delivered the goods, but the one that went down some twenty-five miles off our starboard bow hadn't. Neither had many others. The man-made goods and weapons they carried rotted and rusted in their holds on the sea's bottom.

Our long voyage ended late one night when we sighted the lights of Cape Town. Most of the passengers were, like their shipmate, young Dr. Bunny Loots, South Africans of Boer extraction homeward bound to safety and abundance from the perils and privations of wartime England, and there was great excitement aboard the *Themistocles.*

Dr. Loots ran about the decks rounding up friends and urging them forward to see Cape Town. He was twenty-six years old but almost childishly agitated.

"Look," he shouted, "that's South Africa. See? See that cluster of lights there on the slope that's marked by the smaller string of lights of the funicular that climbs Table Mountain? That's the Chevrolet sign, the biggest in the whole world. . . ." He glanced sheepishly at me, fearing, perhaps, that as the only American on board I might contradict him. I didn't, of course.

I had come to know Bunny Loots rather well during the enforced intimacy of the long journey and knew him to be, like all South Africans, intensely nationalistic. A big, bulky fellow with blue eyes and an unruly shock of blond hair, he had recently received his degree in medicine from Edinburgh University and was returning home after a long absence. He told me he hadn't seen his mother in more than six years, but he evidently missed his motherland at least as much as his mother.

Loots personified the antagonism all Boers felt toward the British ever since they had surrendered to them in 1902, thus ending the independent existence of the Boer Republic. The resentment he expressed was akin to that of many Americans toward the British, a resentment which years of talk about "common heritage" and "common language" had failed to quench.

Bunny's folks owned a ranch in the union's northern rangelands and apparently were very wealthy. He said he had recently bought a deluxe Plymouth sports roadster, which was waiting for him in Cape Town. In South Africa an American car cost twice its Detroit price.

Bunny's grandfather had died in the Boer War, and he spoke with bitterness of the concentration camps and privations the Afrikaners endured in their struggle against the British. He talked vaguely of "social justice" but admitted that in his country social equality was only for whites, not for the people to whom he referred as "Cape niggahs," "Coloreds," or "Hottentots." He also fumed against the "international Jews" as the people mainly responsible for the war and otherwise echoed the gibberish of Dr. Joseph Goebbels.

Bunny was too far removed in ancestry from the early Dutch settlers of South Africa to have been emotionally disturbed by the German invasion of Holland or by the appalling mass murder of Rotterdam committed by the Luftwaffe. He said he was prepared to fight for South Africa's independence from the British Empire, but not to save Britain. I tried but failed to make him see that if Hitler won the war, South Africa would merely become an adjunct of a new German empire. He reminded me very much of many American isolationists I had known and unknowingly prepared me to detest South Africa if I found that his countrymen shared his views.

The *Themistocles* was warped to her dock by a tug in the early morning of the thirty-first day of her journey. A white mist lay like a tablecloth on Table Mountain, rising some thirty-five hundred feet above the magnificent harbor. Around three sides of the "table" rose twelve conelike peaks. They suggested the Twelve Apostles at a phantasmagoric Last Supper—or, considering the hour, Last Breakfast!

I saw an Admiralty official come aboard, and the grapevine informed me that he had brought a cable for our Englishwoman. It said that her husband was safe. I was glad for her and her son, but I recalled there were several hundred others aboard his ship, and what of them?

34

THE RELUCTANT ALLY

Foreigners entering the Union of South Africa were required to post a bond of from five to fifteen hundred dollars. This, I was informed, was to prevent the country from being "filled up with undesirables." For a correspondent en route to the war in the Middle East, however, the five-dollar bond was considered adequate. I paid it in the crowded smoking room of the *Themistocles,* received a receipt, and ten minutes later I was in the long gray shed on the dock.

Behind a pile of packing cases stenciled "Britain Delivers the Goods," customs officers went through my luggage and turned me over to a dour police official. He stamped my passport and exacted sixpence, a sort of head tax, for which he gave me a pink slip of paper explaining it was both a receipt and a check to retrieve my baggage. I stuffed it into one of my pockets but couldn't find it later when I was leaving the shed and had to pay another sixpence for another pink slip. The fact that the officer who had given me the original receipt remembered I had already paid him made no difference. "No pink slippee, no leavee," he said sourly, and waved me on. Afrikaner officials were a mirthless, rule-ridden lot.

The lineup of taxis parked outside the dock was composed entirely of American cars: Chevrolets, Buicks, Fords, even a couple of Lincolns. As I was on my way to the Mount Nelson Hotel in a Chevy sedan driven by a gruff middle-aged Boer with red hair, Cape Town's port side outskirts reminded me of Jersey City or Hoboken. The stateside look was accentuated by billboards extolling the virtues of American breakfast foods, radios, automobiles, farm machinery, electric refrigerators. The port bore a striking resemblance to any American seaport south of the Mason-Dixon Line. In its big-port sights and sounds and smells and in the fact that its menial tasks were being performed entirely by blacks—Herren Doktor Loots's "Cape niggahs"—it might have been Baltimore, Charleston, or New Orleans.

The harbor was alive with war-related activities. Ships loaded and unloaded troops, weapons, munitions, and supplies. Booms rose and fell in the wilderness of funnels and cranes. Our sometime "collie" of the long voyage, the *Winchester Castle,* sleek, pale green, and lovely in spite of the tarpaulined guns that had converted her into an armed merchant cruiser, had mysteriously preceded us into Cape Town and strained at her hawsers in one of the numerous docks while being refueled and revictualed. At another wharf the aircraft carrier *Ark Royal,* under repair after having been damaged by German bombs in the North Sea months earlier, was aswarm with riggers, fitters, mechanics, and welders whose torches produced spectacular showers of white-hot metal. The old liner *Georgic* lay alongside, undergoing similar treatment.

Trains of freight cars stood on sidings, and long rows of black men, bent under bales and boxes, moved like so many caravans of indefatigable ants between ships and warehouses and trains. More blacks jostled crates on squeaky dollies. Others sat about smoking foot-long pipes with thimble-size bowls and drew an unsolicited disdainful comment from my driver.

"They're resting," he growled. "These Cape niggahs are always resting, every chance they get."

On the outer walls of the port's buildings, posters showed suntanned South African soldiers—called Springboks after the national animal, a sort of gazelle—making the familiar thumbs-up sign behind the legend "If It's Worth Having—It's Worth Fighting For." Other posters warned against "Loose Talk—It Sinks Ships" and advertised the might of the British Empire. The empire's naval power, meanwhile, was represented by two capital ships, a battleship and a cruiser, anchored offshore, their blue-black silhouettes barely visible in the mist that still lay on the harbor's smooth gray waters.

But although evidence of his country's involvement in the great war was everywhere, my surly driver never once mentioned it, not even after we had swung onto Adderley Street, Cape Town's Fifth Avenue, past sidewalks crowded with uniformed New Zealanders, Aussies, Canadians, and Springboks, troops enjoying a spot of leave before embarking for the Middle East. Hoping to elicit a patriotic reply by remarking that they were a fine-looking lot of men, I was stunned by the answer.

"Yes," my Chevy's Afrikaner pilot growled, "and they'll probably make fine-looking corpses up there in the Egyptian desert. Old men make wars, but young bucks die fighting them."

"I gather," I said weakly, "you don't agree with those posters that say South Africa's worth fighting for."

"South Africa, yes, but Britain, no. This is a war to save the British their bloody empire, that's all, and I'm against *that.*"

By then we had climbed a hill and pulled up to the imposing entrance of the rambling Mount Nelson, the epitome of Victorian colonial architecture.

"What, then, are you *for*?" I asked, handing him a one-pound note for my fare.

"Independence," he replied, looking me in the eye as he gave me change. "The freedom my ancestors fought and died for in the Transvaal, the Orange Free State, on the veldt and the karroo."

For once in our brief antagonistic relationship he smiled, and he was off in his Chevy after refusing a tip. He had confirmed my impression of South Africa, formed aboard the *Themistocles* in my talks with Bunny Loots, as a racist, unwilling British ally, politically as well as geographically remote from its putative mother country.

The sense of South Africa's remoteness from the struggle was accentuated by the good life its white citizens enjoyed. There was plenty of everything, including food, and I was reminded of preinvasion Holland. Breakfast at the Mount Nelson included butter, eggs, cheese, and bacon, Dutch style. There was real coffee and rich cream and all the sugar one could desire. Fruit—apples, pears, luscious grapes, bananas—was in my room at all times, and when it began to wilt, the black servant brought more.

There was plenty of gasoline for those big American cars that every well-to-do white South African seemed to own, and Cape Town's smart restaurants were always crowded. Meals ran from hors d'oeuvres to baked Alaskas, properly paced with the right wines. Men and women dressed for dinner and attended concerts, the opera, cinemas, and theaters. The rhythm of their lives hadn't missed a beat since September 1939, and the uniforms of the empire's various armies merely lent a romantic touch to their luncheons, teas, dinners, and parties.

To remind the city's citizens that their country was at war, a cannon boomed daily at high noon. Traffic stopped, and pedestrians stood at attention for two full minutes in tribute to Britons who were dying in North Africa and in Britain in the struggle against Hitler. Then life resumed its normal brisk tempo.

The very day I landed in South Africa, April 12, 1941, nineteen months after the war began, the English-language *Cape Times* carried an astonishing front-page article declaring that while Germany's national socialism might not entirely suit South Africa as a system of government, nazism contained "much that could usefully be applied to running the Union." Similar articles in Afrikaner newspapers frankly appealed to South Africans to use the war as a means of attaining the goal of all nationalists: total independence from the British Empire.

There were antiwar demonstrations in Johannesburg and Durban, and prowar newspapers had to barricade their offices to prevent isolationist mobs from smashing the presses. An Afrikaner merchant in Cape Town told me that in his opinion the Jews should have been "ostracized from the life of the nation." Shades of Goebbels and Farinacci.

The Afrikaners were mostly followers of the Germanophile former prime minister James B. M. Hertzog and his equally pro-Nazi foreign minister Oswald Pirow, both of whom had borrowed heavily from *Mein Kampf.* But while the Afrikaners were numerically dominant, constituting about 1.6 million of South Africa's white population of 2 million—the country's 8 million blacks and racially mixed "Coloreds" had no voice in government—they were no longer politically dominant in the Union's affairs.

South Africa was maneuvered into siding with Britain in the war by the politically skillful General Jan Christiaan Smuts, who became prime minister on September 5, 1939, two days after the British Parliament declared war against Germany, and by a narrow margin persuaded the South African Parliament to follow suit. Within twelve months Smuts had raised and equipped an army of 150,000 men with its own air force, artillery, armor, and transport.

Smuts's countrymen referred to him behind his back as "Slim Jannie," some lovingly, others with a gentle sneer that implied slyness and opportunism. To most fellow countrymen, however, he was simply *Oubaas,* Afrikaans for "Old Boss," meaning anything from beloved patriarch to political tyrant, and he was probably a bit of both. As prime minister he was his own United party whip, rarely asked advice, and never accepted unbidden counsel. His skills as a politician rivaled those of Roosevelt and Churchill, and as a member of the British Imperial War Council he was undoubtedly one of the towering figures of World War II.

Physically, however, the seventy-one-year-old Smuts looked less like the consummate politician he really was than an aging Shakespearean actor or scholar. He was tallish and slightly built, with a ruddy oval face, a well-shaped head sparsely thatched with straight white hair, a neatly trimmed goatee with matching mustache, and a strong, longish, thin-nostriled nose. His most compelling feature was his eyes. Steel blue, they reminded me of Hitler's, but the resemblance ended there: Smuts's eyes mirrored inner qualities of compassion and goodness utterly lacking in the Führer's gaze.

I met Field Marshal Smuts soon after I arrived in South Africa, and on April 22, shortly before I entrained for Durban to fly to Cairo, he invited me to lunch in the luxurious dining room of the Senate in Cape Town. During the simple meal, and for more than an hour afterward, he exuded optimism about the war's eventual outcome and assured me that the Union's war effort was gaining momentum daily, citing as proof the substantial contribution his Springboks were making to the successful British campaign against the Italians in Ethiopia. South Africa, he said, realized increasingly that a German victory would mean indefinite postponement of the its desire for independence from the British Empire. Afrikaner isolationism, he said, was on the wane despite outward evidence to the contrary. Above all, he was supremely confident that Germany and its Italian ally would be defeated.

"We will win the war," he declared. "We will win because God is on our side." I could see he meant it so sincerely that I resisted a temptation to remind him that Adolf Hitler had invoked the Almighty in Germany's cause when *he* went to war.

The general's voice was rather high-pitched, though not unpleasantly so, and his manner of speech was typically Afrikaner, jerky and frequently punctuated with the question "You follow?" This was a trick to compel attention, and for the same purpose Smuts leaned across the luncheon table from time to time to grab my arm or to poke a sharp forefinger into my breastbone. He had beautiful hands, long-fingered and fragile-loooking, the well-kept hands of an aristocrat.

Apart from his faith in the support of Divine Providence, Smuts's confidence in democracy's ultimate victory was based on his conviction that America would soon enter the struggle on Britain's side.

"America can't afford to stay out of it," he said. "Americans are a highly moral people. They have a profound consciousness of right and wrong, and they know—whatever their fears might be about who will win the peace to follow, or how much the war will cost, or the justice of Britain's cause— Americans know that Hitler is in the wrong. They won't let 'freedom perish from this earth.'

"And we can't win without American intervention, which is as necessary to the survival of freedom and democracy as it is to ensure a just and lasting peace. America can't afford to lose the war. She can afford even less to lose the peace. . . ."

There was a dramatic pause as though to allow time for his words to sink in.

"Besides all that," Smuts resumed, "the future belongs to the United States. Europe—continental Europe—is dead. Gone. This war, this horrible thing that's happening today, is destroying Europe. She's in her last spasms now. Yes, the future belongs to America."

Smuts believed that America would enter the war "within the year" and that Germany would be defeated "within eighteen months or so." History— and the Japanese—proved him right in the first instance but wrong in the second. The Germans would be fighting until the spring of 1945.

In another prophecy, however, the general proved uncannily correct. He predicted that Hitler would soon turn against Russia. "But the Germans," he said, obviously relishing the prospect, "will never conquer the Russians." He was visibly cheered by the thought that Hitler's invasion of the Soviet Union would ensure a British victory and democracy's survival. (I was in Cairo two months later, when the Germans invaded Russia in June, and I cabled General Smuts asking him to reaffirm his conviction that Germany couldn't defeat the Russians. He replied immediately but cautiously with a cable saying, "All that has happened is to the advantage of democracy.")

Smuts, who described himself as "a Boer of the Boers," outlined what he called his "dream of the Africa of the future," describing a kind of pan-African entity, a continent of member nations bound politically and economically to one another in "a sort of United States of Africa."

I respectfully reminded him that one of his eminent predecessors, Cecil

Rhodes, had dreamed a similar dream, to which Smuts replied: "Ah, yes. But Rhodes envisioned a united Africa merely as another jewel, bigger and richer than India, to be set in Britain's imperial crown."

Smuts indicated that in what he called his "African confederation" the member states would not be "serf nations digging the continent's riches out of its mountains and harvesting wealth from its broad plains and forests for the reward of a few absentee landowners and stockholders in London. No major *outside* power would dominate the confederation, nor even any part of it." (Accent his.)

Smuts's stress on the word "outside" led me to believe that if the *Oubaas* had his way, postwar Africa would be dominated by the Union of South Africa, then (as now) the economically, industrially, and culturally most advanced nation of the former "Dark Continent."

Clearly this was Smuts the internationalist speaking, the Smuts who had contributed so much to the creation of the League of Nations. But his internationalism never outweighed his nationalism. It was Smuts the nationalist who, when asked to join the British Commonwealth Air Training Plan in which Australia and New Zealand had readily agreed to participate, said, in effect, "No, thanks." He trained his own pilots, and they were already fighting in the Middle East, flying American Tomahawks, as a South African Air Force.

Smuts, furthermore, had insisted that his Springboks fight only in Africa. Before they went to the front, South African soldiers signed an agreement with the government stipulating that they would not be required to serve outside the geographical limits of the African continent.

The general sidestepped all questions relating to South Africa's racial problem. His attitude toward his country's huge black majority was one of master toward servants. It seemed to bother him not at all that South Africa's blacks were virtual slaves earning as little as eighteen cents a day mining gold and diamonds and even less as domestics in the amply staffed villas of Cape Town's all-white residential suburbs. Mindful of the low estate of our own blacks back home, I did not pursue the subject.

Smuts devoted most of his time to the war rather than to internal politics and problems. As head of the United party, a fusion of the Dominion party, the pro-British elements of the old Nationalist and Union parties, and the Labour party, he held a comfortable majority of about eighteen seats in Parliament and had the power to carry out reforms that would have given the Union's blacks and Coloreds some measure of that democracy the general loved so well. But history would show that Smuts failed to appreciate the needs and aspirations of his vast country's large, and growing, nonwhite majority.

Two days after lunching with Smuts I was on a train bound for Durban, some nine hundred miles from Cape Town, a distance roughly equal to that between New York and Chicago. But what would have been an overnight ride in a Pullman car in the United States was a journey of three nights and two days in South Africa—sixty hours of tortuous winding from the Cape plain up to the barren plateau known as the Great Karroo, then across the lush country that skirts Basutoland, and through the Drakensberg Mountains to Durban, the Union's port on the Indian Ocean.

The railroad, one of South Africa's main lines, was double-tracked for only short stretches and comparable to an American railway of the days when American pioneers still fought Indians in the West and locomotives burned logs for fuel. Part of the trip might have been a journey across much of Texas and the American Southwest: mesquite, sagebrush, yellow-green plains of tallish grasses, and roadside natives in brightly colored blankets. With its beaches and swank high-rise resort hotels, Durban itself might have been Miami.

I could have made the trip to Egypt on a ship out of Cape Town, but this would have entailed waiting two or three weeks for a convoy to be assembled, then another monthlong voyage through the "combat waters" of the Indian Ocean and the Red Sea. The *Themistocles* had cured me of wartime shipboard travel for a while, and I chose to fly via British Imperial Airways, which operated a service linking Cairo to the Far East with Sunderland flying boats.

Our flight path northward called for overnight stops at Beira, in Portuguese East Africa; Nairobi, in Kenya; and Khartoum, in the Sudan. Flying overland in an amphibious plane was a bit spooky, but I soon became accustomed to the idea and actually enjoyed the sights. We often flew low over herds of elephants, and twice we saw hippos awash on the mudbanks of jungle streams.

At Khartoum, where the Blue and White Niles meet, the heat was so intense that when we stepped from the plane and walked up the bank of the Nile to the riverside customs-police station—a corrugated iron shack better suited to baking bread than to human habitation—one of our twenty-odd passengers collapsed although he wore a pith helmet against the fiery sun. The air was thick with a fine, talclike sand that induced a throat-searing thirst. None of us, however, dared drink from the earthen pots in the customs shed, where a thermometer registered 132 degrees Fahrenheit in the shade, preferring to wait until we reached the hotel.

But it was cool that night, and some of us walked about the town, a modern city with wide streets and handsome buildings. One of the handsomest was the governor-general's palace, near the river embankment. Inside, on the palace stairs, a plaque marked the spot where General Charles George Gordon, history's "Chinese Gordon," was killed by dervishes on January 26, 1885.

The next day, the third of our journey, we flew deep inland to pick up the lower tributaries of the Nile. The land below changed from green to brown, then to buff, and suddenly we were flying over wretched desert country. From the plane's observation deck, a raised runway on the port side in the ship's smoking compartment, we looked down and wondered that men should have fought and died for possession of that seemingly endless lifeless waste.

Four days and four nights after we took off from Durban, we were over Cairo. The Pyramids looked small from ten thousand feet, and the famous

Sphinx was an indistinguishable lump of rock. The whole suggested decadence and rot. But Cairo's gardens and boulevards were alive with trees speckled with purple blossoms, and the ageless Nile, the sinuous backbone of a nation, was dotted with feluccas with pink sails. We landed on the river at sundown.

35

THE FATEFUL
SUMMER OF '41

Cairo's better hotels were crowded with British officers, newly arrived for impending battles in North Africa and the Balkans. It was the end of April 1941, and in both theaters glorious advances were turning into inglorious defeats at the hands of the Germans, who had come to the aid of their crumbling allies, the Italians.

Earlier General Sir Archibald Wavell, commander in chief of the British forces in the Middle East, had swept the Italians out of Egypt, pushed them back across Libya as far west as Benghazi, captured the strategic port of Tobruk on the Gulf of Sidra, and occupied Bardia and Sidi Barrani. In a brilliant campaign, fifty thousand British troops had virtually destroyed Marshal Rodolfo Graziani's army of half a million Italian and Italian colonial troops.

But the campaign that might well have carried Wavell's forces into Tripoli itself and knocked the Fascists out of the war was rudely interrupted. The Greeks, after having first stoutly resisted, then turned back an Italian invasion, now faced German troops and armor and asked for help. Pledged to assist Greece when attacked by the Nazis, Britain complied by sending soldiers, tanks, and planes—mainly from Wavell's command. But the help was proving insufficient to halt the German advance into Greece, and the withdrawals had substantially reduced Wavell's ability to hold the ground gained in his westward drive.

Meanwhile, the Germans surprised the British by sending Marshal Erwin

Rommel to Libya to salvage what remained of Italy's forces after the battering they had sustained at Wavell's hands. Rommel's Africa Korps, superbly equipped with armor and dive bombers, forced the British to evacuate Benghazi on April 3. It attacked Tobruk, gained a foothold in the battered port's defenses, and by May 1 a historic siege had begun.

The Middle East itself was threatened now, and the British rushed reinforcements to the area. This was why I found Cairo full of British officers and troops—Aussies, New Zealanders, Tommies, and Gurkhas and Sikhs from India—the day I arrived, and the city's hotels filled with field-grade commanders, wealthy Balkan refugees, and war correspondents taking a breather from the fighting in the Western Desert.

After trying Mena House and the Continental Savoy, I managed to obtain a room with bath at Shepheard's, an ornate, four-story Victorian structure built in 1841 around a palm-shaded garden on the site of Napoleon's headquarters in 1798 during his unsuccessful campaign to hold Egypt, which the Corsican believed was "the most important country in the world." From the hotel's high-ceilinged rooms General Gordon had set out on his equally ill-fated mission to Khartoum, and Stanley to find Livingstone in the jungles of Africa. I did not know it on the hot and humid evening of my arrival, of course, but my second-floor room in Shepheard's was to be the base from which I would set out to cover many of the battles waged during World War II on both shores of the Mediterranean, where it seemed that the fate of Western civilization was being decided.

Renowned for its comforts, excellent cuisine, and well-stocked cellar, the hotel was somewhat run-down in 1941 but still one of the world's best. My generation of correspondents cherished it mainly as a haven from the sights and sounds of war, as a place to have contact with some of the men who were running it, and for its mahogany Long Bar, presided over by Joe Shalom, everyone's friend. Always immaculate in white coat and white bow tie, Joe had a ready smile that crinkled the corners of his brown eyes and showed rows of white teeth. A good listener with a retentive mind, he heard many indiscretions from the liquor-loosened tongues of his barside military clients and knew more than he ever told anyone about what was going on in the sprawling Kasr el Nil barracks, headquarters of whomever happened to be commander in chief, Middle East.

Having heard of Joe in London from my friend Harry Craddock, the barman at the Savoy, I introduced myself to him the evening I arrived. He in turn presented me to Shepheard's maître d'hôtel, an Egyptian of Italian origin, who complained bitterly that since the war he had lost most of his good cooks, waiters, and busboys. Nearly all were Italian nationals and were hustled off to a concentration camp when Italy entered the war. The Egyptians and Nubians who had replaced them, he said, had slowed down service, and the cooking was somewhat less than great.

"But our cuisine is still the best in town," he assured me, "and we have a fine cellar left over from the dollar days when Cairo was the mecca of American tourists. And I have a good supply of fine steaks and game in our refrigerators. You will dine well here, sir."

Short of a royal suite, my quarters were Shepheard's best: large bed-sitting room furnished Victorian style, heavy drapes, an enormous armoire, a chest of drawers, a well-worn settee and two comfortable armchairs in faded red damask, a writing desk with a lamp and a straight-backed chair, and a comfortable bed canopied with netting against the clouds of affectionate flies that inhabited the place by day and the mosquitoes that invaded it at night.

Unfortunately my room faced the main street and partially overlooked the spacious garden, which had a dance floor at the far end. The garden became a supper club after dark with fifty or more individually lighted, flower-decked tables whose occupants dawdled over their food and wine, talking and laughing and dancing away the hours to the uncertain but recognizably American rhythms of a nine-piece orchestra. I always knew it was two o'clock in the morning when I heard the familiar "Good night, sweetheart, till we meet tomorrow. . . ."

But the orchestra's sign-off rarely meant that what remained of a moonlit, jasmine-scented Cairo night would be quiet enough for restful sleep. The hours before daybreak were invariably punctuated by the grind and roar of horn-tooting taxis and military vehicles, the clippety-clop of horse-driven gharries and the whip cracks of their fezzed or turbaned jehus, the Arabic babble of Egyptian passersby, or the raucous voices of beer-laden Aussies homeward bound to billets after a night on the town.

By day it was worse. A noisy city even in peacetime, populous wartime Cairo almost floated in noise. Its boulevards and reeking network of narrow streets overflowed with humanity, civilian and military: Egyptians in flowing galabias and red fezzes, refugees in Western dress, fat Levantine merchants wearing pith helmets, turbaned Nubians balancing baskets on their heads, ragged beggars of all ages, and, of course, the sunburned, khaki-clad troops of His Britannic Majesty's various armies.

Through the crowds moved street peddlers, offering the soldiers "feelthee peectures," razor blades, fly whisks, shoelaces, boot polish, swagger sticks, aspirin tablets, coffee from brass urns with long spouts, milk hot from an accompanying goat's udder, and malacca canes. Furtive pimps promised "nice young girls, very young, maybe only thirteen. . . ."

In the roadways aging camels were being led to slaughter, staff cars honked and threaded their way through donkey carts and small herds of goats and sheep, and overloaded buses snorted dense black diesel smoke into the already polluted air that stank of urine and uncollected animal droppings. Here and there a barrel organ grinder added to the bedlam with ding-dongy renditions of the Aussies' favorites: "Waltzing Matilda" and "There's Something About a Soldier."

Night usually brought relief from the roasting daytime heat with cooling Nile breezes and a reduction of the diurnal din, but not much. Although Cairo was in the war zone and subject to the blackout regulations in force in Britain, nocturnal Cairo blazed with light, and while the traffic noises abated somewhat, new ones were added, mainly by the dozen or more midtown open-air movies showing rootin'-tootin' American westerns with their sound tracks turned up to a deafening level. Nightfall, moreover, seldom silenced the ubiquitous coin-hungry organ grinders. At its quietest, in fact, the capital of King Farouk's Egypt—and of Britain's Battle of Africa—always produced noise enough to prevent anything but the kind of sleep induced by a bedtime double scotch or two.

Having arrived at last in an active war theater, I was anxious to go to the front and earn my keep by producing the kind of action story I knew Charley Colebaugh was panting for. Early on the morning after my arrival, bleary-eyed but "eager for the fray," I hurried to the army's Public Relations Office at GHQ to make myself known and ask that I be allowed to spend some time with the troops in the Western Desert.

I had a personal letter to General Wavell which my friend Arthur Greenwood, son of the British Labour party leader, had thoughtfully procured for me in London from the War Office. The letter asked that every courtesy be shown me but was so phrased, as such letters invariably are, that it could mean everything it said or not, as the recipient chose.

I had been instructed to present the letter to Colonel Philip Astley, who was in charge of war correspondents. But the colonel was away on a holiday, and I was received by his assistant, Major Oakshott. He read the letter, shook his head sadly, smiled a thin smile, and I knew at once that I wasn't going to the desert soon, perhaps not ever.

Oakshott informed me with obvious regret that the army's facilities for frontline coverage were limited, hence reserved for the representatives of major radio networks and daily newspapers. No provisions had been made, or would be made, for correspondents representing magazines, weeklies or monthlies. Moreover, he said, if I wished to remain in Cairo as a member of the working press, I would have to be accredited to His Britannic Majesty's armed forces, a process that Oakshott indicated "would take some time." For a moment I thought I was back in London in October 1939, trying to persuade a stuffy War Office PR colonel to allow me to go to France to cover the BEF. Through rising anger I heard the major say that accreditation was "absolutely essential in any case" because anything I wrote, including cables and letters, would be subject to censorship. Until I was accredited, I couldn't attend army briefings or press conferences.

I was furious but held my tongue. Oakshott was obviously a decent chap hogtied by red tape, and I asked him if I could fill out the necessary forms for accreditation to start the ball rolling right away. He said to wait for Astley's return because the papers had to be filled out in his presence. Oakshott promised to telephone me as soon as the colonel was available, and we parted friends; but I was boiling.

The next ten days seemed interminable. I could only wander about Cairo, absorbing atmosphere and spending the evenings eating and drinking and talking with American colleagues at Shepheard's or up the road at the Continental Savoy, where there was a fine roof garden, good food, and a floor show that included a particularly sexy, sinuous belly dancer named Hekmet. Unlike her blubbery counterparts at Madame Badia's, she was young, slender, and beautiful.

The Americans in town at the time were few, but among the best reporters in the business. They included Harold Denny, of the *New York Times;* Edward Angly, of the *New York Herald Tribune;* Richard MacMillan, of the United Press; my old friend Ken Downs, of INS; and Ed Kennedy, of the Associated Press. All complained they could rarely visit the front, and none had a good word for the censorship, which was stupid, arbitrary, and poorly organized. The army, navy, and air force each had separate censors, and a story had to go from one to the other, in offices scattered about town. If, in addition, the piece had political implications, it had to be vetted by a political censor. By the time the various censors had all applied their blue pencils to the copy there was often little left to cable back to home offices.

The Americans agreed that the censorship in Cairo at the time—specifically the months of May, June, and July—was worse than they had experienced in Berlin, Rome, Madrid, or, as in the case of Denny of the *Times,* Moscow. A British defeat could not be reported unless it could be made to sound like "a strategic withdrawal." A British victory, on the other hand, would be withheld by the censors until the news had been made public in London, often rendering useless the Cairo-based reporters' dispatches.

The overriding rule of British censorship was that correspondents could not send information of value to the enemy. A sound rule, but it was interpreted in the censors' offices by men who had their own ideas of what constituted "information of value to the enemy." The word "sulfanilamide," for instance, was excised from one reporter's story because the censor thought it was a code word.

My friends were surprised to learn that magazine correspondents were banned from frontline coverage, but none could explain the taboo. The ban frustrated and mystified me until I met the young representative of *Time-Life,* Alan Michie. A tough, dynamic reporter who had come up through the ranks in journalism before landing a job with the Henry Luce publications, Alan explained the setup to me over a couple of Joe Shalom's libations as we sat at a small round table on Shepheard's famous terrace, a bowl of peanuts between us.

"It's a colossal racket," Alan said. "Britain's newspaper tycoons, through their powerful Publishers' and Proprietors' Association—something like our own National Association of Manufacturers—have got themselves a monopoly on news coming out of the Middle East. They froze out British magazines, like the *London Illustrated News, Punch,* and *Post,* figuring they're competition. With their own periodicals out of the game, the ban was extended to include ours, overlooking the fact that American weeklies represent a vast American readership running into the many millions. Not one of their slicks sells more than four hundred thousand.

"And the army people here are only too happy to cooperate. That way they need fewer vehicles, fewer conducting officers and fewer censors. Best of all, from the army's point of view, the policy means a lighter work load for the old-school-tie boys in public relations. They can sleep later mornings and go home to dinner earlier after drinks at the Gezira Sporting Club. We've got to find a way to beat this racket, Frank."

This was a hell of a way to run a war, Michie and I decided, but the war was being run badly in other ways. The fate of the Middle East hung in the balance, but the men who were running it at staff level seemed not to be taking it very seriously. Many of General Wavell's 254 red-hatted brigadiers, for instance, were popping champagne corks nightly at the swank Auberge des Pyramides and having dinner parties while their younger aides played polo with frenzied enthusiasm in the broiling heat or cricket and tennis at the Turf Club. All were fighting the war much as they and their fathers had fought the last one, in leisurely "we'll muddle through" fashion.

They were, for the most part, gentlemen products of Rugby, Eton, and Harrow and kept gentlemen's hours. They went to their jobs in the Kasr el Nil barracks and in offices elsewhere in town more or less promptly at 9:30 A.M., then disappeared for lunch at about 1:00. At that hour they filled every table at Shepheard's, the Continental, and the dining room of the exclusive— no Egyptians allowed—Gezira Sporting Club. After a very large lunch the officers would take a nap. They'd sleep until about 4:30 P.M., when the war was officially "reopened," so to speak, and kept going until 7:30. Then, no matter what happened, the war was shut down for the night!

Those were the hours also kept by the censors and their boss, Captain Berrick, who believed that all war correspondents, especially Americans with "foreign-sounding names" like mine, were really spies. There were no censors at GHQ to read reporters' dispatches if any news broke after 7:30 or, at the very latest, 8:00 P.M., and the journalists were obliged to wait until Berrick and his blue-pencil pushers returned to duty at 9:30 A.M. Meanwhile, of course, London would break the news, and the men who probably had risked their necks getting their material would be beaten on their own stories.

Early one morning Oakshott summoned Alan Michie and me to a meeting with Colonel Astley, a tall, soldierly, handsome guardsman type and former husband of movie star Madeleine Carroll. He had been to America, knew that weekly magazines like *Time, Life, Collier's, Liberty,* and the *Saturday Evening Post* represented a vast reading public, an audience not to be ignored in Britain's efforts to reach the hearts and minds of the American people, and invited Alan and me to fill out the questionnaires for accreditation. The army required a complete history of our personal, political, and professional backgrounds, including the nationalities of our parents, their national origins if, as in my case, they were naturalized citizens, and *their* political views and religious affiliations.

Colonel Astley won my undying affection. To begin with, he interpreted my War Office letter of introduction to Wavell in my favor and saw to it that I would meet the C in C. Furthermore, Astley didn't even raise an eyebrow when he saw that my father's brother, Uncle Gennaro, was an officer in an enemy army. He was mildly amused, in fact, that he and my uncle held the same rank, and when I joked that Uncle Gennaro was probably "in the bag with other Italian prisoners," he said he would do what he could to help me find him.

Most of all, however, I appreciated the fact that Astley arranged matters so that while I wasn't yet a fully accredited correspondent, I could do everything a licensed reporter could pending final War Office approval. He soon had me on the way to the front.

In the meantime, a brisk new wind was blowing through the bureaucracy that was running the war from the Kasr el Nil barracks. Its first gusts arrived in the person of Major Randolph Churchill, the prime minister's son, who was soon to take charge of public relations in the Middle East. Like his eminent father, Randolph had a way of running roughshod over everybody, disliked advice, and made enemies by the score. But he got things done and quickly injected new life into the British mechanism for handling the foreign press. It was at Randolph's insistence, I later learned, that London eventually gave me full accreditation. Michie and I received our licenses on the same day from Captain Oliver Lyttelton soon after the latter arrived to become Britain's new minister of state in the Middle East.

It was nearly the end of May, almost a month after my arrival in Cairo, that Astley telephoned me late one afternoon, asking me to be ready to leave for the desert the following morning, in uniform and with full field equipment: bedroll, canned food for several days; water bottle; flea powder. A conducting officer, Captain Buzz Hawkins, would call for me with a vehicle at 7:30 A.M. sharp.

Luckily I had equipped myself with everything I needed at Jones's Emporium, a sort of local Moss Bros. down the street from the hotel, on the chance that I might be allowed to see some of the fighting in the Western Desert. I had khaki shorts and bush shirts, a khaki wool sweater for cold desert nights, a down-filled sleeping bag, a blanket, rubber-soled suede desert boots, even an enameled washbasin. And, of course, my field glasses.

Captain Hawkins, red-haired, sturdily built, tanned leather brown, showed up at ten-thirty. Someone down the line had overslept, and someone else had forgotten to arrange for transportation. But he had managed to locate a vehicle, a Ford station wagon that had seen far too many better days, and a driver, Corporal Smythe of the Royal Auxiliary Service Corps.

For the captain and the corporal, May 27 was just another workday, but for me it was the beginning of another adventure, my first experience with actual combat between armies. Until now I had only seen Spaniards shooting at other Spaniards years before in the streets of Madrid.

We headed north out of Cairo along the road to Alexandria, where we would turn west toward a British base at Mersa Matruh, which we hoped to reach by nightfall on the first leg of our journey to the front. I was glad to be leaving Cairo, where for nearly a month the war had made little sense. I felt instinctively that up forward, where men were fighting for a cause in which I profoundly believed, the war would be understandable again, as it had been in England. My hunch was right, but some of the things that happened made no sense at all.

36

THE WAR IN THE DESERT

The road northward from Cairo to Alexandria was a narrow macadam ribbon across the desert margins of the Nile, a strictly peacetime highway built for tourist buses and the speeding limousines of fat pashas. In wartime it was burdened with trucks, tanks, staff cars, and motor-drawn artillery. It demanded careful driving, and Captain Buzz Hawkins and I weren't getting any from Corporal Smythe. He wheeled sharply to avoid a five-tonner that refused to be honked out of the way, and in seconds we were hub-deep in brownish red sand under a blazing sun.

Buzz and I thought that perhaps the heat had got to Corporal Smythe because we had the windows up against the wind and sand, and the thermometer over the driver's seat registered 117 degrees Fahrenheit. But it wasn't the heat. Before leaving Cairo, Corporal Smythe hadn't checked the brakes. We had been doing fifty because we had a rendezvous with a war somewhere west of Alexandria, and when Corporal Smythe pressed down on the brake pedal, the vehicle kept rolling on, unchecked.

During the ensuing delay we discovered that Corporal Smythe wasn't what Ernest Bevin would have called a "double-purpose" soldier. In 1940 Churchill's minister of labor had lamented to the House of Commons the fact that England didn't have a double-purpose army of drivers who could repair the vehicles they used in battle. Bevin said the British were not good mechanics, warned that the Germans were, and urged the immediate creation of training schools. Smythe had attended one of those schools but obviously hadn't learned much. He not only couldn't drive a car very well but, worse, couldn't fix it when something went wrong. And many things went wrong that day.

When you have an appointment with a war, for instance, you fill the five-gallon tins on the iron racks on either side of your vehicle with water, gas, and oil. Ours were all empty. Moreover, Smythe had forgotten the jack and neglected to bring a shovel. You're helpless in the desert without a shovel, and he didn't know what the four-foot studded steel tracks clamped atop the station wagon were for. Buzz and I showed him how to slide them under the rear wheels for traction.

Later, after an obliging Bren gun carrier had tractored us out of the sand, and we were tooling along toward the sunset and the war, Buzz explained. He was driving now, and Corporal Smythe was stretched out on the back seat, soundly and noisily asleep.

"It's not his fault, really," Buzz said. "Six months ago Smythe was a baker's deliveryman in Huddersfield and drove a horse and wagon. He'd never driven a car or a truck until he was called up. He wasn't quite up to the mark, physically, for one of the armed branches of the service, so they put him into RASC. How he got to be a corporal, I don't know. Better education than most, probably, but he doesn't know a blasted thing about machinery. He had about six weeks' training in an auto shop, but I doubt he could change a fouled plug.

"We've been accused of being a nation of shopkeepers, and I'm afraid that's true. We certainly didn't have mechanics when war came. We had a small class of fine craftsmen who made our better motorcars and airplanes, but no great pool of mechanics. So we weren't really ready for war. I don't mean merely that we didn't have tanks and guns and planes, though that was true enough, but we didn't have the people needed to make them. The Germans, on the other hand, are a nation of mechanics. So are you Americans. I'm afraid we aren't. Anyhow, we weren't when we went to war. . . ."

Buzz knew what he was talking about. In private life he was a machinery salesman in Manchester.

There were other indications of British deficiency in the art of desert warfare as we headed west toward Mersa Matruh. The army's engineers had allowed the road to disintegrate under the pounding of trucks, tanks, and heavy guns. The potholed and rutted road tore vehicles to pieces. Good American trucks, Buzz said, lasted only weeks. The toll in broken springs, axles, tires, gears, and bodies was terrific. The supply line stalled and men died up forward because ambulances or much-needed ammunition reached them too late.

Nevertheless, with Buzz Hawkins at the wheel, we made good time westward from the Nile Delta through El Alamein, El Daba, and Fuka to Mersa Matruh, where we arrived bone-weary, hot, and caked with powdery sand. Smythe, fully restored now, foraged for gas and water at an army dump and then, doubling as batman—a British army euphemism for soldier-servant— prepared supper while Buzz and I ambled down to the gleaming beach, stripped, and joined several hundred naked, sunburned troops in the greenish blue waters in which, in Roman times, Mark Antony splashed about with Cleopatra.

Smythe wasn't much of a driver or mechanic, but he had a sure touch with canned bully beef, canned peas, and some potatoes and onions he had scrounged. He produced a fine stew, and while it tasted faintly of gasoline—he had cooked it over a gas-fired Primus stove—it went down well with army hardtack and hot tea, followed by canned pineapple for dessert.

We slept that night in the open under a star-spangled sky, and I awoke in my sleeping bag at sunup, my face wet with dew.

Westward again along the coast road and headed for Sidi Barrani, we traversed the area through which Wavell's forces had driven the Italians out of Egypt months before. The losers' debris of Mussolini's dreams of conquest still littered the desert. For miles on both sides of the road there were abandoned guns, the skeletal remains of staff cars and trucks, and dead, burned-out tanks. The stark brownish pink landscape was strewn with discarded tunics, mess tins, boots, rusting rifles and machine guns, cartridge belts, and empty cans—the detritus of Blackshirt legions in precipitous retreat—now the property of the horned vipers and golden scorpions that inhabit the desert's otherwise lifeless wastes.

With my binoculars I scanned the terrain south of the coast road and the disused single-track railway that ran more or less parallel to it. I saw a vast emptiness of gray earth, yellow rocks and boulders, and dusty clumps of thornbush. There were no houses, no signs of human habitation except for an occasional Bedouin in flowing rags, head wrapped in a kaffiyeh, striding purposefully from somewhere to nowhere.

If men had to fight wars, I thought, the area made an ideal battlefield. There were no population centers, hence no civilian targets for bombs and shells. But the desert, I soon learned, demanded almost superhuman effort of the men who fought in it.

Although mornings and evenings were fresh with light breezes and the nights were cold, the long days were almost unbearably hot, a torment for troops limited to no more than a gallon of water a day, often much less. In addition to the enemy, they had to fight thirst and the khamsin, an Arabic word for "hot wind," actually a wind-driven fog of burning sand. It produced temperatures of 127 degrees Fahrenheit and turned the insides of tanks into crucibles. When it blew, you couldn't see your hand before your face, and it blew for three and four days at a time. You sweated, and the sand caked on you like mud-bath clay, found all the areas between your clothing and your body, and sifted powderlike under tent walls and through tent flaps into your food and bedding. In a khamsin you steered by compass and hoped you didn't blunder into a minefield, the enemy's or your own.

What I would remember best, however, were the desert's purple dawns and magnificent sunsets and the vast, all-pervasive silences of the nights, when the temperature dropped thirty degrees or more and I slept snugly in my downy sleeping bag under a limitless sky jeweled with stars.

Nor would I ever forget the scene in the tented field hospital just east of Sidi Barrani, a former Italian stronghold, where the British treated the wounded, their own and the enemy's.

We passed barbed-wire enclosures that held Italian and German prisoners of war and pulled up near a field dressing station. Outside, the air smelled of the sea, visible in the distance beyond rows of brownish pink tents and a parking area filled with camouflaged trucks and ambulances, but inside the tent, where the wounded lay, it smelled of disinfectant and death.

There were several Tommies and two Italians and a German on camp beds. All had undergone rough-and-ready field surgery. A British corporal in a far corner called for water, and an orderly brought it to him, raising the soldier's bandaged head to help him drink. I squatted beside him, and when he saw the "U.S. War Correspondent" tabs on my shoulders, he asked, "Yank?" I said yes, and he grinned and made a thumbs-up sign.

The two Italians were in an opposite corner, side by side. One was a very young *tenente* (lieutenant), his brown uniform stained darkly with blood and caked with dirt, his head a curly black mop streaked with sand, his abdomen covered with bandages "Shrapnel," the orderly said. "We don't think he'll make it." The officer's eyes were closed, but he was not asleep. The muscles of his face twitched spasmodically.

I leaned across his still form to speak to the man next to him, a corporal. He had lost his right arm to its elbow and cradled the stump in his left hand. He was pale under his tan but managed a feeble smile when I greeted him in his own tongue, and he asked me if I was Italian. He seemed more puzzled than surprised when I said, *"No, americano."* He said his name was Giovanni, shook his head, indicating he knew the officer was dying. *"Morira molto giovane, troppo giovane* [He will die very young, much too young]." Giovanni said. The *tenente* was twenty-two.

The corporal and the lieutenant were in the Bersaglieri, a crack Italian regiment of sharpshooters. They wear plumes in their hats, cockades of blue-black feathers that bounce rhythmically when they run in their quick parade step. I remembered how fine they looked when they marched past Mussolini's balcony in the Piazza Venezia in Rome. Neither the *tenente* nor the *caporale* looked fine now, but they had lived their day as lions. "Better to live one day as a lion," their Duce kept telling them, "than a lifetime as sheep." I could see, however, that both men would have preferred living as sheep than as broken lions, one dying, the other maimed for life.

The *tenente* died while I leaned across him talking with Giovanni. With an agonized cry that brought the camp's padre running, the lieutenant uttered the only two words Italians always say when they're hurt. He didn't shout, "Viva Mussolini," but cried out, *"Mamma mia,"* and then was very still. Giovanni crossed himself with his left hand. The sharp-featured little padre, an Irishman from Dublin, drew a rough gray blanket over the *tenente*'s face after making the sign of the cross over the man's forehead.

I had never before witnessed death at such close quarters. I went out and lighted a cigarette.

The young lieutenant and the corporal and thousands like them were paying with their lives for the consummate vanity of Benito Mussolini, the Duce who for more than twenty years had tried to transform millions of peasants into stalwart warriors and had produced an army of ill-equipped, poorly motivated men whose formations had disintegrated before Wavell's numerically inferior forces. I recalled something that Ciano had once said to me: "We must take the mandolins out of our men's hands and give them rifles. . . ." That was after both he and his father-in-law had visited Germany and seen Hitler's disciplined troops in maneuvers.

The extent of the Italian debacle in the Western Desert was brought home to me later that day, when Buzz Hawkins and I visited one of the prisoner of war enclosures near the hospital complex. Shame and disillusionment were written on the faces of the thousands who stood about listlessly behind the barbed-wire fences, squatted on the ground, or lay asleep on their tunics, sheltering their faces from the sun with forage caps or helmets. They were an unshaven, dusty, dirty, cheerless lot but quick to respond when addressed in Italian.

An older prisoner, who acted as spokesman for the others, told me he had fought in Ethiopia, Spain, and France, and proudly declared he had never fired his rifle. Asked to explain, he gathered together the fingers of both hands in the classical Italian gesture of inquiry and said, "Why should I kill anybody?" Other prisoners said the Germans had deserted them in battle when British tanks advanced, leaving them to face the oncoming armor with only rifles. The Afrika Korps had all the trucks. *"Noi, andavamo a piedi* [We marched on foot]," one of the Italians said.

Later the Irish padre introduced me to Günther, a German prisoner, as an American officer. The German stared at me for a moment, unbelieving. His brown eyes opened wide, and his heavy underlip dropped. Then he smiled. He had seen through my disguise. *"Ach,"* he said. *"Korespondent, nein?"* It was the padre's little joke. He had wanted to startle Günther into believing America had entered the war, but Günther was only momentarily taken in.

Günther was a lance corporal in the Signal Corps, and he'd been in an advanced enemy observation post when taken. He wore the cotton gray-green field uniform of the regular army, and he was an ordinary conscript, which meant he was an average German who had reached maturity under nazism. His gods were Adolf Hitler and Rudolf Hess, the central figure in one of the war's most fantastic episodes.

On May 10, flying a new type of Messerschmitt with unloaded guns, Hess took off from Augsburg at about 6:00 P.M. A few hours later, his fuel tank empty after a 750-mile flight, he parachuted near Glasgow onto the estate of the duke of Hamilton, whom he asked to see when he was captured. The purpose of his mission remained obscured in mystery. A public tendency to hail him as a deserting convert from nazism was squelched by Ernie Bevin, who denounced him in the Commons as "a murderer."

Günther had heard of Hess's flight on his wireless and was puzzled that the super Nazi, next in line to succeed Hitler, should have defected. Hess was the hero of him and his comrades in the Hitler Youth movement, and his desertion was a blow to their faith in nazism and to its prestige at home.

Günther had a broad Berliner's face, light brown hair, a downy chin, and a smooth face burned red by the sun. He said he hated the desert, and so did his comrades, and returned to the subject of Hess. He couldn't understand why his country's number two Nazi had fled to England. Neither did I, and I asked him what he thought of Hitler. Günther's eyes brightened, and he said Hitler had been wonderful in the past, citing the German victories in Poland, the Low Countries, and France. *"Schön,"* Günther said. As for the future, Günther wasn't sure. *"Ich habe ein wenig Angst,"* he said.

I gave him some American cigarettes, and an orderly brought Günther a steaming cup of tea. Minutes later a couple of MPs fetched him back to the German POW enclosure.

Meanwhile, lunch was ready in the mess tent. The inevitable bully this time came smothered in onions, carrots, peas, and potatoes with a side serving of Yorkshire pudding. There was no gasoline flavor and no sand. A miracle. Even when there was no wind, your every movement raised puffs of powdery sand, and it fell from your clothes into your food. After eating a peck or so you got something called Gyppy tummy (Egyptian stomach), a mild but nonetheless unpleasant form of dysentery.

After lunch Smythe couldn't get our vehicle started. The sand had got into the distributor apparently, but Smythe thought he could repair the damage. Buzz Hawkins suggested a walk on the dunes that rose temptingly between us and the cool sea. We'd just started when there was a shout from behind. It was the voice of the camp's Cockney sergeant major, a man who called latrines "latrynes."

"Oi say, sir," he shouted. "Better not go up there. Them dunes is fair alive with mines. More than a hundred of them." And he told us about the "money boxes," "fountain pens," and "thermos bottles" with which the Fascists had sown the dunes during their hasty retreat. The money boxes were hand grenades shaped like penny banks, the fountain pens and the thermos bottles also looked innocent enough, like the real thing, but all were booby traps that blew off hands or feet when picked up or accidentally kicked. A dozen Tommy souvenir hunters had paid the price of curiosity and were in the hospital awaiting transportation home.

Buzz and I canceled our exploration of the dunes, went down to the sea by a clearly marked route through the sand hills, took off our clothes, and lay on the cool, wet sand, telling each other how much we missed our families. The captain talked about his wife in England and their nine-year-old son, who rode so well. The boy could jump his pony already and had "a good seat." And

Author at 10 years of age.

Uncle Gennaro in 1939,
a colonel in the Royal Army of Italy.

Street fighting in Madrid in October 1934 during the nationwide disturbances. (Popperfoto, London)

At Ravello, besieging Garbo, author, Stewart Brown, Michael Chinigo-on the roof of Hotel Colombo.

Two cables from the home office. (top-Garbo cable; bottom-D'Annunzio)

In full dress after interview with Pius XI, from left Michael
Chinigo, author, Sam Shulman, INS photographer.

Galeazzo Ciano and Hitler in Berlin on October 21, 1936.

MINISTERO DELL'INTERNO

VISITA DEL FÜHRER

Lasciapassare N. 1476
rilasciato a *l. Signor*
Gervasi Frank
giornalista

PEL MINISTRO

AVVERTENZE A TERGO

Author's press credentials to cover the Führer's visit to Italy.

Mussolini and Hitler at Munich
in October 1939. (Wide World
Photo)

From left: Bill Hillman, Sir Alfred Noyes, Michael Chinigo, Sir Hugh Walpole, and author waiting for news of election of new Pope. The telescope is trained on the Sistine Chapel's chimney.

The Gervasis and the Shirers, on home leave in New York City, 1940.

Harry Zinder, Quentin Reynolds,
and author, Shepherd's Hotel,
Cairo 1942.

Field Marshall Montgomery in the Western
Desert, 1942. (Official British photo)

Generals Auchinleck, Hughes, and Marshall-Cornwall, 1941. (UPI/Bettmann newsphoto)

With General Brereton in Benghazi, shortly after the Ploiesti Raid.

Press conference, Western Desert, 1943, Chester Morrison, Alex Clifford, Kim Mundy, author, George Lait, Alan Moorehead, buddies throughout the war.

Southern Italy in 1943,
during the Cassino campaign,
watching a flight of bombers and
wondering if they're ours or theirs.

General Mark Clark enters Rome,
1944. (UPI/Bettmann newsphoto)

Manila, 1944. Author at right.

Aboard LST, on the way to southern France, 1944.

With Severaid and Stein. (photo by Carl Mydans, Life Magazine ©Time Inc.)

I told him about Kathryn and Tommy and Sean. We both wondered whether our kids would be fighting another war someday, and we agreed there couldn't possibly be another after this one. Then we rolled onto our bellies and fell asleep.

The sun was a great orange disk in the west when we returned to the hospital. Orderlies were unloading ambulances, and the Irish colonel who commanded the station, his two English surgeon captains, and the padre were busy through the night.

We had made camp alongside our crippled vehicle at some distance from the main hospital tent, but in the still night sounds carry. We had squirmed into out sleeping bags when the heavy nocturnal dew started falling, but I got little sleep. There was no moon, and across the bleak and stricken land came the cries of the wounded—Englishmen and Germans and Italians who'd been brought in from the battlefield fifty miles or more west of where we were, and were now in the postop tent coming out of ether and feeling pain.

The captain on the camp bed beside me was snoring; but the cries kept me awake, and I heard the first faraway arrhythmic drone of German bombers, Ju 88s. I shook Buzz awake to warn him. We rolled into the slit trenches Smythe had dug for us with a borrowed shovel. The trenches were really only shallow graves but good protection against blast and shrapnel.

The bombers were undoubtedly headed for Mersa Matruh, but they dropped a few bombs—I counted four—as they passed overhead, flying high, invisible in the night sky. First, I heard the telltale screams descending bombs make, then I saw and felt the earthshaking explosions as flame-colored geysers of earth flowed upward. The bombs fell on the dunes two or three hundred yards from us and did no harm. None hit the field hospital or the POW enclosures.

But there was something intimate, disturbingly personal, and terrifying about these particular bombs, unlike anything I had experienced in London, where the bombs were never aimed at me. Here I felt I was the target. It was all over in minutes, perhaps only seconds, but they were the longest I had ever known.

Smythe had got the distributor fixed with the help of a more experienced colleague, and in the blue-white light of a desert morning, after a breakfast of canned tomato juice, canned sausages fried in margarine and sand, strong tea, and hardtack smeared with gritty marmalade, we resumed our trip to the front.

The battlefield situation at the time, late spring 1941, was one of stalemate, during which both sides were regrouping forces and replenishing their supplies of gasoline, water, food, and ammunition. This explained the heavy nightly traffic on our coast road. Hundreds of trucks—everything from big six-wheelers down to snub-nosed little half-tonners—flowed westward along the rutted, crater-pocked highway.

The British still held the strategic seaport of Tobruk, where about twenty-four thousand Australians and some twelve thousand refugees and prisoners of war, mostly Italians, were holed up behind a double line of concrete and steel fortifications built by the town's previous occupants, the Fascists. Supplied by the British navy, the Aussies, stout fighters in broad-brimmed campaign hats, made frequent raids on Rommel's vulnerable thousand-mile-long supply route to Tripoli. The Aussie garrison had fiercely resisted three German attempts to break through Tobruk's defensive perimeter, inflicting heavy casualties on the attackers, and remained a thorn in Rommel's exposed left flank.

The British also held Salum, an Egyptian frontier customs post that guarded the western entrance to the coast road, the highway Rommel hoped to use to invade Egypt. Otherwise the ground gained by Wavell earlier in the year had been lost. In ten days the Germans under Rommel had regained terrain which the British had taken ten weeks to conquer from the Italians.

As of May 30, while Buzz Hawkins and I bounced along the coast road through the grayish white rubble of Sidi Barrani toward our destination—Buq Buq and the headquarters of the Western Desert Force—Rommel's forces were deployed along a line roughly parallel to the Libyan-Egyptian frontier. Their positions ran southward from Fort Capuzzo, a former Italian stronghold southwest of Bardia, to Sidi Omar and Fort Maddalena just west of the misnamed Libyan Plateau. Actually the plateau is an enormous escarpment that rises a sheer six hundred feet from sea level at Salum and extends like a great brown glacier more than two hundred miles into Egypt proper to the sub-sea-level Qattara salt marshes.

It was an axiom of desert warfare that whoever controlled the escarpment dominated the coast road and the western approaches to the Nile, Alexandria, Suez, and Cairo itself. At the end of May it was still in the hands of the British who held the zigzag road leading up to its heights from Salum through Halfaya Pass, which the Tommies had aptly renamed Hellfire Pass. British artillery was emplaced on the escarpment, and British tanks patrolled what was really a wilderness of sand, rock, and camel thorn brush. There were no roads, only the often indistinct windswept tracks of trucks and tanks that had passed the day before. Vehicles moved on the plateau by compass and sextant, much like ships fighting a naval battle in Nelson's time.

Traffic was still heavy when we joined the westward flow of vehicles on the coast road that morning, and it struck me how much desert warfare had changed since the days of Colonel Lawrence and General Allenby. Their memoirs, and the more recent writings of my friend Lowell Thomas, the radio broadcaster, had led me to imagine desert warfare as a romantic business fought on camelback and horseback. Caught in the stream of trucks, I found nothing romantic about desert warfare. It had long since come down off the backs of camels and horses, and it now moved on oversize tires and clattering, articulated steel tracks. It was about as glamorous as a very big, very busy, and very noisy garage, and it smelled like one.

At Buq Buq, which was merely a name on a map and a place where the bad road became considerably worse, Buzz Hawkins signaled Smythe to turn right into an almost impassable track leading to the headquarters of the Western Desert Force. There, hidden among the dunes, we found what the British called a caravan but Americans called a bus, and in it sat the commander, General Sir Noel Beresford-Peirse, surrounded by staff officers and poring over the maps on his table.

The general made us welcome, offered tea, and explained that his caravan had once belonged to one of the several Fascist generals captured during Wavell's initial campaign months before. It contained a real bed with a comfortable mattress, a table, two or three chairs, and a curtained dressing room with a washbasin at the rear. It also had green awnings for shade and blue glass windows to filter out the glare of the desert sun. Unlike the British, the Italians never adjusted to the desert. Their top brass, at least, went to war with all the comforts of home: packaged pasta, canned tomato sauces, canned chicken and veal stews, wheels of Parmesan cheese, chocolates, coffee and little aluminum pots for brewing their espressos, bottled mineral water, plenty of Chianti in straw-encased flasks, and toiletries. British officers, troops, and war correspondents lived well for months on captured Italian supplies.

General Beresford-Peirse was tall, with blue eyes, pale yellow hair, and a face that might have been sculptured out of polished red limestone, its ruddiness heightened by the loose white woolen scarf he wore around his neck. He had ordered an attack at dawn that morning, and when we arrived, he dismissed his officers and told us what had happened thus far and what he hoped to accomplish, stressing the word "hope." This was, he said, "to drive Jerry back from his present positions and westward beyond Tobruk."

Did the general hope to relieve Rommel's siege of Tobruk? He said that was his intention, but I thought I detected a note of uncertainty, an impression he later confirmed by indicating that he sorely needed more armor, more manpower, and more vehicles. Oddly he stressed the latter. He said that if he had two thousand more trucks, he knew where he could use every one of them, but he also needed more tanks and planes. Most of all, perhaps, he wanted to gain time. "Given enough time," he said, "we might acquire the weapons and men and transport we need with which to run Jerry right out of North Africa."

The general believed Rommel was assembling the armor and artillery he required for a major attack on the lightly held British positions. He estimated the German's strength at about 80 big tanks of the newly arrived fifteenth Panzer Division, and approximately 120 smaller armored vehicles, in addition to batteries of deadly eighty-eights, antitank guns. The general would not say how many tanks and guns he had, but he knew himself to be mismatched. His orders were, apparently, to break up the Germans' concentrations, inflict the heaviest possible losses, and cause them to lose a lot of that valuable commodity called time.

"This morning," the general said, "we hit them hard. Our forces were inferior to theirs numerically, but we struck so hard and so often and in so many places that Jerry didn't know either how strong or how weak we are. But we must drive the enemy westward. This will oblige Jerry to keep his air bases at a long distance from the Nile and Suez and make it more difficult for him to bomb those objectives.

"Most important, we must disorganize him and oblige him to stay close to his bases farther back. We have, as you know, a large and well-armed force in Tobruk which constantly harasses the enemy's rear and which probably has prevented Jerry from trying to push us back into Egypt along the coast."

I thought of a crude simile and said the general seemed to be in the position of a boxer who knows he's outweighed and must keep jabbing with his left until either his opponent weakens or he himself feels sufficiently strong to land a knockout punch. The general smiled and said, "I do believe you've got it, old boy. It's a matter of punch and counterpunch."

Thus encouraged, I said I found it puzzling that planes, tanks, and guns were being poured into Britain when the weapons were obviously needed in the Western Desert for the defense of Egypt and the vital Suez Canal. I did not know at the time that on April 20 Winston Churchill, alarmed by a report from Wavell that his position in the Middle East had grown precarious after the Greek debacle, had ordered the immediate shipment to Egypt of nearly 250 tanks. They had come via the dangerous but short Mediterranean route instead of the long way round via the Cape and had arrived at Alexandria on May 20. The general probably knew this but gave no sign.

In reply to my observation, he said: "We can't lose the war here. We can always give Jerry hell with very little. But let's assume the worst. Let's assume that we are obliged to withdraw completely from North Africa. That still wouldn't lose the war against the Germans but would merely prolong it. We would fight from Aden, from India, from the interior of Africa itself. I'm not saying that will happen, mind you. I'm simply pointing out that the possibility might arise if we are suddenly overwhelmed by the enemy's superiority in weapons and men.

"We could continue fighting here for years before we were defeated. But in England the war could be lost in a matter of days. We must make the island safe at all costs. Of course, while we couldn't really lose the war here, we could go a long way toward winning it if we had the armor and planes and manpower we need."

At the time, however, the British were holding Egypt with a few planes and a mixed bag of about sixty Matildas and I (for infantry) tanks, supported by improvised mobile artillery—I saw two-pounder guns mounted on trucks go into battle—and batteries of twenty-five-pounder cannons. What the British lacked in weaponry, however, they made up in gallantry and an amazing adaptability to fighting in impossible desert conditions. Even the khamsin seemed to bother them far less than it did the Germans.

The general showed us on his map where we would find gasoline and water in the combat zone, and we pushed on along the scabrous road to Salum.

At Salum we turned left onto the rough, zigzag road that led up to the escarpment, and by the time we gained its heights the engine had overheated, and we stopped to cool it and gain our bearings. Around us was an empty sea of sand, boulders, and mesquitelike brush. Behind us, on the horizon, a column of dust appeared, drew nearer, and materialized into a light tank recognizable as British by the proud little regimental pennant it flew. Its commander stood in its open turret and asked the way to headquarters. "Don't know exactly," Buzz replied, "strangers here ourselves, but we were told we'd find it at—" and gave him the map coordinates. The officer thanked us, the tank clattered away, headed southwest, and we followed in its dusty wake.

We reached our destination just before nightfall while an infantry unit was preparing an attack, one of General Beresford-Peirse's "counterpunches."

That night a call went out for volunteers for a patrol. There was a hunt for corks. They were burned, and the black stumps were used to blacken faces, necks, the backs of hands, shiny buttons. Regimental and divisional insignia came off the men's khaki shirts and shirts, and there was much laughter and joking while this went on. One of the men dropped to one knee and did an imitation of Al Jolson singing "Mammy!" Then they saw to their revolvers, hooked grenades to their belts, had a farewell drink in the officers' mess, and filed out into the darkness, followed by "Cheerio" and "Good luck."

We never saw any of them again because we moved on before they returned the following morning. We were following the infantry toward the front somewhere on the escarpment south of Salum, ahead of a squadron of tanks. At first light a thin ground mist floated over the sea of sand, rock, and scrubby camel thorn; visibility was perhaps a hundred yards, no more. Our Ford slogged through hub-deep sand with difficulty, and I took to calling the car Smoky Joe. I didn't think the vehicle would last much longer.

On either side of us where troops should have been there was only more sand and rock. The sun shone hot and yellow and burned off the mist. The sky caught fire and glared down in a hot, glowing mass. From overhead came the drone of planes, and we prepared to jump out of the car and scatter, but Buzz shouted: "They're ours!" They were Martin bombers, newly arrived from the United States, patrolling and covering the infantry's advance. But where the hell was the infantry?

We found it hours later. About two hundred yards ahead of us we could make out motionless forms lying doggo in the sun behind rocks, mounds of sand, clumps of brush, in windblown depressions, wherever there was cover. Their orders were to lie low by day and move forward at night.

The troops had only what food they could carry, what water was in their bottles. They were told when they started that they couldn't expect supplies. To move trucks up behind them would have given away their positions to enemy planes.

The unit we found were scouts, and on them depended the success or failure of the maneuver—a forced march of several hundred men who moved laterally in a long line across the desert like a gigantic comb, a march that drained men's energies and patience. It was hot work, and the desert's vipers slid from the heat into the empty skulls of long-dead camels.

Up ahead, behind the enemy lines, American Martins and Tomahawks pinned Stukas and Junkers bombers to the ground, while British Blenheim bombers blasted away at tank parks, blowing them about like toys. While we watched, a flurry of Hurricanes sailed into twelve Stukas and six Ju 88s. Three of the latter fell in flames.

Late that evening we saw a flight of Martins bomb Fort Capuzzo. Ten tall columns of black smoke and dirt rose straight into the reddening sky, indicating as many hits. We camped that night on the escarpment, too far from the fighting to hear the machine guns and rifles but near enough to hear the sounds of cannon booming.

After a cold breakfast of sardines and hardtack, we climbed back into Smoky Joe, descended the escarpment, and drove eastward on the coast road. The fighting had been heavy on the plateau, and columns of ambulances filled with wounded passed us. It was well after sundown when we arrived at the hospital complex near Sidi Barrani and cadged a meal at the station's officers' mess. A hurricane lamp swung from the mess tent's ridgepole. At one side there was a crude bar, shining with bottles and real glasses and stacked with cigarettes, English and American. We helped ourselves to the drinks and the smokes.

Medical officers, smelling of formaldehyde, came in from the operating tents with tired eyes. One of them, an older man, sighed deeply, said he didn't care what sort of world it might be after the war. All he wanted, he said, were his wife and dogs, his old car and golf clubs, and a little place in the country. And peace . . .

Big Ben solemnly bonged the hour over the shortwave radio tuned to BBC London.

The next morning, on the way to Mersa Matruh, Smoky Joe died forever. We waited three days by the roadside for a rescue truck. It came just as we had finished our last can of bully beef, but when we got to Matruh, there was no time for food. A hospital train was leaving in a few minutes for Alexandria. We left Smythe at Matruh, and Buzz and I clambered into a compartment occupied by a captain on his way to Cairo on leave. "By the way," he asked, "have you chaps got any food with you?" We hadn't, of course, but he had a package of gingersnaps. We each had two. The spicy cookies only whetted our appetites.

We were contemplating a long hungry ride to Alexandria when the aisle door opened and a soldier incongruously attired in a white apron and a tall white chef's hat over his khaki asked whether we'd like dinner. We followed him to the dining car.

We threaded our way through several cars filled with wounded, about 260 men lying in tiered bunks. Some had lost arms; others, hands or feet. They were Tommies and Germans, Aussies and Italians. The war was over for them, and they no longer hated each other.

"Bloke up 'ere wants water," said a wounded Tommy, pointing to an Italian in the berth above him.

"And 'im and me could do with a fag apiece," said an Aussie, thumbing toward a German across the aisle from him.

Minutes later we were wolfing fried steak, potatoes, spinach, apple tart, and tea and drinking clean, cool water. I gave our rescuer a one-pound note. This bothered the captain, the stranger Buzz and I had found when we boarded the train. "You Americans," he said. "You always tip too much. Five bob would have been plenty."

From Alexandria Buzz and I hitched a ride to Cairo, where we arrived late in the evening, bone-weary.

37

EXIT WAVELL, ENTER AUCHINLECK

On June 21, in the wake of disastrous British defeats in Greece and Crete and yet another setback in the Western Desert, Winston Churchill removed General Wavell as commander in chief in the Middle East and replaced him with General Sir Claude Auchinleck, C in C of British forces in India, where he was to be succeeded, in turn, by Wavell.

But before the two commanders could swap jobs, there occurred an event that dramatically altered the character of the war on all fronts and substantially enhanced the importance of Wavell's new assignment: In the early-morning hours of June 22 Germany invaded Russia. News of the attack was tapped out on the Reuters teleprinter which the management at Shepheard's had installed in the hotel's somber lobby for the convenience of its many journalistic and military residents.

All that morning I watched the news juke, as we called it, pour out the bulletins that chronicled the historic turn of events. I recall an inner sense of relief that at last Britain was no longer fighting alone, although the early reports from the Russian front indicated that the Germans were headed for another quick victory. The Red Army had been mobilized but apparently was caught tactically unprepared, and a large part of the Soviet Air Force was destroyed on the ground on the very first day of hostilities.

The consensus among British officers who followed the battle's progress with me at the teleprinter was that the "Bolshies" would "pack it in" within a fortnight or thirty days. A young intelligence major bet me the price of a dinner at the Continental Savoy that the Germans would be in Moscow by mid-July. I took the bet, but only because it seemed the sporting thing to do. I had no grounds to believe the Russians could successfully resist the evidently powerful German attack.

Obviously Hitler had decided, like Napoleon before him, that before finishing off Britain, he must first dispose of Russia. Napoleon had failed. Could Hitler succeed where the Corsican had not?

That was the question uppermost in my mind when I cabled Smuts in Cape Town for his reaction. At the same time I wired Charley Colebaugh to ask the Russian Embassy in Washington to grant me a visa so that I might go to Moscow to cover the war's new front. I had no immediate reply.

In the meantime, Colonel Astley, the army's PR chief, phoned me that Wavell, in response of my long-standing request for an interview, would see me at his villa. The general was still packing for India when Astley accompanied me to Wavell's residence in Zoheria.

Physically Wavell was broad and stocky, with a strong chin and deeply furrowed face tanned the color of cordovan leather. He had one good eye, having lost the other at Ypres in World War I, and the benign expression of a friendly elderly spaniel. In desert tunic with a splash of ribbons he was an imposing, almost intimidating figure with thinning gray hair parted high on one side and a light, rather nasal voice. He was fifty-eight.

I had been advised that there was never much to be learned from a first conversation with the general and that his silences were proverbial. But he put me instantly at ease by offering me tea and asking me how I liked the desert. I replied that I didn't care much for the khamsin, or the furnacelike daytime heat, but that I had grown fond of the desert's vastness, its nocturnal stillness, its starry skies.

He apparently had been told that I had visited the front and surprised me by asking my impression of such action as I had witnessed. I said that I did not feel qualified to pass judgment but that it had seemed even to my untrained eye that unless new tanks, planes, and trucks arrived from England and the United States in great quantities, and very soon, Britain's position in the Middle East would continue to be, well—I groped for a word—"precarious."

General Wavell fixed me with his good eye and said: "Personally, I have always felt quite secure in Egypt. Rommel will never reach the Nile. But of course, we need more and better weapons. And I do believe they will be forthcoming. Not immediately, perhaps, but in due course. You may be certain it will be a long war. . . ."

Would the German invasion of Russia lengthen or shorten the war?

"Only time can tell," the general said. "But it would be folly to underestimate the Russians. The Germans probably will enjoy early successes, but when the rains begin in late October, they will find themselves in difficulties, and in even greater ones when winter sets in in November. Then they will face grave logistic problems. The weather and the absence of roads and adequate rail facilities will work great hardships on the Germans. However, they'll probably have a good innings until then. . . ."

General Wavell would not hazard a guess on the ultimate outcome of the Russo-German war. "Far too early to say," he reiterated, but it was evident that he believed with Smuts that Germany's involvement in Russia would rebound to democracy's advantage.

On parting the general invited me to visit him at his summer headquarters in Simla should my work take me to India, and I promised I would, a promise I was to keep far sooner than I knew.

At his farewell press conference at GHQ later, Wavell summed up his campaigns with habitual modesty. "We have had some setbacks," he said, "and some successes," and he stressed the need for "more equipment."

On July 7 a Sunderland flying boat took Wavell to India and what would soon become the Battle of Asia. Out of Cairo that day went one of the few truly great commanders of World War II. For I agreed with Alan Moorehead, Alex Clifford, Clare Hollingworth, and other able British journalists whom I had met in the Western Desert, that Sir Archibald Wavell—cautious, methodical, scholarly, modest to a fault—had saved the Middle East during the Battle of Africa as surely as the Royal Air Force had saved England during the Battle of Britain.

Moreover, during his tenure as C in C Middle East General Wavell had put down an Axis-inspired rebellion in Iraq, saved Syria from German occupation, and directed the campaigns that liberated Ethiopia and made secure the whole of East Africa. Thanks to his generalship, more than a quarter of a million Italian and German prisoners of war were in camps in Egypt, India, and South Africa.

Meanwhile, Tobruk remained safely in British hands, and Britain retained control of the vital Suez Canal. It was undoubtedly in grudging recongition of his talents that Churchill sent Wavell to India instead of dismissing him outright or accepting the resignation which General Wavell had generously offered after the disasters in Greece and Crete.

In the Middle East Wavell had been a sort of viceroy as well as a military commander. He had had to consider all the political aspects of the restoration of native rule in liberated Ethiopia; keep the Egyptians and their fat pro-Axis king in hand; deal with the Free French, whose leader, General Charles de Gaulle, was not the easiest man to get on with; and do many other things that did not fall directly within the province of a military commander.

Interestingly enough, to replace him, Churchill appointed not one but three men: Auchinleck, as military commander; Captain Lyttelton, as minister of state, and General Sir Robert Haining as Lyttelton's "intendant general," a title that hadn't been used since Napoleon's time. The one I met first, courtesy of Major Randolph Churchill, was Auchinleck, soon to be widely known in the Middle East as the Auk.

Like Wavell before him, the Auk had the misfortune to bear in the Middle East high responsibility in the early years of a British war, when commanders had to fight a strong, well-prepared enemy with forces numerically weaker and equipped with inferior weapons. Moreover, it was when the tide of war was running strongly against Britain, and at such times political leaders at the center of government are inclined to pressure generals for instant victories.

Randolph Churchill said the Auk would meet me in the lobby of Shepheard's at three o'clock, and at the appointed hour he was there, considerably more than six feet of him in khaki shorts and short-sleeved khaki shirt unbuttoned at the collar, moving on ample feet in the manner of a man who knew exactly where they were taking him. Everything about him bespoke a strong, even daunting personality, the embodiment of soldierly authority. It crossed my mind the moment I laid eyes on him that here was a man who was accustomed to having his way and who probably would not be stampeded into reckless adventures by politicians.

The general hadn't had much sleep; he'd only just arrived from India and at three o'clock that morning had taken over from Wavell. But his eyes were clear, blue-gray and steady, and they looked from under the overhanging ledge of a broad, slightly freckled brow. He was just this side of being a redhead, and his head was set on a powerful neck. A clean jaw suggested the strength of a broad, flat, phosphor-bronze spring.

The Auk chose a cool, shadowy corner of the lobby and made the chair creak as he dropped into it. That he arrived promptly at three o'clock told me the Auk didn't take siestas. The hour was normally a poor one for business appointments in sultry Cairo; but the Auk was there at three, and I had a hunch that many Colonel Blimps and their subordinates would be skipping siestas thereafter in a highly important battlefield of World War II.

Furthermore, the Auk came without a fly whisk, an important accessory in the Middle East. It consists of about eighteen inches of horsetail tufted to a short leather handle with a thong to dangle it from the wrist and is used to keep Egypt's sticky flies at a distance. Every well-dressed British officer carried a fly whisk, the lazy man's way of dealing with the pests. The Auk believed in slapping them dead.

While he talked, the general stealthily stalked a fly. He moved his thumb and third finger along until a fly was directly between them. Then his long, poised forefinger came down with the sure deftness of a gem cutter's hammer—and with just enough pressure to kill but not make a mess. I had asked him how he intended to deal with Rommel.

"A general should choose his battlefield," he was saying, "and oblige his enemy to fight on that battlefield and no other. He must choose his objectives and then prepare. He must prepare thoroughly and engage the enemy, knowing down to the last bullet what he's got and how he's going to use it."

The Auk refused a cigarette. He said he'd discovered on the Northwest Frontier and in the deserts of India and Mesopotamia that smoking accelerated the drying-out process which body tissues undergo when water is scarce, and water was always scarce in those climes. He stalked another fly. Could Britain win the war?

"Sure we can win this war," he said, "but not in the Middle East. Here we can only win a battle, not the war. It's got to be won in Germany, perhaps in Austria. We've got to bring the war to the enemy. Our battlefield is his own backyard. Napoleon was beaten that way. And it's the only way. Anything short of the decisive, total defeat of Germany would mean what?" He looked up and stuck out his chin. "It would mean a patched-up peace. Germany in control of all of Europe will turn around and offer peace. You wait and see. And that will be a decisive moment. Acceptance of any peace would be nothing but an armistice, and then it would begin all over again."

His forefinger came down. Splat. A miss. But where could Germany be attacked?

"I don't know now how we will get at her," he replied. "But there will be a way. Something will turn up, and if nothing does, then we'll just have to make a battlefield."

History would judge whether or not the Auk was an able commander, but he arrived in the Middle East with an enviable reputation as one of the British army's leading exponents of mobile, armored warfare. This was why at fifty-seven, an age when most careerists began to hope they might become briga-diers, Sir Claude was a full general entrusted with the defense of Egypt. Back in the late 1920s, Auchinleck had argued in favor of tanks and motorization while Hitler and Göring were still beer hall toughs.

Auchinleck's greatest achievement in India, however, was his Indianiza-tion of the country's army. He was free of the common British prejudice against Indians as an "inferior" race and vigorously opposed the segregationist policy that had long existed in Britain's armed forces overseas. He wanted Indian officers posted with their British equivalents throughout the Indian Army, and by the time World War II erupted he had got his way. By then India's principal enemy was Japan, whose agents and an advance guard of Japanese "tourists" were already infiltrating Asia from Karachi to Manila.

When the Auk was named C in C in the Middle East, Goebbels leaped to the radio in Berlin to announce that the British had "replaced their Napoleon of the deserts with their Napoleon of retreats." This was an allusion to Auchin-leck's withdrawal from Narvik. But Goebbels had it wrong; Auchinleck had been ordered home because France had collapsed and Dunkirk was still being evacuated. The Auk was needed in Britain to help meet what loomed at the time as a certain German invasion of England. The Auk got his men out of shelled and bombed Narvik without a single casualty, and for five months he served as C in C of the Southern Command in England. During that time he helped make the coast secure against invasion. He was subsequently appointed to the Indian command, after which he was summoned to Cairo.

When Auchinleck arrived in Egypt in July 1941, the war in the entire Mediterranean was running strongly in the enemy's favor. The loss of Crete had tilted the strategic balance against Britain.

In German hands the island, which is about 160 miles long and 30 miles wide at its widest, added greatly to the security of Axis communications between Italy and Tripoli. It brought the Luftwaffe's bombers still closer to Alexandria and the Suez Canal. It consolidated the control over the Aegean Sea which the Axis had already established with the conquest of Greece. It opened a possible sea route from the Black Sea to Italy which greatly eased the strain on the Fascists' supply line to the oil of Romania. Lastly, Crete gave the Germans command of the approaches to the Dardanelles, marking a serious advance in the slow encirclement of Turkey which the Axis powers were methodically pursuing in competition with the British.

Auchinleck needed only to look at the maps in his war room at GHQ to perceive the probable development of a new and powerful Axis pincers movement against Egypt and Suez: from Libya in the west and from the Balkans via Crete in the east. Meanwhile, reinforcements for Rommel's Panzerarmee Afrika were arriving unhindered in Tripoli. And while the German buildup was proceeding there, the Luftwaffe was searching out the vital parts of Britain's naval installations at Alexandria.

The Auk, in short, was "back to square one" in planning a successful defense of Egypt and all that it represented: the Suez Canal; the oil lands of the Arab world; the approaches from the west to India and Asia.

Unlike Wavell before him, however, the Auk had help. He was the undisputed star of what the British insisted on calling the show in the Middle East, but it had a new "producer" in Captain Oliver Lyttelton. While the Auk occupied himself with military matters, Captain Lyttelton was to handle the diplomatic chores involved in dealing with the Egyptians, the Free French, the Iraqis, the reestablished Emperor Hailie Selassie in Ethiopia, and all "other measures necessary to the prosecution of the war (in the Middle East) other than the conduct of military movements."

Lyttelton, whom Churchill personally had drafted out of business life to become president of the all-important Board of Trade before making him a member of his war cabinet, tied into his new job in Cairo with enthusiasm, working all hours in his shirt sleeves and startling everyone by actually getting things done. It was Lyttelton upon whom Alan Michie and I descended on his first day in Cairo to complain heatedly about how we magazine correspondents had been treated. He summoned his secretary and in our presence dictated a cable to the war cabinet in London, recommending that Michie and I be "accredited immediately." We apologized for breaking in on him on his first day in office, but he waved an eloquent hand, saying, "Don't apologize. Go home and put on your uniforms."

Among other tasks, it became Lyttelton's responsibility to determine priorities in the distribution of the tons of material being unloaded daily by American ships in Red Sea ports. He also organized transport and set up the organization required to ensure that newly arrived American tanks and planes weren't mishandled. Early dissatisfaction with those weapons was due almost entirely to the fact that they were put into the hands of the inexpert Corporal Smythe breed of mechanics. On the recommendation of Captain James Roosevelt, the president's son, and other American observers who had had a good look at the sloppiness of British workshop methods, the business of preparing American tanks and planes for battle was soon taken over by stateside workers familiar with our machines.

To assist Lyttelton in running logistic and related problems, the captain had his intendant general, Haining. General Haining became the man on the spot who executed Lyttelton's orders and saw to it, for example, that the army got its tanks first if the army needed tanks more urgently than the air force needed planes.

The presence in Cairo of the Auk and Captain Lyttelton worked wonders. The city had wallowed in gloom when I arrived in April. Dejection had permeated the conversations of correspondents, and rich refugees cried it into Joe Shalom's martinis. Even those apostles of reserve, the diplomats, reflected it, and in high places and low the concern for the security of Egypt was as palpable as the brooding solemnity of the Nile. Everyone knew that Wavell was holding the entire Middle East with a scratch force of tanks, planes and guns—everyone, apparently, except Churchill and the Germans.

Contributing to the gloom were rumors that the newly arrived American planes were no good, and some tank commanders predicted the new American tanks wouldn't be any better. By mid-July all this had changed. The Tomahawks were found to be at least the equal of the Hurricanes, maybe even a few revs better. The Martins proved they could outrun the Me-110s, and tankers, after seeing some of the new Shermans arriving from America, admitted they "might do very well indeed in the desert."

Meanwhile, the South Africans, who had helped pull Mussolini's Ethiopian empire down around his ears, arrived in Cairo with their American trucks, tanks, and planes to take over much of the desert from weary Aussies, New Zealanders, and Tommies, and the overall situation brightened considerably, especially after Germany wheeled into Russia.

38

DIVIDED AND VULNERABLE INDIA

In mid-July a cable from Charley Colebaugh advised me that the Russian Embassy in Washington had been ordered by Moscow not to issue visas to war correspondents. I was bitterly disappointed, for I had wanted very much to visit the country which Churchill had aptly described as "a riddle wrapped in a mystery inside an enigma" and discover, if possible, why General Wavell believed the Red Army could contain the Nazis' onslaught.

Thanks to Captain Lyttelton, I was now fully accredited to the British army, hence could have stayed on in Cairo for the duration had I wished. But the war in the Middle East was at a standstill, and there was no telling when it might resume.

Meanwhile, a new threat to the West had developed in the Far East, and there the potential enemy was not Germany but its Oriental ally, Japan. The Japanese were moving into French Indochina, where the Vichyite regime had made them welcome, and were known to be building airfields and land bases there within striking distance of India, Burma, Thailand, the Dutch East Indies, and, perhaps, even the Philippines.

I had come halfway around the world since leaving New York in early February, and I conceived the idea of completing the circumnavigation by visiting the threatened areas, then flying over the Pacific to San Francisco and home. If all went well, I could be in Bronxville with my family for Christmas. *Collier's* approved the journey as I outlined it in a cable and telegraphed me the necessary funds.

On the evening of July 16 I dined at the Continental Savoy at the expense of the British major who had bet me that the Germans would be in Moscow by mid-month, and three days later, on the morning of July 19, I boarded an Imperial Airways flying boat for India.

A two-day flight from Cairo via Basra, at the head of the Persian Gulf, landed me in Karachi, the hot, steamy capital of the predominantly Muslim province of Sind and one of India's three main ports on the Arabian Sea. The thermometer at the airport read 103 in the shade. The harbor was crowded with British and American vessels discharging the weapons and vehicles of war, but there was no war in Karachi. There was only a palpable resentment of the white man in general and of the British in particular. I read dislike and hostility in the glances of Indian civilians and decided to shed my uniform at the earliest opportunity.

Apart from its evident remoteness from the war, Karachi remains firmly fixed in memory for two reasons: my weeklong bout with the Egyptian malady known as Gyppy tummy, a euphemism for dysentery, and Dr. Umar Chanda, the Hindu physician who cured it. More or less confined to bed in an undistinguished midtown hotel room which fortunately had an adjoining bathroom, I might have ended my journey around a world at war in Karachi if the management had not fortunately summoned Dr. Chanda. His evil-tasting potions of a mysterious concoction of his own subdued my fever and curbed the diarrhea.

The doctor, who came to visit me twice daily, was a slender gentleman in his middle fifties with sharp features and straight jet black hair. He was always immaculately attired in loose white cotton trousers and jacket, a stethoscope jammed into one pocket, and a pince-nez dangling from around his neck on a black cord. He had studied at Cambridge and Johns Hopkins and, on ascertaining that I was an American, made no secret of his distrust of the British, whose viceroy, Lord Linlithgow, he said, had "insulted India by declaring war on Germany without consulting Mahatma Gandhi or Pandit Nehru," leaders of the preponderantly Hindu Congress party.

As a follower of the Mahatma, whom he worshiped, Dr. Chanda hoped India would emerge from the war as a "strong, united, independent nation," but he foresaw "trouble ahead" with the Muslims. Their leader, Muhammad Ali Jinnah, had already demanded the postwar creation of an independent Muslim state as his people's price for participating in the war.

"Blood will flow when this war has ended," Dr. Chanda predicted during one of our many talks. "India will never know peace. To emerge as a nation, India must one day flow with blood. . . ."

To look after me between visits, Dr. Chanda insisted that I have a bearer. "No proper pukka sahib in India is ever without one," he said, and on his second visit he was accompanied by a servant, apparently from his own household. He was a big man with a black mustache who brought me morning tea, served my simple meals—mostly boiled rice and unseasoned vegetables, as ordered by Dr. Chanda—did my laundry, pressed the summer-weight Palm

Beach suit I would wear when I resumed my journey, and kept my room tidy. Where or when he slept, I never learned, but he was always outside my door whenever I called, "Bearer!" Without him I could not have coped with India Britannica.

Meanwhile, lying abed most of the time, half naked under mosquito netting and a squeaky ceiling fan that made the humid air tolerable, I read several books on India, including John Gunther's recent *Inside Asia,* a 1939 family Christmas gift. My reading helped bring India into focus as a confused (and confusing) mosaic of races, languages, religions, and customs. It erased the India of Kipling's *Kim* and Hollywood's *Gunga Din* and replaced it with the reality of an India in social, political, and religious turmoil.

In the summer of 1941 India was aquiver with a struggle for power between Hindus and Muslims. In an area as vast as the United States east of the Rockies, lived some 400 million people, about one-fifth of the world's entire population, representing more than 45 races compartmentalized into some 2,400 castes and tribes, speaking more than 200 languages and practicing 9 major religions, the main groupings consisting of 250 million Hindus and 90 million Muslims.

India's politics were as jumbled as its religions. The All-India Congress party, led by Mahatma Gandhi and the brilliant Pandit Jawaharlal Nehru, claimed to be the only political organization free from partisan interests. It demanded total independence from British rule and naively believed it could unite Hindus and Muslims within one government on the basis of proportional representation.

The most militant of India's leaders was Jinnah, the clever Westernized godhead of the Muslim League. In early 1940 he declared his people's postwar objective to be Pakistan, a separate and independent Muslim state. Independence, therefore, not victory over nazism and fascism, was the war aim of India's Muslims, a goal they shared with their coreligionists in Iraq, Syria, Egypt, and Palestine. Unlike the Muslims of those countries, however, the Indian Muslims cheerfully obeyed Britain's summons to war against the Axis powers and constituted the biggest volunteer army the world had ever seen; not a single man in it had been conscripted.

Meanwhile, however, the rest of India's vast starving masses showed little interest in either independence from the British or the outcome of the war itself. To the overwhelming majority the word "freedom" meant as little as democracy, nazism, fascism, or communism. They were concerned only with today's bowl of rice.

By the eighth day after my arrival in Karachi, I had recovered sufficiently to resume my journey. My bearer procured for me a first-class reservation on the Sind Railway, shouldered my bedroll, suitcase box of books, and typewriter, and helped me board the train for Lahore, capital of the Punjab, where Kipling had worked as a reporter on the *Civil and Military Gazette* and where I changed trains for Simla, General Wavell's summer headquarters.

Dr. Chanda saw me off at the station and as a farewell present gave me a vial of large black pills which he said would hasten my recovery from the malady that had left me wobbly in the knees and somewhat light-headed. His bill for fourteen visits came to less than fifty dollars and included the services of my formidable bearer.

Crossing the northwestern province of Sind, I saw from the window of my swaying compartment a landscape of unimaginable poverty. At every stop hordes of people waited to clamber into or onto the arriving trains, many riding on the rooftops when the carriages were full. On the long platforms there were knots of sickly children, ragged beggars, old men with foreheads bearing what I took to be caste marks, and women in flowing cotton saris with jewels in their nostrils and clutching infants. Buzzards wheeled in the cloudless sky, and the air smelled of cinders, cow dung, kerosene, and decay.

Out of Sind, the train chuffed and panted into the Punjab, Kipling country, one of India's great provinces and the heartland of religious tensions among its Muslim, Hindu, and Sikh inhabitants. Mostly a vast plain watered by five great rivers, the Punjab was (and still is) the India of great open spaces, of the tallest men—the Sikhs—and the fiercest forces of nature: torrential rains and devastating floods.

In the open countryside men turned the brownish gray soil behind bullocks that dragged primitive plows. In the distance I glimpsed windowless mud-walled villages much like the poorest I had seen in the Nile Valley south of Cairo. Yet, I learned later, it was Wavell's main source of troops for his Indian Army, mostly Muslims, but also Sikhs.

India had loyally supported Britain during World War I and had sent overseas 1,250,000 of its sons, of whom about 100,000 became casualties. In return the Indians, led by the remarkable Mohandas (later Mahatma) Gandhi had assumed that they would be rewarded with at least the beginnings of home rule. But Britain's postwar concessions proved minimal and unacceptable, and there were riots, demonstrations, and mass protest meetings. The unrest led to the grotesque Amritsar Massacre of the spring of 1919, when British troops fired into a prohibited assembly of tens of thousands of Indian men, women, and children, killing 400 and wounding more than 1,000.

Amritsar established Gandhi as the undisputed leader of the Indian nationalist movement, and when the new war erupted in 1939, he and Nehru refused to cooperate. If the war was being fought for democracy, they said, they wanted a down payment of freedom right away. Congress party administrations in eight provinces resigned. But Muslim League regimes in Bengal and Sind backed the British, as did the mixed administration of Hindus, Muslims, and Sikhs governing the Punjab.

Gandhi encouraged civil disobedience, and the British responded by arresting hundreds, then thousands, of his followers. At Lahore an Indian Civil Service functionary told me that the jails of the Raj (the British) were "full up."

The cool, clean air of Simla, situated on a ridge in the foothills of the awesome Himalayas at an altitude of about eight thousand feet above sea level, was a bracing tonic after the heat, soot, and stenches of the long train ride from Karachi. With my first lungful I understood why every summer the British shifted their government from their capital at torrid Delhi to this sky-high resort town. It reminded me of Cortina, in Italy's Dolomites, until I saw that the only means of transportation was by rickshaw. My baggage was loaded onto the small rear platform of a two-wheeled vehicle, and four coolies, two in front and two behind, conveyed me uphill from the railway station at a surprisingly fast clip to my hotel, the Metropole, as English as Brown's in London.

I was ill at ease throughout the ride, hating being transported by barefooted, turbaned human beings in padded, broad-belted coats who earned the equivalent of twenty-seven cents a day each, hauling white human freight. They were a lean, brown, tubercular-looking lot who smoked water pipes between fares.

General Wavell was away when I arrived, inspecting India's defenses on the Northwest Frontier. For several days I lazed at the Metropole, listening to the war news on the BBC, devouring newspapers and magazine articles, and talking with some of Simla's well-heeled summertime resident guests at the hotel. Most were wealthy businessmen from Calcutta and Bombay, but they included several high-ranking Indian Civil Service functionaries. All seemed glad to have in their midst an American reporter to whom they could defend British policy in India and whom they could chide, more or less goodnaturedly, for America's reluctance to become an all-out belligerent. Few ever refused my invitations to meals or to drinks at the Metropole's well-stocked bar, where excellent whiskey was not rationed. In fact, there was no rationing of any kind in Simla.

Indian insistence on independence was a recurrent topic of conversation. Like many Americans, I couldn't understand why the Indians shouldn't have self-government straightaway. Freedom, it seemed to me, was what the war was all about, and I said so. My barside companions pointedly reminded me, however, that it was "a knotty problem" and one which Britain was unable to tackle while its back was "up against the wall in Europe and the Middle East." The ICS types whom I treated to *burra pegs* (double whiskeys) at the bar were particularly vehement on this point, and I concluded that *their* principal war aim was not liberation of India's masses but preservation of the British Empire.

All seemed grateful, however, that President Roosevelt was keeping imperial Britain afloat with his lend-lease program. America, in fact, had by then become Britain's arsenal; tremendous and increasing quantities of weapons and supplies were being shipped to Britain and the Middle East, much of the tonnage in U.S. vessels.

Meanwhile, life in white India proceeded much as usual. The big businessmen from Bombay and Calcutta were growing rich or richer trading in jute, cotton, and the many other Indian commodities Britain needed for the war effort, and their well-dressed, well-coiffed ladies continued their traditional partying and dining. All the white folks had plenty to eat and drink, and for them the war was something that was happening somewhere far from lovely, reposeful, sybaritic Simla.

Nor did the war touch India's rajas and maharajas. They went boar hunting and tiger shooting as usual and complained of the high cost of maintaining the state armies they contributed to Britain's defense of the subcontinent, but they didn't complain too openly or too loudly. India's feudal lords knew they ruled only so long as Britain ruled. Once India attained independence, they would no longer receive in taxes or tribute their weights in gold or jewels.

On the morning of July 28 a telephone call from a major in charge of Wavell's public relations advised me that the general had just returned from the Northwest Frontier and would see me at his residence at four o'clock that afternoon. "No interview," the caller said. "Just a cup of tea and a friendly chat. Sir Archie is very busy these days, but he can spare you fifteen minutes or so."

I felt let down. I had counted on an extensive interview as part of a *Collier's* piece about the great soldier to whom Churchill had entrusted the defense of the British Empire in Asia after having dimissed him as commander in chief in the Middle East.

When the general greeted me in the airy drawing room of his hilltop home, he looked travel-weary and downright gloomy and years older than when I had last seen him in Cairo barely three weeks before. Wavell motioned me toward an armchair and settled himself opposite on a capacious divan upholstered in faded chartreuse. An Indian manservant poured the tea.

Sir Archibald volunteered the information that he had found "everything shipshape" on the Northwest Frontier and fell into one of those silences for which he was renowned as he stirred the pale brew in his cup. I asked if he still believed the Russians could contain the German attack, for in late July the evidence was all to the contrary. The Nazis had plunged deeply into Russian territory along a two-thousand-mile front extending from the Baltic to the Black Sea, crossed the Dnestr River, and entered Smolensk, less than two hundred road miles from Moscow.

Wavell replied that he was confident the Germans would never reach Moscow. He predicted that before long they would be mired in the mud produced by autumn's rains and later would be immobilized by the ice and snow of "the bitter Russian winter." He said Britain and the United States owed the Russians "a debt of gratitude." The fierce resistance of the Red Army, he said, had provided a "respite" during which the democracies could produce the weapons and train the men needed for "ultimate victory over the Axis aggressors."

After another of his silences Wavell said, "No, I don't believe the Germans will conquer Russia. Heaven help us if they did. Russia is an inexhaustible storehouse of raw materials. Combined with German industrial skills, well, Germany could fight a long, long war. . . . But it won't happen. I'm fairly certain of that."

"Now is the time to hit Germany with everything we've got," he continued. "Otherwise the war may last beyond the memory of present generations. . . ." With that Wavell shook his head, as if it had suddenly occurred to him that Britain had neither the manpower nor the weapons required for an all-out offensive against Germany in the West—for that "second front" which Stalin had been demanding almost from the first day of the German invasion.

Britain's supply of manpower, the general said, was "running thin," adding that what men England had and what weapons it was producing were needed at home for the defense of the British Isles. A cross-Channel invasion was less likely now with Germany so heavily involved in Russia, he said, but an attack was still "a possibility" that demanded "vigilance and a high state of preparedness."

Having only recently arrived in India, Wavell had not yet inspected the country's defenses to the southeast. He had last been in India in 1911, and he had never been east of it. Burma, Malaysia, and beyond, he indicated, were unknown to him. Burma, at any rate, was not under India but came under Singapore for defense purposes.

"Vigilance," Wavell said with a mirthless smile, "is the watchword everywhere. From now on, we must look to the east . . ." and again was silent. Then, looking past me with his good right eye, and as though thinking aloud, he said, "I wonder what the Japanese will do now that they are entrenched in Indochina."

At last, I thought, we were getting at the heart of the matter, but at that point an aide entered with a message and, as he handed it to the general, gave me a look that as much as said I had overstayed my welcome. Wavell rose, muttered something about having "business to attend to," shook hands, and wished me "good hunting."

I learned from one of the general's aides what had accounted for Sir Archibald's gloom. He had been shocked by India's slow wartime tempo and the poor state of the country's defenses against a Japanese attack and was urging in vain that contiguous Burma be placed under his command.

Despite everything Auchinleck had done to bolster its defenses, India was no more ready for war in the summer of 1941 than Britain had been at the time of Munich in 1938. Although recruits and volunteers continued to pour into the ranks of the Indian Army, the bulk of them were still in training. For the first two years of the war their divisions were shipped to Egypt, Iraq, and Iran as soon as they had finished basic training and were equipped only with small arms. In India proper, Wavell had fewer than 750,000 men, none of whom was what could be called battle-ready.

Furthermore, neither the Indian Army nor India's small British garrison had much in the way of mechanized equipment. Wavell was appalled when he discovered that the British forces had only a brigade or two of elderly tanks which would be no match for even the light fourteen-ton tanks of the Japanese. He had no modern tanks or armored cars and only about thirty antiaircraft guns in a country that required at least five hundred.

The Indian Air Force was hopelessly weak, equipped with Hawker Audaxes, Harts, and Hinds, planes dating from the early 1930s, good for light bombing operations against rambunctious tribesmen but useless against the modern fighter planes the Japanese were known to possess.

Finally, the Indian Navy was almost nonexistent. It consisted of half a dozen minesweepers and naval patrol boats operating out of Karachi and Calcutta, patrolling the entrances to the Persian Gulf and the Bay of Bengal.

The threat from Japan, however, was only one of the problems Wavell faced. Another was India itself. The country's jails were filled with Indian opponents of the war, and the continuing antiwar demonstrations and periodic strikes undoubtedly contributed to the gloom I had seen reflected in the general's furrowed face.

From his Simla mountaintop, Wavell looked down over the rugged Punjab with the Greater Himalayas brown and purple and whitecapped in the distance. Here, in an area nearly as large as Colorado but constituting only a fragment of the sprawling subcontinent, was India's great manpower reservoir. The Punjab's plains and rolling hills raised nearly two thirds of the men for India's army, but the Punjab was also India's venom sac. Its inhabitants numbered thirteen million Muslims, six million Hindus, and four million Sikhs. The Sikhs provided about 15 percent of the men for the army. But Sikh and Hindu and Muslim felt toward one another a hatred as deep as the province's five rivers in flood and as everlasting as the mountains that watered them. Before Wavell met the enemy, he would be obliged to build an army of such men, a seemingly impossible undertaking.

Even if the tanks and planes and guns he needed arrived in time from the United States, the general was still faced with the task of training farmers who had never even driven a tractor to operate the complex mechanical weapons of modern warfare. In the late 1930s he had studied at first hand the war machine Stalin had built, and he knew that in Russia it had taken twenty years to train the army that was resisting the Germans in the Ukraine. And mechanization of India's army had only begun in 1939 under Auchinleck.

Small wonder that I had found Sir Archibald gloomy and that he seemed to have aged years in less than three weeks. I needed no doctorate in military science to see that Churchill had handed Wavell one of the war's toughest jobs, the defense of a divided and militarily vulnerable India, the flawed jewel in the British imperial crown.

In the meantime, it became increasingly evident that the United States had embarked on a collision course with expansionist Japan. For some time Washington had been pursuing a conciliatory policy toward Tokyo. Japan had been

receiving shipments of oil, lubricants, aviation fuel, and scrap steel from the United States. But on July 25 both Washington and London froze Japanese assets in their respective countries, a step that virtually ended any commercial dealings with Tokyo.

Shortly afterward President Roosevelt, sensing danger to the Philippines, called to the colors the Filipino armed forces, and on August 1 Washington placed an embargo on the export of all strategic materials to the Japanese.

39

THE CRUMBLING ASIAN BASTIONS

I left India by way of Calcutta, the world's fourth most populous city after New York, London, and Tokyo and a sprawling urban monstrosity situated on the turgid Hooghly River, cursed with what is undoubtedly the foulest climate of any metropolis anywhere. The day I arrived by air from Delhi, Calcutta had just had a drenching monsoon rain, and the city steamed like a busy laundry in a sun that drove the temperature up to 103 while the humidity registered 100.

I stayed only two days, long enough to hope I would never again see its filth, poverty, beggars, and sacred cows; its alleys and shantytowns pullulating with hungry humanity; its sidewalks strewn nightly with sleeping figures as inert as the corpses which many would soon become. If too poor for ceremonial Hindu-style burning, they would be cast into the Hooghly to be washed ashore with the ebbing tide and consumed by scavenging dogs or the vultures I saw perched on the city's streetlight standards.

The climate and the sights confirmed everything unpleasant I had heard or read about Calcutta. The slums called bustees of the city's jute workers were worse than anything I had ever seen in Naples, Beirut, or Cairo. Workmen earning three or four rupees a week (about $1.20) lived with no light, no water, no sanitary facilities in hovels that lined both sides of narrow alleyways down which ran open drains; entire families of nine or ten persons were crowded in windowless rooms measuring eight feet by six. Disease, squalor, and degradation bred unrest, and I left Calcutta thinking that India Britannica might well end one day in the city where it more or less began in the days of Clive.

BURMA

From Calcutta I flew to Rangoon, where I discovered that in Burma the United States was already heavily involved in the struggle to contain Japanese imperialism in Asia.

Rangoon was then the southern terminus of the tenuous lifeline that supplied American and British weapons and ammunition to General Chiang Kai-shek, whose armies had been fighting the Japanese in China for years. The supplies went from Rangoon's wharves northward by rail to Mandalay, thence by truck convoys over the tortuous Burma Road through dense jungle and across rugged mountains into neighboring China. The route, highly vulnerable to Japanese bombers based in contiguous French Indochina, was protected by P-40 fighter planes flown by U.S. Army and Navy pilots of the American Volunteer Flying Group. The fliers were allowed to serve the Chinese without losing their American commissions.

What was rapidly becoming one of the war's major battles, the Battle of Asia, had begun back in 1931, when the Japanese invaded Manchuria, which they renamed Manchukuo. But Tokyo's cry of "Asia for the Asiatics" was not taken seriously by Britain and the other Western powers at the time. The result of a decade of neglect was that in the summer of 1941 Burma was utterly unprepared to meet a Japanese attack. When General Wavell finally made his survey of Britain's defenses in Burma and beyond, he was to be horrified by the country's lack of organization, paucity of military intelligence, and lack of planning in general to resist the Japanese.

I saw evidence of the disorganization that would appall Wavell on a wharf in Rangoon, within walking distance of the Strand Hotel, where I stayed pending clearance on a KLM flight to Bangkok. Huge crates covering automobiles, ammunition, and food supplies stenciled with the names of American manufacturers were piled on the dock. They had been there so long that the rain had smudged the stenciling, and a supervisor told me it would take him six months to move into China the lend-lease supplies that had accumulated on his docks.

The arrival of an American trucking expert, Daniel Arnstein, promised to untangle the transportation snarl. He vowed to increase the monthly delivery of supplies to China from the normal six-thousand-ton monthly level to at least fifteen thousand tons. But it seemed to me that Arnstein, like Burma itself, was fighting a losing battle.

Burma would be a rich prize for the Japanese. In addition to valuable deposits of copper, lead, silver, and tungsten, its oil fields were the richest in the British Empire, producing more than a million tons yearly. The British-owned Burma Oil Company was the principal supplier of aviation fuel for the

RAF east of Iraq and Iran. And in Burma, a vast granary that produced an annual *surplus* of three million tons of rice, the Japanese would find food enough to feed all their forces in Southeast Asia.

The invaders would also find a favorable political climate. Since 1937 Burma enjoyed a high degree of self-government. Its prime minister, U Saw, a pro-Japanese Anglophobe, publicly declared in June 1941: "We in Burma are certain that Japan has no designs on our country, hence has no reason for aggression against us." Discovered in a plot to facilitate Japanese penetration of Burma, U Saw and many of his followers were interned for the duration. Burma's jails were as crowded as India's.

THAILAND

A Dutch KLM airliner, Batavia bound out of Rangoon, dropped me out of war into peace at Bangkok, capital of this neutral kingdom of Muang Thai, previously known as Siam. The effect was startling, like flying out of stormy, wind-tormented darkness into smooth air and sunlight.

The only sign of war on the grassy airport was a Chinese National Airways DC-3 which was being refueled for its return trip to Chongqing with mail, money, and vitamins for General Chiang. The plane was splotched with camouflage paint, contrasted sharply with the silvery Douglas of the Dutch airline, and looked the way I felt: shabby, tired, war-weary.

I arrived in Bangkok in a confused, disturbed state of mind. India, especially Calcutta, had been depressing. General Wavell had not been too reassuring, and Burma had only deepened a growing premonition that the West's "bastions" in Asia were crumbling.

Thailand's climate was not conducive to optimism. Bangkok is where the real heat of the East begins, hot with the terrible, debilitating heat of the tropics, hotter than India, certainly, and the blast of hot air that swept into the plane when the exit door was opened almost beat me to my knees. But it smelled clean, and it was good to feel the spring of turf underfoot on the grass of the big Don Muang Airport. The Thais kept the grass clipped and rolled as though the landing field were one enormous tennis court.

For one fleeting moment I thought I had landed in Palm Beach, Florida, after a midsummer flight from New York. The low-lying white buildings of the airport's offices, waiting rooms, and restaurant were modern, well ventilated, scrupulously clean, and inviting. A Thai customs officer in a freshly laundered khaki uniform that smelled of soap, starch, and the work of a hot iron broke the spell.

Using the data in my passport, he surprised me by filling out a long pink blank and a long white one, work I normally did myself. He asked me how long I intended staying, adding, before I could reply, that he hoped I would stay a month or two. "You can't see much of Thailand in less than a month," he said. I nodded agreement and thought, *What a cinch for the Japanese.*

(When I left Bangkok ten days later, the same policeman looked at me reproachfully.)

Most of Thailand, about the size of France and inhabited by some fourteen million smilingly pleasant people, is, like most of Holland, barely one hand high above water. From the bus en route to the Oriental Hotel I saw miles of rice paddies, wetly green, yellow, and brown, and the country made me think of a freshly laid decalcomania. Bamboo huts with thatched roofs stood on stilts. I caught glimpses of gleaming floors and bare-breasted women playing with fat, naked babies. Sampans poled by coolies in conical straw hats floated in the canals. Oxen pulling crude plows dwarfed the tiny Thai peasants. Swayback pigs with long snouts rooted about under the stilted houses. The farmers' yards were a profusion of flowers.

The passing of the bus through villages was an intrusion. Women came to their doors, holding up their infants to be seen, and coolies set down their burdens by the roadside to look up at the bus, smiling broad smiles that revealed teeth stained purple with betel nut juice. The Thai businessman sitting next to me said betel nut chewing was being discouraged and that schoolchildren were being taught to brush their teeth daily, "Western style."

As the bus neared the city, traffic thickened. Most of it consisted of bicycles and of rickshaws drawn by bicycles. The trams and buses were painted bright yellow. The pedestrians included swarms of Buddhist priests with shaved heads and dressed in flowing saffron and orange robes. There were temples everywhere, architectural confections that might have been designed by Walt Disney's more imaginative draftsmen.

What caught the eye, however, were the small, well-built, beautiful women. They had long, straight, glossy black hair and clear, cocoa-tinted skins. Many wore close-fitting short white vests and black panungs, bloomerlike skirts which draped about the waist and around each leg and tied in a loose knot below the navel. The panung, I was told, had been banned as part of the "Westernization" process that had begun in 1931, when the country had a mild revolution, its only casualty an obstreperous colonel who was shot in one leg. Until then Siam, as it was still known, was an absolute monarchy under kindly King Prajadhipok, who obligingly quit the throne when the revolt erupted, then resumed by popular demand as a constitutional monarch, and Siam became Prathet Thai, or Thailand, which means "land of the free." In the summer of 1941 Thailand was the only free and independent country in Asia between Tokyo and Teheran. But as I registered at the Oriental Hotel and saw the nationality of the guests who had signed in before me, I began doubting that Thailand would be free and independent much longer. Thailand was already inundated with Japanese "tourists," the vanguard of the mikado's armies.

I spotted them easily in Bangkok. They filled the bar at the Oriental, and they crowded the shops, where they bought nielloware ornaments, jade jewelry, and silver-plated tiger skulls used as ashtrays. The Japanese population of Thailand had increased steadily since 1935, when only sixty-seven were listed as residents in Bangkok and none anywhere else in the country. Now there were three thousand, and Europeans had difficulty renting houses.

The influx was partly due to the fact that the world's markets were closed to Japan, and Tokyo had been obliged to turn increasingly elsewhere for money and raw materials. This had meant expansion of the staffs of such Japanese trading companies as the powerful firm of Mitsubishi. A number of new agencies selling machinery and manufactured goods of all kinds had sprung up along Bangkok's business streets, and I saw Japanese signs on the fronts of many buildings with English translations under each, usually a reminder that the firm previously had been Swiss, French, Belgian, or Dutch.

At least six of Thailand's seventeen newspapers had come under direct Axis influence. They received the wire services of Germany's Transocean News or Japan's Domei, and Britain's Reuters was unable to compete with the enormous volume of pro-Axis propaganda which the wire services of Berlin and Tokyo poured into the country. The Japanese also maintained a daily plane service with Tokyo, and every day it brought between twelve and twenty-four new arrivals. The passengers were always Japanese. Americans couldn't obtain passage on their plane. I tried several times. It was always "full up." The best the British and the Dutch could manage from their Asian bases was two services weekly.

From Thailand the Japanese obtained rice, rubber, tin, and teak. Thailand produced an exportable surplus of 1.6 million tons of rice yearly. When that was added to the 1.2 million-ton supply ensured by the occupation of French Indochina, the Japanese had all the rice they would need to feed their far-flung armies, and Thailand's 40,000-ton annual output of natural rubber would help keep the mikado's army vehicles shod.

Measured by such yardsticks as power, wealth, and prestige, Thailand was no more important than a bush-league Balkan country, much of it unexplored jungle. Its army was puny, its navy a marine absurdity, and its air force wouldn't cause a potential aggressor like Japan any great concern.

Nevertheless, the more I studied the map, listened to the news on the BBC, and talked with diplomats like Sir Josiah Crosby, Britain's minister plenipotentiary in Bangkok, the more convinced I became that Thailand would be the Poland of the Battle of Asia.

Geographically the country lay wedged between British Burma and French Indochina. On the map it is shaped like a crudely drawn, floppy-eared elephant with a long trunk dangling southward between the Bay of Bengal and the Gulf of Siam toward the South China Sea. The trunk dips into the Malay Peninsula, below which stood Britain's "fortress city in Asia," Singapore. So long as Indochina was really French, Thailand was a sort of spring between the jaws of the Anglo-French pincer of Western imperialism in Southeast Asia. But one jaw of that pincer had broken when France and Vichy capitulated to Berlin and to Berlin's partners in Tokyo. The Japanese replaced the French in Indochina, where by now they had 150,000 troops and had built air bases from which to strike at the Burma Road, at Singapore, the Dutch East Indies, and Bangkok itself.

Sir Josiah Crosby, in mid-August, counted in mere weeks the period of peace remaining to Thailand and the Far East, but American observers were less pessimistic. "It will be three months," they said, "maybe six before the Japs [their word] strike." They would be proved wrong.

The Thais themselves—I talked with the undersecretaries of the ministries of Foreign Affairs and Propaganda and with businessmen who were getting richer daily trading with the Japanese—felt insecure. They resented the inroads of the Japanese but felt powerless to prevent their country's economic absorption by Tokyo's agents, who burrowed and bribed, browbeat and flattered their way into positions of power over their Thai victims.

The Japanese legation was raised to the status of an embassy, and pro-Japanese Thais suddenly were injected into the cabinet. Japan demanded and obtained a loan of ten million ticals and a few weeks later prepared to ask for more credit from what was then probably the only country in the world with a balanced budget and no external debt.

I had come to Thailand to write a biographical sketch of a distant, little-known independent country that stood in the path of foreseeable Japanese aggression, but I soon saw I was writing an obituary. Neither Britain nor the United States was prepared to go to Thailand's defense, and the country itself had little with which to oppose the Japanese.

To oppose Japan's formidable military machine, the country had thirty or forty thousand troops who had never held maneuvers and who believed their red undershirts would make them impervious to bullets. Its small gunboat navy included three submarines which had never submerged because their crews weren't certain they would return to the surface. Their tanks were old British three- and seven-tonners. Their artillery rolled on wooden wheels, and their air force consisted of fifty old Japanese-built Curtisses and a hodgepodge of other makes, British and American, which would not cause Japan much trouble.

The British minister, Sir Josiah, was an amiable man, short, stout, and addicted to port and good food. He was, however, an astute diplomat and had calipered to within a diplomatic millimeter Thailand's willingness and ability to resist the Japanese with its puny military forces. Nevertheless, he said he had persuaded the Thais to resist and had promised them that Britain would come to their assistance if they were attacked by the Japanese from Indochina.

"I do believe," he said casually over dinner at the Oriental Hotel one evening, "that we have sold the Thais the idea that they are to commit hara-kiri on behalf of the British Empire."

It was a particularly hot and muggy night, I recall, and we dined under a pergola in the fragrant garden with our feet and legs encased in gunnysacks up to our thighs against the pestiferous mosquitoes that carried malaria and dengue fever. Sir Josiah was convinced, however, that Thailand, despite heavy British investments in the country's tin mines, was really an American responsibility.

"This is your show, old boy," he kept saying. "You've really got to fight for Thailand. Without America's immediate, direct intervention, Thailand will be lost, and perhaps Burma and all Southeast Asia as well."

I replied that I thought President Roosevelt would have difficulty convincing the people of Kansas and Oklahoma of the need to defend Thailand, a place they probably had never heard of, and suggested that perhaps British troops should undertake the job instead of parading for the newsreels in Rangoon and Singapore.

Sir Josiah smiled and nodded knowingly. He was the elder statesman of the Bangkok diplomatic corps, a professional with two and a half decades of experience in Southeast Asia. He knew the military as well as the political facts of the situation and, in parting, confided that Britain probably had "missed the bus in Asia."

"Perhaps," he said over a farewell glass of fine old port, "your country and mine have both missed the bus, old boy."

I soon learned what he meant.

SINGAPORE

When I left Bangkok for Singapore, the facts of Japan's colossal preparations for an attack were at hand. They were known to every alert young British officer in Southeast Asia but ignored by their older superiors who remained wedded to the traditional "we'll muddle through somehow" attitude prevalent among the area's profusion of Colonel Blimps.

The truth of the matter was, of course, that the British simply did not have the men and weapons needed to impede Japanese expansion in Asia. What I found worrisome however, was the widespread unawareness of danger and the complacency that accompanied it. In mid-August 1941 Britain was losing the war, but no one in this remote part of the world seemed aware of it. Worse, no one seemed to care very much except Wavell, who inspected the defenses in Singapore and found the "fortress city" very far from keyed up to war pitch.

Smugness and ignorance of the realities were dramatically illustrated one night in an incident outside Singapore's Raffles Hotel. Leland Stowe, the roving correspondent of the *Chicago Daily News,* who had distinguished himself for his coverage of the British fiasco in Norway, and I were returning from a late dinner party in another part of town. The fine old hotel was alight, and the band was struggling with a Cole Porter tune while couples danced on the hotel's long veranda. The men were in white mess jackets and black trousers; the women, in long dresses. There was a babble of merriment punctuated by the voices of bearded Sikh doormen calling for the guests' cars or for taxis, for it was nearing closing time.

At the foot of the steps leading up to the hotel stood a small, wooden-faced, silent Chinese boy holding a bundle of newspapers. To Leland and me, the appearance of a newspaper at that hour—it was well after midnight—was an event of major importance and should have electrified the departing couples.

Sir Josiah Crosby, in mid-August, counted in mere weeks the period of peace remaining to Thailand and the Far East, but American observers were less pessimistic. "It will be three months," they said, "maybe six before the Japs [their word] strike." They would be proved wrong.

The Thais themselves—I talked with the undersecretaries of the ministries of Foreign Affairs and Propaganda and with businessmen who were getting richer daily trading with the Japanese—felt insecure. They resented the inroads of the Japanese but felt powerless to prevent their country's economic absorption by Tokyo's agents, who burrowed and bribed, browbeat and flattered their way into positions of power over their Thai victims.

The Japanese legation was raised to the status of an embassy, and pro-Japanese Thais suddenly were injected into the cabinet. Japan demanded and obtained a loan of ten million ticals and a few weeks later prepared to ask for more credit from what was then probably the only country in the world with a balanced budget and no external debt.

I had come to Thailand to write a biographical sketch of a distant, little-known independent country that stood in the path of foreseeable Japanese aggression, but I soon saw I was writing an obituary. Neither Britain nor the United States was prepared to go to Thailand's defense, and the country itself had little with which to oppose the Japanese.

To oppose Japan's formidable military machine, the country had thirty or forty thousand troops who had never held maneuvers and who believed their red undershirts would make them impervious to bullets. Its small gunboat navy included three submarines which had never submerged because their crews weren't certain they would return to the surface. Their tanks were old British three- and seven-tonners. Their artillery rolled on wooden wheels, and their air force consisted of fifty old Japanese-built Curtisses and a hodgepodge of other makes, British and American, which would not cause Japan much trouble.

The British minister, Sir Josiah, was an amiable man, short, stout, and addicted to port and good food. He was, however, an astute diplomat and had calipered to within a diplomatic millimeter Thailand's willingness and ability to resist the Japanese with its puny military forces. Nevertheless, he said he had persuaded the Thais to resist and had promised them that Britain would come to their assistance if they were attacked by the Japanese from Indochina.

"I do believe," he said casually over dinner at the Oriental Hotel one evening, "that we have sold the Thais the idea that they are to commit hara-kiri on behalf of the British Empire."

It was a particularly hot and muggy night, I recall, and we dined under a pergola in the fragrant garden with our feet and legs encased in gunnysacks up to our thighs against the pestiferous mosquitoes that carried malaria and dengue fever. Sir Josiah was convinced, however, that Thailand, despite heavy British investments in the country's tin mines, was really an American responsibility.

"This is your show, old boy," he kept saying. "You've really got to fight for Thailand. Without America's immediate, direct intervention, Thailand will be lost, and perhaps Burma and all Southeast Asia as well."

I replied that I thought President Roosevelt would have difficulty convincing the people of Kansas and Oklahoma of the need to defend Thailand, a place they probably had never heard of, and suggested that perhaps British troops should undertake the job instead of parading for the newsreels in Rangoon and Singapore.

Sir Josiah smiled and nodded knowingly. He was the elder statesman of the Bangkok diplomatic corps, a professional with two and a half decades of experience in Southeast Asia. He knew the military as well as the political facts of the situation and, in parting, confided that Britain probably had "missed the bus in Asia."

"Perhaps," he said over a farewell glass of fine old port, "your country and mine have both missed the bus, old boy."

I soon learned what he meant.

SINGAPORE

When I left Bangkok for Singapore, the facts of Japan's colossal preparations for an attack were at hand. They were known to every alert young British officer in Southeast Asia but ignored by their older superiors who remained wedded to the traditional "we'll muddle through somehow" attitude prevalent among the area's profusion of Colonel Blimps.

The truth of the matter was, of course, that the British simply did not have the men and weapons needed to impede Japanese expansion in Asia. What I found worrisome however, was the widespread unawareness of danger and the complacency that accompanied it. In mid-August 1941 Britain was losing the war, but no one in this remote part of the world seemed aware of it. Worse, no one seemed to care very much except Wavell, who inspected the defenses in Singapore and found the "fortress city" very far from keyed up to war pitch.

Smugness and ignorance of the realities were dramatically illustrated one night in an incident outside Singapore's Raffles Hotel. Leland Stowe, the roving correspondent of the *Chicago Daily News,* who had distinguished himself for his coverage of the British fiasco in Norway, and I were returning from a late dinner party in another part of town. The fine old hotel was alight, and the band was struggling with a Cole Porter tune while couples danced on the hotel's long veranda. The men were in white mess jackets and black trousers; the women, in long dresses. There was a babble of merriment punctuated by the voices of bearded Sikh doormen calling for the guests' cars or for taxis, for it was nearing closing time.

At the foot of the steps leading up to the hotel stood a small, wooden-faced, silent Chinese boy holding a bundle of newspapers. To Leland and me, the appearance of a newspaper at that hour—it was well after midnight—was an event of major importance and should have electrified the departing couples.

The Chinese boy either couldn't read or was too lazy to call attention to the extra, but he shouldn't have needed to shout in any case.

Leland and I saw the fat black headline, ROOSEVELT AND CHURCHILL MEET AT SEA, and in terse boldface bulletins under the streamer was the story of the historic meeting between the American president and the British prime minister aboard a warship in the waters off Newfoundland. It was a story of vital importance in the lives of everyone, the story of the eight-point Atlantic Charter and the impeccable principles of the Four Freedoms, the Anglo-American moral blueprint for the postwar world.

We grabbed for the papers. Of the people around us few bought papers; most of them merely glanced at the headline and moved on. We heard one mess jacket tell one evening gown: "Oh, I say. They really did meet after all. Boy, my car, please . . ."

Nothing made sense in Singapore, Britain's most important naval base in the Far East, rated second only to Gibraltar in impregnability. The C in C, however, was not a naval officer but Air Chief Marshal Robert Brooke-Popham, a fatuous old fuddy-duddy who should have been retired years earlier. The naval C in C was Vice Admiral Sir Geoffrey Layton, whose feelings had been bruised when Whitehall sent out an airman to take charge, and the two men were not on speaking terms.

I tried for days to see Brooke-Popham, but he hated reporters and was always "too busy." His public relations were handled by a naval lieutenant commander whose only qualification for the job was that he had served as a magistrate in the Fiji Islands for twenty years. He thought *Collier's* was a trade journal for the American coal-mining industry.

Friendly army and navy officers who frequented the bars at Raffles and the Adelphi Hotel, however, told me over *stengahs* what I needed to know about Singapore. Its powerful naval guns, for instance, pointed seaward and could not be turned around to meet an attack from the landward side. Brooke-Popham, or "Brookham," as his officers called him, counted on the base's jungle hinterland to protect it from the rear.

Although the base was big enough to handle the entire American Pacific Fleet as well as Britain's warships in Far Eastern waters, there wasn't a ship in sight. Squadrons of outdated American Brewster Buffaloes and British Hurricane fighters roared overhead daily in practice flights, but knowledge-able airmen told me Singapore's aerial defenses were more facade than reality.

Meanwhile, for the British inhabitants of Singapore (they numbered about eight thousand in a mixed population of seven hundred thousand yellow Chinese, brown Malayans, black Tamils, and bearded Sikhs), it was business as usual. (While I was there, some two thousand Japanese residents were left undisturbed.) It seemed not to occur to anyone that the Japanese might attack by air from Thailand, fewer than four hundred miles to the north, or come down the Malayan Peninsula in force. Brooke-Popham had publicly declared that Singapore was "secure" behind its "Maginot Line" of Malayan jungles, and that was that.

The rich rubber and tea planters from upcountry, and the natty British officers at the base, regularly took their wives and girl friends to tea and cocktails at Raffles and the Adelphi. Meanwhile, the troops of the small Australian and British garrison and the sailors stationed at the base danced nightly with jitterbugging little Chinese girls at Singapore's many taxi dance halls.

I spent the last several days in Singapore fighting off an attack of dengue fever in a hot room in the Raffles Hotel. One of Bangkok's mosquitoes had got me despite the sacking that covered my legs while I dined with Sir Josiah at the Oriental. Quinine, cold compresses, and the ministrations of a British doctor got me through the nasty business, during which I learned why the disease is also known as breakbone fever. The pain was at times almost unbearable.

I stepped on American soil for the first time in months when I boarded a Pan American Airways Clipper at Singapore for Manila. Flying over Britain's "Pacific Gibraltar" as we took off, I was sure that from what I had seen and heard before the fever sent me to bed, Malaya would be another Greece and Singapore another Crete.

40

MACARTHUR'S PHILIPPINE DEFENSES

B etween catnaps and pleasurable thoughts of home by Christmas during the Clipper's ten-hour flight across the South China Sea, I wondered whether I would find Manila as complacent and undefended as Singapore. The capital of the Philippines, a vast archipelago of nearly seventy-one hundred islands, was America's bastion in the Far East and as liable to Japanese attack as any Western stronghold in Asia.

Since 1935 the man in charge of the vulnerable islands' defenses was the flamboyant general Douglas MacArthur, a brilliant soldier and a longtime proponent of the Philippines' defendability. I looked forward to seeing what he had done to make them secure against invasion.

I had met General MacArthur in Washington in 1934, while I was still working for Hearst's Universal Service covering the State, War, and Navy departments, then housed in the gray rococo Executive Office Building on Pennsylvania Avenue across a side street from the White House. The general was serving the third of his four-year tour of duty as U.S. chief of staff. He was fifty-four at the time, tall, trim, strikingly handsome, imperious, the youngest officer ever to hold the post.

I remember him striding the halls of the old building in glossy cavalry boots, fawn-colored riding breeches, and form-fitting khaki tunic complete with polished Sam Browne belt and campaign ribbons. He rarely held press conferences and spent most of his time on Capitol Hill, trying to persuade a reluctant Congress to appropriate more money for the army. After the advent

of Hitler he foresaw another war in Europe and the possibility of eventual
American involvement. His admirers compared him favorably with Jesus
Christ, and his critics were nearly as extravagant in their denunciations.

I saw General MacArthur a few days after my arrival in Manila in his office
in La Fortaleza, his headquarters in the old walled city. I cannot truthfully
say I "interviewed" him, because he did all the talking as he strode back and
forth between two flags—the Stars and Stripes and the flag of the Philippine
Commonwealth—behind an uncluttered desk almost as big as Mussolini's in
Rome. He spoke in resonant and confident tones about what he had done, and
what he still hoped to do, to make the islands' defenses so formidable that the
Japanese would "think twice" about attacking them.

Although seven years had passed since I had last seen him, the general
looked much as I remembered him: tall, handsome as a matinee idol, and
flat-hipped, a decidedly charismatic soldier. Only his uniform had changed; it
was decidedly "nonreg." He wore a freshly laundered khaki shirt open at the
throat and sharply creased, pleated-front khaki trousers cut to disguise the
suggestion of a paunch. But what caught my eye was the heavily gold-braided
visored hat lying on his desk. I had never seen one quite like it.

The burden of the general's definitely one-sided "interview" was that in
recent years, as Japanese penetration pressed south into Indochina, Washington's top brass had increasingly accepted his view that the Philippines were
defendable. He intended making the islands defensively so costly to the "prospective invaders" that they would be deterred from attempting an invasion.
He believed that an attack would cost the Japanese "at least half a million
casualties and upwards of five billion dollars." He said he was sure the Japanese had studied the lesson of Gallipoli, hence would never launch an attack
against a coast heavily defended by modern weapons.

MacArthur seemed certain, in any event, that the Philippines held no
strategic or economic value for the Japanese. "Those who fear a Japanese
attack," he said, "fail duly to credit the logic of the Japanese mind." He
admitted, however, that while the islands were "defendable," they were not
"impregnable."

"Any position, even a machine-gun nest," he said by way of explanation,
"can be captured if the attacker is willing to pay the price. So can the Philippines be captured if the enemy is willing to write off the losses. . . ."

"But what if—" That was as far as I got. The man was intuitive. He
answered my unspoken question.

"Yes," he said. "The Japanese might well decide that possession of the
Philippines, with their vast human and natural resources, might be worth the
heavy cost in lives and matériel which conquest of the islands would entail.
Should they so decide, the Japanese could conceivably conquer the islands. . . ."

MacArthur stopped pacing and stood alongside the American flag. He
sensed that I was about to ask another question and answered before I could
utter it.

"In that event," he said, "we would retake the Philippines . . . island by island if necessary."

The general admitted that much remained to be done to make the islands secure and that he had asked Washington for more troops, planes, guns, tanks. Some help, he indicated, had already arrived: a few B-17 bombers, a shipment of guns, mostly 75s and 105s, and the battleship *Houston*.

We chatted briefly about what I had seen of the war in the Middle East, and MacArthur wore a faraway look when I told him that Wavell didn't believe the Germans could defeat the Russians, but he made no comment. I said I had seen many tanks in Libya—Italian, German, British, and American—and asked to see the ones the general had in the Philippines.

"I'm ashamed to tell you," he said with a long face, "I haven't a tank in the place. I expect some any day now, though. . . ."

But he said I could go where I pleased and see for myself what had been accomplished to make the islands secure. For starters, the general suggested the naval base at Cavite, Clark Field, and the Philippine Army Staff School at Baguio.

As I was about to leave, General MacArthur said he didn't expect anything much to happen before spring, "if then." History would prove him dead wrong about if or when the Japanese would attack.

I confess that the war had aroused the chauvinist in me, and I was heartened by what I saw of the military preparations during my monthlong stay in and around Manila, where I was comfortably housed in the Manila Hotel, though on a much lower floor than the one occupied by the general, his wife—the former Jean Faircloth, a wealthy southern belle whom he had married in 1937—and their three-year-old son, Arthur.

Most of the activity centered on Corregidor, the island fortress at the entrance to Manila Bay, just south of the Bataan Peninsula; on Cavite, the naval base; and on Baguio.

At Cavite I was reminded of Admiral Dewey's victory by a bronze tablet set in a rock in the shade of some palm trees just off the narrow concrete walk that ran past the screened verandas of the officers' billets. It said the U.S. Marines had hoisted the American flag over the place on May 3, 1898.

The naval base was a scene of hurried, almost frantic preparations for the islands' defense, comforting to see after the somnolent indifference I had witnessed at Singapore. Mammoth bulldozers and excavators were at work preparing the foundations for new buildings. Pile drivers drove steel stanchions into the soggy soil at the water's edge for the bunkers that would store the fuel for American warships. Buzz saws growled through seasoned logs, slicing off planks and studs for scaffolding, making lumber for new barracks.

Four thousand Filipinos were building mess halls and a field hospital. New docks already stood where six months before, I was told, there had been muddy flats or coconut groves. Supervised by a corps of American engineers, the Filipinos dug, sawed, and hammered around the clock and were, a foreman said, three months or more ahead of schedule.

Big PBY flying boats—long-range patrol bombers like the one in which I had flown the Atlantic from Bermuda to Britain in February and which now patrolled the South China Sea, the Sulu Sea, and the Malacca Strait—lay on the water at Cavite, their bodies and stubby wings painted the color of whalehide. I saw others on ramps, in hangars, or on cradles in the repair shops. Some were painted dark green and bore the bright triangular orange insignia of the Dutch East Indies. American warships in battle paint were anchored in the harbor; others were on patrol in Philippine waters.

At Clark Field, "one of many airfields," I was told, scattered through the islands, there were P-40 fighters and B-17 bombers in what seemed considerable numbers. But they were either clustered in hangars or neatly lined up, wing tip to wing tip, on the field. Protective revetments were built, and others were under construction, but were not being used. I found this strange, in the circumstances, and said so. "There'll be plenty of time to disperse them if we get into a shooting war," said a noncom who should have known better. A veteran with several hash marks on his sleeve, he seemed to think the Japanese would precede an attack with a formal declaration of war. I reminded him that Hitler hadn't sent Stalin an engraved invitation to a war when he attacked on June 22.

Word had got around that a *Collier's* correspondent who had been covering the war in Europe and the Middle East was in town, and I was invited to visit the Philippine Army Staff School at Baguio to speak to several hundred Filipino officers in training. The colonel in charge asked me to come in uniform and "give the boys the lowdown on how the British are fighting the war." My audience listened with obvious interest to what I had to say about London under the bombs, the difficulties of desert warfare, and the lessons learned from the Nazis' parachute blitz of Crete.

Another visit at a camp where Filipino recruits were being inducted into the U.S. Army after completing training produced one of the most embarrassing moments of my life. I was invited by the commanding officer to join him and his staff on the reviewing stand as his battalions did a march-past in the closing ceremony of their induction proceedings. There I stood, on the colonel's right, in my British war correspondent's uniform, when he nudged me and whispered, "You take the salute."

I was terrified. I had no idea what he meant but responded instinctively when the band struck up a familiar Sousa march and the parade started. At approximately the right moment, when the flags moved by and the marchers did an "eyes right," I came to attention and waggled my very British-style salute, my knees knocking together nervously. I hoped they wouldn't be visible to the newsreel cameras facing me and prayed none of my colleagues would ever see that particular bit of footage.

But while Manila buzzed with activity and looked more like a genuine bastion than Singapore, even a layman could see that the islands' defenses were far from ready to meet a Japanese attack. Presumably the initial strike would come from the sky; but all the available antiaircraft guns were concentrated on the fortifications at Corregidor, and so was all the ground artillery. There were no radar stations, though several, I was told, were "under construction."

In the opinion of most regular army officers, the mobilization and training schedules were based on the assumption that the Japanese couldn't possibly mount an invasion "much before April 1, 1942." Time, they believed, was on their side.

Meanwhile, however, the army had completed the evacuation of all wives and children. Of the important officers' wives, only Mrs. MacArthur remained. The wives of American civilian residents were exempted from the evacuation orders and, while I was in Manila, were organizing what they called a civil defense program. Compared with what I had seen in London, it was a joke. The menu to be served in eventual field kitchens, for instance, was arroz con pollo, a complicated chicken dish with rice.

The city's socially "elite," many of whom descended from the plain sailors and soldiers who had arrived with Dewey, carried on as though there were no threat of war. Every night the Jai Alai Club was crowded with Americans who gambled on the crooked play of the imported Spanish and Cuban players in the fronton. At the Manila Hotel there was nightly drinking, dining, and dancing much as there had been in Singapore. At the hotel's bar U.S. officers arrived in mufti to ease the pain of wifeless loneliness by picking up available "hostesses." The capital's whoreladies prospered; they were obtainable in every hotel from bellboy pimps.

The atmosphere everywhere else in town was one of business and pleasure as usual. Filipino and American entrepreneurs were fattening their purses with lucrative army and navy contracts, and cooperation between the civil authorities and the armed services was virtually nonexistent. The commonwealth reluctantly, and then only after much pressure from MacArthur and the American high commissioner, Francis B. Sayre, appropriated funds for civilian defense projects.

By the time I was getting ready to leave Manila in mid-September, the islands were probably as defendable as MacArthur had been able to make them with the weapons and manpower at his disposal. But the Philippines were morally and spiritually weak. I recall dancing one night at the swank Jai Alai Club with a lovely American matron, the spirited wife of a prosperous used-car salesman.

"Do you really think we'll go to war?" she asked.

"No, madam," I said. "We will not go to war, the war will come to us, particularly to you, here in Manila. . . ."

"Oh, dear." She sighed. "Whatever will I do with my silver?"

One of her forebears, in the Revolutionary War, she said, had sunk her silver in a well and had returned to fetch it when the British were beaten. It was a lovely, brave little story, but I doubted that the spirit of that certain great-great-grandparent of my dancing partner was still alive within the soft, pampered body I held in my arms as the band played "Begin the Beguine."

One afternoon I gave a talk to an assembly of Manila's ladies in the garden of the home of a prominent journalist friend who thought it might be a good idea if the local clubwomen were told a few of the facts of wartime life. The high commissioner's tall, handsome wife was among those present for tea and cookies. Apparently Mrs. Sayre didn't like what I said concerning the low state of civilian unpreparedness in the Filipino capital. She must have quoted me to her husband, for Sayre sent for me the next day.

Sayre, a big man with a heavy jaw and the look and manner of a reformist preacher, was cordial and attentive while we discussed the imminence of war. I told him what I had seen and heard here and there during my months-long travels, and then, with a preliminary "ahumph" or two, he came to the point. He had summoned me, he said, because he feared I might return to the States with the "mistaken notion that the authorities in Manila have done nothing to protect the civilian population of the Philippines in the event of war."

It was quite all right for me to go about Manila making speeches on the imminence of war, he said, and the necessity for awareness of the dangers they faced. But, he said, it would be unfair for me to return to America and to say nothing had been done on behalf of civilian defense.

"We have done a great deal," he said, solemnly, and with that he pulled open the top drawer on the left side of his large, flat-topped desk and extracted from it a thick sheaf of papers. They were a compendium of reports, recommendations, plans, and counterplans about three inches thick. I skimmed through its several hundred pages. Impressive stuff.

"But have you translated any of this into the recommended realities?" I asked.

He confessed that "very little" had been done. No, there were no air-raid shelters. No, the doctors, nurses, and first-aid workers had not actually been mobilized. An evacuation camp, long, contiguous barracks constructed of siwali and bamboo, had been built in the hills. "They will make a merry blaze when bombed," I said.

The following day one of Sayre's assistants came to see me at the Manila Hotel. We sat in the garden overlooking Manila Bay and talked for hours about what the British had done in the way of civilian defense. Apparently none of the reports available in Washington on civil defense in London had been forwarded to Manila. Sayre's aide had never heard of a slit trench and was only vaguely familiar with an Anderson shelter such as Londoners used. One of the few practical schemes that had been put into operation was to encourage civilians to grow vegetables to supplement existing supplies in case of war and to lay by canned food for emergency use. Few paid any attention to Sayre's recommendations.

There were no ration cards or fire buckets filled with sand, no trained civilian defense workers in Manila or anywhere else in the Philippines. The Civil Emergency Administration in charge of such matters jealously refused to buy equipment for the Fire Department. The two organizations were squabbling over who should put out incendiary bombs.

Air-raid shelters, I was told by a CEA official, couldn't be dug because the water table was only a few feet underground. Yet no attempt was made to create shelters in the existing waterproof basements of private homes and Manila's big buildings.

In fairness to Sayre, he had no official funds available to promote a large-scale program of education of the population, native and white, in civilian defense. For what little was done, the high commissioner had to juggle appropriations from one budget to another to keep within the financial limits set by the unimaginative old-boy network in the State Department, whose members still believed, in the early autumn of 1941, that the Japanese could be appeased.

Finally, security was lax in Manila and everywhere else in the Philippines. The islands had a closely knit, well-to-do community of about fifteen thousand Japanese. It was not inconceivable that agents among them were informing Tokyo on the location and defenses of every airfield, on the comings and goings of patrol ships and bombers, on the strength and whereabouts of every army unit, on the arrival of ships carrying weapons and war supplies.

There were prominent Japanese businessmen present at a luncheon of the Rotary Club—or was it the Kiwanis?—at which I was invited to speak shortly before I left Manila. I said I believed we and they, Americans and Japanese, would soon be at war and that they, not we, would be the aggressors. I said I thought there might still be time to avert what would undoubtedly be a disastrous war for all concerned and hoped the many Japanese guests in the room would use whatever influence they possessed with Tokyo in the interests of peace. My remarks were greeted with stony silence.

Seated at the head table with me was Clare Boothe Luce, wife of the publisher of *Time* magazine and future congresswoman from Connecticut, who knew far more about the situation than I did. She asked to be heard after my speech and rebuked me for what I had said. She said I reminded her of the schoolboy who stood by a railroad track while two trains were hurtling toward each other on the same rails and cried, "Look, there's going to be one hell of a crash!" I believe she said I had demonstrated a firm grip of the obvious but had offered no solutions for the crisis. I don't recall that she did, either, but I do remember feeling crushed. I forgave her, however, for she was stunningly beautiful in her very special blond fairness.

A few days later, I boarded Pan Am's Pacific Clipper for San Francisco by way of Wake Island, Midway, and Honolulu.

41

A FATEFUL DAY
IN DECEMBER

My more or less unsentimental journey around a world more or less at war ended in San Francisco on a golden late-September afternoon in 1941 two months and seven days before the Japanese attacked Pearl Harbor. Nearly half a century has elapsed since the day I returned to my own country from the battlefields, active and inactive, of Europe, Africa, the Middle East, and Asia. But I remember still the elation, the unalloyed joy of my homecoming.

I had never before been west of Pittsburgh, and San Francisco excited me. The city was evocative of pioneer days, of the gold rush of the forty-niners and the great earthquake and fire of 1906, a metropolis at once European and Oriental, yet somehow uniquely American, a cool, handsome, worldly city whose uphill-downhill streets reminded me of Baltimore but were cleaner, far less smugly middle-class.

In the early autumn of 1941 San Francisco had not yet become exposed to the common urban problems of a later time: pollution of both air and water; the uglification that would result from unregulated building, violence, and vandalism; and the decay that would afflict all inner cities. The city of my homecoming was a magic place, and I fell in love with it long before a pop singer named Tony Bennett left his heart there.

In 1890 Rudyard Kipling had found San Francisco "a mad city, inhabited for the most part by perfectly insane people whose women are of remarkable beauty." The San Francisco shown me by Hub Keenan, the *Collier's* West

Coast man who met me when I landed and took me at once to the Bohemian Club for dry martinis and dinner with some leading citizens, had none of the razzle-dazzle of Bret Harte's wonderful yarns about the miners and the swindlers who preyed upon them, but it had many of Kipling's women of "remarkable beauty." How desirable they looked after the horse-faced British women I had met in Cairo, the puckered, heat-drained matrons of Simla, their gin-soaked counterparts in Singapore, and the comely little Filipino professionals of Manila.

The San Franciscans I met at the Bohemian Club and, next day, at a bibulous press luncheon which Keenan arranged at the Fairmont on Nob Hill, asked intelligent questions about the war, and while they weren't much interested in Germany, they were ready to fight the Japanese anytime. They looked westward across the Pacific with apprehension, and none reflected the hard-nosed isolationism I had encountered in their East Coast counterparts nine months before although one of their senators, Hiram Johnson, was as vociferously antiwar as the editorials of their leading West Coast publisher, William Randolph Hearst.

Most, though not all, shared my distress that Britain might be defeated unless America threw its entire weight into the military balance against the Axis powers. I had become an incorrigible Anglophile and subscribed whole-heartedly to the closing quatrain of Alice Duer Miller's immensely popular "The White Cliffs of Dover":

> I am American bred,
> I have seen here much to hate—much to forgive,
> But in a world where England is finished and dead,
> I do not wish to live.

Having found kindred spirits in San Francisco, I left the city in a glow of renewed confidence that mobilization and industrial production would soon be sped up to the pitch required for ultimate victory. But during the long haul to New York, changing planes twice, I gradually emerged from the gold and purple mist of my seventy-two hours in San Francisco.

By the time I reached Denver on the first leg of my homeward flight, I realized that isolationism was still alive and well. My seatmate didn't want to talk about the war. He complained about high taxes and the rising cost of living, but mostly he let off steam about "that man in the White House," whom he depicted as the devil incarnate.

My traveling companion from Denver to Chicago waxed bitter about lend-lease: "It's practically a declaration of war by the same SOB who promised us during the election that he wasn't going to get us involved in any war, wasn't going to send our boys overseas to pull Britain's chestnuts out of the fire." He echoed the views of another renowned isolationist, Colonel Robert McCormick, publisher of the *Chicago Tribune* and a leading supporter of the still-active America First movement.

I was puzzled. Midwesterners read the same agency news bulletins as the people on the West Coast, heard much the same radio commentators, yet they held totally different views toward the most important event of our time, the war. Hurrah for freedom of speech!

The Chicagoan who sat next to me on the way to New York was far more concerned with the price of corn futures and the fluctuations of the stock market than with the fate of the nation, much less the future of the world in the event of an Axis victory. About the war the Germans were waging in Russia, he said he hoped the Nazis would "kill a lot of Bolsheviks and vice versa." He, too, hated FDR, and a hostile silence followed when I said I thought Mr. Roosevelt was probably our greatest president since Lincoln.

And so home at last to Bronxville, the arms of a waiting wife and children—the boys had grown amazingly—and the delighted yappings of Christopher, the frisky fox terrier I had given the boys before departing on my thirty-six-thousand-mile odyssey. The gladsome homecoming was marred only by a scolding for my not having written oftener, and days passed before my explanation—the uncertainty of the mails in wartime—was reluctantly accepted. Actually I had written fairly regularly, but most of my letters—like my expense accounts, as I learned on my first day at the office—had journeyed by surface mail even when stamped "Airmail" and were probably at the bottom of the sea. Hitler's U-boats had been busy during 1941.

Tommy, who had turned four in July, looked sturdy enough, but I sensed in him an inner emotional disturbance, an unspoken but palpable resentment that I had been away so long. Sean had celebrated his tenth birthday in August but looked older, more self-reliant. Their mother had retained her Irish good looks and figure, smiled ineffably, and went about running the household with equanimity.

Kathryn had help now: Walter Brooks, a middle-aged black houseman who cooked dinner and did the heavy housework. He lived in nearby Fleetwood, came early, and stayed late for only twenty dollars a week, with Saturday afternoons and Sundays off. Kathryn thus had time for Bundles for Britain, Russian War Relief, and the recently organized USO to entertain servicemen at teas, buffet suppers, and dances.

Bronxville, I soon discovered, remained what it had always been: Republican, white, Protestant, country club-oriented, anti-Semitic, and isolationist. The townspeople had voted overwhelmingly for Willkie and were bitter that FDR had succeeded in winning a third term. The America First movement numbered many followers among the villagers despite the fact that during the campaign Willkie had proved himself as much an interventionist as Roosevelt. They tended to funnel charity into the Community Chest rather than Bundles for Britain, and Russian War Relief was anathema. Anyone connected with it, Kathryn included, was labeled a "fellow traveler" or a "Communist."

The village's flannel-suited male breadwinners were characters out of a John P. Marquand novel, and their wives were of the behatted, tailored breed caricatured in *The New Yorker* by Helen Hokinson. Astonished by the prevalence of anti-British sentiment among them, I traced it (with Kathryn's help) to an incident at a USO "social" to which a number of British seamen on shore leave were invited. The sailors had been at sea for many months and were, after all, men with men's appetites. A few casually hinted that the entertainment hadn't gone far enough. This outraged the ladies, who decided the British were "a barbaric lot." Men who would openly hint it might be more fun to go to bed than to munch cold roast turkey and potato salad couldn't be worth helping. There was a limit, after all, to lend-lease!

Meanwhile, the patriotic local manager of the village's movie theater stopped playing the national anthem at the end of performances, as was done in England, and played it before the show started. His customers, he discovered, had taken to walking out if "The Star-Spangled Banner" was played when the screening ended. Clever manager. Now his clients had to stand before the lights came down and the screen lit up. When the lights went on again, the audiences left the theater to the strains of "God Bless America," a tune Kate Smith had made her own.

Apart from the village's Episcopalian pastor, Father Hohly, and two or three youngish couples, the town was an intellectual desert. What made social life tolerable for Kathryn and me was the fact that Bronxville was also the home of the William L. Shirers, the Leland Stowes, and the Kyle Crichtons.

Kyle, my *Collier's* colleague, was a gregarious extrovert and a fine host. Weekend parties at his big, rambling stone house were festive occasions with plenty of "good talk" about war and peace, politics and books, and Kyle's specialty, the theater.

My first chore at *Collier's* when I resumed my daily commutes to the office was to reconstruct as best I could the missing expense accounts. I had sent monthly accountings—bulky envelopes containing receipted bills and vouchers—but they undoubtedly had shared the fate of many of my letters home. The magazine had cabled me about $10,000 during my travels, but with the help of a few notes, a fairly good memory, and a lively imagination, I managed to account for all of it—plus $485.85! It was the biggest expense account ever submitted at *Collier's,* and the additional $485.85 was paid without a murmur, although the treasurer, an Irishman named Dinny, couldn't resist remarking that I hadn't satisfactorily explained the eighty-five cents.

The editorial room buzzed with the story of my huge expense account, and rumors spread that I was the magazine's "best writer of fiction after Faith Baldwin," whose novels we often serialized. A few years later I relinquished my dubious fame as *Collier's* most expensive reporter to Ernest Hemingway, whom the weekly hired to cover the liberation of Paris, something for which I never forgave it.

Restless weeks followed. I loved my wife, our boys, our comfortable home; but I was a born wanderer, and restlessness had become an occupational malady. Ships, trains, planes, hotels, and the better bars and restaurants were now my natural habitat.

A journey was almost invariably distasteful, and I often detested certain cities while working there. Later, however, I waxed nostalgic about them.

When I first saw Cairo, for instance, I loathed the place for its foul-smelling slums, its noise, the flies crawling undisturbed on the trachomatous eyes of Arab babies and on the open, running sores of beggars. I was revolted by the hunger and pain of the people and the utter dreariness of their seemingly pointless lives. But in retrospect, I recalled only feluccas sailing on the Nile under pastel-tinted lateen sails, the fragrance of jasmine-scented nights, the majesty of the Pyramids luminescent in the moonlight, and the choreography of turbaned figures in flowing robes mingling in the crowded streets with British soldiers and Egyptians in galabias and tarbooshes, a soundless tableau bereft in memory of its earsplitting sounds and repellent stinks. I yearned to return to Cairo.

Of course, it was good to be home again, watching Bronxville's leaves turn as the hot summer gave way to a crisp autumn. On Saturday afternoons I enjoyed kicking a soccer ball around with the boys on our leaf-strewn lawn and relished even more the hilarious times with them listening to Fred Allen, Fibber McGee and Molly, and Jack Benny on the radio. And there were memorable quiet evenings with Kathryn, reading or listening to symphonic music while a friendly fire crackled in the living-room fireplace. But I itched to be back in action somewhere, almost anywhere—except Calcutta!

My restlessness stemmed from an overwhelming curiosity about the world and its people and the war that had condemned millions of them to death, injury, and deprivation. After a period of idleness the urge to be moving again to a new warfront or to an old one to see what had happened since I was there last became almost unbearable. On my return from Manila I was more aware than ever of the enormousness of the story that was breaking in Europe, Russia, the Middle East, and the Orient, and I felt driven to witness whatever was happening.

My recent travels had profoundly influenced my view of the war. I now saw it not only as a colossal struggle between the forces of democracy and those of the nihilistic Axis powers but also as the first stage of a global revolution. It seemed to me that far-reaching changes in the world's social, political, and economic landscape would result from the ongoing conflict—a far better world if we won, an unimaginable one if we lost—but in either case a world in which nothing would ever be the same again.

Everywhere I had been during the past eight months—England, South Africa, the Middle East, India, the Philippines—I had heard people cry out for a better life when the fighting ended, a world in which distinctions of class and race would be obliterated, and the national aspirations of subject peoples recognized. Imperialism and colonialism, I reasoned, could not possibly survive the bloodletting and the tremendous outlay of treasure by all concerned.

Englishmen, I recalled, were fighting not only to defeat Germany, but also to create a postwar England wherein they would enjoy a fairer share of their country's wealth. They looked forward to an end to domination of their social and economic lives by a wealthy privileged class. They were determined to preserve their political democracy, but they also wanted what they called economic democracy.

In South Africa the country's huge black majority stirred with a desire to end the oppressive color bar imposed by a white minority. In the Middle East Arab nationalists wanted independence from British and French colonialism. In Palestine the Jews yearned for nationhood in the land of their origins. In India the people agitated for an end to British imperial rule. In the Philippines the masses looked forward to promised independence.

In my impatience for action, I proposed to Colebaugh that I be reassigned to the Middle East because I felt it to be the decisive battlefield of the war pending the eventual opening of a second front against Germany in Europe proper. But the magazine's advertising and publicity departments had other ideas. Their managers borrowed me from the editorial staff for a lecture tour to promote the magazine.

My first assignment—and my last—was to speak at a luncheon at the very exclusive—meaning no Jews allowed—Athletic Club in Detroit, the capital of the nation's automotive industry.

In my speech I said, among other things, that unless America's industrialists retooled and began turning out the tanks, guns, planes, and vehicles President Roosevelt demanded, the war with Germany would be lost. My audience included the top-drawer executives of the major manufacturers of automobiles, tires, and electronic equipment, all of whom were important advertisers in *Collier's*.

As the clatter of polite applause that greeted my remarks died down, a short man with gray hair and a country-club tan leaped to his feet and shouted: "You sound just like that man *Rosenfeldt*. Now you listen to me—"

I interrupted and angrily shouted back: "No, you listen to me, sir. The last time I ever heard the name of the president of the United States so purposefully mispronounced was in Berlin . . . by a Nazi named Goebbels. . . ."

The portly dissenter was the chief executive officer of Studebaker Motors, one of my magazine's major advertisers. He canceled his company's space contract with *Collier's*, and it took the combined diplomacy and salesmanship of Tom Beck, our publisher, and Bill Chenery, our editor in chief, to set matters right. Neither Beck nor Chenery, however, ever expressed disapproval of what I had done—beyond canceling the rest of my "lecture tour."

Then came Sunday, December 7.

It was a day the fathers and mothers of my generation and all but the smallest of their children would never forget. We would remember always where we were, what we were doing, and how we reacted to the shocking news.

The radio in the living room was tuned to a running account of a professional football game. There was a fire in the hearth, for winter had come quickly on the heels of a fine golden autumn. Sunlight streamed through the casement windows and made a block pattern on the rug where Tommy and his dog pulled and pushed at each other, making a great din. Sean was sprawled on the sofa with the funnies.

It was the houseman's day off, and Kathryn was in the kitchen, preparing tea, making a clatter and singing off key. A player named Manders was running with the ball and had just been tackled deep in his opponents' territory when a calm, strong voice broke into the sports announcer's account.

"We are interrupting for a news flash," he said. "Here it is: Japanese planes have attacked Pearl Harbor. Unconfirmed reports also say that the Philippines have been attacked. . . ."

Sean, startled, looked up from his comics. I ran into the kitchen and told Kathryn what had happened. Wide-eyed, white-faced, she returned with me to the radio, running. I glanced down at Tommy and the terrier; they were wrestling contentedly. Sean looked dejected, chin on chest, frown creases furrowing his smooth child's forehead. An advertisement on the radio had said something about Christmas only seconds after the first bulletin about Pearl Harbor and the Philippines.

"What a Christmas," Sean said, lapsing into gloomy silence.

Charley Colebaugh telephoned moments after the first announcement and again a bit later. He was calm enough, though he had good reason to be agitated: *Collier's* was on the newsstands that week with an article by Walter Davenport entitled "Impregnable Pearl Harbor." He made no reference to it, and neither did I. He merely said he thought I'd better be moving on—in the direction of Manila.

"Where the bullets fly," he said, "there fly we, *n'est-ce pas?*" He had a French wife. "See you tomorrow. We'll make plans. . . ."

I told Kathryn what Colebaugh had said. She nodded, tight-lipped and pale.

Not knowing then, and not for some time, the extent of the death and destruction the Japanese had wrought, I felt a sense of relief that America had passed from bystander to participant. It would be easier, now, to produce the 125,000 planes and tens of thousands of guns and tanks President Roosevelt had demanded of American industry by 1944 in the $100 billion program he had outlined in a message to Congress in October.

Before nightfall that fateful Sunday in December it was clear that the Japanese had attacked all British as well as American bases in the Pacific. The war between East and West that had brooded over Asia like a black, low-lying cloud ever since the Japanese invaded China in 1931 had burst with the sudden fury of a typhoon.

I mentally pictured Manila being bombed, could visualize the big red circles under the Japanese bombers' wings and people scurrying for shelter where no shelters existed. I wondered dimly whether that Daughter of the American Revolution with whom I had danced one fairly recent night at the Jai Alai Club had had time to hide her silver. . . .

Images crowded my mind like the frames in a fast-moving film: the ack-ack batteries on Corregidor blasting away at the attackers; the planes on Clark

Field rising to meet the attack; General MacArthur at his telephone directing the defense of Manila and the Philippines. It would be days before my imaginings were proved chimerical. . . .

At noon the next day President Roosevelt addressed the Congress. His voice thick with emotion, he said: "Yesterday, December 7, 1941—a date which will live in infamy—the United States of America was suddenly and deliberately attacked by the naval and air forces of the Empire of Japan. . . .

"The attack yesterday on the Hawaiian Islands has caused severe damage to American naval and military forces. Very many American lives have been lost. . . ."

"I ask that the Congress declare . . . a state of war. . . ."

The resultant roll call lacked only one vote for unanimity. The lone nay was cast in a tremulous voice by Representative Jeannette Rankin of Montana, a motherly lady deeply devoted to peace, who had also voted against war with Kaiser Wilhelm's Germany in 1917.

America was at war again after twenty-three years and twenty-nine days of peace. Japan had turned a corner in history, but so had the United States.

42

UNITY AND A GRAND ALLIANCE

Although on Black Sunday Charley Colebaugh had indicated he wanted me to return to the Philippines, he reconsidered and sent me to Washington instead, to "feel the pulse," as he put it, and "find out what went wrong in Hawaii." I was immensely relieved, frankly, for I had no desire ever to see the Far East again.

The capital was cold and blustery when I arrived on the morning of December 11 by overnight sleeper on a train crowded with uniformed men reporting to camps, ships, and shore stations. The normally relaxed, easygoing city was in a grim mood, with more uniforms in evidence than I had ever seen in Washington. Government buildings were guarded by marines with bayonets on their rifles, and long lines of young men, some mere boys, formed outside downtown recruiting stations, waiting their turn to volunteer. Squads of civil defense workers scurried about town, locating sites for air-raid shelters and laying in supplies of sand, buckets, shovels, and first-aid equipment.

Later that same day Mussolini and Hitler spared Congress a possibly agonizing debate by declaring war on the United States, and the dictators' challenge was promptly accepted by unanimous votes in both the House and the Senate.

The Japanese bombs that savaged Hawaii had blasted the isolationist bloc into silence, in some cases even grudging acquiescence. Growled Senator Burton K. Wheeler of Montana, one of the panjandrums of isolationism, "The only thing left to do now is to lick the hell out of those Japs," which was how the Japanese would be known thereafter when they weren't called "little yellow bastards."

Meanwhile, throughout the country special agents of the FBI, reinforced by squads of armed police, were rounding up Japanese, yanking them out of houses, shops, and restaurants, even off trains, buses, and planes. The authorities, fearing these people might act as saboteurs for the mikado, had hastily decided to herd them all into detention camps, although of the nation's 110,000 Japanese about two thirds were Nisei, American-born citizens. This somewhat brutal precaution turned out to be unnecessary, but during the early days of the war anti-Japanese feelings ran so high that some Asians found it prudent to wear hand-lettered signs reading CHINESE—NOT JAP. I saw several in Penn Station, in New York, and two or three in Washington.

The hatred of the Japanese born of Pearl Harbor endured through the war years. Probably never in our history was an enemy so thoroughly detested.

Unity of sentiment and purpose is all-important in war, but until Black Sunday the United States had not achieved it. The sectional diversities of our large country of 132 million people; the mixture of many national stocks; the strong pacifist traditions; the devotion to freedom of speech, which made for dissent; the sharp differences of outlook on foreign policy between the seaboards and the interior—all were factors that militated strongly against unity.

The stealthy attack on Pearl Harbor, however, aroused in every citizen, on the West coast and on the East Coast and in between, a sense of deepest outrage. It produced what Arthur Krock, the veteran Washington correspondent of the *New York Times,* called "instant national unity." He wrote on December 8, "You could almost hear it click into place."

The millions of ordinary citizens who heard President Roosevelt's call to arms in his "Day of Infamy" speech exulted. Few, if any, had wanted war. When it came, however, there was a a mighty consensus of national purpose.

The apparent ease with which the Japanese had been able to evade detection puzzled Secretary of the Navy Frank Knox. When I called at his office in the barrackslike Munitions and Navy buildings on Constitution Avenue on Friday morning, December 12, the secretary had gone; he had left for Honolulu two days before with his aides to make inquiries.

Secretary of War Henry Stimson, meanwhile, had sent a mission to Hawaii to investigate the army's behavior during the attack.* At the White House President Roosevelt, cigarette at its usual jaunty angle, artfully dodged all reporters' questions. He urged us correspondents to await Secretary Knox's return.

When Knox returned on Monday, December 15, he admitted that the armed services of the United States "were not on the alert against the surprise

* The plane carrying Stimson's team of investigators took off from Phoenix, Arizona, for Hamilton Field, California, and crashed in the snow and ice of the High Sierras. The wreckage wasn't found until the spring of 1942.

attack on Hawaii. This fact calls for a formal investigation which will be initiated immediately by the President." The losses as he enumerated them, however, while serious, were not as grave as the public had imagined. Knox listed as lost the twenty-six-year-old battleship *Arizona*, sunk by a bomb that "literally passed down through a smokestack," and the equally ancient *Utah*, a target-training ship, as well as three destroyers—*Cassin, Shaw*, and *Downes*—and a minelayer, an old passenger ship converted for combat during World War I.

Other damage, Knox said, ranged from "ships which have already been repaired, and are ready for sea, or which have gone to sea, to a few ships which will take from a week to several months to repair." In the latter category Knox mistakenly placed the battleship *Oklahoma*, which actually had capsized. Harbor approaches, he said, had received little damage, and the vast spread of oil storage tanks was unscathed.

The Japanese lost only two of their little-known, tiny two-man submarines—one sunk, one captured—one full-size submarine, and forty-one aircraft, including those shot down and some forced down for lack of fuel.

Observers and a clutch of analysts found the limited extent of matériel losses as reported by the secretary of the navy most heartening; the Japanese high command had claimed destruction of the entire U.S. Pacific Fleet.

Bit by bit, however, the agonizing truth emerged: Pearl Harbor was the worst military disaster in the country's history. The Japanese had not destroyed the Pacific Fleet but had come close enough to cause widespread concern.

When the carrier-launched Japanese planes came out of the clear blue sky over Hawaii at 7:55 A.M. on sunlit December 7, they found ninety-four combat and auxiliary ships tied up two by two at their berths in Pearl Harbor, including eight battleships, twenty-nine destroyers, and five submarines. The navy was operating under relaxed peacetime conditions with most of its crews on weekend shore leave. None of the vessels' main batteries was manned. Antiaircraft guns had only skeleton crews that morning, and their ammunition was stored in locked compartments.

The approximately two hundred serviceable combat planes of the army and the Marine Corps were tied down wing to wing at the airfields at Wheeler, Hickam, and Ewa like so many shiny butterfly specimens on pinboards. The Japanese attackers had good shooting wherever they looked.

Of the eight capital ships anchored along Battleship Row—the backbone of the Pacific Fleet—four were sunk or capsized. The remaining four were heavily damaged, and the *Arizona* was still burning when Knox arrived. Lost, in addition to the three destroyers already indicated, were three cruisers and four auxiliary vessels.

Fortunately three priceless aircraft carriers were at sea when the Japanese attacked. One hundred and eighty-eight planes were destroyed on the ground, and contrary to Knox's official report, most of the hangars and repair shops were demolished. Saddest of all, the casualty figures dwarfed previous estimates: 2,403 dead and 1,178 wounded. Among those killed was Rear Admiral Isaac Campbell Kidd, commander of a battleship division.

The American people were stunned anew by the unfolding magnitude of the disaster and more than ever wanted to know who was to blame. For diehard Republican isolationists the answer was simple: Franklin Delano Roosevelt. But for most people it was the men in charge at Hawaii: Lieutenant General Walter C. Short and Admiral Husband Kimmel, the military and naval commanders in the islands. Both were immediately relieved of their commands, for they had been warned of the imminence of an attack but had not taken the required precautions against surprise. Kimmel retired and became a resident of Bronxville. (We never met.)

But the outcry to know how and why the costly, humiliating defeat at Pearl Harbor happened persisted. Within days of the disaster a presidential commission headed by Supreme Court Justice Owen J. Roberts began the monumental task of questioning witnesses and sifting through documents in an attempt to fix responsibility.

In the meantime, the news from the areas I had recently visited in the Far East was as unnerving as everything I learned in Washington. The outbreak of war in the Pacific brought a repetition of what had become an all-too-familiar pattern: the swift overwhelming of the area's Allied defenders by enemy forces that had been consistently underrated. December proved to be a month of disasters. One by one British, American, and Dutch positions in Asia fell or came under ultimately irresistible Japanese attack.

On December 10, in the waters northeast of Singapore, bombers from a Japanese carrier sank the *Prince of Wales* (aboard which Roosevelt and Churchill had drafted the Atlantic Charter in August while anchored off Newfoundland) and the *Repulse*.

Three days later the island of Guam surrendered to the Japanese after stiff resistance. For the first time since the flag was raised after the Spanish-American War, the Stars and Stripes came down over Agana, and the strutting, arrogant conquerors shouted the word that was to become odiously familiar to Americans in the years ahead: *"Banzai!"*

Wake was next. When I stopped there on my way home in late September, it was still mainly a refueling station for Pan American Clippers and for westbound B-17s en route to the Philippines. The island fell on December 23, but not before the defenders had sunk two Japanese destroyers, damaged two light cruisers, hit and set afire one transport, and disabled another. The Japanese lost an estimated seven hundred dead and a lot of "face." But the marines and the civilians who had pitched in on the defense also suffered heavy casualties.

Midway Island remained in American hands and struck back effectively at the occasional Japanese raiders that approached from the sea and the air. But with Wake and Guam lost, the chance of reinforcing the Philippines in the face of Japanese naval and air superiority virtually disappeared. Their continued resistance against overwhelming odds provided one of the few bright spots in the gloomy record of the early weeks of the struggle in the Pacific.

General MacArthur's prewar assessments of the defendability of the Philippines and the combat capabilities of his Filipino forces proved to be almost ridiculously overoptimistic. Coincident with the attack on Pearl Harbor, Japanese bombers based on Formosa and aircraft carriers blanketed all the main airfields on the islands. The B-17s on Clark Field and the P-40 fighters at other airdromes were hit with devastating effect.

The full story of what happened in the Philippines was not known until after the war. But it was evident even from the sketchy, heavily censored reports emanating from MacArthur's headquarters in Manila that the general's dream of holding the islands had been shattered. While American fliers claimed to have damaged a number of Japanese transports as well as escorting warships, and while they launched several bombing raids against invading troops on the beaches of Luzon, neither these efforts nor the resistance of the ill-trained, poorly equipped Filipino units could prevent the establishment of beachheads by the Japanese.

On Christmas Eve MacArthur moved his headquarters to the fortified island of Corregidor and the hastily prepared defenses on the Bataan Peninsula. Manila, although publicly declared an open undefended city, was subjected to a savage two-day bombing on December 27 and 28, and the city was occupied by the invaders on January 2. On Corregidor and Bataan resistance continued until the early spring. By then MacArthur himself was in Australia, preparing to fight another day, having left command to his close friend General Jonathan Wainwright, to whom would fall the onerous task of surrendering what was left of American forces.

On December 22 Churchill, accompanied by a staff of military and technical advisers, arrived in Washington to meet with Roosevelt and his generals and admirals in the first of the great Anglo-American wartime conferences which were to chart Allied strategy in World War II, determine joint policies, and map the kind of peace to come. It was Churchill's first state visit to the United States, and he spent five days as a guest at the White House, during which he and the president and their staffs worked out problems of military and naval collaboration.

To millions of Americans the British prime minister was already a figure of legend. His stubby frame, his grumpily cherubic features, his enormous cigar, the imagery of his speech had become as familiar to them as the physical characteristics, speaking style, and mannerisms of their own president. The war had driven from the minds of most of us the old and beautiful words of Christmas—"Peace on earth; good will towards men"—but Churchill revived them on Christmas Eve with an impromptu performance from the White House.

Some twenty thousand men, women, and children gathered on the south lawn around a towering fir for the traditional lighting of the nation's Christmas tree. The Marine Band played, and massed choirs sang carols, and as the sunset gun from across the river at Fort Myer sounded, the president and his guest stepped out onto the mansion's south portico. Mr. Roosevelt pressed a button, and the tree sprang alive with the gay reds and blues and golds of the season.

Then the President introduced his guest and moved aside. Churchill's face was nearly hidden behind batteries of microphones, but his voice, strong, resonant, mellow with sentiment, easily identified him.

"I spend this anniversary and festival far from my country," he said, "far from my family, yet I cannot truthfully say that I feel far from home. . . . I cannot feel myself a stranger here in the center and at the summit of the United States. I feel a sense of unity and fraternal association which, added to the kindliness of your welcome, convinces me that I have a right to sit at your fireside and share your Christmas joys. . . . And so, in God's mercy, a happy Christmas to you all."

I had returned to New York two days before, and I heard the speech on the radio. It helped make the solemn Christmas of 1941 more meaningful and somewhat more cheerful. It made the historic bond between our two countries more than ever a personal kinship, and at that moment my thoughts went to the many friends I had in England. Some would be spending Christmas in London's underground, seeking shelter from Hitler's bombs.

The meeting of Roosevelt and Churchill, which came to be known as the Arcadia Conference, was the brainchild of the prime minister, who had feared a shifting of the main American effort to the Pacific as a result of Pearl Harbor. The conference reaffirmed the principle, already agreed to before Japan thrust the United States into the war, that Germany was the main enemy and had to be defeated first.

There were some stormy sessions and disagreements, notably between Churchill and General George C. Marshall, the U.S. chief of staff, but Arcadia produced the beginnings of a unified Allied command. It appointed Field Marshal Wavell, then still in India, commander in chief of all American-British-Dutch-Australian (ABDA) forces in the Southwest Pacific, the first step toward what later became a recognized system of unified theater commands around the world.

From a political and spiritual point of view, however, probably the most important result of the conference was the formulation and promulgation of the Declaration of the United Nations. It embodied the famous Four Freedoms enunciated by President Roosevelt in his annual message to Congress in January 1941 as constituting the "moral foundation" for whatever role the United States, then still technically at peace, might be obliged to play in world affairs.

In his historic speech the president had invoked "for people everywhere in the world . . . (1) freedom of speech and expression . . . (2) freedom to worship God each in his own way . . . (3) freedom from want . . . [and] (4) freedom from fear [to the end] that no nation anywhere will be in a position to commit an act of physical aggression against any neighbor." It was the seminal concept for a new world society reminiscent of the one envisioned by the idealistic Woodrow Wilson a generation earlier and much in Roosevelt's mind when he met with Churchill at sea in August off Newfoundland to draft the eight-point Atlantic Charter. Four months later, in Washington, the concept was incorporated and given new meaning in the declaration which created a genuine grand alliance.

On the afternoon of January 1, 1942, in a brief ceremony in the Oval Office, the declaration was formally signed by the president, by Churchill, by Ambassador Maksim Litvinov of the Soviet Union (he had arrived in Washington on Pearl Harbor Day) and Ambassador T. V. Soong of the Republic of China, in that order, who would be known thereafter as the Big Four. On the following day, at a similar ceremony at the State Department, the declaration was signed by the representatives of twenty-two other governments formally at war with the Axis.*

The declaration pledged the signatories to a "common program of purposes and principles" in the "struggle against savage and brutal forces seeking to subjugate the world." The signers committed themselves to the defense of "life, liberty, independence and religious freedom" and to the preservation of "human rights and justice in their own as well as other lands." Each signatory also promised not to make a separate armistice or peace with its Axis enemies in the struggle for "victory over Hitlerism."

Thus the seed of Roosevelt's Four Freedoms speech became, in a year almost to the day, the living organism that would be known as the United Nations, the grand alliance that was to save the world from domination by the unholy coalition known as the Rome-Berlin-Tokyo Axis.

In the tumult of other events the historic occasion passed almost unnoticed. The American people were still dazed by Pearl Harbor and were being traumatized anew almost daily by reminders of the viciousness of the war in which they suddenly found themselves. The Japanese were battering into submission democracy's bastions everywhere in the Pacific. In the Atlantic, Allied ships were being sunk by German U-boats faster than the vessels, their crews, and their cargoes could be replaced. In North Africa, Rommel and Auchinleck were indecisively holding each other at bay.

The only encouraging war news came from the Russian front, where, as General Wavell had predicted, Hitler's armies were immobilized at the gates of Moscow by snow and ice.

Early in the new year 1942 the American people could draw little comfort from the report of the Roberts Commission, which painted an appalling picture of complacency and divided authority between the army and navy com-

---

* They were: Australia, Belgium, Canada, Costa Rica, Cuba, Czechoslovakia, Dominican Republic, El Salvador, Greece, Guatemala, Haiti, Honduras, India, Luxembourg, Netherlands, New Zealand, Nicaragua, Norway, Panama, Poland, South Africa, and Yugoslavia.

mands at Pearl Harbor. It accused both Short and Kimmel of failure to react promptly and appropriately to war warnings sent to them from Washington. Washington, the report indicated, had done everything that could have been expected of it in detecting and interpreting the Japanese threat, but in Hawaii interservice rivalry prevented the army from knowing or caring what the navy did about the warnings, and vice versa.

The report maintained that if war warnings sent to both Short and Kimmel on November 27, 1941, had been complied with promptly, the aircraft warning system would have been operating; the reconnaissance of the navy and the inshore patrol of the army would have been maintained; the antiaircraft units of the army and similar shore batteries of the navy, as well as antiaircraft artillery on fleet vessels, would have been manned and equipped with ammunition; and a high state of aircraft readiness would have been in effect.

"None of these conditions," the report said, "was in fact inaugurated or maintained because the respective commanders failed to consult and cooperate in adopting the measures enjoined in the orders given them by the chiefs of the Army and Navy commands in Washington. . . ."

The commission had labored for more than a month. Its members had interviewed behind closed doors nearly 130 witnesses and gathered more than five thousand pages of testimony and documents, and most people were satisfied with the commission's findings, which confirmed suppositions already formed. There were immediate demands that General Short and Admiral Kimmel be court-martialed. They weren't.

The administration's many critics, however, insisted the commission had failed to uncover all the facts and hinted darkly that the investigators had merely contrived to whitewash the real culprits: the president and the responsible members of his cabinet. Particularly vocal were the isolationists, who, bereft of a cause, charged that the Japanese were successful at Pearl Harbor mainly because Roosevelt had weakened the navy by sending fifty destroyers to the British in exchange for bases in the Western Hemisphere.

Colonel McCormick's *Chicago Tribune* accused the president of actually having encouraged the Japanese attack as a means of involving the United States in the war. This was poppycock, but a movement developed in Congress for a more sweeping investigation of the entire affair. Fortunately it was quickly suppressed by the imperatives of fighting what was rapidly becoming a desperate war of survival in a world threatened by the imperialistic ambitions of the Axis powers.

Those ambitions extended to Latin America, whose twenty-one nations were being intensely wooed by Germany and Italy to support their Nazi-Fascist plans for world domination. In Washington, I learned enough about Axis infiltration of Mexico, Argentina, Brazil, and other key countries south of the Rio Grande to cause Colebaugh to send me on a swing through the nether continent early in 1942.

At a conference of the foreign ministers of the Latin American republics, held at Rio de Janeiro in mid-January, the United States pressed for a general rupture of diplomatic relations with the Axis. The "good neighbors" were asked, in effect, to regard Japan's attack against the United States as an aggression committed against all the Americas and to remove from the continent the Axis embassies, consulates, and other institutions known to be centers of hostile intrigue.

Most of the countries rallied behind the once-hated Colossus of the North and declared war against Italy, Germany, and Japan. But Fascist-minded Argentina, with its large Italian and German populations and its burning jealousy of rich Uncle Sam, showed a stubborn reluctance to go that far. Brazil also dragged its feet but in the end was instrumental in rallying support among the conferees behind a compromise resolution recommending severance of relations with the Axis. All proceeded to act on the recommendation except Argentina. If uniformity of policy in the Americas was incomplete, there was nonetheless a large measure of hostility toward the Axis, enough to ensure the industries of the United States the tin, copper, molybdenum, nitrates, and other raw materials they needed to produce the weapons of war.

Soon after my return from South America sometime in April *Collier's* decided it was high time I returned to the Middle East. For once, however, I was reluctant to go back to the war. I had hoped to spend the spring with my family following my long absence from home in 1941.

I temporized, aided in my delaying tactics by the fact that transportation to the Middle East was difficult to obtain. Since Pearl Harbor, the War Department had taken over the airline that carried essential passengers and freight to Egypt, and places for civilians, even war correspondents, were hard to come by.

Management intervened on my behalf, however, and in mid-May I left New York by Clipper to Natal, in Brazil, and from there by military plane to Cairo via Ascension Island, Lagos, in West Africa, thence to Khartoum and up the Nile Valley to Cairo.

43

THE BATTLE FOR
EGYPT RESUMES

Cairo was infernally hot, noisy, smelly, and crowded when I arrived in the late afternoon of May 24, 1942. *Same old Cairo,* I thought as I stepped out of the airline's bus at the curbside entrance to Shepheard's Hotel and was instantly surrounded by several dragomans offering their services as guides.

I was wrong. Cairo had changed, far more than I had ever believed possible.

At the reception desk the clerk said the hotel was "nearly empty," and I had no difficulty reclaiming my former room. The customers at Sam Shalom's bar and in Rossier's dining room were nearly all civilians, British, American, and European. There were a few officers, not headquarters types but men grabbing a few hours' leave before returning to the desert.

It was immediately evident that General Auchinleck had succeeded in ending the peacetime life that Cairo's Colonel Blimps had enjoyed prior to his arrival in July 1941. The Auk had deprived them of their comfortable billets in the capital's smart hotels and obliged them to live in regimental messes. Some, I learned later, were actually living under canvas with their troops in the field. Many more had been sent home.

Moreover, a 10:00 P.M. curfew was in force, and the blackout, for once, was being rigorously respected. There were fewer soldiers in the streets, scotch and gin were rationed, and many of the more popular bars were posted with Out of Bounds signs.

Cairo, by Jove, had gone to war!

This was confirmed the following morning, when I checked in at army public relations. All officers at headquarters now worked a minimum of twelve hours daily with no time off for a "quick one" at nearby bars, the Turf Club, or the Sporting Club. Furthermore, there was no more closing shop at 7:30 or 8:00 P.M. and hurrying away to dinner parties or assignations. Even the censors worked around the clock in twelve-hour shifts.

The change in atmosphere was surprising. But the biggest surprise came when I asked how soon I could go to the front. The reply stunned me: "Can you be ready to leave by eight o'clock tomorrow morning?" That gave me less than twenty-four hours to retrieve my desert gear from storage and buy rations, but I said yes. What a change from the delays and red tape of former times.

Elated, I hurried back to the hotel only to find that the management had lost my kit: camp bed; bedroll; everything except uniforms, which I had with me. But Jones's Emporium was just down the road, and by sundown I had replaced the missing items and shopped for rations: a canned ham; canned potatoes and fruit juices; flea powder. I bought scotch and gin on the lively black market that had sprung up since my previous visit.

This done, I rushed back to GHQ for a briefing on how matters stood in the Western Desert, the disposition of forces, the location of army, corps, and divisional headquarters, and a fill-in on what had happened since last July. Among other things I learned that Auchinleck's command was now as vast as the empire Alexander the Great once ruled. It included Egypt, Palestine, Syria, Iran, Iraq, and Malta, after Tobruk the most bomb-harassed place on earth.

There was no doubt whatever in Cairo that another major and perhaps decisive battle was about to begin in the Western Desert although chairborne experts in Britain and the United States insisted the weather was far too hot for any serious fighting.

During the winter of 1941–1942 Auchinleck's Eighth Army, commanded in the field by General Neil Ritchie, had surged westward from Salum across the scarped deserts of Cyrenaica deep into Libya to beyond Benghazi. But it lost its impetus and ebbed back to El Gazala. That forward thrust had exhausted Ritchie's forces, and the gallant Eighth dug in along a line extanding from El Gazala southward about fifty miles to Bir Hacheim and established what came to be known as the Gazala Line, consisting of a succession of deep minefields enclosed in barbed wire. Meanwhile, Tobruk, the stronghold Rommel coveted in the battle for Egypt, remained securely in British hands.

Just east of the unmanned minefields, at a point where two almost indistinguishable desert tracks met, on desert as smooth as a sow's belly, Auchinleck's sappers drove a stake into the ground and nailed to it a sign reading KNIGHTS-BRIDGE. There they built what is euphemistically called in desert warfare a strongpoint, meaning a boxlike area roughly a mile or two long on each of four sides, garrisoned with troops, equipped with artillery, and supplied with enough ammunition, food, and water to withstand a longish attack from any side.

Knightsbridge Box was the central stronghold of the Gazala Line, a modern application of the old nineteenth-century British square used at Waterloo and Omdurman. Ritchie sealed up his troops within a series of such boxes at El Gazala and Bir Hacheim as well as Knightsbridge. Narrow lanes led into each through their protective mines and wire so that their garrisons could be supplied or reinforced.

Meanwhile, Rommel's forces had halted, too. His panzers, motorized troops, and Italian infantry were also battle-weary after having rolled back the British during the winter campaign and used the early months of 1942 to refit and reorganize. But they had one advantage: They were close to their supply bases and could receive new equipment, ammunition, and fresh troops over the short route across the Mediterranean. It required only some forty-eight hours for a new tank to reach the Afrika Korps from German supply depots in southern Italy or Sicily, whereas it was still at least a six weeks' journey around the Cape of Good Hope from democracy's arsenals to its North African battlefield.

By early May both sides were roughly equal in strength. Auchinleck's demands for more and better weapons before he attempted to comply with Churchill's renewed insistence on a "decisive victory" in the Western Desert had largely been met. The British, however, still had nothing in the way of artillery to match Rommel's deadly eighty-eight millimeter guns although as far as numbers went, they were in better shape than they had ever been. They enjoyed *quantitative* superiority in both tanks and artillery and the ascendancy in the air, which the RAF continued to maintain with the addition of American Boston medium bombers. Along the Gazala Line west of Tobruk, a hundred thousand British troops faced an Axis force composed of fifty thousand Germans and forty thousand Italians.

On the afternoon of May 26 Rommel's forces attacked. "The battle has begun," we were told at a briefing at GHQ that evening, and the next morning, May 27, I was on my way to the front.

The conducting officer who came to fetch me was my old friend Captain Buzz Hawkins. The vehicle he brought, however, was no ramshackle Smoky Joe this time, but a sturdy, Jeep-like truck made in Canada and fully equipped with extra cans of gas, oil, and water. Sand tracks and a shovel were strapped on the top.

We stopped at the Continental to pick up two colleagues, Chester ("Chet") Morrison, of the *Chicago Sun,* whom I hadn't met before, and George Lait, of International News Service, an old friend from my own INS days. We made a joyous party, with Chet reciting ribald limericks he had composed during recent trips to the desert. One went as follows:

There was a young whore from Bagush
Who shat in a pasha's tarboosh,
And as she polished her arsehole
With the little black tassel, she cried
"Down with the Arabs. I'm Joosh. . . ."

Chet was a small, spare man in his mid-forties, who wore his correspondent's uniform so well he was often mistaken for a genuine officer. George was a tall, gangly athletic type and a born collector. His eye caught every bit of metal, paper, wood—anything not native to the desert. He was fond of discarded weapons and owned an amazing collection of enemy pistols, cartridge belts, insignia, a helmet or two, even a machine pistol.

"Watch this guy," Morrison warned Hawkins. "He'll hitch a captured Nazi field gun to our truck if you'll let him. One of these days he'll pick up some bauble the Jerries have left behind and blow us all to hell. . . ."

On the way to Ritchie's camp at Gambut, the road unrolled smoothly under our vehicle. Much of it was the same route I had traveled many times before, and I remembered its scabby surface, its huge patches of rough white stones showing through the worn macadam like enormous sores. The potholes used to bounce you off your seat, broke springs and axles, and slowed the flow of supplies and reinforcements to the front. Now the road might almost have been a highway back home.

I recalled those detours around impassable stretches. Brown dust filled the air so you couldn't breathe and couldn't see and left you caked with a layer of talclike sand. Those detours were rare now, and the broken areas were being repaired by Cape Town blacks of the South African Labor Battalion.

The South African blacks, with some help from Indian labor battalions, kept the lifeline of Britain's desert armies in good repair all the way to the most advanced areas, in some places to within a thousand yards of the enemy. They worked where signs warned against low-flying enemy aircraft.

Westward from Mersa Matruh to Sidi Barrani we averaged an unheard-of forty-five or fifty miles an hour. Hawkins recalled that Smoky Joe had broken down on this particular stretch, and we both remembered how convoys were held up by the roadside waiting for overheated engines to cool or for spare parts to arrive. Up forward, in those not-too-distant days, troops waited for ammunition that never came or for ambulances that arrived too late.

We rarely saw ambulances in the torrid summer of 1941; now they passed us frequently on their way to the front or returned at speed with wounded. Many bore the markings of the American Field Service. There were at least 150 AFS vehicles operating in the Western Desert, substantially supplementing the work of the British and South African medical services.

Apparently, however, neither the searing heat nor the April sandstorms had prevented Auchinleck's engineers from pushing the railroad westward from Mersa Matruh, its previous terminus. We had crossed and recrossed it all the way to Bardia, a good 130 miles west of Matruh. The sappers had laid ties—the British called them sleepers—and rails deep into Libya, across impossible terrain, often under enemy bombing and strafing, leveling the ground as they went with pneumatic rock drills, dynamite, and bulldozers. The building of the railroad almost to the outskirts of Tobruk was one of the epics of the desert war.

The smooth roads with their bypasses and network of connecting tracks across the desert, the extension of the railway, and the speedy removal of the wounded from the battlefield were signs of progress on the all-important Middle Eastern front, source of the oil the Allies needed and the vital territorial link with Russia by way of Iran. But there were other indications of an improved British position. From the Nile Delta westward to Bardia and beyond we passed tidy supply dumps, water stations, munitions depots, emergency repair shops for tanks and vehicles, and airstrips from which the RAF could provide support for infantry or armor.

All was visible evidence of a successful British effort to overcome those deficiencies which had handicapped the army in its duel with a better organized, better equipped enemy the year before. It remained to be seen, however, whether there had been any improvement in the quality of leadership in the field.

On the way to Gambut, a hummocky coastal ridge where General Ritchie had his headquarters, Hawkins explained for my benefit the British order of battle. The Eighth Army was now composed of the XIII Corps, under General W. H. E. ("Strafer") Gott, and the XXX Corps, commanded by General Willoughby Norrie. Gott held the line's northern anchor at Gazala with two infantry divisions, the First South African on his right facing the enemy, and the Fiftieth Division on his left.

Bir Hacheim, the line's southern anchor, was held by a brigade of Free French who liked to be known, Hawkins said, as *les soldats de la France combattante* (the Fighting French), commanded by the energetic General Pierre Koenig, reputedly one of the ablest officers in the field. Between El Gazala and Bir Hacheim ranged Norrie's Thirtieth Corps, which had most of the armor and was positioned to cover the Eighth Army's exposed southern flank or counter any panzer thrusts in the center.

George Lait, who knew more about desert warfare than most conducting officers, had a question. "Why is it," he asked, "that Strafer Gott, one of your best tank commanders, is commanding infantry, while Willoughby Norrie, who has had little experience with armor, is commanding the tanks?" In reply, Hawkins gave him a blank look and a shrug.

So far, except for distant sounds of bombs being dropped west of us and some gunfire from that direction, there had been little evidence that a battle was in progress. But at Gambut, where we arrived May 31, according to my sketchy diary, we were told that the bombing we heard was the pounding Rommel's forces were taking in their attack on the strongpoint called Knightsbridge Box. Rommel's position was described as "becoming critical by the minute." His losses were estimated at "upwards of 260 tanks."

"Seems like a hell of a lot of tanks to me," said George Lait later, when we had reassembled in our truck and headed west again toward Gazala. Hawkins frowned at George's obvious skepticism but made no comment.

Chet was audibly composing a limerick. "Beyond the barbed wire at Salum," he intoned, "General Rommel awaited his doom." But General Ritchie . . ." He gave up.

We pulled up by the roadside behind a pile of rocks for lunch. The driver brewed tea, and we had some of my canned ham, canned fruit, and cookies, after which Hawkins said we couldn't make El Gazala by nightfall, as originally planned, and had better head for Tobruk. "It's on our way, anyhow," he said, "and we can camp there for the night."

Late that afternoon on the outskirts of Tobruk an Arab boy stood by the roadside, offering an egg in a dirty brown hand. The hot wind pressed his loose garment to his body, and he looked like a small, slim statue bronzed by the desert dust. Two girls smaller than he but fuller in their bodies almost to the point of miniature womanliness, clothed in faded purple dresses that covered them from neck to toe, held up canisters of small, bright red tomatoes. Where, we wondered, had they come from? There was no sign of human habitation anywhere.

Their father squatted uninterestedly off the road beside a large shallow basket of eggs. He came suddenly to life, however, when we stopped to bargain with his kids, not for the eggs, which were probably days old and ready to hatch, but for the tomatoes, which looked edible. None of us had enough Arabic to make a deal, but the father had lived at least half his lifetime under Fascist rule and spoke passable pidgin Italian.

The Arab, a thin, hawklike man with a beaked nose who might have been in his mid-forties but looked sixty, contemptuously refused Egyptian paper money for his wares, demanding silver. He said he'd heard the British were retreating. Paper money would be useless when the Italians reoccupied Cyrenaica. He had obviously been listening to Radio Bari, the powerful Fascist propaganda station, which had been predicting the return of il Duce, the self-styled Protector of Islam.

"*Niente carta,*" the Arab kept repeating, "*solo argento* [No paper, only silver]." His meaning was clear enough: Silver coins would retain their value or could be smelted for their metal. We left him with his tomatoes.

"I wonder," mused George Lait, "if Old Spareribs knows something we don't know. . . ."

There was no sign that Old Spareribs, which was how we remembered the Arab thereafter, might be right. Tobruk was still solidly in British hands, and there was no visible or audible indication that the British were cracking under the renewed German attack. On the contrary, the defenders seemed strong and confident. Our planes held the skies; Bostons roared overhead in echeloned triads toward enemy targets; fighters whoomed low, snarling like terriers, westbound to strafe Rommel's troops and tanks; bombers flew high, making white vapor trails across a sky as smooth and brilliant as bright blue tinfoil.

Trucks loaded with ammunition, gasoline, and other supplies moved forward in endless, rarely challenged convoys. The traffic tore the road into sticky ribbons of sun-softened macadam, but work parties repaired them as fast as any serious damage occurred.

Old Spareribs, we decided, had to be wrong about a British retreat.

A refreshing current of sea air caught us as we rounded a turn and sighted Tobruk just beyond a ridge. On seeing it, I experienced a curious sensation of having seen it before although I knew I hadn't. Then I realized why it looked familiar. Cities and towns, like human beings, acquire personalities of their own through struggle and suffering. Physically, and in some indefinable way, Tobruk resembled Madrid or Barcelona or any other bombed, shelled, burned collection of dwellings, shops, and places of worship built by human hands.

Tobruk wasn't much of a town. It was built for a population of from twenty to thirty thousand Italian settlers. Its architecture was that heavy modernistic style Mussolini fancied, and as we dipped down from the escarpment toward the curve of the deep blue harbor that lay between us and the town, it presented a geometry of white, sienna brown, and robin's-egg blue walls tiered up the brown slope of the hill behind it. A minaret, a church steeple, and a tall water tower emerged seemingly unscathed from the mass of flat-roofed masonry.

Men bathed naked in the sun-warmed, shallow water at the harbor's edge. As we drew nearer, we saw many dead vessels in the bay beyond the bathers. Nearest to view, on the bay's eastern margin, were the hulks of Italian merchant ships, two or three of perhaps ten thousand tons each, beached and blasted, their entrails spilling into the sea, their prows protruding absurdly onto the shore.

Now we were on the edge of the shovel-shaped harbor and could see other ships, twenty or more small cutters, which had been sunk by enemy bombers while the British held Tobruk and by the British before the Australians captured the town in January 1941. At the far northwestern end of the bay lay the fused, fire-blackened wreckage of the Italian battleship *San Giorgio,* which the Italians had anchored there as a fortress to protect the town and which the British had sunk at its berth.

While we surveyed this graveyard of dead ships, we had drawn closer to Tobruk itself. Then I saw that the minaret was gnawed, that the church steeple was pocked by shrapnel, and that the shell-bitten water tower stood only by some miracle that defied the laws of physics; its underpinnings had been all but blown away. The tower's tank would never again hold water; a huge ragged patch of blue sky showed through it.

An MP in a red hat with white gauntlets reaching to his elbows directed traffic at the town's gate. Inside Tobruk we made for the central square. En route there was too much for mind to register or eyes to see. Houses that looked whole turned out to be dead and roofless, hollow behind battered walls, with ragged window casements and doorways.

I found it remarkable at first that a town with a physical population of some twenty-five thousand fighting men seemed deserted. Then I realized that the garrison lived underground in the caverns and tunnels the besieged troops had dug.

A few MPs, clean-shaven and ready for inspection, came around a corner, marching in twos toward a building whose lintel identified it, in English, as the POLICE STATION and, in Italian, as the previous headquarters of the CARABINIERI REALE. It was late afternoon now, and Tobruk was changing the guard for the night.

More troops, a few Indians, numerous sturdy-legged South Africans, and a variety of British soldiers, came into view, marching off in squads to relieve the units guarding the perimeter. No one paid any attention to us newcomers seeking water and information about where to camp for the night. There was a camaraderie of aloofness among Tobruk's defenders, as though they felt they belonged to an exclusive other-world society of their own.

In the main hallway of the town hospital South African soldiers slept on the floor and on benches. A few, half awake, regarded us coldly. In a dormitory wing we met four or five Americans of the AFS; Tobruk was the clearinghouse for wounded from the front. The men talked eagerly enough about the job they were doing, about how they lugged between two and three hundred wounded daily to embarkation points along the coast or to Mersa Matruh for the hospital train that would take them to Alexandria. They all were as phenomenally young and dedicated as Ernest Hemingway must have been when he drove an ambulance on the Italian front in World War I.

I asked a South African medic if they'd had many casualties from the nightly bombing. He said they hadn't. Night after night, he said, the enemy dumped tons of bombs on the town without actually killing many people, though many were wounded.

"But," he said, "we've got a lot of bomb-happy ones. They're what makes the bombing hard to take. Some scream and flail about, but others just sit and stare with glazed eyes and won't talk. We move them out as fast as we can. Home to Blighty, most of them . . ."

Tobruk smelled sweetly of the sea and heavily of death and pain and sweat. It smelled, too, of powdery plaster and broken masonry. It had the many smells of old buildings being torn down by wreckers. Its untraveled streets were carpeted with shell fragments, fallen bits of flak, and chunks of bombs.

We filled our water cans from cisterns hung with signs that warned "This Water Must Be Chlorinated" and our canteens from tanks labeled "Potable," wetting the felt coverings of our bottles to keep the brackish contents cool.

At the orange-colored moment before twilight we pulled out of Tobruk proper and headed toward the spot inside the perimeter where we would camp for the night.

It was nearly dark by the time we reached the site Hawkins had chosen on the way in, a sandbagged dugout in a shallow wadi just inside Tobruk's outer defenses. The rough ground where we camped was filthy with the excrement of war. A couple of Tommies who appeared out of nowhere warned us the area was littered with antipersonnel mines and not to go about in the dark.

George, Chet, and I laid our sleeping bags out on our cots outside a two-room sandbagged hutment. An inspection by flashlight had shown the dugout to be uninhabitable, and anyhow we preferred sleeping in the open. There was comfort in being able to look up at the stars, watch them fall in long, luminous arcs, and dream of home, family, and friends.

We slept fully clothed and were awakened about midnight by the bright yellow light of enemy flares. They were accompanied by the familiar whoom-whoom-whoom of Junkers bombers, which made a peculiar arrythmic sound in flight.

The moon hadn't yet appeared, and it was a pitch-black night, which explained the flares, though the enemy must have known, by now, where Tobruk was located. He'd bombed it often enough. Just north of us, where the town lay, searchlights reached upward, their beams desperately scanning the sky. Directly overhead, ack-ack shells burst, hung momentarily like golden balls on a Christmas tree, and died. As they snuffed out, we could hear the sharp corresponding reports of the guns that had fired them.

More ack-ack came into play. The sound was deafening. There was an aurora borealis of light over Tobruk itself, so intense it hurt the eyes. Machine guns fired at the flares, trying to extinguish them, rarely succeeding. Yellow, red, and green tracers streamed toward those yellow lamps the devils had hung in the black sky, and while Tobruk's defenders fired at these, still more flares appeared just to the left of us, due south of the town.

We put on our tin hats. A few machine guns nearby started shooting at the new flares, and we cursed the gunners for giving away their position. It was exactly what the enemy wanted, which was to ascertain where every gun had been relocated after the previous night's action. The planes that night were obviously on a survey flight; plane after plane rode over the town and Tobruk's defensive areas, flying high, beyond the reach of the eager searchlights and the futile flak. Their job was to spot where the guns were emplaced.

Although Tobruk was not the bombers' primary target, the town didn't escape unscathed. The Germans dropped a few bombs before turning away. We could hear and see the resultant explosions that shook the earth under us in a prolonged quivering of earth, sky and air.

The whoom-whoom-whoom came lower and lower, and we knew that this time the bombers were headed in our direction. We waited, tense and expectant. Then the unmistakable sound of falling bombs that began as a whistle and became a scream. Two bombs—five hundred-pounders by the sound of the explosions—threw up enormous geysers of red-yellow flame five hundred yards from us along the perimeter. The bursts were awesomely, hideously beautiful. The spent fragments whistled distantly, and very suddenly the world was quiet.

We slept soundly until daybreak, then hurriedly packed our gear after tea and biscuits. We had a rendezvous with a battle farther west.

44

THE FALL OF TOBRUK

azala was a two-hour trek west from Gambut along the coast road, the Mediterranean innocently blue on our right, the rugged Libyan escarpment ominously brown on our left. We scanned its ridge carefully. Enemy tanks might be moving up there, for Rommel was obviously preparing to attack Tobruk. There were no telltale trails of dust on the ridge, but we proceeded cautiously nevertheless, pausing whenever we heard firing to try to gauge direction and distance. The gunfire, we decided, originated well to the south of us, probably in the vicinity of Knightsbridge Box, and was carried on the light offshore wind like the rolling, faraway thunder of a summer storm.

Knightsbridge held the key to Rommel's success or failure. If he broke through there and overcame the British defenses at intervening minefields around El Adem and Acroma, Tobruk would be at his mercy. The "box" at Knightsbridge was garrisoned by the Coldstream Guards, one of Britain's finest units, and it was against them that Rommel, after failing in his first attempt to flank Bir Hacheim, hurled his panzers. But Knightsbridge held.

The "box" was still resisting when we arrived at General Daniel Pienaar's headquarters in his iron-roofed dugout high on the cliffs at Gazala. From his digs Pienaar had a view of the sea framed in a rear "window," and from his "front porch," a small area enclosed almost head-high with sandbags, he could look southward and westward across the desert where German armor and Italian infantry were hiding.

"Old Danny," as he was affectionately known to his South African troops, wasn't old at all. He was a lean gray wolf of a man in his late forties with ears bigger than Clark Gable's and blue-gray eyes. A commander often doesn't deserve the antipathy of his men. It seldom happens, however, that he doesn't merit their devotion. To his soldiers of the First South African Division, Danny Pienaar was *bobaas,* Afrikaans for the "tops" in bosses. They loved him because he never asked them to do anything he wouldn't do himself and never sacrificed men when guns could do the job for them.

Pienaar, in shorts and bush jacket, had the muscled, skinny legs of a distance runner and was deeply tanned wherever he was exposed to the sun. His nose was large, but his face improved enormously when he smiled. When he inclined his head forward, urged his bushy eyebrows upward, and crinkled his wide brow, he looked like a mischievous satyr. His speech had the precise quality of a man who had thought out what he was going to say before he said it, and it bore an unmistakable Afrikaaner accent, for Danny Pienaar was a Boer. When he was five years old he was in a British concentration camp while his father and thirteen-year-old brother were fighting the British. "And a bloody good go we gave them, too," he said.

Pienaar's origins and the shape of his career—he had risen to general from the ranks, a remarkable achievement in any army—explained much about his nearness to his men. He had what in a politician would be called the common touch. The events of his life, he said, had been "thrice disturbed by war: My childhood was wrecked by the Boer War, my young manhood by World War I, and my middle age by this resumption of the last one.

"But you chaps," he said, interrupting himself, "haven't come up here to listen to the story of my life. If it's a battle you want to see, better head back toward Tobruk, then down to around El Adem. Plenty of shooting there."

Morrison and I were so taken with this unusual man that we decided to spend the rest of the day with him while Lait, needing spot news for his INS wires, excused himself and went off to El Adem with Hawkins, promising to return to pick us up before nightfall. The British-oriented corps of correspondents had neglected Pienaar, and it was evident he wanted to talk. Chet and I stayed for a hot lunch in the officers' mess and more talk with Old Danny. It proved to be an instructive afternoon, during which we learned a great deal about the art of desert warfare as practiced by the British, things we were never told at press briefings back in Cairo. In the process Pienaar unwittingly demolished my illusion that the British could successfully defend the Gazala Line.

Pienaar, we discovered, was, among other attributes, a first-class, grade-A hater. An aptitude for hatred was rare in the Libyan graveyard of British generals. Other Eighth Army officers hated, but they were rather polite about it, always referring to the Germans as Jerry or simply "he" or the enemy. Pienaar called them Huns or the Boche, or those "bastards the Nazis." He hated well and directly and distributed his intense dislike almost equally among Germans and Italians, not because they were Germans or Italians but because they were Nazis and Fascists and "allied," he said, "in an ignoble mission." It rankled, of course, that they had interfered with what might have been a pleasant squirehood in the hills about Pretoria, but that was not the only reason for Pienaar's eloquent loathing of his Axis enemies.

"They've stopped the clock of progress in man's evolution toward a good life in a good world," he said. "The Nazis and the Fascists must be destroyed before they destroy us. Let me put it this way. If some animals in your herd become infected with, say, hoof-and-mouth disease, you destroy them and all other cattle with which they've come into contact. You may kill a few healthy ones in the process, of course. That's regrettable. But only by destroying the infected cattle can you save your own herd and your neighbors' herds."

Pienaar's animosity toward his enemies wasn't merely verbal. It expressed itself in many ways. One was to prevent the Axis troops, especially the Germans, from enjoying the nightly programs of their beloved Lili Marlene. She sang an ethereal tune called "Marlene," her theme song, with lyrics cribbed from a poem composed by Nils Andersen, a descendant of the Hans Christian Andersen who wrote fairy tales, and it was first heard in Belgium early in the war. It was as popular with the Desert Rats of the Eighth Army as it was with the Germans, and it was actually a haunting, sentimental melody evocative of home and loved ones.

Marlene sang in a fruity, flute-toned voice that reminded me of Lucienne Boyer, who used to sing in a lesbian Paris nightclub called Chez Elle back in the days when Paris was still the enchanting City of Light. The song was a great morale builder, but not in any sector opposite Old Danny's guns. The moment Lili came on the air, and at twilight every field radio in the desert was tuned to her transmission from Berlin, Pienaar began shelling enemy positions. "It's a fine tune," he said, "but I'm damned if the Huns are going to enjoy it." Incidentally many of Pienaar's guns were pieces captured from the Italians, and he took perverse pleasure in shelling them and their German allies with their own weapons and ammunition, although every third Italian shell, he noted, turned out a dud. "Apparently," he said, "some workers in the Duce's arsenals don't want him to win the war. . . ."

Essentially an artilleryman, Pienaar was a master of the art of deploying his guns where they would do the most damage yet remain comparatively safe from enemy counterfire. His artillery was expertly emplaced and artfully camouflaged, and his methods, we learned later, were being studied in London, Moscow, and Washington.

Pienaar believed that enemy tanks could not be beaten by other tanks with inferior firepower, which happened to be a shortcoming of British and American tanks. The newly arrived Grants, he said, were fine tanks, armed with a seventy-five-millimeter gun.

"But the gun," he pointed out, "is mounted on one side, below the turret, and is limited in its command of terrain. German tanks mount an eighty-eight-millimeter gun in their turrets and cover a three-hundred-and-sixty-degree range laterally and nearly one hundred and eighty degrees longitudinally. The

Grant must turn to face its opponent, offering a bigger target, and can cover only a lateral hundred-and-eighty-degree area, if that."

The best weapon against tanks, Pienaar insisted, was a self-propelled or motor-drawn gun of heavier caliber than the cannon carried by the enemy.

"That's how the Boche has been fighting us," he said. "He uses his tanks mainly against our soft-skinned stuff—armored cars, Bren gun carriers, vehicles—and whips our tanks with antitank guns of a progressively heavier caliber than ours. He's been mauling us with his eighty-eights, bigger than anything we've got. Give me a good self-propelled gun—never mind the armor—and I'll chase Rommel out of Libya."

Pienaar's lecture on how to fight the "Hun" was rudely interrupted by the unmistakable whistle of incoming shell fire. "That would be Tmimi Tom," the general said, glancing at his watch. "Four o'clock. Right on time."

We had been sitting outside Pienaar's dugout, Chet and I on folding campstools, the general on one of those chair canes British sportsmen used for watching polo matches and field games. When the first shell burst somewhere on the outer edge of the Gazala Box, we withdrew into the general's little cave; it lacked only potted geraniums to make it homey. Inside, we had gins with Rose's lime juice, and our genial host told us about Tmimi Tom.

Tmimi was a German coastal base about fifteen or twenty miles west of Gazala, where the enemy had a mobile long-range fieldpiece that fired at Pienaar's area half a dozen times every day. It rarely did much damage and was more of a nuisance than a danger, "but it's best to be under cover when Tmimi Tom speaks," he said.

Inside, while Tmimi Tom continued speaking in a shrill voice, Pienaar resumed what had become a revealing (and eventually prophetic) critique of how the battle for Egypt was being fought by the British. He was scornful of the minefields and boxes Ritchie and his generals had created. They were reflective, he said, of "a purely defensive mentality."

"Minefields are all right," Pienaar said, "if they are manned—that is, if you can keep them under artillery fire when the enemy runs onto them. Otherwise the enemy's sappers can move into your minefields with magnetic locators, lift up the mines, cart them away or toss them aside, and clear a path through them for their tanks and infantry. Alternatively, the enemy can explode the mines by bombing the fields from the air or shelling them. Anyhow, they're not an impenetrable obstacle. It's dangerous to rely on them overmuch as we seem to be doing. . . ."

Pienaar confirmed our impression that Tobruk was about to be attacked in force and surprised us by expressing doubt that the fortress, vital to the British defense of Egypt, could hold out. At the time Tobruk was garrisoned by the Second South African Division—about fourteen thousand men commanded by General H. B. Klopper—and roughly an equal number of British troops, mostly tired soldiers from various units who'd been fighting a long time.

"Klopper can hold Tobruk," Pienaar said, "if he is reinforced and if his communications aren't severed, if Knightsbridge resists, if . . . there are many ifs in this battle, too many. . . ." He was gloomy about his own chances of holding Gazala, and we were about to pursue the subject with him when Hawkins returned with Lait.

We said good-bye to Old Danny and backtracked east to Acroma, where George could write his story and send it on to Cairo with a motorcycle dispatch rider for censorship before transmission to New York. At Acroma we joined forces with two British correspondents, Alan Moorehead of the *Daily Express* and Alex Clifford of the *Daily Mail.* Their conducting officer was Captain Kim Mundy, one of the best in the tedious business of shepherding journalists about the battlefields.

Kim, an unflappable officer of medium height and few words, was known to reporters as the Flying Tank because he had served in the RAF in the First World War and had joined the Tank Corps in the Second. Too old for active duty, he was assigned to the care, feeding, and transportation of reporters and was famous in the desert for never having lost a correspondent and for his skill in converting bully beef, canned potatoes, onions, and whatever else he could scrounge into the finest curry ever served in war or peace.

We camped at Acroma that night and spent most of the next day touring the line, trying to make some sense out of what was happening. There was heavy gunfire from the German side, each salvo producing thunderous explosions. At times shells fell so close we thought our little convoy—Kim Mundy's vehicle in the lead, ours directly behind, and a third bringing up the rear with provisions—was being bracketed by Rommel's artillery.

Gradually a picture of how matters stood emerged. The Germans had been pouring shells onto the minefields and had succeeded in destroying most of them between Gazala and Bir Hacheim. They were now apparently regrouping for a major attack behind a defensive line of their own roughly parallel to ours. The British faced, therefore, a virtual ring of steel composed of tanks and those lethal eighty-eight-millimeter guns the Germans used so well. The German forces had been thwarted at Knightsbridge but obviously were far from defeated.

Late that afternoon, during a lull in the battle, we came upon a brigade of the Fourth Armored Division drawn up on the flat desert behind a high ridge beyond which, no more than a thousand yards away, lay the German armor. An observer reported by field telephone that the enemy's tanks seemed to be massing preparatory to an attempt to outflank the Fourth Division by moving south, the direction in which their vehicles were pointed.

Meanwhile, mobile British artillery was circling behind us and speeding along to counter the anticipated German maneuver. The colonel in command of the Fourth Division's brigade, composed mostly of Grants and Matildas, had deployed his tanks in battle formation, and I asked him if he intended to attack when the artillery was in position.

"No," he said. "We're waiting for Jerry to shoot first. We expect to make contact at about six-thirty tonight. But we're ready for him. . . ."

The colonel was obviously ready to give battle. Why didn't he strike first instead of leaving the initiative to the enemy? "We have our orders," he replied curtly, in upper-class tones that said, "Mind your own business, little man." Someone else, way back there beyond the sounds of gunfire and the screams of men roasting in burning tanks, had decided when and how the pieces in the deadly game of chess should be moved.

Along the telephone lines laid on the desert floor connecting headquarters with hundreds of subheadquarters and observation posts, orders and replies were passing back and forth—in code. The Germans, meanwhile, were barking out their commands on shortwave radios in the clear and wasting no time. Our side was still playing the game the old way, "by the book," sending and receiving messages in complicated, ever-changing codes, using the radio only in emergencies.

While British signalmen coded and decoded messages, the Germans, apparently confident that even if their signals were intercepted, their opponents wouldn't have time to react effectively, shifted their pieces on the battlefield with dazzling skill and rapidity.

The mirages that had baffled us all day subsided with the setting sun, and we prudently pulled out of what soon would become a killing ground for tanks and men. We headed for El Adem, south of Tobruk, and made camp on the rugged escarpment overlooking the coastal plain. Below us, in the desert behind a minefield, were the vehicles of the rear elements of an Indian division of Gurkhas.

We camped close to a regimental headquarters where a pipy, mustachioed British colonel assured us there was positively no enemy within miles and "guaranteed" us "a good night's undisturbed sleep."

I chose a waist-deep trench someone else had dug before me, long enough for my camp bed but too narrow for my taste; I hated sleeping in a grave. I widened it somewhat and cleaned it out with a pick and shovel, poured half my gallon ration of brownish water into a basin, shaved, and enjoyed a reasonably thorough washup.

All looked forward to a good supper. Kim Mundy had promised us his curried bully and a special treat, *fried* potatoes.

By the time we had supped on Kim's incredibly hot curry, only a faint orange glow showed in the west, and an unusually cold wind was blowing inland from the sea. The dew was heavy enough to qualify as a light rain.

Nightfall was sudden, starless and black, and at that precise moment, west of us at a distance of two or three miles from our ridge, a column of flame shot skyward and burned with undiminished intensity like the distant torch of an exploded gas or oil well. Moments later we heard the muted sound of the explosion that had caused it.

Then to the right of it, and closer, spouted another identical pillar of fire, followed by others in rapid succession. We counted seven, each nearer, each followed by a corresponding contrapuntal explosion. We couldn't make out what had caused them, and we huddled, talking in low, almost awed tones.

"Looks like a stick of bombs," someone said.

"Impossible," responded a gravelly voice instantly recognizable as belonging to George Lait. "We'd have heard the planes."

Finally, it dawned on us that those pillars of fire were trucks burning, vehicles of the Indian division which had blundered onto our own mines. Mundy and Hawkins hurried to regimental headquarters for an explanation. They returned to say the pipy colonel and his vehicles—a communications van and a couple of trucks—had decamped.

Meanwhile, the Indian division was in full retreat. We couldn't see them clearly, but we could hear their vehicles speeding eastward through the night, trailing grayish, faintly visible clouds of dust. "Maybe," muttered Lait, "that son of Allah knew what he was talking about." He meant Old Spareribs, the Sanusi tribesman on the road to Tobruk who had refused paper money for his tomatoes because he had heard the British were retreating from Cyrenaica.

During the thirty minutes or so that followed the first explosion, as darkness thickened into an almost gelatinous blackness, menacing and impenetrable, we witnessed the blind headlong flight of troops in retreat, and we became a part of it. The rest of the night was one of sounds and smells, for we could see nothing. There was no moon.

Purely by touch we gathered up equipment, piled it into our vehicles, and drove off, Mundy's truck in the lead, ours directly behind it. We almost ran into Kim's vehicle several times. He was steering by compass toward the road that led to Sidi Rezegh, where it joined the coast road leading to Alexandria.

Soon after we started, I glimpsed a wire fence, then heard wood splintering under the wheels of our truck. We were in soft ground, and I feared we were in a minefield. We stopped and peered about but saw nothing. I stepped down from the truck and on hands and knees crawled cautiously about in the vicinity of our vehicle. My hand encountered a wooden upright. Exploring it, I realized with horror that it was a cross. We had stumbled into a frontline cemetery. Broken wooden crosses lay under the wheels, and the truck bringing up the rear was blundering into other graves.

Our vehicles struggled out of the soft mounds of sand to more solid ground in three or four frenzied minutes that seemed hours, and we soon reached a crossroads. One led north to Tobruk; the other, east across the desert to Salum and Alexandria.

What proved to be the final siege of Tobruk, the citadel that had withstood many sieges, was under way. Axis bombers were dropping flares, and from the citadel's entire perimeter tracer bullets were arching upward in the familiar pyrotechnics of antiaircraft guns trying to extinguish the enemy's airborne torches. The noise the guns made mingled with the explosions of the Luftwaffe's bombs in one continuous roar that rendered mental processes impossible. Instinctively we turned east, away from the fury raging in and around Tobruk.

An hour or more later we found ourselves in the midst of growling, whimpering, grinding trucks also headed east; they were the vehicles of the retreating Gurkhas. They halted, and so did we. With motors switched off, there was an awesome silence, broken only by the sounds about us of picks and shovels, the chunk-chunk of hundreds of men digging desperately into the ground, like the sounds ants might make if magnified several million times in an enormous chorus of systematic labor.

We had no idea where we were. Although we realized that if the enemy were advancing in our direction, we'd be bombed and strafed when the sun rose, we all were cold and wet with dew and weary to the point of collapse. Buzz Hawkins decided we should camp where we were within reach of help, if needed, from the Gurkhas. In the melee after leaving the cemetery we had become separated from Kim Mundy's party and were very conscious of being on our own in a potentially dangerous situation.

Without bothering to unfold our camp beds, we laid our bedrolls out on the ground, and Hawkins set watches. I drew the first watch, and soon after the others were asleep, I spotted, west of us and off to my left, a green flare. I took it to be some sort of signal, for it was answered immediately by a yellow flare from a moving object to my right. When a red light appeared between the two, I became alarmed and quietly shook George Lait awake. Together we studied the lights and decided they were not Very lights, which would have shot high into the air, whereas those we saw were fairly close to the ground and constant, though they flickered in the distance.

"Thousand yards, maybe," said the knowledgeable Lait. "I say they're German tanks snooping around out there."

We debated briefly whether to wake up the others and take off but decided to wait and see what developed.

"Anyhow, better stay here," George said. "There may be mines east of us. Get some sleep, and I'll rouse everybody if those lights come any closer."

North of us Tobruk was still being bombarded; but the wind was blowing in the opposite direction, and we couldn't hear the explosions. However, we could see the tracers climbing skyward in rapid red, green, and orange pulses and the geometry of intersecting angles made by the slender beams of the searchlights.

As I squirmed into my sleeping bag, shoes and all, I saw there were now four flares on the horizon, probing the darkness this way and that, but receding, not advancing. They were at least a mile or two away. There would be plenty of time to cut and run if they advanced in our direction.

Morning came with a slap of sunlight in our faces, and we found we had the field to ourselves. The Gurkhas had departed during the night, probably alarmed by the flares George and I had seen. There were distant sounds of firing west of us; otherwise the surrounding terrain was as quiet and desolate as a midwestern dust bowl.

We breakfasted on canned fruit, hardtack, and tea and returned to the press camp at Ritchie's headquarters at Gambut. There we were told that the previous night's retreat had been merely "a bit of a flap." The Gurkhas apparently had mistaken an enemy probe to ascertain our strength between Gazala and Tobruk in the Acroma-El Adem sector for an impending attack and had fled.

We were outraged. The omniscient colonel, the one with the pipe and the mustache, whose job it was to know what was happening on his front, should have known that enemy columns were practically under his nose. He had assured us that there were no enemy in our area and had even guaranteed us a good night's sleep. Well, there had been enemy enough around to scare the hell out of the normally unflappable Gurkhas and to cause the colonel himself to decamp hastily without informing us he was leaving.

Something was terribly wrong. There seemed to be an appalling lack of intelligence and coordination of information up forward and, perhaps, poor generalship. The morning after the "flap" we saw the burned-out vehicles of the trucks which had run onto our own mines in their flight. Men had died in them. Obviously their commanders hadn't been given maps indicating the passages through the minefields. "Incredible," said Hawkins as we came away from Gambut that morning.

There was worse in store. On the morning of June 6 Rommel launched an armored division against the British left flank. The British tanks, lighter than Rommel's Mark IVs, found themselves seriously outgunned, and it was only by throwing in all available reserves that General Norrie was able to repel the attack and force the Germans back west of the minefields. Another attack the next day, this time by German infantry with tanks waiting in support, was also repelled. But the British sustained serious losses in men, armor, and vehicles. The battlefield was littered with burned-out tanks, armored cars, Bren gun carriers, and trucks—a junkman's paradise strewn with hundreds of thousands of tons of scrap metal.

Rommel's attention then again turned south toward Bir Hacheim. He concentrated his assault on Bir Hacheim with new intensity. Attacks by tanks and infantry were supported by a heavy artillery bombardment and by persistent pounding by Stuka dive bombers.

British forces drove south from Knightsbridge in an attempt to relieve the pressure on General Koenig's garrison, but not in sufficient strength to dislodge the attackers. After a gallant struggle the bulk of the Free French garrison was successfully withdrawn during the night of June ii, and a major outpost fell to the enemy.

This was a critical development. Bir Hacheim had occupied a substantial portion of Axis strength in armor and artillery as well as foot soldiers. Now Rommel was able to throw his entire weight in a concentrated blow against the main British positions covering the Tobruk area—namely, what remained of the minefields that lay between him and the fortress at El Adem, Acroma, and Knightsbridge.

For the next several days the battle roared furiously, a confusion of burning tanks and vehicles, blowing sand, exploding mines, and deadly shell fire.

British armor repeatedly moved forward to try to halt or slow down Rommel's renewed drive to the coast but ran into concealed German eighty-eight-millimeter guns or heavy Mark III and Mark IV tanks, against which their Valentines and Honeys were useless. Many ran out of fuel and had to be abandoned.

Everywhere on the Libyan escarpment we found battle-weary troops and rumors that the Germans had dropped parachutists. They hadn't, but the effect was the same: panic and fear among the defenders. At Fort Capuzzo, on our way to Halfaya, where we intended to descend the escarpment to the coast road, then turn west toward Tobruk, we found the commissary giving away rum, canned goods, all its stores. Beer, we noticed, was being loaded onto trucks, but all other supplies, including ammunition and weapons, were being destroyed or abandoned. We took on rations, gasoline, and water and continued to Upper Salum, where we halted beyond the old Egyptian barracks to lunch on sardines before descending to the road at Halfaya.

At the top of Halfaya Pass, before descending to the coast road, we heard an explosion behind us and turned to look back in its direction. We saw a straight, tall column of black smoke rising about a thousand yards off. A Honey tank had scored a direct hit on a German armored car that had somehow strayed from its unit. Its funeral pyre accentuated the lonely horror of the scene framed by a tangle of barbed wire and the tall steel stakes that held it protruding askew from the rocky soil.

The wire was part of the fence that Mussolini had built from Salum southward along the entire Libyan-Egyptian frontier, a monumental piece of expensive and utterly futile Fascist engineering. British sappers had long since pierced it at several places.

It was while we prepared to skirt the wire's northern end that Chet Morrison announced he had completed his Ritchie limerick. We stopped at the top of the pass and gave Chet our undivided attention as he recited:

> Beyond the barbed wire at Salum,
> General Rommel awaited his doom.
> But General Ritchie,
> The son of a bitchie,
> Was retreating right back to Faiyum.

It wasn't one of Chet's best efforts, perhaps, but the limerick came closer to the truth than any of us realized at the time. What we saw thereafter was the disorganized retreat of a gallant but thoroughly beaten Eighth Army, defeated by the tactics which General Pienaar had anticipated in his talk with Morrison and me a few days before.

Determined to reach Tobruk, we descended the escarpment at Halfaya and found ourselves bucking a retreating tide of men and machines. We had been told earlier that preparations were being made to defend Tobruk and that the fortress could hold out "for months if necessary" as it had before. But Tobruk was not destined to repeat its previous triumphs.

The bulk of Rommel's forces had been driving northward in a determined effort to break through to the coast beyond Acroma, a few miles southwest of Tobruk. The violence of the assault had forced the British to give ground in the Knightsbridge area, and on June 13 General Ritchie, in an attempt to redress the situation, had broken out to the southwest with a strong tank force to strike at Rommel's flank. The results had proved disastrous.

Rommel succeeded in drawing the British tanks into an ambush. Of the 300 British tanks in action that day, 230 were lost with no corresponding damage to the enemy. It was the heaviest blow yet struck by Rommel. To add to the gravity of the defeat, those British tanks which managed to escape found themselves separated into two columns, and their inability to effect a junction made it possible for a strong German force to defeat each of them separately.

June 13 had marked the turning point of the campaign. The heavy reduction in British striking power enabled Rommel to break through to the coast at a point just west of Tobruk. Only a stubborn defensive action at Acroma by British infantry supported by armor had made possible the withdrawal of Pienaar's forces from Gazala with minimal losses.

On June 15 the Axis forces had cut the coastal road west of Tobruk and reached the sea. The British were forced back to a defensive line behind El Adem and Acroma, where their stand was of short duration. Having broken through to the coast, Rommel wheeled in an effort to encircle Tobruk and attack it from the east. In four days of heavy fighting that began on June 14, the British succeeded—at great cost in men and armor—in barring the way, but once again the pressure had proved too great for them.

On June 18 the British abandoned El Adem, and it was evident that their main force now had to withdraw all the way back to the Egyptian frontier to avoid encirclement. Involved in this prospect was the problem of whether to abandon Tobruk or try to repeat its successful defense of the year before. It was decided to hold the fortress with the Second South African Division under General Klopper, whatever other British forces remained inside the perimeter, and with about seventy tanks. Meanwhile, the Eighth Army withdrew eastward to the Egyptian frontier.

The delay in reaching the final decision about holding Tobruk probably helped prevent its defenses from being put in adequate shape. In any case the final assault came before they were fully consolidated and before the minefield gaps through which the British retreated had been completely closed. At daybreak on June 20 Rommel launched a heavy assault under cover of a bombardment from heavy guns and dive bombers.

At that moment we were on the coast road just beyond Lower Salum, where we found the road to Gambut blocked. It had been closed by sappers with mines two hours earlier, when eleven enemy tanks and a number of armored cars were reported headed that way. We turned back as ordered and became part of the bumper-to-bumper eastward retreat toward Alexandria.

Four hours later Tobruk fell. At field camps, in officers' messes, wherever sundown found us, we heard nightly broadcasts by the BBC assuring us that we were really winning, not losing, the war. The night we learned of Tobruk's fall, we heard London broadcasting that the fortress was still resisting. BBC maintained this fiction for fully two days. In the noise of racing motors and clattering vehicles in disorderly retreat it was almost too much to bear the unctuous blather being broadcast from London.

45

RETREAT TO EL ALAMEIN

We had joined the retreating forces somewhere east of Gambut. Our truck became merely another vehicle among the hundreds of others crawling eastward, noses to tailboards, through clouds of lung-stinging, choking, blinding desert dust, enveloped in noise and exhaust fumes. Defeat hung in the air like a pall of smoke over a burning town; we could smell it and taste it and feel it all around us. Every mile was another episode in a seemingly endless nightmare of blurred images.

The rules governing military traffic no longer held. Trucks moved two abreast, sometimes three. Many, trying to pass in their haste to reach safety from a pursuing enemy, slipped off the road and became stuck in the sand. Road repairers' tools lay scattered about along the verges. I remembered Wavell's promise—"Rommel will never reach the Nile"—and silently prayed he would be proved right. If he wasn't, the British had lost not only Tobruk but Egypt and, perhaps, the war itself. The dismal possibility kept running through my mind as we reached Sidi Barrani, where we stopped for gas, water, rations, and whatever information we could get about what was happening.

We drove on through the night, Hawkins and his driver taking turns at the wheel, and on the morning of June 22 reached Mersa Matruh. There we found no indication that General Ritchie, who was still in command of the disintegrating Eighth Army, intended to reactivate the old fortifications from which Wavell had sprung his victorious drive against the Italians in 1940. The place wore an air of abandoned neglect: Its deep tank traps were nearly filled with drifting sand; wire fences sagged; empty beer cans and tins that had held gasoline and water littered open spaces. We pushed on and at nightfall camped in the desert, well off the road, but within sound of the growling, groaning vehicles that continued moving through the starlit night.

The next morning, at the roadside encampment of a Coldstream Guards unit that had fought its way out of Tobruk, a fellow officer told Hawkins that Rommel probably would be coming on fast. The Desert Fox, he said, had apparently won the desert war's richest prize: some twenty-eight thousand prisoners—General Klopper's entire Second South African Division plus about ten thousand other British troops—and enormous quantities of everything he needed to reequip his own depleted forces with which to resume his drive to the Nile Delta.

At Tobruk the end had come too quickly for General Klopper to complete demolitions, and Rommel found stacks of canned food, beer, and gasoline, mountains of medical supplies, and supply huts bursting with flour, cigarettes, khaki clothing, even whiskey. More important, he acquired a fleet of trucks, plus tanks and guns in working condition or easily repairable, and whatever ammunition he required to use the weapons against their former owners.

When the fighting began in late May, Rommel's forces were roughly equal to those of the British, perhaps even slightly inferior numerically. But with the fall of Tobruk he was twice as strong. He still had eight divisions, approximately a hundred thousand men, and about a hundred tanks. The British now had no more than four divisions and very little in the way of battleworthy armor. We saw few tanks during the nightmarish retreat; we saw, instead, a disorganized army composed of dispirited troops glassy-eyed with fatigue.

The guardsman made what we interpreted as an educated guess that Rommel would move swiftly to capitalize on his victory at Tobruk, for which, incidentally, Hitler was to award him a field marshal's baton. The guards' officer's conjecture proved correct. With characteristic speed Rommel resumed his pursuit of the Eighth Army at daybreak on June 23, three days after storming into the fortress town. He left several battalions of Italians there to reopen the port and look after the prisoners, and he set out in force to conquer Egypt, key to control of the entire Middle East. Before departing, however, Rommel took time to review and address his prisoners. He assembled them in Tobruk's central square and praised them as "fine troops led by goats."

Bardia, Salum, and Halfaya fell to Rommel without a fight. The way to the Nile Delta, Alexandria, and Cairo lay open. On the morning of June 25, less than a week after taking Tobruk, Marshal Rommel, riding atop his Mammoth, a captured British tank, reached the outskirts of Mersa Matruh, more than two hundred miles east of his starting point. The performance astonished the British and caught them unprepared to make an organized stand.

Rommel's forces rode mostly in British trucks, and many of his troops wore British clothing. Their tanks, with their distinctive black-and-white crosses, were mainly German and included a number of newly arrived Mark

IVFs mounting long seventy-five-millimeter guns capable of piercing even heavy armor. A goodly number of the "German" tanks, however, had been manufactured in England and the United States, part of the booty taken at Tobruk.

By June 25, the day Rommel arrived before Mersa Matruh, Auchinleck had dismissed Ritchie and personally assumed command of the Eighth Army along with responsibility for whatever new disasters might befall it. The Auk had hoped that the difficulties of the many miles of intervening desert would delay Rommel sufficiently to give the Eighth Army a breathing space of at least ten days, time enough to reorganize a defensive line. But it was a cardinal principle of Rommel's never to allow his opponent a respite. The only serious resistance he encountered at Matruh when he launched his attack the next day came from General Bernard Cyril Freyberg's New Zealand Division. It had been rushed to the front from the Nile Delta, where it had been resting and refitting after its fierce but losing battles in Greece and Crete.

Schooled in Freyberg's gospel of the bayonet charge, the New Zealanders made a bloody fight of it against Rommel's infantry; but bayonets could not break the tanks of the Panzerarmee, and they were forced back in the wake of other British troops. Mersa Matruh fell, and in quick succession so did Bagush, Fuka, and Daba with yet more British losses in men, vehicles, and guns as well as valuable stores of gasoline, food, and ammunition for Rommel's British weapons.

The time Auchinleck had needed to reorganize and rally his army was denied him, but reinforcements had begun to arrive. They included Australian troops fresh from the transports that had landed them at Suez and planes and tanks from America.

By sundown, June 29, when my friends and I arrived in jittery Alexandria and checked into the Cecil Hotel, Auchinleck had gathered all his forces for a stand on a line extending from the sea at El Alamein southward about forty miles to the edge of the Qattara Depression, a torrid wasteland of salt marshes and quicksands inhospitable to man or beast and impassable to vehicles, wheeled or tracked.

The El Alamein Line, barely 150 miles from Cairo and only some 60 miles from Alexandria, was the last natural barrier of rocky ridges interspersed with irregular desert areas along which Auchinleck could possibly prevent an Axis sweep into the green flatlands of the Nile Delta. Here the coastal corridor narrowed to a bottleneck between the sea and the treacherous Qattara marshlands, and here the Auk made his last-ditch stand to save not only Egypt, strategically important though it was, but the Eighth Army. If he lost Egypt, he could presumably continue fighting elsewhere—in the Nile Valley, in the Sudan—but if he lost the army, he would have lost everything.

Auchinleck hurriedly mined the line's desert areas and hastily fortified the ridges from Tel el Eisa in the north to Bab el Qattara in the south and in between the Miteiriya Ridge and the central Ruweisat Ridge, the most important of several others. This time, furthermore, every minefield was covered by artillery positioned to keep Rommel in a straitjacket of shell fire whenever he moved. Auchinleck, like Pienaar, hated boxes and made sure such defensive contrivances could be turned into traps for the enemy.

Among the many other changes he made, the commander in chief joined his troops in the field. In a sliding, melting world of rout and defeatism, Auchinleck stood a lonely and defiant figure, a rock in a turbulent stream, and the troops rallied to him.

I didn't know at the time, but learned later, that while the race to El Alamein between Panzerarmee Afrika and the retreating wreckage of two British corps was still going on, Auchinleck left his headquarters in the delta, and drove back toward the enemy, against the tide of defeat, to Daba, on the coast road. First he supervised the destruction of the immense stores at Daba; then he went and stood alongside the coast road leading into El Alamein. "He wanted to see for himself," a bearded young tank captain told me, "the general state of morale and discipline of his troops. What he saw shook him."

And what Auchinleck, standing bareheaded in the sand, saw by the road-side was what I had seen during nearly a month's wanderings at the front: the profiles of heavily laden British trucks; disabled tanks on transporters; supply trucks; troop carriers; towed bombers without wings looking like maimed prehistoric insects; guns; and more trucks, loaded not with men and valuable weapons but with stores, mostly beer and cigarettes and furnishings for officers' messes.

What he saw was more like a gigantic circus on the move to its next performance than an army, its vehicles wearing the yellow-brown patina of the desert's dust under sunshine enough to warm a travel agent's heart, against a backdrop of white dunes, beyond them the cobalt blue waters of the Mediterranean. As a scene of disastrous defeat it was superb but incongruous, utterly lacking in the characteristics of historic defeats: the starvation and frostbite of Napoleon's withdrawal from Moscow or Washington's ragged troops at Valley Forge. The faces of these soldiers were brown as the hardtack they lived on, visages powdered thickly with dust, frozen in weariness.

Angered by what he saw during his roadside vigil, Auchinleck resolved to strip the army down to what it needed for action and, most of all, to establish personal contact with his men. Standing hatless in his car, he chatted with as many as he could, from as many different formations as possible—British, Indians, South Africans. Big and square-jawed, he looked the fighter that he was, and the men could tell from the way he spoke to them that he was "a regular chap—no bullshit about him." The Auk could look severe, and often was, but he had great charm and innate kindness. The men liked what they heard and saw.

Meanwhile, the Afrika Korps toiled on through the heat and the clouds of sand, its troops wanting sleep and probably dreaming of swimming in the creamy little breakers that curled endlessly along the Egyptian shoreline. Over them, however, the sky belonged to the RAF and the newly arrived American air force, whose planes were dropping a moving curtain of bombs between the Eighth Army and its pursuers. With its gasoline and ammunition trucks burning, and its men physically and mentally exhausted, the Panzerarmee slowed down. It reached El Alamein like a spent long-distance runner, incapable of responding to its brilliant commander's urgings for just one more final effort.

During the morning of June 30, the British X Corps was still streaming east along the coast road past El Alamein and through General Pienaar's First South African Division, which held the Eighth Army's coastal flank. Then the stream of vehicles dried up at last. The road finally stretched empty in the midmorning haze before the eyes of the army's gunners. Somewhere in the near distance was Rommel. As long as he was there, the situation demanded the utmost in alert vigilance. Rommel, however, had met his match at last, and his name was Auchinleck.

The Auk was ensconced now in a niche behind the line's Ruweisat Ridge with his small headquarters staff: General Dorman-Smith, a couple of aides, and an intelligence and communications team. Auchinleck himself was housed in an unpretentious van from which he would direct the battle. The only warlike sounds now were those made all along the line by pneumatic drills boring out gun emplacements and storage pits in the hard gray-brown rock. To his soldiers Auchinleck issued a calm and heartening order of the day:

> You have fought hard and continuously for over a month. No troops could have fought better. The situation now calls for a supreme effort on the part of all. We are fighting the Battle of Egypt, a battle in which the enemy must be destroyed. The battle is not over yet and will not be over until we have defeated the enemy and defeat him we will. The enemy is stretching to his limit and thinks we are a broken army. He hopes to take Egypt by bluff. Show him where he gets off.

About noon a sandstorm developed, thick as a London pea-souper but oven-hot. Whirling dust filled men's eyes and nostrils and clogged the mechanisms of their guns. Eighth Army gunners peered into the murk, waiting tensely for the tanks that would be crawling toward Alexandria.

Then something moved out there in the swirling clouds of sand. It was Rommel's Ninetieth Light Infantry. A British battery of fifty-millimeter howitzers fired a salvo. They were the first shots of the First Battle of El Alamein, although history would remember only the Second Battle of El Alamein, the one fought by the "insufferable"—the adjective was Winston Churchill's—General Sir Bernard Law Montgomery later.

The Auk had won a little time. Rommel, after his initial assault, withdrew and began laying minefields of his own, a sign of exhaustion. His troops, it later developed, were as bone-weary and dazed with fatigue as the men of the Eighth Army.

For once, luck was with the British, and Auchinleck had a precious twenty-four hours or so to bolster his positions with fresh troops and new weapons, safe at last from an enemy flanking maneuver around his line's southern flank. Not even the audacious Rommel would attempt to move through the quicksands of the Qattara Depression. Had the Desert Fox come onto the Alamein Line with the power with which he had assaulted Tobruk, it would have collapsed. But he didn't. He couldn't. His men were too tired.

We saw no more Germans that day, but they were there, and in force. As long as they remained, the situation continued critical and only now, with Rommel somewhere in the scraggly fig groves west of the Nile Delta, was the full extent of the danger realized. Churchill was in Washington when Tobruk fell, talking with Roosevelt, and together they heard the shocking news that the British position in the Middle East was perilously close to collapse.

London and Washington as well as Cairo had ample cause for alarm. Should Egypt fall to the puissant Panzerarmee *Afrika,* as seemed possible in light of the Eighth Army's performance at the Gazala Line, it would be the greatest disaster since the fall of France.

For Egypt was the keystone of the strategic arch formed by the Middle East which joined Britain to India and the Far East and linked British and American factories (via Iran) with the soldiers of the Red Army fighting in the Caucasus and with Allied troops fighting in Africa and Asia. The Allied presence in the Middle East kept wobbly Turkey neutral and out of alignment with the Axis. Finally, the Middle East contained in Iraq and Iran the oil fields without which the British armed forces would be paralyzed.

The fall of Egypt would terminate British control of the Mediterranean. It would mean loss of the Suez Canal and with it stores and equipment worth many Tobruks. Bereft of troops, Palestine and Syria could not hope to survive, and once in Jerusalem and Damascus, the Germans would be within easy reach of the oil fields, while Turkey, surrounded, would be unable to resist the heavy German pressure to enter the war on the side of the Axis. With Turkish Anatolia and Iran in German hands, Russia's extreme left flank would be uncovered, and Iran's wells would soon start pumping oil for the Axis. India, too, might be exposed to attack by a German force from Iran while the Japanese repeated in the Far East the easy triumphs in Rangoon, Singapore, and Manila.

Indeed, the consequences of a British defeat in the First Battle of El Alamein were almost too disastrous to contemplate. Yet all were distinctly possible as the Afrika Korps came up to the Alamein Line on June 30. On that day, and for several subsequent days, the line was in no condition to resist the kind of all-out attack such as Rommel had launched against Tobruk. It was ready to crumple. Behind Alamein the road lay open to Alexandria, a mere two-hour drive, and there was nothing much to prevent Rommel from cutting the Cairo road and driving straight on to the Egyptian capital.

In the meantime, the news from Russia was far from encouraging. The second German summer offensive, timed to coincide with Rommel's lunge at

Tobruk, was already a few days old and moving fast. Sevastopol was tottering, and Kupyansk, about three hundred miles west of Stalingrad, was being wrested from Russian hands. A deadly pincer was closing in on the vital Middle East, and in my diary for June 30, I wrote, "Unless America commits a large, well-equipped army to the task of helping our British allies, the Middle East is doomed."

That evening I wrote a gloomy letter to my wife in which I said I thought the time had come for me to "return home, quit journalism, and join the army for the duration."

Alexandria had a severe case of jitters. The Cecil Hotel, normally gay with naval officers and highly available women, was practically deserted. What was left of the Mediterranean Fleet after the Battle of Crete had sailed to safety in the Red Sea via Suez. Demolition squads were ready to go to work. The city was nearly empty of troops. The remaining few were confined to barracks under curfew, and all officers were on notice to rejoin their units immediately. Barrage balloons still floated lazily in the sky, but the feeling was general that the city would soon be occupied by Axis troops.

Members of the Italian community made little cakes for the expected Axis visitors. Shopkeepers removed from their display windows the faded photographs of King George and Winston Churchill (I don't recall ever seeing any of Franklin Roosevelt), presumably to be replaced at the proper time by those of Hitler and Mussolini. Il Duce was known to have landed in North Africa, complete with white horse and spurious golden "Sword of Islam" for a triumphal march into Cairo. Alexandria's polyglot Levantine population would have welcomed Rommel and his Axis troops.

The fat, oily dragoman in a Western suit, Turkish tarboosh, and dirty shirt who helped me buy a new bedroll—I had lost mine during the frantic final days of the retreat from Mersa Matruh—endlessly muttered his indignation against "these people who have made for us this war." He meant the British, of course, but prudently did not identify them. He lived off tourists and, with a glance at my green shoulder tabs with "U.S. War Correspondent" embroidered on them in gold thread, decided he "loved the Americans." He told me of generous tips he had received from Gary Cooper and other Hollywood stars whose names he spoke with sycophantic reverence. A disgusting type, but for a price he found me the bedroll I needed for my planned return to the front.

Axis agents had circulated rumors that Alexandria was about to fall to the Afrika Korps. The result was a mass exodus of European refugees and bourgeois Egyptians. The avenues leading to the main road to Cairo were jammed with cars filled with passengers and with trucks packed with household furnishings. The scene as we drove along the broad waterfront corniche, seeking a favorite Greek restaurant of ours famous for its fish menu, reminded me of Paris in early September 1939, when France went to war.

The Greek proprietor and his comely Egyptian wife greeted us warmly, apologized that their restaurant had so few customers, and overcharged us outrageously for a simple meal. We had fish broiled over charcoal, French-fried potatoes, a tomato salad, and a good dry white wine. The bill for the four of us—Hawkins was our guest—came to nearly a hundred dollars, more than double the normal cost. But it was the first decent meal we had had in some time, and we paid the check gladly.

At the Cecil, where Hawkins dropped us before driving off to his own digs in town, the bar normally would have been crowded at that hour, buzzing with conversation and lively with movement. Now it was nearly empty. The few who were there sat in small groups around their beers, discussing the news or bemoaning the lack of it. The usually gossipy Irish barkeep, whose name I've forgotten, was solemn as a priest at a wake.

Morrison, Lait, and I were having after-dinner brandies at the bar when two burly military police entered, mistook us for officers, and ordered us to rejoin our units at once. "Sorry, chaps," one said after he had identified us as correspondents, "but mind you stay inside until morning. Curfew, you know."

That night the sirens wailed, and Alexandria got its first real bombing of the war. The Luftwaffe's targets were the installations at the naval base, but the bombs fell mostly on the city's poorer, thickly populated sections. Early the next morning we saw considerable damage, with firemen digging through the wreckage and ambulances hauling away victims.

It made no sense to us to remain in Alexandria, where there was no headquarters of any kind, press or military. If Rommel succeeded in cutting the road to Cairo and captured Alexandria, we would spend the rest of the war in a German POW camp. The decision to head for Cairo was unanimous. There news could be gathered, written, and cabled, and from there we could return to the front—wherever it might be. I was anxious to see the letters from home that surely awaited me at Shepheard's or any communications from *Collier's*. I had been out of touch with my office for nearly a month.

46

THE GREAT FLIGHT
FROM EGYPT

In Cairo, when my colleagues and I arrived around noon on July 1, the streets were jammed with military traffic from the front and with tooting, honking civilian vehicles from Alexandria. It was bedlam.

Long lines formed at the entrances to banks, travel agencies, stores that sold luggage, and photo supply shops that advertised "24-Hour Service" on passport photographs. The headlines of the capital's two foreign-language papers—one French, the other English—assured their readers that all was well at the front, describing the ongoing retreat of the Eighth Army as a "strategic withdrawal to prepared positions" and the military situation as "stable," but apparently no one believed what they said.

Thousands of British and European residents had fled, and thousands more were making frantic preparations for flight. The atmosphere in Cairo was one of panic born of fear that at any moment Rommel and his Afrika Korps would descend upon the capital.

After stopping briefly at our respective hotels to deposit our gear and pick up mail from home and messages from our offices—there were none for me at Shepheard's, where the lobby was thronged with new arrivals from Alexandria—Morrison, Lait, and I parted company with Hawkins and prowled the jittery city.

The Egyptians seemed calm enough; they went about their business with their customary patience and resigned acceptance of their menial roles in the city's life, secure in their belief that whatever was happening "up north" was "the will of Allah." But fear and apprehension were apparent in the behavior of the capital's foreign population, including the normally unflappable British, who clearly "had the wind up," as they say, and were preparing to abandon Cairo.

The air in the vicinity of the British Embassy by the Nile and the sprawling buildings of GHQ's Kasr el Nil barracks smelled strongly of burning paper. The sky there was gray with smoke and fine ash from the bonfires that were destroying secret documents, war maps, reports, and sensitive files.

Throughout the city army trucks backed up to offices and hauled away desks, filing cabinets, typewriters, mimeograph machines, furnishings, and personal belongings—the impedimenta of years of British residence as masters of Egypt. Every military unit not involved in the preparations for the defense of Auchinleck's El Alamein Line was under orders to evacuate Cairo immediately. Everything was being done systematically enough, but the evidence that the British were preparing for the worst was overwhelming.

We found the British Consulate besieged with foreigners seeking visas for Palestine. The central railroad station teemed with women and children waiting for eastbound trains for Tel Aviv and Haifa and southbound trains for Khartoum. Most of the passengers were the families of British civil servants and South African officers. Truck and bus convoys formed up at midtown collection centers and departed for Suez with the dependents of British officials to be embarked for South African ports.

The mass exodus apparently began with the fall of Mersa Matruh on June 29. Until then the capital had remained what it had always been: physically and spiritually remote from the war, a safe haven for its foreign residents. They had assumed that the Eighth Army would halt Rommel along the fortified defenses which Wavell had built at Matruh in 1940 soon after the war started.

But when the British abandoned Matruh and retreated precipitously to El Alamein, fear spread through Cairo with the speed of heat lightning, and the flight from Egypt began. It gained momentum with the arrival of evacuees from Alexandria and was encouraged by highly effective German propaganda. The night Matruh fell, the Afrika Korps's field transmitter announced that Marshal Rommel intended dining at Shepheard's with his staff within a day or two and invited Cairo's ladies to greet him at a reception attired in their gayest gowns. At the time Rommel's triumphal entry into the Egyptian capital loomed as a distinct possibility.

Cairo's growing colony of American military and technical personnel was not immune to the quasi-hysteria that followed the British retreat. For some time, long before Pearl Harbor, in fact, Alexander Kirk, the tall, imperturbable American minister to Egypt, whom I had known in Rome as counselor to Ambassador William Phillips, had urged U.S. citizens to go home unless they had substantial reasons for staying on, but few heeded his advice. America was still neutral then, and ships had still been available to transport them; but this was no longer true.

Now the only means of escape for Americans was the trans-African, transatlantic route previously established by Pan American Airways and militarized after Pearl Harbor. When my colleagues and I arrived at the legation to call on Kirk on the afternoon of July 1, charred paper whirled about in the lazy breeze. Here, too, documents were being burned, while scores of U.S. citizens crowded the outer offices of the adjoining consulate to have their passports validated for travel and, in many cases, to demand priority approval for air transportation to Brazil and home along the route I had traveled in the opposite direction in the spring.

Americans were experiencing for the first time what Poles, Czechs, French, Yugoslavs, Greeks, and others had experienced before them. Overnight they had become refugees, saying hasty farewells to relatives and friends they might never see again, parting with homes and familiar things, and facing the many problems common to uprooted people. Upwards of four hundred Americans fled during those critical days preceding the Auk's stand at El Alamein, and hundreds more followed, most going south by air to Khartoum, others to Aswan, and still others to Asmara, the new American base in formerly Italian Somaliland. They were to spend Independence Day in the blistering heat of unfamiliar African surroundings thousands of miles from hot dogs and Cokes, backyard barbecues, picnics, parades, and whatever else contributed to celebration of the national holiday, herded into temporary quarters like so many head of cattle, experiencing the fears, humiliations, and heartbreaks of flight before an enemy.

Cairo's most frightened inhabitants, my companions and I discovered, were the people least able to escape, the city's several thousand Jews. We learned about the seemingly insurmountable difficulties they faced when we stopped in at Hachette's, a bookstore in the Sharia Adly Pasha, where I had once found an unexpurgated copy of James Joyce's *Ulysees,* and struck up a friendship with one of the shop's clerks, a handsome young Egyptian Jew who thereafter reserved for me the weeks-old copies of *Collier's* he received sporadically by boat mail. He looked worried and distracted, and when I inquired what seemed to be bothering him, he said he and his bride of a few months wanted to emigrate to Palestine but as Egyptian citizens by birth were finding it impossible to obtain from the corrupt Egyptian authorities the exit permits they required before obtaining Palestinian visas from the British.

"We don't want to be here when Rommel arrives," he said. "But it takes more baksheesh than we can afford to get exit permits from the Egyptians. You've got to be a rich man to bribe your way through their bureaucracy, and I'm not a rich man. . . ."

Quoting Wavell, I tried to assure him that Rommel "would never reach the Nile," but my young friend would not be comforted.

"If that is so," he said, "then why are the British leaving? Only this morning, on my way to work, I saw convoys of lorries carrying their people to Palestine. And they are burning documents at the embassy and at their headquarters on the Nile. . . ."

We shook hands all around, wished him luck, and left. Outside, Lait, who was Jewish, said, "What my people here need right now is another Moses." We made a date to dine that night at the Continental and separated.

At Shepheard's, where I arrived at nightfall at the end of a hard day's prowling about the city, the lobby was still crowded with new arrivals from Alexandria, and I had to elbow my way to the reception desk for the key to my room. There I filled my enormous bathtub, stripped off the dirty, smelly uniform I'd been wearing for what seemed an eternity, and luxuriated in warm soapsuds until every grain of sand was out of my hair, ears, nostrils, and the rest of my body. Relaxing in the tepid water, I became deliciously aware of how good it felt to be alive.

The dimly remembered line from a poem by Rupert Brooke that I had memorized as a schoolboy but had long since forgotten flickered tantalizingly through my mind: "The benison of hot water. . . ." Brooke was the poet of another generation and of an earlier war. It had killed him long before his time, when he was not yet thirty years old and on his way to the Dardanelles and Gallipoli. I dearly hoped I would survive my war, one that was really only a continuation of his and that had engulfed hundreds of millions of men, women, and children throughout the world.

Clean linen and a fresh uniform heightened my sense of well-being as I descended to the lobby on my way to the Continental and my dinner engagement with my pals. The lobby was still buzzing with people. They gathered in small, tight groups to discuss the latest rumors and to share their many grievances, among them the growing scarcity of gasoline and tires for their cars and the sudden rise in the cost of everything. Some of the older, well-dressed gentlemen in the crowd at Sam Shalom's bar worried about the sharp downturn on the Cairo Stock Exchange, where selling was high, apparently, and prices had fallen steadily with every despairing report from the front.

Sam mixed me a Pimm's and read me the text of the latest Radio Rome broadcast in Arabic, one of the several languages he understood and spoke fluently. It was addressed to the Egyptian people, and it said: "Don't worry. Lay in a week's supply of food and remain indoors. No harm will come to you, but see to it that the Greeks and the Jews don't get away." Sam delighted me with his reaction.

"As a Jew," he said, "I'm a congenital pessimist. But about what's happening in the north, I'm an optimist. A lot of my Jewish friends, those who can afford to pay the fees, are clearing out for Palestine. But not me. I'm staying. I think General Auchinleck's going to stop Rommel in his tracks. How about a refill? This one's on me. . . ."

I begged off and went into the crowded, blacked-out street. Cairo's night life continued unabated throughout those critical days. What uneasiness there was during daylight receded every evening at sundown. People dined, wined, and danced at the usual places, with only occasional air-raid alerts to remind them that a battle for Egypt's survival was in progress only about 150 miles away, a distance the enemy could cover in two days or less.

The lobby of the Continental was also crowded with evacuees from Alexandria, but it was a somewhat less distinguished-looking clientele than the one at Shepheard's: elderly couples, middle-class, the men in rumpled tropical suits, the hatted women in flowered dresses. They had the look of British civil servants who had made their homes in balmy Alex after retirement instead of Spain's Costa Brava or some other Mediterranean haven where the sun shone and the living was cheap. Their luggage—well-worn gladstone bags, golf clubs, tennis rackets, huge round hat bags, all much traveled—lined the passageway to the elevator.

The Roof Garden, where my friends had prudently reserved a table as far as possible from the raised platform at one end that held an out-of-tune piano and half a dozen musicians in tacky tuxedos, was livelier and busier than I had ever seen it. My companions hadn't yet arrived, and while waiting, I sipped a very dry martini and watched couples dancing to a waltz. The only uniforms present were those worn by Polish, Greek, and French officers who held their partners with old-fashioned European decorum. Their women were heavily lacquered blondes whom I recognized as belonging to a troupe of Hungarian refugee dancers who often performed at the Continental and who probably were on the bill that night after dinner.

The atmosphere was decidedly old-world, nostalgic of times long past. The subdued lighting came mainly from the shielded lamps on the garden's fifty or sixty tables arranged along the four sides of the rectangular dance floor and was very kind to the somewhat shopworn blondes dancing with the officers. The other couples were a nondescript lot, Turkish, Greek, and Armenian refugees, all of whom were vaguely familiar. I had seen them before here and there in Cairo's restaurants.

My dinner partners were still in their working clothes when they finally showed up, and both wore the expressions of frustrated reporters who had argued long and vainly with uncooperative censors. While I was loafing in my tub, Chet and George had written powerful pieces about the final days of the retreat from Gazala and apparently had had every line questioned or deleted. George was steaming, but Chet was inclined to sympathize with the censors.

"Berlin monitors every word radioed or cabled out of here," he said after he and George had ordered drinks. "Those copy killers at GHQ just wanted to make sure our dispatches didn't contain anything that Rommel might use to his advantage. So they struck out the stuff about documents being burned and the flight from Cairo and changed 'precipitous retreat from Gazala' to 'strategic withdrawal.' Can't blame 'em."

" 'Strategic withdrawal,' my ass," grumbled Lait. "What we saw was the rout of a beaten, broken army. If the Brits don't hold Rommel at El Alamein, they'll lose Cairo, maybe Egypt, maybe even a hell of a lot more, and readers back home ought to know what's going on. Rommel could be here in no time. From Alex it's only a taxi ride to the front. . . ."

"In the circumstances," said Morrison, "this might be our last dinner together for some time. So let's make a night of it. Let's order something to go with a good Burgundy. Afterward we'll have crepes suzette and champagne."

Shared dangers had knitted us closely during our time together, and we made a cheery dinner of it. After we had enjoyed a fine rack of lamb and done justice to the Burgundy, the headwaiter made a great show of flaming the crepes. While he poured the champagne, we settled back to enjoy the garden's nightly entertainment.

The main act was to have featured Hekmet Fathma, the sinuous belly dancer who had become the toast of Cairo and the after-work bedmate of many a British officer. In Hekmet's place, however, appeared a substitute, a fat Syrian lady with a large fake ruby in her navel, and as she began her traditional undulations, Lait summoned the headwaiter, pointed to the hefty performer, and asked, "How come?"

"Mademoiselle Hekmet," the man replied sotto voce, "has been arrested. I believe the charge was espionage. . . ."

Hekmet was, in fact, as George and Chet said they had long suspected, a German agent, indeed, a double agent who also worked for the Egyptians. She spent the rest of the war in a British concentration camp along with a number of pro-Axis Egyptian army officers, including one named Anwar el Sadat.

The next day, July 2, the flight of Britons and other foreigners continued unabated. The atmosphere in the capital remained tense and uncertain.

Among those preparing to depart was John Jones, the wealthy English proprietor of Cairo's biggest tailoring and military equipment supply house down the street from Shepheard's. I stopped in his shop to replace a pair of goggles I had lost in the desert and found Jones at his usual station, behind the cash register, mopping his round, beefy face with an oversize khaki handkerchief and bemoaning the slump in the value of the Egyptian pound.

Jones said he was selling off whatever goods remained on his racks and shelves and "clearing out." He was moving to South Africa, where he hoped to reestablish himself in Durban or Cape Town. His big problem, he said, was converting his cash—some hundred thousand Egyptian pounds, then worth about three hundred thousand dollars—into "real money," meaning dollars or sterling. The local currency had fallen steadily in value with every mile the British retreated and with some help from the Luftwaffe, which had been dropping leaflets. Jones handed me a sample. The rectangular piece of paper was a perfect facsimile of a British one-pound note, but on the obverse a message in Arabic said that while this note was once valuable, now it wasn't worth "a beggar's trouble" to pick it up.

Except for the heavy traffic, the steady outward movement of evacuees, and the crowds at the banks, there was nothing to indicate that Rommel might at any moment arrive in Cairo. Although the army was moving out excess personnel and dependents, the British Embassy indicated it was staying on whatever happened. Ambassador Sir Miles Lampson, a huge man—physically he personified the John Bull of *Punch*'s cartoons—remained at his post. Pretty, petite Lady Lampson, meanwhile, shopped for trinkets in the native souk, her way of showing the Egyptians all was well with the world. And as though to underscore Britain's determination not to give up Cairo, Richard Casey arrived as minister of state—with war cabinet ranking—in the midst of the crisis.

What the average Egyptian thought of the hullabaloo swirling about him I had no idea, for I didn't know any average Egyptians. Those with whom I came into daily contact were either servants or shopkeepers. The former—like the big black Nubian who made my bed and brought me breakfast every morning at Shepheard's—maintained a stoic calm. The merchants, on the other hand, enjoyed the current boom in sales, though they worried about what might happen when the British left. They realized they were not likely to enjoy much freedom and prosperity under Nazi rule.

All the Egyptian officials I had met were decidedly pro-British. Their country had achieved national identity under the British, and they were not ready to exchange the measure of independence they had attained as a British protectorate for colonial status under the Germans. Although their king, Farouk, reputedly liked the Italians and probably would have welcomed them with open arms, he knew he would become at best only a Nazi puppet if Rommel took Cairo, and palace sources told me His Majesty was packing his bags to depart for England, where he had been educated and where he would join Europe's other monarchs in exile.

Meanwhile, however, Farouk's pro-Allied prime minister, Nahas Pasha, whom the British had obliged Farouk to appoint premier in place of the pro-German Hussein Sirry Pasha when Axis troops invaded Egypt in 1940, remained at his villa in Cairo and carried on the increasingly difficult task of running the country. His predecessor had opposed Egyptian military participation in the defense of Egypt, a policy, incidentally, that remained in force.

That afternoon, July 2, while I was packing to return to the front with Morrison and Lait, I received a cable from Bill Chenery, my magazine's editor in chief, ordering me to proceed at once to Lourenço Marques, a port in Portuguese East Africa, where I was to await the arrival on July 10 of a Japanese vessel, the *Asama Maru,* carrying American diplomats and civilians trapped in Japan after Pearl Harbor. Among the returning Americans was our ambassador to Tokyo, Joseph C. Grew, to whom I was authorized to offer up to twenty-five thousand dollars, a most generous sum in those days, for the exclusive rights to any book, diary, or other papers he intended publishing about his experiences.

The cable infuriated me. Didn't Chenery read the papers? Didn't he realize that we were in the midst of one of the biggest stories of the war, an event at least as important historically as the fall of France? If the British lost Egypt, as seemed distinctly possible, even probable, at the time, they might lose their empire. I sent Chenery an urgent telegram suggesting that I had better remain in Cairo for what promised to be a story of utmost importance and indicating that I might have difficulty making the necessary travel arrangements. His reply early the next morning left me no alternative: I was to leave immediately for Lourenço Marques. But how to arrive there by July 10? And would Cairo still be in British hands when I returned?

For answers to both questions I went to see Major General Russell Maxwell, commander of American military forces in Egypt and in charge of air transportation out of Egypt. Maxwell, who wore steel-rimmed eyeglasses and looked more like a bank manager than a general, was most helpful. He assured me that "the situation at El Alamein" was, "for the present, anyway, most satisfactory" and, after reading Chenery's cables, authorized my departure for Khartoum on one of the army's "sky trucks" out of the capital's airport at Heliopolis. "Don't worry," he said meaningfully. "Cairo will still be ours when you come back."

Clearly the general knew something he wasn't telling me. What he didn't tell me, but what I learned from my friend Ed Kennedy, of the Associated Press, who was waiting to see Maxwell, was that Major General Lewis H. Brereton had just arrived to organize an American air force in the Middle East, a development that proved to be decisive in Auchinleck's defense of Egypt. I sensed an important story but had no time to pursue it, and I rushed to the offices of the British Overseas Airways to book a flight from Khartoum to Lourenço Marques.

Assured by BOAC of a flight to my destination out of Khartoum, I hurried back to Shepheard's to pack and at the entrance met Major Randolph Churchill. He greeted me warmly and introduced me to his friend (and future brother-in-law) Captain Christopher Soames. I was anxious to interview Randolph about reports that his distinguished papa was being pressed to take Wavell into his cabinet as war minister and about rumors of impending changes in the Middle East high command. But before I could say a word, Randolph said he was having a small dinner party at the Mohammed Ali Club that night and invited me to join him. The dinner, he said, was in the nature of a "birthday party," but whose anniversary was being celebrated he didn't say.

There were only five of us at dinner on the rooftop restaurant of the Mohammed Ali Club that starry, jasmine-scented night, my last in Cairo for some time, it turned out. Randolph's guests included Brigadier General John Marriott, of the Coldstream Guards, and his vivacious brunette wife, Maud, daughter of banker Otto Kahn, and a gentleman, a high-ranking civil servant, whose name I didn't catch.

The dinner was superb—consommé gelé, sole meunière, and poulet en casserole followed by fresh strawberries with cream, Turkish coffee, and fragile little cakes—accompanied throughout by well-chilled Moselle, then champagne cold enough, though the night was fiercely hot, to crack a hot stone. Randolph was his ebullient, talkative self throughout the meal and eloquent in defense of his father's policies, which, after the fall of Tobruk, were under heavy attack at home. In fact, it was believed in Cairo that the prime minister might not survive the political consequences of the military debacle in Egypt.

Brigadier Marriott and I exchanged reminiscences about the behavior of

the Tommies in the desert, their courage and patience and willingness to work
hard under difficult circumstances. We both deplored, however, their inclina-
tion to "brew up"—pause to make tea at the oddest moments, sometimes in
the midst of battle.

The next day, after hasty telephoned farewells to Morrison and Lait before
they took off for the front, I became, in effect, another American refugee. It
seemed one hell of a way to celebrate the Fourth of July.

The sky truck, a DC-3, rose at dawn from the airport at Heliopolis with
forty passengers. They occupied the bucket seats, squatted or sprawled in the
aisle, and filled the baggage compartment of a plane built for only twenty-three
passengers and three crew. How that pilot got his overloaded plane off the
tarmac I don't know.

The passengers were mainly U.S. Army personnel, legation secretaries,
airplane mechanics, and American Red Cross fieldworkers. Five passengers
were women; one was a three-year-old boy. All wore identity tags on their
outer clothing and were experiencing for the first time in their lives the igno-
miny of enforced displacement.

Many hadn't realized the seriousness of what was happening or the importance of the Battle of Egypt. They were tense and subdued as they strained for
a last look at the irregular Nile-side splotch of buildings that was Cairo. By
the time the plane landed at Luxor to refuel, the people had relaxed considerably. In fact, after being mauled about in the rough air over desert sands that
had begun to warm up under the hot morning sun, some of the passengers
complained that perhaps the evacuation had been unnecessary. The same
persons who had pleaded for seats on a plane to take them out of Cairo and
danger now said they had been "stampeded" into leaving, but when pressed
to explain, they mumbled that flight hadn't seemed "really necessary" and
vaguely blamed "pressure from higher-ups." Actually they were merely bewildered and decidedly unhappy refugees.

For all of us the Fourth of July in Khartoum was very dull indeed.
Watching the Nile flow northward as we sipped lemonades laced with gin
while sitting in wicker chairs on the veranda of the not-so-Grand Hotel seemed
a poor way for Americans to celebrate Independence Day. I envisioned Kathryn and the boys barbecuing hamburgers and franks on the charcoal grill
in our backyard and hoped they were having a wonderful time.

Sean, now ten years old, would be wearing his new blue and gold Cub Scout
uniform for the occasion. I prayed he would never need wear another. Surely
this war would be over before he reached military age. Or would it? When,
I wondered, would we start winning it? So far, there had been only costly
retreats. These, even when called strategic withdrawals and measured in so
many miles lost on generals' maps, were also measured in thousands of dead
and wounded.

Those were the thoughts with which I went to bed that night in a Nile-side
BOAC "rest house" room near the hotel. The room had an earthen floor, and

the walls crawled with small gray lizards. "Harmless," I was told, but not conducive to sleep though I was protected by a canopy of mosquito netting. I tossed and turned for hours, then fell into an uneasy sleep. I awakened with a start from a nightmare during which I crawled endlessly on all fours in the stygian darkness of a desert night over the fresh graves of a burial ground of battle dead. . . .

The BOAC's flying boat took off on the Nile at dawn on July 5. Two days later it landed me in Lourenço Marques, half seaport, half resort, where I checked in at the Polana Hotel, which seemed to be the center of the town's social life. There, that evening at cocktail time, I met the American consul, Austin Roe Preston, who informed me that the *Asama Maru* with Ambassador Grew on board would not be arriving until July 15, and I resigned myself to a holiday from war.

Austin and his Australian-born wife, Marjorie, helped make life tolerable during my stay in Mozambique. But the high point of my enforced vacation was meeting Malcolm Muggeridge, the English historian, a lathy, tweedy, gentle man whose mildness, however, was limited to his voice and manner. He had merry blue eyes, unkempt graying blond hair, and a large, expressive mouth. He had long, bony, nervous hands and one of the most incisive minds I had ever encountered.

Malcolm was on an intelligence mission for his country, and we had long talks about war and peace. He never made the mistake of glossing over British retreats or defeats. Although in every sense a Liberal, he was disinclined to consider the Soviets' remarkable military feats against the Germans as a determining factor in the war or the peace to come. We had, therefore, some lively but always good-natured debates. They would often begin over tea at his office and continue at dinner in the Polana's dining room or while watching Roe and his wife playing tennis. On one point we were in total agreement: Nazism and fascism were iniquities that had to be destroyed root and branch.

I had had misgivings about being able to persuade Ambassador Grew to write for *Collier's,* and they proved to be well founded. When they finally arrived, Ambassador and Mrs. Grew—a handsome woman and a lineal descendant of the Commodore Perry who had opened the Orient to Western commerce—accepted my invitation to lunch at the Polana. At an appropriate moment I made Mr. Grew the offer Chenery had outlined in his cable, but the ambassador politely declined. He said he could not accept until he had cleared the matter with his boss, Secretary of State Cordell Hull.

Mr. Grew was a tall man, a beardless Lincoln with a bushy black mustache and courtly manners. He indicated that he and Mrs. Grew had had a difficult time as internees of the Japanese, but he was under instructions not to reveal the details until he had been debriefed by the State Department. It was what I had anticipated. Nevertheless, I was bitterly disappointed at having failed in my first specific assignment from *Collier's.* I felt I had wasted the cost of the trip—about two thousand dollars—and more than a month's time during which I might have been covering Auchinleck's defense of the El Alamein Line.

I returned to Cairo by way of Johannesburg, Bulawayo, Nairobi, Mombasa, and Khartoum with stopovers en route. On virtually every airfield I saw evidence of the mounting American contribution to the British war effort in the Middle East: planes, both heavy and medium bombers, and fighters. Meanwhile, our sky trucks carried a flow of spare parts, instruments, ammunition, and medical supplies to Auchinleck's forces.

At Khartoum, where I was obliged to lay over two days before I was assigned a seat on one of our DC-3s for Cairo, I saw squadrons of twin-motor A-26 medium bombers, which we called Havocs but the British had renamed Bostons, lying wing to wing while being serviced for their flights to air bases in Egypt and Palestine. Clearly the Auk would at last have the air power he needed to halt Rommel.

Cairo seemed not to have changed much when I returned on a hot day in mid-August. I noticed, however, that there were new troops in the streets, red-faced, sunburned men just off the transports at Suez. They wore the insignia of the Fifty-first Highlanders, fresh British blood for new battles to come. But the big surprise was the prevalence of Americans in the city, instantly recognizable not only by their U.S. Army insignia but also by the cut of their shiny khaki-drill uniforms. They were mostly fliers and technicians, evidence that American manpower as well as machines had entered the crucial battle for Egypt and the Mediterranean.

47

HOW U.S. AIR POWER HELPED SAVE EGYPT

When Rommel reached El Alamein on June 30 and publicly boasted he would soon make his headquarters in Shepheard's Hotel, most people in Cairo believed him. "Only a miracle can stop him," some said, for they saw the Eighth Army's headlong retreat from the Gazala Line as the "beginning of the end" of the Battle of Egypt.

But the "miracle" had happened, and when I visited the headquarters of the newly formed U.S. Middle East Air Force shortly after my return from Lourenço Marques, I learned that it had been an eminently unmetaphysical phenomenon, mostly made in America. It had materialized in Egypt in the form of huge four-engine B-24 bombers. The planes had been headed for India to fight the Japanese but were ordered to remain in the Middle East to help Auchinleck stop Rommel and to keep him where he was until the time came to push him out of North Africa.

The B-24s, which the British promptly and appropriately renamed Liberators, were accompanied by squadrons of B-17s known as Flying Fortresses, twin-engine Boston and Mitchell B-25 medium bombers, and Kittyhawk P-40 fighters, then one of the fastest planes in its class. The addition of the American planes to those of the Royal Air Force, which included Wellington and Halifax bombers, gave the Eighth Army greater striking power from the air than it had ever enjoyed. The RAF commander, Air Marshal Arthur W. Tedder, and General Lewis H. Brereton, who commanded the American force, used their combined strength to wreck Rommel's hope of regaining the initiative in the battle for Egypt. In fact, what had looked like the beginning of the end on June 30 two months later looked more like the end of the beginning. Rommel never won another battle in the deserts of Egypt or Libya.

The arrival of American air power to help Auchinleck hold off the Afrika Korps at El Alamein was part of a far-reaching reorganization of Allied defenses in Egypt, the Middle East, and the entire Mediterranean battlefield in the fateful summer of 1942, the blackest time of the war for the Allies, particularly for the British.

The citadel of Tobruk had become the symbol of British resistance in the Mediterranean and the Middle East, and its loss had created a public ground swell of criticism of Churchill's handling of the war, for it was common knowledge that the prime minister made the major strategic decisions about when and where offensives should be initiated, even who should command them. To Churchill, with his nineteenth-century view of history as a procession of great names and great events, the fall of a legendary fortress like Tobruk rang louder in his mind than the complicated truths of strategy.

So Churchill flew into Cairo from London in mid-August to hold a conference after Auchinleck had halted Rommel at El Alamein. He had with him Averell Harriman, Roosevelt's lend-lease administrator; General Sir Alan Brooke, chief of the imperial general staff; and several other military minds. Wavell flew in from India, and Smuts from South Africa. All the eagles—the generals and senior admirals and air marshals—were gathered in a momentous conference that was to change the course of the war. It would make the Middle East the second front Stalin was demanding, the place where the Allies were immediately in contact with the enemy and in a position to buttress Russia's left flank.

The conference resulted in a purge of generals: Sir Harold Alexander, the dynamic little hero of Dunkirk, replaced Auchinleck as commander in chief Middle East, and General Henry Maitland ("Jumbo") Wilson was given a separate command in Syria and Palestine. Most important of all, however, was the appointment as commander in the desert of a new and unfamiliar leader, General Sir Bernard Law Montgomery. After the fall of Tobruk Churchill had demanded a new offensive against Rommel, and when the Auk said he couldn't possibly mount one for at least another six weeks, Churchill fired him.

But the changes were even more far-reaching. The conference produced a new army in the Middle East, an army that for the first time would include Americans as well as British. An era in the war, a bad era of successive defeats, was over. A new era in which great victories were to spring was born, and a key element was Brereton's Ninth Air Force. But its role in the Battle of Egypt was somewhat obscured, first by the Eighth Army's gallant stand at El Alamein, then by the advent of Monty the Magnificent, whose appointment was announced on August 18.

There was no reticence at Brereton's headquarters, however, about telling me how Yank planes and pilots had helped the British save Egypt during the

July and August fighting. Due credit was given the Auk and his revived army, but I was pointedly reminded that the battle might well have gone the other way if our bombers and fighters hadn't arrived in time.

During those final days in June when Rommel was advancing on Alexandria, our Bostons dumped thousands of tons of high explosives on his troops, tanks, vehicles, and supply depots. Meanwhile, our B-17s and B-24s, as well as British Wellingtons and Halifaxes, battered Rommel's two main Libyan ports, Benghazi and Tobruk, and attacked his Mediterranean convoys. One out of every three Axis ships bringing reinforcements and supplies from Italy was sunk. In the first nineteen days of July Rommel was deprived of fifty-three vessels, many of them carrying precious fuel for his tanks and vehicles.

Yank pilots flew the B-17s, and both American and British crews manned the B-24s. Benghazi and Tobruk were bombed so often that such missions were called milk runs or mail trips. By the end of August Rommel sorely needed troops, tanks, guns, food, and fuel merely to sustain his Afrika Korps in the field. He received some supplies and fresh troops, including a new Italian armored division and a division of paratroopers which he was obliged to deploy as infantry, but not enough men and supplies with which to resume his drive on Alexandria and Cairo. Moreover, the Luftwaffe had been swept from the skies.

In the meantime, huge Allied convoys provided the men and equipment the Eighth Army required, including hundreds of guns, British late-model Crusader tanks, and the latest American Sherman tanks, some of which were taken from U.S. Army units in process of being trained back home.

Of all our bombers, the one the British most fancied was the B-24, the one they had aptly renamed the Liberator. They were so fond of it and so anxious to demonstrate how well their pilots used it that when I asked the RAF public relations people to allow me to fly in one on a raid on Tobruk, they readily granted me permission.

It was a strictly British raid, so the B-24 involved was a Liberator and its name was *Kathleen.* It was flown by an Irishman named Terry, an Ulsterman from Armagh with china blue eyes and a frankly handsome face that smiled without smiling, one of the "few" who had done "so much for so many" during the Battle of Britain.

We met in the briefing room of an RAF desert base near Tel Aviv in Palestine. Pilots, navigators, gunners, and radiomen—all phenomenally young, all survivors of innumerable raids—listened intently as their wing commander diagrammed their order of takeoff, their targets, and their courses to and from their objectives, poking with a pointer at a huge intelligence map chalked on a blackboard.

Terry supplied me with a parachute, a Mae West, warm flying clothing, a helmet, and an oxygen mask. He also handed me a box containing two bars of chocolate, a thermos flask of hot tea, hardtack, and chewing gum. "Here," he said, "you'll need this. We'll be gone a long time."

We loafed about in the mess, reading and writing "last" letters home, until dinner, after which we dozed, waiting for takeoff time. Talk subsided. A ground crew chief with a cockeyed sense of humor wanted to know where we wanted our mail sent "just in case." Nobody laughed.

It was my first combat mission, and an Australian pilot, a leathery veteran of many raids, must have read my thoughts. "Why in heaven's name would you want to go on one of these rides?" he asked. I said I knew of no other way of telling my readers what fliers did and felt when bombing the enemy. I had experienced war on the ground; now I wanted to experience it in the air. "I see," he said, and smiled as though he understood, but I sensed he didn't.

Trucks carried us to our various ships. *Kathleen* loomed hugely in the gathering darkness, a dim oblong of yellow light from her open belly showing on the tarmac. Crew members and ground staff were making last-minute checks of the planes' weapons, bomb racks, instruments. After what seemed an interminable wait, Terry said we'd better climb aboard. Everything happened quickly after that.

We took our places in a blue-black darkness. The only light was the faint glow from the luminous dials of the instrument panel. I sat in the jump seat on the flight deck directly behind and between Terry and his copilot, a chap named Jack.

Kathleen was a big plane, about two stories tall, more than sixty feet long, with a hundred-foot wingspan, blunt-nosed and stubby-looking on the ground, more like a flying boxcar than a plane.

Terry warmed up the four Pratt & Whitney motors. At full throttle they made *Kathleen* shudder and tremble. But they sang smoothly with power, and I thought with a surge of pride, *Americans made these engines, Americans who grew up making model airplanes, tinkering with motors, turning jalopies into vehicles fit for drag racing.*

Terry released the Liberator's brakes, and *Kathleen* moved forward, swung into position on the runway, and with a deafening roar, when the pilot gunned the motors, we were suddenly airborne.

I must have slept for an hour or two, vaguely conscious of noise, the faint smell of lubricating oil and gasoline, and the peculiar odor produced by the warming Bakelite panels that held the instruments, like the smell of a brand-new car.

We had taken off before moonrise, and when I came fully awake, I saw the moon hanging like an orange disk low on the horizon, framed between the Wellsian silhouettes of Terry and his copilot. Terry's voice was saying in the intercom receivers in my helmet, "Put on your oxygen mask, Frank. We are at nine thousand feet and climbing. Please acknowledge."

I switched on the mike on my chest and said, "Okay, pal."

"Attaboy," Terry said. "It won't be long now. . . ."

For me the minutes that seemed hours were filled with penetrating flashes of fear that enemy ack-ack might get us, that we might be intercepted by a German night fighter, and, worst of all, that we might be set afire, the fears intermingling with anxiety that I might betray them to the seemingly nerveless men about me. Thoughts of fire, of being burned alive, were the worst. But there were other imaginings. Of being caught in the starlit sky in a sea of hot steel from the ack-ack guns while drifting down in a parachute. Ah, yes. The parachute. Would it open? I had been briefly instructed in its use but couldn't remember a word of what I had been told.

Voices over the intercom steadied me. They were conversational, human, like office talk between the boss in the front office and one of his employees.

"Captain," a voice said, "navigator here. We're coming onto our target. There's flak up ahead. Lots of it."

"Yes," Terry replied. "I can see it. Gunners, test your weapons."

There were short bursts from the guns forward, amidships and the tail. Several of the shells burst brightly in the sky ahead of us, beyond the cockpit.

By raising myself to a half-standing position between Terry and Jack, I could see bright bursts of orange flak ahead over Tobruk. The bursts were like poppies that bloomed and died in fractions of seconds. I smelled cordite. *Kathleen* bounced about in the air roughened by the explosions.

Again, Terry's calm voice: "Will one of the rear gunners please come forward and conduct our American passenger to the bomb bay, where he can observe the effects of the bombing? Other ships ahead of us are already on target. I can see their hits."

The gunner grabbed my wrist and led me aft through the bomb racks in the plane's big belly. In my cumbersome chute it was a tight squeeze between the stanchions that held tons of death and destruction.

Suddenly I was in a world filled with more noise than I had believed machinery and wind and bursting ack-ack could make. In the bomb bay there was only a thin skin of metal between us and the chaos outside. Added to the roar of the engines, the racket numbed the brain. I adjusted my oxygen mask and plugged in my intercom just in time to catch the voice of the navigator asking Terry whether he should open the bomb bay doors and the pilot's response: "Yes. Now."

There was a low, angry whir of motors, and a blast of air tore into the plane's innards. Moments later the bombs spilled from their racks. I watched them drop and saw the distant bursts below. The exploding bombs, five hundred-pounders, made thick rings that glowed momentarily like enormous, hollow-centered blobs of incandescent lava.

I had been in Tobruk on the receiving end, and now I watched fascinated, surprised, and a little disturbed by the exultant surge of adrenaline. It never occurred to me at the time that we were killing and maiming men. No, we were surgeons removing a cancerous growth, the enemy. I wondered how my companions felt about what we were doing. I made a mental note to ask them, later, whether they ever saw the results of their "operations." That's what the raids were called: operations.

Kathleen behaved beautifully. An ungainly thing on the ground, the plane was graceful as a sea gull in the air. The ack-ack rocked us but never touched us. No Nazi night fighter caught us when we came off our target, banked, turned, and headed east toward home and the dawn.

Everybody relaxed. I slept. I must have slept a long time, for when I awoke, the light stung my eyes. We were flying low, and the Mediterranean was bright blue and cool below us. Terry said, "I didn't have the heart to waken you, but you missed a magnificent sunrise."

We poured tea, ate our hardtack and shouted pleasantries at each other above the noise. It was hot inside the plane. I struggled out of my chute and Mae West and looked out the window of the copilot's seat. Very soon we were flying over ocher-colored sand that rippled endlessly from the blue rim of the sea toward the horizon. Then came the green of the Nile Delta. Men and women paused in their work to look up and wave at us. Minutes later we were in southern Palestine, gliding down toward the complex geometry of the RAF base, *Kathleen*'s home.

Later that morning we sat around in the RAF mess and talked about bombers and their role in war. There was an easy, democratic atmosphere in RAF messes that I'd rarely found in the Eighth Army's messes, where officers and men ate separately, divided by rank and class. Rank mattered little in the RAF. Pilots and their crews shared the same dangers on every mission and the same food and drink when they were on the ground.

The men with whom I flew that morning had great faith in themselves and in their machines. They knew the bomber to be a good weapon. They disagreed with the traditionalists who insisted that air power "couldn't win battles." They didn't claim that the planes themselves were a decisive weapon, only that properly used in sufficient numbers, they were indispensable to victory.

Terry pointed out that the effectiveness of warships at sea was limited unless supported by air power and that the strength of land armies was directly proportionate to the strength of the air force overhead.

"We're artillery," he said, "flying artillery. We can't win battles outright for the generals and the admirals, but we certainly can help. . . ."

All our planes had returned safely, and Terry characterized the night's raid as "a piece of cake." The reconnaissance photos later showed that our "flying artillery" had hit all the squadron's assigned targets. Our bombs demolished dockside dumps of supplies, obliterated already damaged harbor facilities, and further reduced the port's capacity to provide the Afrika Korps with gas and diesel oil, the blood and plasma of Rommel's tanks, planes, and vehicles.

Rommel had lost many tankers to British and American bombers during June and July, and by the end of August his stocks of aviation gasoline were dangerously low, and his Luftwaffe remained pinned to the ground, where it was systematically destroyed by medium bombers, while the heavies battered the Axis supply lines to Sicily and Italy, Crete and Greece. The Desert Fox was learning what a captured fellow officer, General von Ravenstein, had meant when he told his British captors that the war in the desert was "a tactician's delight and a quartermaster's nightmare."

Intelligence intercepts indicated that Rommel had desperately signaled

Berlin demanding planes, pilots, and gas. At the time, late August, German forces were making their most vigorous effort of the war against the Russians in the Caucasus. So urgent was Rommel's need, however, that planes and pilots were flown down to him via Greece and Crete. But Rommel never got enough gas, and the "quartermaster's nightmare" became for him a round-the-clock reality.

The public relations department of the Royal Air Force attributed Rommel's plight that summer to the fine work of Air Marshal Tedder and his deputy, Air Vice Marshal Arthur Coningham. But both Tedder and Coningham knew the truth. They privately acknowledged that their success would not have been possible without the presence in their Western Desert Air Force of the Americans and their commander, General Brereton.

Brereton was in India on June 20, the day Tobruk fell, when he received orders to rush to the Middle East to help Auchinleck stop Rommel. At the time the embittered veteran of the debacles in the Philippines, Java, and Burma commanded the U.S. Tenth Air Force, which he had created to fight the oncoming Japanese. His orders came from General Henry H. ("Hap") Arnold, commanding general of the U.S. Army Air Forces, but actually emanated from the White House, where President Roosevelt had just informed his visitor, Winston Churchill, of the fall of Tobruk, after having jointly decided on a "Europe first" strategy in the United Nations' struggle against the Axis.

On June 28, the day Brereton arrived in Cairo, Auchinleck had assumed personal command of the Eighth Army in the field, but the situation at the front remained critical. In fact, Brereton's first report to Hap Arnold had included a plan for the strategic dispersal of American air forces in the event the Eighth Army was "defeated or destroyed." But on the Fourth of July, appropriately enough, Brereton was in Auchinleck's GHQ in the desert and heard the Auk order a counterattack at El Alamein.

"I knew then," Brereton told me later, "that the Eighth Army had stopped moving backward and was moving forward. I went to work right away organizing the U.S. Middle East Air Force. But I had to start from scratch."

Until then, the mission of the U.S. Army forces in the Middle East under General Maxwell was to funnel American aid to the British in Egypt and the Russians in the Caucasus via the Persian Gulf. An organization to support an American combat air force was nonexistent. Brereton created one almost overnight.

The nucleus of what quickly became a powerful adjunct to the RAF's Western Desert Air Force was the special unit of B-24 heavy bombers which had been trained to bomb Tokyo and other targets in Japan from Chinese bases but had been diverted to the Middle East while en route to India. Commanded by Colonel Harry Halverson, the detachment consisted of twenty-three Liberators, which had arrived in Egypt in mid-June and on July 6 belatedly celebrated Independence Day by sinking one of Rommel's precious cargo vessels in a raid on the harbor at Benghazi.

To the Halverson detachment, Brereton added a bombardment squadron from the Tenth Air Force in India, a fighter group composed of P-40s, and a medium-bombardment group of B-25 Mitchells. He organized his arsenal into two task forces: (1) a strategic striking force of heavy bombers under his immediate command and (2) a tactical striking force of medium bombers and fighters operating under American command but subject to RAF operational control in direct support of the Eighth Army. Most important, perhaps, the gregarious Brereton established cordial relations with Tedder and Coningham. The result was a team that was soon functioning with maximum efficiency.

Physically Brereton, a Hoosier, was of sturdy Napoleonic stature but possessed none of the arrogant characteristics of short men endowed with power. He was blunt in manner and speech, always kept his word, and owned the gift of command, that indefinable something that distinguishes great generals from mediocrities.

I met him the day after the Tobruk raid at a dinner party in his unpretentious brownstone villa in a Cairo suburb. Friendships develop quickly in wartime, and we soon became close friends. Over games of gin rummy, at which the general excelled, lunches in air force messes, or meals at his villa, he often shared his inner thoughts. He confided to me his annoyance, for instance, that Montgomery, in his dispatches to the War Office, invariably credited the RAF for the air support he was getting never once mentioning the role the Americans were playing. "As far as Monty's concerned," Brereton muttered, "we just don't exist, dammit."

Brereton was a disciple of the late General William ("Billy") Mitchell. Like his mentor, Brereton believed that battles could be won by planes, and he put into practice many of Billy Mitchell's ideas in the Battle of Egypt. To his air force in the Middle East, therefore, must go a substantial share of the credit for General Montgomery's subsequent successes against the Afrika Korps not only in Egypt but in all North Africa. The Americans provided the bulk of the strategic as well as tactical air power that gave Monty his highly publicized victories.

Montgomery, incidentally, was Churchill's second choice as Eighth Army commander. His first had been the seasoned Lieutenant General Strafer Gott, but he was killed in an absurd incident on July 7 while flying from Alexandria to Cairo for a brief holiday before assuming command. The slow, cumbersome Bombay troop carrier carrying him to Cairo from Alexandria was shot down in flames by two lurking Me-109s returning from a raid.

Then, less than a fortnight after fate and Winston Churchill had decreed that Montgomery should lead the Eight Army, the new commander faced his first test in the Western Desert. Monty, as he soon became known to us all, appropriated as his own the defensive plans prepared earlier by Auchinleck and emerged the victor in what proved to be Rommel's last desperate attempt to reach the Nile Delta and Suez.

48

ALAM HALFA AND THE GENESIS OF A LEGEND

Rommel's attack on August 30, 1942, was not unexpected. Several days before he launched it, air reconnaissance photos showed heavy traffic on the Afrika Korps's tracks leading east and southeast toward the front. But the British army was ready, readier, in fact, than at any time since the fighting in the Middle East began back in Wavell's time when the Eighth Army was merely a hastily assembled Western Desert Force.

On a visit to the front with Morrison and Lait on August 28 (my first since my return from Portuguese East Africa and the chaos we had witnessed during the final days of June) we found a revitalized Eighth Army deployed in the strong positions Auchinleck had prepared. As Americans, however, we were particularly impressed by the presence in the field of many new tanks from the United States, heavy well-armed General Grants.

Equally impressive was the high morale of the British troops, which officers took pains to attribute to frequent visits and pep talks by their new commander, General Montgomery, whose gifts as a leader included an extraordinary ability to inspire confidence in his soldiers. After touring the front from north to south, the perceptive Chet Morrison put into words what George Lait and I both felt. "Methinks," said Morrison, "I smell the sweet scent of impending victory."

We had learned earlier, in Cairo, that at a meeting of his staff, in which General Brereton had participated, Montgomery had indicated that he was determined to hold the El Alamein Line at all costs. "There will be no with-

drawals," Brereton quoted him as having said. "Absolutely none. None whatever. None!" Monty then described Rommel as a "very able commander, but
he has weaknesses, among them a tendency to repeat his tactics. In fact, he
has a one-track mind. . . ."

Developments proved Montgomery right. What the military historians
recorded as the Battle of Alam Halfa—a mined-in ridge that rose from the
desert at a point roughly twenty miles east of the El Alamein Line midway
between the sea and the great Qattara Depression—unfolded much as Monty
had anticipated, for Rommel employed the same tactics he had used successfully many times before.

The battle started in the blue-black light of the moonless midnight of
August 30 with a massive assault by three armored divisions against the
southern end of the El Alamein Line. There the British had laid a deep barrier
of minefields behind which the Seventh Armored Division was poised to attack
Rommel's flank when he turned north toward Alam Halfa, the core position
of the British defenses.

We followed the battle's progress from Brereton's desert headquarters
situated in the dunes near a tactical airfield east of El Alamein. The crayoned
overlays on the war maps showed the moves Monty and Rommel made in their
deadly military game of chess, and G-2 (American intelligence) officers briefed
us on the forces involved. The Eighth Army had available more than 700 tanks,
of which about 160 were our new Grants. Against this powerful array of armor,
which was well dug in defensively and supported by hundreds of new British
six-pounder antitank guns, Rommel could muster an estimated total of barely
200 Mark III and Mark IV tanks, plus possibly 240 obsolete Italian tanks.

An even more important factor, however, our G-2 reminded us, was that
the British enjoyed for the first time complete air supremacy over the entire
battlefield. There was no German air cover. Monty faced a comparatively easy
task. He had everything he required for victory: more troops than the enemy,
more tanks, more guns, and total command of the air.

Rommel ran into difficulties right from the start. Those British minefields
covering the southern one third of the El Alamein Line proved far deeper than
he had expected, and his armor made slow progress. Ten hours after his attack
began, Rommel's Panzerarmee had moved only about ten miles into British
terrain and was trapped in the minefields.

Meanwhile, the enemy forces were swept by murderous fire from British
artillery and came under heavy attack by Allied fighters and medium bombers.
By noon, however, the dust raised by the milling tanks and the explosion was
as thick as a sandstorm, and all air operations stopped. But close by we saw
black smoke rise from burning German tanks and supply vehicles.

Late that afternoon, using the swirling dust as a screen, Rommel wheeled
his forces sharply north toward the Alam Halfa Ridge. There his panzers met
stiff resistance from the Twenty-second and Twenty-third Armored brigades
of the Seventh Armored Division in their prepared, mined-in battle stations
just south of the ridge. Rommel broke off the engagement and withdrew to the

southwest with a loss of from thirty to forty tanks. Of these, fifteen were left disabled in the combat zone and were destroyed during the night by British tank-hunting units.

The next day, September 1, air action by British and American fighters and medium bombers so hindered and destroyed supply vehicles that Rommel was obliged to land ammunition to his forward artillery areas by aircraft. Throughout the day the Panzerarmee tried repeatedly to break through the British defenses to reach the Alam Halfa Ridge but each time was thrown back. That night decoded radio intercepts indicated that Rommel's crack Fifteenth Panzer Division was "paralyzed" for lack of fuel. The remaining two German armored divisions were not much better off, and in the morning of September 2 Rommel ordered a retreat.

Rommel's attacks had not been pressed with his old-time skill and resolution, and we later learned why: Casualties had disrupted the German command structure. General von Bismarck, commander of the Twenty-first Panzer Division, had been killed and General Nehring, field commander of the Afrika Korps, wounded. In the subsequent reorganization, the Afrika Korps itself and one of its three armored divisions found themselves in the middle of a major battle with new commanders.

Later still we also learned that Rommel himself had been seriously ill. He took the field against Monty enfeebled from the effects of a nose infection and a swollen liver. His defeat, however, was not due to poor health. It was more directly attributable to the devastating effects of Allied air power so skillfully employed by Tedder and Brereton.

September 3 marked the end of the third year of World War II and the end of Rommel's hopes of reaching the Nile Delta. The Afrika Korps retreated southwestward into an area of soft sand known as the Bargiel Depression at the southern end of the El Alamein Line, where the Desert Fox lagered his remaining tanks and some three thousand vehicles for a last stand. Rommel was in a situation of greatest peril, with his armor and transport under intensive Allied bombardment from the air and shell fire from British mobile artillery. Air reconnaissance revealed that more than two thousand vehicles and many tanks were destroyed.

Much of the destruction resulted from action by the American Twelfth Medium Bomb Group and the Fighter Command, both units operating as part of the RAF's Western Desert Air Force. Air Vice Marshal Coningham acknowledged the American contribution in private messages to the units' respective commanders, Colonel Charles Goodrich and Brigadier General Auby Strickland. But as far as Monty was concerned, the attacks that demolished whatever chances Rommel might have had of obtaining the gas, ammunition, and water he needed to continue the battle were made by the RAF.

I was not (and still am not) journalism's greatest expert on matters military, but it seemed to me at the time that the Desert Fox had been driven into a trap and could have been destroyed. But there was no annihilating pursuit. Monty allowed Rommel to withdraw southwestward, and the moment passed.

The Germans, with their aptitude for swift recovery, staged a well-conducted retreat behind a screen of fire from their deadly eighty-eight-millimeter guns.

By nightfall on September 6, Rommel had brought his troops and remaining armor safely out of danger into a sort of beachhead at El Himeimat, a hill on the eastern side of the British minefields at the southwestern end of the El Alamein Line close to the Qattara Depression. Monty made no attempt to turn Rommel out, though if he had, the subsequent Second Battle of El Alamein, which cost the British eighteen thousand casualties, might have been rendered unnecessary.

Nevertheless, Alam Halfa was one of the major turning points of the battle for Egypt. It exploded the myth of Rommel's invincibility, restored British faith in the Eighth Army, and set its commander, General Montgomery, on the first step of his climb to fame. Years later, in his *Memoirs,* Monty admitted that the battle had been "very important for the Eighth Army, and particularly for me."

Although Monty's successful conduct of the Battle of Alam Halfa was based on plans drawn up by Auchinleck and had been facilitated to a possibly decisive extent by the timely arrival of American help in the form of air power and armor, the credit for the victory devolved upon the Eighth Army's newly arrived leader, who soon became the symbol of British successes in the Middle East so passionately desired by Winston Churchill.

Both his predecessors, Wavell and Auchinleck, had been inclined to keep the press at arm's length and kept to themselves during major engagements in the field. But not Monty; he actually liked having reporters watch him in action. To that end, he maintained a large, handpicked staff of public relations men to arrange "photo opportunities," interviews, and visits even while he and his troops were under fire. Cairo-based accredited correspondents were invariably welcome at the front to see for themselves how Monty conducted desert warfare and how he had transformed the "brave but baffled" Eighth Army into a confident, surefooted unit capable of winning battles.

Montgomery rightly attached great importance to the matter of troop morale, and in this department he was more of an innovator than either of his predecessors. Monty, in fact, was probably history's first British general to project himself to his "audience"—meaning his soldiers—much like an office-seeking politician, by means of personal contact and studied efforts to become the focus of their attention and loyalty. Wavell, I remembered, was loved by his men, and the Auk was respected. But Monty was adored. Very soon the Eighth Army was *his* army, and my colleagues and I were given every opportunity to see how he accomplished this.

The Battle of Alam Halfa was in its final stages early in September, when my colleagues and I were invited to accompany Monty on a tour of the rear areas directly behind the front, near enough to hear the incessant roar of artillery and the crash of Allied bombs on the retreating Axis forces a few miles west. By then Monty had already done much to make the Eighth Army over in his own image, and the legend of "Monty the Invincible" was already gestating in the dispatches of Cairo correspondents.

Monty's black beret, with its gold badges denoting rank and regimental affiliation and worn at a jaunty angle, identified him as clearly as Patton's ivory-handled brace of pistols and MacArthur's specially designed nonregulation hat. He was of medium height but looked taller than he really was in khaki shorts and shirt worn open at the collar, knee-length socks, and suede desert boots, for he was spare and wiry with knobby knees. He seemed to enjoy all the contrived adulation and went to considerable trouble to attract the soldiers' attention and draw their salutes.

We witnessed two instances of this. The first was when he inspected a recently arrived division which had assembled in the desert well to the east of the Alam Halfa Ridge. At the time the men were routinely engaged in the process known as digging in. Monty strode up to them and, hands on hips, inquired what they were doing. Looking up from their task, the men instantly recognized the army commander, snapped to attention, and saluted. One of the number replied, "Digging in, sir!"

"No need to dig too deeply," Monty said curtly. "We're moving forward!"

The men instantly broke into cheers and saluted smartly once more. Monty returned their salute and strode on.

Later, inspecting an Australian unit, he told the men to remove their hats. "All soldiers look alike in hats," he said. "I want to see what you really look like." Off came the Aussies' broad-brimmed campaign hats, and into the air they went with a mighty shout. "That's better," said Monty, much pleased, then made a short talk before saluting and departing to more cheers.

To whatever talents Montgomery possessed as a tactician or strategist must be added the skills of a master psychologist and showman. He was also a perfectionist who launched himself into the task of reorganizing and training the battle-weary Eighth Army with relentless energy. He was determined to have an efficient, highly professional, tidy army, and he pursued his goal with icy fire. He toured endlessly throughout his command, seeking out the gold-brickers and the incompetent, his somewhat metallic voice questioning, denouncing, dismissing, ordering changes in personnel and methods. He was much like the superintendent who had been appointed to reorganize a previously mismanaged school.

Meanwhile, Montgomery was receiving a veritable flood of men and weapons for the offensive that would sweep Rommel and the Afrika Korps permanently out of Egypt, Libya, and North Africa. Two new armored divisions, as well as fresh infantry divisions, arrived. All were undergoing intensive training in desert warfare as September became October. Monty never moved unless he enjoyed qualitative numerical superiority over his opponents. By the end of September it was abundantly evident that Monty was preparing the major offensive against Rommel which Churchill had demanded but which Monty would not undertake until he was good and ready.

At Suez, in the course of yet another visit to the front, my friends and I saw freighters unloading scores of American Sherman tanks and guns, including a new self-propelled 105-millimeter cannon which the British appropriately dubbed the Priest. It soon helped administer last rites to Rommel's fading hopes of ever reaching the Nile.

The enemy, on the other hand, was being systematically weakened by Allied air power. Bombing had reduced the intake capacity of Rommel's main intake port, Tobruk, from forty-seven hundred tons daily to fewer than four hundred tons. By mid-October the Afrika Korps was in extremely reduced circumstances; Rommel could obtain less than 10 percent of the munitions, food, and fuel he needed merely to maintain his forces in the field, much less mount a successful offensive.

But while the British were inordinately generous with information about how badly off the Germans were, they tightened censorship on all references to their own mounting striking power, a clear indication that "something big" was in the air. One of the most closely guarded secrets was the arrival of the American Shermans, and all references to them were deleted from correspondents' dispatches.

Indeed, at about the time the Sherman tanks began arriving, British security was tighter than it had been at any time since the war started, and Axis spies, as numerous in Egypt as scorpions in the desert, resorted to unusual methods to signal the presence of the new tanks in the British arsenal.

Our old friend General Danny Pienaar, posted at Tel el Eisa with his First South African Division, called our attention to one of the clumsier German efforts at espionage when Morrison, Lait, and I visited him sometime during the latter part of October, about four weeks after the Battle of Alam Halfa. We found Uncle Danny in his portable hut in the dunes just east of the fortified positions at the northern extremity of the El Alamein Line. He was brooding over a copy of that morning's *Egyptian Mail,* Cairo's English-language daily.

The newspaper lay open on his table, opened and folded to a page containing a line drawing illustrating a premature advertisement for Christmas cards. The ad showed an artist's rendition of a tank whose profile roughly but unmistakably suggested a Sherman tank. Out of the tank's turret emerged an overburdened jolly old Santa Claus, his right hand pointing to the gun. From Santa's bag spilled a profusion of letters, some stamped, other unstamped. The first seven were stamped, a string of many were not, and the last five bore markings indicating stamps.

"Seven and five," the general said. "That's seventy-five, and dear old Santa is pointing to the gun. What is that but an indication of its seventy-five-millimeter caliber? And look at the sprockets. Three teeth are missing from the front drive gear and eight from the rear idler. That happens to be the exact number of the first batch of Shermans that arrived at Suez: thirty-eight."

The lanky general saw the advertisement as evidence of the continued existence of a spy ring within Egypt. He brought the matter to the attention of British intelligence, which launched an investigation.

While we talked, we were bombed, a rare occurrence in those early autumn days of 1942. A few bombs fell close enough to Pienaar's hut to shake it, scaring hell out of me, but Pienaar seemed not to hear them. At one point during the brief attack he coolly turned to straighten a framed photograph of his daughter which had been jarred askew by the explosions.

My friends and I never saw Uncle Danny Pienaar again. He was killed in an air crash later while on his way home on leave to see his family.

By the time the Eighth Army was ready to launch its big offensive late in October, Montgomery had 1,300 tanks, including 300 powerful Shermans; 220,000 well-trained troops; 800 planes and several batteries of those 105-millimeter guns—the American Priests—that would exorcise the Germans' 88-millimeter antitank cannon. Rommel faced Monty with only about 200 good Mark III tanks and 50 superior Mark IVs. His troops numbered about 110,000, and he had an air force of fewer than 300 aircraft. What additional armor Rommel possessed consisted of some 300 hardly battleworthy Italian tanks.

I must leave to the military historians an account of of the Second Battle of El Alamein (if Alam Halfa was counted, it was really the *third*), which established the enduring legend of Montgomery's greatness as a field commander. When it began on the night of October 23, shortly after my visit with General Pienaar, I wasn't in Egypt. I had hurriedly departed for Accra on a tip that an American force had landed in British West Africa for an Anglo-American attack on strategically important Dakar in what I was misled into believing might be the beginning of the much-rumored second front in Africa.

I arrived in malaria-infested Accra in the early afternoon of October 25 or 26, hurting in every joint from a recurrence of the dengue fever I had contracted the previous year in Singapore. I had been warned this would happen periodically. I had no actual fever, only the breakbone effect common to the disease, pain that aspirin did little to alleviate. Double scotches were the best antidote.

Shortly after my arrival in Accra I discovered that the Americans who had landed in British West Africa were not the vanguard of a second front against strategic Dakar, but a detachment of black troops who were to be employed in expanding the local airfield to accommodate the increasing numbers of B-17 and B-24 bombers arriving almost daily from American factories.

A friendly pilot offered me a ride back to the States in his returning sky truck, and I gratefully accepted. Anything to get out of the hellhole called Accra.

I made a number of regrettable errors of judgment during those first three years of the war, but missing the final Battle of El Alamein was one I regretted most of all. For I had witnessed several British reverses and was sorry not to have been present at what proved to be the final and most decisive of their desert victories, comparable in importance, some authorities were to say, with Blenheim or Waterloo.

The bitter battle, with its heavy losses, was to restore British military prestige after many disastrous defeats, but when Monty pierced the Axis defenses on October 30, I was in the air in a bucket-seat cargo version of a B-17 headed for Natal, on the east coast of Brazil, the first stop of a four-day homeward flight to New York. The pain in my joints had subsided but had given way to almost equally painful feelings of guilt at having left Egypt on the eve of a big story.

49

HOME FRONT, WINTER OF 1942-1943

The flight ended at Floyd Bennett Field, in Brooklyn, in the early afternoon of Wednesday, November 4, and it was instantly evident that New York had gone to war. There were no porters at the airport. The GI crewman who extracted my baggage from the plane's cargo hold said the skycaps were "all in the army now or making good dough in defense plants" and helped me carry my gear to the waiting room.

The place was blue with tobacco smoke and crowded with uniformed young Americans, male and female. The few civilians I saw were mostly men, older, jowly, paunchy, who looked frustrated, tired, out of place, and out of sorts. Long lines formed at the several telephone booths.

There were also queues at the various airline counters. At one of them a middle-aged man in a business suit complained loudly to the harassed clerk about having been "bumped" from a flight to Washington, where, he shouted, he had an important engagement. "I just gotta be there tonight," I heard him say, to which the clerk replied, "Look, mister, I'm sorry. But dontcha know there's a war on? Next, please."

"Next" was a trim little WAC lieutenant. Behind her came a U.S. Navy Wave in blue wearing a perky little blue and white hat, then a GI in stiff, brand-new khaki, and behind him a stalwart marine looking very military indeed in olive drab.

At the newsstand, where I bought a copy of that morning's *Times,* a hand-lettered sign said: NO CHOCOLATE. Shades of wartime London, I thought, and asked for Chesterfields. The clerk was all out of "name brands" and gave me a pack of Fleetwoods. I lighted one, took a puff, gasped, and asked the beefy fellow behind the counter what they were using for tobacco these days. He shrugged and said, "Search me. There's a war on, ya know. . . ." I joined the queue at a nearby telephone to call Charley Colebaugh at the office. It was nearly four-thirty.

As I waited my turn, a glance at my paper told me Montgomery's attack was going well after early difficulties with the Germans' minefields. But Monty's battle was not the lead story. Most of the front page dealt with the results of the previous day's elections.

The Republicans had won the governorship of the state of New York—the smugly handsome visage of the youthful-looking winner, Thomas E. Dewey, stared at me from page one—and had made important gains in both houses of Congress. Although the Democrats retained control of the legislative process, their opponents had increased their membership in the House by forty-seven votes and their representation in the Senate by ten seats. Their successes were interpreted as an expression of widespread discontent with wartime restrictions and shortages and popular dissatisfaction with the way Roosevelt was running the war.

I noticed also that in nearby Connecticut, wealthy Fairfield County had sent to the House of Representatives the state's first female member, Clare Boothe Luce, author, playwright, globe-girdling journalist, and wife of the publisher of *Time* and *Life*. The beautiful Clare, had campaigned in favor of "fighting a hard war [was there any other kind? I asked myself], not a soft war." I recalled that she had taken me to task in Manila in the autumn of 1941 for urging the Filipinos to be prepared to fight a very hard war indeed against the Japanese.

Nearly half an hour elapsed before my turn came to use the phone. I caught Colebaugh just as he was preparing to leave. I guiltily expected a reprimand for having left Cairo on the eve of Monty's big offensive but was greeted instead with a cheery "Welcome home, stranger," a scolding for having flown a combat mission over Tobruk—"We don't mind paying the premiums on your war risk insurance but would hate to collect on it"—and a gratifying suggestion that I not show my face at the office until Monday. Four days at home with Kay and the kids! I felt a surge of gratitude and made a clumsy attempt to explain my hasty departure from the Middle East, but Charley would have none of it.

"Forget it," he said. "We're running a magazine, not a news agency. Actually I'm glad you're back. The book is top-heavy with pieces from the fighting fronts. I think we'll keep you here for a while to help cover the home front. I'll see you Monday. . . ."

The man behind me was breathing down my neck in his anxiety to use the phone, and I asked Charley to alert the family that I was on my way home.

Group riding was the rule at the taxi stand in the semidarkness of the wartime dimout outside, and cabs were scarce. Drivers were reluctant to undertake long trips to the suburbs with individual passengers, but luck was with me. A suburban cab had deposited a fare and was returning to its base in White Plains. Bronxville was on the cabby's way back, and he agreed to take me home for twenty dollars, which, I reminded him, was double the usual fare. "Yeah," he said, as I slid in beside him, "everything's gone up. The war, ya know . . ."

The driver was a corpulent, middle-aged crosspatch who complained endlessly about how hard it was to find tires and spare parts to keep his hack running, the scarcity of gasoline, and the disappearance of alcohol. "That whiskey they make from potatoes," he said, "ain't fit to drink." He blamed his troubles on "them bureaucrats down in Washington," especially "those guys running the lousy draft." It had snared his nineteen-year-old son, and he denounced his town's Selective Service Board as "a bunch of crooks" who chose only poor men's sons for the army. "They don't touch those rich college kids," he said.

Mainly to shut him up, I asked the cabby to tune in a news broadcast on his car radio, but all he got was someone singing "Don't sit under the apple tree with anyone else but me," somebody else warbling "I've got spurs that jingle, jangle, jingle," followed by a stentorian announcement that "Lucky Strike *green*" had "gone to *war*!" I turned the radio off myself and feigned sleep until the cab drew up in front of 36 Homedale Road, Bronxville. I was home.

Kathryn opened the door to my ring in the uniform of a Red Cross Gray Lady. It was nearly six o'clock, and the boys were upstairs doing their homework; but they heard their mother shriek, "Daddy's home," and came thumping downstairs, yelling like a couple of Comanches. During the ensuing hubbub they took turns telling me what they were doing to "help win the war." Tommy was collecting tinfoil; Sean spent his after-school hours scrounging the neighborhood for discarded aluminum pots and pans; jointly they were earning money for war savings stamps by delivering *Collier's* to village subscribers. They were visibly disappointed that I hadn't brought them any souvenirs from the desert but listened attentively and seemed to understand when I explained my reluctance to touch anything left behind by dead men. I didn't tell them the real reason: An enemy corpse, a cartridge belt, even a helmet might be booby-trapped.

Their mother bribed them back to their homework with a promise that when they finished their lessons, thcy could listen to *Amos 'n Andy* on our bedroom radio and have dinner with us afterward. They clumped upstairs in a party mood. Kathryn had written me that Walter, our black houseman, had quit to take a better-paying job in a White Plains defense plant, and I asked who was making dinner. I could hear sounds from the kitchen and caught the unmistakable fragrance of something roasting in the oven. My wife smiled and led me into our cozy study, where she had laid a fire and set out the makings of scotch old-fashioneds on a butler's tray.

"That would be Agnes," Kathryn said while I mixed the drinks. "Mrs. Agnes Walsh. She's elderly, a widow, about sixty, Irish, a devout Catholic, and wonderful with the children. I took her on as a live-in cook-housekeeper when Walter left. I had to have someone to look after the boys when I became involved with Red Cross work. We all love her, but she's a monster about her red stamps. . . ."

Kathryn saw I was puzzled and briefed me on the complexities of the rationing system: red stamps for meat, cheese, butter, and other fats; blue stamps for most processed foods; special stamps for sugar, shoes, woolen clothing, nylon stockings. But Agnes Walsh stubbornly refused to contribute her red stamps to the family larder, hoarding them to give to a married daughter she visited on her Sundays off.

"But bless her old heart, she relented when I told her you were coming home, and her red stamps made possible the roast beef you're having tonight," she said. "I asked her to join us at dinner, but she refused. She's very shy, for an Irish lady. . . ."

While she talked, Kay drew the curtains and turned the key in the door. She had read the months-old hunger in me, and we made urgent, passionate love on the rug before the fire, after which we talked about many things but mostly about the traumatic effect the war was having on young Tommy.

"He cries a lot," Kay said, "and is having nightmares. Almost every day, when he isn't otherwise occupied, he marches back and forth across the front lawn, shouldering a broomstick for a gun. When I ask him what he's doing, he says he's guarding the house against those Japs. I can't persuade him there's no danger, and he's forever asking when you're coming home. Dr. Sullivan suggested a good child psychologist, but I have a hunch that if you'll stick around awhile, Tommy's demons will go away. . . ."

She was elated when I told her that Colebaugh planned to keep me home for a spell on domestic assignments. There was a discreet knock on the door, and a small voice said, "Dinner is almost ready, Mrs. Gurvayzie. . . ."

"We'll be right with you," said Kay brightly, and turned to me. "She'll never learn to pronounce our name. Come. Let's wash up and corral the boys. . . ."

Mrs. Walsh was small, on the stout side, with a pink face, blue eyes behind steel-rimmed spectacles, straight white hair that might once have been red neatly caught up in a frilly white cap. She wore a light blue dress under a neck-to-toe white apron and looked more like a nurse than a cook-housekeeper. She said, "Pleased to meet you," when Kathryn introduced us, laid the roast before me, refused my invitation to join us at dinner, and hurried back to fetch the vegetables.

My homecomings were always happy affairs, but this one was particularly joyous. Agnes had laid out our best silver and the company crystal, and as we gathered about the table, I was profoundly conscious of our good fortune. We were in America, safe from bombs, and I thought of the thousands of men, women, and children who at that very hour (it was well after midnight in England) were sleeping in the stagnant air of London's underground.

It crossed my mind, too, that I owed a great deal to the country of my birth and upbringing and inwardly blessed my immigrant parents for having had the courage to leave their native Sicily for a new life in the New World.

After the apple turnovers we had for dessert, I proposed a toast to victory, in which the boys joined with well-watered Burgundy, and Kathryn announced I would be home for a while, "maybe a long while." This elicited from Tommy an explosive "Gee, Dad, that's *neat*. Real *neat,*" his highest form of praise for anything that really pleased him.

Sean, always reserved, said, "That's the best news yet, Papa." For a ten-year-old, he was much too solemn.

I had never before realized how much I was missed at home and did my best to repair the evident damage caused by my long absences. I spent as much time with the boys as their homework and wartime chores allowed, explaining the war to them as an unpleasant task that had to be done to ensure their future freedom and laughing with them at their favorite radio programs. These included *Fibber McGee and Molly, The Aldrich Family,* and many more, among them *The Shadow,* a scary program of doubtful therapeutic value in Tommy's case, but he loved it. A good one they never missed, of course, was *The Lone Ranger,* wholesome cowboy stuff that I enjoyed almost as much as they did.

Occasionally, on Saturday afternoons, I took the boys to the movies. Armed with bags of popcorn—candy bars had virtually disappeared, and the ersatz chocolate tasted like candle wax—we sat through *A Yank in the RAF, I Wanted Wings,* and other films that depicted war as a dashingly romantic business. What the kids and I liked most were the pictures Bud Abbott and Lou Costello made—*Buck Privates* and *In the Navy*—kidding the experiences of men newly inducted in the armed services. War as it really was came through in snatches in the censored newsreels that accompanied the films.

Sunday mornings were usually devoted to the comic sections that came with the *New York Herald Tribune* and the *New York American,* the Hearst paper. Joe Palooka, Blondie and Dagwood, L'il Abner, Dick Tracy, and a host of other cartoon strip characters were as much a part of the boys' lives as radio's Charlie McCarthy, Hop Harrigan, or Superman. After supper on Sundays there were rollicking good variety comedy radio shows featuring the acidulous Fred Allen and the inimitable Jack Benny.

Everybody listened to the radio. The medium was now the main source of entertainment and information, occupying the place in the lives of Americans that was filled later by television, then still incubating in the laboratories. By the winter of 1942 radio had become a billion-dollar industry vital to both the war front and the home front, providing news "every hour on the hour" and fun and solace to millions of listeners almost around the clock.

There were programs for all ages, tastes, and interests. It was the time of swing music and the big bands—Guy Lombardo, Jimmy Dorsey, Fred Waring—and for highbrows there was symphonic music by the New York Philharmonic, the Detroit Symphony, and NBC's Symphony of the Air. On Saturday afternoons there were live performances by the Metropolitan Opera Company. Quiz shows enjoyed wide popularity, and one of the best was *Information, Please.*

Meanwhile, a horde of newscasters and commentators never let anyone forget there was a war on. Their names were household words, and some made no pretense at objective reporting, often airing biased, even irresponsible judgments. They included H. V. Kaltenborn, Fulton Lewis, Boake Carter, Earl Godwin, and many more. They were generally hostile to the New Deal, to the Roosevelt administration, Russia, and sometimes even to Britain. Offsetting them were the saner voices of Ed Murrow, Bill Shirer, Eric Sevareid, Ned Calmer, Drew Pearson, and the dean of them all, Raymond Gram Swing. World War II was radio's first war, and not even the most hostile critics could deny that the medium performed important service in bringing to the listening public war news promptly, effectively, and conscientiously.

It was on our bedside radio that on Sunday morning, November 8, I heard that American troops under the command of General Dwight David Eisenhower had landed in French Africa. The landings were not made at Dakar, as I had heard whispered in Cairo, but at Casablanca, Oran, and Algiers on the road to Southern Europe. Evidently the Allies intended attacking Hitler's vaunted *Festung Europa* not from the north, as everyone had assumed, but from the south in what Winston Churchill was to call its "soft underbelly."

The landings transformed the character of the war dramatically. Democracy passed from the defensive to the offensive in the great struggle against the Nazi-Fascists, and leadership therein moved from British to American hands. It rested thereafter with Franklin Delano Roosevelt and the disarmingly genial soldier and future president whom the West would know as Ike.*

I read the accounts in the *Times* and the *Herald Tribune* that Sunday morning and listened to the reports of the radio correspondents. I envisioned the Afrika Korps being crushed between the Yanks advancing along the North African coast from the west and the Eighth Army thundering on Rommel's heels from the East.

I was furious at myself for having missed such a big story, and the next

---

* I had met Ike shortly after my return from the Orient the year before in an officers' dining room somewhere in the labyrinthine Pentagon, where my colleague Walter Davenport had arranged for me to meet General Joseph ("Vinegar Joe") Stilwell, fresh from the jungle fighting in Burma. The three of us were sitting at a table talking over cups of coffee when Eisenhower entered. He was in civvies, tweedy gray jacket and flannel slacks, and seated himself nearby next to a window. Stilwell greeted him with a "Hello, Ike," and introduced Walter and me. I was unaware, of course, that I had met the future commander of the Allied forces in the greatest war ever fought. Our paths never crossed again, but I never forgot the man's firm handclasp, the trick he had of making instant eye contact, his quick smile, and the resonance in his voice when he said, "Pleased to meet you." He didn't stay to chat but returned to his table and sat looking thoughtfully out the window.

day, at the office, I begged Colebaugh to allow me to return to where the action was, but in vain.

"Get out into the boondocks," he said, "and do us a piece or two about how our war plants are meeting the country's wartime production needs. In the long run, that's where this war will be won, in our factories and shipyards. . . ."

I spent the rest of 1942 and the early months of 1943 watching America become the mightiest maker of deadly weapons the world had ever known. I visited arms factories in New England, textile mills in the Deep South, plants making planes and tanks and guns in and around Detroit, and shipyards in California and Oregon.

The wartime achievements of American industry, I found, bordered on the miraculous. During the winter of 1942–1943, despite serious shortages in vital raw materials, the armaments output of our war plants reportedly equaled the combined production of the arms makers of all three Axis powers.

At Willow Run, near Detroit, Henry Ford built an assembly line that was half a mile long and cranked out one B-24 bomber every hour. The planes came off the line so fast that they were taxied to an adjacent airfield, test-flown there, then ferried directly to wherever they were needed.

In his shipyards in the San Francisco Bay area, Henry J. Kaiser, using assembly-line techniques he had developed building bridges, was constructing ten-thousand-ton Liberty ships at a phenomenal rate, twenty-eight days from keel laying to launching, a performance that reduced the "record" construction time achieved in World War I by an astounding two hundred days, and crusty old Henry J. became known as "Sir Launchalot" Kaiser.

Our new motorized army ran on wheels and required millions of tires, but the Japanese had deprived us of natural rubber that came from the Orient. Before 1942 ended, however, synthetic rubber was being produced in quantity in a new industrial complex created virtually overnight under the direction of "Rubber Czar" William M. Jeffers, president of the Union Pacific Railroad. It was a triumph of American technology, ingenuity, and managerial skills.

The production "miracles" of Kaiser, Ford, Jeffers, and their fellow captains of American industry were made possible by the toil and sweat of about sixty-five million workers of whom some four or five million were women. I saw them everywhere I went. Clad in one-piece overalls, their hair wrapped in bandannas, they operated lathes and drill presses in machine shops, wired the innards of walkie-talkies, assembled small arms and bombsights, and performed innumerable other tasks normally performed by men. They worked as riveters in shipyards and aircraft factories, and Tin Pan Alley's "Rosie the Riveter" rivaled in popularity that other wartime classic "Praise the Lord, and Pass the Ammunition."

Many of the women I interviewed on the assembly lines were service wives fresh from household chores. Some were merely eking out family allotments, but others had taken jobs because work made it easier to endure the anxiety of waiting for their husbands to come home from the war. A few were much older women, service mothers who couldn't bear waiting at home for the mailman or who already knew their sons would never return.

Most of the women with whom I talked, however, were young and unmarried and worked out of an inner psychological need for self-fulfillment. They seemed to want to prove to society and perhaps also to themselves that they were the equals of men in whatever they were doing. They were, in fact, interchangeable with men in many jobs and in the factories I visited were receiving "equal pay for equal work."

The postwar emergence of women as a formidable factor in our society was predictable. For in addition to acquiring workaday skills that enabled them for the first time to earn decent wages, they were learning how to preside at meetings, manage departments, and organize political campaigns.

Meanwhile, the government was pumping an estimated three hundred million dollars a day into the national economy, and the massive infusion of cash generated an unprecedented economic boom, a bonanza for tens of millions of workers and their employers, a Depression dream come true. Unemployment virtually disappeared, and corporate profits in 1943 exceeded those of 1929. The country's precrash confidence in itself revived, and "God Bless America" acquired new meaning when Kate Smith sang it on the radio. It reminded Americans that of all the people in the war only they lived in relative comfort and in complete security.

But while fathers were being drafted in steadily increasing numbers and mothers were drawn from their homes to work on the production lines, the traditional unity of family life broke down. Unshepherded children of high school and college age who left their classrooms to work in the war factories were inclined to run wild. The crowded big cities to which they were attracted by well-paid jobs experienced waves of juvenile delinquency.

The big-city dimouts and blackouts spawned a new crime called mugging. New York, normally ablaze with lights at night, became a ghostly place after dark, where citizens were frequently hauled into shadowy doorways or deserted side streets, knocked unconscious and robbed.

Prostitution flourished in all the wartime centers, with little hindrance from the authorities. The institution enjoyed the dubious status of an "unpleasant necessity" of wartime living. Their pockets filled for the first time with their very own money to spend as they pleased, those in the footloose younger generation found fun and romance in the cheap bars, nightclubs, "skin shows," and other allurements available wherever war plants drew large numbers of workers.

Vast migrations of youthful as well as older job seekers from rural communities to the big cities were a major phenomenon of the war years. Another was the emergence of the bobby-soxers, a predominantly female subculture of teenagers whose idol was a frail crooner from New Jersey named Frank ("The Voice") Sinatra. The girls, in sweaters, skirts, and socks that slopped over rubber-soled shoes, mobbed him in the streets and sighed, screamed, and swooned in quasi-sexual ecstasy wherever and whenever he sang. Sinatra, who was twenty-six years old at the time but looked barely nineteen, a skinny fellow with big ears and an oversize Adam's apple, generated the nearest thing to mass hysteria in the country, a phenomenon which I leave to psychiatrists to explain.

The convulsive transformation of the national economy from peacetime to wartime production gave us an unimaginable prosperity from which sprang far-reaching changes in our society. Social revolution is the by-product of every great war, and the very magnitude of World War II was bound to alter America greatly, far more than anyone realized at the time.

We were criminally unjust in our wartime treatment of American-born Japanese, and we were still light-years away from recognizing our blacks as equal citizens. Nevertheless, during my travels about the country on my home front assignment I detected a national trend toward a new egalitarianism between the sexes and the social classes as they worked shoulder to shoulder to help win the war. The sharp lines between the have and the have-nots of our society became blurred in the national mobilization for victory, and by the time I completed my assignment I was sure I had seen a new and greater America aborning as the mighty leader of the "one world" Wendell Willkie eloquently advocated in his best-selling book.

50

THE SHADY "DARLAN DEAL"

hile working on my home front assignment, I was increasingly tempted to enlist. From time to time throughout the war I had felt the urge to switch from reporting to soldiering; but the commonsense realities of obligations to my family had prevailed, and I decided to await a formal invitation from Uncle Sam to join up.

By the time I turned thirty-five in February 1943 this hadn't happened, and the compulsion to become an active participant rather than a well-paid on-looker in democracy's struggle against Nazi-Fascist totalitarianism became irresistible. The Axis forces in North Africa were being herded into the north-eastern corner of Tunisia by the Americans from the west and the British from the east, and an ultimate Allied victory seemed certain. Sooner or later, I reasoned, the enemy would be cleared out of the area and the Allies would surely press on to Sicily, my ancestral homeland, then Italy.

When this happened, as seemed likely after the dramatic meeting between Roosevelt and Churchill at Casablanca in mid-January 1943, it occurred to me that considering my background, I might be useful in some intelligence capacity or other to the recently created Office of Strategic Services, perhaps as an agent behind Italian lines. Discreet inquiries at the Pentagon indicated that the man who had the final word in choosing OSS personnel was its commander, General William ("Wild Bill") Donovan, an elusive officer whose comings and goings were shrouded in secrecy. No one could or would tell me where to find him.

I had never met Donovan, but I knew that my colleague Walter Davenport had served with him in World War I, was on friendly terms with him, and often saw him whenever he happened to be in Washington. Sometime late in March, when I was in the capital to talk with some of the bureaucrats who were running the war on the production front, I prevailed on Davvy to arrange for me to meet the general.

"You're nuts," he said when I confided why I wanted to see Donovan, but some days later he telephoned me in New York to meet him in the lobby of a Washington hotel near the White House the following morning. I don't recall the exact date, but it must have been in early April because the capital's famous cherry blossoms were in full bloom and the city wore springtime green and smelled sweetly of newly mown grass.

Normally a talkative, good-natured fellow, Davvy was silent and surly that morning, barely acknowledged my greeting, and never said a word even as we rode up to Donovan's floor in the elevator. He spoke only when he introduced me to the general gruffly as "The feller I told you about, Bill." Not an auspicious start for an interview that might change my life.

Donovan, a burly man with a massive round head, heavily tanned broad Irish face, and an inscrutable smile, listened attentively to what I believed were my special qualifications for a job in the OSS: fluency in Italian, a knowledge of the Sicilian dialect learned in childhood from a mother who spoke nothing else, and a familiarity born of long residence and travel with Italian geography, politics, mores, folkways. My recital included my hunch that after bagging what remained of Axis forces in Tunisia, the Allies would probably invade Sicily, then use it as a base from which to attack Italy or southern France.

Ear cocked to everything I said, Donovan looked like a lawyer deciding whether or not to accept the case of a prospective client. I remember thinking at the time that he would be a hard taskmaster, and when I had finished, I knew at once I had been rejected. I didn't make notes, but this is approximately what he said: "Well, now, Walter here has told me a lot about you. [Long pause; exchange of knowing glances between him and Davenport.] Information is an important part of our war effort. I suggest you keep on doing what you have been doing. Frankly I think you would be more valuable to our cause as a correspondent than as an intelligence officer. But thanks for volunteering. . . ."

Outside in the hallway after Donovan had shown us out and the door closed behind us, Davvy saw I was crestfallen.

"Cheer up, Frankie," he said. "You can get yourself killed just as easily covering the war as fighting in it, you dumb son of a bitch. Come on, I'll buy you a drink. . . ."

On our way to the National Press Club I was the quiet one, deep in soul-searching. What had motivated my desire for an active role in the ongoing drama? Was it, I asked myself, a subconscious wish to atone for the fact that quite probably my Italian and very military uncle Gennaro was fighting on the other side? Over drinks at the press club bar Davvy suggested it was "just a crazy idea, an aberration."

I didn't argue. I had no rational explanation for my behavior beyond a sincere desire to serve my country as so many others were doing on the assembly lines at home and in North Africa and the Pacific.

Shortly afterward I was drafted and classified 1-A but was immediately deferred as a "journalist doing essential war work." I hadn't requested deferment and never learned how it was managed. I surmised that *Collier's* had intervened in some way.

By mid-April I was impatient to return to the Mediterranean front. I missed the excitement and adventure of battle, the comradeship of fellow reporters, and, most of all, the sense of participation, if only as an observer, in what had become democracy's "war of survival." Anyhow, *Collier's* had hired me to cover a war, not to sit at home.

This time, however, I knew I would find it more difficult than ever before to leave my family. My recent assignment had allowed me to spend frequent long weekends in Bronxville with Kathryn and the boys, and we had had many happy times together or with friends.

Our Tommy had emerged from his nightmares and fears; he no longer found it necessary to mount guard on the front lawn to protect the house from the Japanese and slept the dreamless sleep of a healthy, active six-year-old who spent his free time romping with Christopher, the frisky fox terrier, now full grown. The older boy, Sean, was no longer the moody, withdrawn child he had become, and their mother glowed with contentment. We were a close-knit family once more, and I was loath to disturb the tranquillity it had attained during the five months since my return from Cairo.

And it was to Cairo that I planned to return. There were a thousand things I wanted to know about the North African campaign, and I believed I would get the answers there, where I had friends in the British Middle East Command, knew my way around, and could most easily reach Eighth Army headquarters wherever it might be when I arrived.

I had followed closely the course of the star-crossed North African campaign as it was reported by the newspapers and the radio and had seen with dismay that the Eighth Army had failed to destroy the Afrika Korps before its remnants joined forces with General Jürgen von Arnim's army in Tunisia. But Monty's failure to trap Rommel was only one of the many puzzling aspects of an offensive that had cost many Allied lives, especially among the inexperienced and often poorly led Americans.

Above all, I wanted to know, as did many fellow Americans, why we had sought and accepted the help of the representatives in North Africa of the pro-Nazi regime in Vichy. General de Gaulle, the leader of the Free French movement, was pointedly excluded from the preparations for Eisenhower's November landings; he wasn't even told about them until after they had occurred. Since the fall of France in 1940 de Gaulle's name had stood for the ideals of antifascism, democracy, the willingness of Frenchmen to fight for principles, for everything the great American enterprise in the Mediterranean represented. Yet when the time came to begin the liberation of German-occupied Europe, de Gaulle was ignored, mainly because he represented France's revolutionary forces, an odd mixture of royalist, Communist, and Socialist elements.

Admittedly an acceptable French leader was absolutely necessary in Morocco and Algeria, where about 120,000 French and colonial troops in the pay and service of the Pétain regime in Vichy represented a potential military and political opposition. When France fell, the United States had recognized the government which Pétain set up in Vichy in unoccupied France, and Roosevelt had named as his ambassador crusty old Admiral William D. Leahy, a man of known conservative views who subsequently established a network of American agents throughout occupied France and North Africa. When the time came to carry freedom's torch into the Mediterranean, the State Department, personified by the canny Adolf A. Berle, Jr., believed the way to resurrect France was not through de Gaulle and his underground irredentist movement—it included too many Communists—but through France's existing leaders.

The American early choice to run things in North Africa was Henri Giraud, an elderly French general who had escaped from a German prison—practically his only qualification for the job—and been brought out of France in a submarine. He proved to be eminently unsuitable. Apart from the fact that only about 25 percent of the Vichyite commanders and civil servants would acknowledge his leadership, the stiff-necked Giraud wanted an immediate invasion of France—with himself as supreme commander of Allied forces! Eisenhower had him stashed away in Gibraltar.

Meanwhile, a far more amenable Frenchman turned up mysteriously in Algiers. He was the notorious Admiral Jean François Darlan, at the time the most important man in the Vichy government after Marshal Pétain himself. Ostensibly in the Algerian capital to visit a son, an officer in the Fusiliers Marin, stricken with infantile paralysis, he was readily persuaded by Eisenhower to become high commissioner of the French colonies in North Africa.

His appointment about a week after the landings raised a storm of protest in Great Britain and widespread dismay in the United States. The months I had spent at home had sharpened my perception of America as the avatar of freedom, and it seemed to me that something of great value had been lost with what the newspapers called the Darlan deal. What were our troops fighting and dying for in North Africa if not for the Atlantic Charter and the Four Freedoms it so eloquently proclaimed?

I had never met Darlan, but in Cairo I had compiled over the years a dossier on him based on numerous conversations with French officers and diplomats who had escaped from France and arrived in the Middle East to serve with de Gaulle's Free French forces. All knew Darlan well, some having actually served under him, and without exception they characterized him as an unscrupulous, ambitious Nazi collaborator almost as iniquitous as the unspeakable Pierre Laval, with whom Darlan had collaborated in France's downfall and in drafting and enforcing Vichy's anti-Jewish laws.

Darlan, my Cairo informants had told me, blamed the British, the Jews, the Communists, and the Socialists for the fall of France. He freely consented to Berlin's demands for the persecution of his country's Jewish citizens and for mass arrests of the Vichy regime's opponents, many of whom wound up on Nazi gallows or in Hitler's concentration camps.

The Germans had no difficulty persuading Darlan to turn over control of 1.5 million tons of French merchant shipping and to grant Germany the use of approximately 80 percent of France's available locomotives and rolling stock. There was enough in my notes about the "Little Admiral"—he was a Napoleonic five feet five inches with an explosive temper—to have qualified him later as a major war criminal, and his appointment cast a shadow over the North African campaign.

I happened to be in Washington when the furor over the Darlan deal erupted. Roosevelt tried to calm the storm by pleading that the arrangement was "only a temporary expedient, justified by the stress of battle." His use of the word "expedient" only made the situation worse. It meant that doing what was convenient but not necessarily right had become a tenet of American policy, and those of us who knew Darlan's history as a persistent and virulent Nazi collaborator were incensed. We saw it as a triumph of pragmatism over idealism. Longtime friends at the State Department were clearly embarrassed when questioned about the deal with Darlan, but military officials defended it, saying they were interested only in "winning the war and to hell with the moral niceties."

In North Africa Darlan's order to the Vichy commanders and troops in Morocco and Algiers to cease all resistance was obeyed and may have saved some British and American lives. But on November 27, when the Germans reached Toulon, the French admiral there disregarded Darlan's secret signal to come over to the Allied side and scuttled his fleet.

It had seemed a stroke of luck that Darlan happened to be in Algiers when Eisenhower's forces landed in the western Mediterranean. It soon become known, however, that he was not in the Algerian capital by chance. State Department and military envoys had been negotiating secretly with him as well as with Giraud. Darlan's intention all along was to wind up on the winning side, and after much persuasion he agreed to collaborate with us as fully as he had collaborated with the Nazis. The Germans helped him make up his mind when they swarmed into unoccupied southern France after the Allied landings in North Africa and the Vichy government lost its already dubious independence.

Meanwhile, through what remained of the winter of 1942–1943 and for some time thereafter, Italian and German troops, plus large quantities of weapons, including giant new German supertanks weighing sixty tons and armed with 88 mm guns, were arriving in Tunisia from Sicily. By the middle of December the Axis had in Tunisia under General von Arnim an army of about twenty-five thousand soldiers, well fortified in rugged terrain.

In the west Eisenhower acquired as allies the French troops in Morocco and Algeria, but they were ill armed and poorly trained. Organizational delays in Algiers, then torrential rains and gluey mud slowed the Allied attempt to reach the vital ports of Tunis and Bizerte before the enemy, and on Christmas Eve Eisenhower called off his offensive to regroup, train the untrained, and arm the unarmed.

Earlier that day, December 24, a slender, dark young Frenchman named Fernand Bonnier de la Chapelle managed to gain entry to the Hôtel St. Georges, where Darlan had his headquarters in Algiers, and killed Admiral Darlan with three quick shots from a revolver. The twenty-year-old assassin was promptly caught, tried by a French court-martial, and executed by a French firing squad. Who or what the young man represented was never clearly determined, though at the time it was reported that he had royalist and/or Gaullist affiliations. Whatever his connections or motives, Bonnier helped solve what had become for the Allies a vexing political problem.

Giraud was brought out of storage and appointed high commissioner to succeed Darlan as the least objectionable of the available candidates pending a better solution.

The matter was finally resolved by Roosevelt and Churchill at Casablanca. Before their eleven-day conference ended on January 24, de Gaulle was flown in from London and with some difficulty was persuaded to shake hands with Giraud for the newsreels. Later, in Washington, I learned that a consultative assembly of Free French former deputies and politicians who had escaped from France would be formed to govern North Africa. Giraud, I was told at the State Department, was "on his way out." I also learned, however, that the president had developed an intense dislike for the stiff-necked de Gaulle. I was not surprised.

The general—*"La France, c'est moi!"*—was a most forbidding individual physically and in other ways. He maintained a suite at Shepheard's, in Cairo, where I saw him often enough to observe his aloofness of manner, his tendency to play a male version of Joan of Arc. He stood fully six feet six inches in his well-polished boots and had a huge, slightly beaked nose, a level, penetrating gaze, dark eyes, and dark, slicked-down hair, which he wore somewhat in the style of the Gay Nineties. He was as imposing in a plain double-breasted suit as he was in his unadorned uniform and possessed the quality to which all leaders aspire: charisma.

The recognition accorded de Gaulle as the moral force behind the regeneration of France as a democracy was one of the most important results of the Casablanca Conference. It restored people's faith in the justice of the Allied cause.

Militarily, however, the Allies were stuck in Tunisia for months during which the Axis ferried additional troops and weapons into the area. By mid-April General von Arnim's army included what remained of the Afrika Korps (by then the ailing Rommel had returned to Berlin) and numbered upwards of 250,000 troops deployed along a well-fortified hundred-mile arc in the hills defending Tunis and Bizerte. The Germans and their Italian allies were fighting desperately to hold on to their North African bridgehead, but the end was approaching. The American Fifth Army in the west and the British Eighth Army in the south and east were poised for the kill. The enemy was caught in an Allied pincer.

On or about April 20 I went to Washington to arrange for War Department transportation back to the Middle East. I now had an additional reason to head for Cairo. A New York publishing house, Appleton-Century, had commissioned me to write a biography of General Montgomery, whose pursuit of Rommel from El Alamein to Tunisia had made headlines in the United States. Monty, in fact, was almost as popular in America at the time as he was in England, where his popularity was second only to that of Winston Churchill. And my shortest route to the Eighth Army's commander lay through Cairo.

Transportation, however, proved to be far more difficult to obtain than I had imagined. Air passage to the Middle East was out of the question. The best I could do after several days of "waiting room duty" in various offices was a berth on an unnamed troopship sailing from San Francisco on an unspecified date. Beyond assurances that the vessel would deposit me "somewhere in Egypt," I could extract no additional information from the officious army PR officer who arranged everything. "Be in Frisco before May first," he said. Armed with what looked like a steamship ticket and other papers, I returned home to spend what time remained with my family.

When I left a few days later to fly to the West Coast, I was inwardly certain I would not see my family again for a long time, probably not before the war ended in Europe. I didn't tell my wife I was sailing to Egypt; to spare her anxiety, I allowed her to believe I was flying. I took care, however, to warn her she might not hear from me for a month or more because of the uncertainties of communications from the war zone.

I was apprehensive about another long wartime voyage through submarine-infested waters, this time those of the wider, bluer Pacific, "Jap country" alive with newsreel memories of Pearl Harbor. I envisioned the "troopship" I had been promised as another scruffy old vessel like the *Themistocles,* which had carried me from Liverpool to Cape Town earlier in the war. I was reassured, however, when I saw my ship at her berth in San Francisco Bay at boarding time in the late afternoon of May 1.

It was the *Nieuw Amsterdam,* the long, sleek-hulled pride of the Dutch merchant fleet, one of the last of those wonderful luxury liners of the prewar 1930s that sailed the oceans when only fish still inhabited their depths.

Built to carry about 250 passengers in high style in first class, and perhaps an additional 1,000 in less comfort with a huge crew to look after them all, *Nieuw Amsterdam* had recently been stripped of her opulent furnishings and converted into a floating military barracks to transport about 6,400 American troops to the Middle East. Antiaircraft guns were mounted fore and aft; the swimming pool served as a vast storage pit for cartons of Spam, bully beef, and canned goods. Dutch crewmen in blue fatigues were struggling to cover the pool with a billowing tarpaulin as I made my way to the office of the billeting officer on the main deck amidships.

The man in line directly ahead of me also awaiting assignment to quarters looked vaguely familiar: stocky; "War Correspondent" embroidered in gold on green epaulets; the China-Burma theater insignia on his left sleeve. "Hazy!" I shouted, causing him to whirl about. It was Harry Zinder, the AP man I had met in Jerusalem in 1940. The delight and surprise were mutual. Zinder had since joined the staff of *Time-Life,* had just returned from covering the disastrous Burma campaign, and was on his way to Cairo for reassignment there, nearer Jerusalem and his family.

The resumption of what became an enduring, lifelong friendship went uncelebrated; *Nieuw Amsterdam,* we discovered to our horror, was a dry ship. But the young billeting officer who saw our exuberant reunion obligingly assigned us to a small stateroom to ourselves on one of the lower decks. Once a "single with shower" in second class, it now had two bunks separated by a chest of drawers. We swapped family news while stowing our gear, then explored the ship that would be our home for many more days than we had anticipated.

The men were still coming aboard, lugging duffel bags and dangling steel helmets, as we elbowed our way topside along the corridors. They were mostly technicians and Special Services personnel ranging in ranks from lowly privates to majors. Their commander on board was Colonel William A. Aird, an "old army" type on whom we called to pay our respects in his upper-deck office. The hat on his desk was vintage World War I: round, broad-brimmed, and peaked. Its owner had a sharp nose, thin lips, and cold blue-gray eyes behind steel-rimmed spectacles. His dry voice and manner suggested he was determined to run "a tight ship," but it was evident he would have his hands full.

Among the passengers coming aboard were about sixty female volunteers of the American Red Cross in natty gray uniforms. They had the men whistling and drooling as they were shepherded to quarters on B deck forward, beyond a cross-corridor chain from which hung a sign that said OFF LIMITS.

The main dining salon, where fat Dutch burghers and their stout wives had sat over their filet dc sole and Liebfraumilch and watched the sea go past a better than thirty knots an hour through plate glass windows was now a mess hall with refectory tables and benches, the rows of plate glass windows boarded over and painted a neutral gray. Tiered bunks doubled and tripled the sleeping space in all staterooms and cabins throughout the ship. Farther down in the vessel's bowels slept her crew and the hundred or so veteran British soldiers who manned *Amsterdam*'s ack-ack guns.

Somewhere aft of the spick-and-span engine room, in a steel-walled cubicle reachable only by a steep iron ladder, Zinder and I found what we had been looking for: a small, power-operated printing press, several type fonts, and a stock of coated paper. We had the makings of a newspaper. We called it *The*

Flying Dutchman and, in view of its size, subtitled it *All The News That Fits We Print.* A notice pinned up on the bulletin board next to the purser's office that evening produced a printer, several reporters, typists, a copy reader, and a sports editor in the person of Captain George Kirksey, a United Press veteran on his way to Cairo to become General Brereton's public relations officer.

We sailed with the tide on the morning of May 2, not in convoy but alone, *Amsterdam*'s cruising speed of twenty-six knots being deemed sufficient to outrun the fastest Japanese subs, and the first edition of *The Flying Dutchman* was distributed on Wednesday morning, May 5. On Sunday, May 9, we put out a special edition complete with two pages of comics drawn with a stylus on mimeograph paper by a shy, spectacled naval rating named Saul Steinberg, the artist whose work enlivened the pages of *The New Yorker.*

Our "daily" was only a single sheet, printed on both sides, three columns wide, but it managed to contain all the international news that came down from the ship's radio room. Surviving copies of *The Flying Dutchman,* especially the one with the talented Steinberg's drawings, ought to be collectors' items. My own collection, which I sent home from Cairo by boat mail, probably was sunk somewhere in the Atlantic.

Although segregated in their own quarters, well guarded by military police, and supervised by a bossy, prissy little middle-aged ARC officer, the Red Cross girls were not entirely safe from the advances of the several hundred commissioned personnel on board. Early in the voyage, as *Amsterdam* breasted the long Pacific swells under starlit skies, romance flourished, vigilance relaxed, and inevitable couplings occurred. Most went unreported, though not unnoticed, but one night the MPs were summoned to raid one of main deck staterooms where half a dozen officers and as many ARC girls staged a well-liquored party.

This resulted in a ship-wide summons from Colonel Aird to a topside roll call, a stern lecture on morals, and a thorough search of all quarters by the MPs for hidden liquor. Enough was found to fill a washtub with the contents of the confiscated bottles. The resultant cocktail was then ceremoniously dumped overboard, as sad a sight as I've ever witnessed.

Our first port of call after zigzagging across most of the Pacific was Wellington, New Zealand, which we reached on or about May 16. There we marched all our troops through the streets to prove to our allies that the Yanks were really in the war, and there Zinder and I replenished our dwindling stocks of coated paper for the *Dutchman.*

Amsterdam then sailed across the Great Australian Bight to Perth, as dull a place as I'd ever seen, memorable mainly as a gloomy agglutination of waterfront warehouses and sailors' pubs. Nevertheless, it was in Perth that a bevy of our ARC beauties—they became more desirable with every league we sailed—participated in a stupendous Aussie-style pub crawl with their officer escorts that brought swift retribution. At our third stop, Colombo, in Ceylon (now unhappy Sri Lanka, then still a reasonably peaceful British colony), all hands were confined to the ship.

Our fourth and last port of call on this bizarre crossing of the vast Pacific was Karachi, on the west coast of India, where we discharged troops destined for service in the Persian Gulf Command, roughly half the ship's passengers. This done, *Amsterdam* sailed southwest across the Arabian Sea, then swung north into the Red Sea toward our destination, Suez.

Although the air conditioning didn't always work and the food was what might be expected from galleys whose omelets were made with powdered eggs and whose stews consisted mainly of Spam and canned vegetables, the journey remained unforgettable for the smiling weather, the star-punctured night skies, the shoals of flying fish, the occasional albatross that swung back and forth across our wake, and, above all, the sense of utter safety in *Amsterdam*'s ability to outrun enemy submarines. It never crossed my mind that we might be torpedoed, much less bombed.

Between ports we saw no other signs of life, nothing to suggest we were not the only ship afloat, indeed, the only living creatures on earth, so profound was the sense of remoteness on the vastness of the Pacific.

When *Amsterdam*'s passengers disembarked at Suez in the early afternoon of June 13, after forty-one days at sea, they knew, thanks to *The Flying Dutchman,* that the Allies had won the Battle of North Africa and were preparing to invade Sicily.

51

WINGS OVER SICILY

B y mid-June 1943, in the fifth summer of the Second World War, the
Allies had cleared North Africa of all Axis forces and were at last
masters of the Mediterranean sea-lanes. Meanwhile, it was common
knowledge among correspondents accredited to Montgomery's
Eighth Army that our next big story would be the invasion of Sicily, the
mountainous island doorstep to Italy.

For reasons atavistic as well as journalistic, the invasion of Sicily was one
story I was determined not to miss. Accordingly I asked Major Oakshott, the
Eighth Army public relations officer, to be sure to include me among the
reporters who would cover the eventual landings. To make certain I was not
overlooked, I also informed Geoffrey Keating, chief of Monty's sizable corps
of press photographers, that I had been commissioned to write a book about
his general, then at the peak of his popularity as Rommel's conqueror, and
Keating, who idolized Monty, promised me as frequent access to the general
as possible during the forthcoming campaign.

Montgomery himself at the time was not in Cairo but in Tunis or Malta,
conferring with Eisenhower, the commander in chief of Allied forces in the
Mediterranean, and the other British and American commanders who were
putting the finishing touches on what turned out to be the biggest, most
powerful seaborne attack ever mounted.

When, however, the invasion of Sicily was launched in the early morning
of July 10, I was not with Monty's forces on a Sicilian beach, but several
hundred miles away in Benghazi, the Libyan desert base of the Bomber Com-

mand of General Brereton's Ninth U.S. Air Force, climbing into the belly of one of his B-24 Liberators to cover the attack from the air. Thus, while the correspondents who accompanied the British Eighth Army into battle were splashing ashore from DUKWs, the new amphibious vessels we knew thereafter as ducks, I was flying across Sicily with an American crew to dump bombs on Axis targets in Calabria, the "toe" of the boot-shaped Italian peninsula.

The change in my plans for reporting the first major allied assault on Fortress Europe resulted from a dinner party, complete with wine and belly dancers, on the roof of Cairo's Hotel Continental on the evening of June 29, when D day for Sicily still lay in the uncertain future. And the person responsible for my presence in Benghazi during the countdown to zero hour instead of in Cairo, where I should have been, was friend Brereton, the feisty little two-star commander of American air power in the Mediterranean.

We were four at dinner that hot, airless June night: our host, Frank Lynch, the resident representative of General Motors; Brereton and I; and my colleague Quentin Reynolds, who happened to be in town on his way to Moscow. Lynch, a longtime friend of the general's, was a compact gray man who, since he had no GM cars to sell in wartime Egypt, I assumed was probably one of Wild Bill Donovan's agents; no one stationed in Cairo knew more about Egyptian politics than suave, self-contained Frank Lynch.

Over the food and wine, after the belly dancers had done their act, Quent told us the story of the Dieppe raid, which he had covered for our magazine and which had proved a bloody failure at least partly because the venture was inadequately supported from the air. The big, affable Irishman's moving account of the Dieppe fiasco held even Brereton's attention and prompted the general to expound on his favorite subject: the importance of air power in modern warfare.

Unlike Montgomery, Hotfoot Louie Brereton shunned personal publicity, but he was proud of his air force. In his view, the Ninth had made a substantial, perhaps even decisive contribution to the ousting of the Axis forces from North Africa. He believed, in fact, that air power in general, and the Ninth in particular, had beaten Rommel and Arnim logistically in Tunisia even before they were defeated on the ground by the American and British armies commanded respectively by Patton and Montgomery. It had irked Brereton that in the dispatches of the correspondents who covered the Tunisian campaign the rambunctious Patton and the methodical Monty, whom Brereton disliked, had emerged as the heroes of the struggle for Tunis and Bizerte.

"Reading the papers," Brereton said in his clipped Hoosier speech, "you'd think Georgie and Monty won the fight for Tunisia. Hell's bells, they'd still be fighting around Tunis and Bizerte if our mediums and heavies hadn't pounded the daylights out of the enemy's supply lines to Sicily and Italy, sunk his transports, hammered his airfields, and demolished his fortifications."

Sensing a story—I badly needed one at the time—I asked the general whether his G-2 (intelligence) could prove that the Ninth's participation had been not merely supportive but decisive.

"Come out to Bomber Command, and we'll give you the facts and figures," he replied. "And you can talk to the men who did the job."

"Is that an invitation, General?" I asked.

"It is," Brereton said crisply. "Tell you what. I'm flying out to Benghazi in a couple of days. You can come along. I'll pick you up."

I was on the verge of saying I'd made arrangements to go to Sicily with Monty's army come D day but chickened. The invitation came from my only close friend among Allied commanders, and I couldn't think of a graceful refusal. Besides, I really needed a story; except for a cable saying I'd arrived in Cairo, my magazine hadn't heard from me since the day I sailed on the *Amsterdam.*

I thanked the general and said I'd be ready to leave whenever he was.

Sweltering June became torrid July with no indication from Brereton's headquarters that the proposed trip to Benghazi was imminent. I looked forward to celebrating Independence Day with Quent Reynolds and Harry Zinder, who shared my quarters at Shepheard's. We bought black-market booze and planned a proper shindig with Chet Morrison, George Lait, and half a dozen other American correspondents who happened to be in town, among them Joel Sayre, of *The New Yorker* and the AP's George Tucker.

But on the morning of the Fourth a phone call from Brereton's aide, Colonel Louis Hobbs, roused me shortly after daybreak and advised me to be ready to be picked up outside the hotel at seven o'clock. "Not a word about where you're going or why," Hobbs cautioned. "Just get yourself downstairs in time, okay?" and rang off.

General Brereton swung open the rear car door when his black Chevy sedan drew up at the sidewalk, and he motioned me to sit beside him. Hobbs was in the front seat with the driver. Except for perfunctory good mornings, neither spoke a word, and Hotfoot Louie was silent all the way to the airfield, as though pondering some weighty secret problem, tight-lipped and inscrutable behind his tinted aviator's glasses.

Brereton was like that whenever he was about to send his men on a particularly dangerous mission, and I knew him well enough not to intrude on his thoughts. I craved a cigarette but refrained from asking permission to light up. Both the general and Hobbs were nonsmokers and had chided me about my habit often enough to inhibit me.

As a major general Brereton rated a private DC-3. Instead of bucket seats in the forward half of the plane, there were four upholstered chairs, two on each side of the aisle, which could be swiveled to face each other across tables for meals or cards.

Hobbs motioned me to one of the port side seats while he and the general sat opposite each other on the starboard side. The navigator, who doubled as steward, served hot black coffee in enameled cups from the tiny galley, said the plane was ready for takeoff, and vanished behind curtains into the cockpit.

The general and Hobbs started playing gin rummy as soon as we became airborne, and after watching the play for a while, I fell asleep, as I invariably did in flight. It was a four- or five-hour trip to Benghazi, and I probably would have slept all the way but was awakened by a roaring "Damn!" from Brereton that indicated Hobbs had probably schneidered him for a big loss.

Hobbs always won at gin. He was a dark-eyed, black-haired man with a black mustache and a deep tan, a Texan who looked like perfect casting to play a devilishly handsome Mexican bad man in a Hollywood western. He was, as I had learned from having consistently lost to him at poker and gin rummy, very good at cards.

While Hobbs was putting away the cards, the general seemed disposed at last to talk, and I told him that I planned going to Sicily with Monty's army.

"I hope," I said, "that I'll be able to get back to Cairo in time."

"No problem," said Brereton. "We're nowhere near D day yet. Takes time, you know, to plan a big amphibious operation . . ."

And for the next hour or so the general schooled me in the complexities involved in assembling the elements of a seaborne operation like the one the Allies were completing for the invasion of Sicily. Nothing in war, he said, is more complicated or less tolerant of error than an amphibious attack on a fortified, well-defended enemy objective. Such operations are extremely dangerous, he said, even when Mother Nature cooperates with good sailing and flying weather.

They mean, Brereton said, assembling hundreds of ships and landing craft, collecting tens of thousands of men, and gathering innumerable items of equipment at designated embarkation ports, securing the required mix of troops—infantry, artillery, armor, engineers, signalmen, medics, drivers—and assigning them to vessels and amphibious landing craft.

The Allies, Brereton indicated, had no experience with an opposed landing. Their virtually unopposed landings in Morocco and Algeria in November had been difficult enough, and they were making certain that their attack on Sicily—appropriately code-named Husky, the general revealed—was being meticulously planned to the last-minute detail to ensure its success. Clearly, they wanted to avoid a World War II version of Gallipoli.

At one point in his dissertation Brereton interrupted himself to ask whether I was sure I wanted to cover the invasion with the ground forces. I assured him I did, adding I knew of no other way of covering the action, and told him I'd asked to be included in the Eighth Army's press corps. Brereton made no comment, but as the plane made a turn and leveled off for its approach to the landing strip, he sprang a surprise.

"I'm going right on to Tunis after we gas up," he said, "and won't be back for a day or two. We'll talk again when I return, and maybe I can persuade you to report Husky from the air. . . ."

"Not a chance," I said.

We landed smoothly on one of the Ninth's desert airfields south of Benghazi, and while the DC-3's tanks were being topped off and the mechanics checked its tires and landing gear, Brereton and Hobbs held a head-to-head parley beyond earshot. I felt that I was the subject of their conversation, an impression Hobbs confirmed by occasionally glancing in my direction as though to make certain I was at a safe distance.

When the plane was ready, Brereton turned, waved a cheery good-bye, returned his aide's sharp salute, clambered aboard his aircraft, and took off in a swirl of stinging sand.

It was well past lunchtime, and the waiting Jeep drove Hobbs and me about two miles to the huge tent that served as the officers' mess at the base camp. It was hot, crowded, and noisy inside, and lunch was the standard fare of "the world's best-fed army": fried hamburgers with mashed potatoes and brown gravy, buttered peas and carrots, thick slices of white bread, and canned fruit cocktail for desert. I would have preferred one of Kim Mundy's bully beef stews to the greasy burgers, but I had to admit the bread, baked daily by the GI bakers, was a vast improvement over the British army's jaw-breaking "biscuits."

After lunch Hobbs walked me about a hundred yards to my quarters, the walled tent I was to share with him during my stay in Benghazi. It smelled strongly of insecticide and the colonel's shaving lotion, but I didn't mind. I liked living under canvas, and our tent was pitched at the end of a short row of officers' tents under the scraggly shade of the palms of a small oasis, hence was reasonably cool. Netting kept out most of the pestiferous Libyan flies, and the insecticide took care of intruders. The latrines, I was happy to see, were downwind from us, and the route to them was clearly marked with white-washed rocks; they'd be easy to find even on moonless nights.

That afternoon Hobbs introduced me to the various commanders—Brigadier General Pat Timberlake, Colonels P. D. ("Dutch") Ent, John ("Killer") Kane, Leon Johnson, Keith Compton—and a number of captains and lieutenants of the closely knit family of Bomber Command, as well as members of the flight crews. Some were just in from raids over Messina, Gerbino, Catania, Comiso, and Gela, Sicilian targets being softened up before D day. I was allowed to sit in on the fliers' postraid debriefings and listened to the pilots' reports of hits on airfields, marshaling yards, and communications centers.

Although I had the run of the place, I soon became aware of something going on from which I was being studiously excluded. I heard enough, however, to know that in the desert well to the south and west of Benghazi, flights of B-24s were rehearsing low-level attacks for which the boxlike Liberators were not intended. They were designed to fly high, above the ack-ack, not swoop down on targets in the manner of Mitchells or fighter-bombers. Now and then I overheard the name Ploieşti in pilots' discussions of the day's maneuvers, but inquiries met stony silence, even from Hobbs.

Pending Brereton's return, I interviewed his flight leaders and crews and soon had several notebooks full of data which confirmed the general's contention that the bomber and fighter squadrons of the Ninth Air Force had played a decisive role not only in the Allied victory in North Africa but also in terminating Axis domination of the Mediterranean.

The commanders I talked with freely admitted having received substantial help from the RAF and the British navy. But it was the Ninth's bombers— mediums and heavies—which, they said, were largely responsible for the defeat of Rommel and Arnim during the critical final stages of the struggle in Tunisia, from the cracking of the Mareth Line in late March to the ultimate triumph over the Axis forces in mid-May.

During that time the Ninth's bombers—among them those B-24 Liberators I had seen coming off the assembly line at Willow Run months before—severed the Axis supply routes to Sicily and Italy and deprived the enemy defenders of their Tunisian stronghold of everything they needed to continue resistance: fuel for their vehicles and tanks, reinforcements, ammunition, food, medical supplies, even water. Finally, it was American air power, my informants said, operating in conjunction with the British fleet, that prevented the enemy from staging an Axis "Dunkirk" which would have released important numbers of troops and weapons for the defense of Sicily. During the climactic phase of the battle for Tunisia, forty-two ships were sunk in the narrow waters between Tunisia and Sicily, mostly by the Ninth's Mitchells and Liberators.

As a result, although Hitler had ordered Tunisia held "to the last man and the last cartridge," the end there was an utter collapse. The "bag" when the fighting ended included General von Arnim and 14 other German generals, and 4 Italian; 260,000 German and Italian soldiers; 250 German tanks and 100 Italian; and more than 1,200 guns, troops and weapons enough to have made Sicily even stronger than the Allies would find it on D day.

Among the Ninth's individual achievements was the conquest of the geographically insignificant but strategically important island of Pantelleria. This volcanic outcrop, measuring barely six miles by four but powerfully fortified with antiaircraft batteries and fifteen-inch naval guns, lay in the center of the channel between Tunisia and Sicily. Its armament, and the Luftwaffe's fighter-bombers operating from the island's airstrip, effectively commanded the narrow east-west passage through the Mediterranean.

Throughout the war the island fortress had obliged British convoys headed for the Middle East from England to take the long sea route around Africa instead of the shortcut through the sea the Italians called *mare nostrum.*

The elimination of Pantelleria and two nearby satellite islands, Lampedusa and Linosa, both also heavily fortified, was deemed essential to complete Allied control of the sea-lanes to Sicily and Italy, and the task of eliminating them was assigned to the Ninth Air Force. From May 30 onward Pantelleria and its sister islands were subjected to intensive, almost continuous bombardment. The defenders on Pantelleria raised a white flag on June 11; Lampedusa fell the next day; and Linosa, the day after.

It seemed to me that with the surrender of those three little islands the dismantling of the outer defenses of Fortress Europe had begun. Moreover, it was the first time since the war began that an Axis foe had surrendered European territory.

I had material, now, for at least one good piece for my magazine; but there were no transmission facilities for correspondents at Benghazi, and at supper that evening I asked Hobbs if he could arrange for me to return to Cairo in the morning. The colonel hemmed and hawed, smiled his best "bad man" smile, then confirmed a growing suspicion.

"My orders are," he said, "to keep you here until D day, whenever that might be. Anyhow, Pops'll be here sometime tomorrow, and you can take it up with him. Maybe he'll let you go, but I doubt it. He's got something laid on for you. Don't worry, you won't miss the invasion, that much I can tell you. . . ."

I felt I had been manipulated and freely denounced Major General Lewis Hyde Brereton as a first-class, double-crossing, no-good Hoosier so-and-so. I stalked off alone to the officers' club, a low one-story building that had somehow survived the shellings and bombings of both sides. Over a lukewarm Coke, I rehearsed the speech I would make to Hotfoot Louie the next day.

Brereton returned in the late afternoon of July 9, in time to attend the interrogation of the crew that that morning had attacked Taormina, the Sicilian winter resort I had often heard my father describe as a spectacularly beautiful place rich in Greek and Roman antiquities. The bombers' objective was the town's San Domenico Hotel, once a monastery, which the Germans were using as their Sicilian headquarters and main communications center. The crew of the 376th Group, which had carried out the attack, reported "at least ten direct hits" on the target. One of the fliers said he had seen part of the hotel, situated on the edge of a high bluff, roll down into the sea.

During the debriefing Hobbs slid onto the stool next to me and whispered, "Pops wants to see you at supper tonight." I gave him what I hoped was a withering look.

Alone with Brereton and Hobbs in a comparatively quiet corner of the officers' mess, I found the general wasn't even faintly contrite about having gulled me into coming out to Benghazi to publicize his Ninth Air Force. He asked me why I was so "all-fired keen on landing in Sicily with Monty." I suddenly realized the general was unaware of my Sicilian background, and I gave him the essential details, the pertinent entries in what Oscar Wilde called "the diary we all carry around with us."

"Messina," I said, defiantly lighting a Chesterfield, "the city our bombers have been blasting almost every day, was where my father was born, sir, and would have been my birthplace, too, had my parents not had the good sense to emigrate to America. And somewhere in a cemetery on Messina's outskirts lie the bones of my paternal grandparents, who perished in the earthquake of 1908. . . ."

And Sicily, I reminded Brereton, was where Garibaldi had begun the liberation of Italy from Spanish tyranny in 1860, landing at Marsala with his immortal One Thousand volunteers, conquering the island in three months, then crossing the strait to wage war against the armies of the Bourbon king Francis. I had waited three years and seven months, I said, to participate in Sicily's—and Italy's—second liberation, this time from Fascist oppression.

Brereton removed his glasses and listened unblinkingly to my somewhat emotional account, and when I had finished, he said he was "truly sorry" he had isolated me in Benghazi during the countdown to D day, which, he now disclosed, was set for the next day, July 10. In fact, the first contingent of about 160,000 troops had probably already sailed from its embarkation ports at Tunis, Tripoli, Tobruk, and Alexandria, and with it the correspondents accompanying Montgomery's forces.

Apparently, the general indicated, D day had not yet been decided when we left Cairo, partly because of uncertainty about the capricious Mediterranean weather. Sudden gale-force winds and heaving seas had caused Eisenhower to consider a postponement.

There had been other delays because of Monty's insistence on a single powerful landing in Sicily under his command, with Patton relegated to the somewhat humble function of protecting his left flank. Monty had a low opinion of the military talents of American generals and of the fighting qualities of Yank troops. And in those days what Monty wanted, Monty got. The changes he demanded delayed an attack that had been originally planned for mid-June at the latest.

General Brereton then filled me in on the hitherto secret details of Husky. The vessels involved were not mere hundreds, but "more than three thousand," he said, some coming from as far away as England. That was why Pantelleria and its satellite islands had had to be eliminated as obstacles in the vital Sicilian Channel.

Ultimately some 378,000 men would be involved in Husky, divided into two armies, the American Seventh, under Patton, and the British Eighth, commanded, of course, by Montgomery. The operation's objective was total envelopment of the southeastern corner of triangular-shaped Sicily, the Trinacria of the ancient Greeks, with Patton attacking from the southwest and Monty from the southeast. Patton was assigned the beaches to the right and left of the important port of Gela, and Monty the shoreline south of the equally essential harbor of Syracuse. Clearly Monty had largely got his way: Patton was on Monty's left, protecting the Eighth Army's flank.

"But since it seems to mean so much to you," Brereton concluded, "you can still cover the invasion—from the air. Vertical envelopment* begins to-

* By "vertical envelopment" Brereton meant the airdrops of gliderborne troops on Sicilian communications centers and tactical features which had been decided by Patton and Montgomery. But poor training, inexpert navigation, and unexpected concentrations of antiaircraft fire, I learned later, made a botch of the whole show.

   Out of the 134 British gliders that took off that night, 47 were released prematurely and fell into the sea, 75 landed off targets on Sicily, and only a dozen reached

night; but it's mainly a British operation, and you can't go. Too damn dangerous, anyhow. You'll go tomorrow. Be ready by oh-three-hundred hours. Somebody will pick you up. . . ."

I was awakened at the appointed hour by a young major I'd not met before.
He waited while I dressed and splashed my face in water chilled by the desert's
night wind. The air was sweet, as though filtered through distant groves of
lemon and orange trees.

Wind and water revived me, and my escort walked me to the crews' mess
tent. On the way he said, "I wonder if Hitler knows what's going to hit him
this morning." There it was again. I had heard it a thousand times before from
British officers: Hitler was the enemy. I argued that Mussolini was our enemy,
too, that it had all begun with his March on Rome way back in 1922, Western
Europe's first revolt against democracy. Hitler, I said, merely took Italian
fascism and elevated it to the new frightfulness we had come to know as
nazism. I made no impression.

"Maybe so," the major said, "but the Eyeties are such nice people."

The mess tent was crowded but, except for the clatter of metal utensils,
curiously quiet. We ate double helpings of fried bacon and eggs and flapjacks
swimming in maple syrup and drank several cups of hot black coffee, well
sugared.

The briefing room later was filled with eager young men with old faces.
They were the pilots and crews for the day's mission, about two hundred men
seated in rows on low, square metal stools. Captain John J. Dore, of Garden
City, Long Island, a veteran of twenty-seven missions over enemy targets, was
introduced to me as my pilot. He was a Yale man and only twenty-four years
old, but he looked thirty-five: seamed face; crow's-feet about the startlingly
blue eyes; a stubble of beard on his lean jaws and sharp chin. "I never shave,"
he said, "before a mission."

Dore accepted me instantly. Apparently he had been told that I was not
a reporter bent on riding a bomber for the mere thrill of it all. He introduced
me to the rest of the crew, a warm, friendly lot.

Dore's copilot was Major Delbert Hahan, a Milwaukee boy; the navigator
was Lieutenant Worthing A. Franks, from Galveston, Texas; Joseph Finneran,
a Boston Irishman, was bombardier; Technical Sergeant A. Lower, of Lewis-
ton, Utah, was the radio operator; the engineer was another Texan, Sergeant
Frank Norris; and Sergeants Stanley Packer, of Spokane, and Wesley J. Jones,
of Wichita, were the gunners.

The target for the day was confirmed as Vibo Valentia, on Italy's Calabrian
"toe"; but it was broad daylight, and the sun was a ball of hot fire by the time

---

their objectives. The Americans fared no better. The airborne operation was a fiasco
in which the Allies wasted some of their most carefully chosen and best-trained
troops mainly because of inexperienced and inadequately trained air crews.

we were togged out in parachutes and Mae Wests and had squirmed into our assigned places aboard Dore's plane. I was placed in the waist of the ship, on a jump seat near the port side gunner, next to the bomb bay.

The plane, heavily loaded with fuel and bombs, roared down the runway almost to the very end before it lifted. Suddenly we crossed the irregular edge of the brown desert and were over the Mediterranean, opalescent blue below us. The gunners cleared their guns, firing a few bursts to test their efficiency, and we settled down for the long haul ahead. For an hour or two I dozed while the gunners and everyone else on board scanned the skies for enemy fighters.

My neighbor the gunner shook me awake and pointed downward through the Plexiglas bubble in which he sat. And I saw Messina. It was a great, gray, battered glob of a city sprawled on the foothills of majestic Mount Etna, the volcano that had brought so much tragedy to my own family and to tens of thousands of other Sicilian families in 1908. Captain Dore must have read my mind at that moment, for his voice came over the intercom: "Bet those poor bums in Messina think we're going to hit them again. Maybe, though, it wouldn't make much difference to them if we did. They've been hit twenty times in the last twenty-four hours."

Some flak rose to greet us, but our squadron was flying well above its outer range, and except for a bit of turbulence, it did no damage. At least twenty vessels were anchored just outside Messina's harbor, with steam up. We could see plumes of smoke rising from their stacks and guessed they were evacuating Axis troops. Over the harbor works proper lay a heavy cloud of grayish black smoke rising from fires which other bombers before us had set.

Up ahead, at high noon, the Calabrian coast was an irregular, faintly visible line of demarcation between blue sky and purplish blue water. In a few minutes we could distinguish the outlines of the towering mountains of Calabria, with the city of Reggio di Calabria a splatter of buildings on the picturesque shoreline.

The bomb bay doors opened with a low, rumbling sound, and the ship quivered expectantly. In the racks there were nearly three hundred fragmentation bombs, painted black and yellow, and looking like so many innocent items in a hardware store, beautifully turned out but deadly marvels of craftsmanship. Dore asked me to open the trapdoor in the floor of the flight deck.

We bored through dense clouds, and when we emerged, the target area was in full view. Framed in the outlines of the trapdoor, which measured about two feet wide by four feet long, was the arid, tumbled Calabrian countryside, unfertile earth which, though diligently tilled, had failed to ease the grinding poverty that had driven so many of its inhabitants to new lives in America.

Minutes later the target itself—the airdrome and installations of Vibo Valentia—slid like film into the oblong below, and the bombardier released our bombs. The missiles left the ship in a pinging flurry of snapping wires and the sharp crackle of detonating primers. The bombs seemed to jostle one another in a downward race to the target. The first bursts I saw were the bombs from a plane immediately ahead of us on the target.

Two enemy planes, like snipe flushed from a brown beach, tried to get away. Only one succeeded. Others in a covey of fighters clustered behind a revetment were destroyed on the ground. I could see them collapse like so many crushed dragonflies. One burned at the end of a landing strip as though hit at point of takeoff.

Our bombs now exploded among hangars and administration buildings. But our attack was only one of many that had hit Vibo Valentia earlier. There was no ack-ack; the antiaircraft batteries had been knocked out in previous raids.

Mission completed. A big turn, and we headed for home. Now, however, there might be German Messerschmitts to face—the tough Me-109s.

Clouds ahead. Captain Dore knew that clouds often hid attackers, and he swung around them, the other elements in our formation falling in behind him.

A second formation of B-24s went into the cloud mass. When it emerged at the other side, somewhat to the left of us, ten Me-109s met it. The B-24s fought them off. One of the bombers was hit but not enough to bring it down; it lost an engine but kept on going.

The Messerschmitts then turned on us. At first they were mere dots before my eyes, uncertainly placed in vision, but they quickly became very real. All our guns—the one in the tail and those in each of the two side blisters—opened up. The noise was deafening, blotting out thoughts, inspiring only—in me, at least—breathless, paralyzing fear.

But when both formations of B-24s formed into a stacked and staggered unit, the Messerschmitts failed to close for combat. Over the intercom a relieved Captain Dore said, "Long way from base. They're probably running out of gas. Just as well. Let's go home, too."

Within a half an hour we were out of danger. We lighted cigarettes, turned the switches of our intercoms to "liaison," and listened to music from the Armed Forces Network. Fred MacMurray was emceeing a show in San Francisco. I had never met Mr. MacMurray, but his voice was as welcome as that of an old friend. Lou Holtz told one of his funnier stories, and a girl named Ginny Simms sang a few songs.

Up in the cockpit Captain Dore twisted his head around, smiled broadly, and raised his right hand in the airman's symbol for "All's well," the thumb and index finger forming an O.

Homeward bound there was time to reflect. We had left behind us a chaos of broken buildings, cracked water mains, devastated hangars, blasted roads, burning railway stations, and crippled vehicles. I wondered, dimly, how many people we had killed or maimed. Hundreds? Thousands? I tried to shake off a sudden, new appreciation of the utter horror of war. Until then I had seen only desert war in the uninhabited wastelands of Egypt and Libya. But this was different. Now we were striking at a heavily populated land. Was I being squeamish because the target was Italy, ancestral Italia?

I pushed the thoughts out of my mind, but they recurred in the months ahead, over and over again.

Ours was not the only raid of the day. Other bombers, heavies and mediums from our own Ninth Air Force and from the U.S. Twelfth Air Force in North Africa, plus units of the Royal Air Force—some four thousand first-line Allied aircraft massed along the southern littoral of the Mediterranean for democracy's first major counterblow against the Axis heartland—had also done their work. They had hit Pachino, and they had hammered Trapani, Catania, Marsala, Sciacca, Licata, Vittoria, Comiso, Noto, and, of course, Messina. They were names familiar from childhood, heard when I was growing up in South Philadelphia's Little Italy, whose residents had come to America from precisely those towns. They were all, in a sense, my *paesani.*

I wondered what the citizens of my boyhood neighborhood would think or feel when they read the news of what our bombers had done to their old homeland. Of one thing I was certain: They would not be playing "Giovinezza" on their blaring Victrolas on summer Sunday afternoons as they had before the war, and they would no longer be singing the praises of il Duce, for having made Italy's trains run on time.

Meanwhile, along the miles of Sicilian coastline that formed the island's southeastern corner, hundreds of landing craft, mainly ducks and LSTs, surged through the rolling swells, reached their appointed positions and spilled antlike files of troops ashore, the men clutching weapons and struggling through the surf under battle-loaded backpacks. Overhead, flights of fighter planes provided protective cover.

At his headquarters on Malta, Eisenhower, I learned later at Bomber Command, had had his bad moments, arising mainly out of fears that the weather would foul the operation. But the wind dropped, as though in answer to his prayers, and the sea leveled off into a broad swell. In fact, the unseasonable weather helped rather than hindered the Allies: The Italian and German shore watchers mistook the numerous blips on their radar screens for atmospheric deviltries during the night of July 9 until it was too late for them to face the realities effectively.

Hence the Allies achieved a measure of surprise, as important an element in warfare as overwhelming power and luck, and the initial landings were comparatively easy with minimal losses in men and weapons. But plenty of hard fighting lay ahead, especially for Patton's Seventh Army, aiming at Gela, the port the American forces needed to supply the subsequent thrust inland in the race to Messina.

Back at Bomber Command on the evening of July 10 there was jubilation that all aircraft had returned safely from the raid on Vibo Valentia. For the time being, at least, the Luftwaffe had been swept from the air, and the Ninth's participation in the mighty endeavor to crack Hitler's Fortress Europe had been a resounding success.

But for the foot soldiers, the tankers, and the seamen of Operation

Husky—the biggest amphibious attack ever mounted, bigger even than the one that was to be hurled at Normandy's beaches eleven months later—the fighting and the bloodletting had only just begun.

"After Sicily," Brereton told me at Benghazi, "will come Italy and a long, hard struggle up that mountainous peninsula. Whether the Italians will fight or not—and I don't think they will—is irrelevant. Hitler can't afford to yield Italy and will defend it with everything he's got."

The next day, July 11, I flew back to Cairo with Brereton and Hobbs. As usual the two played cards during the flight while I pecked away at my Hermès trying to compose a lead for my piece about the Ninth Air Force and the D day flight over Sicily that wouldn't be hopelessly dated by the time it appeared in *Collier's* in from three to six weeks. I made half a dozen or more false starts, ripping out and crumpling page after page. The cardplayers across the aisle were amused by my struggle with the English language.

Brereton's car was waiting at the airport, and on the way into town the general asked me what my plans were. I told him I hoped to go to Sicily after I had finished my article. This brought guffaws from both. "By that time," Brereton said, "the war will be over in Sicily."

We dropped the general at his villa, where he and Hobbs held a brief conference in low tones at the foot of the steps, but I heard the colonel say, saluting, "Okay, sir, I'll tell him." Hobbs got in beside me and told the driver to take us to Shepheard's. As the car drew up at the hotel, Hobbs grabbed my arm.

"I suggest you don't leave Cairo for a while," he said. "Forget Sicily and stick around. Pops told me to tell you there's a big one coming up, and he thinks you'll want to cover it. You'd have an exclusive, a real scoop. What'll I tell him?"

"I'm not in the scoop business anymore," I said. "Okay, Lou, but it better be good."

"It will be," Hobbs replied airily. "I'll call you. . . ."

52

SICILIAN INTERLUDE

After having flown over the island in a bomber, I wanted more than ever to set foot on Sicilian soil, and on the morning of July 13—three days after D day—I telephoned Hobbs to ask whether I could absent myself from Cairo "for a much-needed holiday in another climate."

Hobbs, as intuitive as he was handsome, knew instantly what I meant. "No problem," he said, "but be sure to be back before the end of the month. If anything develops before then, however, I'll know where to reach you. . . ."

The next morning I flew to Sicily in an RAF transport plane that landed me on an airfield near shattered Licata, just west of Patton's headquarters at Gela, but far from my destination: the Eighth Army's public relations camp at Cassibile, on the east coast of Sicily south of Syracuse, the port city Montgomery had captured the very first day of the invasion.

From the airfield where I landed shortly before midday, July 14, I hitch-hiked to my destination toting a bedroll, typewriter, and musette bag. It was a long, hot trek in the quasi-African sun through gluey clouds of the dust raised by the Allies' truck convoys, half-tracks, tanks, staff cars, and Jeeps, and I remembered every torrid mile of the journey.

Fortunately the war had moved inland by D day plus four. The sky was clear of enemy aircraft, and I had no trouble getting lifts along the 150-mile southern coastal route to Cassibile through Gela, Scoglitti, Vittoria, and Comiso, then Ragusa and Noto. At Gela, where I stopped at Patton's press headquarters for information, I was strongly tempted to stay on and hook up with our Seventh Army. If I had, I might have met Two-Gun Patton and followed him into Palermo. But I felt compelled to push on to rejoin the Eighth Army, moved more by loyalty than by sound news sense.

Comradeship is one of the few worthwhile by-products of the unspeakably brutal trade called war. I missed my friends Morrison and Lait and the easy ways of the Eighth Army. The three of us wore with pride the Eighth's Crusader patch, which made us members of an elite element within the British armed forces. In retrospect, I believe the informality of our military dress had something to do with it; it was comfortable and casual, almost raffish in contrast with the Americans, who were required to wear GI regulation pants stuffed into heavy combat boots, long-sleeved shirts, and bucketlike steel helmets at all times in the blazing Sicilian sun.

My GI countrymen were not as comfortable as I, but far better protected against Sicily's endemic scourge, the malaria that took thousands of Sicilian lives annually. As a precaution against it the Sicilians built their villages and hamlets high on mountainsides and hilltops. For centuries they believed the chills and fever that periodically assailed them with often fatal results was due to the *mal aria* (bad air) of the plains and marshes where the deadly carrier, the anopheles mosquito, bred. The Sicilians dosed themselves with quinine, but we had Atabrine, an antimalarial drug that yellowed the skin and made us all look "liverish."

It was my first time with American ground troops. They were friendly as puppies toward a fellow countryman, generous with their cigarettes and K rations and with lifts to my destination. In the Seventh Army sector, which extended eastward to Ragusa, where the British took over, I rode in Forty-fifth Division trucks. My first driver, who hauled me and my gear as far as Scoglitti, was from Oklahoma. A drawling, soft-spoken farm boy, he was very young, very homesick, and very anxious to "get this lousy war over with as quick as possible."

At Scoglitti I was picked up by a Texan, a tall, wiry youth from Dallas, where he had worked as a mechanic in a garage. "The Eyeties," he said, "don't seem to want to fight much, and they're surrendering by the thousands. Those krauts in the hills are doing all the fighting. They're real sonsabitches and fight like maniacs. We don't have many of *them* in our POW camps. . . ."

The Texan dropped me off at a crossroads somewhere below Ragusa, where I had a longish wait for anything on wheels. I sat on my bedroll by the roadside, ate the cheese and crackers contained in my K rations, and scribbled in my notebook what I had seen, smelled, and felt during the hundred miles or so I had traveled, a journey through chaos in the dust and heat of a dry Sicilian afternoon in July.

The recurrent insanity called war is never a humane, reasonable undertaking but is a dirty, repulsive business wherever it happens. Even when con-

ducted in uninhabited desert, the only kind of war I had known until I landed
in Sicily, it is an incredibly noisy, smelly confusion of men and machines and
of thirst and squalor and acute discomfort.

Sicily, however, was neither a desert nor uninhabited. It was a triangular
island about the size of New Jersey, studded with towering mountains, slashed
by deep valleys and tortuous bad roads, and splattered with the cities, towns,
villages, and hamlets of more than four million people. Here the war seemed
noisier, smellier, more inhuman, and infinitely more squalid than it had been
in Egypt or Libya, where civilians rarely were involved in the fighting. In Sicily
they were everywhere.

The route I traveled along the southern coast road took me through those
towns in southeastern Sicily which my Ninth Air Force friends and the RAF
had drenched with bombs before D day and which Allied warships had shelled
from the sea. All were heavily damaged, and in each the air was heavy with
the stench of putrescent bodies, human and animal. A civilization that had
endured since the time of the Carthaginians appeared to have been obliterated.

The Sicily I saw that first day bore no resemblance, therefore, to the green
and fragrant Sicily with which my parents, especially my unassimilable mama,
had filled the picture books of my imagination when I was a boy. What I saw
was a brown, drab country littered with the enemy's burned-out tanks and
personnel carriers, wrecked trucks and staff cars, and dead farm animals
swollen with the gases of their decomposing innards.

The fields had been harvested, but the vineyards looked neglected. There
were few trees, and those were naked, stripped of leaves by bomb blast, their
bare branches making stark, surreal designs against the blue sky. As I looked
north from the road, all was havoc and ruin; the distant hills were blotched
with great black patches where fires had burned.

Yet life went on. In a field at some distance from the road a peasant and
his women were scratching the brown earth between rows of sickly-looking
maize. In an adjoining field a team of donkeys yoked to a central post was being
led around and around in a circle. Peasants tossed sheafs of grain under the
animals' hooves with wooden pitchforks, and I surmised they were threshing
wheat. I saw only older people and children.

No Sicilians used the road, where the traffic was constant and heavy in both
directions. The few passersby I saw crossed the fields afoot well beyond the
verges, which were strung with barbed wire hung with signs denoting the
presence of mines. They were poorly dressed, the men shouldering farm imple-
ments and the women carrying bundles on their heads, followed by children
leading goats or heavily burdened burros. They were Siciliani, a short, dark-
haired, olive-skinned people, a Mediterranean mélange. I saw myself in them,
and an inner voice kept saying over and over again, "There but for the grace
of God, go I."

There was a sudden lull in the traffic, and from some distant campanile
came the tinny sound of bells ringing vespers, a sign of approaching evening.
It was nearly six o'clock, and I began wondering whether I'd make it to

Cassibile by nightfall. If not, where would I spend the night? I was still turning the question over in my mind when a most unlikely vehicle, a heavy motorbike with a sidecar, swung off the coast road and stopped in a swirl of dust where I stood frantically waving my cap and goggles.

The knobby-kneed, helmeted, and gauntleted jockey who dismounted turned out to be Sergeant Miller, an Eighth Army courier, who willingly rescued me from my predicament. Miller lashed my bedroll and typewriter into his sidecar and rode me the sixty miles or so through ravaged Ragusa and battered Noto to Cassibile, where the Eighth Army's public relations people had "liberated" a villa. It was a rough ride; Miller almost lost me several times when we hit potholes or swerved to avoid them. I was barely able to stagger up the broad stone steps of the villa's terrace to grasp the outstretched hand of Major Oakshott. "You look awful," he said. "Come have a drink."

I hurt in every bone and muscle. My face, bare knees, and forearms were sunburned over their tan and caked with sweat and dirt. The major poured me a stiff gin and lime and showed me where I could wash up for dinner, a bench at the far end of the broad *terrazza,* where there was water in jerricans, a washbasin, and yellow soap.

"The bloody house is baronial," Oakshott said, "but there's no bathroom, not even an indoor privy. The facilities, old chap, are in the garden."

My friends Morrison and Lait, the major said, were "up forward" with Monty, and so were the other correspondents, all British. With them, also, was Major Keating, Monty's personal PR man, whom I had to see about arranging an interview with the general whose biography I was writing.* What had emptied the villa of correspondents was a sudden outbreak of fierce fighting on the Eighth Army's front.

Oakshott explained that after capturing Augusta the day before (July 13), Monty pushed on north toward Catania but was stopped where the coast road crossed the Simeto River at the Primasole Bridge, halfway to his objective. Apparently a complicated military situation had developed about which the major had little information. It was evident, however, that the invincible Montgomery's days of easy progress were over.

The major and I, and several of his junior officers, dined that night on an excellent bully beef stew made with fresh potatoes, carrots, onions, and peas bought locally. With it we had an assertive red Sicilian wine that made me so drowsy I almost fell asleep at the table. I was exhausted from the long trip to the villa but with coffee and brandy revived sufficiently to type a few notes on the day's experiences, working by candlelight on the mess table.

Apart from enemy fire and craftily hidden mines and booby traps, exhaus-

---

* It was to have been an "authorized" biography, and I had secured the cooperation of members of Monty's family. But after writing four chapters, I abandoned the project and returned to Appleton-Century the initial advance involved. By then I had concluded that Monty was a vastly overrated general. He was subsequently apotheosized by Alan Moorehead and others.

tion was war's greatest hazard. In time it overcame everyone, officers and men in all branches—infantrymen, especially, but also artillerymen, tankers, engineers, doctors, even reporters. We lived almost as primitively as the troops, but in addition, at the end of a day's work, we had to sit at typewriters and be "creative." Sometimes I was wearier than a footslogging soldier. Tonight was one of those times.

I recalled having visited Sicily only once before, early in 1937 as one of a party of Rome correspondents who accompanied Mussolini on his brief tour of the island during the Spanish Civil War. Mussolini needed the support of the reluctant Sicilians then, and I remembered that he had made them many promises about improving living conditions.

But from what I saw on my way to Cassibile, Sicily's peasants still lived in one-room stone hovels, usually with their goats and donkeys. From the walls of the towns and hamlets through which I had passed, the Sicilians had erased the Fascist mottoes that for a generation had urged them to "Believe! Obey! Fight!" In many places they had defaced or obliterated the oversize stenciled portrait of the warlike helmeted Duce that had stared at them from every convenient space.

I was bleary-eyed after about an hour's work, and everyone else had turned in. The villa was blacked out and silent as a mausoleum. Preferring the open air to the musty indoors, I laid my bedroll out on the *terrazza* and slipped into my sleeping bag in my shorts, taking care, however, to rig a tentlike hood of mosquito netting over my head.

I slept until awakened in the purple dawn by a distant cock's crow and the lewd heehawing of a passing donkey. I revived with a mugful of strong, hot tea provided by the thoughtful Sergeant Miller. He handed it to me gingerly with good news. "Looks like we'll be moving up soon," he said. "Today or tomorrow . . ."

I needed a bath, but at the communal washstand there was barely water enough to shave with. I reeked, but so did everyone else in the great brotherhood of weary British troops, who complained that Sicily was "worse than the fuckin' desert in every fuckin' way."

Usually the field correspondents came back to base after a day's action to write their pieces and be briefed on the overall situation, but on the morning of July 15 (D plus five) none had returned from whatever was happening north of us. Oakshott and I had the villa practically to ourselves, and after breakfast the major led me into the press room, spread a map on the table, and gave me a detailed account of the Eighth Army's movements since the landings.

The composition of Monty's forces had changed somewhat since my time with them in the Western Desert. The general still had the 5th and 50th divisions, to which had been added the crack 231st Infantry Brigade, and the 51st Highland Division. A newcomer was the 1st Canadian Division, which had come all the way from Britain, having sailed from the Clyde after Pantelleria surrendered and the Sicilian Channel was cleared.

Against the predominantly Italian defenders of the Pachino Peninsula,

Oakshott said, Monty probably had the finest troops Britain could field. They were divided into two corps: XIII Corps, commanded by General Miles Dempsey, and XXX Corps under General Oliver Leese. Their objective, the major said, was to "straddle and inundate" the Pachino Peninsula to ensure early capture of the fighter airfields clustered there.

The seasick men who had stumbled ashore on both coasts on D day encountered comparatively weak resistance. There were some local clashes with Italian troops, but there was little prolonged opposition. By nightfall Dempsey's men had captured Syracuse, an excellent harbor for the landing of equipment and supplies.

The Canadians, meanwhile, captured Pachino, with its small fighter air-field, and fanned out both inland and westward along the coast. The American right flank below Gela extended to meet them, and on July 12 the two forces made contact at Ragusa. The southeastern tip of the island was now firmly in Allied hands. The penetration inland placed the beaches beyond range of enemy artillery, and from their starting points the spearheads struck toward the center of Sicily, pressing along the coasts toward Agrigento and Catania.

Thus, three days after the first landing, it seemed that Sicily was ours. The capture of some six thousand prisoners indicated the complete collapse of the Italian will to resist. Five airfields, from some of which Allied fighter planes were already operating, had fallen to the invaders. A complete Allied conquest seemed certain.

In the circumstances, the Germans determined on a delaying action. Abandoning all efforts to hold the western and central portions, they concentrated their forces to cover the northeast corner of the island and the approaches to Messina, their escape hatch to the Italian mainland. Although some Italian units were thrust into various parts of the line, the defense thereafter was almost entirely a German affair. Upon three and a half German divisions fell the main burden of opposing the full Allied strength of nine divisions—two more than would be used in Normandy eleven months later—during the remainder of the Sicilian campaign.

At this point there arose the first of the many clashes over strategy and tactics that were to bedevil Anglo-American military relationships throughout the Sicilian campaign and beyond. The nasty situation arose from Montgomery's quasi-pathological desire to dominate the scene. It was no secret even then that Monty, Husky's putative parent, had wanted to be made overall commander and was bitterly disappointed when relegated to the relatively minor role of commander of the Eighth Army.

Monty's behavior at this critical juncture in the Sicilian campaign revealed flaws in both his generalship and his character worthy of more than passing attention. They resulted in heavy Allied casualties and friction with General Omar Bradley, commander of the U.S. II Corps, whose Seventh Army was protecting Monty's left flank.

The situation was clearly crayoned on the overlays of the maps Oakshott used to brief me, and the story as I was able to reconstruct it more fully later did Monty little credit. It went as follows: The coastal road along which

Dempsey pushed north toward Augusta and Catania hugged the sea all the way to Messina, Monty's ultimate objective. Augusta fell early on July 13, but midway to Catania, the next important port city, the road crossed the Simeto River at the Prima Sole Bridge, then strongly held by the Germans. To capture that vital crossing, Monty ordered the British First Parachute Brigade to be dropped on it the night of July 13–14 and to "take it and hold it."

Like several previous Allied drops of paratroopers, however, everything went wrong. Of the nearly 150 planes involved, fewer than 90 managed to thread their way through heavy enemy antiaircraft fire and only about 40 released their troops within a mile or so of the drop zone. Some landed as far away from the Prima Sole Bridge as the slopes of Mount Etna, about twenty miles northwest of the target. More than a dozen planes carrying parachutists were shot down in error by the Royal Navy.

Of the nearly two thousand British parachutists involved, fewer than two hundred, armed with three light antitank guns, managed to reach and seize the bridge itself, a pitifully small force for holding it. The Germans reacted fiercely to the intrusion, and the result was the daylong battle of July 14.

After taking heavy losses, the British withdrew at nightfall but took up positions on the high ground overlooking the bridge. From there they kept up a heavy covering fire that prevented the Germans from using or sabotaging the structure, but Monty's way to Catania and Messina remained solidly blocked.

In the meantime, entirely on his own, Montgomery conceived a strategic plan for conquering Sicily practically single-handedly. Leese's XXX Corps, which had had a very easy time of it after landing and pushing inland to Ragusa, stood virtually idle. Monty decided to circle Leese's forces around the west side of Mount Etna, then converge on Messina, entrapping the Axis defenders. In so doing, Leese's troops would displace the role assigned to the Seventh Army, using the only good road available for a northward thrust west of Mount Etna, Bradley's Route 124.

What followed was the most arrogant, selfish, egotistical, and dangerous move in the whole of Anglo-American combined operations in World War II. Without consulting even General Sir Harold Alexander, whom Eisenhower had deputized to supervise all ground operations, Monty ordered Leese to advance on the morning of July 13 and head for Enna on Route 124. By that time Bradley's troops had advanced to within a thousand yards of the road. Monty had ordered Leese's XXX Corps directly across the Americans' immediate front without prior notice or permission.

Having set Leese's forces in motion, Monty flew that same morning to Allied headquarters in Tunis and presented his plan to Alexander. He demanded that the army boundaries be changed by moving Seventh Army west to make room for Leese's oncoming troops. The pliable Alexander, more British gentleman than tough soldier, agreed to Monty's demands without taking into account the impact his decision would have on American tactics and sensibilities. Alexander, who shared Monty's low opinion of the Americans, then flew to Gela to announce the plan to Patton, the other prima donna of the Sicilian campaign.

At stake were Allied strategy for the conquest of Sicily, as well as American military honor, pride, and prestige, and many soldiers' lives. The Seventh Army was ready to strike for the only strategic prize of the campaign, Messina. Monty intended to deny the Americans this and relegate them to the inconsequential role of protecting his flank and rear. Yet, inexplicably, Patton, "Old Blood and Guts," who could have been expected to make strenuous objections, "took it," as Bradley said later, "like a lamb."

Bradley, on the other hand, was furious. He and his staff perceived at once the full import of Patton's acceptance of the decision: Monty had nominated himself for the starring role in Sicily, leaving the Americans to eat his dust. The decision involved giving up Route 124, which Bradley's corps had fought hard to take; repositioning his Forty-fifth Division to the left of the First Division; regrouping all support units (artillery, engineers, signalmen, medics); and slowing down the momentum of Seventh Army's attack, which had reached the northern coast road and was poised to turn eastward and drive on to Messina.

Meanwhile, the Germans had gained the time they needed to organize a firm defense. Montgomery's "plan" had misfired completely. The parachute drop had been a costly fiasco, and so had his "left hook" around Mount Etna to encircle and trap the enemy. As of the morning of July 15, when I was being briefed on the situation at Cassibile, the Eighth Army's northward progress was blocked at the Prima Sole Bridge and at the southern edge of the Catanian plain.

Montgomery apparently had misread the difficulty of carrying out his strategy against stiffening German opposition and had grievously riled the Americans by suggesting that there was room for only one offensive army in Sicily. Worst of all, perhaps, Monty the desert fighter seemed to have mislaid his genius when confronted by mountains instead of by the relatively flat expanses of the Egyptian and Libyan battlefields.

Opposite the Eighth Army a potentially firm line of resistance was taking shape in the spiky foothills of Mount Etna. The line was formed by top-notch German soldiers and some of the better Italian units. The defenders' chances of delaying the Allied campaign were evident enough when they were explained by a British intelligence major who joined Oakshott and me that morning. "It would appear," he said, "that our beloved Monty has got himself into a jar, and he is the pickle."

That evening word came, however, that the Fiftieth Division, driving up the coastal highway, had renewed the attack on the bridge in force and that the Fifth Division was striking inland toward Lentini. The next morning, July 16 (D plus six), the press headquarters at Cassibile packed up and started northward up the coast to find Major Keating and his mixed bag of American and British correspondents.

Traffic on the coastal highway was heavy in both directions. The men in the southbound vehicles were visibly tired, exhausted by the fighting in mountainous terrain, the torrid Sicilian sun, the recurrent water shortages. The weather conditions were similar to those that Monty's men had overcome in the Western Desert, but the topography was different; now there was always one more rugged hill to take, one more rock-strewn ravine to cross.

And there were far more casualties than I had ever seen in the desert. Ambulances bearing wounded came down the road and turned off to a field hospital in a hillside olive grove. We followed, and I had a chance to watch the surgeons at work. Five doctors were operating under canvas in the tropical heat. Some, I learned, had been at it as many as fourteen hours at a stretch and looked it. Their robes were blood-splattered, and what faces were not covered by surgical masks were pale and drawn.

Although the surgeons seemed outwardly impersonal at their often gruesome tasks, their fatigue and inner strain were apparent. A dozen times or more every day they had to decide whether to amputate a limb or remove an eye that had been pierced by a steel splinter from an exploding grenade, shell, or bomb, awesome decisions made on the spur of the moment.

The tent reeked of unwashed bodies, disinfectants, and morphia. I stood it for about an hour, long enough to decide that the surgeons and their teams of orderlies, not the infantrymen, were the war's hardest-working men. *Dulce bellum inexpertis:* Sweet is war to those who have never experienced it. Some of the prostrate, motionless, swathed figures on the operating tables were survivors of the fighting at the Prima Sole Bridge. A chaplain, masked, spectacled, solemn, moved about. . . . I escaped to the clean air outside.

Farther up the road we stopped at Syracuse. When Monty entered the city at the end of the first day's fighting, he ordered the streets cleared "within the hour." Officers went down into the malodorous shelters where much of the population lived during the pre-D day bombing and shelling and put all able-bodied men to work clearing the debris. They were still working, with the help of British bulldozers, when we arrived six days later.

On the northern outskirts of the city I made my way afoot to the Greek theater, which I knew to be a rewardingly beautiful sight. I found a guide, a scrawny little old man with a furrowed face and startlingly blue eyes, something not as rare among Sicilians as might be supposed. The name on the license tag pinned on the lapel of his oversize double-breasted gray jacket was F. Sparaceni. Removing his cloth cap, he said for me to call him Filippo.

The ruins, he said, had been miraculously spared. The theater, hollowed out of the solid rock of the promontory above the city by the early Greeks in the fifth century B.C., was built to seat fifteen thousand spectators. From the topmost of its more than sixty tiers, Filippo showed me a magnificent view of *la bella Siracusa,* which, he proudly reminded me, was the birthplace of Archimedes. From the height the city was still *bella* indeed, an agglomeration of seemingly unhurt tile-roofed buildings, church spires, and bell towers gleaming in the brilliant Sicilian sunshine against the blue Mediterranean beyond.

Filippo then led me down to the man-made grotto known as the Ear of Dionysius. Its name, given to it by Caravaggio in the sixteenth century, refers to a legend according to which Dionysius, the autocratic ruler of Syracuse in the fourth century B.C., secretly listened to his Carthaginian prisoners' conversations by means of the "ear's" strange acoustical properties. My guide drew an interesting parallel.

"I sometimes imagine," he said, "that this is where il Duce's spies listen to the people in his Fascist Sicilian prison. Mussolini therefore must know by now how much his prisoners have hated him all these years. Perhaps if *he* wins instead of *you,* we will be thrown to the lions in the Colosseum in Rome, just like the Carthaginian prisoners of Dionysius. . . ."

Would Mussolini win the war? Filippo looked at me as though he thought I had taken sudden leave of my senses, smiled a broad, rather toothless smile, and chuckled, his skinny concave chest heaving with each chuckle.

I gave him two packs of Chesterfields, worth their weight in gold on the black market, and a crisp dollar bill from my wallet. At parting, Filippo said he was sixty. He looked eighty.

Below Augusta we turned left and inland off the coastal road toward Lentini along a narrow, much-traveled secondary route through hilly country. The area seemed to be saturated with British troops and vehicles. It was slow going through sworls of dust, and it was nearly sundown when we arrived at our destination, the villa on the outskirts of Lentini, on the southern edge of the rich and decidedly malarial Catanian plain, where Major Keating had established Eighth Army's new press headquarters.

The place was full of tired-looking newsmen, all British, who had come to follow a triumphant Monty into Messina. The only two I knew were Alex Clifford, of the *Daily Mail,* and his friend Alan Moorehead, of the *Daily Express,* two of Fleet Street's best. My American friends Morrison and Lait had left and were either back in Cairo, I was told, or had joined the press corps covering Patton, Monty's rival for journalistic attention.

Keating, aware of my special interest in Monty, said the general was too busy to see me right away but promised to bring us together "at the earliest opportunity." Meanwhile, I was to make myself at home.

The several large upstairs bedrooms were crowded with the reporters' bedrolls, and I chose to bed down in a corner of the huge *terrazza* where the air was scented by flowering jasmine in clay urns.

Before Monty shelled it—his battles were invariably preceded by heavy artillery fire—Lentini had been one of southern Sicily's more prosperous agricultural centers with a population of more than twenty thousand. Now it was mostly a heap of abandoned ruins. Where had all the inhabitants gone?

The morning after my arrival I intercepted the grizzled farmer named Nino who brought daily supplies of fresh vegetables and fruit to the correspondents' mess. He looked more like an Arab than an Italian and spoke only dialectal Sicilian. He was taciturn and reserved at first, but his black eyes widened when

I told him that despite my uniform, I was not British but *un americano d'origine siciliana* (an American of Sicilian origin). He flung his long, strong arms about me and kissed me on both cheeks, muttering, *"Fighiu mio, fighiu mio, chi gioia mi porti.* [My son, my son, what joy you bring me]." He smelled strongly but not unpleasantly of sweat, strong tobacco, and garlic.

When I asked him what had happened to Lentini's citizens during the fighting, he performed a pantomime of controlled but eloquent gestures indicating that while some Lentinesi had remained in their underground shelters, most had fled to the nearby hills.

Nino dismissed Mussolini with a knowing smile and yet another gesture, a meaningful twirling of the thumb and first two fingers of his right hand alongside his temple, indicating that he had long considered the Duce a candidate for the *manicomio,* the local booby hatch.

When I awoke next day at sunup, I found alongside my bedroll a small panier lined with grape leaves and covered with a clean square of white cloth. The tiny basket contained a Sicilian delicacy, ripe, golden prickly pears, the fruit of the island's ubiquitous cacti. Nino was gone. He must have known, or sensed, that fierce fighting was about to resume.

In the dusty, sweltering final days of July the battle lines of the impending struggle for the northeastern corner of Sicily were sharply drawn. They formed an almost perfect isosceles triangle within which the opposing armies were deployed in a race for its apex, Messina, though for totally different reasons: the Allies to terminate the Sicilian campaign as quickly as possible; the Axis forces to delay the invaders long enough to facilitate their escape to the mainland.

Germany's General Hans-Valentin Hube, now master of all Axis troops and weapons within his steadily shrinking zone of operations, was skillfully completing the defenses essential to his phased withdrawal to Calabria, on the toe of the Italian mainland, so near yet so far. It lay across the narrow Strait of Messina, the ribbon of opalescent blue water immortalized in Homer's *Iliad* as the scene of the most tragic of the many adventures of Odysseus in his legendary wanderings while homeward bound to Ithaca after conquering Troy with his wooden horse.

Hube needed much of the wisdom, resourcefulness, and courage that Homer attributed to Odysseus to complete successfully the task with which Hitler had entrusted him. Homer's hero had had to cope with crises in personal relations among the ancient Greeks; Hube faced similar difficulties in dealing with the Italians, who saw little to be gained from helping the *tedeschi* evade the trap being set by the *anglo-americani.*

Low morale among the *macaroni,* as most Germans disdainfully referred to their allies, however, was the least of the many problems Hube faced. Actually, he had the best of the remaining Italian formations. But even these were gradually disintegrating through desertions, and Hube relied far more on the topographical help provided by nature. His area contained some of the most defensible terrain in the entire Mediterranean: the convulsed and convoluted volcanic arrowhead of land shaped by Mount Etna and its satellites, Mounts Soro and Nebrodi, and their rugged foothills.

With fewer than a hundred thousand German and Italian troops, Hube faced some three hundred thousand superbly equipped American and British forces who could count on the support of their massive air power and the guns of Allied warships patrolling the coasts. The German commander intended reaching the Italian mainland with his army and the bulk of its armaments intact to continue the war on the peninsula that was soon to become merely a southern province of the Third Reich.

Opposite Hube, Patton's forces held the northern coast road with the sea at its left and on its right the craggy cliffs of Le Madonie, the mountain range rising from the lush but narrow plains of Palermo and Messina along the Sicilian *Conca d'Oro* (Golden Horn). Monty's Eighth Army meanwhile possessed the eastern coast road with the sea at its right and controlled the spacious plain, though not the city, of Catania, his troops reaching westward up to the foothills of Mount Etna itself.

The "base" linking the two "legs" of the "triangle" was formed by Bradley's II Corps, its elements reaching from just below San Stefano on the northern coast and deployed along a line running roughly southeast to the formidable natural defenses of Troina. Bradley's forces, in place to protect Patton's right flank and rear, were also prepared for a forward thrust.

Those were the positions crayoned on the overlay maps in the villa's press room on the night of July 25 when, at eleven o'clock, Radio Roma broadcast electrifying news: Victor Emmanuel III of Italy, the "little king" who had acquiesced to Fascist rule of his country for twenty-one years and nine months, had at last found the courage to dismiss Mussolini as prime minister.

Moreover, the broadcast said in Italian, the king had placed the Duce under arrest and turned the government over to Field Marshal Badoglio. Following this cryptic announcement, Badoglio himself came on the air. Speaking in his gravelly, decidedly Piedmontese Italian, he said: "I have assumed the military government of the country with full powers. The war will continue. Whoever believes he can interrupt the normal course of events, or whoever seeks to disturb internal order, will be struck down without mercy."

No sooner had I finished translating for the others clustered about the press room's field wireless than BBC came on from London and confirmed the news. I would have given much to have been in Rome or Milan or any other major Italian city and witnessed the reaction of the people to the sudden, dramatic turn of events. Would the Italians feel liberated, I wondered, or betrayed, or both? If what I had seen and heard in Sicily was any indication, there would be cheers in the piazzas.

On the evening of July 28 I was handed a message from Cairo that said simply COME HOME SOONEST—LOU. I flew back to Cairo the next morning in an RAF plane from an airfield near Pachino.

53

AERIAL BALACLAVA AT PLOIEȘTI

eneral Brereton and Colonel Hobbs resumed their duel at cards, sitting cross-legged on the flight deck, on our way to Benghazi in the early afternoon of July 30, 1943. The general seemed more pensive than usual, his bronzed, sharp-featured face reflecting emotions ranging from habitual premission concern to outright anxiety.

My thoughts were still in Sicily. I had come away from the front elated that the Sicilian campaign had produced the downfall of Benito Mussolini, but shocked by the devastation I had seen, the terrible cost in Allied casualties, the poverty and suffering of the civilian population.

Moreover, I was annoyed with myself. I had rushed back to Cairo on what might be a fool's errand, before the Allies resumed their offensive and before Major Keating had been able to arrange a meeting with Montgomery. I resolved to return to Sicily as soon as I had finished covering the "important" story Lou Hobbs had promised.

I was wondering just what the story might be and hoping it was as "important" as Hobbs had indicated when, suddenly, Brereton pushed away the cards and said: "Well, Frank, this is it. This is where the Ninth Air Force makes history or wishes it had never been born. Hap Arnold has handed us a tough one. And when it's over, I'll be a hero or one first-class bastard. . . ."

Still, however, no hint of what the "tough one" might be, but I could guess. On my previous visit to Bomber Command I had seen the Ninth's B-24s practicing low-level bombing runs on mock targets in the desert south of the

base, and I had overheard whispered references to Ploieşti. I sensed, now, that
I hadn't come on a wild-goose chase. Ploieşti was Hitler's Romanian oil barrel.

Brigadier General P.D. Ent, commander of the Ninth's five bomber squadrons, met our plane. He was a tall, lean, blond man with blue eyes and a quiet
manner whose real name was Uzal; but he was of Pennsylvania Dutch ancestry, and everyone knew him as Dutch or P.D. His first words to Brereton were
"Well, sir, everything's all set," and the two walked off together toward the
gate to the walled-in compound that held Bomber Command's various headquarters buildings, Hobbs and I close behind. P.D. towered over the Napoleon-
size Pops, who listened attentively to whatever his taller subordinate was
saying, head cocked toward him, hands clasped behind his back, gripping the
riding crop he always carried on duty.

Benina Airport, located at the sea's edge about twenty miles east of battered Benghazi, was Italy's principal African air base until Montgomery captured it in November while chasing Rommel across Libya from El Alamein.
It had changed hands five times during the war, but it was ours now with the
Stars and Stripes lazing in the light evening breeze over the main headquarters
building, a shell-pocked two-story structure at the far end of the compound,
splotched with ugly gray, brown, and green camouflage paint.

At some distance from the main runway were heaped the carcasses of
Italian and German warplanes that had been cleared off the field when the
Ninth took over the base in March. Now Benina was about to become the
springboard for the raid that would carry the air war deep into Hitler's
Fortress Europe.

Within the brown-walled compound and its periphery of scraggly palm
trees, Jeeps and staff cars were directed to parking spaces by MPs whose
salutes and gestures had an extra snap as they managed traffic. I could feel the
rising amperage of premission tensions even before Hobbs and I entered headquarters behind Pops and P.D.

Inside, the two were met by the base maintenance chief, Colonel Sam Nero,
a short, stocky, dark-complexioned fellow, who told his superiors that all
planes were "tuned and ready." Yes, he said in reply to a question from
Brereton, the delayed-action bombs had been loaded. "Plenty of incendiaries,
too, sir," Nero said.

None of the group commanders was at mess that night. They and their
pilots, navigators, bombardiers, and gunners were restricted to their quarters
at the base's several airfields. After three weeks of rehearsals and trial runs over
dummy targets the crews were learning for the first time that D day had been
set for August 1.

Until that July 30 evening, only General Ent; his chief of staff, Colonel
Richard Sanders; and a few persons in operations and intelligence knew the
starting date. But I was "safe" now, "inside the reservation," and Brereton
talked freely about Operation Tidal Wave over our supper of cold cuts and
potato salad.

53

The decision to attack Ploieşti, the general disclosed, was made in Washington in mid-May, when Roosevelt and Churchill met to formulate Allied strategy in the Mediterranean after the victory in North Africa. The planning was entrusted to Brereton, who, like General Hap Arnold and General Carl ("Tooey") Spaatz, believed oil to be the Achilles' heel of the German war machine.

At the time American air strategists thought the course of the war in Russia and the success of the impending campaign in Italy depended on depriving the Germans of oil and high-octane gasoline. Intelligence reports indicated that from Ploieşti the Nazis extracted the oil and refined oil products which maintained the entire German and Italian navies, one third of the Wehrmacht, and most of the German Air Force in Russia. The reports also revealed, however, that the Germans had raised a forest of antiaircraft guns surrounding the Ploieşti installations, had built blast walls around the plants' vital parts, and located airdromes from which the Luftwaffe's fighter planes could rise to intercept Allied bombers.

Ploieşti is situated about thirty-five miles north of Bucharest on the Dambul River, which flows through Romania's Wallachian plain. Lying at the foot of the Buzau Mountains, the town nestles in a deep valley formed by two ridges descending in a southeasterly direction that were bristling with antiaircraft guns.

With the possible exception of Germany's well-dispersed and strongly defended synthetic gasoline plants, Ploieşti had become the enemy's most difficult single target to attack successfully. Nevertheless, Brereton and his commanders set to work. In the desert south of Benghazi they found an area which topographically approximated the environs of Ploieşti. Engineers blocked out with whitewash and pylons the contours of Tidal Wave's principal targets and the outlines of the town itself.

The objectives included the Phoenix, Orion, and Astra-Romana refineries owned by British Shell; the Colombia plant, formerly French-owned; Vega-Concordia, built by the Belgians; the refineries and cracking stills owned by the so-called Petrol Bloc (German and British); and the installations of Romano-Americana, property of Standard Oil of New Jersey. The engineers also laid out the nearby town of Brasov with its Creditul-Minier high-octane plant, the newest and best in the region.

In addition to the full-scale mock-up in the desert, a tabletop replica of the city and the refineries was constructed for study by the navigators, bombardiers, and pilots. The model was built from information supplied by British and American oil engineers and from prewar photos and blueprints.

When planning began, Brereton had to decide whether the raid was to be conducted at high altitude or at low level. It was a difficult decision. He knew that his Liberators were "definitely not suited" for low-level operations. But he also knew that because of the long distance involved—about twenty-four hundred miles to and from the targets—the formations might become dispersed and not hit their objectives from a high altitude. He decided, therefore, that the raid should be a "low-level, horizontal bombing attack in daylight hours."

It took Brereton two weeks to make up his mind, and when he announced his decision, he invited no discussion from the commanders, all of whom, no doubt, would have preferred a high-level raid of the kind they had been making in the past. The general was taking what he defined as "a calculated risk" to ensure the raid's success, but what he risked were the lives of several hundred men, not to mention planes worth tens of millions of dollars.

Now, after three weeks' preparation, including two "successful" low-level attacks with dummy bombs on the mock Ploieşti, the planes and their crews were ready.

On the morning of July 31 Brereton spent the day talking to each group in turn. He stressed the importance of the mission and outlined the difficulties they would meet.

When Brereton had finished speaking, the men knew what they were up against and that some of them wouldn't be coming back. They were told they would encounter the dangling cables of barrage balloons, smoke screens, ack-ack batteries estimated to number between one hundred and four hundred guns, and enemy fighter planes, perhaps as many as one hundred, in the vicinity.

August 1, 1943, D day for Tidal Wave, fell on a Sunday, and like everyone else, I was awake long before dawn.

When Hobbs invited me to cover the story, I assumed that I was to participate in the raid as a passenger. At a predawn breakfast in the officers' mess I asked Brereton for permission to fly in the *Hail Columbia,* piloted by Colonel John ("Killer") Kane, a burly Texan whom I had met and knew to be one of the ablest, most daring of the Ninth's pilots. The general gave me a stony stare. "Not a chance," he said brusquely, and left to attend to more urgent business.

Determined to fly anyhow, I scrounged flying gear and randomly joined one of the crews on their way to their plane. The ship was the *Daisy Mae,* for I distinctly recall the image of the voluptuous heroine of the popular comic strip *L'il Abner,* painted on the aircraft's fuselage near the nose.

Just before daybreak I was struggling up the ladder into the ship's bowels, burdened with a parachute, Mae West, water bottle, and canvas bag containing Spam sandwiches, notebook, and pencils, when a Jeep roared up the runway and screeched to a stop a few yards from the plane. In it was Brereton in a towering rage.

"Where the hell do you think you're going?" he shouted, waggling his riding crop at me. "Get your ass down off that ladder. That's an order."

Brereton drove me back to headquarters in silence, dismissing me there with a stern "See you later."

Within minutes the air trembled with the engine roar of planes taking off from Benina and its satellite fields. The noise numbed the mind; the desert sand raised by the prop wash stung with needle-point sharpness.

The mission's 177 Liberators were heavy with the extra gas in the tanks that had been built into their bomb bays for the long round trip across the Mediterranean and over the Balkan mountains. Each of the B-24s used every foot of runway to lumber into the purple sky of the hot, windless August morning. By sunrise all were airborne. They would arrive over Ploieşti in full daylight.

An ominous silence descended upon the base as the sun rose on what would be the longest, most nerve-racking day I had ever known. Brereton, apparently in forgiving mood, allowed me to rejoin him and Hobbs outside the command radio shack. Hobbs admitted he had spotted me on my way to the *Daisy Mae* and had alerted the general.

"There's nothing left to do now," said Brereton when the last plane was in the air, "but pray for them."

A few minutes later, while the main Benina runway was still clouded with sandy prop wash, engine trouble caused one of the Liberators to return to base. The pilot, in trying to land, slid off the tarmac and hit a concrete telephone pole. His plane crashed and instantly caught fire. Only two of the crew of ten were saved.

Tidal Wave had counted its first casualties.

Now the hours dragged. Brereton, Hobbs, and I went to a nearby beach for a swim, had lunch in the officers' club, then tried playing a round of gin rummy, but nothing eased the tension. Late that afternoon the almost unbearable anxiety was relieved by a radio signal from General Ent, who was in the lead formation with Colonel Compton. It said, simply, "Mission successful."

Brereton smiled, then laughed aloud for the first time in about seventy-two hours. "Well, Frank," he said, "I told you I'd be a hero or a bastard before the day was over. Anyhow, I ain't a bastard," and fell silent again. He knew he wasn't a hero either. He had sent nearly eighteen hundred good men on a hazardous mission, and a number of them—we didn't know how many as yet—wouldn't be coming back.

Finally, that evening, the first formations signaled they were less than a hundred miles away. We piled into staff cars and Jeeps and headed for the runways to watch them come in. The sun had set, and we were in that long twilight that turns the desert into a magic land of tawny brown earth and indigo sky. All the ground crews were out, scanning the horizon for their own ships.

"There's *Old Baldy*," said one, and, "That's *Vulgar Virgin* coming in now," and "Looka them bomb doors swingin'." There were planes with dead engines and others with holes in wings and fuselages. One ship fired a colored flare: It wanted an ambulance; there were wounded on board. One by one they landed, some without gas enough left in their tanks to fill a Zippo lighter.

Colonel Compton, with Ent on board, landed first. Dutch Ent looked grave. His formation, he said, had missed its assigned target. Major Norman Appold, a tall, thin young man with a prominent Adam's apple, was close behind Compton. He wasn't happy either; he had seen one of his closest friends shot down in flames. An ack-ack shell pierced his buddy's plane from nose to tail and set it afire.

From the incoming planes the crews staggered on to the hut, where they were interrogated while Brereton, Ent, and I listened in. Many of the men were in shock or numb with fatigue and were released to stumble off to sleep. What I heard, however, led me to conclude that whatever was gained had come at a high price in men and machines.

Some of the accounts were fantastic. The force of 164 bombers which actually reached the target area roared down at it at treetop level and even lower altitudes through curtains of ground fire and, in some cases, concentrated attacks by enemy fighters. Explosions of boilers and gas storage tanks on the ground spread flame and smoke. Colonel Leon Johnson, who led one of the bombardment groups, said, "We flew through sheets of flame, and our airplanes were everywhere, some of them on fire and others exploding."

The Liberators flew so low that they dipped their wings through treetops and hit the guy wires of smokestacks. One plane actually brought back cornstalks in its bomb bay. Many fire fights took place between the gunners in the Liberators and machine-gun batteries on enemy flak towers hidden in haystacks, in farm buildings, and on railway flatcars.

One of the last of the late arrivals was the *Daisy Mae,* its props chewing the air, nose wheel gone, top and tail turrets wrecked, flak holes splattered all over the wings and fuselage. Somehow the pilot managed to keep his ship level. The plane coasted silently and swiftly through the gritty fog of swirling sand until it buried its nose gently in the ground at the far end of the runway.

An ambulance rushed out to the ship, and I saw it bring back four badly wounded men. One of them, Lieutenant Guido Gioana, *Daisy Mae*'s bombardier, was carried off in a litter unconscious. It took flight surgeons at the base hospital most of the night and four blood transfusions to save his life.

At nightfall I staggered off to my tent emotionally spent. What had happened on the *Daisy Mae* made me realize that by grounding me, Brereton probably had saved me from serious injury or death. I crawled into my cot under the mosquito netting but slept fitfully, reliving a raid I hadn't made.

Two or three times I left my bed and sat outside the tent on a campstool to gaze at the thin, intermittent, swordlike blue flashes of the searchlight that split the darkness of the moonless night beckoning home the stragglers. Out there somewhere was Killer Kane in *Hail Columbia.* Before takeoff he had written last letters home to his wife, Pansy, to his father and mother in Eagle Springs, Texas, and to the lawyer who had drafted his will.

At the radio shack the next morning one of the operators told me several Liberators had made it to an RAF airfield at Nicosia, on Cyprus. Among them was *Hail Columbia,* but Kane had inadvertently hit an embankment on land-

ing and was coming home on one of the other ships. *Hail Columbia* had been
badly shot up and was practically unflyable even before the pileup.

Several hours later, in midafternoon, a nameless, battered B-24 wobbled
onto the runway at Benina. Kane and his crew deplaned and went directly to
interrogation.

I found Killer later in his Quonset hut with most of his crew, the wind
blowing through the square window at the far end, funneling Libyan dust into
the room and covering Killer, his desk, maps, and papers with a reddish,
talclike coating. It was hot, and the flies were bothersome, and Kane wielded
a dime-store flyswatter with practiced precision. He killed one and flicked it
onto the earthen floor. He was in a talkative mood and gave me the first lucid,
coherent account of what had happened over Ploieşti. I took notes.

"It was a rough show," he said. "It was a sight I'll never forget, seeing those
B-twenty-fours falling like flies to the right and left of us. From below, ack-ack
batteries were firing at us point-blank. I'll never forget those big Libs going
down"—Killer's swatter thwacked again—"like flies."

The hut, about seven feet wide by twenty feet long, was quiet except for
Killer's soft Texan drawl and the sound of the wind sloshing sand on the tin
structure's curved surface. The others sat on low iron stools, looking at their
feet or up at the ceiling or staring at Killer's square, impassive face with its
dust-laden lids and black mustache.

"It was hazy on the way out over the sea, and we couldn't maintain contact
with all the other groups," he said. "We arrived at our target—it was the
Astra-Romana high-octane plant—at about three-fifteen P.M. Everything
worked out just as we had planned it up to here, except for the smoke from
burning oil tanks and the flames over the target. We could see reservoir tanks
exploding, with fire shooting up like great greedy red tongues in the middle
of the smoke. It was so hot the hair on my arms was singed."

"Yeah." Hubbard, the radio operator broke in. "It was flying through hell,
that's what it was. I guess we will go straight to heaven when we die. We've
had our purgatory."

"Young, there"—Killer indicated his copilot with a nod—"yelled at me
that our number four motor was hit just as we came over the target. We
feathered it and increased power on the other three but dropped to about
treetop level. We were right in the middle of our group, and as we lost speed,
I could see other ships slipping past us like weird fish behind plate glass in an
aquarium.

"We finally got our speed up to about one eighty-five. Then the fighters got
to work on us. We took everything they had. There's no question about that.
There were ten or a dozen fighters on top of us, I guess. We got five hits from
forty-millimeter shells. An inboard engine and the underside of the right wing
were hit. The top was shot off the number one prop; it had a hole in it big
enough to pass a silver dollar through it. There was a hole in the left aileron,
and another, a big one, through the bomb bay doors. Then we made our turn
leaving the target and headed for the Aegean Sea. We had to climb to get over

the mountains. We found we could climb, but it was quite a struggle. We threw out everything we could tear loose from the ship. We ditched one empty bomb bay tank, our heavy flying clothes, all our shot-up useless guns, tools, a ladder, everything except food, water, and the ammo we would need to fire the few guns we could still work.

"It was steaming hot in the plane from the heat over the burning target. The wind flung blasts of hot air at us, and we had a hell of a time trying to climb. The mountains in our vicinity rose to about forty-five hundred feet, and their crests were about two hundred feet above our flight level. But the ship kept rising. There was nothing we could do but wait and see if we'd make it. . . ."

They made it, although some of the crew swore they felt *Hail Columbia*'s broad belly scrape the mountaintops. With all loose gear overboard, however, the plane cleared the mountains and staggered up to seven thousand feet.

"After that," said Kane, "it was just a case of flying home, and I headed for Nicosia. Our tail gunner reported that three or four planes had picked us up and were following us in. Now we had to show them the way home, too. But we were running low on gas. Frankly, I figured we had about as much chance of making it home as a snowball in hell. We used every drop we had by the time we set down on Nicosia. . . ."

The adventures of *Hail Columbia* and its crew were not over yet. Killer hadn't been told there was an embankment alongside the runway at Nicosia ten feet off the strip and about five feet high. His ship hit the hump. The impact knocked one wheel off and ripped the prop off the number three motor.

"We bounced about fifty feet into the air," Killer said, "and came straight down, managed to level off, and hit the ground with a bang. The RAF airport control officer fired a flare, which meant danger. To us, it meant that we were on fire."

With a shout Copilot Young ripped off his parachute harness and leaped for the escape hatch on top of the flight deck. Then he checked himself, turned, and said to Kane, "Oh, sorry! After you, Colonel."

Kane pushed him through the hatch and followed. They slid down the nose of the plane to the ground. They saw the others, tail gunner, waist gunners, radio operator, and engineer kneeling some distance away, kissing the ground. Kane and Young kissed the ground, too.

That night, Killer and Young had pork chops and a bottle of wine in a Nicosia nightclub, the only place they could get anything to eat.

"And that," said Kane, "is the story of our flight to Ploieşti. It isn't the whole story, of course. Some of our boys may be wandering about in Romania, Bulgaria, or even Yugoslavia. Some may be prisoners. Some may be having the adventures of their lives. Anyhow, I couldn't sleep last night. I kept thinking about those guys going down, some of them in flames—big Libs like so many broken flies."

Other Liberators landed, and the next day Killer and his crew patched one up and flew it to Palestine and from there to their home base in Libya. The biggest low-level raid by heavy bombers in aviation history was behind them.

While Kane talked, the image that kept flashing through my mind was the charge of the Light Brigade at Balaclava, planes instead of horses charging into an aerial valley of death. Had someone blundered? Had the results justified the losses in men and machines? Of Tidal Wave's seven targets, two—Romana-Americana and Concordia-Vega—were missed completely or only slightly damaged.

At first Brereton insisted that the "German oil machine," as he called it, had been dealt "a crippling blow as a result of one of the greatest feats in the history of military aviation." Four days later, however, he admitted he was "somewhat disappointed" in the results. "We did not achieve the sixty-five to seventy-five percent destruction we had hoped for," he said. "Nevertheless, we have put a serious dent in Germany's oil supply."

That night, August 4, Berlin's radio siren, Lili Marlene, dedicated one of her haunting melodies to the Ninth Air Force and ended it with a spoken message for the commander: "Fine job on Ploieşti, Brereton, but you lost too many."

I stayed long enough at Benghazi to learn that of the 1,620 men who actually reached Ploieşti, 446 were killed or missing and 54 wounded. Of the 164 Liberators in the fray, at least 41 were lost to enemy action.

When the Ninth closed the casualty books on Tidal Wave, President Roosevelt gave the figures to Congress, saying that the losses might seem disastrously high. "But I am certain," he added, "that the German or Japanese High Commands would cheerfully sacrifice tens of thousands of men to do the same damage to us, if they could."

The participants all received medals and commendations. Five Congressional Medals of Honor were awarded, one of them to Killer Kane. Brereton got his third star, and he and his staff were transformed into a new British-based fighter-bomber support command for the invasion of Normandy. I never saw Brereton again but would remember him always as the man who very probably saved my life.

54

MONTY BREACHES FORTRESS EUROPE

After the fighting ended in Sicily, General Montgomery moved into a princely palazzo on the bluffs above Taormina, where he could look directly across the blue Strait of Messina to the gray-brown Calabrian toe of the Italian mainland, his objective in the impending Battle of Reggio. He was having a tea party when I arrived from Cairo on the afternoon of September 1, and he invited me to join his guests, aides, and junior officers, to whom Major Keating introduced me.

The talk over the teacups indicated that no one present, with the possible exception of Monty himself, anticipated much of a struggle ahead. The consensus seemed to be that with Mussolini toppled from his perch, Sicily cleared of the enemy, and the Italians already secretly negotiating for an armistice, the war in Italy might well be "over by Christmas."

Keating had told the general that I was doing a book about him, and Monty apparently felt that he had to tell me what a splendid lot of officers and men he commanded. He spent a good five minutes describing the courage, fortitude, and skill of the Eighth Army, which, he said, was "the finest in the world." I heartily agreed and said so, adding that I believed its successes were obviously due to "excellent leadership at the top," an assessment of his talents in which the general, deep-set blue eyes aglow with pride, unabashedly concurred.

"Quite so," he said, smiling. False modesty was not one of Monty's faults, and he gave me chapter and verse on the Eighth Army's victorious two-thousand-mile march across North Africa, then its triumph over the Germans in Sicily. I told him I regretted not having been with him at El Alamein but looked forward to being with the Eighth Army when it landed at Reggio.

"Yes," he said. "The time has come to carry the battle to the mainland of Italy. The Eighth Army has been given the great honor of being the first troops of the Allied armies to land on the continent of Europe. There can be only one end to the next battle, and that is another victory."

Although Monty gave no sign of inner turmoil, he was nursing a grievance. He was "damned unhappy," a senior member of the general's staff confided at dinner that evening, with the invasion plan which Allied headquarters in Algiers had handed him.

Monty had seen himself as the commander best qualified to lead the assault on Italy and in Algiers had said so to Eisenhower, Alexander, and anyone else who would listen. But he had riled Eisenhower by his single-minded conduct of the fighting on the Sicilian front, and Monty, though granted the signal honor of being the first Allied commander to set foot on the crumbling southern bastion of Hitler's Fortress Europe, was relegated to a minor role in the Italian campaign.

Montgomery's plea for one single powerful attack was disregarded, and it was decided, instead, that the invading Allied forces should make several landings to split the enemy concentrations in southern Italy. The points chosen were Reggio on the toe of the Italian foot, Taranto on the base of the foot, and Salerno on Italy's ankle. After the landings the two armies were to continue northward separately on either side of Italy's spinal column, the Apennines, presumably until they reached the Plain of Lombardy, where, it was thought, the Germans would make their stand.

The plan's goals, as outlined to me by General Francis de Guingand, Monty's devoted chief of staff, were threefold: (1) to knock Italy out of the war; (2) to seize the Foggia airfields with such nearby seaports as Bari and Naples; and (3) to pursue the Germans through Rome to the Plain of Lombardy. The simultaneous Reggio and Taranto landings were called Baytown, and the Salerno landing Avalanche.

To command the Fifth Army for the attack on Salerno, Eisenhower chose General Mark Wayne Clark, a tall, handsome West Pointer who had never led large bodies of troops in combat. His main claim to fame lay in the fact that in October 1942 he had secretly landed in Algiers from a submarine to make contact with friendly French officials in North Africa. D day for Baytown was September 3. D day for Avalanche was September 9.

From the outset Monty was opposed to both the overall plan and his own limited part therein. He knew better than most that the Sicilian campaign had not been the smashing success everyone pretended it was. Some forty thousand Germans and sixty-thousand Italians had escaped to Italy across the narrow Strait of Messina with enough tanks, guns, and vehicles to continue the struggle on the mainland.

Moreover, two of Monty's best divisions, the Fiftieth and the Fifty-first, were going home on leave. Others, like the Seventh Armored, had been taken away from him and given to Clark. He demanded, and got, additional troops and landing craft for Baytown, for unlike his superiors in Algiers, he was by no means certain that the Italians would do an about-face and fight the Germans when the armistice was finally announced. He knew, furthermore, that there were fifteen or sixteen German divisions in Italy. The splitting of the Allied forces in multiple landings laid the invaders open to serious counter-attack.

In the end, however, Monty swallowed his objections and followed orders, content that he would be the first Allied commander to set foot on the territorial fringes of Fortress Europe and this on the fourth anniversary of Britain's declaration of war against Germany. He prepared for Reggio a fire storm of artillery shells of unprecedented ferocity and moved his tactical headquarters to a convenient spot on the Sicilian shore just south of Messina opposite his objective, Reggio di Calabria.

On the morning of September 2 I joined an artillery battery emplaced on the furrowed hills above Mili and a cluster of other tile-roofed fishing villages. Groves of lemon and olive trees concealed the Eighth Army's guns, their muzzles aimed at the mainland.

That afternoon the battery commander—a tall, lean colonel who had been a don at Oxford before the war—and I climbed to a forward observation post to gaze across the strait at the target area. On the opposite shore and slightly to the right of our positions glittered Reggio di Calabria, and to the left we could see the splash of buff-colored buildings which we knew to be the bombed and shelled remains of Villa San Giovanni.

Lordly Aspromonte towered some six thousand feet into a corona of white clouds, motionless in an innocent, peaceful blue sky. The pale pearl cliffs of Bagnara shone bright gold within what seemed swimming distance. Through glasses I could see vehicles moving along the winding Calabrian roads.

"Tonight," said the commander, almost regretfully, "we attack."

"Yes," I said. "Tonight Italy gets a hotfoot."

The colonel looked puzzled. I explained. He smiled wanly, not quite getting it.

We climbed down from the OP to where he had rigged a sort of camp behind a low stone wall. There in the twilight, under a tarpaulin stretched between two silvery green olive trees, we ate half-cooked beans and bully beef stewed with fresh tomatoes, drank hot tea, and smoked. We tried to talk about everything except the war.

"The attack has been set for three forty-five in the morning," the colonel said, and suggested we get some sleep.

My conducting officer and I groped our way to where we had laid our beds in the lee of the wall of what had been headquarters for an Eyetie ack-ack battery. We slept under mosquito netting, for even in the hills Sicily was alive with malaria. An old bell in the village sounded ten o'clock in a tinny voice as we turned in.

The colonel called us at three. It was dark still, and damp. Somewhere a dog barked; a faraway truck's motor growled, then was silent. The sky was a midnight blue bowl splattered with brilliants. Here in the hills the sky and stars were distant, impersonal, and aloof, and it was cold. We looked toward the mainland, and it was like looking into an interminable black void.

The silence was almost tangible, and yet to the left and right of the observation post, from which the barrage was to be directed, men worked feverishly passing and piling shells for their guns and drinking hot, sweet, dark tea to keep awake. The village bell sounded the quarter hour, and suddenly, for an hour and a half, hell came to live in the hills above Mili and all along the marina.

The batteries directly below us spoke first in a salvo that was like a summer storm's thunderclap close by. Bright yellow flames spit from our guns toward Calabria. Had it been possible to shut off sounds completely, the scene would have been a Disney color choreography for fantastic music. Tracer shells described long, low yellow and orange arcs to the opposite shore. Through my glasses I saw explosions mushrooming one within another on their targets.

But we were harpooning a dead whale. There was no answering fire from the enemy. Round after round tore across the intervening darkness without reply. The ground shook beneath us with each salvo from the nearer batteries, and for ninety minutes, the earth quivered.

Four beams of blue-white light were directed immediately above us from searchlights placed equidistantly about half a mile behind and ahead of the observation post, and the light beams intersected overhead. It was like standing inside an enormous star sapphire. The point of intersection of the four beams, about a mile above us, was to serve as a guide for the waiting invasion fleet, deployed along the coast.

The objective of the barrage and of the invasion force was a stretch of gray beach about five hundred yards long and a hundred deep directly opposite where we stood. On this beach, its mines, pillboxes, and barbed wire, we poured some of the two hundred thousand rounds our batteries fired. The rest were directed against positions in the hills commanding the bridgehead the Eighth Army had to secure.

All day the Eighth Army waited to be, as General Montgomery had told me, "deservedly first to set foot on the continent of Europe and so begin the liberation of four hundred million people. We have come two thousand miles across Africa to do this and we shall not fail."

Monty was sleeping now in his caravan somewhere along the coast south of Messina. His work was done for the time being. My colonel's battery, and a hundred others, continued shelling enemy targets.

To the east, far behind Aspromonte, the sun was rising, and a dim light illuminated the edges of Calabria's mountains. Suddenly it was still. The air that for an hour and a half had been a tortured sea of sound was again quiet.

I hurried away to pack my bedroll and drive with my conducting officer to Monty's headquarters. For I was going to Italy with Monty four years to the day, almost to the hour, after Neville Chamberlain declared war on Germany.

The barrage ended at 5:15 A.M. In the uncertain light the strait between us and the mainland looked like a slow-flowing river of molten lead, and Calabria was a dark blur. But we could see the landing craft headed in formation toward the opposite shore. They were hulls down with tanks, infantry, trucks, supplies, and ammunition.

Behind the landing craft streamed long lines of ducks, huge amphibious trucks, and behind these their smaller counterparts, "ducklings." Cruisers, destroyers, and gunboats shepherded the invasion fleet. It was a regatta, for the strait had been swept of mines. Of the three hundred ducks and several hundred landing craft and scores of warships involved, not one was lost from enemy action.

When we arrived at Monty's headquarters, the general was in the act of completing the recording of a proclamation to his army. He stood beside the sound truck listening to a playback. He was pleased; he cocked his head toward me and said, "I think that's all right, don't you? Good recording! Good recording!" And then: "Come in and I'll tell you about the battle."

I followed him into his caravan, a ten-ton truck chassis mounted with a one-room apartment complete from toilet to dinette. He showed me his battle plan and told me how he intended to secure the bridgehead nearly two hundred square miles in area on the mainland before pursuing the enemy northward. He was confident the Italians would fold up "within six weeks."

"A good hard knock now," he said, "may very well cause them to say they've had enough. Of course, there are Germans, and they will fight. They have some sixteen divisions in Italy—a considerable force. But I don't anticipate any real difficulty until we strike the main body of the German Army, which will be in strong defensive positions much farther north. Now"—and he couldn't disguise his delight—"let's go to Italy!"

At ten-fifteen on the morning of September 3 Monty and I climbed into a duck and set off across the strait for the beach between Reggio and San Giovanni, which his troops had secured. With us were Alex Clifford and Alan Moorehead.

Monty, standing in the bow of the squat craft, as ungainly in water as it was incongruous on land, was a strange figure for a great military commander. His angular elbows protruded from the short sleeves of his plain khaki shirt; his thin legs stuck out of his shorts. Nevertheless, his lean body suggested strength and endurance. He wore his beret at a jaunty angle, and his strong hands rested firmly on his bony hips when they weren't busy steadying him against the roll and surge of the duck or waving to troops who cheered him from the nearby landing craft, ducks, and ducklings as we passed.

They instantly recognized his unique profile—high forehead with deeply indented eyes and great hooked nose. His outstanding feature however, was one they couldn't see but perhaps could feel, the magnetic power in his blue eyes.

We reached a corvette for crossing the strait, and Monty, his aide and I and the others transshipped. We went below, and Monty exploded the myth that he never touched coffee, for he drank three cups in the wardroom. Knowing his distaste for the smell of tobacco smoke, we refrained from smoking.

I asked him how it felt to lead an army onto an enemy shore. He said simply, "It's a great satisfaction," and the smile creases on either side of his small, mustache-adorned mouth deepened. It was obvious he was happy. The night before, he had dined on roasted peacock, which the prankish General Freyberg, the New Zealander, had sent him as a present, perhaps with overtones of irony, for Monty had a well-founded reputation for vanity.

Nevertheless, few generals commanded the love and admiration of their troops as did this short, long-armed, scrawny crusader in khaki, this pious Billy Sunday in a tank, Britain's most successful general.

Anyway, Monty dined on peacock.

Off the Calabrian shore we transshipped again to a duck. It growled out of the water onto the gray sand of a Calabrian beach and up a wire-mesh track at ten minutes after twelve, and as we landed, three German fighter-bombers dropped three five-hundred-pound bombs. Two landed harmlessly in the water; one hit the beach, raised an enormous cloud of dust, and killed a half dozen troops, wounding several others, the only casualties of the first day's fighting. There was no resistance except for some wild, sporadic machine-gun fire.

Several hundred Italian soldiers, abandoned by their German allies, rushed down to the beach with hands upraised, shouting, laughing, and obviously glad the British had come. Later I talked to many Italian soldier-prisoners. Their hatred for the Germans matched only their shame at their plight and their relief at being rid at last of a corrupt Fascist hierarchy. They were weary men, exhausted spiritually and broken physically.

We entered Reggio, walked through its bombed and shell-torn streets, and inspected the wrecked port, where the air was heavy with the familiar stench of unburied dead. Reggio would have to be rebuilt from foundations to rooftops.

While Monty stopped to confer with his divisional commander, I talked with grubby civilians, who clustered about when they found I spoke their language. Most had just come down out of the hills above Reggio to search among the ruins for bedding and cooking utensils. They said they lived in caves and stables or crowded in with peasants in villages. An old man with watery eyes and quavering chin told me, however, that not all the civilians had taken to the hills.

"Go see them," he said. "There are thousands living like animals in shelters near the port."

As in Taormina, Messina, and other towns, the Germans had looted Reggio before they evacuated in civilian transport confiscated over the protests and opposition of the carabinieri. The Germans, they said, backed their trucks to the doors of shops, lashed the locks to the chassis with ropes, pulled down the doors, and pillaged the stores. "We killed three and wounded six out of fifteen," said a carabiniere officer who had taken part in the fighting.

I listened to their hatred of Nazis and asked them, "Why did you fight us?"

Almost in unison they cried, *"Chi? Noi?* [Who? Us?] We didn't fight you." And there was an embarrassed silence. Finally one of them spoke up. "Most of us attend to our work and are friends of all and enemies of none," he said. "Tell me, *signor capitano,* the war is over for us, isn't it? Surely you will drive the Germans out of Italy."

I assured him we would.

What apparently shocked the Italians most was the utter collapse of the Fascist administration. It was unable to cope with the problems that bombs and shells brought. Transportation broke down; food rapidly vanished from the markets; after the first year of war, clothing became unobtainable; prices spiraled upward except for such rationed staples as bread, rice, oil, and beans. Bomb-damage clearance and the restoration of gas, electricity, and transportation were demoralizingly slow.

Gradually the Nazis became overlords, and Italy an occupied country like others of Europe. None of the people with whom I talked mentioned Mussolini. Few were more than vaguely interested in Badoglio or King Victor Emmanuel. They only wanted peace as quickly as possible and a quick return to normality. They wanted, they said, only *lavoro e pane* (work and bread).

The sudden sound of our twenty-five-pounders shelling the heights above Reggio to clear the way for our advancing columns dispersed the crowd and brought Monty out of his conference. In the amphibious duck, Monty and his guests inspected the total area of about fifty square miles that we had conquered that day. Up forward, the Eighth Army's columns were trying to make contact with the retreating Germans.

For half an hour or so the roads and streets of Reggio were crowded with hundreds of Italian prisoners—Alpini, customs guards, and militiamen—routed out of air-raid shelters. All were burdened with suitcases and bundles of personal belongings; all seemed small, very young, or old beyond military utility. Many limped, but few were depressed.

Major Keating stood up in our duck to photograph one of the prisoner columns. A bearded young soldier looked up and shouted a photo caption back at the major, *"Sì, sì, 'Prigionieri italiani,'"* and laughed ironically. The older men turned their faces from the camera or looked straight before them.

It was nearly six o'clock when our duck turned back toward the beach through the roaring traffic of tanks, laden ducks, trucks, Jeeps, ambulances, and guns. On either hand, men cheered Monty, and Monty gave some of them cigarettes—awful Woodbines—always with the remark "I don't smoke myself, and I've got thousands here."

As we transshipped from our duck to a corvette, a hundred yards from shore, enemy planes came out of the blue and attacked us. It was almost as though they had known Monty was there.

There were knocks on the corvette's hull, bumps from bombs exploding less than a hundred yards from our vessel. Three bombs were dropped from three Nazi fighter-bombers which had dived from thirteen thousand to six thousand feet to release them. The harbor was crowded with ships, but none was hit. Our corvette and other vessels had opened an umbrella of flak.

Monty lay on his back beside a bulkhead on deck during the attack, calmly watching the proceedings. He waved away the steel helmet which an aide tried to press on him, yelling thinly, "They've gone, see," and he pointed to silver planes high overhead skimming through the flak. It all happened within the space of minutes. The bearded skipper of our corvette signaled the engines, and we headed for Sicily. Monty posed for a picture in the bow.

So ended a strange battle, remarkable for its one-sidedness and perfection of execution, later described to me by Montgomery as a "set piece," an exercise in pure military tactics. The Eighth Army had driven its tank-tipped columns into Italy with the ease with which you might prod your finger into a putrid melon and found there corruption and rot.

After Reggio, where I had talked with many hungry Italians sick of war, ashamed of their Fascist past, and frightened of the future, I lacked both the energy and the desire to go to Messina. I had wanted to visit the city and perhaps find the graves of my ancestors, but the thought of prowling among more ruins in what might well be a vain search discouraged me. I flew back to Cairo on September 9, immediately after learning that Mark Clark had attacked at Salerno. I wanted now to hurry on to Algiers and become accredited to the American Army.

The Allies had adopted a strategy, the conquest of Italy from south to north, discarded by the country's foreign previous conquerors: Hannibal, Attila, and Napoleon. All three had entered Italy from the north. I began wondering whether our great leaders hadn't blundered, whether, in fact, the Italian campaign was even necessary. In Algiers, where sat the mighty of the "great endeavor," I might get the answers.

55

WITH MARK CLARK IN ITALY

I t took the ponderous American military bureaucracy at Allied headquarters in Algiers three weeks to accredit me to the U.S. Army before authorizing my flight to the Salerno beachhead. But the delay gave me time to outfit myself in woolen GI khaki and replace the field equipment which an officious boarding officer obliged me to leave behind when I left Cairo.

I landed at Montecorvino, a grassy airfield on the southern edge of the broad Salerno plain shortly before noon on September 29 and was met by one of General Clark's aides, a tall, blond, boyish-looking parachutist named Bill with blue eyes and a soldierly manner.

It had rained the night before, and a chill wind swept down from the brown slopes of the Apennines as I stepped onto the soggy ground. Autumn was in the air, a harbinger of the rain and mud to come, and I was glad I wasn't wearing desert shorts and a bush jacket.

It felt good to be in a warm American uniform for another reason. In the early spring of 1939, on the eve of my departure from Rome, I told Count Ciano that if and when I returned to Italy, it would probably be in the uniform of an American soldier. Sheer bravado, at the time, to dispute the Fascist foreign minister's contention that the democracies dared not go to war against the mighty Axis powers. But here we were, tens of thousands of Americans, marching on Rome.

On the way south to Fifth Army's press camp in Bill's Jeep we passed through Battipaglia, a town I remembered as a thriving community of perhaps twenty thousand people in the heart of the rich coastal campagna south of Salerno. It was one of fascism's showplaces, a geometric arrangement of squat, ugly, "modernistic" buildings erected on land reclaimed from a malarial swamp as an example of Fascist progress against misery and poverty in southern Italy. The town's only adornment was a bronze statue of an infantryman in the central square, a memorial to Italy's dead in the First World War.

But of the tidy community I knew in the late 1930s only the soldier remained—intact on his high stone pedestal, facing north toward where his generation of Italians fought the Austrians and Germans on the Piave and in the Alps from 1914 to 1918. Bombed and shelled by both sides in the new war, Battipaglia had virtually disappeared. Not a single building remained recognizable as a shop, workplace, or human habitation. It was worse than anything I had seen in Sicily, or Calabria, and the few civilians in the piazza looked dirtier, poorer, and hungrier than the Calabresi who had survived Monty's tempest of fire on September 3.

"Anybody who wants to fight another war someday," Bill said above the roar of the traffic, "ought to see this place. A lot of people died here."

The reminder wasn't necessary. The stench that rose from the debris was overpowering.

"Yes," I said. "And I'm beginning to miss the desert already. It was a clean war there. Only soldiers got hurt, and there were few cities to shell and bomb and burn. . . ."

Battipaglia soon was behind us and the air was sweet again. We were in the green flat, open campagna. Peasants plowed the fields behind bullocks, and a few cows grazed on a rising slope in the distance, a momentary illusion of peace.

My diary for September 29 reminds me that the Fifth Army's forward public relations office was located in an old pre-Fascist two-story brick *fattoria* (farm building) set on spongy ground shaded by walnut trees. In charge of it, I was surprised to find, was Lieutenant Colonel Ken Clark, chief of the Universal Service Washington Bureau and my boss when I worked there in 1934. I hadn't seen him since the farewell cocktail party he gave for my wife and me before we sailed for Spain on my first overseas assignment. The years had changed him little; he was as brisk of speech and curt in manner as ever.

The *fattoria* was a damp, gloomy, primitive place crowded with reporters, among them two former Rome correspondents, both old friends: Bill Stoneman, of the *Chicago Daily News,* and Reynolds Packard, of the United Press. Stoneman had good news for me from home; he had visited Kathryn and the boys in Bronxville before leaving for the front and reported them "happy and well."

The ground floor of the *fattoria* served as Clark's office and as the correspondents' combination mess and workplace, where at night we worked by candlelight. Colonel Clark (he was not related to the general but plainly idolized him) admitted that Salerno had been a "rough show" despite its ultimate success. There was fierce fighting, and at one point General Clark proposed reembarking his men but was deterred by the British admiral in command of the supporting Allied naval forces. Their well-directed fire on the German positions had helped save Mark Clark's bacon in his first important battle.

After a few other alarming moments, when it seemed the Fifth Army might have to abandon Salerno after all, Monty's troops arrived from Calabria on September 16, and the Germans fell back. Ken Clark confirmed that casualties had been heavy on the beachhead—at least thirteen hundred American and British dead, not to speak of wounded.

But the reporters were virtually unanimous that the enemy would retreat to the Po. The Fifth Army would take Naples *en passant,* they believed, and reach Rome within a "matter of weeks." One of the few skeptics was Mark Watson, of the *Baltimore Sun.* He saw plenty of hard fighting ahead, a view I shared because I knew the country's geography.

I told Watson what I had seen at Battipaglia, and as we worked side by side that night—he on his dispatch for the *Sun,* I on my notes for future use—he turned to the map on the wall behind him and said, "The shocking truth about this stupid campaign is that every name we see on that map is the name of a city, town, or village that will be razed to the ground by bombs and shells, theirs and ours, before it's over. This wonderful warehouse of Western civilization called Italy will look like Battipaglia. . . ."

The sleeping quarters were in the *fattoria*'s upper story, but when I staggered upstairs that first night, I found every foot of space occupied by the cots and gear of the other correspondents. I laid my bedroll out on the floor, but sacks of walnuts were stored at the far end of the room. They emitted a strong, tannic stink that kept me awake most of the night.

If everything had gone according to plan, Mark Clark was to have captured and occupied Naples on September 12, three days after the Fifth Army landed at Salerno. But here it was September 30, nearly three weeks later, and the Fifth Army—"Mark Clark's Fifth Army," as his well-drilled corps of public relations people kept urging us reporters to call it—was only just beginning its lunge toward the great seaport on its way to Rome.

General Clark had found the "soft underbelly"—Churchill's term—strongly defended by some of those Germans who had been allowed to escape from Sicily. They included the Nineteenth and Twenty-ninth Panzer Grenadier divisions, and the Fifth Army's troops of the Thirty-sixth and Forty-fifth divisions found themselves overmatched when they landed on September 9 in the vicinity of Paestum. The Thirty-sixth, composed of Texans, was badly chewed up by enemy artillery. Its commander, General E. J. Dawley, went to pieces from overwork and was replaced by General John P. Lucas. But Clark emerged from the near debacle at Salerno, his first combat command, as something of a hero.

The correspondents joined the drive on Naples en masse. I shared a Jeep with burly Reynolds Packard and followed our infantry northward by way of Salerno, where we stopped at the beach to watch bivouacked British troops unload mountains of supplies. Hungry Salernitani swarmed about them, bargaining grapes for canned bully beef, tea, matches, and cigarettes.

The devastation in Salerno was awesome. Power lines and telephone wires hung like limp spaghetti from the battered facades of the buildings facing the port. The destruction was bad enough, but the visible evidence of widespread hunger was worse. The very old and the very young contested refuse heaps with hungry dogs.

Relief was on its way, and the Allied Military Government (AMG) had moved into what remained of Salerno's *municipio,* the city hall, where a huge crowd of women, nearly all in the traditional black which widows and bereaved mothers wore, gathered outside the entrance. Word had spread that food was being distributed, and all had come with baskets or string bags to take it away. But the AMG officials were merely registering the needy and issuing ration books for future use. The women came away tearful and angry. Twenty or more, enough to be dangerous, rushed toward our vehicle, all talking at once, gesticulating, pleading for food. Packard explained in his pidgin Italian that we were merely *giornalisti* and had no *mangiare.*

Behind me someone tugged at my sleeve. I turned and looked into the eyes of a young woman in black, who held up to me a half-clad infant with running sores on its face and head. Two toddlers with swollen bellies hung on to the woman's long skirt. The appeal in their big black eyes was too much for me. Against my better judgment, and as surreptitiously as possible, I slipped the woman two cans of meat and vegetables from my C rations, and ordered our GI driver to get us the hell out of there before a mob descended.

Thirst along the way was almost as bad as the hunger. There was no clean, potable water anywhere. The retreating Huns—the word for the enemy on the American front—had destroyed the water mains, and there was no fuel to boil what water there was. At Torre Annunziata I saw people slurping the murky stuff they scooped out of stagnant pools and ditches. A priest hovered over them making the sign of the cross. He wasn't practicing divine prophylaxis; he was merely blessing those who drank.

In deserted Pompeii, a bit farther on, I had the driver stop at a roadside curio shop I knew from previous visits. The store's steel shutters were partly drawn, and I guessed, correctly, that the proprietor was open for business. While I bargained over the price of a small bronze replica of the *Dancing Faun,* our artillery engaged a German reconnaissance unit a few hundred yards up the road. Had we not stopped, we would almost certainly have run into the rear guard of the retreating Germans. We were well ahead of our occupational troops, directly behind our reconnaissance forces.

Only the day before, in approximately the same area, the Germans had hit a Jeepload of four audacious British correspondents with a shell from a Mark III tank. Stewart Sale, of the *London Daily Herald,* A. B. Austin, of Reuters, and Bill Mundy, of the Australian AP, were killed outright, and B. H. T. Gingell, of the British Exchange Telegraph, was wounded. We passed the temporary roadside graves of the dead on our way up the road to Torre del Greco.

On both sides of the road, refugees, laden with personal belongings, clothing, and bedding, wearily trudged Indian file. Those on our left came from Naples, and those on our right were returning to *la bella Napoli.* Many were the ragged, ill-shod remnants of Italy's army, free now to return to their homes.

On the steps of what was once a palace, a mother searched her child's hair for lice. A pregnant woman carried a heavy wicker basket on her head and an infant cradled in her arms. The baby suckled as the mother trudged on, urging before her two other small children.

Once, as we passed through the village of Portici just this side of San Giovanni—almost at the gates of Naples—our Jeep nearly hit a stringy-haired child who was carrying her infant brother in her arms. The streets and sidewalks and sagging balconies of the remaining buildings—those whose innards weren't spilled in masses of dusty gray debris across the road—were black with people.

Portici was in a quiet hiatus between war and peace. The street was a valley of human voices all talking at once. But with one voice they screamed at us and at the child. Their screams coincided with the screech of our brakes and were followed by a unanimous sigh of relief and a fleeting silence. Then came the strident overloud voices of Neapolitan women scolding the child while thanking us for having spared her.

We emerged from Portici into San Giovanni, another lively people's forum. Throughout the night, all the way from Scafati and Pompei, there had been street fighting, with the Germans defending each town street by street. Where all the people had gone, it was impossible to guess, for there seemed to be no place for them to go. But now here they were. Children came out to throw bundles of flowers at us. Barefooted women and men in rummage-sale garments stopped to cheer and clap their hands and to shout, *"Viva l'americani, viva gli inglesi."*

For a quarter of a mile or more the town of San Giovanni was clean and wholesome and undamaged. The cheers of the people were embarrassing. We were greeted like conquering heroes. We hadn't done anything to deserve cheers, but we waved feeble acknowledgments because the people expected us to.

Less than a hundred yards farther on, a large blue sign announced NAPOLI in white letters. A horde of armed civilians rushed wildly out to stop us. One red-eyed man held a nickel-plated revolver in one hand and, with the other, waved behind him and shouted, *"Tedeschi."* He made himself heard above the babble to inform us that the Germans were nearby with armored cars. He said they were shooting civilians: *"Anche donne e bambini* [women and children]."

This was nothing new. All the way from Salerno we heard stories of

German outrages, but we had no means of confirming or denying the claims of the excited crowds. The burden of such tales was that the Germans executed known or suspected anti-Fascists or those who listened to American or English radio broadcasts.

In Torre Annunziata a man named Mario Guerriero said he was arrested and jailed for listening to Fiorello La Guardia, the New York mayor who regularly broadcast to the Italians in their own language. Entering the town ahead of our troops behind the retreating Germans, we received an ovation. The mayor made a twenty-minute speech of welcome, and when he finished, he turned to me and said in amazement, "I haven't talked so long in twenty years." In the excitement one man in the crowd gave the Fascist salute from force of habit, and his neighbor nearly broke the unfortunate fellow's arm knocking it down.

Along the road to Naples, hatred for the Germans was as evident as something like love for the Americans and the British. Everywhere there were reports of German looting. In every town they destroyed supplies and carried away valuables and food, and the people's bitterness against their Fascist officials equaled their hatred of the Hun.

We entered Naples from the south. It seemed a dead city. The enemy had retreated beyond Castel San Martino and the Vomero Hill to the north. We found only three small boys, so dirty they didn't look human. Each dragged a gunnysack behind him. They stopped to wave at us and cheer.

We drove up the Via Garibaldi to the piazza where the grizzled old hero of the Risorgimento looked down in bronze grandeur on the desolate public square and the wreckage of what was once one of the most glamorous and, in some respects, most beautiful cities in the world. But it wasn't the same city that tourists remembered. Only Vesuvius was the same.

We had three second-rate hotels on our list as possible billets. We found all three—the Londres, the Royal Palace, and the Park—burned out. The Excelsior and the other grand hotels along Santa Lucia were badly damaged. Zia Teresa's restaurant, where before the war the fish was good and the Chianti heady and the boatmen sang of Naples' charms, was barely recognizable.

For a thousand yards or more inward from the sea, Naples was a shambles. The old Castel del l'Uovo was gnawed by shell fire; one of its crenellated towers, which faced the new, ugly, but efficient principal dock, was nearly demolished. Only the main streets—Via Garibaldi and Corso Umberto—were clear. Side streets, down which we caught glimpses of the havoc wrought by German dynamiters, our own bombers, and the enemy's shell fire, were torn up and otherwise impassable.

We entered Naples at about 10:30 A.M., and by noon our occupation troops began arriving. The roar of their motors brought out the people, who streamed down the narrow, winding streets. They were the happiest people I had ever seen. Most were on the edge of hysteria. The older women wept, knelt, and crossed themselves in thanksgiving.

Under the trees in the square before Naples's medieval city hall, we met an efficient American lieutenant colonel named Craigie. He denied rumors of rampant cholera but admitted there was typhus and considerable typhoid. He planned to restore the water supply sufficiently to enable the population to obtain water at the public fountains.

In the harbor we had a shipload of flour, enough for only a few days, but other supplies were on the way. Brigadier General Frank McSherry, who had been the first official to enter the city, brought with him quantities of food and representatives of law and order. They installed themselves in the city hall, and while the sound of guns could still be heard in the city's northern outskirts, the Allied Military Government tackled its biggest job since the war began: feeding 1.5 million hungry Neapolitans and bringing order out of the chaos the Germans had left.

The Piazza del Municipio was filled with thousands of animated, cheering, happy Neapolitans. They had come not to beg but to demonstrate their joy at having been liberated. It was as big a crowd as I had ever seen assembled for one of Mussolini's speeches but with an important difference: There was laughter and undisciplined, unrestrained elation.

We stopped at the edge of the crowd and were immediately engulfed by Neapolitans who reached up to touch us and shake our hands. A dozen or more wanted to know how they could communicate with relatives in the *Stati Uniti*. They said they had brothers, fathers, uncles, and cousins in Boston, Baltimore, Brooklyn, and Philadelphia.

Inevitably there were stories of German outrages and tales of atrocities evocative of scenes from Goya. Oddly, no one in the crowd that surrounded us begged for food, though hunger was plainly written in their pinched, pale faces. But at the end of that first day's long journey, what I remembered most vividly, and would never forget, was the plea in the luminous black eyes of the woman who had silently begged me for food in the piazza outside the *municipio* in Salerno.

Unable to find billets in any of the hotels on our list, we established press headquarters in an empty villa on the Via Partenope facing the Bay of Naples and Mount Vesuvius. The view was magnificent, and the house had good modern plumbing but no water except what we had brought in jerricans—not nearly enough to flush the toilets!

The departing Germans had wrecked the city's water supply and sewerage systems and had destroyed the port with ruthless efficiency. Every berth at the docks was obstructed by sunken ships. Many tugs and harbor craft were sunk; cranes and gear for handling cargo were sabotaged; power lines and pipelines were ripped out; power stations were blown up, and the waters of the harbor itself were sown with mines. Naples, in other words, was rendered inoperable.

Ashore, time bombs were hidden in such places as the main post office, hotels, and barracks buildings—anywhere likely to be used by Allied soldiers and Italian civilians after the city fell—and many exploded with deadly effect days after we occupied the city.

The worst of the explosions occurred on October 10 in the central post office, where some of our troops were billeted and facilities had been set up to handle correspondents' cables and GI mail. The main ground floor hall was full of GIs when an enormous time bomb blew up, killing dozens of our soldiers and wounding dozens more. I had left the place only minutes before the blast and had just reached the villa when it happened.

The delayed-action mines, though they killed more civilians than soldiers, could have been considered legitimate weapons of warfare. But the wanton vandalism was inexcusable on any grounds. Not content with making Naples virtually uninhabitable, the Germans looted the city's National Museum—one of the world's finest—burned the Royal Society's priceless library of two hundred thousand volumes in the University of Naples, and set fire to the incalculably valuable Neapolitan archives at Nola. The blind, senseless destruction of cultural monuments and priceless art treasures compiled a Nazi record in Naples that would be forever shameful.

In each case the destruction was simply retaliation for the killing or wounding of a German soldier or some other act of sabotage by anti-Nazi Italians. Personally, I found it difficult to believe that the German high command would allow a few brutal officers to punish Italy for quitting the war by looting and burning its art treasures. The Vandals and the Huns knew no better, but I had hoped for more from men of the people who had produced Goethe and Kant.

By their outrageous behavior, however, the Germans aroused the resistance of a growing underground movement, even among the very young. In Naples some of the most effective guerrilla warfare against the Germans was waged by the *scugnizzi,* gangs of street toughs in their early teens and under. They stole and hid rifles, ammunition and grenades, stealthily roamed the streets at night, and sniped at enemy vehicles.

Our engineers soon had the port functioning again, and Liberty ships loaded with sugar, wheat, rice, and other foods began arriving to relieve the universal hunger. Except for feeble trickles of water at public fountains, however, Naples remained waterless and sewerless for weeks.

Nevertheless, the city gradually regained a measure of its traditional vitality. The streets filled with people, and the shops reopened along the Via Roma and the Corso Umberto. The luxury goods they displayed indicated the feebleness of the Italian war effort. There were silver fox capes in furriers' windows, and some tailoring establishments offered British textiles.

Allied soldiers bought ladies' hats, shoes, gloves, manicuring files and scissors, bath sponges, cooking pots and pans, embroidered infants' layettes, Venetian lace, jewelry, watches, perfume by weight, and, for a nation renowned for its art and culture, some of the ugliest "modernistic" furniture in existence. Our British friends purchased items which had disappeared in England within a year after the war started. Our GIs bought sheer silk stockings, negligees, scarfs, and lingerie to send home for Christmas, and shopkeepers' stocks were soon exhausted. Scarcity brought in its wake a thriving black market, in which American cigarettes became a substitute for money. They

could be exchanged for almost anything, including the sexual favors of prostitutes.

It became increasingly evident to those of us who had worked and lived
in Italy before the war that the Allied occupation had brought with it political
problems far more complex than those in North Africa. The Allies operated
without any clear plan for the country's postwar governance. They casually
assumed that they could work through Badoglio and the king.

The aging marshal (seventy-two at the time) and the diminutive monarch
hurriedly and ignominiously scuttled out of Rome on September 10, the day
after the armistice was announced, and fled to Brindisi. There Badoglio established a "government" to rule what was left of Italy—four miserable provinces
in the heel of the boot—which was immediately "recognized" by a hastily
formed Allied Military Mission that subsequently became the Allied Military
Government.

The Americans would have preferred dealing only with Badoglio, as they
had with Darlan in North Africa, but the British, notably the promonarchist
Churchill, insisted on including King Victor Emmanuel. The State Department took the position that Italy was infinitely more important to the British
than to the Americans, and the decision about recognizing the king's participation in Badoglio's regime was left to Eisenhower. The general didn't care one
way or another, so the king, recognized and supported by the Allies, began an
eventually successful fight to save the throne for his son, Prince Umberto.

On October 13 the Badoglio regime declared war against Germany, and
Italy became a "cobelligerent." But the marshal had no constituency or real
authority. In the south the reviving political parties openly agitated against
him. They wanted a republic, not the restoration of a monarchy that had
allowed fascism to displace, to suppress, and ultimately to destroy Italian
democratic institutions.

In Italy, as in Yugoslavia and Greece, the Allies were content merely to
remove Nazi and Fascist rule, but the left-wing resistance movements wanted
far more radical and meaningful social, political, and economic change. In
Italy, as elsewhere, the war had unleashed revolutionary forces which the
Allies, their eyes fixed solely on military victory, either did not see or failed
to understand.

56

THE ROAD TO ROME

Italy provided the most difficult terrain imaginable for modern mechanized warfare: a succession of jagged mountains and swift-flowing streams. Moreover, soon after Mark Clark captured Naples, two new factors complicated his hoped-for quick march on Rome.

The first factor was the weather. It had been raining sporadically since the end of September, but starting early in October, the autumn rains became an almost daily occurrence, producing thick yellow-brown mud that mired the Fifth Army's tanks and heavy vehicles and brought acute discomfort to the men. The autumn rains and a touch of winter arrived with extraordinary abruptness. Blinding dust and sunshine suddenly turned into cold rain and mud.

The second factor was a sudden 180-degree turn in German strategy. Far from evacuating to the Plain of Lombardy, the enemy began reinforcing his armies and building what was to be called the Gustav Line, a fortified barrier across the narrowest part of the Italian peninsula in the mountains above the Garigliano and Sangro rivers about seventy-five or eighty miles south of Rome.

And with the bad weather the real fighting started, not skirmishes with the rearguard elements of a retreating enemy, but pitched battles against entrenched Germans holding the high ground; deaths not in batches of a dozen or two, but in hundreds, with the survivors struggling in cold wetness, rarely knowing a dry night's sleep or a hot meal, slogging through gooey mud, lying in damp foxholes day in, day out, their forward movement checked by the deplorable state of the roads.

Even in fine summer weather the road network in southern Italy would have been barely adequate for Clark's army of more than a hundred thousand men with modern motorized equipment. In the autumn rains, with the land turning to mud, the forward motion of men and machines, already complicated by German demolitions, became virtually impossible. The retreating enemy destroyed every bridge and culvert, and torrents of water gushing from rain-swollen streams and rivulets created impassable quagmires at crossing points that had already been churned by tanks and vehicles.

Four main roads ran up the peninsula. Two lay on the eastern Adriatic side of the Apennines and were assigned to Montgomery's Eighth Army. On the western side, the main road was Route 7, which forked just above Caserta and thereafter provided two roads to Rome. The left fork, the old Via Appia, continued as Route 7, ran along the Tyrrhenian Sea, crossed the Pontine Marshes, and passed close to the beaches at Anzio. The right fork, which above Caserta became Route 6, the Via Casilina, crossed the Volturno River beyond Capua and continued northward to Rome via Cassino and the Liri Valley.

During my prewar years in Italy I had frequently made the 190-mile trip between Rome and Naples in fewer than four hours in my Fiat. It was to take an unimaginable and very bloody eight *months* for the Fifth Army to cover the same distance. Forward movement was possible only during brief pauses when the sun shone sufficiently to dry out the tracks and the engineers could bridge culverts or bulldoze new tracks around mudholes.

Huge convoys were bogged along the roads and sometimes remained motionless for days. Meanwhile, a piercing wind kept sweeping down from the Apennines, and the Tyrrhenian Sea turned from cobalt blue to sullen gray. The men wrapped themselves in blankets and ponchos and shivered in their foxholes. There was only one answer to the problem—wait until the rain stopped—but few commanders, least of all Mark Clark, hell-bent on reaching Rome by Christmas, were willing to do so.

Men and vehicles struggled on until eventually forced to halt. The rain then stopped, the sun dried out the tracks somewhat, and once more full of hope, the commanders pushed their units forward. Down came the rain again, and the whole dreary, disillusioning process was repeated. Only when the units were too exhausted to move any farther was a halt ever called.

Eager to push on to Rome, Mark Clark twice scheduled H hour for the Fifth Army's first opposed crossing of a river, the Volturno, and twice postponed it. Then, on Sunday, October 10, the sun made a welcome appearance, and the attempt to cross the Volturno was rescheduled for the night of October 12–13. To be there in good time, Bill Stoneman and I took off for the front on the surprisingly sunny, though cold and windy, morning of October 11.

We loaded field gear and rations into a Jeep and headed for the forward positions of General Lucian Truscott's crack Third Division, reputedly the finest infantry in the line. It had fought well at Salerno and taken heavy casualties—one in every ten of its approximately fifteen thousand men. I had visited the front twice before, on October 6 and 8—each time in driving rain and in vain because the attacks were postponed—but I had made friends at the headquarters of the Second Battalion of the Third Division's Seventh Infantry and headed the Jeep in their direction.

Driving northward through Caserta along the winding Casilina (Route 6) past long lines of trucks, we climbed the Abruzzi mountains to Capua, then descended to the flat campagna and passed through what the Germans had left of the town called Maddaloni. The once-pleasant farming community was a total ruin, its main street littered with debris and the swollen, rotting carcasses of mules and donkeys, a grisly sight.

We found the Second Battalion bivouacked among olive trees in a gorge in the hills beyond the town, a few hundred yards from the southern bank of the Volturno. Although the men were encamped under the trajectory of our own artillery and hadn't slept much during the previous night's incessant cannonading of the Germans' positions on Mount Monticello north of the river, they were a cheerful, hospitable lot and made us welcome.

Their commander was Captain Andrew Leaming, a tall, tough soldier with unruly blondish hair and a strong, pockmarked neck. We had met before, on October 8, when I had come up to cover the scheduled (but postponed) crossing of the Volturno. That night, in a driving rain, the captain and I had listened to seven innings of the World Series game between the Yankees and the Cardinals on the field radio in his staff car. But we never learned who won. At the bottom of the seventh inning, we came under heavy German artillery fire and spent the rest of the night in our foxholes. I returned to Naples wet to the skin and nursing a bad cold.

Andy Leaming gave us hot coffee on arrival and, when he discovered we were not too well equipped for the muddy terrain and whatever lay ahead, provided us with leggings, extra GI pants and shirts, underwear, woolen socks, blankets, and shelter tents complete with groundsheets. The unit's American Red Cross man, a genial volunteer named Joe Cappiello—like myself, from South Philly and of Italian origin—showered us with welcome gifts: soap, towels, toothbrushes, toothpaste, and shaving gear. "By the way," Leaming asked when we had settled in, "who won the World Series?" Neither Stoneman nor I could tell him.

Nothing in war is "enjoyable," yet I can think of no other word to describe my time with the battalion, my first experience with GIs in the field. In the cliquey atmosphere of the Eighth Army, I had often encountered British reserve; but among my fellow countrymen I found only genuine, unrestrained comradeship, and I quickly acquired a new vocabulary.

In the American Army a first sergeant was a "top kick," canned condensed milk was "armored cow," a shovel was an "army banjo," and a Ph.D. was not an academic degree but a "post-hole digger." A "sad sack" was an unfortunate fellow who never did anything right, always had bad luck, and was often the butt of pranks. The Second Battalion, like all other units, had one, a runty redhead from Seattle who constantly complained of the rain and the mud and was regularly admonished to "Tell it to the chaplain!"

The battalion also had its hero, a man everyone else looked up to, big, cheerful First Sergeant James Kemp, an almond farmer from Chico, California, with a chest like a beer barrel and hands the size of hams. On the moonlit night of October 12 Sergeant Kemp made it possible for his unit to cross the Volturno, and behind it an entire regiment, one of several that crossed when H hour struck at 3:45 A.M. on October 13. He had, of course, volunteered for the job.

Two hours before the attack, Sergeant Kemp was wading in the Volturno where the river flattened out and made a quarter circle at the base of Monte Castellone about four straight-line miles upriver from Capua. It was a clear night with a three-quarter moon, and it was cold. The wind needled through the men's blankets and officers' combat jackets, whenever they halted on the laborious march up the ravines and goat paths of the mountain, then down the forward slope to the river's edge toward battle with its promise of injury or death.

In the springtime, those rocky, uncertain mountain paths flowed with the melted snows of Castellone. On the night of October 12–13 they flowed with silent men bearing thirty-pound battle packs, hugging bazookas and ammunition, machine guns, automatic rifles, and coils of wire for telephone lines and shouldering heavy, cumbersome boats—seventeen men to each boat. Nobody talked. Commands were given in undertones, acknowledged in grunts and executed as silently as hobnailed boots and the uncertain footing allowed. During halts the men relieved themselves—some unintentionally—and on the forward slopes of the mountain the air was foul.

In the grotesque shadows, faces were indistinguishable one from the other. There was no drama except that created by the eerie setting and the indisputable fact that we were going into battle just as soon as Sergeant Kemp finished his job some three hundred yards below.

The dirty gray-brown waters of the Volturno swirled about Sergeant Kemp's knees, then his waist. It reached his neck before he arrived on the northern bank, dragging a steel cable. It weighed two hundred pounds for every 100 feet, and where he crossed, the Volturno was about 150 feet wide. Noiselessly he anchored the cable on the enemy bank. It was to serve as a guide for assault troops and to carry telephone wire for communications. The sergeant made the cable secure and waded back.

South of the tortuous Volturno elements of the Fifth Army were poised for attack. Every regiment assigned to cross the Volturno had its Sergeant Kemp, but ours was the first. To those of us who waited and shivered with the painful cold in the phantasmagoric silence of Monte Castellone, he was all the Sergeant Kemps of this world rolled into one, a brave man of gigantic proportions alone in an unfriendly river, moving surely toward an enemy shore, the free end of the heavy wire wrapped around his waist, swinging his huge fists to balance himself against the uncertainties of current and mud.

The next day he said simply, "The river wasn't so cold. But those krauts over there must all have been asleep. I made lots of noise, I guess. That cable was heavy, and I was thrashing around in the bushes, trying to find a place to anchor the damn thing."

That was all Sergeant Kemp had to say on the subject. But for an electric hour or so in the deep mountain stillness, an entire regiment waited on the southern riverbank and on the mountain that bulked enormously below it, while he completed his mission.

Shortly after midnight on the morning of October 13 (just about the time Sergeant Kemp was scrambling back up the southern bank of the Volturno, dripping water and mud), the artillery opened up. Our big guns were firing from behind us over two mountain ridges and toward primary objectives on the opposite bank. Our mortars, meanwhile, were firing from just above and behind us. The heavier guns were aimed at Monticello, a stumpy, pyramidal mountain at the edge of the Volturno Plain opposite us.

Bursting shells raised showers of incandescent earth on the mountain targets. Every minute for an hour and a half fifty shells fell on Monticello. Few dropped on the broad plain itself, the trajectory of the projectiles being too flat and too long. Only mortars could reach the plain, which had once been a malarial swamp but was now ditched and drained and dotted with peasants' houses and haystacks and cooperative farms. One of these, La Fagianeria, was a huge place with tall silos and rows of workers' houses and buildings. All— ditches, houses, haystacks, culverts, walls, and even corn shocks—hid Germans armed with machine pistols, machine guns, rifles, and rifle grenades. The swamp's drainage system constituted ready-made trenches, and the enemy had dug himself in well.

Our batteries fired in chaotic rhythm. At times the noise was almost beyond human endurance, a primordial noise in which great hammers swung against gargantuan, varitoned gongs, and their echoes bounced from mountain to mountain in the vast natural amphitheater. The shells tore the sky with the sound of silk being slit by sharp knives, and the tortured air protested with loud, echoing groans and moans down the valley.

Under this arcade of screaming steel, two battalions waded the river, some along the cable that Kemp had strung, others along still other cables that the first assault troops carried. And all the while not a sound from the enemy. Then the barrage ceased. It was H hour.

The silence was almost tangible. On the opposite bank wet, muddy doughboys crawled on elbows and bellies toward they didn't know what, with their heads well down, their faces often in the oozy mud of the Volturno Plain. A German machine pistol broke the quiet. This weapon made a sound like a small high-speed riveting gun—*trrrrrrrt.* Then came the slower-paced answering fire from a Yank machine gun, and we knew that the doughboy who manned it was on the ball. Once, in a moment of quiet, there was a burst from a German pistol. Then another and another, and one determined splut-splut-splut from an American weapon. The German failed to reply.

The sounds of firing from the German side were surprising. It had seemed certain that no living thing could have survived our shells. But the enemy had survived. Our barrage had largely gone over the Germans' heads. When it subsided, they came out of their holes, manned their weapons and met our troops with a deadly crossfire of automatic weapons and grenades and mortars.

On our left, in Capua, the attack by the British Forty-sixth Division had run headlong into a German counterattack on the southern side of the river. Some of the British boats were smashed by the Germans almost before they had been put into the water. One battalion suffered heavy losses.

On our right an American division, the Thirty-fourth Infantry, encountered stiff resistance before it reached the river. Twenty-four hours later both outfits were across the stream and into the battle that raged up and down the Volturno Valley, but just as the first light limned the blue-black Apennines in the north beyond that absurd ribbon of river, only our two battalions of the Third Division had crossed. Dawn came as though a stage electrician had turned up the blue lights, and with it, a great, soundless desolation. On the plain there wasn't a sign of life or movement, only a great mist of smoke.

Down at the water's edge engineers were hurrying to throw a bridge across the river. A sufficient number of British tanks to support the infantry had already crossed the stream, but there were guns and trucks with ammunition and supply units, ambulances, and hundreds of vehicles, from Jeeps to bulldozers, yet to go.

Behind the bridgehead along the narrow road toward the rear area, men, material, and weapons were crowded in the valley as far back as our headquarters at Caserta and beyond. A hundred times a day we were thankful that the enemy had lost supremacy in the air. A few German bombers could have turned the Allied crossing of the Volturno into a debacle of the first magnitude. But in the first twenty-four hours of battle enemy air power was remarkable for its absence.

Some hours after we had crossed, while we broke open some K ration breakfast units at a regimental forward command post and heated water in canteen cups over cans of gasoline set in the mud, a Messerschmitt came over on a reconnaissance mission. It flew low enough for me to distinguish the black cross on the underside of its blunt wings. It was the only enemy plane we saw until late in the afternoon, when two fighter-bombers came over the bridgehead. One dumped an ineffectual bomb, and the other gave us a harmless burst of machine-gun fire. Both got away before our mobile ack-ack units could draw beads on them.

Enemy shell fire delayed the engineers. The men worked waist-deep and neck-deep in water. They worked like demons and in a few hours managed to throw a light pontoon bridge over the river, strong enough to support loaded Jeeps with trailers. Somehow, they got a bulldozer across, too, to gnaw out the approaches for a heavier bridge. I saw shells bursting about trucks loaded with deflated pontoons, girders, steel track, and planking, which were growling up a narrow road in the steep gorge toward the river. None was hit. The attack, however, caused several hours' delay.

German batteries of eighty-eights stung in on a position where the trucks were bound to pass and intermittently shelled the place all day long. With Stoneman and two other correspondents—Merrill Mueller, of NBC, and Homer Bigart, of the *New York Herald Tribune*—I climbed a mountain to watch the bombardment. Shells came from the enemy side of the river over our heads and dropped in the gorge below.

A thousand feet below us, on our left, our trucks milled about like bewildered oxen backing out of danger. Jeeps darted about buglike off the road into the shelter of ditches. Shells tore up the road and hit one truck, killing at least one man and injuring others. Later German fighter-bombers attacked a heavier bridge farther up the river. A bomb hit a half-track. It killed three men and hurt six. Several big pontoons were punctured by shrapnel, but the bridge held up. One of the first trucks to cross it hit a three-decker German Teller mine on the opposite shore. The explosion demolished the truck, killed one of its riders, and tied up traffic.

The engineers worked on through the day, overcoming mud and bombs, shells, shortages of materials held up on the mucky, crowded roads, and enemy mines in unexpected places. The men worked until they were so weary that their movements were automatic, and their faces became the dull, dirty, unshaved masks of automatons. They were wet. They dried. They were wet again. They ate cold C rations out of cans and smoked when they could. There was no time for hot coffee.

At 9:20 P.M. the bridge was finished, and the caissons were rolling across it.

My friend, General William ("Bill") Eagles, the commanding officer of the regiment to which I was attached for the Battle of the Volturno, was one of those COs who wanted their command posts within walking distance of the firing line. We moved three times in two days and we moved again at H hour plus five, which meant at seven o'clock on the morning of the battle.

By nine o'clock I was sweating in a Jeep heavily loaded with half the command post equipment going across a light pontoon bridge over the Volturno. By that time the rain, which had begun to fall intermittently after a clear, dry night, had settled into a steady downpour. The approaches to the bridge on the other side were hog wallows two feet deep. Only Jeeps could make it—those incredible Jeeps that had the dogged persistence of mules when you slipped into low gear with all four wheels activated. What a machine!

The new command post was somewhere in the lee of the mountain we had blasted a few hours before. The way lay through fields where Americans had fought Germans, across ditches the enemy had held, and around foxholes our Yanks had dug. In one ditch lay two blond young Germans on their backs, waxen faces and dead eyes to the sky. In another, a tall Yank lay face downward; the graves registration officer had not yet arrived. At a small crossroads farther on, under a rude pergola of grapevines half in, half out of a trench he had dug, lay a mangled German, a machine gunner. Unaccountably, there was a stout rope tied around his body under his armpits.

I drove through La Fagianeria. Amazingly the silos still stood. Several of the peasants' houses were intact. Weary GIs, wary of booby traps, moved cautiously in and out of houses and prowled in gardens. Where the doors of houses were closed, nobody bothered to enter. It was a common trick of the enemy to attach trip mines to doors, windows, anything movable. The Germans even planted booby traps on their dead. La Fagianeria smelled of decaying bodies, and I got out as quickly as possible.

The command post site was several thousand yards farther on, in the debris the enemy had left behind. The Germans were once well-disciplined, well-equipped, meticulous soldiers, but they had grown careless with a carelessness born of weariness and defeatism. Formerly they buried their dead or carried them away. It was rare now to find neat German graves with wooden crosses. Instead, we found the broken, rotting bodies of supermen who had died for the Führer. And we saw the holes they used as latrines within fly range of where they lived and ate and slept. Their cans were discarded where used. Only their weapons showed soldierly care.

Four white Leghorn pullets huddled aimlessly near where the CO pitched his pup tent beside a ditch. Somehow they had survived, but not for long; we had them for dinner, roasted on spits over a campfire.

Three German prisoners were brought in toward noon. Two were under twenty years old but had seen eighteen months of service. They were small, frightened boys. The third was in his thirties and had fought in Spain, France, and Russia. He said Germany was headed for communism as soon as Russia won on the eastern front. He said only the Nazi party members and the wealthy feared communism. He said he didn't care one way or another, "The poor man is interested only in work and bread, and it matters little who rules him in Germany, only let it not be the Nazis." When asked why he and his comrades continued to fight, he shrugged and made a pained smile. "We are soldiers," he said.

Up at battalion headquarters, within sound of blurping machine guns and bursting grenades, we found the remains of sixteen Germans. They were sprawled on the ground at the base of a hill. There were no blankets to cover them, and they lay with flies and wasps buzzing around them. One was bandaged heavily about the neck and face. Yank medics had found him in a ditch, burbling blood out of a hole in his throat, and had tried to patch him up, but he lived only three hours.

Arranged in rows and covered with blankets were our own dead, almost as many as there were Germans. From some, white identification tags fluttered, with their names and serial numbers and details of how they died.

Nearby was an impressive pile of German weapons guarded by an unshaven GI with an expressionless, tired face. We nodded to each other, and he gave me a mirthless smile. He was huddled in a blanket against the cold rain and stared down at the pile of rifles, pistols, bayonets, grenades, and machine guns.

"How goes it?" I asked.

"Just tell them," he replied, "we're doing our best."

57

STALEMATE AT THE RAPIDO

orth of the Volturno the Fifth Army encountered more mountains, more Germans, more diabolical roadblocks, more rain, and
more rivers to be crossed. First it was the broad Garigliano, then
the narrower but icy, swift-flowing Rapido, which crossed Route
6 at Cassino and which actually ran red with Allied blood when Mark Clark's
forces attempted to bridge it after reaching the Germans' *Winterstellungen*,
their "winter line" south of the Gustav Line.

Italy had to be fought for thereafter mile by bloody mile, and nowhere
along the way was there the faintest hope of a hot bath. Indeed, by the end
of October the original conception of the attack on the "soft underbelly"—the
rapid withdrawal of the Germans northward to the Plain of Lombardy—had
proved fallacious. The Allies found themselves twisting and turning, compro-
mising with short-term gains, taking a hill here and another there, and in the
maze of minor operations the overall plan lost its original purpose. "Rome by
Christmas" became an impossible dream.

In fact, the entire Italian campaign took on a chimerical quality. Success
seemed forever within the grasp of Clark's army along the west coast and
Monty's forces on the other side of the Apennines. Yet each time the generals
reached forward to grasp what seemed like certain victory something went
wrong. Usually it was the weather. The rain fell in torrents, vehicles were
mired above their hubcaps, the lowlands became quagmires, and the cleverly
entrenched German rear guard effectively delayed Allied progress.

The breach in Fortress Europe which Montgomery had opened on September 3 was effectively closed after the Fifth Army crossed the Volturno in mid-October. Had the commanders been content with the capture of Foggia— the air base from which the Allies could bomb Germany's industrial heart- land—and possession of the excellent port at Naples, then gone into winter quarters until spring, many lives might have been spared.

But General Alexander, in his comfortable headquarters in sunny Bari, and Eisenhower, six hundred miles away in warm Algiers, apparently believed they had to secure Foggia and Naples from German counterattacks by advancing to the north. After a few small gains the generals deemed it necessary to capture Rome itself, a goal difficult enough in the rainy autumn and impossible when winter came ahead of schedule.

But Rome didn't seem to be beyond reach at the time, so the northward push continued. In the process, thousands of Britons and Americans were killed or wounded. As of the end of October, the Fifth Army's British dead and wounded totaled eight thousand, and its American casualties numbered six thousand. The Eighth Army, thanks to Monty's more cautious ways in slightly less formidable terrain, lost only a thousand. But the slaughter was far from over. The worst was yet to come along the Rapido below Cassino.

After crossing the Volturno, I accompanied the infantrymen of the Third Division up the Casilina under incredibly difficult conditions. The rain never slackened as the troops slogged northward to create the supply dumps their commanders needed as far forward as possible before an attack could be mounted. For the men, this was hard work, usually done under enemy artillery fire, with the frequent added heartbreak of having the results of their labors blown sky-high by German shells. The enemy gunners had every trail, gully, and draw on the slopes registered on their maps and zeroed in on them at will when bad weather grounded our air forces.

I had read about the mud of Flanders in World War I, but I doubt that it was deeper, stickier, or more loathsomely persistent than the mud of Italy. On flat ground you sloshed disgustedly through it, often over your ankles, and it was worse on the slopes, where you found yourself slipping and falling into it. When you fell, you were almost too weary to get up, but you did, and trudged on.

The men marched in mud, slept in it, and never really got rid of it, not even in most "rest areas" behind the lines, for they, too, were usually seas of mud. The supply problem was so critical that there often was not enough water for drinking, much less for washing off the mud. Your face, ears, and hair were caked with it, and so were your clothes. Uniforms were never really dry and stiffened uncomfortably on those windy days when it didn't rain.

The nights were so cold that I was unable to keep warm in a sleeping bag covered with two blankets and a poncho. I devised a stove by igniting charcoal in a perforated empty oil tin, but it was of little help. Nevertheless, I was far better off then the men. I was under canvas, in a wall tent of my own, and slept on a cot. The troops bedded down on groundsheets in foxholes under shelter halves. Many developed pneumonia, a major cause of casualties; all of us had bad colds.

For the footsore GIs of the Fifth Army, the phrase "Sunny Italy" soon held the same hollow sound that the words *La Belle France* acquired for their fathers in World War I. In terms of misery, rain, and mud Italy was, in fact, the France of World War II—France, however, minus the "Gay Paree" and the "wine, women, and song" American doughboys knew in the old war. The only major city the Fifth Army had captured by the time winter arrived was Naples, a dark, sad city where the wine the men drank was popskull "dago red" spiked with raw alcohol, where the women they slept with were pathetic creatures obtainable for a bar of chocolate, and where the songs they heard came from the raspy throats of tired waterfront hacks with warped guitars and cracked mandolins.

Rome was the next big town on Route 6—"Victory Road"—but it promised only more waterless toilets, ragged children begging for *biscotti* and *caramelle,* and black-market prices spiraling out of an inflation attributable partly to the Allied Military Government's arbitrary pegging of the lira at a hundred to the dollar and partly to the traditional merchants' aptitude for gouging foreigners.

After nearly a year of fighting in North Africa, Sicily, and Italy the tired and muddy and freezing men of the Fifth Army nourished only two desires. These were: (1) to "beat the ass off the fuckin' Germans" and (2) to return home to double features, baseball, hamburgers, beer, girl friends, families, firesides, and Sunday clothes. I talked with hundreds, and they made their yearnings abundantly clear. They evinced little interest in what kind of world would result from their monumental efforts and were of one voice in declaring, "Let's get it over with and go home."

Even the most inarticulate British Tommies expressed yearnings, though often only vague, for the creation of a postwar world in which there would be peace and justice and "jobs for everybody," a world so organized, moreover, that opportunities for tyrants to reemerge would be reduced to a safe minimum. They seemed to understand that war and politics were inseparable. But the Americans fought much as they played baseball or football—intensely and for the sole purpose of *winning*.

Englishmen knew they were not going to find the "same old England" when they returned to London or Liverpool, and they weren't at all sorry. The Americans, however, wanted nothing changed. To them "social gains" or change of any kind smacked of communism, and they wanted no part of that. They preferred their own "free enterprise system," a euphemism for capitalism. As one muddy young lieutenant put it after we had crossed the Volturno, "At least, under our system, every guy's got the same chance of becoming president, if you know what I mean. Yeah, sure, it's dog eat dog, but you can be the dog that wins. *That's* democracy."

It was late October—and far too late for a major offensive—before the Fifth Army's infantry reached within striking distance of the Germans' *Winterstellungen*, whose major stronghold at the time was at Cassino astride Route 6. At Naples we were roughly ninety or ninety-five road miles from Rome, but the distance might as well have been a thousand. We were definitely, irretrievably stuck at the Rapido.

I was still with the Third Division's Seventh Infantry when it arrived in the hills just south of the river and was deployed along a line extending from Calabritto on the left to Mignano on the right. The Second Battalion, to which I had attached myself, made camp in an olive grove on a hillside overlooking the Casilina to the south and facing Monte Cassino to the north.

From the battalion's forwardmost OP I had a fine view of Monte Cassino, rising 1,340 feet, its summit crowned by the massively impressive Benedictine abbey founded by the good St. Benedict in the year 529. In the Middle Ages the abbey served as a refuge for the priceless manuscripts, paintings, and sculptures of the time. In those days it was virtually inaccessible; now, however, it was reachable by a winding, narrow road hacked out of the mountain's granite flanks.

In the town—or what remained of it after we had bombed and shelled it repeatedly since early September—German tanks and tank destroyers were secreted among the ruins of the thick-walled stone houses. From their positions the enemy commanded Route 6, the Via Casilina, the more inland of the two west coast roads to Rome and the one Mark Clark needed most to keep his Fifth Army supplied.

In peacetime Cassino held about twenty thousand inhabitants, nice people who lived well off the tourist traffic of devout European Catholics who came to visit the abbey and to see the Roman ruins of ancient *Casinum*. In the late 1930s it was a fine halfway house between Rome and Naples, a 190-mile trip I had often made in my Fiat, a place where you could refill your gas tank and have your tires checked while you lunched on an omelet, freshly baked bread, goat cheese, and a local wine. It was then a reasonably clean town whose nubile girls promenaded in gay frocks in the small central square on Sunday afternoons. If you were headed for Rome after a weekend in southern Italy, at Cassino you felt you had left the poverty and misery of the backward south and were returning to civilization.

There were certainly no omelets to be had in Cassino in the wintry autumn of 1943, and no decorative signorinas to be seen in the town's *piazzetta*. Now there was only the all-too-familiar devastation we had caused with our bombs and shells—stony ruins amid which the enemy waited with deadly eighty-eights, heavy mortars, and machine guns.

We were certain then that the Germans were using the abbey and its mountaintop environs as vantage points from which their spotters directed artillery fire down on our positions. Their field guns were emplaced on a forbidding range of mountains that ran northeastward across our front from the Tyrrhenian coast to the high Apennines, barring our way to Rome via Cassino, Frosinone, and the Alban Hills.

Every clear day meant an artillery duel from sunup to sundown, and on one such morning the guns were pounding so hard at daybreak that the steel mirror hanging from the open flap of my tent shivered while I shaved, sending meaningless heliographic messages southward along Route 6. From the sound of it the stuff was mostly ours, outbound toward Cassino, but there was also inbound fire from German long-range cannon groping for our positions south of the Rapido.

A roadside marker along the Casilina where it wound past our olive grove read: CASSINO—KM 20.5. That wasn't very far, a twenty-minute run or less in a Jeep. But it was to take the Fifth Army all winter to break through the Germans' barrier. Rome had been captured from the south only once in history, by the Byzantine general Belisarius in the year 536, and the Germans were doing their expert best to prevent Mark Clark from being the second.

On October 24 or thereabouts General Clark had advanced his headquarters northward some twenty-five miles from Naples to Caserta, a miserable town with a splendiferous palace. Shunning palatial grandeur—and in the interest of mobility—the publicity-wise Clark set up his headquarters in a wooded area behind the royal palace, using trailers and wall tents for himself and his staff. The palace itself eventually housed the commander and staff of the Allied forces in Italy, General Alexander. Clark himself lived in a trailer, which, he made sure the world knew, had room for only a bunk, a small desk, and a bucket of water.

It was at Caserta, when summoned there for a press conference, that I first met Mark Clark. Tall (six feet two inches) with a biggish nose of the kind usually described as "Roman," youthful, and energetic, he was physically impressive. At forty-seven he was the youngest lieutenant general the U.S. Army had ever known. Among his fellow officers only his close friend and mentor Dwight Eisenhower had risen faster than he.

An entire chapter would only begin to do justice to Clark's career, but a few details about his rise to the second-highest rank in the U.S. Army are essential to an understanding of the Italian campaign as it developed in the bitter winter of 1943–1944. Born of a military family, he was graduated from West Point in 1917 in time to see brief combat in World War I. Between the wars Clark was for sixteen years just another captain, but as World War II loomed, he rose to the rank of lieutenant colonel and was assigned to drafting training plans for our expanding ground forces. His superiors were so impressed by the diligence and competence which he demonstrated in that assignment that when the United States entered the war, he was jumped to brigadier general. He never wore a colonel's eagle.

Later, when Eisenhower went to England to plan the November 1942 landings in North Africa, he asked for Clark, and the two shared living quarters in London's Grosvenor Square. Then came Clark's secret, dramatic trip by submarine to Vichy-ruled Algiers to make contact with friendly French officials and his narrow escape from capture by the Vichy security police. His daring escapade won him his third star and command of the Fifth Army under Britain's Alexander and over half a dozen British and American generals older than he, all far more experienced in the business of fighting battles. Major General Fred Walker, commander of the Fifth Army's Thirty-sixth Division, for instance, had once been Clark's instructor. Clark early acquired a well-deserved reputation for monopolizing the limelight, and his attention-getting ways were understandably resented by senior generals under his command.

On at least one occasion, at the crossing of the Volturno, Clark's orders for a simultaneous attack by all forces, British and American, were sternly disputed by Major General Sir Robert McCreery, commander of the British X Corps, which included the Forty-sixth and Sixty-fifth Infantry divisions and the Seventh Armored Division and which constituted the left wing of the Fifth Army.

At the time McCreery's troops were on flat ground facing the Volturno, and the British general pointed out that after crossing the river, they would be on a plain facing strong German mountain defenses. He thought that the Americans on his right should attack first, permitting the British to attack a day later when the enemy presumably would be outflanked by the Americans and less able to shoot up his X Corps. Clark went to McCreery's headquarters to "talk things out." The British commander was blunt.

"I want to make it quite plain," he said, "as the commander responsible for British troops and with my experience against Rommel in Egypt, that this is the most difficult job I've faced. You know how I feel about a simultaneous attack. I am opposed to it. I accept your orders, of course, and we will go all out; but I have to say that I am embarrassed when an American gives British troops orders that we don't like."

In the end, McCreery followed Clark's orders, but his X Corps, especially the Seventh Armored Division, took needlessly heavy casualties during and immediately after the crossing. In any event, by nightfall of October 13 the Fifth Army as a whole had secured its bridgeheads and forced the Germans back so rapidly that in some places they did not have time to complete demolitions. Clark's simultaneous attack all along the river was deemed a success and was heartily endorsed by Alexander after the fact.

Clark's popularity with the American press rose considerably the day the general played host to General Giraud during the latter's late October visit to Caserta in connection with preparations for putting French troops into the field as part of the Fifth Army. After inspecting the front, Giraud returned to headquarters at Caserta to talk to us correspondents. A map showing the front lines was set up under a tree, and while photographers and reporters formed a semicircle, Clark explained the positions. When he finished, Giraud asked if he could make "an observation."

"Certainly," said Clark.

"Your headquarters is too far back from the front lines," the Frenchman said. "In the First World War, when I commanded a regiment, my headquarters was only half a kilometer back of the front lines. In the beginning of this war, in 1940, my headquarters was only two kilometers behind the front lines."

Clark's jaw dropped at Giraud's remarks. We all were scribbling furiously on our notebooks and waiting to hear what our general would say.

"Yes, General," Clark replied, "and as I recall, you were taken prisoner by the Germans on both those occasions."

Giraud's elegant handlebar mustache bristled, and the session ended rather abruptly.

Shortly afterward we correspondents were transported en masse by air to Bari for a press conference with General Alexander. Most of us had first met him in Cairo in the febrile days before El Alamein. At the time we were not impressed. A "hitter" was needed in the Middle East, and we had been sent a man who already had struck out twice—at Dunkirk and in Burma.

Physically he looked small, slight, harassed, and altogether inadequate. We mentally compared him with the magnetic Wavell and the imposing, virile Auchinleck. Alexander, in well-tailored slacks, short-sleeved bush shirt, and burnished Sam Browne, although handsomer by far than either of his predecessors, suffered by comparison. And when the gorgeous little guardsman outlined his views on military tactics in precise Harrovian accents—"Attack, attack, and attack again, even when you are on the defensive"—some of us inwardly snickered.

In Italy, Alexander was still the gorgeous guardsman. He looked as though he had just had a steam bath, a massage, a good breakfast, and a letter from home, all the things we craved as we gathered to hear what he had to say about the new campaign. His well-shaped face, with its fine thin-nostriled nose, level eyes, and well-trimmed mustache, was plainly pinkish under its tan. His chestnut hair was sleekly brushed and parted high on the left side, graying a bit about the hollows of his temples. There was a pouchiness under his eyes, however, that made one realize he was fifty-three, not thirty-five.

Alex wore a freshly laundered bush jacket, its elegant severity relieved only by a long red ribbon over his left breast pocket. It meant that he was a Knight of the Grand Cross in the Order of the Bath. He wore buff-colored riding breeches and brown boots which sparkled in the morning sun that shafted through the wide doors of the walled modern villa where he lived and worked.

In dress and manner the jaunty Alexander personified the gallant, charming, and highly professional British commander. He had an enviable track record. He had twice saved a British army from annihilation—at Dunkirk and in Burma—and in Tunisia had forced the capitulation of an entire German army group. Moreover, he was the strategist behind the Eighth Army's victories in Egypt, Libya, North Africa, and Sicily for which the credit went almost entirely to a subordinate named Montgomery.

Now, as commander in chief of Allied ground forces in the Mediterranean, Alexander was the general most directly responsible for the conduct of the

Italian campaign, and all of us wanted to know why it was going so badly. Given his performance to date, he could not be accused of insipid leadership. But why had he failed in Italy? The reporters fired a barrage of pointed questions. Alexander replied calmly and with disarming candor. He began by admitting that his plan's maximum goals—the rapid march to Rome and the German withdrawal northward before the onset of winter—had not been realized and probably wouldn't be for some time.

"But we cannot say that the campaign thus far has been a failure," he said. "True, when we landed at Salerno, the idea was to drive straight across the Italian leg to Barletta, on the Adriatic coast, and trap those German divisions contained in southern Italy. We had expected a few Germans in the Salerno area, but certainly not more than one division. We no sooner landed, however, than we found ourselves with a four-division front on our hands. The enemy moved one division down from the north and as we attacked, they pulled two others down into the region, and about September 15 our situation was, frankly, critical indeed."

In fact, as noted, the Germans came close to pushing the Fifth Army back into the sea at Salerno, and Mark Clark had seriously considered abandoning the beachhead. "But General Clark," said Alexander with characteristic generosity, "handled the situation and his troops well. After some stiff fighting, he broke out of the German encirclement."

One of the many factors that had complicated his conduct of the Italian campaign, Alexander said, was the September 3 armistice with the Italians. "The armistice," he disclosed, "was to have created such difficulties for the Germans that they would have been forced to flee northward, perhaps even to evacuate Italy all the way up to the Alps. Instead, the armistice became for the men of the Italian Army merely a signal to return to their homes. Its formations simply disintegrated."

Alexander doubted that as a "cobelligerent" Italy would produce units which could be brought into the line against the Germans but admitted that the carabinieri were policing the four liberated provinces in southern Italy and that Italian troops were being used as labor battalions repairing roads, railways, and power lines and restoring the water supply, tasks which would otherwise have required ill-spared Allied manpower.

The general relaxed when the press conference broke up, and he privately confessed to some of us that he would have conducted the Italian campaign differently had he been allowed to do so. His original idea was to take Foggia and Naples, then strike across the Adriatic in the Balkans to support the active Yugoslav and Greek resistance movements, and attack Germany from the south via the Danube Valley. The concept had Churchill's support but was frowned upon by the American general staff and vetoed by Stalin.

"And now," Alexander concluded somewhat ruefully, "we'll just have to punch, punch, punch, and keep Jerry on the run until we reach Rome. For he who holds Rome holds the hearts of the Italian people, as well as the country's road and rail network. . . ."

In Bari, in a local hotel, I had my first "overall" bath in tepid water in weeks and my first haircut in two months in an unhygienic-looking barber-shop. And at the Villa Aurora, where the Eighth Army press corps had established headquarters, I learned from an intelligence officer friend that preparations were being made in Cairo for a high-level conference that would include Roosevelt, Churchill, Generalissimo Chiang Kai-shek, and, possibly, Uncle Joe Stalin. Captain Bill Warrener, often my conducting officer during the campaigns in the Western Desert, arranged for me to fly to Cairo.

58

THE WINDS OF CHANGE

The Cairo to which I returned from the dismal Italian front was no longer the embattled capital it had been thirteen months before, when Rommel stood at El Alamein, only 150 miles away. Gone were the fear and trembling, the sense of imminent disaster, the all-pervasive defeatism. The atmosphere had changed even in the two months since I had left for Sicily.

The noisy, bustling city was less grim, less warlike. More and more lights were turned on at night, and the blackout, never fully respected by the Cairenes anyhow, was a thing of the past. Moreover, the unsightly sandbags that had protected public buildings and had begun to disintegrate were disappearing.

The refugees who had fled east and south to safety during the critical late summer of 1942 were returning. The crowds along the main street, the Sharia Ibrahim Pasha, were bigger than ever, their numbers swelled by newly arrived soldiers from Poland, Denmark, Belgium, Holland, France, even Brazil. The newcomers provided fresh customers for the sidewalk hawkers of fly whisks, razor blades, fountain pens, picture postcards, and Zippo lighters, one of America's ubiquitous contributions to GI equipment.

The warmth of Cairo's autumnal sunshine and the city's upbeat mood lifted my spirits. A hot bath, a good night's sleep between clean-smelling sheets in my comfortable bed at Shepheard's, and the fine breakfast which the Nubian *safraghi* brought me with a welcoming smile of recognition the morning after my arrival from Bari heightened my sense of well-being and led me to hope I would soon shake off what I thought was bronchitis. But no such luck.

A sudden onset of fever quickly ripened into what an elderly English doctor—hastily summoned late one night by my roommate Harry Zinder—diagnosed as pneumonia. I spent the next ten days or so in Cairo's old Anglo-Egyptian Hospital, a shabby relic of Victorian times. The food was inedible, the scabrous bluish walls needed paint, the crowded corridors reeked, and the treatment for what ailed me bordered on the medieval.

The therapy was called cupping and was meant to stimulate the circulation and reduce the inflammation in the lungs. About twenty small, heavy ceramic vessels were applied hot to my back from the shoulders to the waist, becoming powerful suction cups as they cooled, and producing corresponding blue-black circular welts fearsome to behold, like so many enormous discolored eyes. Zinder, Chet Morrison, and other friends who regularly brought me mail and newspapers, were appalled when they saw the weird design the cuppings made.

But the old-fashioned treatment proved effective. I was able to return to work in time to deal with the frustrating business of trying to cover the five-day meeting of Roosevelt, Churchill, and Chiang, which opened in Cairo on November 22, but from which correspondents were effectively and inexplicably excluded.

Shortly before the conference began, Zinder and I learned it was to be held at the Mena House, a small, walled-in luxury hotel on the city's outskirts at the end of the road leading to the Pyramids and the Sphinx. We taxied out to the area and found that the hotel, plus more than twenty nearby villas to house the entourages of the three leaders, was enclosed in barbed-wire barricades and guarded by troops. The approaches bristled with gun emplacements, antiaircraft batteries, pillboxes, powerful searchlights, even watch towers.

The meeting was being run entirely by American and British security experts obsessed with protecting the lives of the principals and with ensuring the total secrecy of their deliberations. Reporters were denied access not only to the conference area, but also to the conferees themselves. A hastily formed Allied Press Committee headed by Cyrus Sulzberger, of the *New York Times,* cabled our protests to the authorities in charge of information in Washington and London, but the replies were negative. A total blackout on news had been mandated in the name of security.

A subsequent appeal to Richard Casey, the British minister of state in Cairo, produced a small concession: He authorized periodic briefings by minor underlings of the principals. The one Zinder and I attended was a disaster. The U.S. army major who was supposed to discuss American policy showed up in our press room drunk, leered foolishly, and began by saying, "I thought all you guys would be Ay-rabs." Through Sulzberger, we sent message after message to Roosevelt and Churchill and to their main advisers—respectively Harry Hopkins and Anthony Eden—but they remained effectively isolated by guards and barbed wire at Mena House. Cy might as well have addressed our appeals to the Sphinx.

The official communiqué issued when the Cairo meeting ended said that the Allied leaders had agreed to punish Japan for its aggression by stripping it of its empire and reducing its territorial holdings to what they were before 1895. The same day, November 27, Chiang returned to Chongqing, and Churchill and Roosevelt flew to Teheran for their historic four-day meeting with Stalin, to whom they promised an Anglo-American invasion of France in 1944.

Some correspondents flew to Teheran, but I didn't. I saw no point in facing what would almost certainly be an even tighter censorship than the one that had prevailed in Cairo. Moreover, reports from across the Mediterranean indicated a new ferment in the Balkans, where the Germans had sown the wind and were now reaping the whirlwind.

In Yugoslavia the Communist leader who called himself Tito was making history. His powerful guerrilla army of some 250,000 leftist-oriented partisans was tying down in the Balkans no fewer than sixteen crack German divisions— eight in Yugoslavia itself, five in Greece, and three in Bulgaria—and was fighting for revolutionary goals of its own, which did not include the country's return to monarchist rule.

I spent much of my time talking with Tito's representatives in Cairo and with delegates of his royalist Chetnik opponents, meanwhile trying, in vain, to persuade the British Special Operations Executive, which directed subversive activities in occupied Europe, to allow me to go to Yugoslavia. I wanted to interview Tito to determine, if possible, whether he was merely "a tool of Stalin," as his Chetnik critics claimed, or was really the freedom-loving Social Democrat described by his representatives. From my vantage point in Cairo, it seemed that Tito would permanently alter the political landscape in the Balkans and might influence revolutionary movements in Italy, France, and elsewhere.

Meanwhile, on December 4, Churchill returned to Cairo to meet with Turkey's President Ismet Inönü, whom the prime minister had summoned from Ankara to scold him for the meagerness of his country's help to the Allied cause. Churchill subsequently held a press conference which we correspondents eagerly attended.

After the meetings in Cairo and Teheran we expected an upbeat account of the plans he had helped so much to bring to fruition not only for victory in Europe and the Pacific but also for ensuring a lasting peace. Instead, we got from the prime minister a rather gloomy view of the immediate future.

It was the first time I saw the great British war leader in action in person, but he was clearly not at his best. He appeared before us in his zippered navy blue jump suit, his travel attire, visibly fatigued, and he spoke in a tired voice. He had probably taxed it in long hours of debate with Stalin at Teheran, for the Russian "man of steel" was known to have become increasingly assertive in the wake of the Red Army's summer successes against the Germans on the eastern front, victories that had contrasted unfavorably with the deadlock in Italy.

"If the Germans hold on through February," a pale and subdued Churchill said in his opening remarks, "we shall have a heavy summer's fighting. As long as Hitler's central government stands, [his] army will continue to fight. It is counterattacking sharply in Italy. There we must beat the enemy with the least amount of undue slaughter, but without flinching. Meanwhile, the life of the world is flowing away and the wealth of the world is melting fast. . . ."

Churchill paused and shook his massive round head as though suddenly aware of the gravity of what he had said. I stood less than six feet away from him and observed him closely as he fielded questions from the forty or fifty correspondents present. At times his replies were barely audible.

Asked whether Chiang Kai-shek was "anything more than a pious hope" in the Allied scheme of things, Churchill sensed a challenge and countered by saying he considered the generalissimo "an extraordinarily able man." He must have known that British and American liberals were criticizing Chiang as the inept and inordinately ambitious leader of a corrupt Kuomintang (Nationalist) regime.

Questioned about Palestine, where a resurgence of antagonisms between Arabs and Jews threatened a reprise of their bloody prewar struggle over respective rights to the land, Churchill gave halting and disappointingly vague replies. "In Palestine," he said, "there should be room for both. There is enough for all." He reminded us that in the past he had helped the Arabs by placing Faisal on the throne in Iraq and Abdullah in Trans-Jordan. But as a "Zionist from the beginning," he said, he was aware of the "tremendous contribution" the Jews had made in the Holy Land. "They have built cities where there were only hamlets," he said, "and made orange groves bloom where there was only sand."

The prime minister then touched briefly on the "maelstrom in the Balkans." Romania was "quaking," he said, and Bulgaria was "split wide open." After characterizing the civil war raging in Greece as "very unfortunate," he surprised us by indicating that he supported Tito's left-wing movement in Yugoslavia. "All I hear about Tito and his partisans," he said, "is much in their favor," a startling position for a statesman who had opposed communism in any form throughout his long career.

Churchill's friendly remarks about Tito indicated a dramatic about-face in Allied policy. London and Washington had long supported Tito's royalist rival and bitter enemy the Chetnik leader General Draza Mikhajlovic, a regular army officer who appealed to old-style Serb nationalism and served the interests of the exiled royal government.

Tito, on the other hand, had built up a movement of another kind. From all accounts, he intended to create a united *Communist* Yugoslavia. If that were true, there would be howls of protest from Mikhajlovic's anti-Communist American supporters, for they believed the bearded, charismatic Chetnik commander to be God's gift to democracy and freedom.

In the early winter of 1943–1944 little was known about the partisan leader, and even less about what he really stood for. From a number of partisan representatives who suddenly appeared in Cairo, however, it was not difficult to assemble a sketch of the man, his policy and his political objectives.

Tito was the nom de guerre of Josip Broz, born near Zagreb in 1892, when his native land was still part of the Austro-Hungarian Empire. He fought in World War I as a conscript in the emperor's army, was captured by the Russians, became a Communist, and participated in the Russian Revolution of 1917.

After the war Josip Broz returned to his homeland, newly constituted as Yugoslavia, a confirmed revolutionary and was hunted as a Communist criminal by the secret agents of the tyrannical king Alexander for having organized the country's electrical workers' union and for conspiring against Alexander's dictatorship.

Caught in 1929, he was jailed, and when released four years later, he had gray in his wavy brown hair, ulcers in his stomach, and a dream in his head to free his country from Serbian monarchist tyranny. He loved freedom well enough to fight for it in Spain against the Fascist and Nazi supporters of Franco in 1936 and against the Germans as a soldier in the Yugoslav Army five years later. When Yugoslavia surrendered in the early spring of 1941, Broz took his dream, and his politics, into the mountains, where he organized guerrilla groups to fight his country's Nazi conquerors and their Fascist allies.

Although earlier Tito had stressed the role of communism in the liberation of his country, in the autumn of 1943 he sang democratic-sounding variations on the Soviet theme. Tito's envoys to Cairo who came to see me at my hotel stressed that in the emerging Yugoslavia the people (1) retained the right to own property, (2) were free to engage in private industrial and commercial enterprise, and (3) enjoyed the protection of a representative federal government in full compliance with the Four Freedoms, including freedom of religion.

Tito's emergence in the winter of 1943–1944 as the dominant *political* as well as military figure in Yugoslavia seemed to me at the time to be one of the most significant events of World War II. It was largely due to him that the war, which the Allies were still fighting merely to defeat the Germans and to liberate Europe from Fascist-Nazi rule, became a revolutionary "people's war" with far-reaching consequences.

True, I failed to see in the Yugoslav drama as it unfolded in the winter of 1943–1944 a future dictatorship under Josip Broz. In that I was wrong. I was right, however, in assuming that Tito was far too independent a spirit to be dragooned into either the Soviet or the Allied camp after the war.

Meanwhile, as 1943 approached its end, the Italian front, to which I felt attached as though by an umbilical cord, remained frozen at the formidable Gustav Line. I had seen the German defenses on my last visit to the Fifth Army and knew that few Allied soldiers could wish themselves a Merry Christmas and a Happy New Year, for they faced a masterpiece of fortifications bristling with tank traps, gun emplacements, extensive minefields, steel-encased pillboxes, barbed-wire concertinas, and ruined villages which had been converted into miniforts.

The Gustav Line's pivotal center was the awesome mountain mass at Cassino, the towering rock capped by the gaunt, fortresslike abbey of Monte Cassino. This forbidding eminence dominated the Liri Valley and the Via Casilina, General Mark Clark's only direct route to Rome, and seemed to say, "Thou Shalt Not Pass."

The line of German defenses formed the southern boundary of Hitler's shrinking but still extensive Fortress Europe, and it was evident that to reach the Italian capital, the defensive border had to be pierced. In fact, if the Allies were to win the war in Western Europe, they simply had to break into Fortress Europe. In Cairo we were certain that the Allies could not lose the war; but it was plain enough that they had yet to win it, and to win it, they had to invade the European continent itself.

What we didn't know in Cairo was that the invasion of the German heartland was coming sooner than had seemed likely. Its commanders had already been chosen, and the timetable set. In fact, the weapon itself—the invasion force—was in the process of being forged. All had been decided at Teheran, where Roosevelt and Churchill had met with Stalin in November. The president and the prime minister had agreed to the Soviet leader's demands for a second front to be launched in France, simultaneously from north and south, a strategy that relegated the Mediterranean to a subordinate position in the scheme of things.

The downgrading of the Mediterranean campaign was virtually confirmed on Christmas morning, when the Reuters teleprinter in Shepheard's lobby tapped out the overnight news of the dramatic changes in the composition of the high command. From his home at Hyde Park President Roosevelt announced on Christmas Eve that General Ike Eisenhower had been chosen as supreme commander of Allied forces for the assault on Fortress Europe.

From London, at the same time, came word that Ike's team for the toughest job of military coordination since Marshal Foch took supreme command over the stalemated western front in 1918 included the stars of the Mediterranean campaign: General Montgomery, Admiral Sir Andrew Cunningham, and Air Chief Marshal Tedder. General Alexander remained in command of Allied forces in Italy, and General Jumbo Wilson was to succeed Eisenhower as commander in chief of Mediterranean operations.

Messrs. Roosevelt and Churchill had good reason for choosing Eisenhower to lead the invasion of Fortress Europe. He was the only commander with experience in large-scale coordination of British and American forces, having brilliantly managed the amphibious operations that had led to the invasions of French North Africa, Sicily, and southern Italy.

But his departure along with the other stars of the Mediterranean campaign indicated that what the British had long considered the big show of World War II had suddenly been downgraded to the status of a mere sideshow.

The Allies had apparently decided to call it a day in Italy and intended to stabilize a front which, in the grim icy weather that prevailed along the mountainous Gustav Line, seemed already to have put itself into cold storage.

However, early in January the Italian front suddenly came alive again as the Fifth Army launched a new offensive against the Gustav Line. The news juke in Shepheard's lobby reported that British forces had crossed the Garigliano at the seaward end of the German defenses and that the Americans were attacking fiercely at Cassino.

My efforts to join Tito's guerrillas in Yugoslavia having come to naught, and having wearied of tiresome parties attended by too few pretty girls and far too many stuffy, red-hatted British staff officers with nothing better to do when their boss, Jumbo Wilson, moved his headquarters to Algiers, I decided to return to Italy. This took longer to arrange than I had expected, and I was unable to leave Cairo for Algiers and a connecting flight to Naples until the morning of January 20.

59

ALMOST ANOTHER GALLIPOLI

In the cold small hours after midnight on January 22, 1944, two divisions of the Fifth Army's hastily formed Sixth Corps—one British, one American—landed at Anzio, on Italy's west coast about thirty miles southwest of Rome, and some seventy miles behind the Germans' stubbornly defended Gustav Line. It was the military equivalent of an end run, the stratagem used in football when progress through the line becomes impossible. It was intended to break a stalemate in the Italian campaign that had lasted 141 days and had cost far too many thousands of Allied lives, mostly American.

It was nearly noon, and I was still at Dar-el-Beida Airport on the outskirts of Algiers, waiting to board a plane for Naples, when I heard of the landing, the third of the Allied campaign in Italy and potentially the most important. If it succeeded, the Fifth Army would be marching into Rome within a matter of days, a few weeks at most, and I took off for Naples in a DC-4 in high spirits.

Long before Anzio entered the history of World War II, it had become part of my life when I was Hearst's correspondent in Italy. I remembered it as a pleasant resort town with a fine harbor, a wide beach of gray sand edged with gaily painted bathhouses, and waterfront restaurants renowned for their zuppa di pesce, a sort of Italian bouillabaisse, that went down very well with the wines from the nearby Castelli Romani, better known as the Alban Hills.

Anzio, moreover, was where my friend Dr. Giorgio Mattoli had a villa on a hillside overlooking the harbor's blue-green waters, and I had often taken my family there to escape Rome's fierce summer heat or on sunny early autumn weekends to taste the new wine from the Castelli. I would drive south along the Via Appia to Albano, in the graceful Alban Hills, then west to the coast through a fragrant forest of umbrella pines. As we approached the town itself, the air suddenly smelled of the sea and of fishnets drying in the sun.

And it was at Anzio that in July 1936 I had convalesced from the surgery for appendicitis that prevented me from going to Spain when the Civil War erupted. Part of the therapy was a daily walk along the glistening sands of the broad mile-long crescent-shaped beach that linked Anzio with its picturesque twin village of Nettuno, whose cool underground caves, carved out of the volcanic rock called *tufo,* were filled with casks of maturing local wines.

Snug, friendly, prosperous Anzio was ancient Antium, the birthplace of Nero and Caligula, in whose theater the former is supposed to have fiddled while Rome burned. I remembered it, however, as a place to sit and laze in the shade of the orange trees in the walled garden of Villa Mattoli on sunny afternoons. In the evenings there was good talk with Giorgio, Ercole Graziadei, and a raffish fellow I knew only as il Comandante who had an inexhaustible stock of anti-Fascist jokes. Sitting with our families in deck chairs on the villa's terrace under starlit Mediterranean skies, we could hear the town band playing in the square below and on Saturday nights watch the fireworks that celebrated the anniversary or name day of some saint or other.

Fireworks of an entirely different kind, I imagined, were taking place now along the beach I knew so well. I mentally pictured our troops being swept by German machine-gun and artillery fire, Tommies and GIs scrambling for cover where none existed, falling and staining the sands with their blood.

About twenty hours had elapsed since the landings by the time I arrived at Fifth Army headquarters, in the tented area within the grounds of the royal palace at Caserta, on the evening of January 22 just as the correspondents were being briefed on the day's operations. None of the slaughter I had imagined during the long flight from Algiers had occurred. The bloodletting was at Cassino, where the Fifth Army had attacked in force in an attempt to cross the Rapido River, crack the Gustav Line, and enter the Liri Valley.

General Clark was away, presumably visiting General John Lucas, the VI Corps commander, aboard his command ship USS *Biscayne,* and the briefing was conducted by Clark's chief of staff, General Alfred Gruenther, a mild-mannered, scholarly officer with a pale face, thinning reddish brown hair, and long sideburns. He described the Anzio operation with much enthusiasm as a stratagem that would be studied by future generals at our War College.

"We prevented the Germans from knowing of our expedition in advance," he said, "and achieved complete surprise. Our forces met virtually no opposition. What few casualties we had were caused not by enemy fire but by mines on the beaches. So far the operation has been a total success."

As Gruenther explained it, the Anzio landing was really only half of a "pincer movement" to break the stalemate in southern Italy. While the troops were being landed "deep in the rear of the present enemy front lines," the bulk of the Fifth Army was attacking northward in a massive land operation against the Gustav Line in the vicinity of Cassino.

Ostensibly, whichever way the Germans moved would leave the way open for a quick Allied victory: If they defended against the frontal attack at Cassino, the troops on the beachhead would be able to penetrate the enemy's lines of communication between Rome and Anzio; if they counterattacked against the landing, their Gustav Line defenses would be weakened, enabling the Fifth Army to break out into the Liri Valley and drive up Route 6, the Via Casilina, to Frosinone, the Alban Hills, and Rome.

Reports from the beachhead continued bullish. The only Germans the invaders found on D day were four drunks in a stalled staff car and four others asleep in a dugout under a machine-gun emplacement. Interrogated, they said they were troops of a battalion of engineers of a Panzer Grenadier Division sent to Anzio to rest and refit and to practice demolitions in the harbor.

Gruenther admitted, however, that the Germans had been "very skillful" and had somehow managed to bring reinforcements up to the high ground above Anzio, where they were massing but "probably were not yet ready to attack." In the meantime, tanks and Bren gun carriers were already ashore in support of some thirty-six thousand fighting men. Most important, perhaps, Allied airmen controlled the skies over a beachhead that by nightfall on D day plus one was already nearly eight miles deep and about fifteen miles wide at the base.

In other words, the Anzio landing had survived the first crucial forty-eight hours and could be judged a "complete success." If the German commander in Italy, General Albert Kesselring, contemplated a strong counterattack, there was no hint of it as yet. For the first time since Mark Clark's triumphal entry into Naples on October 1, Rome seemed at last within his reach.

Colonel Ken Clark, the Fifth Army's public relations chief, promised me a trip to the beachhead as soon as it could be arranged, and I prepared myself for it by studying the G-2 maps in the press tent and learning all I could about the commanders involved. I saw that General Lucas had two of the Fifth Army's best divisions under him. They were the British First Infantry Division, which had proved its worth in the Tunisian campaign, and the American Third Infantry Division, which had distinguished itself in Sicily.

Both, moreover, boasted top-notch commanders of the breed known as frontline generals, officers who actually led their men in battle and not from command posts well back from the actual fighting. The British were led by the experienced General W. R. C. Penney, a World War I hero, and the Americans were commanded by General Truscott, a forthright, confident gray-haired man of forty-nine known to his troops with affection and considerable esteem as "Old Gravel Mouth." In leather battle jacket, steel helmet, and high boots, Truscott looked as tough as he was.

Penney was a bit younger than Truscott but was considered one of Montgomery's most promising students. He had much of Monty's directness of speech and manner and a good deal of his tactlessness, but he was generally regarded as a highly effective field commander. Truscott, on the other hand, had Patton's "flair for terrain" without his appetite for publicity, and he could be counted on to undertake the kinds of daring moves the beachhead demanded for ultimate success.

From all accounts, however, their commanding officer, General Lucas, was a man of a totally different stamp. He was fifty-four, patient, thorough, and cautious to a fault. He wore steel-rimmed spectacles, was rarely to be seen without a corncob pipe—somewhat à la MacArthur, but the similarity ended there—and had a double chin and closely cropped sparse hair. I had met him at Caserta while he was still commanding the II Corps before his new assignment and remembered him as a friendly, avuncular gentleman who looked ill suited to the war business. He had served as Eisenhower's deputy in North Africa and so far in the Italian campaign had participated only in the quasi-disastrous struggle at Salerno as commander of the II Corps.

Lucas seemed a strange choice for a task that demanded imaginative leadership and daring. Instead of striking out boldly from the beachhead when he found the area empty of Germans, Lucas chose to build up and consolidate a firm defensive position and soon found himself hemmed in by no fewer than seven German divisions. Some elements of the seasoned Hermann Göring Division were diverted to Anzio from the main front at Cassino, but most of the forces which the Germans gathered to oppose Lucas at Anzio came from northern Italy, France, and the Balkans. The landing, therefore, neither undermined the German defenses along the Rapido nor prevented the arrival of enemy reserves to meet the new situation at Anzio.

In other words, the end run had been stopped dead in its tracks, and on January 27, D day plus five, General Clark, urged by his superior, General Alexander, decided to go to Anzio to prod Lucas into whatever offensive action might prevent a looming disaster at the beachhead. Clark invited me to go along.

That evening I played poker with several members of the general's staff—mostly G-2 types—including a lieutenant colonel from whom I won four hundred dollars. He gave me his marker for the sum, but I never saw him again. He knew I was going to Anzio in the morning and may have figured I might not return! I very nearly didn't.

Long before dawn January 28 an orderly awakened me in my tent somewhere within the headquarters compound at Caserta. It was colder than I had ever known it to be in Italy and as dark as the inside of a hall closet. By the light of a flashlight I dressed far more warmly than usual, something I was eternally grateful for later that awful day, the most harrowing I had ever experienced.

Over the long johns I slept in, I put on heavy trousers, a shirt, a sweater, a woolen Eighth Army combat jacket, and a flannel-lined mackinaw bound at the waist by my wide webbed army belt. I tucked my trousers into combat boots and followed the orderly across rough ground to a waiting Jeep that drove me to the mouth of the Garigliano River.

At the river's muddy edge, I boarded a cockleshell assault boat powered by a tiny, high-revving outboard motor which sounded like a monstrous mosquito and propelled the fragile craft at high speed through choppy waters that threatened to swamp us with every bounce. The splashy, bumpy ride ended alongside the first of two PT boats which, with engines idling, were waiting at the far bank. I clambered aboard PT 201 wet about the head and shoulders but otherwise miraculously dry.

There were buns and hot coffee in the tiny wardroom below, where I met the boat's commander, Lieutenant Patterson; his second-in-command, Ensign Benson; Ensign Donald; and other members of the small crew. On deck, topside, were Colonel Howard, General Clark's G-2, and Colonel Bowman, his staff engineering officer.

General Clark himself arrived minutes later with General Don Brann, his G-3 in charge of operations and training, and Captain Jack Beardwood, his aide. All three were drenched. Their boat had hit a sandbar en route, nearly capsized and shipped a great deal of water.

The weather had turned foul during the night with rain, sleet, and a cold, piercing wind. Mark Clark shielded himself from it by sitting on a stool beside the helmsman, Ensign Benson, where the bridge's cowling offered some protection. It was a scene out of a wartime film, with the tall, angular Clark playing Gary Cooper, as Benson swung PT 201 into the restless, surly waters of the Tyrrhenian Sea, gunned the boat's engines, and roared north along the coast to Anzio in the semidarkness, followed by the second PT boat carrying a few reporters.

I found shelter from the wind and spray behind the bulkhead of the deckhouse on the port side of the gangway that led down to Lieutenant Patterson's station below. This was high adventure, my first action at sea and, frankly, I relished every moment of it until . . .

Suddenly, somewhere off Anzio, we were challenged by an Allied warship, later identified as U.S. minesweeper AM 120. Patterson responded by firing green and yellow flares while his signalman blinkered the flashes that indicated we were "friendly." The minesweeper's response, however, was decidedly unfriendly. Her skipper either misread our signals or, like everyone else in the area on that dark, windy, ill-starred morning, had a bad case of nerves. His gunners cut loose with forty-millimeter and five-inch shells and, unfortunately for us, proved to be good marksmen.

I had been shot at before, but this time I felt that I personally was the target. I was stupefied with fear; I could feel my hair thrusting upward under my helmet, and my voice stuck in my throat as I tried to cry out.

Machine-gun bullets and heavier stuff tore the air overhead, making whistling sounds and swooshes that chilled the blood. I heard a shell explode behind me toward the bow. I turned and saw that it had smashed the stool Clark had been sitting on, but the general evidently had stood up and moved away when the minesweeper challenged us, because there he was, unhurt, helping Benson, who had been hit. I flung myself facedown on the deck and crawled toward the gangway, thinking to go below for greater safety.

I had just reached it when a second shell exploded below and wounded Lieutenant Patterson. There was blood on his trouser legs as he staggered up the ladder, muttering, "Red, yellow, red," and pointing to the Very pistol and flare cartridges hanging in receptacles on the bulkhead beside him out of his reach. I understood instinctively, loaded the pistol, and stood up on deck to fire it. In that instant something hit me in the pit of my stomach with the force of a slugger's errant baseball bat and knocked me flat on my back. I clutched at the spot with both hands, felt something hard and hot; but there was no pain, no blood, and I knew I wasn't hurt.

Turning to retrieve the Very pistol I had dropped, I found myself lying next to Ensign Donald. He was bleeding from an ugly wound in the upper part of his right leg. I stuffed it with the scarf I always wore and lay there beside him, looking about for help.

Mark Clark had found the Very gun and was firing the appropriate signals, but to no avail. He fired a second round of flares, but the firing from the minesweeper continued. AM 120 seemed determined to sink us but scored no more hits, although bullets and shells agitated the air around us and came audibly close to doing more damage.

I doubt that the attack lasted more than a few minutes, but in that time it had caused damage enough. The boat's three naval officers and two of her sailors were casualties. At the helm Benson had leg wounds. Lieutenant Patterson had managed to crawl up on deck and lay there, inert but conscious. Clark knelt beside him, and I heard him ask, "What do we do now, Skipper?"

Patterson's reply was barely audible. "I don't know," he said, and tried to regain his feet.

"Well, let's run for it," Clark said, and bodily lifted the slender, pale-faced Patterson so he could see what was happening and direct the boat's movements. Benson swung the boat around a full 180 degrees. Shells were still splattering around us as we ran southward away from the minesweeper, followed closely by the other PT boat, which had escaped damage.

By the time we were out of range, our deck was littered with wounded and slippery with blood. Clark moved about, pouring sulfa powder into people's wounds; he could do nothing about their pain. The most seriously hurt was Ensign Donald, beside whom I lay, trying to stem the blood burbling from a hole the size of my fist in his thigh just below the hip. Patterson had wounds in both legs, one of which was fractured. Benson had shell fragments in both legs. One of the naval ratings had his kneecap blown off and was in great pain. The fifth man, who was below when we were attacked, had stomach wounds and a fractured pelvis.

As we sped southward to get help, Clark saw me groggy and bloodstained lying alongside Ensign Donald. He turned me over and exclaimed, "My God, you, too?" I insisted I wasn't hurt, but he spotted a large, irregular tear in my mackinaw just above the belt. There was blood down the entire front of my uniform, and together he and I unbuttoned the several layers of clothing down to my bare skin. We found only a large reddish purple bruise. I saw a look of relief on Clark's face; the blood on my clothing was Ensign Donald's.

Out of the lining of the torn mackinaw fell a curved, mean-looking, jagged piece of steel four or five inches square, obviously a spent fragment that had had force enough to knock me down but not enough to penetrate the cocoon in which I had fortunately encased myself that morning.

There were more anxious moments half an hour later as we approached the British minesweeper *Acute,* but her skipper recognized our signals, said he had a doctor on board, and took our casualties. While the wounded were being transferred, the commander of the second boat took charge of ours, and Clark ordered both boats to return to Anzio over the objections of General Donald W. Brann, who plainly disapproved, arguing it was "too dangerous."

When we reached the point where we had been shelled, about eight miles off Anzio, we again approached AM 120. This time we were recognized and drew up under the minesweeper's bow close enough for our new skipper, using his megaphone, to take the vessel's captain to task for having "just fired on General Clark." The minesweeper's commander made no apology for having tried to blow us out of the water. Leaning over his bow rail, he shouted that he had no advance notice that the general had intended "using a patrol boat of the United States Navy to taxi him to Anzio." He said he had been alerted to hostile boats in the area and had decided to "take no chances" when we approached.

"You came on like a couple of [German] E-boats moving in for an attack," he shouted. "You had no business approaching us in battle formation. The goddamn light was bad, and we couldn't read your goddamn signals. We had every reason to believe you were hostile. There was a goddamn red alert over Anzio when you showed up. . . ."

The three-striper aboard the minesweeper was still shouting down at our three-star general when we turned away and headed toward Anzio, but as we entered the harbor, German planes were bombing the beachhead. Turning quickly, we headed back out to sea and cruised about for a while, watching the action.

A curtain of antiaircraft fire rose from the beachhead to meet the invaders. I could see the flashes made by the exploding enemy bombs and heard their delayed booms, but if the Luftwaffe did any serious damage that morning, it was not visible from the unsteady deck of PT 201.

It was nearly noon before we entered and docked at Anzio's inner port, the one fishermen used in prewar days. Clark, Brann, and the others went immediately in Jeeps to see Lucas at his command post in Nettuno, and I wandered off on my own, hoping to find some familiar landmark that would lead me uphill to the Villa Mattoli.

From a point on the cluttered beach roughly midway between Anzio and Nettuno, nothing was recognizable. The three- and four-story apartment houses and buildings that had lined the waterfront were hollow ruins, the work of German bombers and enemy shells from artillery emplaced on the high ground above the beachhead. It was a depressing sight.

All around me, the buildup on the beach continued at a furious, almost frenzied pace. Masses of supplies and equipment were piled in an organized chaos. Lucas had asked for more of everything to make his beachhead secure before launching an attack, and he was getting whatever he wanted, including more men.

Already ashore were elements of General Eagles's Forty-fifth Infantry Division, and I watched LSTs discharging the tanks of General Ernest Harmon's U.S. First Armored Division. The tough sergeant who was directing traffic, tally sheets in hand, told me the beach was receiving thousands of tons of supplies a day. "Mostly ammo," he said. "And we're gonna need it. Any minute now, Foxy Grandpa's gonna bust outta here. . . ." "Foxy Grandpa," I knew, was what the men called General Lucas.

A fleet of Liberty ships lay offshore, discharging their cargoes onto lighters. On the beach, trucks backed up to the heaps of crates and mounds of boxes, were loaded, and growled away on the metallic road matting with which the engineers had laced the sands.

At no time during the war, not even in southern Sicily, had I seen so many troops and weapons crowded into so small an area. Among them Anzio and Nettuno and the immediate hinterland had never held more than eight thousand inhabitants—at most only double that number during the tourist season. Now, in the early afternoon of D day plus six, the same area contained about seventy thousand troops, some five hundred pieces of artillery, and at least 240 tanks, plus hundreds of Bren gun carriers, trucks, bulldozers, and Jeeps.

What I saw that afternoon indicated that Lucas was preparing to attack in force, something he should have done, perhaps, no later than D day plus two. For it was common knowledge even among the lowliest private that during the first forty-eight hours of the landing the road to Rome had lain wide open. Everything spelled an imminent offensive. I assumed Clark had come to Anzio to order "Foxy Grandpa" to get off his duff and push out, and the activity indicated Lucas was getting ready to do just that.

Somewhere along the waterfront row of ruined buildings, and quite by chance as I stumbled through rubble past troops stringing signal wires and clearing debris from potentially habitable dwellings—shelter was in desperately short supply on the crowded beachhead—I found the villa where the Fifth Army had established press headquarters. It was a huge, rambling, four-story structure inhabited by four or five officers, a dozen or more enlisted men, and about as many British and American correspondents.

Among the Americans were friends of many years—Packard, of the UP; George Tucker, of the AP; Homer Bigart, of the *New York Herald Tribune*— and a reporter I had never met before: Ernie Pyle. He was a small, thin, nervous man with a haunted look in his eyes. All had been covering the war much the way infantrymen fought it: on the ground and on the move, subject to fear and squalor and the same capricious fates that decided death for some men, life for others. They had been under fire on the various fronts for a long time and the strain showed. Pyle, apparently, had had more narrow escapes in North Africa and Italy than the others, and his colleagues had dubbed him "Old Indestructible."

With Major Jay Vessels, the PR officer in charge of the villa, I scanned the war map in the press room. It was splattered with place-names I knew and traversed by roads I had traveled. One went straight up from Anzio past Carroceto, Aprilia, and the railway station at Campoleone and joined the Via Appia just beyond Albano; the other ran northeastward along the seashore to Ostia, the bathing resort at the mouth of the Tiber. From there an *autostrada* ran eastward arrow-straight to the capital. It was Mussolini's favorite forty-minute ride on summer afternoons in his apple red Alfa Romeo roadster with his mistress, Claretta Petacci.

Major Vessels agreed that quick thrusts along those roads by armored columns while the area was still free of Germans during the first two days after the landings might have succeeded in capturing undefended Rome or, at the very least, might have totally disorganized German defenses. "But we missed the bus," he said ruefully, and while General Lucas built up his forces on the beachhead, the enemy encircled it with an estimated forty thousand troops, batteries of 8 mm guns, howitzers, self-propelled guns, Tiger tanks, and armored cars. The entire German Fourteenth Army was now deployed around the perimeter, and two key towns—Aprilia, due north of Anzio, and Cisterna, to the southeast on the edge of the Pontine Marshes—lay in enemy hands.

Aprilia was one of the several big agricultural centers Mussolini had built for the peasants he had resettled in the new farms on or near the reclaimed Pontine Marshes. Behind its stern red-brick and stucco outer walls, I recalled, lay a village square, a church, a town hall, and Fascist headquarters together with a row of shops, a health center, and a wineshop. The town was a natural stronghold for whoever possessed it, for it dominated the flat, surrounding countryside.

Cisterna, astride the railway and the Via Appia leading to Rome, was equally important for much the same reasons. I imagined—correctly, it later developed—that the Germans had already turned every house and building in both towns into semifortresses, as they had done at Cassino and elsewhere.

It was evident to anyone with even minimal knowledge of warfare that the impending battle, due to begin before the month ran out, would be a long and bloody one.

I needed a Jeep to reach the Villa Mattoli, but Major Vessels couldn't spare one for a visiting correspondent, so I hurried back to the dock where PT 201 was waiting to take Clark and his party back to Fifth Army headquarters. The other boat had already left.

I believe General Clark remained on the beachhead, for he was not on board PT 201 for the uneventful return trip. I learned from General Brann, however, that Clark had ordered Lucas to take "bold and aggressive action" to capture Cisterna and the highway leading to Velletri, in the Alban Hills, the gates to Rome. Simultaneously equally strenuous efforts were to be made to occupy Aprilia.

While at Anzio, Clark decided to set up his own advance command post on the beachhead in the pine grove of the Villa Borghese near Nettuno. This indicated that he considered the situation there at least as dangerous as the one at Cassino. There a defeat would merely prolong the agony of costly stalemate, while a reversal at Anzio might prove calamitous.

Instead of one front to deal with, Mark Clark now had two, and he evidently intended dividing his time between them. To be closer to the Cassino front, he moved his Fifth Army headquarters from Caserta to a hillside below the rocky village of Presenzano in the foothills of the Abruzzi mountains, where, in an olive grove, the general's public relations section made camp. One of its two-man wall tents became my home for several weeks of the coldest winter southern Italy had ever known.

During that time I covered the noisy, messy, and very bloody fighting along the Rapido in what became known as the Battle of Cassino. It was the most grueling, most harrowing, and in some respects the most tragic episode of the Italian campaign, a searing struggle fought in biting cold, torrents of rain and snow, and lakes of mud that sucked down men and machines.

The Anzio landing failed to fulfill its bright promise of a quick capture of Rome. What was to have been a mortal Allied thrust into the Germans' flank degenerated into static trench warfare that called to mind the terrible battles of the First World War. In one four-day battle on the beachhead in mid-February, the Allies lost 404 killed, 1,982 wounded, and 1,025 captured or missing, plus 1,637 nonbattle casualties caused by exposure, exhaustion, and trench foot.

What went wrong with one of the boldest, most adventurous Allied strokes of World War II became known only years later, after the responsible generals and war leaders had published their memoirs. Only then did we learn that Anzio was launched at the insistence of Winston Churchill, who, back in 1915, when he was first lord of the admiralty, ordered a similar amphibious assault made at Gallipoli, in the Dardanelles, with catastrophic results.

Like Gallipoli, the Anzio landing would have been immensely useful had everything gone according to plan. Had the outcome been thoroughly successful, it would have brought Churchill the praise for the inspired strategic thinking he coveted and that success deserves but that failure denies. Fortunately, unlike Gallipoli, the outcome at Anzio was not ignominious withdrawal. Although the Germans very nearly succeeded in driving the Allies off the beachhead, Operation Shingle, as the landing was called, ended in an eventual breakthrough that led to the fall of Rome. But at what a cost! Success came only after nearly five months of savage fighting in the malodorous mud of the Pontine Marshes, during which the Fifth Army lost about thirty-five thousand men, of whom some twenty-one thousand were Americans.

After the war Churchill took full credit for the Anzio stratagem and ungenerously blamed the commanders who executed it for "frittering away a brilliant opening." He did not criticize General Alexander, who improvised

Shingle to please his prime minister, but he did blame Mark Clark and Lucas for what went wrong after the troops landed.

We know now that the Anzio adventure was launched to satisfy Churchill's desire to "keep the Mediterranean ablaze with action" while the cross-Channel invasion, code-named Overlord, was being planned. We also know that it was launched under divided counsels and against the inner convictions of the Americans, including Clark and Lucas, who opposed the idea when it was first launched in the autumn of 1943. The British generals believed in Anzio; the Americans did not. In the end the two sides compromised, but compromise never won a battle. Lucas, for one, left the final January 9 conference on the subject muttering, "This is going to be worse than Gallipoli!" And he came closer than anyone else to being right.

Of the many postwar memoirs dealing with the Anzio landing, one of the most revealing was Lucas's diary. The aging general seemed to be far more aware than the planners and proponents of the risks involved in the operation. He knew that ships and men were being withdrawn from the Mediterranean for Overlord, hence were in short supply for Shingle. "Unless we can get what we want, the operation becomes such a desperate undertaking that it should not . . . be attempted." To Lucas, the whole affair had "a strong odor of Gallipoli, and apparently the same amateur was still on the coach's bench." Nevertheless, always the professional soldier who would obey orders, he agreed to lead the Sixth Corps into battle knowing that "a failure now would ruin Clark, probably kill me, and certainly prolong the war."

After the conference on January 9 Lucas summarized both the event and his own forebodings:

> Apparently SHINGLE has become the most important operation in the present scheme of things. Alexander started the conference by stating that the operation would take place on January 22 with the troops (only two divisions) as scheduled and that there would be no more discussion of these points. He quoted Mr. Churchill as saying, "It will astonish the world . . . and will certainly frighten Kesselring." I feel like a lamb being led to the slaughter but thought I was entitled to one bleat so I registered a protest against the target date as it gave me too little time for rehearsal. . . . I was ruled down, as I knew I would be, many reasons being advanced as to the necessity for this speed. *The real reasons cannot be military* [emphasis added].

Mistakes undoubtedly were made in planning and executing the Anzio affair, and one of them quite probably was Clark's choice of Lucas as commander of the VI Corps, for he must have known that "Foxy Grandpa" harbored misgivings and objections. With a gung ho general like Patton in command on the beachhead, the venture might have had a different, more spectacular, and far happier outcome. At the time, however, Lucas was the only corps commander available.

Moreover, I later learned from my friend Gordon Gaskill, a correspondent who was present on board the command ship *Biscayne* on the morning of January 22 and overheard the unreported exchange, it was Clark himself who counseled Lucas to be "cautious" on the beachhead. "Don't stick your neck out, John," Clark told the worried Lucas. "I did at Salerno, and you know what nearly happened to me there. . . ."

Mistakes were made also in the Battle of Cassino, and here, too, the blame fell heavily on Clark.

60

RED FLOWED THE RAPIDO

owhere in Italy was the war more violent than along the banks of
the Rapido River in the vicinity of Cassino where the Fifth Army
tried to pierce the Gustav Line, first to ensure the success of the
end run at Anzio by drawing enemy forces southward away from
the vulnerable beachhead, then to break out into the Liri Valley to reach the
coveted prize, Rome.

But Cassino, as I have already indicated, was the centerpiece of the Gustav
Line, probably modern warfare's most effective defenses, comparable with
those erected by the Russians at Stalingrad: a murderous maze of concrete-
and-steel pillboxes, overlapping minefields, and barbed-wire barricades backed
by artillery, dug-in tanks, howitzers, and batteries of Nebelwerfers, a new
weapon that launched screaming salvos of deadly rockets from multiple barrels. Behind the fortifications, furthermore, the Germans had deployed some
of their best troops: four divisions of their XIV Panzer Corps, plus the Ninetieth Panzer Grenadiers Division of armored infantry, a highly mobile unit
prepared to reinforce the line wherever needed.

Yet it was against this array that in the late evening of January 20, while
General Lucas and his II Corps were approaching Anzio unobserved in a fleet
of nearly three hundred ships, that General Mark Clark flung a series of
attacks distinguished mainly by the sufferings of the troops involved, hundreds
of whom died in attempting to cross the Rapido. In the intervals between
assaults, thousands more endured almost unimaginable privations, shivering

in shallow foxholes under torrents of enemy shells while awaiting orders for their next scramble to drive the Germans off yet another hill or mountaintop along the rugged Italian frontier of Hitler's Fortress Europe.

The hardships sustained by the infantry during what became known as the Battle of Cassino cannot be overstated. In the rough terrain and appalling winter weather, supply shortages were chronic. It frequently became impossible to move up to the front relief units, hot food, winter clothing, and medical supplies to alleviate the men's sufferings. If Anzio very nearly became the Gallipoli of World War II, Cassino was its Passchendaele.

In the end the Rapido was crossed, Cassino fell, and Mark Clark marched into Rome at the head of his victorious troops. But at Cassino, as at Anzio, success came only after *months* of vicious combat which cost the lives of many thousands who died to satisfy the objectives of a battle plan designed by Alexander but actually born of the restless mind of Winston Churchill while he was recovering from pneumonia at Marrakesh in December 1943.

The Battle of Cassino was really a succession of engagements involving not only the Fifth Army's Anglo-American forces but also New Zealand and Indian formations and the North African troops of the newly formed French Expeditionary Corps (FEC). The responsibility for the slaughter probably should have been shared by the entire high command but ultimately fell primarily on Mark Clark although he acted on orders from his immediate superior, General Alexander, who, in turn, was under pressure from 10 Downing Street, London, to hasten the capture of Rome.

Clark later acknowledged that he had made mistakes in the conduct of the Battle of Cassino, and his first error, perhaps, was in having chosen General Fred Walker's Thirty-sixth (Texas) Division for the dicey task of crossing the Rapido on both sides of San Angelo, an enemy-held village on a forty-foot bluff just south of heavily fortified Cassino. The Thirty-sixth had already fought long and hard at Salerno, then slogged its way northward to Monte Trocchio, a mountainous lump across the river from San Angelo and diagonally opposite Cassino. The Texans had known months of cold, mud, hunger, rain, and sleepless nights. Its three regiments were under strength from earlier casualties, demoralized, and badly in need of replacements and rest.

Another mistake was to have ordered the Thirty-sixth to attack on the heels of the failure of the British Forty-sixth Infantry Division to establish a bridgehead at San Ambroglio, south of San Angelo, where the Rapido become the broader, slower-moving Garigliano near the confluence of the Gari and Liri rivers. The failure caused the British front to swing back sharply by several miles, exposed the left flank of the adjacent Thirty-sixth Division, and greatly complicated General Walker's job. But Clark deemed it imperative that the Fifth Army attack in strength in the south in order to facilitate the Anzio landing.

General Gruenther, Clark's chief of staff, had indicated to me that the fate of the Anzio beachhead depended on what happened on the southern front, and on January 29, the day after my adventure in the murky waters off Anzio,

I decided to visit the Thirty-sixth Division at Monte Trocchio. I persuaded the amiable Hal Boyle, of the AP, to come along. On the way there through snowy mountainous terrain previously held by the Germans, we saw examples of how they had improved on Italy's natural defenses with fortified strongpoints.

The one we examined along the Via Casilina looked from a distance like merely another pile of rocks overlooking the road. Built under trees that made it impossible to spot from the air, it measured twenty by twenty feet at the base, rose about ten feet, and was approximately ten feet by ten square at the top, like a truncated pyramid. The German engineers had first dug a huge pit about eight feet deep by sixteen feet long, lined its walls with telephone poles a foot in diameter, laid lengthwise and close together like logs in a cabin wall, then placed enough roughhewn foot-square beams across them as rafters for the roof. Earth and rocks were piled around the walls and over the rafters. An opening was left on the south side facing the road that wound up from Naples.

Boyle and I crawled inside and found the gun which the Germans had left after spiking it, a 57 mm high-muzzle-velocity antitank weapon. The enemy gunners had a fine view down the road for about a mile and a half. Allied tanks and vehicles coming up the highway must have looked like little iron ducks on the slow-moving belt of a carnival shooting gallery. And what targets the gun on one side of the road missed, its equivalent on the opposite side, just as cannily placed, would be certain to hit.

The Germans had plenty of time—from early September, when the Allies signed an armistice with the Italians, until at least the end of November—to build hundreds of such strongpoints, and they built them well. Direct hits from our antitank guns or field artillery would bounce off them harmlessly. We didn't drive the Germans out of their miniforts; they just left when they found it necessary to retreat into their Gustav Line, leaving behind a devilish assortment of mines and booby traps that took time to locate and disarm.

We arrived at the Thirty-sixth's headquarters at Monte Trocchio at about sundown on January 29 in time for a hot supper in the huge mess tent, six days after the division's desperate battle at the Rapido. General Walker was at Fifth Army headquarters at Presenzano conferring with Mark Clark, but by interviewing officers and men, we were able to reconstruct most of the tragic episodes of one of the worst defeats the Americans had suffered in the Italian campaign.

To a man, those with whom we talked mourned buddies lost in the debacle. All were sullen and angry and openly critical of the way the battle had been run. Oddly enough, their anger was not aimed at their own commander, General Walker, or against General Geoffrey Keyes, who had replaced Lucas as commander of the II Corps (which included General Charles Ryder's Thirty-fourth Infantry Division as well as Walker's Thirty-sixth), but was directed entirely at Mark Clark. They accused him of having sent them into a "meat grinder" of a battle without sufficient artillery support, and minus the equipment they needed for crossing "that goddamned Ra-PEE-do."

Indeed, for the first time in my experience I heard American soldiers muttering to each other of mutiny, and I was shocked to learn that certain nameless engineers had refused to obey orders to attempt to build a Bailey bridge under fire.

From all accounts by the participants, the battle was mismanaged from the outset. At the designated crossing points to the left and right of San Angelo, for instance, the Rapido was a formidable obstacle with steep, slippery banks, an unfordable twelve to fifteen feet deep and from thirty to thirty-five feet wide with an icy current that flowed at that time of the year—after a January thaw—at better than ten miles an hour. A captain of engineers said that General Walker had requested a dozen ducks for the crossing, but they weren't available because more than forty of those amphibious trucks—together with scores of precious 105 mm howitzers and antitank guns—had been lost in the sea off Salerno during a disastrous rehearsal for the Anzio landing.

The Thirty-sixth was therefore obliged to use big, clumsy wooden boats, which were heavy and hard to handle, and inflatable rafts. These, along with pontoons and other matériel, were moved under cover of night to forward dumps between Monte Trocchio and the muddy riverbank. Engineers also located the minefields which the Germans had laid on terrain they had held before withdrawing to their Gustav Line and marked lanes through them with tapes.

Shortly before the attack began in the dark, foggy evening of January 20 Allied artillery subjected the enemy positions across the river to an intensive barrage, and surprise became impossible. The Germans responded instantly with a deadly rain of shells and rockets from their nefarious Nebelwerfers. When the Texans arrived at their dumps, they found many of their boats destroyed; others were so badly holed by shrapnel that they sank when placed in the water. Men weighted down with backpacks and weapons were swept downstream and drowned in the swift current.

Moreover, the heavy enemy fire had obliterated the tapes that marked the safe lanes through the minefields. Troops, hunched under the weight of the remaining boats, struggled blindly through the dark across the muddy approaches to the riverbank. Some staggered off the lanes, stumbled on mines, and were blown to bits with their burdens. Shells and rockets fell on the assembly areas as well as on the crossing troops, and the attack became disorganized before it began.

Nevertheless, despite the confusion, low visibility, and the incessant enemy fire, elements of the A and B companies of the 141st Regiment's First Battalion—about 480 men—struggled across the river in boats and rafts north of San Angelo. Although subjected to intensive machine-gun fire by the waiting Germans, they succeeded in establishing a precarious bridgehead about a thousand yards from the riverbank. They dug in as best they could and fought back with grenades and rifle fire, but they took heavy casualties. With their men scattered in small units all over the place, the commanders couldn't call in artillery support, nor could they safely move about to regroup amid the enemy's mines

and concertinas of barbed wire. To hold their positions until reinforcements arrived, the embattled Texans fought as fiercely as their ancestors at the Alamo, but in the end theirs, too, proved to be a lost cause.

Meanwhile, in the river, which the Germans had thoughtfully mined, engineers struggled to build footbridges. Four were destroyed by mines and mortar fire before one could be improvised from the damaged remnants of the others to permit the rest of the men of the A and B companies to cross. Only a few made it, and a subsequent attempt by the First Battalion's C Company to reach its comrades on the enemy side of the Rapido proved disastrous. Its rubber rafts were sunk by enemy rifle fire, and its assault boats were destroyed in midstream by mortar shells.

The simultaneous attack by the 143d Regiment south of San Angelo ran into even greater trouble, if possible, than the 141st. Three platoons of Company C crossed the river with many casualties before the Germans destroyed their boats, and the rest of the battalion reached the other side on two hastily made footbridges, one of which was knocked out and the other damaged. The battalion was herded into a pocket barely five hundred yards from the bank, and its commander ordered a withdrawal. Only remnants managed to swim back to their own side of the river.

When daylight came on January 21, the Thirty-sixth Division had only two depleted companies across the Rapido, both north of San Angelo and being steadily whittled down by withering enemy fire. Men were blown out of their foxholes by mortar bombs and artillery shells and cut down by machine-gun bullets as they scrambled for cover. It proved impossible to reinforce them during the daylight hours of January 21, but by early morning of the next day the enemy machine-gun positions covering the crossing were eliminated and two footbridges were erected. The Second and Third battalions crossed to the German side under enemy shell fire, and more men were lost in what soon proved to be a futile effort.

On the afternoon of January 22 the Germans attacked the positions of the 141st in force and were driven off. But the embattled regiment was running out of ammunition. A second German attack met lessened resistance, and by nightfall the men on the American side of the river realized the end had come.

"We knew it was all over," a young lieutenant told me, "when we heard no more answering fire from our guys." Late that night about forty survivors returned to the south bank of the Rapido. All the others had been killed, wounded, or captured. A scheduled attack by the division's 142d Regiment was wisely canceled.

After a three-day battle nothing had been gained and many good Texans were dead, wounded, or missing. The official casualty count that I was given at Fifth Army headquarters later for the period January 20–31 was 155 killed, 1,052 wounded, and 921 missing, a total of 2,128. The "missing," of course, could be presumed dead or captured, but the Germans took few prisoners at Cassino.

What I saw at Monte Trocchio, however, had convinced me that the losses

were considerably greater than those eventually made public. In a cold, muddy
ravine behind the mountain I entered the tent of a Medical Corps dressing
station filled with at least a hundred wounded awaiting transfer to a field
hospital. The strangely silent place smelled like a slaughterhouse.

What remained forever imprinted in memory were the contents of a nearby
cave scooped out of a hillside. It was the most gruesome sight I had ever
beheld. Under a crudely lettered sign that read PIECES lay several burlap bags
containing the unidentified—and probably unidentifiable—arms, legs, hands,
and feet of Texans dismembered on their own side of the Rapido by enemy
mines, shells, and rockets. I had seen many wounded, but never before gunnysacks lumpy with the bloody *remains* of men.

I had long since come to detest war, but at Monte Trocchio I learned to
loathe it and longed to escape from it. Yet, like the men who fought it, I stayed
with it out of an inner, obsessive need to share their dangers. The horror of
the scene in that damp, murky, malodorous cave recurred in the nightmares
that troubled me for several years after the war. Burdened with guilt that I had
somehow survived when so many good men had not, I sought the help of
psychiatrists, who in time helped me rationalize the butchery as the inevitable
price of ridding the world of the evil personified in Adolf Hitler and his Fascist
ally.

At the time the shocking details of the grim tableau in the cave and of the
mismanagement of the battle by the Fifth Army command were suppressed
by censorship. Newspaper readers and radio listeners back home never learned
what officers and men of the Thirty-sixth Division told Hal Boyle and me at
Monte Trocchio. We could not get past the censors, for instance, the fact that
at the assembly areas not all the boats to be used in the crossing were provided
with paddles.

Nor were we permitted to describe the utter futility of the battle itself. Not
a single Texan ever seriously threatened the enemy's positions on the other side
of the Rapido, and not one tank was taken across because the engineers
couldn't, and in some cases wouldn't, build the necessary Bailey bridges under
the incessant hail of artillery, mortar, and rocket fire.

Many stories about the fighting at the Rapido remained untold. Among
them was one about the truce arranged on January 25, three days after resistance ceased in the 141st Regiment's sector, to enable the Americans to collect
their dead on the German side of the river. A graves registration officer who
supervised the grisly operation said the Germans helped to find and collect the
bodies and carry them to the riverbank.

"Altogether, we found about eighty," the officer said. "Most of them had
got direct hits from mortar shells and had no heads, shoulders, or arms. They
must have been standing in their holes when they were hit. Anyhow, they
proved hard to identify. . . ."

Yet, on the night of January 30–31, in the olive groves on the southern slope
of Monte Trocchio, the men of Walker's Thirty-sixth Division waited discon-
solately for orders to resume the attack. The horrifying details of what had

happened during the initial attack were known to the men, and from their talk of mutiny it was evident they feared another attempt to cross the river. Fortunately the attack was canceled, and on the morning of February 1 Boyle and I decided to visit a forward observation post for a good look at the scene of the previous debacle.

We followed the rough trail around the right side of the mountain and entered the woods which the 141st had used as a staging area, taking care to stay within trodden ground that we hoped was free of mines. There had been intermittent exchanges of artillery fire the night before, but it was quiet now as we passed smashed boats and a litter of helmets, empty ammo boxes, and other gear. We walked as men do in a cow pasture, placing each foot carefully on a preselected spot, Boyle a few yards ahead of me.

At a sudden random burst of enemy machine-gun fire, we both dropped to the ground, and I saw Boyle shaking as though he had been hit. I snaked up to him as fast as I could, but he wasn't hurt; he was laughing. Before I could cuss him out for scaring me out of my wits, he chortled, "It just occurred to me, Frank, that you and I are a bit too old for this sort of thing. . . ."

And perhaps we were. I was just four days short of thirty-six, and the rather corpulent Boyle several years my senior. We both smoked more than was good for us and were not in the best of shape for crawling over a stinking battlefield. Nevertheless, we continued forward and emerged on the flat ground which its previous German tenants had cleared of trees and underbrush to obtain a clear field of fire.

Standing in a soggy hole some Texan had dug days before, we had a fine view of San Angelo on our left and, in the distance to our right, the forbidding eminence we knew to be Monte Cassino. There was no sign of life. The great wall of mountains that rose beyond the river looked like the painted backdrop of a stage set. It was a gray, overcast day, but the abbey on Monte Cassino glowed golden in a halo of light where the morning sun had momentarily broken through the clouds as though to illuminate the monastery's importance in the strategic scheme of things.

Left of the mountain mass there was an open space in the gently serrated skyline indicating the entrance to the valley of the Liri River, along which ran the highway to Rome. From the direction of Monte Cairo, on our right, beyond Monte Cassino, came the sound of heavy gunfire like the distant rumble of thunder during a violent summer storm, and we knew that the Battle of Cassino had resumed on yet another front.

Thinking the firing might spread to our sector and feeling naked under the enemy OPs on the bluff that held San Angelo, we scuttled back to regimental headquarters, arriving in time for lunch. At the kitchen tent the cooks were ladling out hot chili, a special treat for the tired Texans of the Thirty-sixth Division.

Before leaving the Thirty-sixth Division, Boyle and I visited the Eleventh Field Hospital about six miles behind the front. Situated in a ravine that led off the Via Casilina, it consisted of a line of tents marked with huge red crosses.

The colonel in charge of the place confirmed that the division had suffered upwards of 65 percent casualties; some units, he said, were virtually wiped out.

Many of the hospital's patients were being treated not for battle wounds but for trench foot, the cold numbness which, if ignored, turned the feet into blue-green gangrenous lumps. Trench foot ranked with pneumonia as a major cause of casualties among the troops who lay in damp foxholes day in, day out under enemy fire and unable to take proper care of feet that needed warmth and dry socks.

At the height of the battle from January 20 to 23, the wounded arrived in such numbers that the supplies of blood and plasma ran dangerously low. The entire staff-nurses, orderlies, cooks, stretcher-bearers, ambulance drivers, even doctors—donated blood. Word was sent to a field artillery battery about a mile and a half back, and its gunners came in to give blood, then returned to their posts.

Hospitals were usually good billets for a night or two; the food was better than in the line, and a spare tent was always available for a more or less peaceful night's sleep. But not the Eleventh; it was in plain sight of the German observers on Monte Cassino and on a line with our battery of Long Toms. The night we spent there the air was filled with the scream and whistle of shells, outbound and incoming. Two of the latter landed close enough to shake the ground under our cots.

In the morning, when we emerged from the ravine onto the Via Casilini and looked north, up the Liri Valley—the GIs now called it Purple Heart Valley—there was Monte Cassino. I, for one, experienced more strongly than ever before the uncanny, daunting feeling that I was being watched from the huge, barrackslike monastery on its summit.

Hal Boyle read my thoughts. "Sooner or later," he said cheerfully, "somebody's going to have to blow that place all to hell. . . ."

Down the road we stopped to talk with the gunners of the battery of 155 mm guns emplaced behind a craggy knoll seemingly out of the abbey's line of sight. Its commander, however, was aware of its presence. He echoed Hal's prediction that something had to be done about it despite orders from the high command to "respect the buildings and monuments of the Roman Catholic Church."

"I have Catholic gunners in this battery," he said, "and they've begged me for permission to zero in on it; but I haven't been able to give it to them, and they don't like it. We get heavy counterbattery every time we fire, and it's only because the krauts have spotters up there in that damned monastery."

The officer led the way to the top of his knoll, and sure enough, there was the abbey in full view. Its rows of cell windows, its immense brooding length, its massive, battlemented base made a splendid but inviolate target. I could see the artilleryman was itching to put a few rounds into those distant walls; his Long Toms could reach it easily, but his hands were tied.

The Texans, however, were not the only Americans who fought and bled in the misbegotten Battle of Cassino. On the night of January 24, only two days after the Thirty-sixth Division had failed in its attempt to force the Rapido south of Cassino, General Clark ordered its sister division, the Thirty-fourth Infantry, to try to pinch out the town from the north. And for the first two or three days the river flowed red with the blood of Iowans, Kansans, and other farm boys from the Middle West.

But the division, whose symbol was the head of a bull and whose commander was the tall, scholarly General Ryder, got the job done though the cost came high. By the time I arrived at divisional headquarters on February 5, my thirty-sixth birthday, Doc Ryder's outfit had lost about 65 percent of his riflemen killed, wounded, or missing, among them members of the division's 100th Battalion, a unit of Nisei who fought like devils to prove they were at least as good as their white comrades.

But the division had crossed the river, captured Cairo, a stony village located in a defile leading up to Monte Cairo, taken many German prisoners, occupied the headquarters of the enemy's 131st Grenadier Regiment, and begun the long, hard fight to dominate the snowy peaks around Cassino before descending upon the town itself. In other words, the Thirty-fourth had breached the Gustav Line and established a bridgehead on the enemy's side of the river *behind* Cassino in a maneuver that was to rank with the finest feats of arms carried out by any Allied soldiers during the whole of World War II.

Not to draw an invidious comparison but merely to set the record straight, the only advantage the Thirty-fourth had over the Thirty-sixth was that north of Cassino the Rapido was fordable and boats were not needed. Otherwise the task Clark had handed Doc Ryder was every bit as difficult, if not more so. The Germans had blown a dam upriver from Cassino and turned the section of the three-mile-wide valley that the division had to cross into a mined quasi-quagmire difficult for the heavily burdened troops to negotiate and virtually impassable to tanks.

During the initial phase of the attack—in incessant rain that turned to sleet and under torrents of German artillery and mortar fire—each of the three battalions of Colonel Charles Marshall's 133d Infantry Regiment lost more than a hundred men. For a while, with tanks helpless in the muddy ground and unable to support the foot soldiers, another debacle was in prospect.

But the engineers, working desperately under heavy fire, managed to lay tank tracks across the muddy approaches to the river with strips of the wire matting used by the air forces for the construction of temporary landing fields on soggy ground. The tracks were completed during the night of January 29, and tanks were able to cross in strength. With the help of the infantry, the armor reached all the division's objectives: Cairo village, the strongly fortified former Italian military barracks some two thousand yards upriver from Cassino, and the mountains behind Cassino—Monte Castellone and Monte Maiola—from which the troops could *descend* on Cassino itself. One company of the 133d Regiment even reached the outskirts of the town but was pushed back.

It took the Thirty-fourth eight days to gain its bridgehead—a mere nibble into the mountain wall—and secure passage into the hills. Now the infantrymen had to force their way up those huge, barren mountainsides, then turn southward and fight along the craggy mountaintops toward Cassino, always under the watchful eyes up there in that abbey. Gradually it dawned on the men that the key to victory in their sector was Monte Cassino rather than the town itself.

What I saw of the terrain on a quick visit to the regimental headquarters of Colonel Marshall's 133d Infantry in the hills beyond the Italian barracks filled me with wonder that men could endure the hardships created by the terrain nature had devised. The hills and mountains were strewn with boulders and gorse thickets, veined with ravines and gullies, and where clumps of trees had stood there were only stumps blasted by shell fire.

The Germans had had plenty of time to blast holes in the hard, volcanic rock, enlarge existing caves, and create new ones. But the American attackers had to rely for cover on loose stones scraped together with their bare hands to build protective breastworks. There were no trails, only goat paths, and all supplies had to be brought up to the men by mules.

The Nisei, men from sunny California and tropical Hawaii, suffered most from the cold in that inhospitable terrain. Their undersize boots were scattered about as they tried to massage warmth into their frostbitten feet.

The men slept, when they slept at all, during the usually quiet midday spells, wrapped in their blankets, munching K rations which had been slipped to them the night before. At night patrols prowled the crags and defiles, seeking prisoners or scouting enemy positions. It was dangerous work; challenging a dark figure in the normal way was to tempt death from an enemy bullet or grenade. The Americans used a code of whistled recognition signals. The Germans, on the other hand, seemed to be using various catcalls. Sometimes patrols never returned.

Meanwhile, the Germans, far from withdrawing troops from the Rapido front to bolster their defenses at Anzio, were reinforcing hard and were mounting fierce counterattacks. On February 7 a battalion of the Thirty-fourth's 133d Regiment reached Colle San Angelo, about three miles behind Cassino but was thrown off it. Another battalion reached a hill immediately below the monastery but was driven back by overwhelming machine-gun fire from the slopes of Monte Cassino.

The wounded, when they could be reached, had to be carried down the slopes in litters or on muleback and were often killed by German rifle fire or mortar bombs on the way down. The dead, alas, remained where they were; they could not be removed in daylight, much less buried in ground that rendered useless the spades of their comrades. Meanwhile, platoons became squads, and squads were whittled down to teams of twos and threes numbed with cold, fatigue, and exposure, but obstinately clinging to their positions.

What motivated them? I wondered. Their selflessness, their acceptance of their lot as they waded rivers, scrambled up craggy hills, and exposed themselves to enemy fire filled me with a sense of deep obligation. They were fighting my battle. I had talked to enough of them to know they neither hated the Germans nor fully understood the evil the Nazi enemy represented. Why, then, did they fight? I confess I never found a satisfactory answer. I knew only that I felt deeply indebted to them and sought to repay my debt by sharing their hardships insofar as possible short of getting myself killed.

I came away from the Cassino front with a deepening conviction that the Italian campaign had been ill conceived, undertaken with insufficient forces, and executed to satisfy the vainglorious goals of politicians far removed from the scene of battle for whom divisions were not flesh-and-blood men but symbols on a gigantic war map.

It was snowing when we left the Cassino front, and wounded men were being brought down the mountain on litters. But relief for the exhausted troops of the Thirty-fourth Division was at hand. On our way back to the press camp at Presenzano, we saw New Zealanders moving into the line. They were coming westward from the static Eighth Army front in hundreds of vehicles with their own artillery and tanks. The Battle of Cassino was entering a new phase.

61

DEATH OF A MONUMENT

The news from Anzio, even in the somewhat sanitized versions made available to us at the Presenzano press camp, was all bad. Truscott's crucial drive on Cisterna had failed, and the British were pushed out of their salient at Aprilia. The beachhead's three and a half Allied divisions were hemmed in by seven of Field Marshal Kesselring's best divisions and were being hammered daily by German artillery and a reborn Luftwaffe, which even bombed a clearly marked field hospital, killing six American nurses. In less than a month the Allies had suffered more than six thousand casualties, and a repetition of the World War I disaster at Gallipoli remained a distinct possibility.

As February wore on, and indications multiplied that the Germans were determined to force an Allied withdrawal, it became increasingly evident to Mark Clark and to his superior, General Alexander, that the most they could hope for at Anzio was a successful defense. To save the beachhead and salvage victory from defeat in what had become a decisive phase in the Italian campaign, both men realized they had to make something truly dramatic happen on the main front along the Rapido.

For this, however, they needed more of everything: fresh troops, artillery, tanks, and, perhaps most of all, imaginative leadership in the field. To provide it, Alexander left the static, snowbound Adriatic front to a holding force and moved three of the Eighth Army's divisions westward to reinforce the Fifth Army. They were the Second New Zealand and Fourth Indian divisions, with the British Seventy-eighth Infantry to come later. With these units, plus about half of the U.S. First Armored Division (the other half was at Anzio), Alexander formed the II New Zealand Corps under Lieutenant General Sir Bernard Freyberg, a prestigious World War I hero. He had served at Gallipoli and then in France, where he had won the Victoria Cross, the highest British service decoration for conspicuous acts of heroism, a medal usually awarded posthumously.

Well over six feet tall and still physically powerful at fifty-five, Freyberg was an imposing figure with searching gray eyes and a hard jawline. He owned a well-deserved reputation for independence of thought and action, was almost as popular in Britain as Monty, and in the eyes of his adoring fellow countrymen in New Zealand could do no wrong. He was, in short, a sort of British composite of our own MacArthur and "Old Blood and Guts" Patton.

Freyberg and his New Zealanders had fought valiantly against overwhelming odds on Crete in the spring of 1941 and had distinguished themselves later under Montgomery in the Middle East and North Africa. The dour, tough, battle-hardened troops I saw moving into the line on my way back to Presenzano from the Cassino front seemed to be just what was needed to break the Gustav Line where it was strongest and to open the way up the Liri Valley for our tanks. They looked clean, fresh, and eager and contrasted sharply with the tired, dirty, disconsolate GIs they were replacing.

Many New Zealanders were men who had operated remote farms and sheep ranches in their distant homeland, an island nation of about two million people. They were a self-reliant lot, capable of thinking for themselves in the heat of battle and ideally suited, therefore, to the business of modern warfare. In addition to raw courage, they possessed the high degree of farm-bred mechanical aptitude required to maintain the trucks, tanks, mobile artillery, and other machinery used in the killing industry called war. Tractor drivers made fine tank pilots.

Like Montgomery, Freyberg enjoyed the trust and affection of his troops, though without Monty's insistence on the salutes and other formalities of a spit-and-polish corps. Freyberg was not above joining his men in a pint or two in a barracks-room jamboree, and I remembered that in Cairo, after the debacle on Crete, he had opened for his troops the biggest beer bar in town. The general was renowned for his disregard of the outward appearances of discipline, and once, when Monty asked him why his men never saluted, Freyberg replied, "Try waving to them. They always wave back." Captain Geoffrey Cox, one of Freyberg's intelligence officers, had described him to me in Cairo as "unique in many ways, a crusty old cuss sometimes, but we love him because he'd never ask us to do anything dangerous that he wouldn't do himself."

The big New Zealander was unique among Allied commanders in another important respect. Unlike Alexander or Montgomery, Freyberg was responsible not to Winston Churchill but to his own prime minister and government. He possessed, therefore, far greater freedom of action than any other divisional commander, British or American, and was rarely shy about asserting it. Usually what Freyberg wanted, Freyberg got.

Nevertheless, Freyberg reluctantly allowed himself to be inserted into a seamless Fifth Army command under Mark Clark and coolly accepted the difficult dual task Alexander assigned to him: (1) to relieve the exhausted Americans of the Thirty-fourth and Thirty-sixth Divisions in the hills around Cassino and (2) to break out into the Liri Valley, a challenging mission which, if successful, would redound to the credit of New Zealand, its expeditionary force, and, of course, its commander.

Freyberg's chances of success were greatly enhanced by the inclusion in his corps of the Fourth Indian Division, probably the most professional of the Allied formations in Italy. One third British and two thirds Indian—mostly Nepalese Gurkhas, plus Sikhs and Punjabis, all troops who loved soldiering for its own sake—the division had proved itself first in the mountains of Eritrea in 1940, when it helped bring down Mussolini's short-lived African empire, then in the Middle East and in North Africa under Montgomery.

Like the New Zealanders, the Fourth Indian boasted an exceptional commander. Major General Francis I. S. Tuker was as strong-minded as Freyberg and a renowned scholar in the arcane art of warfare who had written several books on the subject. In the view of many Indian Army officers, Tuker was "the brains that the brawny Freyberg lacks."

When Tuker arrived in Italy with his Indians in December 1943, he immediately immersed himself in the problems involved in fighting a war in mountainous territory. Unwilling to squander lives for impossible military targets situated on inaccessible peaks, he concluded that fortified places like the battlemented high-walled abbey on Monte Cassino could not be taken by ground forces without the help of massive aerial bombardment, and he lost no time advising Freyberg of the fact.

This was a delicate subject. It was Allied policy to respect and preserve "all religious institutions, local archives, historical and classical monuments and objects of art," unless, of course, "military necessity necessitated their destruction." The Fifth Army repeatedly warned its air forces to avoid bombing the abbey on Monte Cassino.

Life under canvas at the Presenzano press camp in the rain, sleet, and snow of February 1944 was no picnic, but it had the advantage of nearness to the various headquarters of the Fifth Army's polyglot components. It was a relatively simple matter to move from one to the other, and I regularly visited in turn the New Zealanders, the Indians, and the French farther on at Venafro, high in the icy Abruzzi mountains.

Nearest were the New Zealanders. Their fifteen thousand vehicles, more than any other unit of comparable size possessed, cluttered the Liri Valley south of Cassino, bivouacked among the revolting evidence of previous combat: clusters of shallow roadside graves; burned-out Allied and German tanks and trucks; tangles of power lines dangling from poles leaning askew; splintered trees; and craters filled with black, oily, smelly stagnant water that reminded the older British officers of the French battlefields of the First World War. What I would always remember, however, was the all-pervasive stench of decaying corpses, human and animal, that mingled with the pungent stink of cordite, burning rubber, and exhaust fumes.

The New Zealanders seemed undismayed by their repulsive environment. They brought to the Cassino front the high morale and easy confidence born of previous successes, and they regarded the impending battle as merely another opportunity to demonstrate their invincibility. One of their officers, a lieutenant colonel of infantry whom I had known in Cairo when he was three years younger and still a major, unabashedly reminded me that his troops were, after all, "this bloody war's best bloody soldiers." As proof, he cited the fact that the Germans were shifting units from the Adriatic front to the defense of Cassino, and he showed me their positions on the celluloid overlay on his field map.

I wondered, but refrained from asking, whether he had personally inspected the terrain in which his men would be fighting. I was sure he hadn't, at least not yet, or he wouldn't have been so cheery.

Freyberg, however, had seen the flooded Rapido Valley that extended across his front like a natural tank trap, studied the gray-brown desolation of mountains that rose beyond it, and, after glimpsing for the first time the buff-colored fortresslike eminence atop Monte Cassino, began having doubts about his chances of success. His plan of attack, as it unfolded following the withdrawal of the GIs of the Thirty-fourth Division, was essentially the one tried twice before by Mark Clark. It differed in only one respect: Cassino was to be assaulted simultaneously from the north and the southeast, but with more troops than were previously employed. Moreover, they were men who had been virtually resting on the Adriatic front following Monty's departure to join Eisenhower in London to prepare Overlord, the cross-Channel invasion.

The Indians and some New Zealanders were to occupy the precarious bridgehead which the Americans had established behind the town, then storm Monastery Hill and the abbey itself, and sweep down the steep slopes to the Via Casilina north of the Rapido. At Fifth Army headquarters I learned later that when Al Gruenther, Clark's chief of staff, asked Freyberg how he figured his chances of success, the general had replied, "About fifty-fifty," not ideal odds in the deadly game of war.

General Tuker's Indians, I found, were fully aware of the difficulties they faced. From those precarious forward positions on Snakeshead Ridge and other heights formerly held by the Americans came reports that the troops were having trouble establishing themselves in the moonscape terrain. They particularly complained of being constantly under direct German observation from Monte Cassino and its adjacent peaks. Enemy occupation of all the commanding heights, especially Monte Cassino, sharply limited such routine operations as normal reconnaissance and movement of supplies during day-light hours. Every movement drew German mortar fire. "Wherever we turn," the British officer commanding a platoon of Gurkhas told me, "there's the monastery staring down at us."

In their new positions the troops of the Fourth Indian Division held what was virtually a separate battlefield miles ahead of the main Fifth Army front and were experiencing logistical difficulties even before any serious fighting started. Relief units, ammunition, food, everything they needed had to come to them over a winding, highly vulnerable route some seven or eight miles long from San Michele, their base on the Allied side of the river about two miles north of the Via Casilina.

After crossing the Rapido Valley, which had become a sort of no-man's-land, the route lay up slopes along a succession of tortuous, icy trails that were little more than goat paths, impassable to the smallest four-wheeled vehicles, difficult even for mules, which were in short supply.

The only other means of supplying the Gurkhas in those mountains was by airdrops. Early one morning I watched planes zoom down low over their positions to drop supplies from varicolored parachutes. Every drop drew enemy fire while the Gurkhas scrambled to recover whatever the various boxes and bundles contained, and the Germans tried to prevent them. The Gurkhas got even by distributing highly spiced bits of meat among the dogs the Germans employed on night patrols and on counterforays released among them bitches in heat.

The Gurkhas, whom I had first met in the desert, were ferocious and skillful night fighters. They fought with kukris, curved knives that resembled sickles, useful for eliminating somnolent sentinels and in close combat. Their skill with their kukris gave rise to a widely circulated tale of a Nazi who, believing he had evaded the swipe of one of those razor-sharp weapons, shouted exultantly: "Ha! You missed me."

The Gurkha was supposed to have replied: "Well then, just try shaking your head!"

The presence of the Indians created problems for the Eighth Army quarter-master who provisioned them. He had difficulty finding enough beef for the Muslims, rum for the Sikhs, pork for some of the Hindus, and for everybody enough ghee, a butterlike fat used as a spread on bread or in cooking and derived from buffalo milk. Muslims liked it as a dressing for boiled rice.

The curry I had in the British officers' mess at San Michele was as good as any Kim Mundy ever made in the desert, and its main ingredient was not bully beef but American Spam. By far the most imaginative cuisine, however, was to be found at Venafro, the headquarters of the French Expeditionary Force.

Venafro was a town much like Cassino, an agglutination of stony ruins nestling on the slope of a huge mountain in the cold, snowbound Abruzzi about twenty-five miles northeast of Presenzano. We reached it by a crowded secondary road that turned off the Via Casilina south of the press camp, then wound up a valley between forested hills furry with fresh snow.

In its upper reaches, on the outskirts of Venafro, the road might have been French. The roadside signs read: SENS INTERDIT, DIRECTION UNIQUE, QUARTIER GÉNÉRAL. American drivers daubed girls' names on their vehicles, but those we passed, or saw parked in ravines, were named *Quo Vadis, Je m'en fou, N'Importe,* or, more expressively, *Merde Alors!*

Had I covered the North African campaign, I would have known that the French Expeditionary Force was not really French, but was composed largely of Arabs—goums, Algerians, and Moroccans—with French officers and technicians. I knew that tens of thousands of Jews were fighting in the Allied armies, including Russia's, but until I saw those fezzed and turbaned North African troops in their rest camp on the outskirts of Venafro, I had been unaware that our armies included Arabs and that they were being employed as frontline troops.

The Arabs I had known in the Middle East, Palestinians and Egyptians, were decidedly pro-Axis in sentiment, and the few who had volunteered for service in the British Royal Army were used as labor battalions far behind the front lines. I was amazed to find Arabs fighting in what the editorialists back home now called "democracy's war of survival." What were the Arabs of the French Expeditionary Corps fighting for? I wondered.

The Arabs that caught the eye were the goums, big, tough, fierce-looking Berbers from the Atlas Mountains of North Africa, attired in odds and ends of British, French, and American uniforms, the whole covered in ankle-length homespun burnouses striped lengthwise in gray-brown and black, colors that blended well with the terrain. Most were shod in heavy regulation hobnailed boots, but a few wrapped their feet against the cold with strips cut from blankets. They wore the oval, crested helmets of the poilus of World War I and carried long, mean-looking knives in scabbards dangling from their belts.

At the headquarters of General (later Marshal) Alphonse-Pierre Juin, commander of the French Expeditionary Corps, which he had formed in North Africa, trained, and brought to Italy in November–December 1943, I was saluted smartly by spahi guards and met Brigadier General Theodore Roosevelt, Jr., son of our "Rough Rider" president and the Fifth Army's liaison officer with the French forces. A short, wiry, assertive, hard-drinking man in his mid-fifties, Roosevelt took charge of me at once, gave me a welcome tot of excellent brandy from his private stock, and conducted me to lunch in the officers' mess in the common room of what must have been a local tavern or wineshop, a decidely rustic but pleasant place warmed by a log fire.

General Juin—as was his habit, I was told—was in the field somewhere, scouting the terrain, but I met a number of his officers at lunch. They were a proud lot, with whom the niceties of military courtesy were second nature, and made me instantly aware of an even sterner discipline than I had encountered among Tuker's elite Anglo-Indian regiments. Many were survivors of Dunkirk. None took the war more seriously, it seemed to me, than the Frenchmen who led their colonial troops on the right wing of Mark Clark's Fifth Army.

About twenty field-grade officers sat facing each other, ten on each side, across a wooden refectory table, scrubbed clean, set with battered tin plates and primitive cutlery, and at each end holding a huge earthenware pitcher of local red wine. What the place lacked in appointments, it more than made up for in the excellence of the food which was prepared with care and served with a Gallic flourish.

Before the meal was brought on by fezzed Arab orderlies, the burly mess sergeant, in tall white chef's hat and gravy-stained apron, emerged from the kitchen, announced the bill of fare, and wished us all a throaty *"Bon appetit, messieurs! Bon appetit!"* There was a hearty soup in which I thought I detected C ration vegetables, then a meat course with potatoes. There was plenty of freshly baked white bread, and for dessert we had oranges, peeled, sliced, and flavored with a touch of Grand Marnier.

Roosevelt's French was worse than mine, but most of our tablemates spoke passable English, having learned it in England after Dunkirk before joining the FEC in North Africa. I sat between Roosevelt and a Captain Duhamel, whom I interviewed concerning the goums.

Duhamel said they were "excellent troops for night operations requiring stealth, patience, and endurance." They could crawl on elbows and bellies to within striking distance of an enemy position, knife the outposts, and attack with grenades before the defenders were even aware of their presence. "They are very efficient with grenades," he said. "They love grenades and keep the mule packs busy bringing them grenades. They are very good also with the bayonet."

When not fighting, Duhamel said, the goums were really a docile lot, happiest just sitting on a rock holding the tether of a mule or donkey, talking with the animals as though in serious conversation for hours on end or singing their diatonal tribal songs softly to themselves, slapping their feet on the ground, and clapping hands in rhythm. "But I would not like to be the Boche who meets one of them in the mountains in the dark," Duhamel added.

What motivated them? The captain wasn't sure. He supposed they fought because they liked army life, which fed and clothed them well and paid them for their services. The married troops' families regularly received allowances. *"Mais, après la guerre* [But after the war]?" The captain answered his own question with a shrug.

The French corps, Roosevelt explained later as we Jeeped toward the front to meet General Juin, was composed of two divisions: the Second Moroccan and the Third Algerian, both veterans of the Tunisian campaign. Their *tirailleurs* (riflemen) had swept away such formidable obstacles as Monte Pentano and Monte Mainarde that had held up the Americans on their northward march to the Rapido from Naples, feats that established them as the Fifth Army's finest mountain fighters.

It was nearly sundown when we reached Juin's forward command post in the hills overlooking the Rapido Valley and the desolate mountainscape in which the general's troops were deployed. Diagonally opposite, on the right, was towering Monte Cifalco, rising snowcapped some three thousand feet, and on our distant left, Monte Cassino. In between lay the challenging outline of more mountains.

Juin was a compact, rosy-faced Breton. His round head was capped by a dark blue beret on which shone the five tiny silver stars of his rank, an unlighted cigar was clamped between his teeth, and his bristly mustache was beaded with frost. In his khaki greatcoat, unbuttoned down the front, he epitomized the frontline "soldier's general." His right arm was partly paralyzed by a World War I wound, and he gave me his left hand in greeting, then waved it in a sweeping but undramatic gesture across the narrow gorge of the Rapido, muttering, *"Voilà, notre champ de bataille!"*

Juin looked solemn, disturbed. His troops were struggling to hold their positions on the Colle Belvedere, the peaks northeast of Cassino which they had won at great cost from the pounding they had received from German artillery on all-seeing Monte Cifalco, the Monte Cassino of the French sector. Some units had lost nearly all their officers, many of them Frenchmen who had survived Dunkirk only to die in Italy.

Juin had spent the early morning hours with his troops, at times within a few hundred yards of the enemy, and was visibly indignant at what he had found after the battle that had ended on February 6. The forwardmost French positions were well above and ahead of those of the main Fifth Army, with supply problems even more serious, if possible, than those of General Tuker's Indian regiments. His Algerians on their salient on the Colle Belvedere were in danger of being cut off by General Frido von Senger's heavily reinforced Germans. Some of Juin's men had been fighting for several days without food and water, and their ammunition, especially those indispensable grenades, was running low. One recent night a supply train of eighty pack mules had set out to reach the *tirailleurs* on their peaks, but only two reached their destinations; the rest were cut down by enemy machine-gun and mortar fire or had slipped off the icy tracks and crashed down the slopes into the gorges below.

But statistics were inadequate to describe the trials of the French corps. Everything had to be done at night. Daylight movement brought immediate retribution from the enemy's artillery observers. The rocks splintered, and the pieces had as much power to kill and maim as the metal shards of shells and bombs. The French capture of the Colle Belvedere cost Juin's forces twenty-five hundred casualties.

Like so much about the Italian campaign, the full story of the French struggle in the mountains behind Cassino was not known until after the war. I learned enough at Venafro, however, to come away convinced that the French contribution to the Battle of Cassino had at least equaled that made by the Americans and the British. They fought until they could go no farther and held their positions with the tenacity of men determined to salvage French honor lost in the debacle of 1940.

Nothing Juin actually *said* during his hurried explanation of the military situation as it was reflected on his map suggested that he was displeased with the way in which the battle was being conducted, but his manner and his clipped, almost monosyllabic speech indicated disapproval. I did not know at the time that Juin, like Tuker, on his left, had advocated a wide swing around the right that would have bypassed the elaborate German defenses around Cassino and saved many lives.

Juin and Tuker, I learned later, had urged such a strategy on Freyberg, who at first agreed, then changed his mind in favor of a frontal assault on both Cassino and Monastery Hill. Like everyone else, Freyberg had become uneasy about the abbey on that mountaintop. It exercised an almost hypnotic effect on all concerned, for it dominated physically and psychologically the approaches to the Liri Valley.

Troops stared at it with hatred in their eyes. Officers saw it increasingly as the main obstacle on their way to victory and the principal cause of the heavy casualties among their men. There was an unspoken consensus that the monastery had to be bombed. No one doubted that Germans occupied the place. Whether the enemy occupants were fighting men or mere observers was irrelevant, for we all knew that the mountain's slopes, right up to the base of the abbey itself were honeycombed with German sangars containing mortar squads, machine-gun nests, and hidden antitank guns.

On Saturday, February 12, Mark Clark was away, presumably at Anzio, where the situation, the correspondents were told at Fifth Army GHQ, was "touch and go." Intelligence intercepts had indicated that the Germans were mounting a new, major offensive against the beachhead. The Allies now had seventy thousand men and nearly four hundred tanks there but were still outnumbered and vulnerable. Fellow reporters who had seen Clark in recent days while I was away variously described him as "worried-looking" and "harassed."

There was tension at headquarters, with much coming and going of air force brass. Something was brewing, but what it was no one would say. The presence of the "fly-boys," however, clearly indicated we were preparing to bomb what the troops called "that fuckin' monastery." If so, the weather was decidedly unfavorable. Sunday was a day made hideous by high winds, rain, and sleet that by nightfall had turned to snow.

Monday dawned clear and bright, and early that morning a lone Piper Cub flew low over the monastery. It was not as daring a thing to do as it seemed; the Germans were smart enough not to give away the positions of their antiaircraft guns or defensive sangars by firing on it.

The spotter plane, I learned later, had contained some very high brass indeed: General Ira C. Eaker, commander of the Allied air forces in the Mediterranean, and his close friend General Jacob ("Jake") Devers, General Jumbo Wilson's deputy commander in chief of the Mediterranean theater of operations. Eaker and Devers identified what they believed was a military radio aerial sticking up out of the abbey's inner courtyard and thought they saw German soldiers moving about, entering and leaving the monastery.

A few hours later the monastery was bombarded with leaflets. They were fired by the field artillery in the Liri Valley in canisters that burst in the air over the abbey. The sample I obtained said, in Italian:

Italian Friends

BEWARE!

We have until now been especially careful to avoid shelling the Monte Cassino Monastery. The Germans have known how to benefit from this. But now the fighting has swept closer and closer to its sacred precincts. The time has come when we must train our guns on the Monastery itself.

We give you warning so that you may save yourselves. We warn you urgently to leave the Monastery. Leave it at once. Respect this warning. It is for your benefit.

THE FIFTH ARMY

The stage was set for the darkest episode of the Battle of Cassino, indeed, of the entire Italian campaign. No event of the war would cause more heated and lingering controversy than what happened the next day, February 15, 1944. Some of us, reporters and officers, had grandstand seats for the show on Monte Trocchio, the Allied observation post about four thousand yards south of Monte Cassino as the crow flies.

The fateful day dawned clear and crisp with a light wind, perfect flying weather. The first wave of about a hundred Flying Fortresses, flying high in formation, arrived over the target at 9:28 A.M. Faintly at first, then with rising crescendo, we could hear the screams of the bombs, the faraway muted rumble of their arrhythmic explosions, and the contrapuntal humming of the planes' engines as they passed overhead on their way back to their bases.

From the monastery buildings rose great orange bursts of flame. Then, for some minutes, an immense cloud of dust and smoke enveloped the scene. When it subsided, the abbey's roofline looked jagged and uneven, but the buildings seemed otherwise virtually intact. The centuries-old masonry of the outer walls had withstood the explosive force of more than a hundred tons of five-hundred-pound bombs. Pillars of grayish smoke climbed high into the blue, forming strange, evil-looking arabesques such as I had seen in paintings depicting Dante's version of hell.

Beside me a U.S. Signal Corps officer, peering through a powerful telescope mounted on a tripod, excitedly declared he saw many uniformed Germans—perhaps as many as forty or fifty—leaving the monastery and scurrying down the mountainside as the first bombs fell. Scanning the slopes with my own field glasses, I saw no signs of life, only dust, falling rocks, and debris.

The distant vapor trails of the first flight of B-17s still hovered overhead when a second wave of about one hundred bombers arrived at 9:45 A.M.

Apparently the U.S. Army Air Force was going all out to demonstrate the efficacy of high-level "pinpoint" saturation bombing in battlefield conditions, something never before attempted, and the monastery provided a perfect laboratory case. The planes dropped their bombs with deadly precision.

"Beautiful," shouted one of the observers. "Beautiful precision!"

Someone else growled, "Give 'em hell, boys! Let 'em have it."

Most onlookers merely stared as though hypnotized and said nothing. I heard a neighbor mutter, "My God!"

When the second flight had gone, what had been a monastery was a heap of rubble from which rose the smoke of several fires. The stout outer west wall of the abbey was still virtually intact, but not for long. A flight of eighty or more medium bombers—Mitchells and Marauders—administered the coup de grace with thousand-pound blockbusters. Some of the bombs fell close enough to us on Monte Trocchio to cause the ground to tremble and sent us scrambling for cover.

I watched the awesome spectacle with mixed emotions. It saddened me that one of civilization's sacred monuments was being destroyed before my eyes, and with it the probably irreplaceable frescoes and sculptures I had read about. Inwardly, however, I exulted that at long last a threat to our troops was being eliminated. Like so many officers and men involved in the Battle of Cassino, I had persuaded myself that the destruction of the monastery was indeed "a military necessity."

The Germans made good use of the raid for propaganda purposes. Radio Berlin roundly denounced the bombing as a flagrant example of Anglo-Saxon contempt for the sanctity of civilization's monuments and stoutly maintained there had been no German troops inside the abbey. This subsequently proved to be true, causing moralists in England and the United States to deplore the bombing almost as scathingly as Field Marshal Kesselring, who rejected Allied claims that his troops had occupied the abbey as "cynical and sanctimonious mendacity."

Militarily the demolition of the abbey only helped the Germans. They quickly fortified the resultant ruins and successfully repelled subsequent repeated attacks by Freyberg's troops. After three days and nights of some of the most vicious fighting of the entire Italian campaign, the rugged slopes of Monte Cassino were strewn with the bodies of dead New Zealanders and Indians. Like the Americans before them, Freyberg's troops had failed to break out into the Liri Valley, and when the guns fell silent on February 18, Rome remained as far away as ever.

Mark Clark ordered the demolition of the monastery to hasten his Fifth Army's conquest of Rome. But it didn't; more than three months of combat costly in Allied casualties were required before the general could be photographed entering the Eternal City in triumph. On the face of it, the bombing was yet another command error in the conduct of the bloody Battle of Cassino.

Years later Mark Clark admitted that the bombing had, in fact, been "a tragic mistake.... Not only an unnecessary mistake in the psychological field, but a tactical military mistake of the first magnitude. It only made the job more difficult, more costly in terms of men, machines and time." He said he had strenuously objected to the bombing, warning that the Germans would use the ruins as defensive positions. Nevertheless, he authorized the attack by the air force.

The responsibility, however, was not Clark's alone. He had consented to the bombing only under pressure from his superiors, Jumbo Wilson and the natty Alexander, who, in turn, had yielded to Freyberg's demands for demolition of the Benedictine abbey as the precondition for his attack on Cassino and Monastery Hill. It may fairly be said that the headstrong Freyberg virtually blackmailed Alexander and Clark into bombing the monastery, for he had the power to withdraw his troops from the battle if his demands were not met.

Of all this, however, correspondents covering the Cassino front remained in the dark. We did not know that Mark Clark had objected to the bombing of the abbey but had been overruled by Alexander, who, in turn, was being pressed by Winston Churchill to produce a "British" victory in Italy. We were encouraged to believe that the destruction of the monastery was the logical consequence of the fear that its presence engendered in the hearts and minds of the men who were ordered to capture it.

The bombing's failure to produce the hoped-for breakthrough into the Liri Valley merely deepened the general sense of disillusionment with the Italian campaign and exacerbated the already widespread cynicism among the combat troops about the competence of their high-ranking commanders, including Mark Clark. Remembering that cave somewhere behind Monte Trocchio filled with burlap bags containing the mangled remains of American soldiers, and recalling the disastrous consequences of the crossing of the Rapido by the Thirty-sixth Infantry Division, I, too, decided that General Clark was not quite the Clausewitz his public relations organization sought to paint him. Nor had I forgiven him for having apparently neglected to inform the navy beforehand that he had intended using a certain PT boat, on which I was a passenger, to visit the Anzio beachhead on the morning of January 28.

Shortly after the destruction of the abbey I went to Naples and soon wished I had stayed at the front. The city had become the rest and rehabilitation area of the Allied armies and a glaring example of Anglo-American ineptitude in dealing with the social, economic, and political problems of liberation.

62

PESTHOUSE IN PARADISE

It was late February; but winter was already slipping away, and the vague promise of spring was greeted in Naples by crowds of strollers along the Via Carraciolo, the broad boulevard that runs along the waterfront from Piedigrotta to Santa Lucia. Thousands of Neapolitans walked arm in arm, talking, laughing, crying, arguing, gesticulating, and taking the feeble sun. Most were shabbily dressed and poorly shod, and the women drew their shawls closely about them against the chill wind that came off the bay as they pushed through masses of Allied soldiery against a backdrop of ruined tenements and waterfront hotels.

Possibly because it was a Sunday afternoon, the boulevard's sidewalk cafés all were occupied, mostly by Allied troops and their girls, but also by family groups in their pathetic best, and Naples seemed noisier, busier, and more crowded than I had ever known it in prewar times. The trolleys were running again, as were the smelly diesel-powered buses and the funiculars that climbed the Vomero and Posillipo to the cream and brown villas of the bourgeoisie set in green gardens of myrtle and bougainvillaea high above the hovels of the proletariat. In the distance Vesuvius smoked as softly and solemnly as ever, enhancing the illusion that six months after its liberation Naples was alive again.

The impression that the city had returned to something approximating normality was shattered, however, at the water's edge. Standing on the float that held Zia Teresa's restaurant, badly damaged during the bombings but repaired now and serving as a French officers' mess, I saw the real Naples. The bay was crammed with Liberty ships, LCIs, and LSTs; hospital ships with huge red crosses painted on their sides were anchored in the ways. But the vessels the Germans had sunk at their berths were still there, most of the docks were still littered with the cranes and other machinery they had destroyed, and the harbor's waters had become a vast oil-streaked sewer of floating debris—bottles, beer cans, condoms, garbage, and countless nameless things—the detritus of war's winners and losers.

Meanwhile, Neapolitans and Allied soldiers mingled in a noisy moil in the Via Roma, the once splendid shopping street. The shopwindows, so full of luxury items soon after our victorious entry in October, were virtually empty now, their scanty stocks spread out in feeble attempts to make appealing displays. All advertised SOLDE! (sales) and promised GRANDE RIDUZZIONI in prices. Allied officers on three-day passes, singly or in twos, forage caps jauntily set at an angle and pockets bulging with occupation lire, prowled the Via Roma for female companionship and invariably found it. Prostitution was one of several "cottage industries" the Neapolitans had devised to survive.

Posters warned the troops that "Girls Who Take Boarders Provide Social Disorders," but the warnings had little effect. "PRO" stations where the men could obtain prophylactics and postcoital prophylaxis were as numerous as MP stations and operated around the clock. They could be found in the nightly blackout by lighted orange globes over their entrances. At the Psychological Warfare Board an army major told me that in a nubile population estimated at 150,000 no fewer than 46,000 young women were engaged in full-time or occasional prostitution. The VD rate among our soldiers, he said, was "appalling." Naples, he said, had become a "pesthouse." Syphilis was rampant.

Among the city's most active pimps were the *scugnizzi*, those grimy, ragged, pestiferous boys who were as much a part of the Neapolitan scene as hunger, squalor, and Vesuvius. They threaded through the crowds like ferrets, importuning GIs, Tommies, Frenchies, or Poles for money, cigarettes, candy, food, whatever they could scrounge. They also offered their sisters for a price: "Hey, Joe, wanna piecea arse? Too tousan' lire . . ."

Street-wise and tough, the boys were the product of Europe's biggest baby factory. Ranging in age between ten and fifteen, they hung like leeches, rarely responding to a GI's mere "Scram, you dirty little ginzo, *capeesh*?" and had to be cuffed or kicked out of the way by the annoyed conqueror, especially if the latter was heavily occupied in trying to make it with a signorina on a street corner or across one of the café tables in the teeming Corso Umberto.

Artful begging, mostly by slatterns carrying "rented" babies with hungry eyes and faces with running sores, was another Neapolitan industry. I saw more beggars in Naples, where they were always numerous and exigent, than I had ever seen before. They infested the Via Roma and the *corso*, patrolled the lines forming outside the San Carlo Opera, and badgered customers waiting at the entrances of several movie houses.

By far the most important local "industry," however, was *la borsa nera* (the black market), the biggest, most vicious in all wartime Europe. The illicit traffic in food and consumer goods had existed under fascism and had flourished during the German occupation, but after our arrival in October 1943 it assumed gigantic proportions, and what I had hoped would be a holiday from war turned into a weeks-long study of the failures of the Allied Military Government in its first field test in governing a liberated people.

The Naples I knew in the late 1930s was an overcrowded, exuberant, excessively noisy city, at once gay and touchingly sad, whose approximately one million inhabitants lived intensively in their streets and piazzas, using them as their workshops, marketplaces, and living rooms. In fact, the former capital of Bourbon kings was in those days a sort of vast "people's theater" that produced at times comic opera, at others real-life drama. Its actors were for the most part incredibly poor and lived in squalor without much hope of improving their lot except by emigration, which was forbidden by the Fascist regime, and crime, which flourished even in Mussolini's time.

The ruling criminal element was a secret society known as the Camorra, the Neapolitan equivalent of the Sicilian Mafia, and the Fascists were no more successful in rooting out the camorristi than they were in their efforts to rid Sicily of the mafiosi. Naples remained the neglected capital of neglected southern Italy, a city with one third of its workers permanently unemployed but surviving somehow as street peddlers, organ-grinders, bootblacks, itinerant tinkers, petty thieves, pickpockets, pimps, and prostitutes.

The Neapolitans found relief from hunger in their Catholicism and in making music, much of it gay, all of it sentimental, its lyrics written in a Neapolitan dialect that was virtually a separate language. I acquired a smattering of it in my childhood, listening to the songs and nostalgic conversations of our neighbors in Philadelphia's Little Italy.

"Vedi Napoli e poi muori! [See Naples and die!]" they used to say, and after Rome, the city that shone brightest in my youthful yearnings for ancestral Italia was their Napoli.

Nature endowed Naples with a setting of incomparable beauty. Wonderfully situated on the northern shore of one of the world's most celebrated bays, it forms a multilevel amphitheater on the slopes of the Vomero and Posillipo, the hills facing volcanic Vesuvius and a great harbor open to the blue Tyrrhenian Sea, its wide entrance flanked by the gray-brown islands of Ischia and Capri. I fell in love with the city when I saw it for the first time in 1936, and after exploring its ancient alleys, its narrow stepped streets, its museums, and the life in its animated piazzas and boulevards, I found myself agreeing with Stendhal that Naples, not Rome, was the "real capital of Italy."

It grieved me to see what the war had done to Naples when I returned with the Fifth Army in October 1943. Between us, the Germans and we had wrought irreparable damage to what was always the poorest but also the gayest, most fiercely individualistic city in Mediterranean Europe. From what I saw then of the destruction, and of the hunger and misery of the Neapolitans, I doubted that Naples could ever be restored as a living urban entity. The city lay in ruins. The Allies had bombed it; the retreating Germans had wrecked it and mined it. The people were starving.

To their everlasting credit, the officers of the AMG, with the help of army engineers, quickly restored the city's transportation system, and when I arrived from Cassino, Naples also had electricity, water, even gas to cook with, though very little for its people's cookpots. Schools and universities were open, a few fairly good restaurants were back in business, and there was even a nightclub in Piedigrotta with a barrel organ that played four tunes for dancing.

The American officers of the AMG landed in Italy after a sketchy "orientation course" in a school in Charlottesville, Virginia, and armed with a 278-page volume of plans, proclamations, and instructions on how to rule a conquered people. Unfortunately, the manual contained little or nothing about how to deal with the Neapolitans' penchant for *contrabbandismo*, the art of "dealing in contraband," the kind of banditry that quickly produced the city's black market, which by mid-March was big business even by American standards.

According to figures I obtained at the Psychological Warfare Board, 65 percent of the per capita income of Neapolitans came from transactions in stolen Allied goods, and at least one third of all imported supplies was disappearing in the *borsa nera*. Every single item of Allied food and equipment, short of guns and ammunition—both readily available, however, "under the table"—was openly displayed for sale in stalls along the Via Forcella.

Tailors all over Naples were taking stolen Allied uniforms apart, dying the material a muddy brown or black, and turning it into smart new outfits for civilians able to pay the price. I saw men and women going to the movies or the opera in suits and coats made from stolen U.S. Army blankets. Men and boys were increasingly shod in officers' shoes or GI combat boots. Frequent raids were made; the culprits were tried, found guilty, and sent to jail at Poggio Reale, but they easily bribed their way out.

Everything imaginable was obtainable on the black market. You could buy "imported" cognac, gin, and whiskey for 1,000 lire ($10) a bottle. American corned beef stolen from army stores was available at 120 lire ($1.20), canned ham at 200 lire ($2), fresh eggs at 35 lire (35 cents) *each*. The prices were high and out of reach of Neapolitan workers, those lucky enough to have jobs, who earned an average of 30 lire (30 cents) a day, and famine stalked the working-class districts.

The high prices were partly the fault of the AMG policy of fixing the value of the lira at 100 to the dollar, thereby automatically creating an inflation of 400 percent. The low rate provided plenty of spending money for the GIs, who promptly bought up everything shopkeepers had to sell, but worked hardship on people with fixed incomes. On the Via Roma I paid ten dollars for a two-dollar pair of kidskin ladies' gloves to take home. The salaried middle class found itself in a desperate plight.

Entire shiploads of American supplies disappeared into the black market. I was still in Naples when a shipment of sugar vanished—along with the train that hauled it away from the dock! The sugar wound up in the *borsa nera*, where it was sold for four hundred lire a kilo. The switching engine and the two freight cars involved were eventually traced to a steel mill at nearby Pozzuoli, where they became scrap for the furnaces. The thieves were never caught.

By mid-March the black market was a colossal racket involving victors and vanquished, Americans and Neapolitans. Truth had long since become a casualty of the Italian campaign; but censorship was even stricter in Naples than at the front, and the lurid story of what was happening remained untold. Back home, readers never learned from our wartime dispatches that some of their sons, brothers, husbands, and fiancés were enriching themselves by selling in the black market not only their rations of cigarettes and food but also whatever they could steal from Allied supply depots. Many were living high off the hog in comfortable apartments, complete with servants and mistresses, and riding about in cars illegally commandeered from civilians.

In the meantime, Naples had become the Peninsular Base Section of the Allied armies, the new crossroads of the world for Allied troops and correspondents. It was the Cairo of the Italian campaign minus its luxuries but with much the same feeling that the war, though it was being fought only some fifty miles away, was a remote affair, something happening in a world apart.

The PBS was an agglomeration of smartly uniformed administrators of the AMG, quartermasters, Special Services officers, public relations sections, representatives of the adjutant general's office, military police, British and American security organizations, Red Cross girls—in short, a vast assortment of noncombat personnel who kept regular hours doing desk work and spent their free time going to dinner parties, touring the picturesque countryside in borrowed army vehicles, and having a wonderful time while men bled at Cassino.

For every man at the front there seemed to be twenty or more behind the lines to supply the individual warrior with the essentials of combat and personal welfare and to look after him when he came to Naples for R&R. The amenities for the GI on leave were simple enough, consisting of "snack bars" and USO "clubs" run by Red Cross girls who usually were far more interested in their own social lives than in helping the war's Private First Class Smiths enjoy their brief respites from combat.

For the PBS officers, on the other hand, there were exclusive dining and dancing clubs in which parties were organized well in advance in the calm certainty that the war would not interfere. Social climbers among them did their utmost to find friends among the members of the Italian nobility, Fascist or not, who inhabited the fine villas on the Vomero.

Meanwhile, plain GIs became intimates, almost members, of working-class Neapolitan families, exchanging rations for home cooking and companionship. These were mostly poor boys of immigrant Italian parents homesick for the closely knit family ties of their upbringing. Others—men who had spent their youth in poolrooms—passed their time in Neapolitan bars, picking up girls with whom intercourse meant playing Russian roulette with VD.

Particularly obnoxious was a coterie of officers who served as "special advisers" and "aides" in various headquarters. They were billeted in the best hotels, where they seemed to be well supplied with bubbly wines and whiskey and lavishly entertained visiting movie stars and USO performers. Reporters had difficulty obtaining transportation, but not the socialites; army vehicles seemed to be at their disposal whenever they wanted them for trips to Amalfi, Sorrento, and Ravello, and they often flew off on mysterious "missions" to Cairo, Algiers, Casablanca, or Washington.

There were also Italo-American gangster types from the slums of Chicago, New York, and Philadelphia whose only qualification for service in the AMG was their sketchy knowledge of the Italian language in the Neapolitan, Calabrian, or Sicilian dialects of their parents. They made common cause with the Camorra and traded as viciously in the black market as the camorristi who ran it.

The corruption was at its worst in the dank, smelly, narrow back streets of the Bassi, where the poorest of the poor lived. Into their alleyways *scugnizzi* lured drunken black GIs with promises of sex with white women, then rolled them, stripped them of everything they possessed, and left them naked in the gutter to be collected by MP patrols.

The Bassi was off limits to Allied troops, but it was where the uncontrolled whorehouses were located. In the Via Roma and the *corso* the girls sold themselves for occupation lire, but in the Bassi they traded sex for C rations and canned beef or for cigarettes, silk stockings, lipsticks, and other items exchangeable for food on the black market or salable for many times their real value.

Despite the apparent abundance on the *borsa nera*, famine stalked the back streets of Naples, and Lieutenant Colonel Carl Kraege, the AMG commander of the Naples area, whom I interviewed in his bleak office in a midtown palazzo, admitted no immediate solution for the food shortage was in sight. Kraege, a former Naval Academy footballer and boxer who later became a prosperous Green Bay, Wisconsin, businessman, said he needed at least seventy-six thousand tons of food a month to break the black market but was receiving less than eight thousand. Shipping was in short supply, and the port was busy with military traffic.

Moreover, said Kraege, there seemed to be little understanding at the American end about what foods were required. The Neapolitans understood only bread, pasta, dried beans and peas, olive oil, and cheese. But he had recently received a shipload of dehydrated soup mix. The Neapolitans had no idea what to do with it. His greatest concern, however, was the steady disappearance into the black market of such shipments as did arrive. The colonel passed a despairing hand across a damp brow.

"I'm up against something I just don't understand," he said, "and nothing in my manual gives me a clue to a solution. . . ."

Kraege, one of the ablest of the AMG administrators produced by the crash course in governing liberated peoples at the Charlottesville school, was up against a formidable racket mysteriously run by Americans with Mafia connections who had turned up in Italy as advisers to the AMG.*

Taxpayers back home would have been outraged had they known the truth about how hundreds, indeed, thousands of their soldier sons lived in the "base areas." Many were making more money than they had as civilians, lived in better homes, visited picturesque areas, entertained in great style at government expense, and were entertained in turn by lonely contessas and marchesas who had lost Fascist husbands, permanently or temporarily, in the war. The cushy lives of the PBS men poisoned the hearts and minds of combat troops, and in Naples the togetherness, selflessness, and sense of common purpose that characterized life at the front broke down into bitter antagonisms. Relations between PBS men, who wore tan-colored uniforms, and "real soldiers," who dressed in olive drab, became so strained that on the road GIs would not pick up hitchhiking soldiers attired in tan.

Many PBS men, however, were unhappy with their lot and tried to volunteer for combat duty. None that I knew of ever made it, their fates having been decided by whoever operated the vast impersonal machinery of military life. Few PBS rebels had a good word to say for their area commander, Major General Arthur Wilson, a stern disciplinarian of the spit-and-polish school who emulated his old-school-tie British counterparts to the extent of carrying a swagger stick.

Wilson's inspectors patrolled the streets of Naples and woe to the poor GI who, returning from the front exhausted, failed to salute an officer or whose uniform happened to be in disarray as he strolled the Via Roma. Soldiers called Wilson the Nero of Naples. He was far more unpopular with the troops than Mark Clark, who was, after all, a fighting general.

The enemy rarely disturbed the hectic social life of the PBS men. Our air forces had total control of the air over southern Italy, and the Germans seldom penetrated it with their bombers. But the busy port of Naples remained their occasional target, and one night in mid-March the air-raid sirens sounded. I was staying at the Terminus Hotel, in the Via della Liberta, not far from Santa Lucia, and when the bombs started falling, the place shook as if in the grip of an earthquake; but knowing the air-raid shelters to be foul and crawling with typhus-bearing lice, I stayed in bed.

Early the next morning I went to see the results. As usual, the bombs had fallen on a densely populated waterfront quarter and caused heavy casualties among the poor. Frantic crowds ran through the streets screaming, "Out with

* The name most frequently mentioned as one of the ringleaders of the *borsa nera* by both American and British intelligence officers was that of Vito Genovese, head of one of New York's Mafia "families," but I was never able to confirm their allegations. The head of the AMG after it was succeeded by the Allied Control Commission was Colonel Charles Poletti, a former lieutenant governor of the state of New York and a man above reproach.

the soldiers! Give us peace!" Victims, some of them mere babies, were still being dug out of the ruins when I arrived, and I found myself engulfed by Neapolitans. I had to push and elbow my way through grief-stricken families and the dozens of professional mourners they had hired to underscore their bereavement.

A few days later, on March 19, Vesuvius erupted. It was a majestic sight, and I went up to the top of Posillipo by funicular for a better view. Smoke from the crater rose many thousands of feet into the blue sky and formed a grotesque, seemingly solid white mass, immense and fearsome and shaped like a human brain. As night fell, the volcano's mouth spewed serpentine streaks of fiery lava that streamed down the face of the mountain and formed a wide, golden red river of fire, awesome to behold and in what it portended for anyone or anything in its irregular downward path.

The Neapolitans were certain the eruption was God's vengeance for the destruction of the abbey of Monte Cassino, and I confess that the absurd thought crossed my mind. Whatever the cause, not even the oldest inhabitants I talked with had ever seen anything like it. The newspapers said it was the worst eruption since 1872, and everyone agreed Naples was spared by its patron saint, San Gennaro, revered for sixteen centuries as a worker of miracles on the city's behalf.

The saint's congealed blood is contained in two vials in his cathedral, the Duomo, and is supposed to liquefy on the first Saturday in May and sometime during the seven days that follow September 19, the day of his martyrdom A.D. 305. If the liquefaction fails to occur, the citizens expect dire consequences for their city. When it failed to do so in 1527, there was a plague; in 1569, a famine; and in 1941—the Allied bombings!

Following the Vesuvian pyrotechnics, fears spread that the blood of San Gennaro might not liquefy. High-ranking intelligence officials were alarmed, for such a failure might be exploited by anti-Allied troublemakers to set off large-scale rioting of the kind that frequently had happened in Neapolitan history. But this time the blood liquefied and the crisis passed.

During an exhausting month covering what was essentially a lurid police story of corruption and crime on a vast scale, I rarely glimpsed the mysteriously enchanting Naples I once knew. And only the songs I heard—"O Sole Mio" and "Torna a Sorrento"—and the view from the hilltops suggested *la bella Napoli* so dear to the hearts of my South Philly boyhood's neighbors.

But there were unmistakable stirrings under the rubble, and even in its half-life the city's appeal was irresistible. The Neapolitans were clearly determined not to die. They had survived the Bourbons, fascism, and the Germans. By the time I was ready to leave, I felt fairly certain they would also survive the Anglo-American conquest.

The hopeful signs were mostly political. The arrival of the Allies in 1943 had revived the Camorra and created an even bigger one, but it had also revived, not only in Naples but throughout southern Italy, a desire for freedom by people who had not known any for twenty-one years.

The Italians seemed to be struggling to achieve the republic for which

Mazzini and Garibaldi had fought and bled during the middle decades of the previous century. By the time I left Naples the struggle had only just begun. It would be continued in Rome after the capital finally fell to Mark Clark and the Fifth Army on June 5.

But I wasn't in Rome to attend the general's numerous appearances in his role as conqueror of the first enemy capital to fall to an American army. From Naples I had flown to New York via Algiers and Casablanca in early April, hoping *Collier's* would assign me to the impending cross-Channel invasion. I had begun covering the war in Paris in 1939 and had dreamed of marching up the Champs-Élysées with Eisenhower's forces, but Charley Colebaugh, my good friend and editor, died of a heart attack in May, and his successor, Henry La Cossitt, eager to increase the magazine's circulation, hired Ernest Hemingway for the job.

I wish I could say I took the blow gracefully, but I didn't. While I fully appreciated the fact that Papa Hemingway's signature over dispatches from the front outweighed mine by a ton or two, I sulked for a while before accepting reassignment to the Mediterranean front.

What really irked me even more than having been shunted aside in favor of Hemingway, was Papa's rather arrogant and unfounded assumption, expressed over double whiskeys at the Marguery bar, that I hadn't really coveted the Normandy assignment but had begged off because I believed it too dangerous. "There's a lot of courage in a bottle of gin," he suggested in a smallish voice that somehow didn't match his machismo. I was so flabbergasted by what he said that I made no reply but downed my drink and left him the check. We never met again.

63

AVE, ROMA IMMORTALIS

I returned to Rome, the capital of the Catholic Church, in the company of its archbishop of New York, the Very Reverend Francis J. Spellman. We met on board the transatlantic flying boat that flew us to North Africa, and at Casablanca, where we landed at daybreak one mid-July morning in 1944, the kindly prelate offered me a lift to the Eternal City in his plane, a DC-3 comfortably furnished with upholstered armchairs.

The archbishop was short, almost tubby, with the round face and small mouth of a cherub, intelligent eyes behind steel-rimmed spectacles, and delicate well-kept hands. He smiled easily and conversed in a light, rather high-pitched voice, but behind the bland exterior one sensed courage and an iron will. He would need both in his self-appointed task of becoming, in his words, the "parish priest" of the American troops in Italy.

Spellman was, in a sense, a colleague, for *Collier's* had commissioned him to write a series of articles based on his experiences. In addition to Hemingway, the ruling high priest of American letters, our new editor had hired an archbishop of the Holy Roman Church to help boost the magazine's circulation.

For Spellman the journey was a return to the city of his student days as a seminarian, and he told me he looked forward to an audience with the Holy Father, whom he revered.

For me personally, it was a return to the city I had called home during the violent years that had spanned some of the seminal events of the Second World War: the Ethiopian War, the Spanish Civil War, democracy's sellout at Munich, and the formation of the Rome-Berlin Axis, the marriage of fascism to nazism that had precipitated modern history's longest and bloodiest war.

I had left Rome disenchanted shortly after the coronation of Eugenio Pacelli as pope in the early spring of 1939, hating the city as the capital of fascism and detesting most Romans as a people who had allowed themselves to be manipulated by Benito Mussolini into accepting a regime that denied them freedom of speech, assembly, press, and even thought while he talked peace and plotted war. But returning after an absence of more than half a decade, I forgot how much I had grown to dislike Rome and the Romans—the city and the people of absurd youthful yearnings for kinship with the land of my forefathers—and remembered only Rome's subtle charms, its charisma as the living monument of our long march to civilization, and the home of many friends.

Approaching from the sea, the pilot followed the course of the Tiber, and soon the Eternal City was below us, an irregular pattern of mellow whites, browns, and pastel tints broken by splotches of dark green that I knew to be the pines and cypresses of the Villa Borghese and the gardens of the Pincio. The cupolas of a myriad churches rose russet in the early-afternoon sun, and Spellman gasped when he saw the dome of St. Peter's rising majestically above a great piazza enclosed by the arms of Bernini's colonnades.

The plane overflew the city for the archbishop's benefit, and familiar landmarks came into view: the Vatican with its austere, formal gardens; residential villas with pink-tiled roofs, their ocher walls veined with flowering vines; treelined streets; the Forum of the Caesars; the hulks of giant ruins stripped naked long ago by generations of papal architects greedy for marble for the palazzi of their princes; and one monument to Rome's recent Caesar, the starkly white elongated oval of the Foro Mussolini with its peripheral parade of heroic statues. In the distance we saw green Monte Mario and the guardian Alban Hills, and as the plane turned for its approach to the airport at Ciampino, we glimpsed the pyramid that keeps vigil over the graves of Keats and Shelley in the adjacent Protestant Cemetery.

Rome had been declared an "open city," not to be defended even if attacked, but the great gray-black blob of twisted rails, fused freight cars, and fire-blackened sheds that had been the San Lorenzo marshaling yards reminded us of the massive Allied bombing of Rome of July 19, 1943. There were several hundred casualties, and our bombs had damaged the Basilica of San Lorenzo Fuori le Mura. The pope, Spellman said, had gone at once to the scene to bless the dead and to comfort the wounded and the homeless.

Ciampino Airport, where we landed, was a shambles. Our air forces had bombed it, too, and the Nazis had blown up what was left before they withdrew on the morning of June 4, when Mark Clark and his Fifth Army were at Rome's gates.

Never before had the world's most historic city been conquered in a campaign from south to north. What Hannibal and Napoleon dared not try, Clark and his troops had accomplished, though in about as difficult, bloody, heart-less, and heartbreaking a campaign as military history had ever recorded.

The only transportation at the airport was the black Lancia limousine the Vatican had sent for the archbishop, who saw at once I would be stranded and insisted on taking me into town. We rode along the Via Appia through green-ing fields aglow with buttercups and red poppies, past the stark arches of an ancient Roman aqueduct that someone had dubbed "the ribs of twenty centu-ries," and into the heart of Rome.

The car dropped me off at the Hotel Excelsior, on the Via Veneto. The concierge remembered me and took charge of my baggage, but he couldn't find me a room, not even for a substantial tip, though he made a great show of searching his register. The hotel, he explained, had been taken over by the high brass of Rome's new Anglo-American rulers, and he suggested I try the Albergo de la Ville, in the Via Sistina, where, he said, the American correspon-dents were billeted. He would look after my bags while I investigated.

I knew a shortcut to the de la Ville, but I took the long way, down the Via Veneto to the Piazza Barberini, then up the Via Sistina toward Trinità dei Monti. A good two or three hours of daylight remained before sundown, and the walk would enable me to get the feel of liberated Rome. The outward signs of change were instantly visible and audible. There was no water in the foun-tains whose splash and sparkle had imparted life to the Rome I knew, but there were new sounds: the growl and grind of traffic, horn tooting, and the voices of people talking.

Nearly two months had elapsed since the bells in the campaniles of the city's eight hundred churches had rung their collective greeting to Mark Clark and his troops, but to judge by the volume of noise the Romans generated, they were still celebrating their liberation. The city seemed alive again with a vitality it had not known for almost a quarter of a century, and I took it all in as I threaded my way down the Via Veneto through the sidewalk crowds of Allied soldiers and Romans, the latter walking in twos and threes, talking, arguing, gesticulating, much like the Neapolitans, but mirthless. I heard no laughter.

The tables of the several cafés along the way were fully occupied, for it was *l'ora del aperitivo* (cocktail hour), and while there was no gin or whiskey, there seemed to be plenty of vermouth. At the foot of the Via Veneto where it enters the Piazza Barberini, I stopped at a café, found a place at one of its tables opposite Bernini's lifeless fountain of the *Triton*, ordered a Carpano, and watched the passing parade. The whore ladies were out in force, somewhat shabbily dressed, and wearing too much makeup, but saucy as ever as they sashayed past on the arms of American officers. Some, walking singly or in twos, had shaved heads, the price they had paid for having been too friendly with the enemy, which they tried to disguise with colorful turbans and floppy hats, their eyes darting catlike left and right for prospects.

Under fascism even Rome's pedestrians were regimented and required to use one-way sidewalks. Allowed to cross only at designated points, people often had to walk blocks out of their way to reach their destinations or pay fines for violating the rule. Now the Romans wandered all over the streets, good-naturedly bumping into each other, dodging Jeeps and staff cars, or snaking their way through the traffic on bicycles.

From where I sat, the sculptured face of Bernini's *Triton* seemed to reflect the wonder I felt at Rome's noisy emergence from Mussolinian conformity and silence. The dictator had forbidden all horn tooting, but now the city's dominant sounds were the honkings the traffic produced. GI drivers tooted their way through the crowds and around the few horse-drawn *carrozze*, the only apparent means of public transportation.

Although most of the traffic was military, it included an astonishing number of private vehicles. Sipping my drink, I counted a score of Lancia and Fiat sedans in half an hour, their chauffeurs all uninhibitedly using their horns as they thundered up and down the Via Veneto.

More indicative of change, however, was the fact that the Romans had found their tongues again. Under Mussolini, if they talked at all in public, they whispered. Now they talked, incessantly and at *alta voce*, mainly in *romanaccio*, the wonderfully expressive dialect that is to Italian roughly what Brooklynese is to English. The snatches of sidewalk conversations that I overheard reflected popular concern with problems similar to those that plagued the Neapolitans: the iniquities of the *borsa nera*, the scarcity and high prices of food, the housing shortage, and the shortcomings of the city's Allied administration.

After a generation of Fascist repression the moment of rebirth was at hand. But what I heard and saw in the streets during my first hour in Rome depressed me. Although physically intact, Rome was suffering. The horn tooting and the jaywalking were misleading. The mood of the crowds was not happy. The grumbling indicated Rome might become, perhaps already had become, another Naples.

Hunger was etched on many of the faces I saw, and there was no doubt that a certain class of Roman women was dealing with it by trading sex for money or creature comforts. But were the complaints I overheard justified? The Romans as a whole had not been subjected to the incessant Allied bombings and other hardships the Neapolitans had endured. Then why were the people so visibly unhappy?

Entering the Via Sistina and needing a haircut and shave, I stopped at the barbershop whose *padrone*, Angelo, had trimmed my hair at least once a month for years. I remembered him affectionately for the subtle anti-Fascist jokes with which he sprinkled his barber talk whenever there was no one else in the shop.

A tall, spare man with a beaked nose and wavy gray hair, Angelo was seated in his barber's chair reading a newspaper when I entered. He greeted me warmly, quipped that it was about time I showed up—he said he had already served many of my colleagues—and waved me to his chair. I was soon being lathered with cold water from an earthen jug and the same soap powder, and his troops had accomplished, though in about as difficult, bloody, heartless, and heartbreaking a campaign as military history had ever recorded.

The only transportation at the airport was the black Lancia limousine the Vatican had sent for the archbishop, who saw at once I would be stranded and insisted on taking me into town. We rode along the Via Appia through greening fields aglow with buttercups and red poppies, past the stark arches of an ancient Roman aqueduct that someone had dubbed "the ribs of twenty centuries," and into the heart of Rome.

The car dropped me off at the Hotel Excelsior, on the Via Veneto. The concierge remembered me and took charge of my baggage, but he couldn't find me a room, not even for a substantial tip, though he made a great show of searching his register. The hotel, he explained, had been taken over by the high brass of Rome's new Anglo-American rulers, and he suggested I try the Albergo de la Ville, in the Via Sistina, where, he said, the American correspondents were billeted. He would look after my bags while I investigated.

I knew a shortcut to the de la Ville, but I took the long way, down the Via Veneto to the Piazza Barberini, then up the Via Sistina toward Trinità dei Monti. A good two or three hours of daylight remained before sundown, and the walk would enable me to get the feel of liberated Rome. The outward signs of change were instantly visible and audible. There was no water in the fountains whose splash and sparkle had imparted life to the Rome I knew, but there were new sounds: the growl and grind of traffic, horn tooting, and the voices of people talking.

Nearly two months had elapsed since the bells in the campaniles of the city's eight hundred churches had rung their collective greeting to Mark Clark and his troops, but to judge by the volume of noise the Romans generated, they were still celebrating their liberation. The city seemed alive again with a vitality it had not known for almost a quarter of a century, and I took it all in as I threaded my way down the Via Veneto through the sidewalk crowds of Allied soldiers and Romans, the latter walking in twos and threes, talking, arguing, gesticulating, much like the Neapolitans, but mirthless. I heard no laughter.

The tables of the several cafés along the way were fully occupied, for it was *l'ora del aperitivo* (cocktail hour), and while there was no gin or whiskey, there seemed to be plenty of vermouth. At the foot of the Via Veneto where it enters the Piazza Barberini, I stopped at a café, found a place at one of its tables opposite Bernini's lifeless fountain of the *Triton*, ordered a Carpano, and watched the passing parade. The whore ladies were out in force, somewhat shabbily dressed, and wearing too much makeup, but saucy as ever as they sashayed past on the arms of American officers. Some, walking singly or in twos, had shaved heads, the price they had paid for having been too friendly with the enemy, which they tried to disguise with colorful turbans and floppy hats, their eyes darting catlike left and right for prospects.

Under fascism even Rome's pedestrians were regimented and required to use one-way sidewalks. Allowed to cross only at designated points, people often had to walk blocks out of their way to reach their destinations or pay fines for violating the rule. Now the Romans wandered all over the streets, good-naturedly bumping into each other, dodging Jeeps and staff cars, or snaking their way through the traffic on bicycles.

From where I sat, the sculptured face of Bernini's *Triton* seemed to reflect the wonder I felt at Rome's noisy emergence from Mussolinian conformity and silence. The dictator had forbidden all horn tooting, but now the city's dominant sounds were the honkings the traffic produced. GI drivers tooted their way through the crowds and around the few horse-drawn *carrozze*, the only apparent means of public transportation.

Although most of the traffic was military, it included an astonishing number of private vehicles. Sipping my drink, I counted a score of Lancia and Fiat sedans in half an hour, their chauffeurs all uninhibitedly using their horns as they thundered up and down the Via Veneto.

More indicative of change, however, was the fact that the Romans had found their tongues again. Under Mussolini, if they talked at all in public, they whispered. Now they talked, incessantly and at *alta voce*, mainly in *romanaccio*, the wonderfully expressive dialect that is to Italian roughly what Brooklynese is to English. The snatches of sidewalk conversations that I overheard reflected popular concern with problems similar to those that plagued the Neapolitans: the iniquities of the *borsa nera*, the scarcity and high prices of food, the housing shortage, and the shortcomings of the city's Allied administration.

After a generation of Fascist repression the moment of rebirth was at hand. But what I heard and saw in the streets during my first hour in Rome depressed me. Although physically intact, Rome was suffering. The horn tooting and the jaywalking were misleading. The mood of the crowds was not happy. The grumbling indicated Rome might become, perhaps already had become, another Naples.

Hunger was etched on many of the faces I saw, and there was no doubt that a certain class of Roman women was dealing with it by trading sex for money or creature comforts. But were the complaints I overheard justified? The Romans as a whole had not been subjected to the incessant Allied bombings and other hardships the Neapolitans had endured. Then why were the people so visibly unhappy?

Entering the Via Sistina and needing a haircut and shave, I stopped at the barbershop whose *padrone*, Angelo, had trimmed my hair at least once a month for years. I remembered him affectionately for the subtle anti-Fascist jokes with which he sprinkled his barber talk whenever there was no one else in the shop.

A tall, spare man with a beaked nose and wavy gray hair, Angelo was seated in his barber's chair reading a newspaper when I entered. He greeted me warmly, quipped that it was about time I showed up—he said he had already served many of my colleagues—and waved me to his chair. I was soon being lathered with cold water from an earthen jug and the same soap powder,

faintly scented with lavender, that he had always used. Unless otherwise
ordered, he habitually shaved a customer before cutting his hair, and I remarked that *evidentemente,* nothing had changed. This triggered a torrent of
words.

Angelo was glad the Germans were gone, of course, but he was decidedly
unhappy about what the *alleati* were doing to Rome. Drunken Allied soldiers
were misbehaving in bars and cafés; Rome was becoming *un vero bordello* (a
regular whorehouse). Worst of all, he said, the Allies were not living up to their
promises to end the people's hardships as soon as the *tedeschi* were driven out.

"Nearly two months, and we still have no gas to cook with," he said. "The
electricity is rationed, water is only available at certain public fountains and
has to be carried away in receptacles, and the black market is eating us alive."

Angelo reeled off a list of black-market prices for food more or less the
same as those in Naples, but what irked him most was the high price of
charcoal: thirty-five lire a kilo, and at least six kilos were needed, he said, to
cook a simple meal of pasta and a few vegetables. "Sometimes," he said, "the
charcoal costs more than the food." Olive oil and cheese were scarce, meat had
become a distant memory, and there was no salt to be had at any price. While
plying his whisk broom in the international barber's ritual that precedes paying
the bill, he volunteered more information.

"Some of my old Fascist clients are saying that we were better off when
we were worse off," Angelo said. "But that is not true. We are free now, and
we will make a better Italy, a democratic Italy like the one I knew when my
class was called to the colors in 1914. That's what the newspapers are saying,
and I believe them, though from what I hear we shall have to build our country
all over again, brick by brick, stone by stone. I saw what happened at San
Lorenzo, and a lot of Italy must look like what I saw there."

I glanced at the masthead of the newspaper he had been reading. It was
L'Unità, the organ of the Communist party and of Italy's *partigiani,* the
partisans. Angelo was one of millions who had never joined the Fascist party.

The barber charged me the equivalent of two dollars for his services and
sternly refused the pack of Chesterfields I offered in addition to his gratuity.
He said he preferred his own Nazionali. Clearly, however, what he really
preferred was his self-respect.

I remembered the Albergo de la Ville as a modest "family hotel" where
middle-class European tourists stayed. Recently it had housed German officers, and it was now a somewhat seedy billet for a horde of American newsreel
cameramen, still photographers, and reporters.

As usual, the public relations people who ran the place had taken its best
accommodations for themselves, and the working stiffs of the press corps got
the leavings. The treatment accorded me by the billeting officer—he wore the
silver bar of a first looey—smacked of the arrogance I had encountered among
his kind in Naples.

"Best I can do, mister," he said when I balked at being assigned to a tiny

room facing the noisy inner courtyard. "And no visiting civilians above the
lobby floor," he added. "All interviews must be conducted in the ground-floor
reception room reserved for the purpose. That's the way security wants it."

But my broom closet of a room had a bathroom with tepid water in the
tap that said CALDA and, amazingly, a telephone that worked. I used it to call
the concierge at the Excelsior, who promised to have my baggage delivered
before curfew.

Awaiting its arrival, I went down to the officers' bar off the lobby and
ordered a gin and lime from the white-coated Italian waiter. Someone directly
behind me said, "I'll have the same." Turning, I looked into the welcome,
smiling round face of Ralph Forte, a close friend of many years whom I hadn't
seen since the early days of the blitz in London.

We were discussing where to dine to celebrate our reunion when my
baggage arrived on a handcart drawn coolie fashion by a perspiring elderly
porter in Excelsior livery. The man's eyes widened when I tipped him with a
crisp one-dollar bill instead of the standard hundred-lire occupation money,
and he was so effusive with his thanks that when he left, I turned to Ralph
for an explanation. After all, I had only given the man the equivalent of a
hundred lire.

"Sure, that's the official AMG rate," Ralph said, "but apart from the fact
that that buck represents nearly three times his daily wage, he'll sell it to the
black-market money changers for two hundred, maybe three hundred lire,
enough to buy his family half a kilo of veal. The veal might turn out to be horse,
but it will be meat, something he probably hasn't tasted for months. But I
know where we can have genuine veal cutlets à la milanese. . . ."

Ralph led the way through the now-silent blacked-out streets to the narrow, cobbled Via Mario dei Fiori and one of my favorite restaurants, Ranieri,
where my wife and I had often entertained Roman friends and visitors from
America. We were royally received by Signor Ranieri, the proprietor, looking
thinner, older, and grayer than I remembered him, and Nello, the headwaiter,
elegant as ever in the uniform of his profession: tailcoat, black tie, wing collar,
black vest. *"Che bella sorpresa,"* he said, conducting us ceremoniously to his
best corner table, where Signor Ranieri uncorked a bottle of Asti Spumante,
filled Ralph's glass and mine, poured a few drops into his own, and toasted
"il ritorno di vecchi amici." I was deeply touched by what I took to be a show
of genuine affection, not for me personally, but for what Ralph and I represented: America. Italy's liberator.

The seven or eight other client couples distinguishable in the candlelight
were American and British officers whose dinner partners were ladies drawn
from the *crème de la crème* of Roman society, contessas and marchesas who,
no doubt, had recently dined with staff officers of the Wehrmacht and the SS.
The women were well coiffed and smartly attired, and I doubted they had
suffered unduly during the Nazi occupation.

The menu Nello brought had recently been "translated" into English and
featured: "Preasant With Red Wine Sauce, Brest of Veal Rost; 2 Quailes Devil
Style; Slice of White Fish As You Like; Chustnuts Cake." Nello personally

guaranteed that the veal was the real thing and said the chef could make us costolette à la milanese (breaded veal cutlets). The salad was made of dandelion greens but was dressed with real olive oil. We declined the "Chustnuts Cake" and had sliced oranges flavored with an unidentifiable liqueur instead. The coffee was genuine, and Ralph and I split a check that, with tip (15 percent), came to about thirty dollars each, roughly triple what it would have been before the war. When I looked astonished at the size of the bill, Nello quietly informed me that everything we'd had, even the salt and pepper in the silver shakers and the sugar in the tiny bowl, came from *la borsa nera*.

Ralph had spent most of the war as the United Press correspondent in Madrid and arrived in the wake of the Fifth Army to reactivate the UP's Rome Bureau. Everything he said during dinner confirmed my impression that Rome had become another rear-area base much like Naples. Its new Anglo-American rulers, headed by Colonel Charles Poletti, commandeered private vehicles, requisitioned public buildings without apparent necessity, were intransigent or dismissive in dealing with anti-Fascists, "especially Socialists or Communists," and permitted the oppressive black market to flourish.

Admittedly, the tasks the liberators had faced on June 5 were daunting. They had to feed a population swollen by masses of refugees to about 2.5 million, double its prewar size. They had to restore electric lighting and repair the water supply. Above all, they had the problem of keeping order while introducing democratic freedoms to a people who for twenty-one years had only heard democracy disparaged. In certain respects, the AMG worked wonders: Although still rationed except for use by the army and the hospitals, electricity was restored by June 6, and the telephones began working the next day; many banks, most schools, and the university had reopened; and the bread ration was doubled to two hundred grams (two small rolls) a day.

But there were well-founded and widespread complaints that promised political reforms were not being carried out quickly enough and that the Allies had failed to improve substantially the near-famine conditions prevalent when the Germans withdrew. Over the Armed Forces Radio since June 5 came daily preachments from Colonel Poletti about the benefits of democracy, and he was already the butt of a satirical couplet that went:

Charlie Poletti, Charlie Poletti
Meno ciarle e piu spaghetti [less talk and more spaghetti].

The basement bar of the Excelsior, once Rome's smartest rendezvous, where the city's bourgeoisie gathered for supper and wine after the opera or the theater, was now known as the Snake Pit, frequented by low-grade prostitutes and their officer escorts. The hotel itself, and its luxurious counterparts along the Via Veneto, were nightlong bordellos reserved for officers on leave, guarded by MPs, who turned away enlisted men. The latter were directed to the Foro Mussolini on the edge of town, where, however, they could swim, eat, and loaf in a comparatively wholesome atmosphere.

On the way back to our hotel through the dark streets we were stopped twice by MP patrols because Forte was not in uniform. At night Rome was a silent, lonely city of deep shadows.

In the morning I called the office of Ercole Graziadei, the politically sophisticated anti-Fascist lawyer friend who had schooled me in the darker side of fascism during my early days in Rome and who probably could tell me more about how the Eternal City had managed to survive the German occupation than anyone else. The female secretary who answered my call said the *avvocato* wouldn't be in until after lunch, which meant early afternoon, for like all Romans, Ercolino would be taking a siesta before returning to work. The secretary asked whether I wished to leave a message, but I wanted my visit to be a surprise and told her to say merely that "an old friend from America" had called and to expect me sometime in the early afternoon.

After bolting a GI breakfast of fried Spam, something that approximated an omelet derived from powdered eggs, hot rolls, and real home-style coffee in the stuffy correspondents' mess, I set out in the warm morning sun to revisit familiar streets and places, intending to wind up at the Galleria Colonna, my old workplace. I headed up the Via Sistina to the Trinità dei Monti, descended the rococco Spanish Steps, and stopped at the first landing to gaze nostalgically down at Bernini's boat-shaped fountain, the *Barcaccia*, waterless and lifeless like all the others. I continued down to street level. Missing there were the flower stalls that traditionally flanked the approach to Rome's most famous steps. Until they returned, I thought, and the water flowed again in the fountains, Rome could not really be said to have revived.

Entering the Via dei Condotti, I stopped at number 9, where we had lived for a time before moving to the Via Rovigo. The place held memories of my meeting with Uncle Gennaro, who had visited us in our penthouse apartment that overlooked the Piazza di Spagna. I remembered that on my son Sean's fourth birthday the boy had accidentally dropped a toy wooden truck from our fifth-floor terrace, narrowly missing a pedestrian. The carabinieri came running, and only the timely intervention of old Emilio, our *portiere*, whom I rightly suspected of being an informer for Mussolini's secret police, saved us from paying a huge fine.

On an impulse I pressed the call button of the apartment Emilio occupied on the ground floor. I wanted to revisit our *attico* and perhaps recapture the sense of adventure Rome still held for me in those early days of my apprenticeship as a foreign correspondent. Emilio's fat wife opened the door, recognized me at once, and invited me in, summoning Emilio with a *"Vieni, vieni, vecchio, abbiamo un ospite* [Come, come old man, we have a guest]." Emilio may have been a two-bit spy for the cops in my time, but to judge by the comfortable decor of what was apparently their *salotto*, he and his wife were prospering now. An oriental rug covered the floor; the armchairs and the divan, though garishly upholstered, were what might be found in any middle-class Roman home.

Yes, I could see my old *attico*, which Emilio said had been taken over as a workshop by Bulgari, the famous jewelry firm next door, if I didn't mind climbing five double flights of stairs in the terrible heat of a late July morning. The lift was out of order, kaput ever since the *tedeschi* left. Was Emilio glad the Germans were gone? *"Ah, si, signore."* They were a bad lot, those Germans, making almost nightly raids on people's homes during the final weeks of the occupation, looking for hidden radio transmitters, deserters from the Italian Army, and *ebrei* (Jews) hiding with Catholic families.

Clearly Emilio had moved up in the world by trading on the black market. During the Fascist regime the *portinai*—the doorkeepers of Rome's apartment houses and palazzi—eked out their modest salaries by spying on tenants for the OVRA and by earning gratuities for special services. I had paid Emilio a substantial sum for having spared us the expense and bureaucratic bother of a lawsuit when Sean dropped his wooden toy from our terrace. Now, apparently, Emilio and his kind had found a new source of income. I later learned that it was a bitter joke among middle-class Romans that the doorkeepers were moving up out of their humble, windowless rent-free basement quarters into well-lighted apartments upstairs and renting their own rooms to formerly well-to-do tenants.

The shops along both sides of the Via dei Condotti, Rome's equivalent of New York's Madison Avenue or London's Bond Street, displayed an amazing array of luxury goods. A king's ransom in jewelry sparkled in Bulgari's show window; Gucci showed leather goods and smart accessories; Ferragamo flaunted handmade shoes and riding boots; Cenci's window displayed fine linens for dining rooms and boudoirs. The prices, however, were beyond the reach of the Allied soldiery; in one of the stores a game set for poker containing two decks of cards and the necessary chips, for instance, carried a fifty-thousand-lire price tag, five hundred dollars in American money, a huge sum in those days. I had seen much the same thing in New York for fifty dollars.

Emerging into the Corso Umberto from the Via dei Condotti, I recalled having often seen this handsome street of stately palazzi crowded with Fascists in black boots and black uniforms marching toward the huge white Victor Emmanuel monument in the Piazza Venezia, where they assembled in military formations to voice their loyalty to Benito Mussolini, chanting "Duce! Duce! Duce!" under his balcony.

Now the *corso* was again filled with troops, but they wore the sturdy brown shoes and khaki uniforms of the Allied armies, and the roadway flowed with their Jeeps, trucks, staff cars, and motorcycles. Plain citizens mingled with the uniformed pedestrians, whom the Romans seemed to have accepted as liberators, not conquerors.

The reappearance of hordes of beggars—previously outlawed and relegated to the alleyways and back streets far removed from touristic midtown Rome—indicated the price in poverty the Romans had paid for their longtime subservience to fascism. Out of sight the mendicants were out of mind, and foreign visitors left Italy remembering only that the Duce had made the trains run on time, drained the Pontine Marshes, and "saved Italy from communism." They never saw the hunger and misery of Rome's underclass of homeless unemployed living in caves on the outskirts of the country's gorgeous capital.

When I reached the Largo Chigi and the entrance to the palazzo of the same name that had housed the offices of Count Ciano, it struck me that on the day I said good-bye to him I had unwittingly foreseen just such an end to fascism's dreams of European conquest as I was now witnessing.

What a pity, I thought, turning away to enter the turmoil in the shadowy Galleria Colonna, that neither Mussolini nor Ciano had ever visited the United States and seen for themselves the immense warmaking potential of its industries, mines, fields, and workers. They might never have allied themselves to Germany had they seen Pittsburgh's steel mills and Detroit's assembly lines; they saw America only through the eyes of sycophant envoys who reported what they knew would please their masters in Rome and depicted in their dispatches a "decadent" America neither able nor willing to go to war.

Ciano lived long enough to see America become the "arsenal of democracy" whose troops and weapons helped the British rout the Germans in North Africa and conquer Sicily. He was dead by the time Rome fell, strapped to a chair and shot in the back as a traitor despite the pleas for clemency of his wife, Edda, Mussolini's favorite daughter. So Ciano never knew that on the day after Rome fell to Mark Clark's Fifth Army, the Allies landed on Normandy's beaches the mightiest array of men and weapons ever assembled to begin the liberation of France and the demolition of Hitler's Fortress Europe.

The Galleria Colonna was much as I remembered it. Except for the presence of Allied soldiers sitting at the café tables at Picarozzi's and Biffi's with some of the city's gaudier whores, the place remained what it had always been: the noisy, crowded public living room for Rome's underworld of wheeler-dealers, out-of-work actors and actresses, gamblers, pimps, prostitutes, and black marketeers.

Bootblacks shined their conquerors' shoes; pairs of elderly nuns circulated among the café patrons, soliciting alms, and a cadaverous man in a suit that had seen far better days shuffled about, picking up discarded cigarette butts. The *galleria*'s tobacconist where I used to buy imported Chesterfields for fifty cents a pack, then double the price back home, explained that scavenging for butts had become a minor industry. The scavengers salvaged what tobacco remained in the unsmoked ends to roll cigarettes for themselves or for sale. My expression of disgust brought a wry smile to my former supplier's face. A pack of *americani*, he said, cost a hundred lire (one dollar) or more, and even the inferior domestic brands, when available, cost nearly as much. He sold Camels and Luckies *singly* for ten lire *each*, the equivalent of two dollars a pack!

I entered the dark stairway next to Picarozzi's café leading up to my old offices but turned back at the first landing. The place had been used as an air-raid shelter. It reeked of urine, and I lost all desire to revisit my old offices.

The midsummer heat was bearable in the shadowy *galleria*, but outside, it rose in shimmering waves from the pavements and the cobbled expanse of the Piazza Colonna. White-collar workers lucky enough to have jobs were hurrying home afoot or on bicycles to their *pasta e fagioli*. The vehicular traffic had subsided considerably, and with the thermometer in the upper nineties, a familiar midday torpor that kindled nostalgia had descended upon Rome; on such days I would collect my family and drive happily out to the beach at Ostia.

Deciding it was far too hot to walk, I found a *carrozza* parked among the Jeeps and staff cars in the piazza, the driver dozing under his huge umbrella. He reluctantly agreed to take me to the de la Ville when I offered him double fare for the short ride.

A surprise awaited me in the hotel lobby. There stood Ercole Graziadei, grinning broadly, arms extended in welcome, looking a bit leaner, but otherwise little changed. We embraced like brothers after a long separation. Then, stepping back, he searched my face. "You've gone gray," he said thoughtfully, "but you haven't changed much. Come, let's go home. Emma is waiting lunch. The car's parked down in the Piazza Barberini. . . ."

On the way Ercolino explained that he had telephoned his office at noon, guessed at once who the "friend from America" might be, and, knowing where American correspondents were billeted, rushed to the hotel. He'd been waiting nearly an hour and was about to give up when I arrived.

"I looked for you among the reporters in General Clark's entourage when the Fifth Army arrived," he said, "but found only Michael Chinigo. He said you had left INS and were getting rich writing for an important weekly publication. He sounded critical, I thought, and a bit envious. . . ."

He had never liked Chinigo, the suave little Italo-Albanian who had been my assistant during my INS days, suspecting him, correctly, of pro-Fascist sentiments or worse. Michael, I knew, had since attached himself to Truscott's Third Division as his agency's correspondent, covered the Sicilian campaign, and entered Rome with the Fifth Army, which was now pursuing the Germans northward beyond Leghorn.

At the wheel of Graziadei's old Fiat sedan sat Ettore, my friend's longtime chauffeur-butler, he was touchingly glad to see me and eavesdropped openly as Ercolino and I exchanged family news in the back seat during the drive to the Graziadeis' villa in Parioli. He joined in the laughter when my friend revealed that soon after the war began, Emma became pregnant and produced a baby sister for their teenaged daughter, Paola. The couple were in their late forties and had believed themselves no longer capable of producing children.

"Imagine our surprise," Ercolino said. "We named her Argentina after the silver in our hair. A beautiful child, as you will see. . . ."

Emma met us at the door of the two-story villa with leggy Paola holding the toddler, Argentina, by the hand, a shy little girl whose delicate features held the bright promise of beautiful womanhood. Their handsome mother's abundant hair had gone white, but it crowned the same tall, stately matron I had known as an outspoken feminist and the founder in pre-Fascist days of Italy's Girl Scout movement. Emma and Paola obliged me to repeat what news I had of Kathryn and the boys.

Giorgio Mattoli was well, I was happy to hear, and, like Ercolino, had survived the difficult time of the German occupation by staying out of circulation as much as possible and hiding in secret places during the Nazis' frequent raids on private dwellings. We talked over aperitifs in the comfortable *salotto* until Ettore, now in white coat and gloves, announced luncheon. The children disappeared, and we grown-ups sat down to a plain meal that included buttered taglioline with Parmesan cheese, a roasted fowl, green vegetables, fresh fruit for dessert, and a good wine from the Castelli. My perceptive hostess read my mind.

"Everything but the wine," she said, "comes from the black market. Fortunately we can afford it, but most people cannot. The black market is undermining not only our economy but our morals. Unless the Allied authorities bring it under control, they may have a revolution on their hands—"

"There may be a revolution anyhow," Ercolini interrupted, "for political as well as economic reasons. The people want a republic, but the Allies, especially the British, seem determined to saddle us with a monarchy under the same house of Savoy that gave us fascism, supported Mussolini's adventures in Ethiopia and Spain, then plunged us into this unpopular, disastrous world war. *Ora basta con la monarchia* [We've had enough of monarchy]."

During nearly the whole of August I left coverage of the war to another *Collier's* writer—Hemingway's third wife, Martha Gellhorn—and concentrated on Italian politics, hoping I would discern in the complex situation that developed with the fall of Rome a second Risorgimento, the rebirth of the republican Italy for which Mazzini and Garibaldi had fought but whose libertarian principles the monarchy had betrayed by truckling to fascism.

64

THE BITTER FRUITS OF LIBERATION

I
n the hot, humid summer of 1944 Rome's Anglo-American rulers behaved increasingly more like conquerors than liberators. Allied officers caroused in the luxury hotels on the Via Veneto and turned a city holy to the Catholic Church into Europe's unholiest pleasure palace.

Although liberation brought freedom of the press and assembly, it also brought poverty and near starvation, crime and the black market, rising prices and widespread immorality. With industry paralyzed, and the currency debased daily by uncontrolled inflation, the economic situation in Rome and throughout liberated Italy was desperate.

Although we were bringing in quantities of food, our military occupation increased the economic distress, and a widely publicized promise by President Roosevelt to raise the bread ration immediately from two hundred grams to three hundred, remained unfulfilled. Adding insult to injury were reports that the Italians in the German-occupied north—in Mussolini's puppet Socialist Republic, which was based in Salò, on Lake Garda—were living better than in the Allied zone.

The capital's moneyed aristocracy entertained Allied brass in their palazzi just as they had entertained the German commanders during the occupation. But for the masses, Rome, gasless, largely waterless, and sparsely lighted, was a mirthless place, an unhappy city under nightly curfew, its plain people wretched and bitter. Their bitterness was characteristically expressed in the slum district of Trastevere, where someone daubed on a wall the words

Arivolemo er Puzzone, in dialectal *romanaccio*, meaning "We Want the Stinker Back," the "Stinker" being Benito Mussolini. By the end of July the word "liberation" had a hollow ring for most Romans.

Well-meaning Americans and Britons persisted in believing that the Italians should have been grateful for having had their country used as a battlefield, and had we frankly looked upon the wholesale destruction of Italy as retribution for fascism's shameful policies as an ally of Nazi Germany, it would have made cruel but acceptable sense. But to have shredded the physical and cultural fabric of Italy and then tried to persuade the Italians to be grateful was sheer hypocrisy.

Our deceit was reflected in how we used the word "liberated." We never "sequestered" automobiles or "requisitioned" houses; we "liberated" them. A "liberated" town or village, and I had seen many, invariably meant that we had virtually obliterated it, leaving its inhabitants without homes, schools, churches, or shops.

In Rome the Allies "liberated" private automobiles at a great rate and one day very nearly took over Graziadei's Fiat. Like most correspondents, I had no transportation, and my friend volunteered to drive me from his offices across town to the Ministry of War, where, with his help, I hoped to learn the fate of my soldier uncle, Gennaro. We were stopped at the Porta Pinciana by British MPs and managed to save the car only through the timely intervention of their commander, an Eighth Army major who spotted the Crusader patch on the sleeve of my bush jacket. He ordered his cops to lay off and even treated us to a full tank of gas from a nearby military depot. Fearing that another encounter with MPs might have a less happy ending, we put off the visit to the War Ministry and returned the Fiat to its berth in the courtyard of the building where Ercole had his offices.

I spent many hot August afternoons there talking with Graziadei's anti-Fascist friends. Most were Socialists, men of the underground resistance movement, who believed that only by taking an active part in the fight against the Nazi-Fascists would Italy be able to assume its rightful place at the side of the United Nations. All, moreover, were convinced that the monarchy and Marshal Badoglio, our "Italian Darlan," having failed to organize the country for such a struggle, should vanish and be replaced by a republican government.

All bitterly resented the Anglo-American political obstructionism that hindered the development of a stable, truly democratic republican regime, for Allied political policy in Italy was determined by Winston Churchill and was in no sense calculated to encourage the republican trend of the country's resurgent liberal and democratic forces. Churchill, with the acquiescence of Washington, supported Badoglio and the king, a policy as wrongheaded as the Italian military campaign itself. It precipitated a "constitutional crisis" that lasted many months and laid the groundwork for enduring Italian postwar instability, a complex situation that bears explanation.

Italy's political revival could be said to have begun in September 1943, when Badoglio signed the armistice, then ignobly fled south to safety with his king, leaving Rome without a government. To fill the vacuum, a clandestine Committee of National Liberation (CNL) was formed under the leadership of Ivanoe Bonomi, an elder statesman from pre-Mussolini days, who had been a Socialist deputy in the early 1920s and now headed the small right-wing Labor Democratic party. He lived in hiding in the huge seminary building behind the grand Basilica of San Giovanni in Laterano, a refuge, also, for Pietro Nenni, Alcide de Gasperi, and other anti-Fascists and for many Jews.

In addition to Bonomi's party, the CNL included five other parties: Communist, Socialist, Christian Democrat, Party of Action, and Liberal. Their leaders had suffered persecution, imprisonment, and exile and saw the resistance in terms of a second Risorgimento, which would spiritually, socially, and economically re-create Italy with a well-defined program of agrarian reforms, industrial revival, and redistribution of wealth.

The best organized of the parties was the Communist, headed by Giorgio Amendola, son of Giovanni Amendola, the murdered anti-Fascist, and feared and distrusted by the Vatican as well as by the Anglo-Americans. The Socialist party, led by the prestigious Pietro Nenni, harked back to the original Socialist principles shared by Mussolini himself before his March on Rome. The small Party of Action, led by Count Carlo Sforza, was primarily a party of the exiled anti-Fascist intellectuals of the Justice and Liberty movement.

By far the most powerful of the parties in terms of numbers and popular support throughout Italy was the Christian Democrat party. It was led by de Gasperi and represented conservative and Catholic opinion. The Liberals, farther to the right, owed their inspiration to the Neapolitan senator-philosopher Benedetto Croce. The Christian Democrats and Liberals supported Croce's view that the monarchy should go.

In February 1944, 120 delegates from the various parties met in an old theater in Bari, the first free political meeting in Italy after twenty-one years of fascism.

The delegates declared themselves to be "the only true expression of the will of the people" and sent a letter to King Victor Emmanuel III demanding his abdication. When the stubborn "little king" refused, Croce, the meeting's chairman and moving spirit, suggested a compromise whereby the monarch ceased to be chief of state and transferred power to his son Crown Prince Umberto, not as his successor but as lieutenant general of the realm. The king agreed but insisted that the actual transfer of power await the liberation of Rome, to which he wished to return with slightly more glory than he had left.

At this point, February 22, 1944, Churchill rose in the House of Commons to champion the cause of Badoglio and the king. He was as determined that Italy remain a monarchy as he was to return to their thrones the unwanted kings of Yugoslavia and Greece.

Almost simultaneously, however, a new character entered the Italian political scene: the Soviet Union. Eager to become a major player in the looming struggle for power in the Mediterranean, Stalin dispatched to Bari a representative named Palmiro Togliatti, known in the Italian underground as Ercole

Ercoli, who, like Nenni, had fought fascism in Spain during the Civil War.

Togliatti took charge of the Communist party, whereupon the party, which had been agitating for the king's abdication, declared itself ready to join Badoglio's government. The opportunistic old marshal welcomed it with open arms. The other parties were stunned, and so were the Western Allies. But London and Washington moved quickly to prevent Russia from seizing the advantage in Moscow's first foray into Italian politics. A delegation composed of Robert MacMillan, representing His Majesty's government, and Robert Murphy, representing the United States, called on the king on April 10 and pressured him to abdicate. The next day, in his own hand, Victor Emmanuel drew up an act of abdication in favor of his son Umberto, and on April 22 Badoglio had his new government.

Badoglio managed to hold on to the Ministry of Foreign Affairs, as well as the premiership, with the other portfolios going to such anti-Fascists as Croce, Sforza, and Togliatti. The lame-duck king received the new cabinet at his residence in Ravello, near Naples, but his days were now numbered.

When Rome fell to the Allies, Badoglio was obliged to resign, and an anti-Fascist government was formed by Bonomi as head of the Rome CNL, with Sforza, Croce, Nenni, and other bona fide liberals. Victor Emmanuel was not allowed to set foot in Rome, and the legal machinery was created for an eventual referendum to banish him forever. Churchill, meanwhile, fearing the Communists might get the upper hand in Italian politics, as they had in Yugoslavia, did his utmost to obstruct the anti-Fascists. Under his inspiration the British not only hindered the anti-Fascists' leaders' efforts to make the fall of fascism a reality by projecting reforms and eliminating Fascist officials from the administration but even tried to undo what had already been accomplished.

By his prestige and previous experience, for instance, Count Sforza was the anti-Fascists' choice for foreign minister, but Churchill blackballed him, the British ambassador in Rome letting it be understood to Premier Bonomi that the count would not be "acceptable" to His Britannic Majesty's government.

In July Umberto signed a legislation declaring: "The Fascist Movement from its initial successes to its later developments was always a criminal undertaking directed against the constitutional guarantees of the State and its citizens, for the purposes of personal profit and enrichment." Nevertheless, any spurious "ex-Fascist" who swore to support the monarchy, far from being jailed or prosecuted, was granted an affidavit attesting to his partisan activities on behalf of the Allies.

A generation of fascism, capped by nine months of German terrorism, had left an ineradicable residue of moral weakness, and when the time came to purge Italy of Fascist criminals, the new regime faltered. A law designed to "purify" the nation of Fascists, promulgated in August, was so full of loopholes that all but the guiltiest would escape. I attended the press conference at which Sforza, who became foreign minister despite Churchill's objections, tried to explain it. When I asked him if the law would include those guiltiest of all of having collaborated with fascism, the members of the royal family, he made a ten-minute speech declaring that the "constitutional question" had to be tabled until the end of the war. Even Sforza succumbed to pressure from London and Washington.

The Americans were as upset as the British over the downfall of Badoglio and his king, and to prevent it, our elegant ambassador, Alexander Kirk, had worked as hard as his British counterpart. I found it disturbing to go from a talk with idealistic Italian patriots in Graziadei's office to a meeting with Kirk, who minimized the democratic sincerity of the anti-Fascists and amplified the threat to democracy from the Socialist-Communist left. What I found particularly distressing was his refusal to meet officially in his office with two non-Marxist republicans, friends whom I had met through Graziadei and who wanted Washington's support for the revival of the old pre-Mussolinian Republican party. He agreed to meet with them only if I brought them to his private residence at night, so they might not be seen.

I waited outside in the car my friends had provided for the occasion, and both looked glum when they emerged. They indicated that Kirk had seemed not to understand what they were saying, though one of the two spoke excellent English, and his companion said, "The Anglo-Americans are driving us into the arms of the Communists."

It seemed to me the anti-Fascists, whatever their political coloring, had to be helped, not hindered, if a democratic Italy was to emerge as part of a stable democratic Europe after the war, but with few exceptions, among them Colonel Poletti, our people failed to recognize this.

The revolutionary "people's war" which was already in progress in Yugoslavia and Greece—and in France, as I soon discovered—was also under way in Italy. It found its most militant expression in the partisan movement, which materialized when Badoglio signed the armistice. The Italians' armed resistance, too, had to be encouraged, not hindered, but our policy in dealing with what was essentially a left-wing revolutionary movement born of the cataclysmic consequences of war, and of the Allied pledges contained in the Atlantic Charter and Roosevelt's Four Freedoms, was obstructive rather than helpful. True, many partisans were Communists, and we feared they represented an extension of Russian influence in Italy.

Actually, the partisan movement was an expression of the Italian people's desire to participate directly in their own liberation as they had hoped to do when they became "cobelligerents" under the armistice. The Italians, however, found themselves cobelligerents in name only.

The Allied radio and our secret agents encouraged the partisans north of the front to risk their lives to kill Germans, and for that purpose guns and advisers were dropped to them in their mountain hideouts. Partisan forces known as Gruppi de Azione (GAP) succeeded in liberating scores of cities and towns in the Nazi-occupied north hours, even days before the arrival of our forces. In virtually every one of those communities the Allies found the partisans in control and the essential municipal services—water, gas, and electricity—intact.

Invariably, however, the Allies disbanded and disarmed the partisans and curtly ordered them to return to their farms and workshops. When stories of the partisans' resultant shock and bitterness over the treatment they received at the hands of the "liberators" trickled back to Rome, General Alexander had "certificates" engraved to be ceremoniously awarded to the *partigiani.* The sample I saw looked remarkably like my high school diploma.

Nevertheless, the partisans in the German-occupied north numbered in the tens of thousands and continued rendering invaluable assistance to the Allied armies. Their GAPs ambushed German troops, blew up ammunition dumps and fuel depots, and disrupted enemy communications. Many young *gapisti,* as they were known, were captured, jailed by the Gestapo, tortured and executed. Sometimes German firing squads provided mercifully quick death. Often, however, the end for these ragged heroes of the Italian resistance came less humanely. Some captured *partigiani* were hung by their chins until dead on the meat hooks of butchers' shops.

Of the many daring partisan acts of vengeance against their Fascist and Nazi tormentors, by far the most sensational happened in Rome in the late afternoon of March 23, 1944, on the eve of fascism's twenty-fifth birthday. The incident was so dramatic, and had such tragic consequences, that it was still being talked about in the capital when I arrived in mid-July. The story as I heard it from various sources, mainly Italian journalists who visited the scene, was the most horrendous of the innumerable Nazi atrocities in the occupied areas.

According to my informants, the partisans planted a forty-pound bomb in a street cleaner's rubbish cart in the Via Rasella, near the Palazzo Barberini, timed to explode while a column of about 150 German troops marched through the street to their assigned posts during a routine changing of the guard. The bomb killed 32 German soldiers and wounded many more.

There had been numerous partisan attacks on the city's German occupiers, all resulting in prompt arrests and the execution of known or suspected perpetrators. This time, however, the affront to German power was considered to have been far too great for mere one-for-one reprisal, and the Germans ran amok. Unable to find those actually responsible for the attack, the Gestapo engineered a gruesome retribution involving more than ten victims for each dead soldier.

When the roundup was completed on the night of the bombing, 356 men and women, many in their nightclothes, were taken in trucks to the Ardeatine caves, the ancient Christian catacombs at the city's edge. There they were chained in groups and cut down by machine-gun fire. Then, without waiting to ascertain whether their victims were actually dead, the Germans sealed the caves by dynamiting the entrance. Faint cries from the dying could be heard by passersby throughout the night and the following day.

When I visited the place, the caves were faintly illuminated by the uncertain light of smoky tallow candles. The bodies had been removed, identified, and given decent burials. Chlorinated lime had been liberally spread over the killing floor, but it did not succeed in dispelling the stench of violent death.

Still visible were fragments of clothing and footwear that must have belonged to the victims.

It was not difficult to imagine writhing bodies falling on those that had preceded them, their bowels and bladders emptying, their blood forming pools on the hard ground. Feeling faint, I barely made it to the clean air outside.

Those selected by the Gestapo for "punishment" had had nothing whatever to do with the bombing in the Via Rasella; they were simply suspects languishing in the Regina Coeli Jail or innocent Jews—twenty-six, according to one reliable source—dragged from their homes in Rome's ghetto. The victims also included a number of Socialist partisans who spied for Peter Tompkins, Wild Bill Donovan's daring young OSS operative in Rome.

As the summer wore on, the war continued north of the liberated capital. Alexander and Clark were determined to push on, assaulting the German's new Gothic Line and other defensive obstructions until they conquered the Po Valley. Nor did the generals intend stopping there; they would carry on, we correspondents were told, hoping to enter Germany from the south in order to "beat the Russians into Berlin," an objective I had heard Alexander express in Brindisi months earlier, when the British were still hoping to launch a major campaign in the Balkans in accordance with Churchill's original game plan for attacking Fortress Europe.

The generals' plans for future operations in Italy implied fighting through the Alps in the coming winter, an undertaking that smacked of madness. I was not alone, however, in believing that after the fall of Rome it might have been prudent merely to hold Italy while we diverted as many troops as possible to the impending invasion of southern France, an operation already freely talked about among correspondents. In fact, it was surely the worst-kept secret of World War II, for it was being openly mentioned as the "next big show" by tipsy officers and drunken soldiers in sidewalk conversations with total strangers, any one of whom might have been a Nazi agent.

At the War Ministry, which I visited on the eve of my departure for Naples to embark with General Alexander Patch's forces for the landings on the French Riviera, all was chaos. Most bureaus were closed, and files were sealed. I was shunted from one department to another, but none of the sallow-faced, demoralized Italian officers in charge could tell me the whereabouts or fate of my uncle, Colonel Gennaro Gervasi, last heard from in Tripoli, where he was in command of a motorized unit. I walked out of the gloomy building into the hot August sun burdened with a premonition that my boyhood hero was dead.*

---

* Sometime early in 1946, shortly after the war ended, my father received from the Italian government a black-bordered engraved card informing him that Colonel Gennaro Leone Gervasi was "killed in action" on June 10, 1940. That was the day Italy declared war on Britain and France. Presumably, therefore, Gennaro had died on the French front the very day the Italians invaded France, a fact which somehow didn't ring true.

I spent a sleepless night debating whether I should stay on to determine whether my only living Italian relative was dead, alive, or a prisoner of war, but in the end I decided against the idea. For nearly five years, since that ominous night when Paris had seemed defeated even before the Germans had invaded France, I had looked forward to reentering the city on the day of its liberation, an experience which had been denied me by circumstances beyond my control.

I would have the pleasure, however, of returning to France, of finding out what happened to that wonderful country's people, and perhaps catch a glimpse of its future, which was bound to influence the future of Europe, indeed, of Western civilization.

In 1949, when I was in Rome on an assignment for the *Washington Post*—I had left *Collier's* to return to daily journalism—I learned from a distant cousin, Ottavio Marrota, who came to visit me from Palermo, where he practiced law, that Gennaro had not died in combat but had been found dead at his desk in Verona, an apparent suicide. Marrota was puzzled. The shot that had killed our relative had been fired into his left temple by a German weapon, a Luger; Gennaro was right-handed and always carried a Beretta. "I believe," Marrota said, "he was executed by the Nazis, either for having a Jewish wife or for refusing to obey orders from the German high command." Neither Marrota nor I was able to find any trace of Uncle Gennaro's survivors: his wife, Augusta, or their daughter, Graziella, who might have helped clear up the mystery.

65

THE SWEET SCENT OF VICTORY

Preparations for the invasion of southern France, the last great amphibious operation of the war, were in their final, hectic phase when I arrived at our embarkation point in Naples in the evening of August 11, four days before D day. The coveted assignments with the infantry assault wave went to the correspondents of the major daily newspapers, wire services, and radio networks. I drew a berth on an LST with the 809th Battalion of the Aviation Engineers, charged with building an all-important airstrip for fighter planes on the beach between Le Lavandou and St.-Raphaël, where Major General Patch was to land his Seventh Army.

The LST to which I was assigned was skippered by Commander Mike Mickelson, USN, a huge man with a foghorn voice, who only two years before had been a soap salesman in Minnesota but was already a veteran of seaborne operations in Sicily and Italy. From the bridge deck of his crowded vessel I had a superb view of the complexities involved in assembling and loading the fleet of eight hundred vessels that was to strike what we all hoped would be the decisive blow against Hitler's Fortress Europe, which, incidentally, was already crumbling. While we waited in Naples, the breakthrough in northern France occurred, and Bradley and Patton were smashing their way toward Paris.

Originally planned to coincide with the landings in Normandy but postponed because of the perennial shipping shortage and the vicissitidues of the Italian campaign, the invasion of southern France would be spearheaded by three veteran U.S. divisions—the Third, Thirty-sixth, and Forty-fifth, all blooded and tempered in Sicily and Italy—and would be followed ashore, appropriately enough, by a North African army commanded by French officers. In other words, Frenchmen were to participate directly in the liberation of their own country, and even before we sailed, the war began making more sense to me than it had in Italy. For one thing, the French terrain would be incomparably better suited to tank warfare than the Italian, and for another, we had as commander one of the U.S. Army's best generals.

Sandy Patch was renowned as a "soldier's soldier" cast much in the mold of Patton, including even a touch of his flamboyance. Lean, ramrod straight, he popped up at a preinvasion briefing for correspondents wearing a handsome gold-buckled belt and a sporty silk scarf stamped with the map of southern France. He warned us to expect "tough going" because the French coast, he said, was "heavily defended."

For the next three days I watched LSTs swallow bulldozers, tractors, steamrollers, and power shovels, while others ingested tanks, trucks, Jeeps, guns, and ammo cases. At the same time Liberty ships took on mountains of supplies, weapons, and equipment while huge transports aspirated long columns of helmeted, pack-burdened men. I wondered how many out of every ten I counted would survive the promised ordeal by fire.

Yet never before had I felt so relaxed about going into a battle, possibly because I was in the company of friends I had made in Italy at the Volturno and the Rapido. Among them were Lieutenant Colonel Giles Evans, and Captains Buster Waddell and Choo-Choo Wilson, all engineers, members of a corps whose work was the hardest in our army after that of the surgeons and the infantry. Having studied engineering at Drexel for a year and spent a summer as a surveyor's helper, I could read the plans they showed me for the airfield they would build.

Evans was regular army and had a wife and kids back in Nashville; Waddell had played football at West Virginia University, and Wilson got his nickname because he had driven a locomotive in New England. By the time we sailed, we were as chummy as schoolmates.

The days passed watching the spectacular gathering of the invasion fleet. It included nine aircraft carriers, several battleships, many cruisers, and scads of destroyers and patrol boats, their arrival from distant ports timed to the hour, the minute. In the wardroom of our LST there were breakfasts of flannel cakes, sausages, and highly assertive coffee; lunches of steak with fried onions, and turkey dinners with cranberry sauce—navy grub, a welcome relief from C rations and the ever-drearier K rations.

Finally, one morning in the half-light before dawn, Big Mike Mickelson received a blinkered signal from the *Ancon,* the fleet's command ship, and the skipper's voice bellowed over the ship's public-address system: "Men, you're sailing for France. [Cheers] Thought you'd like to know. Keep your life belts handy, eat heartily, and take it easy. . . ."

The diesels belowdecks came alive, and right after Mike spoke, someone utterly lacking in appreciation of the solemnity of the moment put on a record of Larry Adler playing "Begin the Beguine" on his harmonica. Beethoven's Fifth or "Onward Christian Soldiers" might have been more appropriate.

Then, on our last afternoon on board, we sailed straight into a flaming sunset in perfectly aligned columns of four, with escorting patrol boats ahead of us, on our flanks, and protecting our rear. Nightfall brought clouds through which a crescent moon shone fitfully, and although the sea was calm, many of the men suffered from *mal de mer.* Big Mike allowed me to stretch out in my bedroll alongside the wheelhouse, and I enjoyed the light wind, the sound of water breaking from the vessel's blunt bow, and the steady thrumming of the engines.

At 4:00 A.M. on D day, August 15, the task force assembled off the forty-mile stretch of beaches between Le Lavandou and St.-Raphaël, right on schedule, and we heard the thunderous overture of what Britain's General Jumbo Wilson, C in C Mediterranean, had promised us in Naples would be "a mortal symphony." While the men waited in the darkness, our battle wagons' guns bored noisy yellow holes in the night, dumping tons of high explosives onto predetermined targets. Every German battery, minefield, demolition charge, ammo dump, and pillbox was plotted on our charts. Thanks to the French underground, our fleet's commanders knew precisely where their gunners were to aim their weapons.

Simultaneously, our airborne troops landed inland, far behind the German positions, beyond the Monts des Maures (Moorish Mountains), which rise between Toulon and St.-Raphaël. The parachutists dropped on towns and villages and into the welcoming arms of Frenchmen, who, the night before, had heard the secret coded signal over the BBC and knew that the dawn would bring the long-awaited liberation. To the maquis, the organized clandestine French forces, our airborne soldiers distributed weapons and ammunition, and the invasion became a liberation.

Hitherto every amphibious attack on European shores was made at first light before sunrise or by moonlight. Usually, therefore, the air forces couldn't provide adequate support for the infantry, and deadly pillboxes or other enemy positions remained intact, as at bloody Salerno. On this job, however, H hour was set for broad daylight, 8:00 A.M., to give our tactical bombers—medium and fighter-bombers—an opportunity to cauterize the beaches properly. And they did.

The planes arrived at dawn and began "walking" their explosives through the fringe of water along the beaches, shooting up mines, underwater obstacles, wire barriers, and enemy machine-gun emplacements. Then the rocket ships darted in, searing the black sands with deadly fire. Idling about four miles off shore, we could hear enemy mines detonating seriatim with the rapid pop-pop-pop of so many exploding balloons.

The arrhythmic thunder of our shells and bombs was incessant for four hours. At precisely 8:00 A.M. there was sudden silence, and the men of the Seventh Army began pouring ashore into an area bisected by the mountainous ridge called the Estérel, which divides the Riviera. The Estérel, according to the charts shown me by Colonel Evans, our troop commander, was also the hinge of two German divisions. We strained to hear the familiar sounds of such moments, the rapid splurt-splurt-splurt of German machine pistols and the loathsome yowl of the enemy's Nebelwerfers but heard none though we learned later that some Americans had died on the beaches and that on the far right, in the vicinity of St.-Raphaël, our first three waves were thrown back.

On the whole, German opposition was sporadic, fainthearted, and easily overcome. The defending Nineteenth Army of roughly ten divisions seemed chiefly concerned with extricating itself from an untenable situation. The Germans found themselves caught between two mighty Allied armies, one moving southward from Normandy, the other advancing northward from the Riviera. "The krauts," said Evans, indicating on his map what was happening, "are trapped between an anvil and a hammer. We're the hammer."

Long before I caught my first glimpse of the shoreline, however, I could smell the sweet scent of final, total heartwarming victory. It was in the wind that came off the cobalt-hued sea and that caressed the tall pines on the hills above the Côte d'Azur, the peacetime playground of the rich and famous dotted with resorts and casinos. Only Cannes was still held by the Germans.

Big Mike aimed our LST for a grayish black sandy beach between the flat blue sky and the brown-splotched green hills beyond in the vicinity of St.-Tropez. On our chart the beach looked enormous, but now it seemed absurdly small. Our schedule called for us to land at H hour plus four, or noon, but we were late, delayed by an unexpected, uncharted sandbar. Our shallow-draft vessel struggled over it with a wet, grinding, sucking sound, and a few enemy shells raised geysers around us uncomfortably close; but they helped rock the ship off the sandbar.

We were near the shore, now, close enough to see long lines of prisoners being herded into enclosures. Later I had a closer look. The thousands of prisoners were a strange-looking group; for every German there seemed to be a Czech, a Pole, or a Russian. There were some Italians, even a few renegade Frenchmen, who were sifted out and turned over to Free French officers. The captured troops were the worst-looking lot I had ever seen. All were ragged and either poorly shod or barefoot. Many wore only trousers, faded and torn and incredibly dirty. "Hitler," said Wilson, "seems to be running out of supermen . . ."

After our huge LST slid onto the beach and had begun disgorging the bulldozers, tractors, and power shovels that Waddell and Wilson would be using to make their airstrip, Colonel Evans and I reconnoitered the beachhead, looking for the best possible site.

We drove along the dusty coast road through the vineyards that carpeted the coastal plain between the sea and the Monts des Maures and through pretty St.-Tropez, Cogolin, Cavalaire, Bormes, Fréjus all the way to Hyères, whose palm-lined streets, however, were still held by the Germans. These ancient towns of Provence, bathed in the hot August sun, were astir with excitement. We heard the faint, distant chatter of machine guns, the occasional roar of a big gun, German or ours, and the periodic sharp crack of a sniper's rifle, but otherwise there was peace.

The road was lined with people, who waved friendly welcomes, reached up to shake hands or simply to touch us, and whenever we stopped in the heavy traffic of tanks and trucks and tractor-drawn guns, little girls gave us grapes and pears or limp bunches of wild flowers. People waved from windows or leaned over walls to greet us. They had been as hungry as the Italians ever were, though perhaps the Italians had been hungry longer, but there were no cries from the kids for candy, and there was no begging for food from the grown-ups. The French welcome was warm and dignified, utterly lacking in the wild acclamations we had known in Italy.

It was, however, from a man I came to know as Corlin Jean Baptiste Hébréard and his wife, Simone, that I learned what was really in French hearts. Colonel Evans and I had stopped at a likely-looking expanse of vineyards, and while Evans sat in the Jeep and unfolded his maps and sketches, I wandered off along a path whose dust showed plainly the nail marks of German boots that had passed there only a day or two earlier in headlong retreat.

I saw Monsieur Hébréard before he saw me. He was bent over a vegetable patch near a stone house shaded by trees. I called out to him, and when he stood up, I waved to him to come to me, indicating that the colonel and I wanted to talk to him. He, in turn, beckoned me toward him and his small house, and I strode through the vines in his direction. When I was about a hundred yards from him, he ran toward me on work-bent legs, his stubby arms flapping. He stopped a few paces from me, spread his arms wide like the spars of a small stout ship, and, in the tones of an exasperated schoolmaster, said, "*Enfin, mon enfant, vous êtes venu* [At last, my son, you have come]." His faded, ragged shirt flapped in the gentle breeze like a tattered sail. When he embraced me, he smelled of honest sweat, wine, and tobacco.

Madame was more restrained but no less happy to see me. For both, I was evidently the first American they had seen since the habitués of the Riviera had sailed for home in 1939, perhaps longer, because no one from the fine hotels of the resort towns ever strayed inland very far, and this vineyard was miles from the nearest bar, beach house, or roulette wheel.

Though she must have been sixty, gray-haired Madame Hébréard wore shorts (her suntanned legs were knotty with varicose veins) and one of her husband's shirts, which, like his own shirt and his voluminous denim gray pants, was faded and much patched. They were poor tenant peasants, who shared their two-room house with a cow they called Poochie. Yet they asked for nothing. Madame graciously accepted my gift of K ration chocolate, but Monsieur Hébréard politely refused the cigarettes I offered and lighted from my Zippo the stump of a stogie he extracted from a pants pocket.

They gave me wine from a demijohn which Madame drew up from their well, apologizing that it had not been cooling long enough. They looked at each other and shrugged when I told them that Colonel Evans and his engineers would be coming later with bulldozers to build an airstrip through their vineyard. I had expected lamentations. Instead, both smiled, and Hébréard said, *"C'est la guerre, n'est-ce pas?"* adding that in any case it was better to have *les avions* than *les boches.* Besides, he said, the vines hadn't been making very good wine lately. Not enough rain and too much sun.

While Evans and I were gone, the 809th had set up camp under the umbrellalike pines on a hillside above St.-Tropez, overlooking the plain where Waddell and Wilson, and their crews of chainmen and rodmen, were already sighting a center line for their airfield. Our bivouac was pleasantly situated on a level spot carpeted with fragrant pine needles; but the troops had dug no foxholes, and Evans and I soon wished they had.

A flight of fighter planes arrived, and as we peered upward through the trees' branches, wondering whether those vague shapes in the early evening sky were "theirs" or "ours," the first bombs fell. We clapped on our steel hats, flopped down on the ground, and lay there, motionless, while tracers from our ack-ack on the beaches and surrounding hills drew a geometric pattern of broken red lines which intersected directly overhead. Shells exploded above us in black puffs with yellow kernels, and we heard the snarl of descending flak. When Evans later bawled out Waddell and Wilson for having neglected to dig foxholes, they argued hotly that it had seemed more important to start working on the airfield.

Captain Wilson ran his center line with the transit, staked it, and flagged it with bits of red and white rag. Meanwhile, Waddell measured off half the width of the airstrip on each side, and before his crew of chainmen had driven their first stake, the bulldozers were at work digging deep into the ancient vines and the loamy French soil. Giles Evans fretted about what a shame it was that years of farmers' work was being destroyed by the thundering diesel-driven 'dozers, but he needn't have fussed.

Two French peasants in black berets and blue denim overalls, one barrel-shaped and middle-aged, the other skinny, gray, and elderly, watched the Americans work from the edge of a ditch. I asked the rotund one whether he minded too much, and he said he didn't. *"C'est la guerre,"* he said, echoing their neighbor Hébréard, and, like him, deprecated the quality of the vines. "They make only ordinary wine, and they are in poor health."

The old one nodded agreement, adding, "It does not matter much that *les vignes* should go." He, too, echoed Hébréard. *"Meilleurs les avions des alliés que le boche,"* and he spit. Frenchmen always spat when they said *"boche."* The old one then suggested we all go to his house and have some good wine from last year's grapes, and we did.

Buster and Choo-Choo weren't nearly as sentimental about those vines as their colonel. To them, vines were nasty things that left sharp, spikelike roots, which, unless removed by backbreaking hand labor, could knife a tire and wreck a few hundred thousand dollars' worth of airplane. There were thousands of these roots to be pulled, and RAF ground crews arrived to help out.

By nightfall of D day plus one (August 16), a rough strip had already been hacked out, and Choo-Choo Wilson had completed surveying parking areas for planes, trackways, and approaches. Now the big sheep's-foot rollers went to work. These huge steel monsters had rollers studded with spikes, six inches long and two inches square, that packed the loamy surface down with the help of water sprinkled from fifteen-hundred-gallon tanks mounted on six-wheel, six-drive trucks known as six-by-sixes. Water is an essential ingredient in building an airstrip. It rained on the night of D day plus two, and while the rest of us were cursing it and wondering how we were going to keep dry in our inadequate pup tents, Buster Waddell was down in the field, dancing up and down, yelling, "Rain, beautiful wonderful rain. Hot damn! Hot damn!" Throughout that night the rollers, the sheep's-foot monsters, and other special rolling equipment worked, the drivers sitting up in their exposed cabs, soaked to the skin.

By the morning of D day plus three, we had a landing ground. From our hilltop bivouac it looked as though it had always been there, its center line running smack through Hébréard's vineyard. His well had been sealed to prevent seepage and soft spots, but his tiny stone house had been spared. By 11:00 A.M. we had an airport complete with a rough control tower and wind sock.

The runway wasn't quite smooth yet, but it probably saved the life of one Lieutenant Dinks, a Chicagoan who had worked as a pressman in that city's *Tribune* newspaper before he became a fighter pilot. Dinks was in trouble. There wasn't a friendly airport in all southern France, and there were many miles of open sea between him and his base after he had completed a mission over Cannes. But he spotted our airfield, and he came down on it with the last half pint of gas in his tanks.

Later the next morning RAF Group Captain Duncan Smith brought in his squadron of Spitfires, and we all went down to the field to wave him in, holding our breaths, hoping all the obstacles on the approaches—power lines, odd trees, and those spiky vine roots—had been removed. But Smith, an RAF veteran I'd known in the Middle East, got himself and his planes down okay.

Later, over generous tots of the gin he'd brought, he pronounced unreserved approval of the work of Buster Waddell, Choo-Choo Wilson, Colonel Evans, and the 809th Battalion of the U.S. Engineers. The hills that were silent only four days before, except for the belching splutter of diesel engines and the roar of truck motors, now echoed to the louder, fullthroated voices of Duncan Smith's Spitfires and the woodwind music that the Spits made with their wings and tails when they cut off power to glide in for a landing.

There was little drama except for a couple of halfhearted enemy raids and the capture of three krauts—potential snipers—whom one of our men found asleep in the canebrakes. And in a missed minefield just off the far end of the strip, beyond Hébréard's vineyard, there were three white crosses where three dead GIs were buried. They had stumbled on a mine.

There was plenty of drama, however, elsewhere on the beachhead and in southern France, as we pursued the Germans northwest toward Avignon, and up the Rhône Valley toward Grenoble.

66

REBIRTH OF A NATION

Unlike the much-maligned General Lucas at Anzio, General Patch, tall, slender, energetic, and elegant in riding breeches and boots, was a "thruster." By the end of the first week of the campaign in southern France his Seventh Army had created a huge, firm, and powerful beachhead over which protective fighter planes were flying. Roughly shaped like a triangle, its base was more than forty miles wide and its apex extended inland to Aix-en-Provence, where Cézanne had painted his glorious green and purple landscapes.

But it was in bawdy, revolutionary Marseilles that the battle achieved a climactic denouement. Birthplace of the "War Song of the Rhine Army"—sung by five hundred volunteers marching to Paris during the French Revolution in 1792 and renamed "La Marseillaise" to become the national anthem—the city was outflanked at first. Then, fittingly enough, it was liberated on August 23—D day plus eight—by a French force under General Jean de Lattre de Tassigny after some of the bitterest street-by-street, house-to-house fighting of the invasion. Meanwhile, the Seventh Army swung northward up the Rhône Valley, the Route de Napoléon, to its eventual junction with Patton's forces coming from the north.

In Marseilles, it seemed to me, France rose again from its shameful defeat in 1940, and it was there that I realized that the French themselves, as much as we, were liberating their country. The underground maquis of the French resistance were magnificent, and they, perhaps more than we, were the true liberators. They were brave, joyous young men and women who, though excessively cruel at times, most clearly demonstrated the spirit of a reborn France. Its children were redeeming the shame of their defeated elders.

In southern Italy we had fought what was essentially a war of conquest, treating towns and villages like so many mere military obstacles in our path and ruthlessly obliterating them. In warm, sunny southern France, which had not suffered even remotely comparable physical damage and in fact seemed almost whole, the war became what it should have been from the outset: a splendid act of liberation. In Provence, among groves of cork oak and on hills where the pines scented the air with the clean fragrance of resin, the maquis fought alongside Patch's swiftly moving troops, and I began seeing the war once more as a "good war."

I had hated the war in southern Italy, where all was destruction and despair. But in southern France I found myself actually enjoying the campaign. Apart from the fact that we were everywhere greeted as liberators, not fawned upon as victorious conquerors, the war seemed suddenly to be making good sense again as it had two years before at El Alamein, when Auchinleck and Montgomery demolished the myth of German invincibility.

The French Forces of the Interior (FFI) were particularly effective in Marseilles, where, with other correspondents, I dodged snipers' bullets from windows and doorways along La Cannebière. Many of the snipers were Frenchmen, followers of Jacques Doriot, the ex-Communist who had betrayed his followers and his country to collaborate with the Germans. We saw the signs his men had daubed on the walls of the villages on the outskirts of besieged Toulon. A typical one read: VIVE DORIOT! WE REFUSE TO BE THE SLAVES OF STALIN!

The Vieux Port of Marseilles, a hillside honeycomb of ancient slums ideally suited to underground activities, pullulated with armed, vengeful Frenchmen who were determined to exterminate the followers of Doriot, Laval, and Pétain, the men they held principally responsible for their country's humiliating collapse in the summer of 1940. French hatred of fellow countrymen and women who had collaborated with the enemy exceeded, if possible, their hatred of the Germans, and they hunted down collaborationists relentlessly. Frenchmen who had helped the enemy usually paid with their lives; women who had slept with the Nazis lost their hair. The FFI fighters I met fought in the name of Charles de Gaulle, and it occurred to me that if the Italians had had a de Gaulle to look up to instead of the senescent Pietro Badoglio, they might have done a better job of ridding themselves of their Fascists.

In some towns American soldiers, who did not have the remotest conception of what motivated the guerrillas of the FFI, rescued convicted young women collaborationists at gunpoint and drove off with them after loudly denouncing the epuration process as "A lot of crap!" But higher up the military ladder, the Allied brass apparently realized that Britons and Americans could not apply in France the kind of military government they had imposed in Italy and wisely left France's future in the hands of Frenchmen.

When we entered Marseilles in the glorious morning of August 23, an FFI fighter in black beret and blue denim overalls thrust into my hands a single-sheet clandestine newspaper, the ink still wet, that carried this headline: MAR-SEILLES, CONQUERED BY THE F.F.I., IS ENTERED BY ALLIES TROOPS. Two days later Paris fell, and the same newspaper announced in the biggest type its editors could find: FFI LIBERATES PARIS FROM THE YOKE OF THE INVAD-ERS.

Plainly, the French had taken charge of the war, and I, for one, thought this was as it should be.

Marseilles and Toulon fell days ahead of schedule, and we chased the retreating Germans northwestward along the valley of the Durance River through civilized Provence, golden van Gogh country, toward Avignon, home of the popes for nearly a century. The army and the maquis took thousands of prisoners, and here and there the French treated them abominably. Like the Yugoslavs, the Greeks, the Italians, and others, they had suffered a great deal under German occupation, and the French kept their wounds open with acts of vengeance disallowed by the Geneva Convention. In victory Europe's most civilized people became, at times, barbarians.

One hot August day, shortly after having nervously dodged street-corner duels between FFI patriots and renegade Frenchmen of Doriot's *milice* in Marseilles, four other correspondents and I stopped in a country village. More than a thousand German prisoners crowded a narrow street leading to the town's square, where there was a fountain. I had never seen a dirtier, wearier, more completely beaten lot of German soldiery. Captured somewhere near Toulon, they had been walking all night and throughout the day without pause.

The exhausted prisoners were sprawled all over the roadway, flat on their faces or on their backs, or leaning against the walls with staring bloodshot eyes, mouths agape, gasping for breath. Their clothes were ragged, their shoes worn to the bursting point. They moaned and cried for water. FFI guerrillas in berets and denim overalls patrolled up and down the column, lining them up four abreast by kicking and shoving them into place like so many cattle, using their rifle butts as persuaders.

The villagers filled the square to watch the spectacle. At a signal the Germans were allowed to approach the fountain in fours. They lurched toward the gurgling life-giving water, making strangled, choking cries and greedily plunged their faces into the fountain's basin. When the big, beefy guerrilla in charge decided they'd had enough, he beat them back with the stock of his rifle or bashed their faces with a ham-size fist. I took him to be the village black-smith or butcher.

This went on hour after hour, the Germans taking turns at the water, stumbling on their way to the fountain, staggering to their feet, and struggling on for their small share of the fountain's cooling gift.

Farther down the line a German lay on the ground, twitching. Minutes later the spasmodic movements stopped; the man was dead. On the wide stone steps of the town's gray old church, a priest bent down to comfort three dying Germans. Two or three others, already dead, lay nearby.

Meanwhile, a blond, blue-eyed effeminate young man in immaculate blue shorts, Riviera-style leather sandals, and a canary yellow T-shirt moved up and down the long line of prisoners, randomly beating at them with a long stick. I shouted at him to stop, and he turned on me a look of unblinking hatred that will stay with me the rest of my life. I think he would have struck me had I not been in uniform, but he scuttled off, his fancy sandals going splat-splat-splat on the pavement as he vanished up the road.

Throughout the unlovely spectacle the villagers were strangely undemonstrative, their faces expressionless, though there were gasps and murmurs of disapproval whenever the beefy one at the fountain was needlessly violent with fists or rifle butt. Obviously, no French authorities of the de Gaulle government were present to see that matters were conducted properly. On the way out of town we saw a number of the guerrillas seated at a long wooden table set up in the shade under some plane trees a few feet from the prisoners, drinking wine and singing "Auprès de Ma Blonde."

With me at the time were Eric Sevareid, of CBS, and three other American correspondents. Later we discussed the revolting scenes we had just witnessed. The only justification Eric and I could find for the behavior of those rough Provençal guerrillas was that in these parts the Gestapo almost certainly had never shown mercy to captured French patriots.

War is many things. It is hatred and fear, weariness and filth, cowardice and heroism. It is also, we decided, revenge, and for the French the war seemed to have entered a new phase in which vengeance on their longtime Nazi tormentors and traitors had become a predominant element.

Our party traveled in a bulky command car with a trailer that carried our bedding and rations. At Avignon we turned north up the Rhône Valley toward the Drôme River, which flows westward into the Rhône at Livron. We soon discovered that pursuing a retreating enemy force, in this case the Germans' Eleventh Panzer Division, can be almost as dangerous as participating in a set piece battle in which the relative positions of friend and foe are known.

The Germans apparently were moving north on the west bank of the Rhône with the French Army in hot pursuit, and we were on the east bank without any clear idea of what was happening ahead, behind, or around us. En route maquis warned us of loose bands of Germans preying on the countryside and to beware of ambush; our vehicle, they said, would tempt footsore enemy troops anxious to escape east toward the German frontier.

The American division in the area, the Thirty-sixth, was moving so rapidly that the press camp was invariably too far behind to be of any help, and we did not know, therefore, that the Texans were preparing to trap the fleeing Germans somewhere between the Drôme River and Grenoble, northeast of us. Nor had we any way of knowing that the enemy, to escape the maquis in the hills west of the Rhône, had to cross the river at its confluence with the Drôme at Livron, then proceed eastward along the latter river's valley.

We moved warily up the highway along the Rhône and turned right at Livron. The town's streets were deserted, and its windows shuttered. That should have warned us something was afoot, but we pressed on through the late afternoon and at Crest turned north, crossed a slender bridge over the Drôme, and found ourselves amid the vehicles, weapons, and men of the Thirty-sixth Division deployed in battle formation. The Texans, refitted and reinforced after the mauling they had experienced at the Rapido, were to block the German retreat until the Third Division, coming from the south, could overtake the Eleventh Panzers and help the Thirty-sixth demolish them.

We found the Thirty-sixth's divisional command post in a rambling farmhouse, and a surprised G-2 officer asked: "How the hell did you guys get in here? Is that bridge at Crest still open?" We assured him it was and were told that it was mined for demolition, the charges having been set long before we crossed it. "Well," the officer said, "you're in, but I doubt you'll be able to get out."

Close at hand, our guns were roaring, and German shells were coming in occasionally from enemy positions just north of us. Obviously we had stumbled into a major battle, one of the very few fought in southern France during a campaign which, except for those days of fierce combat in Marseilles and Toulon, had been for us correspondents something of a picnic through some of Europe's loveliest landscape.

The atmosphere at the Thirty-sixth's CP, however, bordered on panic and reminded me of the early desert days, when units of General Wavell's forces, finding themselves outnumbered and outgunned by the enemy, broke into hasty retreats euphemistically called flaps. This one, involving Americans, had the smell of a "flaparoo." Officers gathered in groups, talking among themselves in low voices. Some sat on the farmhouse steps of the CP reading an army instruction manual on what to do when captured.

Urged again by a friendly G-2 officer to "leave while the going's good," we demanded to know why and were amazed to learn that the Thirty-sixth was surrounded. The Texans were trapped between a superior armored force moving down upon them from Valence, to the north, and the approaching Eleventh Panzers, whose tanks, apparently, had been only a mile from the bridge at Crest when we crossed it.

We had no intention of leaving what promised to be a good fight and asked to see the general, but our hearts sank when he stepped out of his trailer. The man who had replaced General Walker as commander of the Thirty-sixth appeared in trousers and undershirt, and "flop sweat" beaded his brow. His decidedly unmilitary appearance, manner, and what he said were almost as disturbing as the prospect of capture by the Germans. He glared at us, counted us off, and grunted: "Well, five more men might help. You may have rifles in your hands before morning."

This was a preposterous idea. If we were captured carrying weapons, the

Germans would be entitled to shoot us. Journalists were never armed. We faced a difficult choice: stay or go. We were too proud to leave and, in the circumstances, too sensible to stay. In the end we took the way of reason and left, hurrying to cross the bridge at Crest before someone blew it up.

The bridge was still intact when we recrossed it in the twilight, turned east on the road that paralleled the Drôme, and made camp among the maquis assembling in the hills to join in the battle that began just before nightfall. We slept on the ground far enough from the Thirty-sixth Division's area to be safe but near enough to hear the guns that pounded the enemy through the night. At dawn the air force joined the slaughter, and by the time we returned to the new divisional CP near Livron in the morning it was all over.

Despite the panic at the top, the Thirty-sixth—with the considerable help of the Third Division arriving from the south and a strong force of maquis coming westward from Grenoble—had turned the tables on the Germans. At Livron the Thirty-sixth occupied the heights commanding the narrow Rhône Valley, along which the Germans had to pass. Their devastating fire blocked the road with the Eleventh Panzers' wrecked tanks and vehicles. Behind those obstacles the stalled German columns were exposed to point-blank artillery fire from the guns of the Third Division behind them and merciless attack from the air.

Eventually a strong German remnant broke through by sheer weight of its remaining armor, but it left behind a twelve-mile stretch of road littered with smashed tanks and trucks, burned-out personnel carriers, abandoned artillery, dead horses, and dead Germans. It was a sight none of us soon forgot.

We followed the victorious Thirty-sixth along the east bank of the Rhône and left it just beyond Valence, where we turned into the pleasant valley of the Isère River. At St.-Nazaire de Royans, beyond Bourg de Péage, we found what looked on our maps like a shortcut to our objective, Grenoble, site of a great university, birthplace of Stendhal, and headquarters of the maquis defenders of the Vercors, an area of high plateaus, cultivated fields, and some of the most magnificent scenery in all France.

German formations were known to be in the vicinity, but we doubted they would be along this narrow, graveled road through mountainous country well defended by the maquis. There were no tracks, no indications of any kind, in fact, that troops of either side had used the road. Nevertheless, we proceeded cautiously and began to be apprehensive when we found the villages along the way shuttered and seemingly deserted. A light rain was falling, and visibility was poor. The road climbed sharply and became little more than a track barely wide enough for vehicles moving in opposite directions to pass each other, on our left sheer rock wall and on our right an eerie void filled with treetops and gray mist.

We rounded a succession of sharp bends carefully, keeping as far to the right as safety allowed, while peering anxiously through the clouded windshield, and were suddenly confronted by a tank instantly recognizable as a German Mark III, its gun swiveling slowly until it pointed directly at us. The enormous vehicle had halted as though waiting for us in ambush, and for several breathless moments we thought we'd had it. The soldier who emerged from the turret to look us over, however, was not a a Boche, but a grinning American sergeant who knew damned well that he had scared the juices out of us. He was riding the captured tank back to his unit's headquarters behind the lines and was still obviously enjoying the situation as we maneuvered around his iron monster, taking care not to skid off the road into the chasm on our right. Passing, I cursed him loudly for being a sadistic son of a bitch.

Meanwhile, it had stopped raining. The warm sun reappeared, shining brightly and turning the countryside into a wonderland of sparkling green fields and quaint farmhouses as we approached the pretty resort town of Villard de Lans. In the square a number of townspeople were gathered attentively about a tall, distinguished-looking Frenchman and his gray-haired wife, who had just arrived from La Chapelle, farther up the valley.

The man, dignified and stylishly dressed in sports clothes, turned out to be a prominent Paris lawyer who was now the judge advocate of the region's maquis forces. His wife was doing most of the talking but was having difficulty controlling her emotions. In La Chapelle she and her husband had just found the grave of their twenty-year-old son, a maquis. He and his fiancée had fought back to back, to their last bullet and grenade, defending a house against German raiders. When the youngsters' bodies were recovered, dead Germans lay all around them.

The lawyer's wife invited us to their chalet, where we sat around a table while she tried to tell us more about her son and the heroic defense of the Vercors by the maquis. Although plainly a woman of great inner resources, she frequently became incoherent, her voice rising to a shout, then breaking into dry sobs. Reluctant to press her for clarification, we decided to continue to La Chapelle to see for ourselves what had happened.

There were abundant indications along the way that terrible events had occurred in that green and pleasant valley. No traffic moved on the country lanes; no cattle grazed on the hillside pastures; in every hamlet furtive figures disappeared into houses or behind farm buildings. The inhabitants had seen no Allied troops and must have thought we were Germans. But when we stopped in a village square and dismounted to look around, people emerged from their homes, running to grasp our hands, and gleeful children clambered all over us or stood before us with uplifted faces to be kissed.

Farther on we saw burned-out farmhouses, fire-blackened barnyard buildings, and the rusting wrecks of private cars and farm machinery. We were in the area where the Germans had struck in a final attempt to destroy the military organization of the maquis in the Vercors.

Of La Chapelle's ninety-odd houses that lined the road on both sides, fewer than half a dozen were intact. The rest were the burned-out stone shells of houses filled with charred rubble. The villagers eagerly gathered about us to tell us what had befallen them at the hands of *les Boches*. Their spokesman was their priest, the abbé Pitavy, a vigorous man in his mid-sixties, of medium height, with a round, open face and thick gray hair cut *en brosse.* He wore World War I decorations and spoke in a resonant voice that thickened with emotion as he related what had happened at La Chapelle when the enemy attacked, referring from time to time to notes he had made, reading through steel-rimmed eyeglasses.

The abbé had been present throughout the horror that began with fire bombs from low-flying planes at 1:00 P.M. on July 15 and ended ten days later in a mass execution of innocent civilians. He conducted us to the spot: the rear wall of the blocklike stone house of Madame Lucie Albert, the side where she kept geraniums in pots arranged in a row along the foot of the wall, where it was moist, the abbé explained, "and at the same time quite sunny in the afternoons."

We saw where the enemy had lined up nineteen boys and men, including two Italian dairy workers and a Polish farmhand, machine-gunned them, and then tossed grenades into the writhing bodies. The whitish marks in the stone wall where the bullets had struck were clearly visible. Madame Albert had since rearranged the potted flowering geraniums in a row along the base of the wall as a sort of memorial to those who had died there.

Standing there facing the execution wall, the five of us had become one with the people of La Chapelle, and when we clambered back into our vehicle, the villagers shook hands with each of us in turn. *"Bon courage,"* they said, instead of *Au revoir,* as though aware we shared their grief. Shouldering shovels and other tools, they returned slowly to the ruins of what had been their family homes for generations. None of us could think of anything appropriate or decent to say beyond *Bonne chance.*

A few kilometers from La Chapelle, we gave a lift to five men. They were bareheaded, clean-shaven, tough, and dressed in baggy threadbare pants and shirts. All carried back packs and cheap cord-bound fiber suitcases. We took them about five miles on their way, and where the road turned off into a wood, they asked us to halt. A great valley swept away downhill to our left, and in the distance, perhaps fifteen miles off, we could see a village.

"We're going there," one of them said, pointing to the cluster of red-tiled roofs around a church spire. They shouldered their packs, picked up their bags, and started off downhill, turning once to wave at us. They were going to report to a French Army post after having fought for nearly four years as maquis.

We sat in our vehicle and watched them go down the green hillside into the valley. We watched for a long time, thinking how different the French were now from the apathetic French we had known in 1939. Then, I recalled, they had been reluctant to take a train to war; now they walked many miles to enlist in the new army of a reborn France.

It was raining lightly when we entered Grenoble late that afternoon. The city's streets were crowded with men, women and children, some under black umbrellas, others defending themselves against the drizzle with newspapers or shawls. They converged on a broad, piazzalike factory yard where six tall steel stakes, the kind the Germans used for stringing their barbed wire, were set before a blank factory wall flecked with bullet marks.

The people seemed to be in holiday mood, laughing, chattering in a hubbub of expectancy. They might have been gaily on their way to a soccer game, but they were gathering to witness the execution of six countrymen who had borne arms against France, condemned men captured earlier by the maquis and tried that very morning by a civilian judge and two military assistant judges in the town's shabby Palais de Justice. An FFI guerrilla assured me the prisoners had been ably defended by two of Grenoble's best lawyers, duly found guilty of treason under the laws of the French Republic, and sentenced to death by a firing squad.

The six, we were told, had not pleaded innocence but merely declared they had been "misled by Vichy propaganda." At the appointed hour they were taken in a police van to the factory yard where, a few weeks before, twenty-three maquis were shot by the servile *milice* of Fascist Vichyite collaborationists.

The yard overflowed with spectators despite the steady drizzle. Others watched from the windows of nearby houses. Boys clambered up lampposts for a better view. Many women in the crowd held infants in their arms.

A tremendous, blood-chilling cry of exultation rose from the crowd when the police van arrived and discharged the six who were to die. They looked very young to me, between eighteen and twenty-five years old, and there were boos and catcalls as they walked, serenely enough, I thought, to their respective places to have their hands bound behind the steel stakes and, with one exception, be blindfolded. He was the one nearest to where I stood, the youngest. He had a shock of reddish hair and might have been a student at Grenoble's university.

There was a sudden deep silence, the metallic click of rifle bolts, then the sharp, climactic crack of the volley. Three of the men died well—which is to say, they died instantly and dropped to their knees. Three did not. They sagged on their stakes, swaying, and one—the one without a blindfold and closest to where I stood—remained erect for what seemed an eternity, shaking his head from side to side as if suddenly understanding, and regretting, what was happening. But an officer with a revolver hastened to him and to each of the others to administer the coup de grace.

With the officer's last shot another tremendous cry sprang from the crowd. It lingered in the air before dissolving into shouts of *"Vive la France,"* then laughter, exclamations, and the kind of loud small talk spectators make when they've seen a good show. People, singly and in groups, including mothers clutching infants, advanced for a closer look at the crumpled figures. Boys ran up, spit at each of the bodies in turn, and scuttled off as though suddenly frightened by what they had seen or ashamed of what they had done.

Two or three of my colleagues were outraged by what they had witnessed and loudly denounced the executions as maquis "drumhead justice." I found myself in total disagreement. The animalistic reaction of the mob had been as distasteful to me as it was to them, but I felt I understood why the French had behaved as they did. The men who died had actually fought fellow Frenchmen on behalf of the Nazis. Traitors had met the end traitors deserve. That morning, at the Palais de Justice, the collaborators who had merely profited financially from contracts for the construction of German barracks or airfields or by selling food, raw materials, or manufactured goods to the enemy had received only prison sentences. French justice, it seemed to me, had behaved with Gallic good sense and fairness.

I pitied only the red-headed youngster whom the volley had failed to kill immediately. In those final, fractional moments of life how he must have regretted the futility of having embraced the Nazi cause!

67

THE "LIBERATION" OF GERTRUDE STEIN

The end of August found the northward thrust of the Seventh Army bogged down in the sudden rains and mud of an early mistral. General Patch's forces, superbly equipped and ably led, had ballooned out into southern France in the fastest development of a Allied beachhead since the landings at Casablanca. Our army had exploded into an apparent vacuum created by an unexpectedly weak German defense and the effective work of the guerrilla forces of the French resistance movement.

Maquis patriots swarmed to the advancing Americans like children to the Pied Piper. They came afoot, on bicycles trailing little wagons, on horse-drawn carts, and in buses, to which they had hitched draft animals when the engines quit. Men of all ages, and many young women, were armed and burning for the revenge for which they had waited since 1940.

By September 1, the fifth anniversary of the beginning of Hitler's war, nearly the whole of southern France was liberated. That morning I wrote my wife that the Battle of France was as good as finished, that the Battle of Germany was about to begin, and that I hoped to be home by Christmas. "I trust," I added, "that the good news which has been coming from all of us here hasn't, however, reduced production or impaired Mr. Roosevelt's chances of reelection." It was an election year, and I knew Kathryn was working hard on the president's behalf in hidebound, Republican Bronxville.

I had good reason for optimism. Our military situation in southern France was fantastically good. On our right a plunge northeastward from Briançon had brought our troops to within five miles of the Italian frontier, and any hopes the Germans might have entertained of evacuating large numbers of their men from southern France into northern Italy had been extinguished. On our left our forces were steadily pursuing the Germans up the Rhône Valley toward Lyons.

It was in the center, and directly northward, however, that the Allied advance had made the swiftest progress. Motorized units led by Brigadier General Fred Butler, kiting up secondary roads in the hills east of the Rhône Valley, including the one on which my colleagues and I traversed the Vercors, had quickly reached Grenoble. They were greeted with flowers, gifts of fruit and vegetables, and warm embraces from the clean, good-looking girls who clambered aboard the Americans' Jeeps and trucks. Our soldiers, I noticed, soon learned not to kiss the girls on their mouths but on both cheeks unless serious developments were contemplated.

Our men loved Grenoble. After southern Italy's smashed towns and villages, the clean, wholesome, virtually undamaged university city on the Isère represented civilization. I heard men of Butler's force say, "This is just like home, almost," an impression subsequently enhanced by the availability of beer and real ice cream made with whole milk from the cows in the green valleys of the Vercors. A few GIs with high school French basked in the friendly warmth of the townspeople who complimented them on how well they spoke *français*.

In Italy our troops called the Italians "wops," "dagos," "Eyeties," even "gooks." In France I rarely heard them use the pejorative "frogs" that came so easily to British lips, and some soldiers of the Forty-fifth Division, lanky youngsters from the Middle West, confided they might "stay over to help these fine people rebuild their country." Many said they intended to return with their brides on their honeymoons, an intention I seldom heard expressed in Italy.

For the first time in my experience our soldiers acted more like members of a professional army rather than as reluctant civilians in uniform. In Italy, their morale shattered by slow progress and, at times, poor leadership, they had been cantankerous and grumbly, even, on occasion, mutinous, wanting only to "get this goddamn war over with and go home." Now their morale was excellent; they were winning soldiers, and victories gained without heavy casualties are the best possible morale builders, better even than Red Cross girls and visiting performers from Hollywood or Broadway.

Meanwhile, the press corps was bivouacked under canvas in the hills above Grenoble, cursing the foul weather, the stupid censors, and the understandable but nonetheless repugnant vengefulness of the French. Frenchmen were killing Frenchmen everywhere in the liberated portions of their country, and I, for one, after the bloodletting in Egypt, Libya, Sicily, and most recently Italy, had wearied of the slaughter.

The executions in the factory square in Grenoble had unnerved me. It is one thing to see men die in the heat of battle, but quite another, even in the name of justice, to see them deliberately killed in cold blood by firing squads. Years later I still envisioned that red-haired boy shaking his head in dumbfounded wonderment at what was happening to him. . . .

On the morning of September 1 I was in my tent working on a piece for my magazine. I had just finished the letter to my wife and was trying to convey to paper what I had seen and heard at La Chapelle, in the deep green silences of the Vercors, and deal sensibly with the shocking business I had witnessed in that bleak, rain-swept factory square in Grenoble when Eric Sevareid stepped through the flap and invited me to join him in a search for Gertrude Stein. I accepted with alacrity. Not only was Eric's invitation a welcome interruption of the tedious business of composing a readable piece, but I had recently met Ernest Hemingway, had formed a thoroughly unfavorable opinion of him as a person—I thought he strove harder than necessary to assert his masculinity—and looked forward to hearing what his onetime friend and mentor might have to say about him.

Moreover, the search promised adventure and for Eric, certainly, the possibility of a major scoop. For me personally, the prospect of meeting an authentic genius, the inventor of a literary style known as Steinese, was irresistible. Miss Stein had influenced several important writers of our time, among them Hemingway and Sherwood Anderson, and was a close friend and early patron of yet another giant, Pablo Picasso.

Gertrude Stein and her companion, Alice Toklas, Eric said, were known to be living in the vicinity of Belley, well to the north of Grenoble, hence probably beyond established Seventh Army boundaries. Eric had cabled CBS in New York to ask Miss Stein's publishers, Random House, where she might be found, but the reply merely gave the address she was known to have had two years before. The uncertainty, however, only added spice to the occasion.

The resourceful Sevareid had wangled a command car like the one that had brought us to Grenoble, a sort of overgrown Jeep with comfortable leather seats, and a top and side curtains to keep out the rain, driven by Sergeant William B. Druggan, a Boston Irishman, who said he had never heard of "this Stein broad." With us went Price Day, of the *Baltimore Sun,* Newbold Noyes, of the *Washington Star,* and Carl Mydans, the distinguished *Time-Life* photographer. None of us could remember anything Stein had written except *The Autobiography of Alice B. Toklas* and could quote (or misquote) only "Rose is a rose is a rose," and "Pigeons on the grass alas."

Our route followed the Isère north toward Chambéry and into the Haute-Savoie, through a region veined with swift-running clear streams, which surely abounded in trout, and past sweet-smelling fields alive with wild flowers. Tall cottonwoods and poplars lined the roads; the air smelled of wet grass, damp earth, and the smoke of distant wood fires. The skies cleared, the sun shone brightly, and the war suddenly became a faraway something that was happening on another planet.

We were in an area where we believed no Allied troops had entered, and shortly before noon, somewhere beyond Chambéry, our vehicle coughed and spluttered to a stop. While Sergeant Druggan fussed with the motor, a Jeep appeared from the opposite direction and drew up alongside, its occupants eyeing us suspiciously. They were Private First Class John Schmaltz and Lieutenant Colonel William Perry of the Forty-fifth Infantry, who wanted to know "where the hell" we thought we were going. He laughed heartily, snickeringly seconded by his driver, Schmaltz, when Eric told the officer we were on our way to Belley to "liberate" Gertrude Stein.

"Forget it," the colonel roared. "Gertrude Stein's already been liberated— by damn near the whole United States Army. We spent the night in her home—in beds the Germans had slept in only a few nights ago."

While Private Schmaltz, a better mechanic than our Sergeant Druggan, tinkered with our engine, we listened, somewhat crestfallen, to Colonel Perry's account of his visit with the Misses Stein and Toklas. He said they lived in Culoz, a few miles north of Belley. The two ladies and their dog, a poodle named Basket, had arrived in Belley in a taxi the day before, found the town full of Americans, and had a grand reunion with them at the hotel where some of our officers were billeted. The colonel had driven the two women and the dog home in his Jeep that evening. He and his driver had stayed for supper, talked until well past midnight—"Miss Stein asked a million questions about America," the colonel said—and remained overnight.

Schmaltz got our engine going again while the colonel traced the route to Culoz on our maps, and advised us to hurry. "If you do," he said, "you might make it in time for lunch, and those girls sure set a swell table. By the way, do any of you know Hemingway, Van Vechten, or Sherwood Anderson? Miss Stein kept asking about them."

This puzzled us. Anderson had died early in the war, in 1941. Was it possible that Gertrude Stein did not know of his death? Or had Colonel Perry confused Sherwood Anderson with Bob Sherwood, who was very much alive and well at the time and active in propaganda work? We should soon know.

Although we were delayed by detours around several small bridges which the maquis had blown up to delay the retreating Germans, we found Culoz without difficulty. The road led directly into the tiny seventeenth-century hamlet, and there, at the entrance to the community, stood its mayor. He was Monsieur Justin Hey, thin, elderly, with a grayish white, tobacco-stained mustache, and wearing a bowler hat and black bow tie. He carried a stout cane, and personally escorted us to the home of "Madame Shstayn." The Château la Colombière was an old two-story stone house cowled by a graceful slate roof set in a well-tonsured garden alongside a crystalline stream that ran volubly through Culoz and provided it with drinking water as well as power for its small flour mill.

We came upon Gertrude Stein and Alice Toklas as they were about to sit down to lunch with two friends, a husband and wife by the name of Schwab, he very professional in a winged collar and she very schoolmistressy in a plain gray dress. Alice fluted out orders to an elderly servant, and soon lunch for four became lunch for eight, with Bill Druggan assigned to the kitchen of a nearby house, where he drank more *vin de la victoire* than was good for him.

Gertrude Stein was seventy when she waddled voluminously across the polished living room floor, spread her arms in a welcoming embrace, and clamped them about me, nearly crushing my ribs, saying over and over again, "You don't know how glad I am to see you." Never having met her before, I was a little taken aback but managed to remark at the strength in her arms, which felt hard and well muscled. She looked like a strong, healthy peasant woman of no more than fifty.

"I've been working hard," she explained. "Gardening, chopping wood, helping Alice with the chores, and walking. My, what a lot of walking I've done these years."

What about writing?

"Oh, yes, yes, yes. But later. We'll talk about that later. Now, let us have lunch."

Lunch was a delicious soup of vegetables, followed by omelets, a crisp lettuce salad, a chocolate soufflé, and strong black coffee served in tiny cups as fragile as Alice, who did little talking during the meal, letting Gertrude Stein carry the conversation. But her deep-set dark eyes followed every word and looked penetratingly into each face, seeming to note every expression, every nuance in our voices. She was as frail and as magnificently unattractive physically as photographs I had seen. "Pussy," as Stein called her, was as warmly attentive as a friendly feline and made disapproving clucking sounds when we said we had seen Hemingway's wife, Martha Gellhorn, in Italy. "That makes his third." She sniffed. "Tch, tch, tch."

The surprise was Gertrude Stein, whose big Picasso portrait of her dominated the spacious, sunlit living room of La Colombière. I had heard and read much about her unwomanliness and her lesbian relationship with Alice, but I found them both quite womanly, especially Gertrude Stein. She had a kindly, inquiring face, merry eyes indeterminately brown, and a strong mouth and nose. Her graying black hair was cropped close and combed mannishly, but her principal feature was her voice, which was musical, pitched low, and smooth as fresh cream.

She was full of questions about Hemingway, whom she obviously disliked, and Thornton Wilder and Carl Van Vechten, both of whom she equally obviously adored. She wanted to know their whereabouts and what they were doing. Yes, she had heard about Anderson's death, and that Alexander Woollcott had died, too, but what was Bob Sherwood up to these days? I was able to inform her that Papa Hemingway, after sitting out most of the war in the waters off the Florida keys, had recently been hired by my magazine to cover the northern front in the Battle of France and that Bob Sherwood was involved with the War Writers' Board and similar activities. I knew nothing about Wilder or Van Vechten.

We, in turn, asked many questions about her four years under the Nazis, and Gertrude Stein did most of the talking thereafter. She told us that in her opinion not all the Vichy people were bad, though some of their leaders were evil men who collaborated freely with the Germans. She had no kind words for the French Vichy militia, of course, but for the most part, she said, the French civil servants and functionaries "and everyone generally" were in the maquis or the FFI and "fooling the Germans the whole of the time."

"The German way," said Gertrude, "was to bang on the door and demand this room and that room and say, 'No answers, please'—not that anybody would ever try to answer them. They were just unpleasant at times but never really bad while they were here, only they were always going off with the keys, and then I would have to go to the locksmith again. It was such a bother."

As an American, and a Jewess to boot, she might have been fair game for the Gestapo, but the French officials never allowed the enemy to discover her identity. Monsieur Justin Hey, the mayor, simply neglected to enter her name and Alice's on the town's list of inhabitants, and the Germans never discovered his purposeful oversight.

Three times Gertrude Stein had had German officers quartered in her house as "nonpaying" guests. She had let her servants deal with them— servants with wonderfully French names like Olympe and Clothilde. Gertrude herself rarely needed to speak to them personally, but when she did, her Nazi boarders never caught her decidedly un-French accent.

"But once," she recalled, "I had an Italian major and his aide as guests. The major remarked on my accent, but if he guessed my identity, he never gave me away as an American, which goes to show the difference between Italians and Germans in more ways than one."

The Germans, it seems, were completely flummoxed by the canny mayor and citizens of Culoz, which, incidentally, was a railway crossroads. About 80 percent of the village's wage earners worked for the railroad and were members of the maquis. Their leader was the station master, who had to work daily with two German assistants in the operations of the railroad center, but the derailments and other acts of sabotage he engineered were never traced to him.

In fact, Miss Stein told me, there was only one collaborationist in Culoz, an old count who lived like a feudal lord in his château and was certain that the Americans would never come and that the Germans would win the war. His was the only house in Culoz where no Allied flags were displayed.

"And under its roof," Miss Stein said, "there is a great tragedy. The count's beautiful only daughter had married a brave young maquis of middle-class parents. Under her father's influence, she has turned against her husband and is even more Vichyite than her sire. The two young people rarely see each other. A great sadness."

While we talked, the sun burst out unexpectedly over the broad front lawn of La Colombière. Village children came to play maquis and Germans, making sounds like machine guns, and I thought of my Tommy guarding our house in Broxville against the Japs, shooting "infiltrators" down out of our maple trees. . . .

After lunch Gertrude Stein drew me aside and asked me if I knew her publisher, Bennett Cerf, of Random House. I said I did, adding that I was certain he would be panting to publish whatever she had written during the occupation. I also told her I thought my magazine might be interested in publishing excerpts from her work. Was her manuscript ready?

"As a matter of fact," she said, "Alice is typing the last pages."

Would I see to it that that the manuscript reached Bennett Cerf? I said I would be delighted, and I asked her permission to show it first to the editors of *Collier's*. She agreed and invited me to return the following day to fetch it. "It will be ready," she said, "if Alice has to type all night. . . ."

That was on Friday, and that evening I cabled *Collier's*, asking whether the magazine would be interested in an autobiographical account of Gertrude Stein's four years under the Nazis, stressing that it would be the first such account by a major author out of occupied France, and suggesting that twenty thousand dollars might be a fair price.

The next day I returned to Culoz, alone, and Gertrude handed me the manuscript of *Wars I Have Seen*. Its final sixty-five pages contained, in my humble opinion, some of the best writing Stein had ever produced. They related the story of the arrival of the Americans as liberators of her country of residence and of her rediscovery, through them, of the depth of her affection for the America of her birth, sentiments that struck a responsive chord, for I, too, had rediscovered America during the war.

At our previous meeting Gertrude apparently had sensed my annoyance that *Collier's* had assigned Hemingway to the Normandy invasion and volunteered her view of him as a creative artist. I made no notes at the time, of course, but I distinctly remember her saying that over the years Papa had not lived up to the great promise he had shown in his early work. In her opinion, he had become less a creative artist than a seeker after success, and she plainly indicated her disillusionment.

"Success, success, success," she said. "That is what drives him, not a search for truth. He prizes acclaim. . . ."

She was certain, furthermore, that Hemingway was tormented by a death wish hidden behind his posture as a hard-boiled character; hence physical courage as the theme of his brilliant short stories and novels. She saw him as a writer with a keen, though narrow, vision of moral dignity but admitted he possessed a supreme gift for staccato vernacular dialogue, a technique of understatement that heralded a revolution in American writing.

The next day, Sunday, September 3, the fourth anniversary of the war, Eric and I drove again to Culoz, lunched with Gertrude and Alice, and took them back to our press camp to meet our colleagues, make a recording for CBS, and have dinner at our mess. The two women seemed to like our C rations and were happy to meet all the reporters. Most of them didn't quite know who Gertrude Stein was, but they all sent pieces to their papers about the author of "Rose is a rose is a rose. . . ."

The ladies were accompanied by their dog, Basket the Second, Basket the First having died in Paris years earlier. Their pet, Gertrude explained, was a woolly French poodle "with twenty generations of German blood in his veins, but we keep it from him so as not to break his spirit."

On parting, Gertrude handed me a closed, unsealed envelope. "This," she said, "is for you. Don't read it now. . . ."

In my tent, later, I withdrew from the envelope nine pages of Air France airmail paper and discovered that Gertrude Stein had written a ballad commemorating our meeting. It was her way, I supposed, of thanking me for having volunteered to carry her manuscript of *Wars I Have Seen* through the wartime censorship to its final destination at *Collier's* and/or Random House.

I saw the ballad less as a "reward," however, than as an act of friendship that reciprocated the deep affection I had so quickly developed for this remarkable woman and her companion. This is what she wrote in her barely decipherable calligraphy, published here for the first time:

A BALLAD

A big bird flying high
In the sky
Makes little birds sitting by
Know they must do or die

It was in the woods and it was dark,
And dogs bark,
But little birds know that dogs are there
Where they cannot stare
Into the nests where birdies are.

But a big bird that flies on high
Even when leaves are everywhere
He can see right down from the sky
And see even nests hidden with care.

And so they do not dare
The little birds do not dare
to let the big bird fly too low
Because he will take the little ones so
Right in his claws and away will go
To give them to eat to his own big
birds which need to eat and have a treat
of littler birds which are so sweet.

And so
As I said
And as you have read

When a big bird flies high
The little birds know they must do or die.

And so they do
And to be true
It is not the little birds that
die but the big bird that flies
high in the sky.

The big bird is there,
The little birds with all care
All together fly over there.
They fly higher and higher
And higher and higher
And they come nearer and nearer
One after the other
Until the big bird begins to feel queer
And wonder what is all the bother
And so the little birds in a big number,
Come hitting the big bird on the head
And hoping he is dead.

And another comes down
And another comes down
And the big bird begins to frown
And he tries to get away,
But there is no way,
The little birds say,
If he gets away he will come back another day
And so one after the other so quickly that they
seem like bees,

They come down and hit the big bird on the crown,
And slowly the big bird sinks lower down,
And down and down,
And the little birds begin to frown
And they begin to know
That the big bird will go down, down,
And down and down
And at last no more
Can the big bird soar
And he falls down and down
And the little birds keep hitting at him
And the big bird at last has fallen down and the
lake is there and he will drown
and all the little birds will fly away

to tell other little birds to stay
all the danger has gone away.

And this does happen every day
Just like I say . . .
For Frank Gervasi
Culoz, September 1, Happy Days, Always
(signed) Gtd St.

Pure "Steinese," obviously, and I leave its interpretation to the reader. Bearing in mind Montaigne's admonition that "It is easier to write a mediocre poem than to understand a good one," I dared interpret the ballad as an expression of its author's joy in the imminent triumph of virtue over evil.

Meeting Gertrude Stein and Alice Toklas was one of the brighter events of my peripatetic journey through the violent decade that began in 1935 with the Fascist invasion of Ethiopia and soon was to end in 1945 in atomic holocaust. I have often wondered why those two women—the sturdy Gertrude and the fragile, birdlike Alice—remain full-bodied and vivid in the dimming gallery of my memory, whereas scores of other famous persons I met in my travels—presidents, dictators, generals—have become mere duo-dimensional, almost insubstantial figures. I have concluded that it is because those two women were genuine human beings, loving and lovable, endowed with a boundless capacity for affection and sincere friendship.

My visit with Stein and Toklas somehow helped assuage the bitter disappointment I had felt at not having completed my wartime assignment in Paris, where it had begun, and when the campaign in southern France bogged down somewhere above Dijon in the Alps in the autumn of 1944, I flew to Cairo, where I had been based during much of the war. In Cairo I walked Stein's manuscript through a series of friendly censors who treated the work with the respect it deserved. Not a word was deleted.

When I arrived in New York just before Christmas—aboard a hospital ship out of Alexandria—I gave the manuscript to *Collier's,* but the new editors weren't interested. The late Charley Colebaugh would have gladly published it; but his successor didn't think its publication would help the magazine's efforts to increase circulation, which, incidentally, had not substantially improved with Hemingway's work. I then took *Wars I Have Seen* to Bennett Cerf at Random House, who published it promptly and profitably to excellent reviews.

EPILOGUE

LEST WE FORGET

Future generations may dismiss the Second World War as "just another war," but some of us who experienced it would strongly disagree. Apart from the fact that it was by far the most murderous and destructive of the thirty-odd previous major wars of modern times, the Second World War was unique in having produced the atomic bomb, the nuclear weapon which ended the war in the Pacific and whose subsequent proliferation now threatens humanity's continued existence.

In the year 1988, forty-three years after the war ended in the fateful summer of 1945, there are enough nuclear weapons in the world to turn our planet into a lifeless, incandescent ball of coke, and the arms race that produced them continues unabated. According to figures made available to me by my late son Tom (the little boy who "guarded" our Bronxville home against the hated "Japs" with a broomstick gun had become, at fifty-one, an author and an established authority on global armaments production), the world bristles with nearly 60,000 nuclear warheads divided as follows: 37,657 in the United States; 17,656 in the Soviet Union; 936 in France; 784 in Great Britain; 389 in China; 200 in Israel; and 36 in South Africa.

In the summer of 1945 only three atomic bombs existed, and we owned all three, the product of four years of secret intensive labor by a coterie of international scientists whose work was authorized in 1940 by President Roosevelt and was nourished by two billion dollars' worth of American taxpayers' money. At the time I was in Washington, my employers having relieved me of further overseas duty and assigned me to the capital's political beat shortly after I came home from the war. I remember with horror the chronology that preceded the surrender of Japan, the end of the Second World War, and the dawn of the nuclear age.

On July 16 we tested one of our three bombs at Alamogordo Air Base in the remote desert lands about 120 miles southeast of Albuquerque, New Mexico, and the damned thing worked. It exploded in a blinding flash more brilliant than the midday sun at its brightest, vaporized the tall steel tower from which the device hung, and left an enormous, sloping crater.

On August 6 we dropped the second of our bombs—a missile with the destructive power of twenty thousand tons of TNT—on Hiroshima, Japan, killing outright an estimated 78,000 of the city's 265,000 inhabitants, mortally wounding some 20,000 more, and incinerating virtually every building as well as every tree and every other living thing within a three-mile radius. Three days later we exploded our third and last bomb over equally populous Nagasaki with similarly lethal results, and on August 14 the Japanese announced their readiness to surrender.

Washington, I recall, erupted into a wild, bacchic victory celebration. Church bells pealed, automobiles paraded through the streets, honking their horns, trucks purposefully backfired salutes, and youngsters set off firecrackers. There was a lot of public and private boozing, and servicemen randomly hugged and kissed the women they passed on the sidewalks.

A huge crowd chanting, "We want Harry!" gathered outside the White House, now occupied by Roosevelt's successor, plain, bespectacled Harry Truman, the failed haberdasher-turned-politician from Independence, Missouri, whom fate had chosen to lead the nation at a critical juncture in its history and who, as commander in chief, had ordered the bombs dropped on Hiroshima and Nagasaki.

Truman, I learned when I interviewed him at his retreat in Key West, Florida, in the spring of 1946, had not even known the A-bomb existed when he took office, for Roosevelt had not told his vice president of its existence. Truman, therefore, probably knew little of the nuclear weapon's lethal powers. He subsequently admitted that he regarded the bomb "as a military weapon, and never had any doubt it should be used."

Hence, like the rest of us, the new president believed that when the final curtain fell on the war in the Pacific, we had survived the worst of all possible wars. Blissfully unaware that the bomb was not "just another weapon," but a device capable of producing something infinitely, unimaginably worse than the war we had just experienced, Americans looked forward hopefully to life in the united, peaceful, and prosperous world promised in the Atlantic Charter and envisioned in the United Nations Organization, the recent war's most important political achievement.

The atomic bomb may or may not have decided the issue in the Pacific; on this point people long would differ, for it was evident for some time before the bombs were dropped on Hiroshima and Nagasaki that Japan's fighting power had been largely crushed. As early as June 22, I remember, diplomatic circles in Washington buzzed with believable reports that Hirohito had been trying to initiate peace negotiations by way of Stockholm and Moscow, the Russians having not yet entered the war in the Pacific.

When the Japanese surrendered, there was no further need for atomic bombs, hence no further use for Los Alamos and its machinery for manufacturing them. In the circumstances our government should have razed the installations at Los Alamos, burned the blueprints for making the bombs, and outlawed forever the use of atomic energy in the production of weapons, all of which might have happened if Roosevelt had lived.

But FDR died on April 12, nearly four months before those two fateful days in August. His successor, no doubt on the advice of the generals who were running the nation's affairs at the time, chose to build more bombs, to share the secret of their construction only with the British, and to deny it to our wartime ally the Soviet Union.

The policy of Anglo-American atomic secrecy, however, rested on a misconception, for the bomb was actually an international achievement. Although American and British scientists had done most of the work, they were helped by Canadian colleagues, a Danish professor, an Italian physicist, and a number of German and Austrian scientists. The results of their work could no more remain the secret of only two powers than had the secret of Faraday's discovery of electromagnetic energy.

Not surprisingly, therefore, Stalin soon learned that the United States possessed the means to obliterate Moscow in the blink of an eye and ordered his physicists and engineers to produce Russian atomic bombs.

So began the most fearsome arms race the world has ever known.

A host of experts—scientists, moralists, even some farsighted soldiers—repeatedly warned that unless arrested, the arms race could only lead to a Third World War and ultimate disaster. For it is axiomatic, they argued, that nations arm only for war, not peace. A world that amasses armaments unrestrainedly, E. M. Forster reminded us, "can no more help discharging its filth in war than an animal which keeps on eating can stop itself from excreting." An inelegant metaphor, perhaps, but an apt one.

Meanwhile, during the years since the Second World War ended, a number of other serious threat to humanity's well-being have developed: widespread poverty, overpopulation, pollution of such life-sustaining elements as the water we drink and the air we breathe, diminishing natural resources, drought, plague, drug abuse—all threats that should be seriously addressed on a global basis but remain sorely neglected in the atmosphere of mutual harassment and hostility that has prevailed since the late summer of 1945.

It is madness for a world community which in 1988 was unable to feed and house all its people to continue spending hundreds of billions of dollars, indeed, trillions, on weapons, both nuclear and conventional. Unless the arms race ceases, and the immense resources thus saved are used to deal with the other dangers humanity faces, a Third World War—and nuclear holocaust—remain distinct possibilities.

The conclusion in December 1987 of a Russo-American treaty reducing their respective intermediate nuclear forces was a welcome first step toward sanity. It should be noted, however, that the INF treaty diminishes the nuclear arsenals of the two superpowers by only 3 percent and that in the meantime plans are already afoot in American military circles to make up the deficit with the introduction of a new tactical nuclear weapons system.

Oddly enough, after two generations of Cold War, the only voice raised in favor of total elimination of nuclear arms comes not from Washington but from Moscow. Mikhail Gorbachev, his thinking possibly influenced by the tragic consequences of the "accident" at Chernobyl and by youthful memories of the horrors of war, has indicated he realizes the utter folly of the costly competition in armaments, and from all accounts sincerely desires to end it. We—and his own hard-liners—should join him, not oppose him, in his efforts to halt the headlong rush to an atomic Armageddon.

If World War II taught us anything it was that there must never be World War III, but the rift that developed between the United States and the Soviet Union in the mid-1940s—even before the guns fell silent in Europe and Asia in the summer of 1945—persists to this day. It deepened into an antagonism so acute as to resemble actual combat and in fact came to be known as the Cold War. The united, warless one world of our wartime yearnings—when Roosevelt's Four Freedoms sounded above the clamor like a second Sermon on the Mount—quickly became two worlds, one Communist and led by Russia, the other composed of the capitalist democracies and led by the United States.

The ideological opposites had been obliged to unite against the common dangers from Germany and Japan, but the moment those threats ceased to exist they reverted to the mutual suspicions with which they had regarded each other ever since the Bolshevik Revolution of 1917. In the relentless, often mindless propaganda spawned by the resultant Cold War, Americans and Russians were schooled to regard each other as enemies destined sooner or later to go to war to settle their differences, and both sides diligently prepared for it. Now both own not only obscene numbers of atomic weapons of all kinds but devil's arsenals of so-called conventional arms far deadlier than those employed in World War II, acquired at tremendous cost in the sacred name of defense, the crutch of politicians in both camps more responsive to the demands of vested interests than to the clamor of ordinary citizens for a cleaner, safer world in which to raise their children.

There is only one way to prevent a holocaust of life and property beyond any historical precedent, and that is to prevent war. But another war can only be prevented by first reducing to zero the enormous stockpiles of atomic weapons already in existence and then forbidding, by international agreement, their future production, admittedly no easy task but surely essential if humanity is to survive.

Ideally, of course, we should also drastically reduce "conventional" weapons as well. Those employed in World War II were lethal enough, killing an estimated twenty million of the seventy million combatants involved and two or three times as many innocent civilians.

Nevertheless, despite the slaughter and the destruction that accompanied it, the Second World War could be rated a "good" war, for it turned back the threat to Western civilization posed by Europe's Nazis and Fascists and Asia's Japanese imperialists, closed the Nazis' gas chambers and crematoria, emptied the concentration camps, and punished most, though by no means all, of the criminals responsible for the crimes committed against humankind.

Of the many crimes perpetrated by the Nazis in the years between September 1, 1939, when the Germans marched into Poland, and May 8, 1945, when their armies surrendered in Europe, by far the most grotesque was the attempted extermination of Europe's nine million Jews, of whom six million perished in the Nazi gas chambers and before firing squads in execution of Adolf Hitler's insane racial doctrine.

In Nuremberg, in a cell in the prisoner of war camp where he awaited trial as a war criminal, Robert Ley, the former Nazi Labor Front boss, confessed that what he and his Führer and their allies had done had been a "mistake." Ley was a swine, a blackmailer, a drunkard, and a swindler. Yet just before he choked himself to death with a gag, he found courage enough and sufficient reason left to write what he chose to call his "political testament" attributing the downfall of nazism to German anti-Semitism.

"We have forsaken God," the creature wrote, "and, therefore, we were forsaken by God. We put our human volition in the place of His godly grace. In anti-Semitism we violated a basic commandment of His creation. Anti-Semitism distorted our outlook, and we made grave errors."

The Second World War was fought to liberate peoples from Nazi and Fascist and Japanese tyranny. In this it succeeded, though the price in human life and property came high. No one can contemplate the present state of the world without admitting that people everywhere are freer, happier, and more prosperous than they would have been if the Allies had lost the war. So, it was a "good" war as wars go.

But the Second World War also produced the atom bomb. A Third World War could never be a "good" war, for it would inevitably involve the use of nuclear weapons, which would multiply exponentially the killing and the devastation. It would know no victors, and its survivors, it has been said, would envy the dead. In this time of unexampled danger, the world needs a universal demand for peace, a global rising of the masses against war and the wasteful expenditure of the fruits of their toil for tools designed only to kill, maim, and destroy.

The world belongs to the people who inhabit it, not to states or the governments that run them. "If people want peace badly enough and demand it," a great American suggested some years ago, "governments will get out of their way and let them have it." That person was Dwight David Eisenhower, who led the Allied forces to victory in Europe, became president of the United States in 1952, and was reelected in 1956.

The other, nonnuclear threats to humankind's well-being and continued existence on this planet—poverty, pollution of the environment, dwindling natural resources—will take time to attain catastrophic proportions; hence remedial measures are possible. No such margin of safety would be allowed us in the event of a nuclear war. World War II lasted six years. World War III might last only the time it takes an intercontinental ballistic missile to cross the Atlantic: thirty minutes.

INDEX